# Choice,
# Welfare and
# Measurement

To Eva

# Choice, Welfare and Measurement

AMARTYA SEN

Harvard University Press

Cambridge, Massachusetts
London, England

First Harvard University Press paperback edition, 1997.
Published by arrangement with Basil Blackwell Publisher.

*Library of Congress Cataloging-in-Publication Data*

Sen, Amartya Kumar.
    Choice, welfare and measurement / Amartya Kumar Sen.
        p.   cm.
    Originally published: Oxford : Blackwell, 1982.
    Includes bibliographical references and indexes.
    ISBN 0-674-12778-1 (alk. paper)
    1. Welfare economics.    2. Social choice.    3. Utility theory.
I. Title.
HB846.S46    1997
330.15'56—dc21                                        97–14986

# Contents

# Preface

The papers included in this volume of essays deal with a number of related topics: choice, preference, rationality, welfare judgements, public decisions, social choice and social measurement. The papers are not arranged chronologically, but divided into five broad groups.

I have added a longish 'Introduction' to place the papers in their context. In fact, the 'Introduction' is not only concerned with the papers themselves but also with the related literature. The problems tackled in the different articles relate — in some cases closely — to each other. They also relate in various ways to the contributions of others. Also, many of the papers included here have provoked extensive discussions — in the form of extensions, applications and criticisms — and some of these discussions have clearly been much more valuable than the papers themselves. I have, therefore, gone well beyond the brief of a standard 'Introduction', and taken this opportunity of examining the underlying issues and the related developments.

One of the papers included here (Essay 7: 'Necessary and Sufficient Conditions for Rational Choice under Majority Decision') was written jointly with Prasanta Pattanaik, and I am grateful to him for permitting me to reproduce it here.

The idea of publishing a selection of essays came from René Olivieri of Basil Blackwell. His advice on what to select and how to arrange has been invaluable, and I am most grateful to him for his sagacious counsel.

A.K.S.

# Introduction

## 1  *Choice and Preference*

### 1.1  *Consistency and revealed preference*

Preference may be seen as 'prior' to choice: we may try to choose what we prefer. This is indeed the natural sequence in reflective choice, seen from the first-person point of view. However, from the point of view of the outside observer the opposite sequence may be the natural one: we observe the person's choices and surmise his or her preferences from these choices. There are, of course, cases that run counter to each of these interpretations. There exist situations—or so we are told by people who keep watching themselves carefully—in which a person 'understands' what he or she 'really' prefers by observing his or her own choices (e.g., 'I didn't think I preferred sweet German wines until I noticed that I always choose them at wine parties!'). And, of course, we may learn about a person's preference by means *other than* observing his or her choices (e.g., through conversation), and on that basis we may advise or predict what the person should or would choose.

In all this both 'choice' and 'preference' are taken as 'primitive' concepts with meanings of their own. The correspondence of choice and preference is seen as an empirical matter, and this is indeed how the correspondence is viewed in the classic framework of demand theory.[1] It is, of course, possible to vary that empirical assumption without descending into incoherence. The picture is, however, quite different with the approach of 'revealed preference'.[2] Preference here is simply *defined* as the binary relation underlying consistent choice. In this case 'counter-preferential' choice is not empirically different, but simply impossible. *Non*-preferential choice is, of course, possible, since the choices may lack the consistency needed for identifying a binary relation of preference, but obviously it cannot be the case

1. See, for example, J. R. Hicks, *Value and Capital* (Oxford: Clarendon Press, 1939); H. O. A. Wold, *Demand Analysis* (New York: Wiley, 1963).
2. See P. A. Samuelson, *Foundations of Economic Analysis* (Cambridge, Mass.: Harvard University Press, 1947).

that such an identified preference relation exists *and* the choices are 'counter' to it.

The four papers in Part I explore and examine different aspects of the correspondence between choice and preference, and investigate some related issues, e.g., linkages with individual welfare, characterization of normative analysis and conduct, and the behavioural foundations of economic theory. They address some of the problems that arise respectively in the definitional, empirical and normative linking of choice with preference.

The revealed preference approach—in its traditional formulation—has two technical limitations of some importance, and Essay 1 addresses itself to these. First, traditional revealed preference theory is almost exclusively concerned with 'transitive' preference relations. Thus the consistency of choice it demands is of an especially exacting variety which makes choices representable by a *transitive* binary relation. However, there are good grounds for expecting the introspective or observed preference relation to be not fully transitive, and indeed the case for admitting intransitivity of indifference has been forcefully argued in various contexts including demand theory.[3]

'Choice Functions and Revealed Preference' (Essay 1) discriminates between three cases, involving increasing regularity: (1) the choice function (telling us what is chosen from each subset) is representable by a binary preference relation (this is called 'normality', but 'binariness' would be a more direct description[4]), (2) *additionally* that the preference relation is quasi-transitive (transitive *strict* preference, not necessarily transitive indifference), and (3) *additionally* that the preference relation is fully transitive. The consistency requirements of each case are axiomatically identified.[5]

The second limitation concerns the restriction in traditional revealed preference theory that consistency of choice is demanded only over a class of convex polyhedra ('budget triangles' in the two-good case). While this is the form in which actual choices are faced by the consumer in competitive

3. See in particular W. E. Armstrong, 'The Determinateness of the Utility Function', *Economic Journal*, 49 (1939); D. Scott and P. Suppes, 'Foundational Aspects of Theories of Measurement', *Journal of Symbolic Logic*, 23 (1958); R. D. Luce, 'Semiorders and a Theory of Utility Discrimination', *Econometrica*, 24 (1956); N. Georgescu-Roegen, 'Threshold in Choice and the Theory of Demand', *Econometrica*, 26 (1958); T. Majumdar, *The Measurement of Utility* (London: Macmillan, 1962); P. C. Fishburn, 'Intransitive Indifference in Preference Theory: A Survey', *Operations Research*, 18 (1970); J. S. Chipman, L. Hurwicz, M. K. Richter and H. F. Sonnenschein, *Preference, Utility and Demand* (New York: Harcourt, 1971).

4. This corresponds to the condition of 'rationalizability' investigated by M. K. Richter, 'Revealed Preference Theory', *Econometrica*, 34 (1966).

5. Case (1) does not require the preference relation to be transitive or quasi-transitive, but it does require it to be 'acyclic', i.e., free from strict preference cycles (e.g., $x_1$ preferred to $x_2$, ..., $x_{n-1}$ preferred to $x_n$, and $x_n$ preferred to $x_1$), which is a less exacting demand. Indeed, for a reflexive and complete binary relation $R$, the *necessary and sufficient* condition for it to generate a choice function, with a non-empty choice set for every finite, non-empty set, is the acyclicity of $R$ (see Lemma 1*1 in my *Collective Choice and Social Welfare* (San Francisco: Holden-Day, 1970; reprinted, Amsterdam: North-Holland, 1980), p. 16)).

markets, the form can be quite different in non-competitive market situations,[6] and in choices other than that of pure consumption, e.g., of voters or of government bureaucracies.[7]

There is, in fact, a deeper methodological issue in the use of consistency axioms for choices over budget sets only. In so far as the consistency conditions represent *axioms* of the system, there is no reason why such consistency should not be demanded over all choices that could, in principle, arise— irrespective of whether such choices could be observed in market behaviour. However, in so far as the consistency conditions are taken as *hypotheses* to be tested, the issue of observation is important. But the possibility of actual testing of these consistency conditions of choice in markets is very limited.[8] Aside from other observational difficulties, there is a temporal problem. Over short periods people may seek variety (fish today and steak tomorrow is not inconsistent), but over longer periods tastes can easily change (apparent inconsistencies may then reflect instead a changing choice function). The popularity of an axiom such as the Weak Axiom of Revealed Preference is not really due to any decisive empirical support it has received— the tests have been very limited—but primarily due to its *intuitive* reasonableness as an axiom of choice behaviour. But as an *axiom* of choice behaviour—rather than as a hypothesis under testing—it is not at all clear why it should be assumed to apply only over choices that can, in fact, be observed (in this case, in individual behaviour in markets), rather than generally over all choices that can, in principle, arise.

If the consistency requirement is not exclusively confined to budget-set choices but applied to choices over all subsets,[9] the structure of revealed preference theory changes a great deal from its traditional format.[10] For

6. See T. Majumdar, 'Revealed Preference and the Demand Theorem in a Not-Necessarily Competitive Market', *Quarterly Journal of Economics,* **83** (1969).

7. For a far-reaching probe into the preferences revealed by governmental decisions, see K. Basu, *Revealed Preference of Governments* (Cambridge: Cambridge University Press, 1979).

8. See J. Kornai, *Anti-Equilibrium* (Amsterdam: North-Holland 1971); Essays 2 and 4 reprinted here; F. Hahn and M. Hollis (eds), *Philosophy and Economic Theory* (Oxford: Oxford University Press, 1979).

9. In fact, for the formal results presented in Essay 1, and many related ones, it is sufficient that the domain of the choice function includes all finite subsets (in most cases it is sufficient to include all pairs and triples), irrespective of whether other subsets are also included.

10. Non-budget-set choice functions were studied by Kenneth Arrow, 'Rational Choice Functions and Orderings', *Economica,* **26** (1959). Essay 1 extends Arrow's investigation and goes into motivational justification and also into factorization. See also H. S. Houthakker, 'On the Logic of Preference and Choice', in A. Tymieniecka (ed.), *Contributions to Logic and Methodology in Honor of J. M. Bochenski* (Amsterdam: North-Holland, 1956); S. Afriat, 'Principles of Choice and Preference', Research Paper No. 160, Department of Economics, Purdue University, 1967; B. Hansson, 'Choice Structures and Preference Relations', *Synthese,* **18** (1968); P. K. Pattanaik, 'A Note on Democratic Decisions and the Existence of Choice Sets', *Review of Economic Studies,* **35** (1968); Essay 6 ('Quasi-transitivity, Rational Choice and Collective Decisions') reprinted in this volume; and my *Collective Choice and Social Welfare* (1970), chapter 1*.

example, the weak axiom of revealed preference can be shown to be *equivalent* to the strong axiom, and quite sufficient for transitivity of the generated preference relation, and in Essay 1 reproduced in this volume, a great many distinct conditions are shown to be exactly equivalent. The requirements of weaker regularity conditions of preference—in particular acyclicity and quasi-transitivity—are also similarly analysed.[11] The exercise is further pursued in Section 4 of Essay 8.

In the context of general choice functions, it is useful to factorize the requirements for the various regularity conditions of preference into constituent parts, and Essay 1 presents such factorizations.[12] One important distinction that emerges in Essay 1 is that between conditions—such as Property $\alpha$—that insist on 'contraction consistency' (in the sense that they require that a chosen alternative must continue to be chosen as the 'menu' from which the choice is to be made is—in some particular way—contracted), and conditions—such as $\beta$ and $\gamma$—that insist on 'expansion consistency' (in the sense that they require that a chosen alternative must continue to be chosen as the menu from which the choice is to be made is—in some particular way—expanded). In fact, in the context of Arrow-type impossibility theorems, this distinction proves to be crucial (as is shown in Essay 8, 'Social Choice Theory: A Re-examination', also reprinted here). Indeed, Arrow's impossibility result and related ones can be shown to be thoroughly dependent on contraction consistency and essentially independent of expansion consistency (see also Section 2.2 below).

Another distinction explored in Essay 1 that proves to be rather central to social-choice impossibility results is that between Samuelson's 'revealed preference' relation $R$ (with $x \, R \, y$ if and only if $x$ is chosen when $y$ is available) and the pair-choice relation $\bar{R}$, sometimes called the 'base relation'[13] (with $x \, \bar{R} \, y$ if and only if $x$ is chosen from the pair $x, y$). It emerges that the regularity properties of the base relation are immediately relevant to impossibility results of the Arrow type, whereas those required of the revealed preference relation can in one sense be satisfied without violating Arrow's conditions and related ones (see Essay 8 reprinted here, and also Section 2.2 of this Introduction).

In these various ways Essay 1 is concerned with some of the most elemen-

11. In recent years these and other regularity properties have come to be extensively investigated in the context of general choice functions by E. Bergstrom, J. H. Blau, D. Blair and R. Pollak, G. Bordes, R. Deb, P. C. Fishburn, H. Herzberger, D. T. Jamison and L. J. Lau, S. Kanger, J. S. Kelly, D. Kelsey, A. Mukherji, R. R. Parks, C. R. Plott, T. Schwartz, T. E. Smith, K. Suzumura, M. Walker, R. Wilson, among others.

12. In recent years these and other types of factorization have been extensively investigated by D. Blair, G. Bordes, P. C. Fishburn, S. Fuchs-Seliger, H. Herzberger, J. S. Kelly, Y. Matsumoto, R. R. Parks, C. R. Plott, J. Richelson, T. Schwartz, M. Sertel and A. van der Bellen, M. Sjöberg, K. Suzumura, among others.

13. See H. G. Herzberger, 'Ordinal Preference and Rational Choice', *Econometrica*, **41** (1973).

tary issues of choice theory. However, it does not view preference as anything other than what transpires from choice, and it belongs to the tradition of seeing preference as tied completely to choice, dispensing with the need for an empirical or normative (and not just logical) investigation of the relation between choice and preference. The other three essays in Part I are concerned with different aspects of those substantive questions.

It is, however, worth mentioning that the technical results in Essay 1—and in contributions by others in a similar framework—are not all lost even when preference is given an existence of its own as an introspective concept. The results then need to be interpreted *either* (1) as dealing exclusively with the *binary relation of choice* which does not necessarily coincide with the introspective notion of 'preference', *or* (2) as dealing with the introspective notion of preference under empirical or normative assumptions guaranteeing 'preferential' choice. The former is, of course, quite the natural format for *institutional* social choice theory, and in that context no introspective social preference need be invoked. There is no obvious inadequacy there. The latter approach, on the other hand, fits in well with the traditional assumptions regarding personal behaviour, especially in economic theory. However, Essays 2, 3 and 4 question the sagacity of that common tradition, and in the next section the latter approach is discussed in the context of personal choice.

## 1.2 *Beyond consistency*

While consistency is taken in economic theory to be a necessary condition of rationality, it is usual to supplement that requirement by some substantive view as to what the individual would maximize. The regularity of consistent pursuit of self-interest is a frequently used assumption of rational behaviour.

Though only a few authors have discussed this assumption explicitly (Edgeworth is one who did),[14] it is implicitly present in much of traditional economic theory. For example, in general equilibrium theory,[15] in establishing the correspondence of equilibria with Pareto optimality, 'preference' plays the dual role of determining individual decisions (it coincides with revealed preference in this role) and serving as the basis of Pareto optimality judgements (it reflects individual welfare in this role). Together this amounts to assuming that individual choices are guided exclusively by the requirements of maximizing the respective individual welfares.

That assumption may not be particularly unrealistic in some types of choices, but there is little evidence that all choices in *economic* matters fall in

14. F. Y. Edgeworth, *Mathematical Psychics: An Essay on the Application of Mathematics to the Moral Sciences* (London, 1881).

15. See, for example, G. Debreu, *Theory of Value* (New York: Wiley, 1959); K. J. Arrow and F. H. Hahn, *General Competitive Analysis* (San Francisco: Holden-Day, 1971; reprinted Amsterdam: North-Holland, 1980).

that category. Decisions regarding work ethics, job choice, where to live, whether to strike, etc., might well be partly influenced by values other than maximization of perceived individual welfare. Essays 2, 3 and 4 go into this question from various perspectives.

There is no point in repeating in this Introduction the arguments that are presented in the reprinted essays, but some general remarks might be useful.

First, it is important to distinguish between the assumption of individual-welfare maximization as a *rationality* condition and that as an *empirical* assumption as to how people actually do behave. Both the uses can be found in traditional economic theory. While both may be—and indeed are—questionable, they are not questionable on the same grounds. Essay 2 ('Behaviour and the Concept of Preference') is mainly concerned with the empirical question, whereas Essay 4 ('Rational Fools') goes into both the questions.[16]

Second, the interdependence between different people's welfare may make the pursuit of individual interests produce inferior results for all, *in terms of those very interests*. This problem, which is nowadays illustrated with the 'Prisoner's Dilemma' game, had been clearly perceived much earlier, and played an important part in—say—Hobbes's and Rousseau's treatment of the state.[17] Since the problem is quite central to many economic

16. On related issues see my *Collective Choice and Social Welfare* (1970), chapter 1; T. Nagel, *The Possibility of Altruism* (Oxford: Clarendon Press, 1970); F. Hirsch, *Social Limits to Growth* (Cambridge, Mass.: Harvard University Press, 1976); H. Leibenstein, *Beyond Economic Man: A New Foundation for Microeconomics* (Cambridge, Mass.: Harvard University Press, 1976); T. Scitovsky, *The Joyless Economy* (Oxford: Oxford University Press, 1976); J. Elster, *Ulysses and the Sirens* (Cambridge: Cambridge University Press, 1979); A. O. Hirschman, *Shifting Involvements* (Princeton: Princeton University Press, 1982); H. Margolis, *Selfishness, Altruism, and Rationality* (Cambridge: Cambridge University Press, 1982).

17. On this see W. J. Baumol, *Welfare Economics and the Theory of the State* (Cambridge, Mass.: Harvard University Press, 1955), and W. G. Runciman and A. K. Sen, 'Games, Justice and the General Will', *Mind*, **74** (1965). The 'prisoner's dilemma' was presented by R. D. Luce and H. Raiffa, *Games and Decisions* (New York: Wiley, 1958). On related issues see A. K. Sen, 'On Optimizing the Rate of Saving', *Economic Journal*,**71** (1961); S.A. Marglin, 'The Social Rate of Discount and the Optimal Rate of Investment', *Quarterly Journal of Economics*, **77** (1963); M. Olson, *The Logic of Collective Action* (Cambridge, Mass.: Harvard University Press, 1965); A. Rapoport and A. M. Chammah, *Prisoner's Dilemma: A Study in Conflict and Cooperation* (Ann Arbor: University of Michigan Press, 1965); A. K. Sen, 'Isolation, Assurance and the Social Rate of Discount', *Quarterly Journal of Economics*, **81** (1967); J. W. N. Watkins, 'Imperfect Rationality', in R. Borger and F. Cioffi (eds), *Explanation in the Behavioural Sciences* (Cambridge: Cambridge University Press, 1970); N. Howard, *Paradoxes of Rationality* (Cambridge, Mass.: MIT Press, 1971); P. J. Hammond, 'Charity: Altruism or Cooperative Egoism?', in E. S. Phelps (ed.), *Altruism, Morality and Economic Theory* (New York: Russell Sage, 1975); K. Basu, 'Information and Strategy in Iterated Prisoner's Dilemma', *Theory and Decision*, **8** (1977); E. Ullman-Margalit, *The Emergence of Norms* (Oxford: Clarendon Press, 1977); M. Black, 'The "Prisoner's Dilemma" and the Limits of Rationality', *International Studies in Philosophy*, **10** (1978); I. Levi, *The Enterprise of Knowledge* (Cambridge, Mass.: MIT Press, 1980); D. H. Regan, *Utilitarianism and Cooperation* (Oxford: Clarendon Press, 1980); D. Parfit, 'Prudence, Morality, and the Prisoner's Dilemma', *Proceedings of the British Academy for 1979* (London: Oxford University Press, 1981).

issues, it is important to consider the use of norms in economic behaviour (see Essays 2 and 3). Indeed, every member of the group might be better off with a norm involving systematic deviation from individual-welfare maximization, and Essay 3 ('Choice, Orderings and Morality') provides a format for analysing and thinking about such interdependence-oriented norms. The concept of meta-rankings (ranking of rankings) is introduced in this context.[18]

Third, while the Chinese attempt at doing away with incentives on an extremely broad front has been abandoned as a failure, the issues involved in that debate—discussed in Essay 3—remain important. Also, as argued in Essay 4, norm-based behaviour is both useful and—to a varying extent— actually used in many different spheres of economic activity—influencing the functioning of cooperatives, unions, business firms, and other organiza-tions, both in socialist and capitalist economies.[19] Variability of such norms is, in fact, often invoked to explain international differences of work behaviour and productivity (e.g., in contrasting Japan and Britain), and while this is typically done in an *ad hoc* way, the underlying issue is a very general one, and requires more systematic treatment.

Fourth, the contrast between 'sympathy' and 'commitment' introduced in Essay 4 ('Rational Fools') is relevant in seeing how others figure in one's actions. Sympathy—including antipathy when it is negative—refers to one

---

18. For discussion, criticism, application and extension of the approach of meta-rankings, see K. Baier, 'Rationality and Morality', *Erkenntnis,* **11** (1977); A. K. Sen, 'Rationality and Morality: A Reply', *Erkenntnis,* **11** (1977); A. K. Sen, 'Informational Analysis of Moral Principles', in R. Harrison (ed.), *Rational Action* (Cambridge:   Cambridge University Press, 1979); R. E. Goodin, 'Censored Utility Functions', Workshop on the General Will and Common Good, ECPR, Brussels, 1979 (Essex University); M. Hollis, 'Rational Man and Social Science', in R. Harrison (ed.), *Rational Action* (Cambridge: Cambridge University Press, 1979); M. S. McPherson, 'Mills Moral Theory and the Problem of Preference Change', *Ethics,* **92** (1982), and 'Want Formation, Morality and the Interpretative Dimension of Economic Inquiry', Research Paper RP–33, Williams College, 1979; G. A. Gigliotti, 'Values, Tastes and Rights Respecting', Discussion Paper 80–20, and 'Higher Pleasures, Values and Tastes', Discussion Paper 80–21, Bureau of Economic Research, Rutgers University, 1980; T. Majumdar, 'The Rationality of Changing Choice', *Analyse und Kritik,* **2** (1980); P. K. Pattanaik, 'A Note on the "Rationality of Becoming" and Revealed Preference', *Analyse und Kritik,* **2**(1980); G. C. Winston, 'Addiction and Backsliding: A Theory of Compulsive Consumption', *Journal of Economic Behaviour and Organization,* **1** (1980); M. Hollis, 'Economic Man and the Original Sin', *Political Studies,* **29** (1981); L. Putterman, 'Incentives and the Kibbutz: Towards an Economics of Communal Work Motivation', Working Paper 81-24, Brown University, 1981; N. Baigent, 'Social Choice Corres-pondences', *Recherches Economiques de Louvain,* **46** (1980), and 'Rational Choice and the Taxation of Sin', *Journal of Public Economics,* **16**(1981); R. J. van der Veen, 'Meta-rankings and Collective Optimality', *Social Science Information,* **20**  (1981); Hirschman, *Shifting Involve-ments* (1982), chapter 4; Margolis, *Selfishness, Altruism, and Rationality* (1982).

19. See, among others, A. K. Sen, 'Labour Allocation in a Cooperative Enterprise', *Review of Economic Studies,* **33** (1966); J. Vanek, *The General Theory of Labour-Managed Market Economies* (Ithaca, NY: Cornell University Press, 1970); B. Ward, 'Organization and Compara-tive Economics', in A. Eckstein (ed.), *Comparison of Economic Systems* (Berkeley, Calif.: University of California Press, 1971); N. E. Cameron, 'Incentives and Labour Supply in

person's welfare being affected by the position of others (e.g., feeling depressed at the sight of misery). Commitment, on the other hand, is concerned with breaking the tight link between individual welfare (with or without sympathy) and the choice of action (e.g., acting to help remove some misery even though one personally does not suffer from it). Sympathy alone does not require any departure from individual-welfare maximization: but commitment does involve rejection of that assumption.

Fifth, while 'commitment' may relate to the working of some universalized morality, it need not necessarily be so broad-based. Indeed, a sense of commitment to one's community, race, class, fellow-workers, fellow-oligopolists, etc., could be important in the choice of actions. Such relations already do, in fact, figure—typically in a rather *ad hoc* way—in various branches of economic theory.

Sixth, there are several related but different statements about a person's interests, actions, etc., that need to be distinguished, even though they are often identified in the literature:

(1)    the person gets more satisfaction in state $x$ than in state $y$ (statement about satisfaction or pleasure);

(2)    the person thinks that he or she is better off with $x$ than with $y$ (statement about introspective welfare);

(3)    the person is better off with $x$ than with $y$ (statement about individual welfare which may or may not be introspective);

(4)    the person prefers that $x$ rather than $y$ occurs (statement about the mental condition of preference, or desire, regarding states);

(5)    the person would like to so choose that $x$ rather than $y$ occurs (statement about desired choice);

Cooperative Enterprises', *Canadian Journal of Economics,* 6 (1973); A. K. Sen, *On Economic Inequality* (Oxford: Clarendon Press, 1973), chapter 4; J. E. Meade, 'Preference Orderings and Economic Policy', in A. Mitra (ed.), *Economic Theory and Planning: Essays in Honour of A. K. Dasgupta* (London: Oxford University Press, 1974); C. Riskin, 'Incentive Systems and Work Motivations: The Experience of China', *Working Papers for a New Society,* 1 (1974); E. S. Phelps (ed.), *Altruism, Morality and Economic Theory* (New York: Russel Sage, 1975); J. M. Montias, *The Structure of Economic Systems* (New Haven: Yale University Press, 1976); T. Wilson and A. S. Skinner (eds), *The Market and the State* (Oxford: Clarendon Press, 1976); M. D. Berman, 'Short-run Efficiency in the Labor-Managed Firm', *Journal of Comparative Economics,* 1 (1977); J. P. Bonin, 'Work Incentives and Uncertainty on a Collective Farm', *Journal of Comparative Economics,* 1 (1977); D. L. Chinn, 'Team Cohesion and Collective Labour Supply in Chinese Agriculture', *Journal of Comparative Economics,* 3 (1979); L. D. Israelson, 'Collectives, Communes, and Incentives', *Journal of Comparative Economics,* 4 (1980); L. Putterman, 'Voluntary Collectivization: A Model of Producers' Institutional Choice', *Journal of Comparative Economics,* 4 (1980); L. Putterman, 'On Optimality in Collective Institutional Choice', *Journal of Comparative Economics,* 5 (1981); T. Ishikawa, 'The Emulation Effect as a Determinant of Work Motivation', mimeographed, University of Tokyo, 1981; R.C.O. Matthews, 'Morality, Competition and Efficiency', *Manchester School,* 49 (1981). See also Michio Morishima's recent study, *Why has Japan 'Succeeded'? Western Technology and Japanese Ethos* (Cambridge: Cambridge University Press, 1982).

(6)    the person believes that it would be right to so choose that $x$ rather than $y$ occurs (statement about normative judgement regarding choice);

(7)    the person believes that it would be better if $x$ were to occur rather than $y$ (statement about normative judgement regarding states of affairs);

(8)    the person so chooses that $x$ rather than $y$ occurs (statement about actual choice).

None of these statements logically entails any of the others, and it is a matter for substantive empirical or normative analysis to check how in particular cases any two of these statements link with each other.[20] The thoroughly methodical person who chooses with impeccable consistency but does not distinguish between different issues (such as those outlined above), has been characterized as the 'rational fool' (Essay 4). In one form or another, the rational fool is invoked a great deal in economic theory.

Seventh, one reason for the tendency in economics to concentrate only on the 'revealed preference' relation is a methodological suspicion regarding introspective concepts. Choice is seen as solid information, whereas introspection is not open to observation. This narrowly behaviourist view is critically scrutinized in Essay 2 ('Behaviour and the Concept of Preference'). Even as behaviourism this is peculiarly limited since *verbal* behaviour (or *writing* behaviour, including response to questionnaires) should not lie outside the scope of the behaviourist approach. Much of economic theory seems to be concerned with strong, silent men who never speak! One has to sneak in behind them to see what they are doing in the market, etc., and deduce from it what they prefer, what makes them better off, what they think is right, and so on. There is, of course, the problem of ascertaining the veracity of communication, e.g., in responses to questionnaires, but the difficulties of *strategic non-verbal* choice behaviour (departing from preference) are serious too.[21] It is argued in Essay 2 that in economic theory 'we have been prone, on the one hand, to overstate the difficulties of introspection and

---

20. In addition to Essays 2 and 4, see also my 'Plural Utility', *Proceedings of the Aristotelian Society,* **81** (1980–81), and 'Rights and Agency', *Philosophy and Public Affairs,* **11** (1982).

21. The possibility (and under some assumptions, the ubiquity) of strategic distortions—originally discussed by Arrow, Dummet, Farquharson, Hurwicz, Samuelson and Vickrey—has recently been probed at great depth in the context of various types of choices, e.g., voting (the Gibbard–Satterthwaite theorem), resource allocation (Hurwicz's impossibility result), and there is an extensive literature in this area. I have discussed some of the more general issues in my 'Strategies and Revelation: Informational Constraints in Public Decisions', in J. J. Laffont (ed.), *Aggregation and Revelation of Preferences* (Amsterdam: North-Holland, 1979). Good technical accounts can be found in P. K. Pattanaik, *Strategy and Group Choice* (Amsterdam: North-Holland, 1978); H. Moulin, *The Strategy of Social Choice* (Amsterdam: North-Holland, forthcoming); B. Peleg, *Some Theoretic Analysis of Voting in Committees* (Cambridge: Cambridge University Press, forthcoming); J. J. Laffont and E. Maskin, 'The Theory of Incentives: An Overview', mimeographed, Université des Sciences Sociales de Toulouse, 1981.

communication, and on the other, to underestimate the problems of studying preferences revealed by observed behaviour'. Finally, even if it were the case that market choice provides the only solid basis of information, it would still be illegitimate to equate fundamentally different questions just on grounds that we have information on one but not on the others. Happily, silent choice is not the only source of information, and Essays 2 and 4 discuss the possibility of expanding the informational base for studying preference, welfare and norms.

## 2   Preference Aggregation

### 2.1   Restricted preferences

Modern welfare economics has been deeply influenced by Kenneth Arrow's 'general possibility theorem', showing the impossibility of aggregating individual preference orderings into a social order satisfying certain conditions of reasonableness.[22] The four essays in Part II deal with that and related aggregation problems. Arrow defines a social welfare function as a functional relation which specifies one social ordering $R$ for any set (in fact, $n$-tuple) of individual preference orderings—one per person (with $n$ people in the society): $R = f(R_1, \ldots, R_n)$. Arrow's four conditions demand, respectively that: (1) the domain of the function should include any conceivable $n$-tuple of individual preference orderings (unrestricted domain); (2) if everyone prefers any $x$ to any $y$, then that $x$ is socially preferred to that $y$ (weak Pareto principle); (3) no individual is a dictator in the sense that whenever he prefers any $x$ to any $y$, it must be the case that $x$ is socially preferred to $y$ (non-dictatorship); and (4) the social ranking of any pair $(x, y)$ depends on individual rankings of that pair only (independence of irrelevant alternatives).[23] An intuitively explained proof of Arrow's theorem can be found in a later essay in this volume, viz., Essay 15 ('Personal Utilities and Public Judgements: Or What's Wrong with Welfare Economics?'), pp. 331–4, which discusses that proof in the context of pursuing a critique of the informational basis of traditional welfare economics—an issue that will be taken up later in this Introduction.

One possible solution, which Arrow himself has explored, is that of dropping the condition of unrestricted domain. The method of majority decision clearly satisifies the three conditions other than unrestricted domain,

---

22. K. J. Arrow, *Social Choice and Individual Values* (New York: Wiley, 1951; 2nd edition, 1963).

23. This is the second version of Arrow's 'impossibility theorem', presented in the second edition of his book. The independence condition is defined here in purely relational terms (like Arrow's other conditions), though Arrow himself used a choice-functional form, which happens to be exactly equivalent, in his framework, to the above relational statement.

but yields intransitive social preferences for some $n$-tuples of individual preference orderings. Duncan Black and Kenneth Arrow showed that if the individual preference combinations are 'single-peaked', then the majority relation must be transitive, if the number of individuals happens to be odd.[24] Single-peakedness is a domain restriction that permits only those individual preference combinations such that the alternatives can be arranged in a way that would make everyone's utility curve (preference intensity) have one peak only. Other sufficient conditions for transitive majority rule were identified by Inada, Vickrey and Ward.

Essay 5 offered a generalization of all these conditions in the form of 'value restricted' preferences. There is no particular point in discussing in this Introduction the exact content of value restriction, or how it relates respectively to the other conditions of which it is a generalization, since all this is discussed extensively in Essay 5.[25]

However, three limitations of the result in Essay 5 are worth noting. First, the result concerns full transitivity of strict preference whereas regularity properties such as quasi-transitivity or acyclicity are adequate for there being a majority *winner* in every finite subset (acyclicity is, in fact, exactly necessary and sufficient for that). Transitivity is not the only interesting issue, and indeed in the context of choice it is in an obvious sense a much less interesting issue than acyclicity of the majority preference relation. Second, the peculiar—almost eerie—requirement in the conditions proposed by Arrow, Inada, Vickrey and Ward that the number of individuals (more strictly the number of non-indifferent individuals) be odd is also present in the generalization offered in Essay 5, and this makes this whole route or solution rather *ad hoc*. Third, value restriction is only a sufficient condition, not also a necessary one. Other sufficiency conditions can be found.

24. R. D. Black, *The Theory of Committees and Elections* (Cambridge: Cambridge University Press, 1958); Arrow, *Social Choice and Individual Values* (1951), chapter VII.

25. There have been many further contributions on related lines. Aside from Essay 6 in this volume published in 1969, see K. Inada, 'On the Simple Majority Decision Rule', *Econometrica,* 37 (1969); K. Inada, 'Majority Rule and Rationality', *Journal of Economic Theory,* 2 (1970); P. K. Pattanaik, *Voting and Collective Choice* (Cambridge: Cambridge University Press, 1971); P. C. Fishburn, *The Theory of Social Choice* (Princeton: Princeton University Press, 1973); R. Saposnik, 'On Transitivity of the Social Preference Relation under simple Majority Rule', *Journal of Economic Theory,* 10 (1975); M. Salles, 'A General Possibility Theorem for Group Decision Rules with Pareto Transitivity', *Journal of Economic Theory,* 11 (1975); C. R. Plott, 'Axiomatic Social Choice Theory: An Overview and Interpretation', *American Journal of Political Science,* 20 (1976); J. S. Kelly, *Arrow Impossibility Theorems* (New York: Academic Press, 1978); J. M. Grandmont, 'Intermediate Preferences and Majority Rule', *Econometrica,* 46 (1978); W. Gaertner and A. Heinecke, 'On Two Sufficient Conditions for Transitivity of the Social Preference Relation', *Nationalokonomie,* 37 (1978); S. Slutsky, 'A Characterisation of Societies with Consistent Majority Decision', *Review of Economic Studies,* 44 (1977). There have been many other interesting contributions as well.

The first two problems are dealt with in Section 3 of Essay 6 ('Quasi-transitivity, Rational Choice and Collective Decisions') where it is shown that value restriction is sufficient for *acyclic* majority relations, i.e., for the existence of majority winners, *irrespective* of whether the number of individuals is odd or even.

The third limitation is removed in Essay 7 ('Necessary and Sufficient Conditions for Rational Choice under Majority Decision'), written jointly with Prasanta Pattanaik. For this class of restrictions, necessary and sufficient conditions for acyclicity of the majority relation are identified (this turns out to be satisfying either 'value restriction', or at least one of two other identified conditions, viz., 'extremal restriction' and 'limited agreement'). Necessary and sufficient conditions are found also for the special case of 'strict' (i.e., antisymmetric) individual preferences (value restriction is exactly the necessary and sufficient condition in this case). The necessary and sufficient condition for fully transitive majority preference is also identified (extremal restriction in this case).[26] Essay 7 also shows that the adequacy of value restriction and limited agreement extend well beyond the majority rule, and they apply to whole classes of rules with certain general characteristics.

It is clear that these results can be interpreted as being 'comforting' typically only in those choice situations in which the set of alternatives is rather limited, e.g., choosing between a few candidates in an election, or deciding in an assembly between some alternative proposals. In the economic problems of allocation and distribution involving a rich commodity space, there is little chance that the required conditions will be fulfilled. Indeed, it is easily checked that even for the elementary problem of the distribution of a given cake between three or more persons (with each preferring more cake for himself), the majority preference relation will be intransitive, and furthermore will violate the milder requirement of acyclicity. (It follows, of course, immediately that these far-from-pathological preferences will violate the identified restrictions since these restrictions are—by virtue of the *sufficiency* parts of the theorems—adequate for guaranteeing acyclicity of the

---

26. This exercise of finding necessary and sufficient domain restrictions for transitivity of social preference can be extended from the case of the majority relation to that of any rule satisfying Arrow's Pareto principle, non-dictatorating and independence. See E. Kalai and E. Muller, 'Characterization Functions and Nonmanipulable Voting Procedures', *Journal of Economic Theory,* **16** (1977); E. Kalai and Z. Ritz, 'Characterization of Private Alternative Domains Admitting Arrow Social Welfare Functions', *Journal of Economic Theory,* **22** (1980); E. Maskin, 'Social Welfare Functions on Restricted Domain', *Review of Economic Studies,* forthcoming; G. Chichilnisky and G. Heal, 'Necessary and Sufficient Conditions for a Resolution of the Social Choice Paradox', mimeographed, University of Essex, 1981.

majority relation.[27]) As a social welfare function to be used in welfare economics, the method of majority decision offers very little. Indeed, the *necessity* parts of the theorems help to show the severity of the required restrictions and their typical unsatisfiability in welfare economic problems. While the domain conditions such as value restriction require only 'a comparatively limited measure of agreement' (as it is put in Essay 5), that agreement is much too ambitious for welfare economics, and offers scope for optimism only in some other contexts, e.g., in some political decision problems involving aggregation of individual judgements concerning the relative merits of a few alternative candidates (or proposals). Essay 7 serves to bring out the demanding preconditions of consistent majority decisions through identifying the *necessity* requirements.

The failure of majority rule to deal consistently with welfare economic problems is not really a cause for mourning. As argued in Essay 8 ('Social Choice Theory: A Re-examination') the method of majority decision is a most peculiar way of dealing with conflicts of interest. Even in ranking just one pair of alternative social states, in which context the problem of intransitivity or cyclicity does not arise, majority rule is a terribly gross method. To illustrate, in the cake division problem, with any given division of the cake, take away half the share of the worst-off person and divide the loot among the rest. We have just made a majority 'improvement'. If we are ambitious and want *more* social improvement, we repeat the exercise! The majority rule cannot really serve as the basis of welfare economic judgements dealing with interest conflicts, and this can be seen even without considering the question of consistency at all. (The basic issue here, which relates to the 'informational basis' of majority rule, and which applies to all Arrovian social welfare rules, is considered more generally in Section 3.1.)

The method of majority decision, then, just isn't a plausible social welfare function for welfare economics, and it wouldn't have been of much interest to welfare economics even if it were consistent. Types of aggregation problems are distinguished in Essay 8, and among the distinctions considered is the one between aggregating individual *interests* (as in, say, the cake-division problem) and aggregating individual *judgements,* e.g., regarding public welfare or institutional policy (as in, say, committee decisions or

---

27. G. H. Kramer shows explicitly—rather than by implication—that 'the Sen–Pattanaik conditions' will be violated over a wide class of welfare economic problems ('On a Class of Equilibrium Conditions for Majority Rule', *Econometrica,* **41** (1973)). There have been a great many contributions on related themes involving majority rule over commodity spaces representing allocation and distribution possibilities. Similar grounds for 'pessimism' hold also for the corresponding conditions for *any* Arrovian rule, e.g., the conditions identified by Maskin, Kalai and Muller, Kalai and Ritz, and Chichilnisky and Heal.

political elections). The gross method of aggregation used by majority rule—
it is argued in Essay 8—is less plausible for the former than possibly for the
latter. It is, therefore, of some interest that the preference restrictions shown
to be necessary and sufficient for consistent majority decision in Essay 6 are
also less plausible for the former than for the latter.

## 2.2   *Social intransitivity and non-binariness*

Essay 6 ('Quasi-transitivity, Rational Choice and Collective Decisions')
explores a different way of avoiding Arrow's impossibility problem. Rather
than restricting the domain of the social welfare function, it is possible to
expand 'the range' of it, by dropping the insistence that social preference be
fully transitive. Since full transitivity is unnecessary for preference-based
choice, the weaker requirement of acyclicity being adequate for it (discussed
already in Section 1.1, 'Consistency and revealed preference'), it is not
entirely unreasonable in the context of social *choice* to demand that Arrow's
requirement of transitivity of social preference be replaced by the milder
condition of acyclicity.[28] This relaxation leads to a more general type of
function, called a 'social decision function' (SDF), of which a social welfare
function is a special case.[29] It is demonstrated in Essay 6 that the four conditions proposed by Arrow can all be satisfied for a social decision function.
Indeed, the weakening of social transitivity need not go as far as acyclicity,
since all the Arrow conditions can be met even with *quasi-transitive* social
preference, dropping only the insistence on transitivity of indifference.

This was seen in Essay 6 as a technical result of some interest—suggesting
the need for further investigation—but very far from a 'resolution' of the
Arrow problem. 'Two notes of caution' were emphasized 'lest we jubilate
too much at the disappearance of Arrow's impossibility result for social
decision functions.' The first of the two notes of caution pointed out that the

28. See A. K. Sen, 'Planner's Preferences: Optimality, Distribution and Social Welfare',
presented at the International Economic Association Roundtable Conference at Biarritz in
1966, published in J. Margolis and H. Guitton (eds), *Public Economics* (London: Macmillan,
1969), and P. K. Pattanaik, 'A Note on Democratic Decisions and the Existence of Choice
Sets', *Review of Economic Studies*, **35** (1968).

29. There is a slight ambiguity here. In fact, in Essay 6 a 'social decision function' was
characterized as a rule 'the range of which is restricted to only those binary relations $R$ each of
which generates a choice function ... over the entire $X$ [the set of social states]' (p. 125). It is
only with the further assumption that $X$ is finite that this becomes equivalent to the definition
used here requiring the generated binary relation $R$ to be reflexive, complete and acyclic. The
difference is not, in fact, very important in the present context since the relevant arguments do
not deal with infinte sets. Indeed, while the concept of a 'social decision function' was first introduced in the literature in Essay 6, the more common definition of it by now is the variant used
here (see, for example, J. H. Blau and R. Deb, 'Social Decision Functions and the Veto',
*Econometrica*, **45** (1977) ).

four Arrow conditions were proposed by him as being '*necessary* for a reasonable social choice mechanism; he did not claim this set to be *sufficient* for it' (Essay 6, p. 128). It was pointed out that the example in terms of which the theorem asserting the satisfiability of the Arrow conditions for a social decision function is proved was, in fact, 'unattractive to most of us', and other conditions must be imposed for a reasonable social choice procedure. The actual example involved everyone having a 'veto' in the sense that if anyone strictly preferred any $x$ to any $y$ that would make $x$ to be socially at least as good as $y$. Allan Gibbard soon proved that for all social decision functions satisfying Arrow's four conditions and yielding quasi-transitive social preference at least one person must have a veto,[30] and thus the noted 'unattractiveness' is, in fact, inescapable. A non-veto condition—in the same spirit as Arrow's non-dictatorship requirement (but stronger)—would re-establish the impossibility.

That veto result re-occurs in subsequent contributions even without quasi-transitivity but with additional conditions (such as 'positive responsiveness') imposed on social decision functions.[31] There was indeed rather limited reason for jubilation at the technical disappearance of Arrow's impossibility. However, the precise role of transitivity and other regularity conditions of social preference in generating Arrow-type impossibility results got fairly thoroughly investigated as a consequence of this line of inquiry, and appropriate axiomatic derivations of various types of *special power* were developed in this context.[32]

The second 'note of caution' introduced in Essay 6 points to the possibility that 'we might wish to impose certain rationality conditions on the choice

30. 'Intransitive Social Indifference and the Arrow Dilemma', unpublished manuscript, 1969; reported in my *Collective Choice and Social Welfare* (1970), pp. 49–50. In fact, Gibbard proved the existence of an 'oligarchy', with every member of the oligarchy having a veto and all members of the oligarchy together being decisive. The example used in the proof of the possibility of a social decision function satisfying all of Arrow's conditions (theorem V in Essay 7) corresponds to an 'oligarchy' of all individuals. Ashok Guha established the existence of a hierarchy of oligarchies, on the basis of slightly stronger assumptions; see A. Guha, 'Neutrality, Monotonicity and the Right of Veto', *Econometrica, 40* (1972), and J. H. Blau, 'Neutrality, Monotonicity and the Right of Veto: A Comment', *Econometrica, 44* (1976).

31. See A. Mas-Colell and H. Sonnenschein, 'General Possibility Theorem for Group Decisions', *Review of Economic Studies, 39* (1972); D. J. Brown, 'Aggregation of Preferences', *Quarterly Journal of Economics, 89* (1975); D. J. Brown, 'Acyclic Aggregation over a Finite Set of Alternatives', Cowles Foundation Discussion Paper No. 391, 1975; B. Hansson, 'The Existence of Group Preferences', *Public Choice, 28* (1976); J. H. Blau and R. Deb, 'Social Decision Functions and the Veto', *Econometrica, 45* (1977).

32. In addition to the oligarchy and veto theorems referred to above, important results have been established recently about partial vetoes and group vetoes on the basis of acyclity itself without the additional assumptions needed for the existence of an individual vetoer (see D. H. Blair and R. A. Pollak, 'Acyclic Collective Choice Rules', mimeographed, University of Pennsylvania, 1980, and D. Kelsey, 'Acyclic Social Choice', M.Phil. thesis, Oxford University, 1981).

functions generated by the SDF' (p. 129). Such 'rationality' conditions might make the underlying social preference transitive, in which case the Arrow result will, of course, re-emerge fully.[33] The insistence on 'rationality' (consistency) conditions becomes particularly significant when social choice takes the form of a choice function which need not necessarily be based on—or be representable by—a binary relation ('preference').

In Essay 8 a 'functional collective choice rule' is defined as a functional relation that determines a choice function $C(\cdot)$ for the society for any $n$-tuple of individual preference orderings: $C(\cdot) = f(R_1, \ldots, R_n)$. This is essentially equivalent to a 'social choice function' as defined by Peter Fishburn,[34] and differs from it only in presentation, in separating out the 'choice function'—in the usual sense—for the society $C(\cdot)$ as the 'value' of the functional collective choice rule. (In contrast, social welfare functions, social decision functions, etc., are examples of *relational* collective choice rules: $R = f(R_1, \ldots, R_n)$, with the 'value' of the function $f$ being a binary preference relation $R$.) Consistency or 'rationality' conditions required of social choice can make $C(\cdot)$ 'binary'. Less demandingly, weaker consistency conditions (e.g., some conditions obtained in Essay 1 through factorization) can permit the use of some—but not all—properties associated with the binariness of choice, and some of these more limited properties can be, in many cases, adequate for re-establishing the impossibility results (see Essay 8).

Schwartz, Plott, Campbell and Bordes have demonstrated that it is possible to have a functional collective choice rule satisfying Arrow's conditions, appropriately redefined, and fulfilling some consistency properties as well.[35] There is an element of ambiguity in what is to count as appropriate redefinition. Take, for example, the weak Pareto principle, which in the case of Arrow's social welfare function (or a social decision function) is defined as requiring that if everyone prefers some $x$ to some $y$, then $x$ is *socially preferred* to $y$. If, however, the notion of social preference is dropped and replaced by

---

33. Arrow's dictatorship result can, in fact, be established even without full transitivity, using only 'semiorder' properties and weaker conditions; see D. H. Blair and R. A. Pollak, 'Collective Rationality and Dictatorship: The Scope of the Arrow Theorem', *Journal of Economic Theory*, 21 (1979); and J. H. Blau, 'Semiorders and Collective Choice', *Journal of Economic Theory*, 21 (1979).

34. P. C. Fishburn, *The Theory of Social Choice* (Princeton: Princeton University Press, 1973). A 'social choice function' specifies the chosen subset of any non-empty subset $S$ of the set of alternative states, for any $n$-tuple of individual preference orderings: $C(S, (R_1, \ldots, R_n))$.

35. See T. Schwartz, 'On the Possibility of Rational Policy Evaluation', *Theory and Decision*, 1 (1970); C. R. Plott, 'Path Independence, Rationality and Social Choice', *Econometrica*, 4 (1973); D. E. Campbell, 'Democratic Preference Functions', *Journal of Economic Theory*, 12 (1976); G. Bordes, 'Consistency, Rationality and Collective Choice', *Review of Economic Studies*, 43 (1976). See also S. Bloomfield, 'An Axiomatic Formulation of Constitutional Games', Technical Report No. 71-18, Operations Research House, Stanford University, 1971; and R. Deb, 'On Schwartz's Rule', *Journal of Economic Theory*, 6 (1977).

that of a choice function for the society, this condition can be translated in several different ways. One simple translation—indeed the one that most authors have used—demands in this case (when everyone prefers $x$ to $y$) that $x$ alone must be chosen from the *pair* $(x, y)$. This can be seen as a condition on the 'base relation' of social choice (see Section 1.1 above). Alternatively, the Pareto principle could have been applied to the 'revealed preference relation' of social choice, requiring that if everyone prefers $x$ to $y$, then $y$ must not be chosen from *any* set that contains $x$. We can refer to these two alternative interpretations as the 'pair interpretation' and the 'general interpretation' respectively of the weak Pareto principle in the context of social choice.

The truth of the claims made by Schwartz, Plott, Campbell and Bordes can be easily checked by taking an example of a suitable social choice procedure. Take the majority rule and convert any majority preference cycle into an indifference class in the context of choice from any set containing all the elements involved in the cycle. If, for example, $x$ beats $y$, which beats $z$, which again beats $x$, then—in choosing from the triple $(x, y, z)$ or from any set containing that triple—proceed to find the subset of best elements treating $x$, $y$ and $z$ as socially indifferent. Schwartz, Campbell and Bordes show that not only do rules of this type satisfy all of Arrow's conditions, as they interpret them, but also such rules have many other attractive properties, including full transitivity of the 'revealed preference relation' associated with the generated choice functions.

Despite its ingenuity and technical merits, this line of resolution has, I believe, an inescapable defect. It works only because the Arrow problem is reinterpreted in the choice context in such a way that some of Arrow's conditions—in particular the Pareto principle and non-dictatorship—are made to work exclusively on the *base relation* thanks to choosing the 'pair interpretation', while some of the other Arrow conditions—in particular regularity in the form of transitivity (or quasi-transitivity, acyclicity, etc., in extensions of the Arrow result)—are made to work exclusively on the *revealed preference relation*. If this 'schizophrenia' is removed, Arrow-type impossibilities would re-occur; see Essay 8.

In fact, there are three distinct ways in which the impossibility results can be revived:

(1) Impose all the requirements on the base relation, including demanding transitivity (or quasi-transitivity, acyclicity, etc.) of that relation.

(2) Impose all the requirements on the revealed preference relation, including choosing the 'general interpretation'—as opposed to the 'pair interpretation'—of the Pareto principle and non-dictatorship.

(3) Maintain the 'schizophrenia'—imposing some conditions on the base relation and some on the revealed preference relation, but directly impose consistency conditions on choices from different sets—in particular impose 'contraction consistency' (see Section 1.1) which will tie up the base relation to the revealed preference relation.

Essay 8 ('Social Choice Theory: A Re-examination') shows how robust the Arrow-type impossibility problems are in preference aggregation.[36] The scepticism expressed in Essay 6 ('Quasi-transitivity, Rational Choice and Collective Decisions'), while proposing this line of inquiry, has unfortunately proved to be quite justified.

## 3    Welfare Comparisons and Social Choice

### 3.1    Informational basis of preference aggregation

In aggregating individual preferences, Arrow's social welfare functions and the related rules (social decision functions, social choice functions, functional collective choice rules, etc.) have to make do with rather limited information, viz., interpersonally non-comparable, ordinal utilities (or orderings). This informational base is expanded in Essays 9 to 16, and that was also one of the main thrusts in my Collective Choice and Social Welfare (chapters 6−9). It is perhaps useful to go a little into the motivation behind these exercises.

The Arrow informational format does not permit the use of cardinal information regarding individual utilities. This, however, proves to be not really a serious limitation, since the Arrow impossibility result can be generalized to cover cases in which the individual preferences are expressed as cardinal utility functions (see Theorem 8*2 in Collective Choice and Social Welfare). However, the absence of interpersonal comparability of individual utilities is a binding limitation, and its removal does indeed permit many rules satisfying all of Arrow's conditions, redefined for such a broader framework (see chapters 7 and 9 in Collective Choice and Social Welfare). It can be argued that it is the imposed poverty of the utility information that dooms Arrow's aggregation exercise to failure.

But this remark is a bit misleading since the informational limitation of the Arrow format relates not merely to the poverty of the utility information but also to the eschewal of non-utility information. Most actual public judgements make extensive use of non-utility information, varying from relative incomes and ownerships to the description of who is doing what to whom. Taking note of non-utility information is not, of course, explicitly ruled out by social welfare functions, etc., despite treating individual

---

36. See also Sen, Collective Choice and Social Welfare (1970), pp. 81−2; J. A. Ferejohn and D. M. Grether, 'On a Class of Rational Social Decision Procedures', Journal of Economic Theory, 8 (1974); P. C. Fishburn, 'On Collective Rationality and a Generalized Impossibility Theorem', Review of Economic Studies, 41 (1974); D. Blair, G. Bordes, K. Suzumura and J. S. Kelly, 'Impossibility Theorems without Collective Rationality', Journal of Economic Theory, 13 (1976); J. A. Ferejohn and D. M. Grether, 'Weak Path Independence', Journal of Economic Theory, 14 (1977); Y. Matsumoto, 'Choice Functions: Preference, Consistency and Neutrality', D. Phil. thesis, Oxford University, 1982.

preference orderings or ordinal utilities as the basis of social judgement or choice. This is because the description of the social state incorporates non-utility information, and the social welfare functions, etc., need not be 'neutral' to the nature of the social state. However, such a neutrality *is*, in fact, precipitated by the combination of the conditions that Arrow—and following him others—have typically used, viz., the Pareto principle, independence, and unrestricted domain. While this consequence was implicitly recognized in the literature for a long time, since Arrow's own proof of his impossibility theorem proceeded by way of some neutrality,[37] the neutrality results were formally established by Guha, Blau, d'Aspremont and Gevers.[38] Essay 15 ('Personal Utilities and Public Judgements: Or What's Wrong with Welfare Economics?') examines the genesis and the exact role of this type of 'neutrality'.

A strong form of such neutrality, which has been called 'welfarism', has been present in the moral philosophical literature for centuries. Indeed, the utilitarian formula of judging the states of affairs by simply summing the individual utilities—used not only by Bentham but also by such economists as Edgeworth, Marshall, Pigou, Robertson and others—illustrates a straightforward case of welfarism. In a less restrictive form, welfarism is present in the general formula for social welfare that can be found in, say, Samuelson's *Foundation of Economic Analysis*, or Graaff's *Theoretical Welfare Economics*: $W = f(\mathbf{u})$, when $\mathbf{u}$ is the vector of individual utilities. This is often called—misleadingly I think—'individualism' (as if individuals must be seen as no more than *locations* of their pleasures or utilities!). Arrow's social welfare functions, constrained by his conditions, produce a slightly weaker form of welfarism—called 'strict ranking welfarism' (see Essay 15)—which requires exclusive reliance on utility information in the special case in which individual preferences happen to be strict, involving no indifference.

The consequences of these information restrictions are indeed severe for public judgements, and this general issue has been discussed in Essays 8, 11 and 15.[39] It may be useful to illustrate the nature of the limitation with an example. Consider again the cake division problem and take two different cases (Figure 1). In case A, person 1 is very rich while 2 and 3 are poor,

37. See Arrow, *Social Choice and Individual Values* (1963) pp. 98–100; and Sen, *Collective Choice and Social Welfare* (1970), Lemma 3*a. See also J. H. Blau, 'The Existence of Social Welfare Functions', *Econometrica,* **25** (1957).

38. Guha, 'Neutrality, Monotonicity and the Right of Veto' (1972); Blau, 'Neutrality, Monotonicity and the Right of Veto: A Comment', (1976); C. d'Aspremont and L. Gevers, 'Equity and Informational Basis of Collective Choice', *Review of Economic Studies,* **46** (1977). See also Essay 11.

39. See also my 'Informational Basis of Alternative Welfare Approaches: Aggregation and Income Distribution', *Journal of Public Economics,* **3** (1974), and 'Informational Analysis of Moral Principles', in R. Harrison (ed.), *Rational Action* (Cambridge: Cambridge University Press, 1979).

     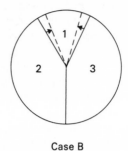

Case A                                    Case B

FIGURE 1

whereas in case B, person 1 is very poor while 2 and 3 are rich. In both cases
we consider a redistribution—cutting out a bit from person 1's share of the
cake and dividing that gain between 2 and 3. If each person prefers more
cake to himself (i.e., if we make the standard assumption for the cake division
exercise), then persons 2 and 3 prefer the change while person 1 disprefers it,
in both cases A and B. Now the question: are the two cases of redistribution
exactly similar? In the Arrow format they have to be. Suppose we want to
say that the redistribution is more justified in case A than in case B, how
would we distinguish the two cases? It is tempting to point out that person 1
is *worse off* than the others in case B but not so in case A. But if by 'worse
off' we mean having lower utility, then that type of statement is ruled out by
the absence of interpersonal comparisons. If, on the other hand, by worse
off we mean having less cake and thus being poorer, that type of non-utility
information cannot be taken into account given the feature of strict-ranking
welfarism, insisting on exclusive reliance on utility information only. Indeed,
in the Arrow format the two cases are *informationally identical,* and exactly
the same judgement must be made about the change in both the cases, since
the individual preference orderings are identical in the two cases.[40]

Arrow's remarkable achievement was to show—though he did not put it
this way—that in such an informational format there are no consistent non-
dictatorial rules. It does not belittle the outstanding importance of this
elegant and far-reaching logical result—it has in fact been the prime mover
of a whole discipline—to note that an informational format that cannot
distinguish between cases A and B is quite unsuitable *anyway* for welfare
economics. More information is needed to deal with interest conflicts. The
unsuitable, it transpires, is also impossible.

40. Majority rule would, of course, support the redistribution in both cases. That is not needed
in the Arrow format generally. What is needed, however, is treating the two cases alike. Either
the redistribution is better in both cases, or worse in both, or indifferent in both.

This informational problem is not quite so compelling in the case of aggregation of conflicting *judgements* (e.g., in combining different people's judgements on whether it would be better for Britain to come out of the EEC, or on whether marijuana should be legalized), as opposed to aggregating conflicting *interests*. Essay 8 explores the distinctions between different aggregation types and shows the varying relevance of Arrow's—and related—results, depending on the precise nature of the aggregation exercise that is involved.

## 3.2   *Utility information: invariance, intersection and partial comparability*

Essays 9 to 12 deal primarily with enriching the utility information, while Essays 13 to 16 are mainly concerned with the use of non-utility information. Since the Arrovian social welfare functions and related structures do not have room for richer utility information, it is necessary to get a suitable format for putting more utility information into the process of social judgement or choice. The procedure used for this purpose in *Collective Choice and Social Welfare* is to define a 'social welfare functional' SWFL as a function of the $n$-tuple of individual utility functions:[41] $R = F(U_1, \ldots, U_n)$, and then to constrain it through identifying different $n$-tuples of utility functions that are 'informationally identical'. The methods are explained and explored in Essays 9 and 11.

Depending on the measurability assumption of individual utility (e.g., ordinality, cardinality, etc.), each person has a *family* of utility functions, e.g., in the case of ordinality each member of a family of utility functions of a person is a positive monotonic transformation of all other members (and the family includes *all* such transformations). If there is no interpersonal comparability, we can pick any $n$-tuple of individual utility functions—one from each person's family. However, interpersonal comparability can be seen as consisting in tying up different people's utility functions with each other, reducing this freedom of choice, e.g., we can't simply blow up the representation of my utility function a million-fold, keeping yours unchanged (overwhelming your utility gains and losses in the utilitarian calculus). So interpersonal comparability specifies some *subset*—called the 'comparability set'—of the set of $n$-tuples of utility functions permitted by the measurability assumption, and all $n$-tuples in a comparability set are informationally identical. Thus, depending on the exact measurability and comparability assumptions that are chosen, for any real utility situation a subset of all possible alternative representations (in the form of alternative $n$-tuples of

41. Note that this does not imply that each state must be judged by the utility *vector* associated with that state, i.e., welfarism is not implied. Welfarism can, of course, be produced by additional restrictions imposed on SWFLs; see Essay 11.

utility functions) are arrived at. A SWFL is thus supplemented by statements on informationally equivalent $n$-tuples of utility functions.

From here we can go in one of two directions. Either we can admit only those rules that yield the *same* social ordering (or choice) for every $n$-tuple in the informationally identical set. This all-or-nothing approach was explored in Chapter 8 of *Collective Choice and Social Welfare* and is explored at some length in Essay 11. Or, alternatively, we can admit any rule whatsoever, but accept only that *partial* ordering of social states which is common to (i.e., is the intersection of) all the social orderings generated by the rule, respectively for all the members of the comparability set. Essay 9 explores this more permissive 'intersection' approach. To illustrate the contrast, for non-interpersonally-comparable individual utilities, the utilitarian rule is simply inadmissible under the all-or-nothing approach, but will yield the Pareto partial ordering in the more permissive approach (since even with no interpersonal comparability a state that is higher in everyone's utility function must yield a higher utility-sum no matter which particular utility representations we choose).

The more permissive 'intersection' approach also allows the use of *partial* interpersonal comparability. This concept was introduced in Essay 9, and reflected the possibility that utility comparisons may be neither impossible, nor—on the other hand—terribly exact. To take up an example presented in Essay 9, we might not be able to put Emperor Nero's utility functions into a one-to-one correspondence with every other Roman's utility function, but we might nevertheless find it absurd to multiply Nero's utility function by a suitably large number—keeping the utility functions of the others unchanged—to produce the result that there was indeed a net gain in the utility-sum from the burning of Rome while Nero played the fiddle.

Partial comparability may either represent a limitation of information regarding the true situation, or be interpreted as reflecting an intrinsic element of vagueness in the very nature of utility comparisons.[42] Essay 9 analyses how partial comparability can be accommodated within a formal structure of utility aggregation, and Essay 12 makes a few further remarks on that problem.[43]

---

42. There is some similarity, in this respect, between the partiality of utility comparisons and Issac Levi's notion of 'indeterminate probabilities' (see I. Levi, 'On Indeterminate Probabilities', *Journal of Philosophy,* **71** (1974), and *The Enterprise of Knowledge* (Cambridge Mass.: MIT Press, 1980)).

43. See also my *Collective Choice and Social Welfare* (1970), chapter 7*; C. Blackorby, 'Degrees of Cardinality and Aggregate Partial Orderings', *Econometrica,* **43** (1975); B. J. Fine, 'A Note on "Interpersonal Aggregation and Partial Comparability"', *Econometrica,* **43** (1975); K. Basu, *Revealed Preference of Governments* (Cambridge: Cambridge University Press, 1979); Th. Bezembinder and P. van Acker, 'A Note on Sen's Partial Comparability Model', Department of Psychology, Katholieke Universiteit, Nijmegen, 1979.

If partial comparability is viewed not as an intrinsic quality of utility comparison, but as a reflection of limitation of information, e.g., availahle tc a person making a political judgement, or to a planner taking policy decisions, then there is a clear similarity between that notion and Abba Lerner's concept of 'ignorance' on the part of the central planners as to who has which particular utility function out of a given set of (interpersonally comparable) utility functions.[44] Lerner had shown that with the assumption of 'equal ignorance', which implies that any person has the same probability of having any given utility function as any other person, the optimal distributional rule for a given total income is equal division, provided (i) the utilitarian formula of social welfare is accepted, and (ii) we maximize the expected social welfare.

Milton Friedman pointed out the limitation of the utilitarian formula in dealing with problems of income distribution when people's 'capacities to enjoy' in fact differ, since we may not be indifferent to the *distribution* of total personal utilities.[45] Essay 10 shows that Lerner's result does not require the utilitarian formula, and indeed any concave group welfare function—no matter how concerned with the distribution of total utilities—will yield Lerner's result. Thus, Friedman's criticism, while valid for Lerner's own proposition, does not affect the case for equal division of income no matter what importance we decide to attach to the question of 'distribution' of total personal utilities. The same consequence holds—in fact with even weaker assumptions—if the approach is focused not on maximizing the *expected value of social welfare,* but on maximizing the *minimal value of social welfare.*[46]

However, while the assumption of 'equal ignorance' imposes a pattern of symmetry on the information we have regarding different people's utility functions, there is no such assumption in the general format of partial comparability. The purpose in this case is to catch a common attitude towards interpersonal comparisons of utility, which involves neither Pigovian precision,[47] nor Robbinsian rejection.[48]

44. A. P. Lerner, *The Economics of Control* (London: Macmillan, 1944).

45. M. Friedman, 'Lerner on the Economics of Control', *Journal of Political Economy,* **55** (1947); reprinted in his *Essays in Positive Economics* (Chicago: Chicago University Press, 1966).

46. Gordon Tullock, in a characteristically spirited note ('On Mathematics as Decoration', *Papers in Economic Criticism,* May 1975), has attacked this last result as trivial. It might well be trivial (the proof is just a few lines anyway), but Tullock's diagnosis is based on a confusion between (1) maximizing the *minimal value of social welfare,* and (2) maximizing the *minimal income that any person* receives ('in the Sen article there is another mathematical proof which is that if you divide the given sum of money equally among people, the minimum amount that any one of those persons can receive is higher than if you divide the money unequally', Tullock, p. 23)! In my response to Professor Tullock, I had to confess my enhanced admiration for his ability to write so much and so well without—evidently—being able to read.

47. A. C. Pigou, *The Economics of Welfare* (London: Macmillan, 1920).

48. L. Robbins, 'Interpersonal Comparisons of Utility', *Economic Journal,* **48** (1938).

## 3.3 Axioms, implications and interpretations

In the format of social welfare functionals it is possible to study various common—and uncommon—social welfare rules (e.g., utilitarianism, Rawlsian maximin,[49] and various other formulas for judging social welfare). That was indeed one of the main purposes in getting away from the informational straitjacket of Arrow's social welfare functions (see Chapters 7 to 9 of my *Collective Choice and Social Welfare*).[50] There have been a number of outstanding contributions in this general area in recent years, providing— among other things—alternative axiomatizations of various social welfare rules.[51]

While cardinality of individual utility functions without interpersonal comparability has no effect on Arrow's impossibility result, interpersonal comparability of the 'ordinal' sort, even without cardinality, does indeed remove the impossibility. An example satisfying all the Arrow conditions in the framework of ordinal comparability is Rawls's rule of judging the welfare of the society by the welfare level of the worst-off individual. This can be made compatible with the stronger version of the Pareto principle by being defined in the lexicographic form—often called 'leximin'—so that if the worst-off persons in two states are equally badly off, then we compare the second worst-off persons, and so on (see chapter 9 of my *Collective Choice and Social Welfare*). While the Arrow conditions are all satisfied by the Rawlsian 'leximin', they do not uniquely define that rule. Peter Hammond, Steven Strasnick, Claude d'Aspremont, Robert Deschamps, Louis Gevers,

49. John Rawls, *A Theory of Justice* (Cambridge, Mass.: Harvard University Press, 1971). See also his 'Social Unity and Primary Goods', in A. Sen and B. Williams (eds), *Utilitarianism and Beyond* (Cambridge: Cambridge University Press, 1982).

50. See also my 'Informational Basis of Alternative Welfare Approaches: Aggregation and Income Distribution' (1974); 'Rawls versus Bentham: An Axiomatic Examination of the Pure Distribution Problem', *Theory and Decision*, 4 (1974); 'Welfare Inequalities and Rawlsian Axiomatics', *Theory and Decision*, 7 (1976); and Essay 11.

51. See P. J. Hammond, 'Equity, Arrow's Conditions and Rawls' Difference Principle', *Econometrica*, 44 (1976); S. Strasnick, 'Social Choice Theory and the Derivation of Rawls' Difference Principle', *Journal of Philosophy*, 73 (1976); d'Aspremont and Gevers, 'Equity and Informational Basis of Collective Choice' (1977); Deschamps and L. Gevers, 'Leximim and Utilitarian Rules: A Joint Characterisation', *Journal of Economic Theory*, 17 (1978); E. Maskin, 'A Theorem on Utilitarianism', *Review of Economic Studies*, 45 (1978); R. Deschamps and L. Gevers, 'Separability, Risk-bearing and Social Welfare Judgements', in J.-J. Laffont (ed.), *Aggregation and Revelation of Preferences* (Amsterdam: North-Holland, 1979); Gevers, 'On Interpersonal Comparability and Social Welfare Orderings'; E. Maskin, 'Decision-Making under Ignorance with Implications for Social Choice', *Theory and Decision*, 11 (1979); K. W. S. Roberts, 'Possibility Theorems with Interpersonally Comparable Welfare Levels', *Review of Economic Studies*, 47 (1980); K. W. S. Roberts, 'Interpersonal Comparability and Social Choice Theory', *Review of Economic Studies*, 47 (1980).

Eric Maskin and Kevin Roberts have produced various alternative ways of tightening the conditions to pinpoint the 'leximin' rule exactly.

Essay 11 provides, among other things, a rather different axiomatic derivation of 'leximin'. Leximin—like the maximin—has the appearance of an 'extremist' criterion in giving priority to the interest of the worst-off even if it goes against the interests of a very large number of others. Its greater plausibility in two-person conflicts has been asserted, and certainly it is not unreasonable to give priority to the interests of the worse-off among exactly two persons when all others are indifferent. Theorem 8 ('Rawls from Inch to Ell') in Essay 11 shows that for any social welfare functional with unrestricted domain and independence, leximin for two-person conflicts logically entails leximin *in general*—no matter how many people are involved in the interest conflict.[52]

While the axiomatic study of interpersonal comparisons and their uses helps to clarify the ways through which utility information can be utilized for social judgement or choice, there are important interpretational issues underlying all these exercises. What do interpersonal comparisons stand for? Are they just value judgements, as is often alleged? If so, how can we systematize these judgements for further use? Or are they factual matters? If so, how do we obtain these facts for our exercises? Essay 12 ('Interpersonal Comparisons of Welfare') investigates these foundational problems, and explores various alternative avenues. Moving far away from the once-fashionable view that interpersonal comparisons are 'meaningless', it is argued in Essay 12 that 'the central problem in the theory of interpersonal comparisons of welfare seems to be an embarrassment of riches—there are many reasonable ways of making such comparisons and they need not coincide'.


## 4  Non-utility Information

### 4.1  Pareto versus rights

Essay 13 ('The Impossibility of a Paretian Liberal') was instrumental in starting a line of inquiry that has led to a rather voluminous literature. The impossibility result indicates a conflict between individual liberty (in the form of a person being 'decisive' over certain personal matters) and the Pareto principle (asserting the priority of unanimous preference rankings). The formal result shows the inconsistency of three conditions, viz.,

---

52. Peter Hammond has provided an alternative proof of this theorem, and in the process proved a very important general property relating two-person equity norms to *n*-person equity norms, of which 'Rawls from Inch to Ell' can be seen as a special case ('Equity in Two Person Situations: Some Consequences', *Econometrica,* **47** (1979)).

unrestricted domain, the weak Pareto principle, and a condition of 'minimal liberty'[53] requiring that *at least* two persons have some 'personal sphere' each, such that if either of them prefers some $x$ to some $y$ in his or her own personal sphere, then $x$ is socially preferred to $y$.[54] A necessary—though quite plausibly not sufficient—condition for a pair $(x, y)$ to be in an individual $i$'s personal sphere is that the states $x$ and $y$ differ from each other exclusively in a matter that is 'personal' to $i$, e.g., whether $i$ reads or does not read a particular book.

Various proposals for avoiding the conflict have been suggested in the literature, and they have respectively involved alternative ways of weakening each of the three conditions: unrestricted domain,[55] minimal liberty,[56] and

53. In Essay 13 the condition was called 'minimal liberalism', though it was also stated: 'The term "liberalism" is elusive and is open to alternative interpretations. Some uses of the term may not embrace the condition defined here. What is relevant is that Condition $L$ represents a value involving individual liberty that many people would subscribe to. Whether such people are best described as liberals is a question that is not crucial to the point of the paper' (p. 286). In Essay 14 the condition was renamed as 'minimal libertarianism'. Neither term is very satisfactory. The expression 'minimal liberty'—used here—has the advantage of focusing directly on 'a value involving individual liberty that many people would subscribe to', rather than on the advocacy of that value in liberalism or libertarianism.

54. For different types of examples of this conflict, see my *Collective Choice and Social Welfare,* chapter 6; Allan Gibbard, 'A Pareto-Consistent Libertarian Claim', *Journal of Economic Theory,* 7 (1974); Jonathan Barnes, 'Freedom, Rationality and Paradox', *Canadian Journal of Philosophy,* 10 (1980); J. Fountain, 'Bowley's Analysis of Bilateral Monopoly and Sen's Liberal Paradox in Collective Choice Theory: A Note', *Quarterly Journal of Economics,* 95 (1980); E. T. Green, 'Libertarian Aggregation of Preferences: What the "Coase Theorem" Might Have Said', Social Science Working Paper 315, California Institute of Technology, 1980.

55. See, among others, J. H. Blau, 'Liberal Values and Independence', *Review of Economic Studies,* 42 (1975); C. Seidl, 'On Liberal Values, *Zeitschrift für Nationalökonomie,* 35 (1975); F. Breyer, 'The Liberal Paradox, Decisiveness over Issues, and Domain Restrictions', *Zeitschrift für Nationalökonomie,* 37 (1977); F. Breyer and G. A. Gigliotti, 'Empathy and the Respect for the Rights of Others', *Zeitschrift für Nationalökonomie,* 40 (1980); D. Austen-Smith, 'Necessary and Sufficient Conditions for Libertarian Collective Choice Rules', mimeographed, University of York, 1981; E. Maskin, B. Nalebuff and A. Sen, unpublished notes on the impossibility of the Paretian liberal.

56. See, among others, K. Ng, 'The Possibility of a Paretian Liberal: Impossibility Theroems and Cardinal Utility', *Journal of Political Economy,* 79 (1971); A. Gibbard, 'A Pareto-Consistent Libertarian Claim', *Journal of Economic Theory,* 7 (1974); P. Bernholz, 'Is a Paretian Liberal Really Impossible?', *Public Choice,* 19 (1974); J. H. Blau, 'Liberal Values and Independence' (1975); D. E. Campbell, 'Democratic Preference Functions', *Journal of Economic Theory,* 12 (1976); J. S. Kelly, 'Rights Exercising and a Pareto-Consistent Libertarian Claim', *Journal of Economic Theory,* 13 (1976); J. S. Kelly, 'The Impossibility of a Just Liberal', *Economica,* 43 (1976); J. Aldrich, 'The Dilemma of a Paretian Liberal: Some Consequences of Sen's Theorem', *Public Choice,* 30 (1977); J. A. Ferejohn, 'The Distribution of Rights in Society', in H. W. Gottinger and W. Leinfellner (eds), *Decision Theory and Social Ethics: Issues in Social Choice* (Dordrecht: Reidel, 1978); E. Karni, 'Collective Rationality, Unanimity and Liberal Ethics', *Review of Economic Studies,* 45 (1978); D. C. Mueller, *Public Choice* (Cambridge: Cambridge University Press, 1979); R. Gardner, 'The Strategic Inconsistency of the Paretian Liberal', *Public Choice,* 35 (1980); F. Breyer and R. Gardner, 'Liberal Paradox,

weak Pareto principle.[57] Essay 14 examines and evaluates some of the proposals which had by then (1976) been put forward, but there have been many others since then. There have also been many interesting extensions of the result to other areas, in particular to group rights (including federalism).[58]

One reason for the attention that Essay 13 has received is the interest that normative 'rights' have recently aroused. The paper departed from the traditional formulations of welfare economics in trying to make room for rights, and it identified a conflict even with the allegedly mildest of the welfare-economic principles, viz., the weak Pareto principle. The lessons drawn from the conflict have, however, varied a great deal. For example, in a powerfully argued contribution, Robert Nozick has claimed that the lesson to be drawn from this result is the impossibility of reflecting rights through a 'social ordering',[59] and he has outlined an alternative, deontological

Game Equilibrium, and Gibbard Optimum', *Public Choice*, 35 (1980); K. Suzumura, 'Liberal Paradox and the Voluntary Exchange of Rights Exercising', *Journal of Economic Theory*, 22 (1980); W. Gaertner and L. Krüger, 'Self-supporting Preferences and Individual Rights: the Possibility of Paretian Libertarianism', *Economica*, 47 (1981); L. Krüger and W. Gaertner, 'Alternative Libertarian Claims and Sen's Paradox', Economics Discussion Paper 81, University of Bielefeld, 1981; K. Suzumura, 'Equity, Efficiency and Rights in Social Choice', Discussion Paper 155, Kyoto Institute of Economic Research, 1981; J. L. Wriglesworth, 'Solution to the Gibbard and Sen Paradoxes Using Information Available from Interpersonal Comparisons', mimeographed, Lincoln College, Oxford, 1981.

57. See, among others, M. J. Farrell, 'Liberalism in the Theory of Social Choice', *Review of Economic Studies*, 43 (1976); K. Suzumura, 'On the Consistency of Libertarian Claims', *Review of Economic Studies*, 45 (1978); P. J. Hammond, 'Liberalism, Independent Rights and the Pareto Principle', forthcoming in the Proceedings of the 6th International Congress of Logic, Methodology and Philosophy of Science, 1979; D. Austen-Smith, 'Restricted Pareto and Rights', *Journal of Economic Theory,* forthcoming; Rawls, 'Social Unity and Primary Goods' (1982); P. Coughlin and A. Sen, unpublished notes on conditional Pareto principles.

58. See R. N. Batra and P. K. Pattanaik, 'On Some Suggestions for Having Non-binary Social Choice Functions', *Theory and Decision*, 3 (1972); D. N. Stevens and J. E. Foster, 'The Possibility of Democratic Pluralism', *Economica,* 45 (1978); J. L. Wriglesworth, 'The Possibility of Democratic Pluralism: A Comment', *Economica,* 49 (1982). For extensions in a different direction, see A. Weale, 'The Impossibility of Liberal Egalitarianism', *Analysis,* 40 (1980); and I. S. McLean, 'Liberty, Equality and the Pareto Principle: A Comment on Weale', *Analysis,* 40 (1980). Gibbard's 'A Pareto-Consistent Libertarian Claim' (1974), pursues problems of internal consistency of libertarianism.

59. R. Nozick, 'Distributive Justice', *Philosophy and Public Affairs,* 3 (1973), and *Anarchy, State and Utopia* (Oxford: Blackwell, 1974), pp. 164–6. On related matters, see C. K. Rowley and A. T. Peacock, *Welfare Economics: A Liberal Restatement* (London: Martin Robertson, 1975); James Buchanan, 'An Ambiguity in Sen's Alleged Proof of the Impossibility of the Paretian Liberal', mimeographed, Virginia Polytechnic, 1976; C. R. Perelli-Minetti, 'Nozick on Sen: A Misunderstanding', *Theory and Decision,* 8 (1977); B. Barry, 'Lady Chatterley's Lover and Doctor Fischer's Bomb Party: Liberalism, Pareto Optimality and the Problem of Objectionable Preferences', presented at the Ustaoset Conference on the Foundations of Social Choice Theory, 1981; P. Gärdenfors, 'Rights, Games and Social Choice', *Nous,* (1981); R. Sugden, *The Political Economy of Public Choice* (Oxford: Martin Robertson, 1981); P. J. Hammond, 'Utilitarianism, Uncertainty and Information', in A. Sen and B. Williams (eds), *Utilitarianism and Beyond* (Cambridge: Cambridge University Press, 1982); B. Chapman, 'Individual Rights and Collective Rationality: Some Implications for Economic Analysis of Law', *Hofstra Law Review*, 10 (Winter 1982).

approach which rejects consequentialism including judging actions by consequences—thereby departing altogether from the format of welfare economics and social choice theory. Essay 14 ('Liberty, Unanimity and Rights') argues—among other things—against this diagnosis, but insists on the need to relax the Pareto principle if rights are to be substantially incorporated in moral or political systems. I have argued elsewhere in favour of the case for retaining consequence-based analysis for moral or political systems involving rights—even purely libertarian rights.[60]

The utilitarian moral approach can be factorized into three distinct elements: (1) *consequentialism* (judging all choice variables, e.g., actions or policies, entirely in terms consequent of states of affairs); (2) *welfarism* (judging states of affairs entirely in terms of personal utility information relating to the respective states); and (3) *sum-ranking* (judging personal utility information entirely in terms of their sum-total).[61] If the last—sum-ranking—is dropped, we get utility-based systems that are not fully utilitarian, e.g., the utility-based 'leximin' or 'maximin' discussed in Section 3.3.[62] To incorporate fulfilment and violation of rights in the evaluation of states of affairs, it is necessary to go further and drop welfarism. Indeed that route, used in Essay 13, is the form that the use of rights in social choice theory has typically taken, and it is that form that is defended in Essay 14, and elsewhere.[63] There is no necessity here to drop consequentialism, even though dropping consequentialism is, in fact, compatible with the approach of social choice theory, provided actions, etc., are judged in a consequence-*sensitive* way (without necessarily relying *entirely* on the evaluation of consequences).[64] While these foundational issues are typically met with absolute silence in welfare economies, they are, in fact, rather important for policy judgements and economic evaluation.

---

60. See my 'A Positive Concept of Negative Freedom', in *Ethics: Foundations, Problems and Applications,* Proceedings of the 5th International Wittgenstein Symposium (Vienna: Holder-Pichler-Tempsky, 1981); 'Rights and Agency', *Philosophy and Public Affairs,* 11 (1982); 'Liberty as Control: An Appraisal', *Midwest Studies in Philosophy,* 8 (1982); 'Liberty and Social Choice', forthcoming in *Journal of Philosophy,* January 1983.

61. See my 'Utilitarianism and Welfarism', *Journal of Philosophy,* 76 (1979).

62. Note, however, that Rawls himself does not interpret these criteria—related to his 'Difference Principle'—in terms of utility data, and chooses instead to judge 'advantage' in terms of 'primary goods' (see his *A Theory of Justice* (1971); and 'Social Unity and Primary Goods' (1982).) In *The Just Economy* (London: Allen & Unwin, 1976), James Meade has provided an illuminating and thorough exploration of the utility-based—but not necessarily utilitarian—welfare economic framework. See also James Mirrlees, 'An Exploration of the Theory of Optimal Income Taxation', *Review of Economic Studies,* 38 (1971).

63. Particularly in 'Rights and Agency' (1982), and 'Liberty and Social Choice' (1983).

64. There are other grounds for eschewing fully consequentialist systems; see especially Bernard Williams, 'A Critique of Utilitarianism', in J. J. C. Smart and B. Williams, *Utilitarianism: For and Against* (Cambridge: Cambridge University Press, 1973). See also 'Introduction', in Sen and Williams, *Utilitarianism and Beyond* (1982).

## 4.2 Utilities, goods and capabilities

The informational limitation of Arrovian social welfare functions and related structures was touched on in Section 3.1. Essay 15 ('Personal Utilities and Public Judgements: Or What's Wrong with Welfare Economics?') goes extensively into this question, discussing the combined impact of having poor utility information *and* eschewing the use of non-utility information. This informational format was not, of course, invented by Arrow, and he had followed the general tradition of welfare economics in this choice. Essays 8 to 12 deal with the possibility of enriching the utility information to be used. With richer utility information, Arrow-type impossibilities are avoided. However, avoiding Arrow-type impossibilities is not the only issue of interest, and the general adequacy of an informational format with rich utility information but no usable non-utility information is open to questioning (see Essays 13 to 15).

The consideration of liberty requires the use of some specific non-utility information, as was discussed in the last section. Other types of non-utility information are crucial for other normative principles, e.g., 'equal pay for equal work', or eliminating or reducing 'exploitation' or respecting privacy. It is difficult to claim that these types of non-utility information are needed only as 'surrogates' for some utility information, or simply for 'instrumental' analysis aimed at some deeper utility-based criteria.[65] The existence of fundamental non-instrumental interest in such non-utility information need not, of course, deny the importance of instrumental considerations as such. Instrumental issues will be typically important in a consequence-based system,[66] but the instruments can be aimed also at non-utility goals and not just at utility objectives (as assumed by utilitarians).

John Rawls has argued in favour of judging efficiency and equality in terms of the personal command over 'primary goods'—goods that everyone seeks no matter what else they seek.[67] There is much of interest and value in that perspective, which takes us well beyond utility information and implies a clear rejection of welfarism.

However, what people get out of goods depends on a variety of factors, and judging personal advantage just by the size of personal ownership of goods and services can be very misleading. For example, the impact of food on nutrition varies with population groups, climatic conditions, age, sex,

---

65. See my 'Utilitarianism and Welfarism', *Journal of Philosophy,* 76 (1979). See also Y.-K. Ng, 'Welfarism: A Defence against Sen's Attack', *Economic Journal,* 91 (1981), and my 'Reply' in the same number.

66. Cf. T. Scanlon, 'Rights, Goals and Fairness', in Stuart Hampshire (ed.), *Public and Private Morality* (Cambridge: Cambridge University Press, 1978), and P. Dasgupta, 'Utilitarianism, Information and Rights', in Sen and Williams, *Utilitarianism and Beyond* (1982).

67. J. Rawls, *A Theory of Justice* (Cambridge, Mass.: Harvard University Press, 1971). See also his 'Social Unity and Primary Goods' (1982).

etc. It seems reasonable to move away from a focus on goods as such to what goods do to human beings.

It might, of course, appear that if we were to take such a step we would senin17 return to the utilitarian—more generally welfarist—arena; but that is not so. Utility is only one aspect of what goods can do for human beings, and it concentrates entirely on the psychological side of the story. There are, however, also non-psychological effects of goods on people, and a comparison of—say—malnutrition of different people is *neither* a comparison of foods they had consumed (they could consume the same food and still have different levels of malnourishment), *nor* a comparison of utility (they could be equally malnourished but their levels of satisfaction or desire-fulfilment could still be quite different). Essay 16 ('Equality of What?') develops and defends this perspective.

The following chart exemplifies the distinction between different categories involved in the relation between a good (say, a bike) and a person.

*Goods* ⟶ characteristics ⟶ functioning ⟶ utility
(e.g., a bike)   (e.g., transport)   (e.g., moving)   (e.g., pleasure)

'Characteristics' are qualities of goods, whereas 'functioning' relates to a person's *use* of those characteristics, e.g., *a bike* provides transport while *a person* moves with it.

Various wealth-based, growth-oriented criteria focus just on goods. This can be made more discriminating and purposive through Rawls's focus on 'primary goods'. The approach can also be refined by bringing in the Gorman–Lancaster[68] translation of commodities into characteristics, and this extension is close to Rawls's own approach. While these approaches deal with goods and characteristics, the focus on utility is common to all welfarist approaches (including, of course, utilitarianism).

What seems to be missing in between is a focus on the category of 'functioning' (e.g., moving, being well-nourished, being in good health, being socially respected). However, it can provide a basis for judging personal advantage which is neither purely commodity-centred, nor purely psychological.

When dealing with adults it seems natural to look not merely at whether a person is functioning in a certain way, but whether he has the *capability* to function in that way—even if he does not choose to do this. This is of course the typical concern of 'rights'—freedom of speech does not require that a person should be continuously speaking, but that he should be able to speak if he were to so choose. For many of the *basic capabilities,* e.g., the capability

68. W. M. Gorman, 'The Demand for Related Goods', *Journal Paper J3/29,* Iowa Experimental Station, Ames, Iowa, 1956; K. J. Lancaster, 'A New Approach to Consumer Theory', *Journal of Political Economy,* **74** (1966).

to be adequately nourished, the choice element may well be unimportant since opportunities if present will be taken up. In other cases the distinction is important.

Essay 16 argues in favour of focusing on basic capabilities (i.e., on the ability of a person to *function*), which reflect what people can actually do.[69] This differs from focusing on goods as such (as in the Rawlsian approach) or on the person's psychological relations only (as under the utilitarian approach). Even after this is accepted, there will remain, of course, various additional issues to consider. Different types of functioning, and correspondingly, different types of capabilities, have to be weighted. Problems of interpersonal conflicts also have to be faced. These problems naturally do remain; but the choice of focus variable is a *prior* requirement, and it is with that issue that Essay 16 is concerned.

## 5 Social Measurement

### 5.1 The axiomatic approach to poverty measurement

Essay 17 ('Poverty: An Ordinal Approach to Measurement') is aimed primarily at providing a more useful measure of poverty than found in the earlier literature. More ambitiously, it is also aimed at developing an axiomatic approach to the measurement of poverty.

The traditional measures of poverty concentrate either on the number of people below the poverty line ('the head-count measure' $H$) or on the aggregate income gap *vis-à-vis* the 'poverty line', of the people below that line ('the poverty gap measure' $I$). Obviously, each is seriously incomplete as a measure of poverty, but so is any combination of $H$ and $I$, since neither takes into account the distribution of incomes below the poverty line. A set of axioms is proposed for an acceptable measure of poverty, and this determines a unique measure $P$ (Theorem 1).[70]

These axioms are not, of course, the only ones that could be reasonably defended. Retaining the axiomatic approach, but varying the exact axioms, a number of other measures of poverty have been developed in the recent

69. It can also be shown that the focus on basic capabilities not only accommodates the perspective of rights, it is also helpful in understanding some earlier classic arguments, e.g., Marx's treatment of 'needs' in a non-subjective framework, Ernst Engel's statistical use of the share of expenditure on food as an indicator of well-being. On the latter and related methods of 'equivalence scales', see A. Deaton and J. Muellbauer, *Economics and Consumer Behaviour* (Cambridge: Cambridge University Press, 1980), chapter 8. The capability approach is further explored in my Hennipman Lecture, 'The Standard of Living', to be published by North-Holland, Amsterdam.

70. An earlier version of this result was presented in my 'Poverty, Inequality and Unemployment: Some Conceptual Issues in Measurement', *Economic and Political Weekly* (Bombay), **8** (1973).

literature.[71] These measures not only take into account the number of people below the poverty line and their income gaps, but they are also sensitive to the distribution of incomes below the poverty line. In Essay 17 the indicator of distributional inequality that emerges from the axioms, and is then incorporated in the measure $P$, happens to be the Gini coefficient. The set of axioms reflects—among other things—the consideration of 'relative deprivation', and that feature combined with 'ordinal' information regarding personal welfares (eschewing cardinality) makes the Gini coefficient emerge as a natural candidate; the Gini coefficient does indeed concentrate on each person's ordinal rank in the order of relative incomes.[72] If that focus on *relative* deprivation is dropped, or if it is thought possible to use a more *demanding* informational format regarding individual welfare (see Essay 12), or if the normalization procedures are altered, the axioms can be legitimately varied, and the axiomatically determined poverty measure will vary with that too.[73]

One particular issue of some contention has been the form of an axiom called the 'transfer axiom', which was mentioned in Essay 17, though it was not used to obtain any results at all. In Essay 8 ('Social Choice Theory: A Re-examination') the transfer axiom was weakened. The original—'strong'—version claims that any transfer of income from a poor person to anyone who is richer must increase the poverty measure. The 'weak' version insists on this *necessarily* only if such a transfer does not reduce the total number of poor people by transporting the recipient of the transfer across the poverty line. In so far as the index of poverty is seen as a representation of the condition of the poor—*how many* and each *how poor*—a plausible case can, in

71. See S. Anand, 'Aspects of Poverty in Malaysia', *Review of Income and Wealth,* 23 (1977); N. Kakwani, 'Measurement of Poverty and the Negative Income Tax', *Australian Economic Papers,* 16 (1977); K. Hamada and N. Takayama, 'Censored Income Distribution and the Measurement of Poverty', *Bulletin of International Statistical Institute,* 47 (1978); N. Takayama, 'Poverty, Income Inequality and Their Measures: Professor Sen's Approach Reconsidered', *Econometrica,* 47 (1979); D. Thon, 'On Measuring Poverty', *Review of Income and Wealth,* 25 (1979); S. Clark, R. Hemming and D. Ulph, 'On Indices for the Measurement of Poverty', *Economic Journal,* 91 (1981); C. Blackorby and D. Donaldson, 'Ethical Indices for the Measurement of Poverty', *Econometrica,* 48 (1980); G. Fields, *Poverty, Inequality, and Development* (Cambridge: Cambridge University Press, 1980); N. Kakwani, 'On a Class of Poverty Measures', *Econometrica,* 48 (1980), S. Chakravarty, 'Some Further Results in the Measurement of Poverty', mimeographed, Indian Statistical Institute, Calcutta, 1981; A. Kundu and T. E. Smith, 'An Impossibility Theorem on Poverty Indices', mimeographed, Regional Science, University of Pennsylvania, 1981; J. Foster, J. Greer and E. Thorbecke, 'A Class of Decomposable Poverty Measure', mimeographed, Cornell University, 1981; S. R. Osmani, *Economic Inequality and Group Welfare* (Oxford: Clarendon Press, forthcoming).

72. See my 'Informational Bases of Alternative Welfare Approaches: Aggregation and Income Distribution', *Journal of Public Economics,* 4 (1974). Also Essay 18.

73. I have discussed the class of these various poverty measures and the methodological and substantive issues underlying the choice of axioms, in my 'Issues in the Measurement of Poverty', *Scandinavian Journal of Economics,* 81 (1979), and in *Poverty and Famines: An Essay on Entitlement and Deprivation* (Oxford: Clarendon Press, 1981), chapters 2 and 3, and Appendix C.

fact, be made for permitting the possibility that a reduction of the number of the poor might under certain circumstances compensate a rise in the extent of penury of those who remain below the poverty line. The 'strong' transfer axiom takes no note whatever of the poverty line, and while that is quite legitimate for a general measure of economic inequality for the *whole* community, it is arguable that this is not so for a measure of poverty as such.

This remains an interesting and rather controversial issue. What is not, however, controversial is the fact that the poverty measure $P$ proposed in Essay 17 satisfies the 'weak' but not the 'strong' version of the transfer axiom.[74] There are variants of that measure proposed by others that do satisfy even the 'strong' version, but of course do not fulfil all the other axiomatic requirements used to obtain the so-called measure $P$. Given the complex nature of the concept of poverty,[75] it seems reasonable to argue that no *one* measure will be able to capture the entire concept. There is nothing particularly defeatist in accepting some 'pluralism', and pointing to a *class* of measures rather than to a unique 'correct' measure of poverty.[76]

The data requirement for empirical computation of measure $P$ and many of its variants is relatively modest, and indeed that was one of the considerations in pursuing this line of investigation.[77] There have been quite a few empirical applications (none, I hasten to add, by this author) of measure $P$ and its variants and the empirical exercises have helped to bring out various features of actual poverty that may be obscured by the more traditional measures.[78] And it is primarily because of these empirical applications that the analytical exercises in the axiomatic approach to the measurement of poverty have not ended up being just a theoretical hiccup in a practical world.

74. The erroneous assertion that the measure $P$ satisfies the strong transfer axiom, made in Essay 17 (though not used in the axiomatic derivation of measure $P$), was corrected in Essay 8 published the following year. The strong axiom is violated under some—rather special—circumstances.

75. On this question, see my 'Issues in the Measurement of Poverty' (1979); Blackorby and Donaldson, 'Ethical Indices for the Measurement of Poverty', (1980); Kakwani, 'On a Class of Poverty Measures' (1980); and Foster, Greer and Thorbecke, 'A Class of Decomposable Poverty Measures' (1981).

76. See Essay 20, 'Description as Choice'.

77. See my 'Poverty, Inequality and Unemployment: Some Conceptual Issues in Measurement' (1973).

78. See, among others, I. Z. Bhatty, 'Inequality and Poverty in Rural India', in T. N. Srinivasan and P. Bardhan (eds), *Poverty and Income Distribution in India* (Calcutta: Statistical Publishing Society, 1974); F. Seastrand and R. Diwan, 'Measurement and Comparison of Poverty and Inequality in the United States', presented at the Third World Econometric Congress, Toronto, 1975; Anand, 'Aspects of Poverty in Malaysia' (1977); S. A. R. Sastry, 'Poverty, Inequality and Development: A Study of Rural Andhra Pradesh', *Anvesak*, 7 (1977); R. J. Szal, 'Poverty: Measurement and Analysis', ILO Working Paper WEP 2–23/WP60, 1977; M. Ahluwalia, 'Rural Poverty and Agricultural Performance in India', *Journal of Development Studies*, 14 (1978); M. Alamgir, *Bangladesh: A Case of Below Poverty Level Equilibrium Trap* (Dacca: Bangladesh Institute of Development Studies, 1978); B. Dutta, 'On the Measurement of

## 5.2  *Real national income and named goods*

Essay 18 ('Real National Income') presents a general approach to comparisons of real national income in terms of social welfare evaluation. The procedure extends the traditional approach of *personal* real income analysis through constant-price comparisons, given convex preferences.[79] The approach yields partial orderings, being able to check only whether a point $x$ is below the tangent to the indifference curve through $y$ (more generally, whether $x$ is below the supporting hyperplane to the at-least-as-good region of $y$). One needs information regarding the 'locally relevant' weights, which with convexity then yields a partial ranking, and this avoids the hopeless task of seeking the indifference map itself.[80]

The extension to *national*—as opposed to *personal*—income and welfare requires the use of 'named goods', treating commodity $j$ going to person $i$ as a distinct named good $ij$. The various technical issues involved in using such a named-good approach to national income evaluation are discussed in Essay 18. One issue that does not get adequately discussed is the underlying basis of social welfare evaluation. It is, of course, common to interpret social welfare as a function of individual utilities (i.e., to assume 'welfarism'). In that context distributional weights can be related to individual utilities, e.g., to marginal utilities (as with utilitarianism), or to total utilities (as with 'Rawlsian' systems). However, welfarism is not the only possible way of making such judgements (see Essay 15), and it is possible to include various non-utility considerations that may be thought to be relevant to social welfare. It is even possible within this general approach to rely on considerations related to 'basic capabilities' and to concentrate on personal 'functioning' (see Essay 16 and Section 4.2 of this Introduction).

Practical applications require some fairly straightforward assumptions

Poverty in Rural India', *Indian Economic Review,* 13 (1978); Fields, *Poverty, Inequality, and Development* (1979); N. Kakwani, *Income, Inequality, and Poverty* (New York: Oxford University Press, 1980); Y. V. Pantulu, 'On Sen's Measure of Poverty', mimeographed, Sardar Patel Institute of Economic and Social Research, 1980; S. A. R. Sastry, 'Poverty: Concepts and Measurement', *Indian Journal of Economics,* 61 (1980); W. van Ginneken, 'Some Methods of Poverty Analysis: An Application to Iranian Data, 1975–1976' *World Development,* 8 (1980); A. Fishlow, 'Who Benefits from Economic Development?: Comment', *American Economic Review,* 70 (1980); G. S. Fields, 'Reply', *American Economic Review,* 70 (1980); Clark, Hemming and Ulph, 'On Indices for the Measurement of Poverty' (1981); Foster, Greer and Thorbecke, 'A Class of Decomposable Poverty Measures' (1981); Osmani, *Economic Inequality and Group Welfare,* forthcoming; R. Gaiha and N. A. Kazmi, 'Aspects of Poverty in Rural India', *Economics of Planning,* forthcoming; K. Sundaram and S. D. Tendulkar, 'Poverty Reduction in the Sixth Plan', Working Paper 233, Delhi School of Economics, 1981.

79. See J. R. Hicks, 'Valuation of Social Income', *Review of Economic Studies,* 7 (1940), and 'Measurement of Real Income', *Oxford Economic Papers,* 10 (1958). See also P. A. Samuelson, 'Evaluation of Real Income', *Oxford Economic Papers,* 2 (1950).

80. On the mechanics and the rationale of the approach, see my 'The Welfare Basis of Real Income Comparisons', *Journal of Economic Literature,* 17 (1979). See also Dan Usher's 'Comments' and my 'Reply' in the same journal, 18 (1980).

regarding the locally relevant weights. In Essay 18 the general approach is illustrated with the special case of 'rank order price weighting', taking the locally relevant weight on the named good $ij$ to be the product of the market price of commodity $j$ and the income rank of person $i$ (so that the poorer a person, the higher the local weights on the goods going to him).[81] There have been several empirical applications,[82] and these all involve integrating distributional considerations within the real income analysis of group welfare.

The approach presented in Essay 18 differs in motivation from the approach underlying the distinguished tradition in national income analysis of seeking a *complete* ordering based on a *partial* view (excluding distributional considerations) of economic welfare. Explicitly or implicitly within the general structure of that tradition, major contributions have been made to the practical measurement of national income by such authors as Kuznets,[83] Usher,[84] Nordhaus and Tobin,[85] Kravis, Heston and Summers,[86] and others.

81. Note, however, that in this particular illustration there is little scope for making any discriminating use of the 'capabilities' approach. Also, if 'rank order price weighting' is to be combined with 'welfarism', then because of the role of market prices, this illustration can be consistently used only under the assumption that individual preferences are identical and homothetic (or at least 'quasi-homothetic' with 'sufficiently high' incomes—the so-called 'Gorman case'), as has been shown by Peter Hammond, 'Economic Welfare with Rank Order Price Weighting', *Review of Economic Studies,* 45 (1978). On related issues, see also J. de V. Graaff, 'Equity and Efficiency as Components of General Welfare', *South African Journal of Economics,* 45 (1977); J. Muellbauer, 'Distributional Aspects of Price Comparisons', in R. Stone and W. Peterson (eds), *Economic Contributions to Public Policy* (London: Macmillan, 1978); K. Roberts, 'Price Independent Welfare Prescriptions', *Journal of Public Economics, 13* (1980); A. B. Atkinson and F. Bourguignon, 'The Comparison of Multi-Dimensional Distributions of Economic Status', *Review of Economic Studies,* 49 (1982).

82. See the Appendix to Essay 18; Sastry, 'Sen's Welfare Measure and the Ranking of Regions: Study of Rural Andhra Pradesh', *Asian Economic Review,* 19 (1977); Kakwani, *Income Inequality and Poverty,* 1980; B. Dutta, 'Intersectoral Disparities and Income Distribution in India: 1960-61 to 1973-74', *Indian Economic Review,* 15 (1980); N. Bhattacharya and G. S. Chatterjee, 'A Further Note on Between State Variations in Levels of Living in Rural India', in P. Bardhan and T. N. Srinivasan (eds), *Rural Poverty in South Asia* (New York: Columbia University Press, forthcoming); I. E. Broder and C. T. Morris, 'Socially Weighted Real Income Comparisons: An Appliation to India', *World Development* , forthcoming; Osmani, *Economic Inequality and Group Welfare,* forthcoming; R. Radhakrishna and A. Sarma, 'Intertemporal Comparisons of Welfare in India', presented at the 4th World Econometric Congress, Aix-en-Provence, 1980; among others. See also R. Marris and H. Theil, 'International Comparisons of Economic Welfare', presented at the American Economic Association meetings at Denver, 1980.

83. S. Kuznets, *Modern Economic Growth: Rate, Structure and Spread* (New Haven: Yale University Press, 1966).

84. D. Usher, *The Price Mechanism and the Meaning of National Income Statistics* (Oxford: Clarendon Press, 1968).

85. W. Nordhaus and J. Tobin, 'Is Growth Obsolete?' in National Bureau of Economic Research, *Economic Growth: Fiftieth Anniversary Colloquium* (New York: NBER, 1972).

86. I. B. Kravis, A. W. Heston and R. Summers, *International Comparisons of Real Product and Purchasing Power* (Baltimore: Johns Hopkins University Press, 1978).

In contrast with seeking a *complete* ordering from a partial view, the approach presented in Essay 18 seeks a *partial* ordering reflecting a *full* assessment of economic welfare of a group. The *former* feature—the partiality or incompleteness of the ordering—follows from the informational economy of invoking only the general assumption of convexity in using locally relevant weights, rather than assuming full knowledge of the complete indifference map (e.g., making the particular assumption of linearity—as opposed to just convexity—to use locally relevant weights).[87] The *latter* feature—the fullness of the economic welfare assessment for the group—follows from operating on named-good vectors rather than on the usual commodity vectors.[88] Even though the possibility of expanding the availability of relevant data for named-good analysis is substantial, the analytical illustrations and empirical applications show that specific types of named-good analysis are quite feasible even within the currently available statistics.

## 5.3  *Measurement, description and prescription*

In Essay 18 ('Real National Income') the evaluation of group income is explicitly related to the notion of the economic welfare of the group. It may be tempting to conclude from this that the exercise of real national income estimation has thus been converted into one of making prescriptive value judgements (through the choice of the group welfare function). This conclusion is misleading for two distinct reasons. First, group welfare can be given a descriptive as opposed to prescriptive interpretation. The notion of the economic welfare of the group, like that of the standard of living, can be related to the common ideas of national prosperity rather than directly to prescriptions as such. Indeed, right from the beginning, the subject of national income estimation has been related to seeking what Antoine Lavoisier called 'a veritable thermometer of national prosperity'.[89] Second, even if the group

87. The method of getting partial orderings from convexity builds on the foundations laid by John Hicks, 'The Valuation of Social Income' (1940).

88. This differs from Ian Little's well-known method of *supplementing* constant-price comparisons of aggregate commodity bundles with additional and distinct 'distributional' judgements, on which see Little, *A Critique of Welfare Economics.* See also A. K. Sen, 'Distribution, Transitivity and Little's Welfare Criterion', *Economic Journal,* 73 (1963); J. S. Chipman and J. C. Moore, 'Aggregate Demand, Real National Income, and the Compensation Principle', *International Economic Review,* 14 (1973); Y.-K. Ng, *Welfare Economics: Introduction and Basic Concepts* (London: Macmillan, 1979), chapter 3; Sen, 'The Welfare Basis of Real Income Comparisons' (1979), pp. 29–30. For a different approach to full assessment including factorization into equity and efficiency components, see Graaff, 'Equity and Efficiency as Components of General Welfare' (1977) and also his 'Tastes, Values and the Foundations of Normative Economics', presented at the 6th Interlaken Seminar on Analysis and Ideology, 1979.

89. A. Lavoisier, *De la richesse territoriale du royaume de France* (Paris, 1791). See also the historical study of P. Studenski, *The Income of Nations* (New York: New York University Press, 1958).

welfare function is interpreted in prescriptive terms, the choice of the group welfare function by the national-income measurer is not so much a matter of uncorking his or her own value judgement, but one of using the accepted value judgements in the society. Describing a prescription is not in itself a prescription.[90]

The scope for making explicit assumptions about values and prescriptions is enhanced in the case of estimation of national income by the fact that national income is largely a 'devised' concept and, obviously, did not have any primitve descriptive meaning in so far as economists 'invented' it. The same is not true of some other concepts used in economics such as inequality, which quite clearly has had primitive descriptive meaning.[91] It is this meaning that can get into a headlong conflict with the 'ethical measurement' of inequality, pioneered by Dalton, Kolm and Atkinson,[92] as is shown in Essay 19. While the 'ethical measures' can be quite useful for welfare-economic analysis,[93] this conflict has to be faced, for methodological clarity as well as for the substantive reason that the interest in inequality comparisons need not arise only from ethical preoccupations.[94] The same applies to the measurement of poverty, and the axioms used for deriving a poverty

90. The distinction is well brought out by Adam Smith's discussion of what counts as 'a necessary of life' (*An Inquiry into the Nature and Causes of the Wealth of Nations,* 1776, Everyman's Library, London: Dent, 1954, volume II, pp. 351–2), or by Karl Marx's discussion of 'the means of subsistence' (*Das Kapital,* volume I, 1867, English translation by S. Moore and E. Aveling, *Capital: A Critical Analysis of Capitalist Production,* London: Allen & Unwin, 1938, pp. 149–50).

91. See my *On Economic Inequality* (Oxford: Blackwell, 1973). The different connotations of 'income inequality' are clarified and investigated by F. Nygård and A. Sandström, *Measuring Income Inequality* (Stockholm: Almqvist & Wiksell International, 1981). See also R. Bentzel, 'The Social Significance of Income Distribution Statistics', *Review of Income and Wealth,* **16** (1970); B. Hansson, 'The Measurement of Social Inequality', in R. Butts and J. Hintikka (eds), *Logic, Methodology and Philosophy of Science* (Dordrecht: Reidel, 1977); F. A. Cowell, *Measuring Inequality* (Oxford: Philip Allan, 1977); A. Krelle and A. F. Shorrocks (eds), *Personal Income Distribution,* (Amsterdam: North-Holland, 1978).

92. H. Dalton, 'The Measurement of the Inequality of Incomes', *Economic Journal,* **30** (1980); S.-Ch. Kolm, 'The Optimum Production of Social Justice', presented at the International Economic Association Roundtable Conference at Biarritz in 1966, published in J. Margolis and H. Guitton (eds), *Public Economics* (London: Macmillan, 1969), and 'Unequal Inequalities', *Journal of Economic Theory,* **12, 13** (1976); A. B. Atkinson, 'On the Measurement of Inequality, *Journal of Economic Theory,* **2** (1970), and *The Economics of Inequality* (Oxford: Clarendon Press, 1976). See also my *On Economic Inequality* (1973).

93. In addition to the works of Atkinson, Dalton and Kolm, there have been several other important contributions in this tradition, e.g., C. Blackorby and D. Donaldson, 'Measures of Relative Equality and Their Meanings in Terms of Social Welfare', *Journal of Economic Theory,* **18** (1978). Descriptive characteristics of inequality can also be *directly* used for normative analysis; see, for example, P. Dasgupta, A. Sen and D. Starrett, 'Notes on the Measurement of Inequality of Incomes', *Journal of Economic Theory,* **6** (1973).

94. For example, one might be interested in the primarily predictive question as to whether greater economic inequality leads typically to more crime. Or one might wish to know more about the causal connections between economic inequality and work incentives in the 'welfare state' (cf. A. Lindbeck, 'Work Disincentives in the Welfare State', in *Nationalökonomische Gesellschaft Lectures 79–80* (Vienna: Manz, 1981)).

measure can be given various descriptive interpretations, of which reflecting the prevailing ethics is only one.[95]

In Essay 20 ('Description as Choice') some methodological issues concerning economic description are investigated.[96] This provides *inter alia* the occasion also for critically evaluating the important controversy between Milton Friedman and Paul Samuelson on the role of realism in economic analysis. While that controversy is primarily concerned with 'truth', many of the interesting issues arise only in the process of selection among alternative ways of truthfully describing the phenomenon in question. Various different motivations behind descriptive exercises in economics are examined in this context. It is also argued that the traditions of descriptive economics have been impoverished by the exclusive methodological concentration *either* on predictive interests (cf. Friedman),[97] *or* on prescriptive interests (cf. Myrdal).[98] These two do not exhaust—either individually or jointly—the motivations underlying descriptions in economics. While any description involves choice, grounds for selection can vary a great deal—much more so than the dominant methodological contributions suggest.

Since quite a few different motivations have been explicitly or implicitly invoked in the rag-bag of essays reprinted in this volume, the methodological position defended in Essay 20 may be seen as unduly comforting to the author. That is indeed a truthful description. But not, I believe, the only truthful one.

95. See my 'Issues in the Measurement of Poverty' (1979), pp. 285–8, and *Poverty and Famines: An Essay on Entitlement and Deprivation* (1981), chapter 2.

96. Some related issues have been explored in my 'Accounts, Actions and Values: Objectivity of Social Science', Wolfson College Lecture, 1981 to be published in Christopher Lloyd (ed.), *Social Theory and Political Practice* (Oxford: Oxford University Press, forthcoming).

97. M. Friedman, *Essays in Positive Economics* (Chicago: Chicago University Press, 1953).

98. G. Myrdal, *Political Elements in the Development of Economic Theory*, ed. by P. Streeten (London: International Library of Sociology, 1953). It is, however, clear that the later Myrdal sees his focus on value elements as a *corrective* to a common bias—a bias that the early Myrdal himself shared. On this question, see my 'Accounts, Actions and Values: Objectivity of Social Science' (1981).

# Part I

# Choice and Preference

# 1

# Choice Functions and Revealed Preference

## 1 *Motivation*

The object of this paper is to provide a systematic treatment of the axiomatic structure of the theory of revealed preference. In particular it is addressed to the following problems in revealed preference theory.

(1) Much of revealed preference theory has been concerned with choices restricted to certain distinguished subsets of alternatives, in particular to a class of convex polyhedra (e.g., 'budget triangles' in the two-commodity case). This restriction may have some rationale for analysing the preferences of competitive consumers, but it makes the results unusable for other types of choices, e.g., of government bureaucracies, of voters, of consumers in an imperfect market. If the restriction is removed, the axiomatic structure of revealed preference theory changes radically. This axiomatic structure is studied in Sections 2–5. In Section 6 the rationale of restricting the domain of choice functions and that of rationality conditions is critically examined.

(2) While some revealed preference theories are concerned with element-valued choice functions (i.e. with choice functions the range of which is restricted to unit sets), others assume set-valued choice functions. It is interesting to analyse the problem generally in terms of set-valued choice functions and then study the consequence of an additional restriction that all choice sets be unit sets. Section 7 is devoted to this additional restriction.

(3) While revealed preference theory has been obsessed with *transitivity*, certain weaker requirements have come to prominence in other branches

For comments and criticisms I am most grateful to Hans Herzberger and Roy Radner.

From *Review of Economic Studies,* **38** (July 1971), 307–17.

of choice theory. It is interesting to investigate the conditions that guarantee that a choice function is representable by a binary relation of preference whether or not that relation is transitive. Also the conditions that ensure transitivity of strict preference though not necessarily of indifference are worth studying because of the relevance of this case to demand theory (see Armstrong [1], Majumdar [14], Luce [13], Georgescu-Roegen [7]) and to the theory of collective choice (see Pattanaik [15], Sen [18], Inada [11], Fishburn [4]). The axiomatic structure of these requirements is studied in Sections 8–10. This also helps to achieve a factorisation of the conditions for full transitivity.

## 2   Choice Functions and Binary Relations

Let $X$ be the set of all alternatives. For any subset $S$ of $X$, a 'choice set' $C(S)$ represents the chosen elements of $S$. A 'choice function' is a functional relation that specifies a choice set $C(S)$ for any $S$ in a particular domain $K$ of non-empty subsets of $X$. We can represent a choice function as $C(\cdot)$, or more loosely as $C(S)$ taking $S$ as a variable within $K$.

*Definition* 1.   A function $C(\cdot)$ that specifies a non-empty choice set for every non-empty set $S$ in $K$ is called a choice function defined over $K$.

It will be assumed for the moment that $K$ includes *all* finite subsets of $X$. This assumption will be examined further in Section 6.

There are many alternative ways of generating binary relations of preference from any choice function. Three different ones will now be introduced. The first is that $x$ is 'at least as good as' $y$ if $x$ is chosen when $y$ is available. This is to be denoted $xRy$. Strict preference $(P)$ and indifference $(I)$ are defined correspondingly. For all $x$, $y$ in $X$:

*Definition* 2.   $xRy$ if and only if for some $S$ in $K$, $x \in C(S)$ and $y \in S$.

*Definition* 3.   $xPy$ if and only if $xRy$ and *not* $yRx$.

*Definition* 4.   $xIy$ if and only if both $xRy$ and $yRx$.

A second interpretation corresponds to Uzawa's [19] and Arrow's [2] definition of a 'relation generated' by the choice function in terms of choice over pairs, and we shall say $x\bar{R}y$ if $x$ is chosen (not necessarily uniquely) in a choice over the pair $[x,y]$. For all $x,y$ in $X$:

*Definition* 5.   $x\bar{R}y$ if and only if $x \in C([x,y])$.

*Definition* 6.   $x\bar{P}y$ if and only if $x\bar{R}y$ and *not* $y\bar{R}x$.

*Definition* 7.   $x\bar{I}y$ if and only if both $x\bar{R}y$ and $y\bar{R}x$.

A third interpretation corresponds to what Arrow [2] calls 'revealed preference' $\tilde{P}$. We say $x\tilde{P}y$ if $x$ is chosen when $y$ is available *and* rejected. We define $R$ and $I$ correspondingly. For all $x,y$ in $X$:

*Definition* 8.   $x\tilde{P}y$ if and only if there is some $S$ in $K$ such that $x \in C(S)$ and
$$y \in [S - C(S)].$$

*Definition* 9.   $x\tilde{R}y$ if and only if *not* $y\tilde{P}x$.

*Definition* 10.   $x\tilde{I}y$ if and only if $x\tilde{R}y$ and $y\tilde{R}x$.

The contrast between the definitions is illustrated in terms of an example.

*Example* 1.   $x = C([x,y])$, $y = C([y,z])$,
$x = C([x,z])$, $y = C([x,y,z])$.

It follows from the definitions that:

(1) $x\underline{I}y$, $y\underline{P}z$, and $x\underline{P}z$;
(2) $x\bar{P}y$, $y\bar{P}z$, and $x\bar{P}z$;
(3) $x\tilde{P}y$, $y\tilde{P}z$, $x\tilde{P}z$, and $y\tilde{P}x$.

All the interpretations have some problem. $R$ has the problem that $x$ and $y$ are treated as indifferent even though $x$ is chosen and $y$ rejected over the pair $[x,y]$. $\bar{R}$ has, on the other hand, the problem that $x$ is declared as strictly preferred to $y$, even though $y$ is chosen and $x$ rejected in the choice over the triple $[x,y,z]$. However, $\tilde{R}$ involves the problem that $\tilde{P}$ is not asymmetric, and $x$ is declared preferred to $y$ and $y$ to $x$. Another way of viewing the problem in (3) is that $\tilde{R}$ is not 'complete' over $[x,y]$. On the other hand, $R$ and $\bar{R}$ are always complete if $K$ includes all finite subsets of $X$, or even if it only includes all pairs in $X$.

It can be established that for any $C(S)$, $(R = \bar{R})$ if and only if $(P = \bar{P}$ & $I = \bar{I})$, $(\bar{R} = \tilde{R})$ if and only if $(\bar{P} = \tilde{P}$ & $I = \tilde{I})$, and $(\tilde{R} = R)$ if and only if $(\tilde{P} = P$ & $\tilde{I} = I)$. The proofs are straightforward.

### 3     *Image, Normality and Binariness*

Corresponding to each choice function $C(S)$ we may define its 'image' $\hat{C}(S)$ as the choice function generated by the binary relation $R$ revealed by $C(S)$.

*Definition* 11.   For any $S$ in $K$, $\hat{C}(S) = [x \in S$ and for all $y$ in $S$, $xRy]$.

That is $C(S)$ consists of the 'best' elements of $S$ in terms of the relation $R$. Clearly, $C(S) \subset \hat{C}(S)$, since $x \in C(S)$ implies that for all $y$ in $S$, $xRy$. But the converse may not hold as is clear from Example 1.

*Definition* 12.   A choice function $C(S)$ is *normal* if and only if $C(S) = \hat{C}(S)$ for all $S$ in $K$.

It is clear that a choice function being normal is equivalent to its being essentially binary in composition. Further, for a normal choice function,

$R = \bar{R}$. But $R = \bar{R}$ does not imply that the choice function is normal. The last is clear from the following example.

*Example* 2.   $[x] = C([x,y])$, $[x,z] = C([x,z])$, $[z] = ([y,z])$, $[x] = C([x,y,z])$.

This implies $xPy$, $xIz$, $zPy$, and $x\bar{P}y$, $x\bar{I}z$, $z\bar{P}y$. But $[x,z] = \hat{C}([x,y,z])$. Note also that a normal choice function does not guarantee that $R = \tilde{R}$, though the converse will be shown to be true (see T.3).


## 4   *Axioms of Revealed Preference and Congruence*

The concept of *indirect* revealed preference discussed by Houthakker [9] makes use of the finite closure of $\tilde{P}$. *Indirect* revealed preference in the 'wide' sense (see Richter [16]) is based on the finite closure of $R$.

*Definition* 13.   For any pair $x,y$ in $X$, $x$ is *indirectly revealed preferred* to $y$ (denoted $xP^*y$) if and only if there exists in $X$ a sequence $x^i$, $i = 0, \ldots, n$, such that $x^0 = x$, $x^n = y$, and for all $i = 1, \ldots, n$, $x^{i-1}\tilde{P}x^i$.

*Definition* 14.   For any pair $x,y$ in $X$, $x$ is *indirectly revealed preferred* to $y$ *in the wide sense* (denoted $xWy$) if and only if there exists in $X$ a sequence $x^i$, $i = 0, \ldots, n$, such that $x^0 = x$, $x^n = y$, and for all $i = 1, \ldots, n$, $x^{i-1}Rx^i$.

The following conditions of rationality have been much discussed in the literature. For all $x,y$ in $X$:

WEAK AXIOM OF REVEALED PREFERENCE (WARP): *If $x\tilde{P}y$, then not $yRx$.*

STRONG AXIOM OF REVEALED PREFERENCE (SARP): *If $xP^*y$, then not $yRx$.*

STRONG CONGRUENCE AXIOM (SCA): *If $xWy$, then for any $S$ in $K$ such that $y \in C(S)$ and $x \in S$, $x$ must also belong to $C(S)$.*

WARP and SARP were respectively proposed by Samuelson [17] and by Houthakker [9], Ville [20] and von Neumann and Morgenstern [21], adapted here as in Arrow [2] to correspond to set-valued choice functions. SCA is Richter's [16] 'Congruence Axiom', renamed to permit a weak version of it to be proposed, which is done below.

WEAK CONGRUENCE AXIOM (WCA): *If $xRy$, then for any $S$ in $K$ such that $y \in C(S)$ and $x \in S$, $x$ must also belong to $C(S)$.*

(T.1)   *The Weak Congruence Axiom implies that the revealed preference $R$ is an ordering, and if the choice function is normal then the converse is also true.*

*Proof.*   Since the domain of the choice function includes all finite sets, $R$ must be complete and reflexive. To prove that *WCA* implies the transitivity of $R$ take any triple $T = [x,y,z]$ such that $xRy$ and $yRz$. In view of WCA if

$z \in C(T)$, then $y \in C(T)$, and if $y \in C(T)$ then $x \in C(T)$. But at least one of $x, y$ and $z$ must be in $C(T)$. Hence $x \in C(T)$ and thus $xRz$. $R$ is, therefore, transitive.

To show the converse, for any $S$ in $K$, let $y \in C(S)$, $x \in S$ and $xRy$. Clearly, $yRz$ for all $z$ in $S$, and in view of $xRy$ and the transitivity of $R$, $xRz$ for all $z$ in $S$. Thus $x \in \hat{C}(S)$. And since the choice function is normal, $x \in C(S)$. Hence WCA holds.

While WCA seems necessary and sufficient for an ordinal preference structure, the same result is guaranteed by the convergence of $R$ and $\tilde{R}$.

(T.2)  *The Weak Congruence Axiom holds if and only if $R = \tilde{R}$.*

*Proof.* Let WCA be violated. Evidently for some $S$ in $K$, for some $x, y \in S$, while $y \in C(S)$ and $xRy$, $x$ does not belong to $C(S)$. Obviously $y\tilde{P}x$, so that *not $x\tilde{R}y$*. Thus $R \neq \tilde{R}$, and therefore $R = \tilde{R}$ implies WCA.

To show the converse it is noted that $x\tilde{R}y$ implies *not $y\tilde{P}x$*, which guarantees that $x \in C([x,y])$ and therefore $xRy$. On the other hand, *not $x\tilde{R}y$* implies $y\tilde{P}x$ so that for some $S$ in $K$, we have $y \in C(S)$ and $x \in [S - C(S)]$. If it is now assumed that $xRy$, then WCA will be violated, and therefore *not $xRy$*. Thus WCA implies $R = \tilde{R}$.

## 5   *Equivalence of Axioms*

This equivalence can be extended to cover all the 'rationality' conditions proposed so far.

(T.3)  *The following conditions are equivalent:*

   *(i)  $R$ is an ordering and C(S) is normal;*
   *(ii)  $\bar{R}$ is an ordering and C(S) is normal;*
   *(iii)  Weak Congruence Axiom;*
   *(iv)  Strong Congruence Axiom;*
   *(v)  Weak Axiom of Revealed Preference;*
   *(vi)  Strong Axiom of Revealed Preference;*
   *(vii)  $R = \tilde{R}$;*
*and (viii)  $\bar{R} = R$ and C(S) is normal.*

*Proof.* The equivalence of (i) and (ii) is immediate since $C(S)$ being normal implies $R = \bar{R}$.

From (T.1), (i) implies (iii) and (iii) implies that $R$ is an ordering. The equivalence of (i) and (iii) is completed by showing that WCA guarantees the normality of the choice function. Since $C(S) \subset \hat{C}(S)$, it is sufficient to show that WCA implies that $\hat{C}(S) \subset C(S)$. Let $y \in C(S)$ while $x \in \hat{C}(S)$. Obviously $xRy$, and hence by WCA, $x \in C(S)$.

By definition (iv) implies (iii). To prove the converse assume that WCA holds and the antecedent of SCA holds, i.e., $y \in C(S)$, $x \in S$, and $xWy$. Since $y \in C(S)$, $yRz$ for all $z$ in $S$. Using the notation of Definition 14, if $x^{n-1}Py$, then $x^{n-1}Rz$ for all $z$ in $S$ since $R$ is transitive given WCA. Thus $x^{n-1} \in \hat{C}(S^1)$, where $S^1$ is the union of $S$ and the unit set $[x^{n-1}]$. Hence $x^{n-1}Py$ implies that $x^{n-1} \in C(S^1)$. If, on the other hand, $yIx^{n-1}$, then $y \in \hat{C}(S^1)$ since $y \in \hat{C}(S)$. Thus by normality $y \in C(S^1)$, and by WCA, $x^{n-1} \in C(S^1)$. Similarly $x^{n-2} \in C(S^2)$ where $S^2$ is the union of $S^1$ and the unit set $[x^{n-2}]$. Proceeding this way $x = x^0$ is in the choice set of $S^n$. But if $x$ is in $\hat{C}(S^n)$, then $x \in \hat{C}(S)$, since $S \subset S^n$. Hence $x \in C(S)$ and SCA must hold.

Next the equivalence of (iii) and (v). If WARP is violated, then for some $x$, $y \in X$, we have $x\widetilde{P}y$ and $yRx$. Since $x\widetilde{P}y$ implies that there is an $S$ in $K$ such that $x \in C(S)$, $y \in S$, and $y$ is not in $C(S)$, WCA must be false in view of $yRx$. Thus WCA implies WARP. Conversely, let WCA be violated. Then for some $x, y \in S$ we have $xRy$, when $y$ is in $C(S)$ but $x$ is not in $C(S)$. Evidently $xRy$ and $y\widetilde{P}x$. This is a violation of WARP.

Next, (vi) is taken up. Obviously, (vi) implies (v), since SARP subsumes WARP. On the other hand, by (T.1), WCA implies that $R$ is an ordering. Hence WARP, which is equivalent to WCA, implies that $R$ is an ordering. But by (T.2), $R = \widetilde{R}$ in view of WCA. Hence WARP guarantees that $\widetilde{R}$ is an ordering and that $xP^*y$ implies $x\widetilde{P}y$ for all $x,y$ in $X$. But then WARP implies SARP.

Equivalence of (vii) and (iii) is given by (T.2) and that of (viii) and (vii) follows from the fact that $R = \bar{R}$ whenever $C(S)$ is normal. This establishes (T.3).

This demonstration of the complete equivalence of all the rationality conditions proposed so far would seem to complete a line of enquiry initiated by Arrow [2] who proved the equivalence of (ii), (v) and (vi).[1] Some of the results contained in (T.3) have *apparently* been denied and it is worth commenting on a few of the corners. For example, Richter [16], who has proved the equivalence of SCA and (i), has argued that 'it can be shown that the Congruence Axiom does not imply the Weak Axiom [of revealed preference] and hence not the Strong' (p. 639). But the difference seems to arise from the fact that Richter applies Samuelson's and Houthakker's definition of the revealed preference axioms, which are made with the assumption of element-valued (as opposed to set-valued) choice functions, to a case where there are a number of best elements in the set (Richter [16], Figure 2, p. 639). Similarly, Houthakker's [9] argument for the necessity of bringing in the Strong Axiom of Revealed Preference, rather than making do with the Weak Axiom, arises from the fact that Houthakker considers a choice function that is defined

---

1. Some weaker rationality conditions will be discussed in the following sections of the paper. See also Herzberger [8] for a vast collection of results involving some rationality axioms not covered here.

over certain distinguished sets only, viz., a class of convex polyhedra representing budget sets, and which is undefined over finite subsets of elements. The same is true of Gale's [6] demonstration that WARP does not imply SARP in a rejoinder to Arrow's paper [2].

Finally, it may be noted that rationality may be identified with the systematic convergence of different interpretations of the preference revealed by a choice function. As is clear from (T.3), $R = \widetilde{R}$ implies complete rationality in the sense of transitivity and normality, and so does $\widetilde{R} = \bar{R}$ if the choice function is normal. That a primitive concept like the coincidence of different interpretations of revealed preference can be taken to be a complete criterion of rationality of choice is of some interest in understanding this problematic concept.

## 6  The Domain of the Choice Function and the Rationality Axioms

It is conventional to assume in revealed preference theory that the domain of the choice function includes only the class of convex polyhedra that represent 'budget sets' in some real (commodity) space, e.g., 'budget triangles' in the two-commodity case. In contrast it has been assumed here that the domain includes all finite subsets of $X$ whether or not it includes any other subset. The difference is significant for Arrow's [2] result on the equivalence of the 'weak' and the 'strong' axioms of revealed preference and more generally for the set of equivalences established here in (T.3).

Evidently if there is some argument for confining the domain to the budget polyhedra, it applies to the study of the competitive consumer and not to choices of other agents, e.g., a non-competitive consumer, a voter or a government bureaucracy. But does it make sense even for the competitive consumer? The question deserves a close examination.

It is certainly the case that the observed behaviour of the competitive consumer will include choices only over budget sets. What can then be the operational significance, it might be asked, of including *other* subsets in the domain of the choice function? The significance lies in the fact that the interpretation of observed choices will depend on whether it is assumed that the rationality axioms would hold over other potential choice situations as well even though these choices cannot be observed in the competitive market. For example if it is assumed that the Weak Congruence Axiom would hold over finite subsets as well, then the observation that $x$ is chosen when $y$ is available in the budget set and $y$ is chosen when $z$ is in the budget set can be used as a basis for deducing that $x$ is regarded as at least as good as $z$ even without observing that $x$ is chosen when $z$ is available. This is because by (T.2) WCA defined over all finite subsets implies that $R$ is transitive. Thus the *interpretation* of observed choices will vary with what is assumed about the applicability of the rationality axioms to unobserved choices.

Thus a real difference with operational significance is involved. But it may be argued that if some choices are never observed how can we postulate rationality axioms for these choices since we cannot *check* whether the rationality axioms assumed would hold? This problem raises important questions about the methodological basis of revealed preference theory. In particular the following two questions are relevant.

(1) Are the rationality axioms to be used only after establishing them to be true?
(2) Are there reasons to expect that some of the rationality axioms will tend to be satisfied in choices over 'budget sets' but not in other choices?

Suppose a certain axiom is shown to guarantee some rationality results if the axiom holds over every element in a certain class of subsets of $X$, i.e., over some domain $K^* \subset K$. In order to *test* this axiom before using, we have to observe choices over every element of $K^*$. Consider $K^*$ as the class of budget sets. We know that any observed choice will be from $K^*$ in the competitive market, but this is not the same thing as saying that choice from every element of $K^*$ will, in fact, be observed. There are an infinite (and uncountable) number of budget sets even for the two-commodity case and choices only over a few will be observed. What is then the status of an axiom that is used in an exercise having been seen to be not violated over a tiny *proper* subset of $K^*$? Clearly it is still an assumption rather than an established fact. There is, of course, nothing profound in this recognition, and it is in the nature of the theory of revealed preference that the exercise consists of taking axioms in the strictly logical sense and then deriving analytical results assuming these axioms to be true. But then the question arises: why assume the axioms to be true only for 'budget sets' and not for others? Such results as the non-equivalence of the 'weak' and the 'strong' axioms relate to this issue.

This takes us to question (2). Are there reasons to expect the fulfilment of these axioms over budget sets but not over other subsets of $K$? No plausible reasoning seems to have been put forward to answer the question in the affirmative. The difference lies in the ability to *observe* violation of axioms and not in any inherent reason to expect violations in one case and not in the other. But even for $K^*$ not all choices will be observed. Why then restrict the domain of an axiom to $K^*$ only and not to entire $K$ when (*a*) verification is possible in fact neither for $K$ nor for $K^*$, and (*b*) there are no *a priori* reasons to expect the axiom to hold over $K^*$ but not over $(K - K^*)$?

The validity of the theorems obtained does not, of course, depend on whether we find the above line of argument to be convincing, but the importance of the results clearly does, especially for demand theory.

Two final remarks may be made. First, while it is not required that the domain includes all *infinite* sets as well, nothing would of course be affected in the results and the proofs even if all infinite sets are included in the domain. Second, it is not really necessary that even all finite sets be included in the domain. All the results and proofs would continue to hold even if the domain includes all pairs and triples but not all finite sets.

## 7  Element-valued Choice Functions

Much of revealed preference theory has been concerned with element-valued choice functions. Certain special results are true for such functions.

(T.4)  *A choice function the range of which is restricted to the class of unit sets is normal if and only if R is an ordering.*

*Proof.* Let $C(S)$ be normal. For some, $x$, $y$, $z$ in $X$ let $xRy$ & $yRz$. Hence $x\bar{R}y$ & $y\bar{R}z$ since $C(S)$ is normal, and $x\bar{P}y$ & $y\bar{P}z$ as the choice sets are unit sets. Thus $xPy$ & $yPz$ due to normality. If we now take $[z] = C([x,z])$, then $zPx$, but that will make $C([x,y,z])$ empty. Since this is impossible, $[x] = C([x,z])$, and hence $xPz$. Thus $R$ is transitive.

It is obvious that choice sets being unit sets would imply $P = R = \tilde{P}$. And if $R$ is an ordering, $R = \tilde{R}$, and this implies that the choice function is normal by (T.3).

Consider now a weak property of rationality originally introduced by Chernoff [3].

*Property α.*  For any pair of sets $S$ and $T$ in $K$ and for any $x \in S$, if $x \in C(T)$ and $S \subset T$, then $x \in C(S)$.

That is, if $x$ is 'best' in a set it is best in all subsets of it to which $x$ belongs.

(T.5)  *Any normal choice function satisfies Property α.*

*Proof.* Let $x \in C(T)$. Then $xRy$ for all $y$ in $T$. If $S \subset T$, then $xRy$ for all $y$ in $S$. Thus, $x \in \hat{C}(S)$. By normality $x \in C(S)$.

(T.6)  *A choice function the range of which is restricted to the class of unit sets satisfies Property α if and only if it satisfies WCA.*

*Proof.* WCA implies normality and by (T.5) this implies Property α. Regarding the converse it is sufficient to show that α implies that the antecedent of WCA must always be false. If it were not false, then for some $S$, $x \in S$, $y \in C(S)$ and $xRy$. Since $y \in C(S)$ and $x \in S$, by Property α, $y \in C([x,y])$. On the other hand, since $xRy$, obviously for some $H$ such that $y \in H$, $x$ belongs to $C(H)$. Then by α, $x \in C([x,y])$. But this is impossible since $C([x,y])$ must be a unit set.

As a corollary to (T.6) it is noted that for element-valued choice functions Property α implies *all* the conditions covered in (T.3).[2]

---

2. For a direct proof that for element-valued choice functions α is equivalent to condition (v) in (T.3), see Houthakker [10].

## 8   *Transitivity and Factorization*

For element-valued choice functions Property $\alpha$ implies complete rationality, but what does $\alpha$ imply in general? Not even normality as is clear from Example 2 in Section 3, but it does guarantee that $R = \bar{R}$.

(T.7)   *For any choice function Property $\alpha$ implies $R = \bar{R}$.*

*Proof.*   $x\bar{R}y$ implies $xRy$ by definition. With $xRy$ we know that for some $S$ in $K$, $x \in C(S)$ and $y \in S$. By $\alpha$, $x \in C([x,y])$. Hence $x\bar{R}y$.

How can $\alpha$ be supplemented in the general case to get complete rationality? Property $\beta$ was introduced for this purpose (see Sen [18]).

*Property $\beta$.*   For all pairs of sets $S$ and $T$ in $K$ and for all pairs of elements $x$ and $y$ belonging to $C(S)$, if $S \subset T$, then $x \in C(T)$ if and only if $y \in C(T)$.

That is, if $x$ and $y$ are both best in $S$, a subset of $T$, then $x$ is best in $T$ if and only if $y$ is best in $T$.

(T.8)   *A choice function satisfies the Weak Congruence Axiom if and only if it satisfies Properties $\alpha$ and $\beta$.*

*Proof.*   By (T.3), WCA implies normality, which in turn implies $\alpha$, by (T.5). Let $\beta$ be violated with $x$ but not $y$ belonging to $C(T)$. But since $x \in S$ and $y \in C(S)$, we have $yRx$. This is a violation of WCA. Thus WCA implies $\alpha$ and $\beta$ both.

Now the converse. Let the antecedent of WCA hold, and for some $S$, $x \in S$, $y \in C(S)$ and $xRy$. By $\alpha$, $y \in C([x,y])$. Since $xRy$, for some $H$, $x \in C(H)$ and $y \in H$. By $\alpha$, $x \in C([x,y])$. Thus $[x,y] = C([x,y])$. But then by $\beta$, $y \in C(S)$ if and only if $x \in C(S)$. Since $y$ is, in fact, in $C(S)$, so must be $x$. Thus WCA must hold and it is shown that $\alpha$ and $\beta$ together imply WCA.

A corollary to (T.8) is that $\alpha$ and $\beta$ together imply all the conditions listed in (T.3) and thus amount to complete rationality in the usual sense.

## 9   *Axioms for Normality and Binariness*

Properties $\alpha$ and $\beta$ imply normality and transitivity of $R$. What implies normality alone?

*Property $\gamma$.*   Let $M$ be any class of sets chosen from $K$ and let $V$ be the union of all sets in $M$. Then any $x$ that belongs to $C(S)$ for all $S$ in $M$ must belong to $C(V)$.

That is, if $x$ is best in each set in a class of sets such that their union is $V$, then $x$ must be best in $V$.

(T.9)   *A choice function is normal if and only if it satisfies Properties $\alpha$ and $\gamma$.*

*Proof.* Let $C(S)$ be normal. By (T.5) it satisfies Property $\alpha$. Let the antecedent of Property $\gamma$ be fulfilled. Thus $xRy$ for all $y$ in $V$. Hence $x \in \hat{C}(V)$. But since $C(S)$ is normal, $x \in C(V)$. Hence Property $\gamma$ is also satisfied.

To prove the converse let $x$ belong to $\hat{C}(V)$. Thus $xRy$ for all $y$ in $V$. By (T.7), $x\bar{R}y$ for all $y$ in $V$. Therefore, $x \in C([x,y])$ for all $y$ in $V$. Therefore by Property $\gamma$, $x \in C(V)$. Hence $C(S)$ is normal.[3]

## 10   *Axioms for Quasi-transitivity*

An intermediate property between normality alone and that with full transitivity is normality coupled with 'quasi-transitivity' of revealed preference (see Sen [18]). Armstrong [1] had shown the plausibility of intransitive indifference combined with transitive strict preference. This possibility has been discussed further by Georgescu-Roegen [7], Majumdar [14] and others in the context of demand theory, and by Pattanaik [15], Sen [18], Inada [11], Fishburn [4] and others in the context of the theory of collective choice.

Luce [12], [13] has studied extensively the case of 'semi-orders' which is a special case of quasi-transitivity.[4] Our concentration here will be on the more general condition. What guarantees quasi-transitivity as such?

*Property $\delta$.*   For any pair of finite sets $S$, $T$ in $K$, for any pair of elements $x$, $y \in C(S)$, if $S \subset T$, then $[x] \neq C(T)$.

That is, if $x$ and $y$ are both best in $S$, a subset of $T$, then neither of them can be *uniquely* best in $T$. However, unlike in the case of Property $\beta$ it is not required that if one of $x$ and $y$ is best in $T$, then so should be the other.

---

3. For any finite class $K$ properties $\alpha$ and $\gamma$ can be redefined in terms of pairs of sets in the following way.

For all $X$ and $Y$ in $K$:

Property $\alpha^*$: $C(X \cup Y) \subset [C(X) \cup C(Y)]$;
Property $\gamma^*$: $[C(X) \cap C(Y)] \subset C(X \cup Y)$.

It is clear that $\alpha^*$ amounts to $\alpha$, and $\gamma$ is the finite closure of $\gamma^*$. This formulation brings out the complementary nature of the two properties in an illuminating way and I am grateful to Hans Herzberger for drawing my attention to this.

4. The axiomatic structure of semiorders has recently been subjected to a searching examination by Dean Jamison and Lawrence Lau in 'Semiorders, Revealed Preference, and the Theory of the Consumer Demand', Technical Report No. 31, Institute for Mathematical studies in the Social Sciences, Stanford University, July 1970, presented at the World Econometric Congress in Cambridge, September 1970. [Revised version published in *Econometrica*, **41** (1973).]

(T.10)   *For a normal choice function, R is quasi-transitive (i.e., strict P is transitive) if and only if Property $\delta$ is satisfied.*

*Proof.*   Let $xPy$ and $yPz$ hold. If *not $xRz$*, then $\hat{C}([x,y,z])$ will be empty, which is impossible since $C(S)$ is normal. Hence $xRz$. If $xIz$, then $[x,z] = C([x,z])$. Property $\delta$ will now imply that $x$ should not be uniquely best in $[x,y,z]$, but we know that

$$[x] = \hat{C}([x,y,z]).$$

This is a contradiction since $C(S)$ is normal. Hence $xPz$. So $R$ is quasi-transitive.

To prove the converse let $\delta$ be violated, and in spite of the antecedent holding, let $[x] = C(T)$. Since $y \in C(S)$, $yRx$ holds, so that $y$ can fail to belong to $\hat{C}(T)$ only if some $z^1$ in $T$ exists such that $z^1Py$. But $z^1$ does not belong to $C(T) = \hat{C}(T)$, so that there exists $z^2$: $z^2Pz^1$, and by quasi-transitivity $z^2Py$. Obviously, $z^2 \neq x$, since $yRx$, and there exists $z^3$: $z^3Pz^2$. Proceeding this way we get a sequence $z^1, z^2, \ldots, z^n$, such that $z^i \neq x$ and $z^{i+1}Pz^i$, for $i = 1, \ldots, n - 1$, and such that all elements of $T$ other than $x$ and $y$ are exhausted.

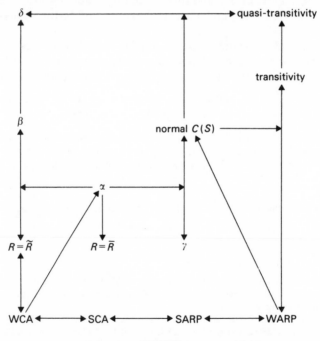

FIGURE 1

5. It may be observed that Property $\delta$ can be apparently relaxed to $\delta^*$ to require that the stated condition should hold for all triples $T$ and subsets $S$ thereof, rather than for all finite sets $S$ and $T$. From the proof of (T.10) it is seen that for a normal choice function $\delta^*$ is sufficient to guarantee quasi-transitivity, but then by (T.10) $\delta^*$ guarantees $\delta$, and thus no real relaxation is involved.

If $xPz^n$, then by quasi-transitivity $xPy$. This is impossible and hence $z^n \in C(T)$. But this is a contradiction since $[x] = C(T)$.[5]

Finally, the main results presented in the paper are represented in an Implication Diagram with the direction of the arrow representing that of implication.

## References

[1] Armstrong, W. E. 'The Determinateness of the Utility Function', *Economic Journal*, **49** (1939).

[2] Arrow, K. J. 'Rational Choice Functions and Orderings', *Economica*, N.S., **26** (1959).

[3] Chernoff, H. 'Rational Selection of Decision Functions', *Economica*, **22** (1954).

[4] Fishburn, P. C. 'Intransitive Individual Indifference and Transitive Majorities', *Econometrica*, **38** (1970).

[5] ____ 'Intransitive Indifference in Preference Theory: A Survey', *Operations Research*, **18** (1970).

[6] Gale, D. 'A Note on Revealed Preference', *Economica*, **27** (1960).

[7] Georgescu-Roegen, N. 'Threshold in Choice and the Theory of Demand', *Econometrica*, **26** (1958).

[8] Herzberger, H. 'Ordinal Choice Structures', mimeographed, 1968. [Revised version published later in *Econometrica*, **41** (1973).]

[9] Houthakker, H. S. 'Revealed Preference and Utility Function', *Economica*, N.S., **17** (1950).

[10] ____ 'On the Logic of Preference and Choice', in A. Tymieniecka, *Contributions to Logic and Methodology in Honor of J. M. Bochenski* (North-Holland, Amsterdam, 1956).

[11] Inada, K. 'Majority Rule and Rationality', *Journal of Economic Theory,* **2** (1970).

[12] Luce, R. D. 'Semiorders and a Theory of Utility Discrimination', *Econometrica*, **24** (1956).

[13] ____ *Individual Choice Behaviour* (Wiley, New York, 1958).

[14] Majumdar, T. *The Measurement of Utility* (Macmillan, London, 2nd ed., 1962).

[15] Pattanaik, P. 'A Note on Democratic Decisions and the Existence of Choice Sets', *Review of Economic Studies,* **35** (1968).

[16] Richter, M. K. 'Revealed Preference Theory', *Econometrica,* **34** (1966).

[17] Samuelson, P. A. 'A Note on the Pure Theory of Consumers' Behaviour', *Economica*, N.S., **5** (1938).

[18] Sen, A. K. 'Quasi-transitivity, Rational Choice and Collective Decisions', *Review of Economic Studies,* **36** (1969). [Essay 6 in this volume.]

[19] Uzawa, H. 'A Note on Preference and Axioms of Choice', *Annals of the Institute of Statistical Mathematics,* **8** (1956).

[20] Ville, J. 'Sur les conditions d'existence d'une ophélimité totale et d'un indice du niveau des prix', *Annales de l'Université de Lyon,* **9** (1946).

[21] von Neumann, J., and Morgenstern, O. *Theory of Games and Economic Behaviour* (Princeton University Press, Princeton, 1944).

[22] Wold, H. O. A. *Demand Analysis* (Wiley, New York, 1963).

# 2

# Behaviour and the Concept of Preference

1

Thirty-five years have passed since Paul Samuelson published in the house journal of the London School of Economics his pioneering contribution to the theory of 'revealed preference'.[1] The term was perhaps not altogether a fortunate one. Revelation conveys something rather dramatic, and the biblical association induced the late Sir Dennis Robertson to wonder whether 'to some latter-day saint, in some new Patmos off the coast of Massachusetts, the final solution to all these mysteries had been revealed in a new apocalypse'.[2] While the appropriateness of the terminology may be debatable, the approach of revealed preference has gradually taken hold of choice theory in general and of demand theory in particular.

My intention in this lecture is to examine the philosophy behind the approach of revealed preference and to raise some queries about its use, and then to go on to discuss the implications of these issues for normative economics. The crux of the question lies in the interpretation of underlying preference from observations of behaviour.

'The individual guinea-pig', wrote Paul Samuelson, 'by his market behaviour, reveals his preference pattern—if there is such a consistent pattern.'[3] If a collection of goods $y$ could have been bought by a certain individual within his budget when he in fact was observed to buy another collection $x$, it is to be presumed that he has revealed a preference for $x$ over $y$. The outside observer notices that this person *chose x* when $y$ was available

1. P. A. Samuelson, 'A Note on the Pure Theory of Consumer's Behaviour', *Economica*, 5 (1938). Also 'A Note on the Pure Theory of Consumer's Behaviour: An Addendum', *Economica,* 5 (1938).
2. D. H. Robertson, *Utility and All That* (London, 1952), p. 19.
3. P. A. Samuelson, 'Consumption Theory in Terms of Revealed Preference', *Economica,* 15 (1948).

An inaugural lecture delivered at the London School of Economics, published in *Economica,* 40 (August 1973), 241–59.

and infers that he *preferred x* to *y*. From the point of view of introspection of the person in question, the process runs from his preference to his choice, but from the point of view of the scientific observer the arrow runs in the opposite direction: choices are observed first and preferences are then presumed from these observations.

The consistency condition that Samuelson based his theory on, which has come to be known as the Weak Axiom of Revealed Preference, says that if a person reveals a preference—in the sense just defined—for *x* over *y*, then he must not also reveal a preference for *y* over *x*. That is, if he chooses *x* when *y* is available, then he will not choose *y* in a situation in which *x* is also obtainable. Armed with this innocuous-looking axiom, Samuelson proceeded to obtain analytically the standard results of the theory of consumer's behaviour with remarkable economy.[4] It also opened up the way for empirical studies of preferences based on observed market behaviour.[5]

The approach of revealed preference need not be confined to market choices only, and indeed it has been used in studying preferences revealed by non-market behaviour such as government decisions, choices of public bodies and political acts like voting. The exact mathematical structure of the problem differs substantially from case to case, and the formulation in the context of preferences revealed by political or bureaucratic decisions will differ from that in the context of consumer's choices. But there are common methodological elements, and I shall be concerned with them in this lecture.

2

Before I proceed to examine the status of the preference revealed by choice, I would like to comment on one very elementary issue that seems to me to have certainly clouded the interpretation of revealed preference theory. This concerns the somewhat surprising claim that has been frequently made that the theory of revealed preference 'frees' demand theory from the concept of preference and *a fortiori* from the concept of utility on which traditional demand theory was based.

In his pioneering paper, Samuelson argued that his object was 'to develop the theory of consumer's behaviour freed from any vestigial traces of the utility concept'.[6] The exact content of the statement was not altogether clear, and in pushing forward the revealed preference approach in a classic paper, Little argued that one of his main aims was to demonstrate 'that a theory of

4. See Samuelson's articles, referred to earlier, and also his *Foundations of Economic Analysis* (Cambridge, Mass., 1947).

5. For a recent survey of the analytical literature in this branch of economics, see A. Brown and A. Deaton, 'Models of Consumer Behaviour: A Survey', *Economic Journal,* **82** (1972).

6. Samuelson, 'A Note on the Pure Theory . . .', p. 71.

consumer's demand can be based solely on consistent behaviour',[7] adding that 'the new formulation is scentifically more respectable [since] if an individual's behaviour is consistent, then it must be possible to explain that behaviour without reference to anything other than behaviour'.[8] In a similar vein, Hicks stated that 'the econometric theory of demand does study human beings, but only as entities having certain patterns of market behaviour; it makes no claim, no pretence, to be able to see inside their heads'.[9]

On this interpretation the use of the word 'preference' in revealed preference would appear to represent an elaborate pun. In saying that $x$ is revealed preferred to $y$, it would not be asserted that $x$ is preferred to $y$ in the usual sense of the word 'preferred'. A redefinition of the expression 'preference' is, of course, possible, but it is then legitimate to ask what does 'consistency' of behaviour stand for and on what basis are the required consistency conditions chosen. The alleged inconsistency between (i) choosing $x$ when $y$ is available and (ii) choosing $y$ when $x$ is available, would seem to have something to do with the surmise about the person's preference underlying his choices.

Preferring $x$ to $y$ is inconsistent with preferring $y$ to $x$, but if it is asserted that choice has nothing to do with preference, then choosing $x$ rather than $y$ in one case and $y$ rather than $x$ in another need not necessarily be at all inconsistent. What makes them look inconsistent is precisely the peep into the head of the consumer, the avoidance of which is alleged to be the aim of the revealed preference approach.

It could, however, be argued that what was at issue was not really whether the axiom of revealed preference represented a requirement of consistency, but whether as a hypothesis it was empirically verified. This line would not take one very far either. Consider the simplest situation of one consumer facing two divisible commodities—the case that figures on blackboards in every Economics Department in the world, and would have, I imagine, adorned the magnificent glass doors of the St Clement's Building but for the greater deference shown by our architects to the even more classic demand-and-supply intersection. Even in this rudimentary case, the set of possible choice situations for any individual is infinite—indeed uncountable. To check whether the Weak Axiom holds for the entire field of all market choices, we have to observe the person's choices under infinitely many price—income configurations. In contrast, the number of actual choices that can be studied is extremely limited. Not only is the ratio of observations to potential choices equal to zero, but moreover the absolute number of cases investigated is also

---

7. I. M. D. Little, 'A Reformulation of the Theory of Consumer's Behaviour', *Oxford Economic Papers*, 1 (1949), p. 90.

8. *Ibid.*, p. 97.

9. J. R. Hicks, *A Revision of Demand Theory* (Oxford, 1956), p. 6. Hicks did not, however, fully subscribe to the revealed preference approach himself. See especially 'The Measurement of Income', *Oxford Economic Papers*, N.S., 10 (1958). [See also the Introduction to his *Wealth and Welfare: Collected Essays on Economic Theory* (Oxford: Basil Blackwell, 1981), pp. xii–xiv.]

fairly small. Comparisons have to be made within a fairly short time to avoid taste change, but the time elapsed must also be sufficiently long so that the mutton purchased last time is not still in the larder, making the choices non-comparable. With durable goods the problem is quite vicious. The actual number of tests carried out have, not surprisingly, been very small. Faith in the axioms of revealed preference arises, therefore, not from empirical verification, but from the intuitive reasonableness of these axioms interpreted precisely in terms of preference. In fact, the concept of taste change is itself a preference-based notion, and the whole framework of revealed preference analysis of behaviour is steeped with implicit ideas about preference and psychology.

I would, therefore, argue that the claim of explaining 'behaviour without reference to anything other than behaviour'[10] is pure rhetoric, and if the theory of revealed preference makes sense it does so not because no psychological assumptions are used but because the psychological assumptions used are sensibly chosen. The use of the word preference in revealed preference must indeed be taken to be more than a pun.

Indeed, the psychological assumptions involved have been discussed explicitly or by implication in all the major contributions to revealed preference theory. There have also been discussions about 'the transition to welfare economics' from revealed preference theory, and even Ian Little has argued that among the possible routes for this transition is the view 'that a person is, on the whole, likely to be happier the more he is able to have what he would choose'.[11] Samuelson had in any case put less emphasis on sticking exclusively to observed behaviour, and his statement, which I quoted earlier, that 'the individual guinea-pig, by his market behaviour, reveals his preference pattern',[12] makes the fundamental assumption of revealed preference theory explicit. The rationale of the revealed preference approach lies in the assumption of revelation and not in doing away with the notion of underlying preferences, despite occasional noises to the contrary. So we would be justified in examining the philosophical foundations of the revealed preference approach precisely in terms of the assumptions of revelation. This is what I shall now go on to do.

3

I shall take up a relatively minor question first. The Weak Axiom of Revealed Preference is a condition of consistency of two choices only. If $x$ is revealed preferred to $y$, then $y$ should not be revealed preferred to $x$. Perhaps because of this concentration on the consistency between any *two* choices and no

10. Little, *op. cit.*, p. 97.
11. *Ibid.*, p. 98.
12. Samuelson, 'Consumption Theory . . .', p. 243.

more, the Weak Axiom has appeared to many to be a condition of what Hicks calls 'two-term consistency'. And it has appeared as if the other well-known requirement of consistency, viz., transitivity, lay outside its scope. Transitivity is a simple condition to state: if $x$ is regarded as at least as good as $y$, and $y$ at least as good as $z$, then $x$ should be regarded as at least as good as $z$. In the case of preference, it implies that if $x$ is preferred to $y$ and $y$ preferred to $z$, then it should also be the case that $x$ is preferred to $z$. Since this condition involves at least three choices and since the Weak Axiom involves a requirement of consistency only over *pairs* of choices, it might look as if the Weak Axiom could not possibly imply transitivity. This has indeed been taken to be so in much of the literature on the subject, and additional conditions for transitivity have been sought. In a very limited sense this point about transitivity is indeed correct. But it can be shown that the limited sense in which this is true ignores precisely the methodological point concerning the *interpretation* of revealed preference theory which I discussed a few minutes ago.

The philosophical issue involved is, therefore, worth discussing in the light of the logical problems raised by revealed preference theory. Consider a case in which we find a consumer choosing $x$ and rejecting $y$, and another in which he is found to choose $y$ and reject $z$. So he has revealed a preference for $x$ over $y$ and also for $y$ over $z$. Of course, even under the assumption of transitivity of the underlying preference, the person is not obliged to *reveal* a preference for $x$ over $z$ since such a choice may not in fact arise in his uneventful life. But suppose we could offer this person choices over *any* combination of alternatives and could thus ensure that he had to choose between $x$ and $z$. Then clearly it would be required by transitivity that he must choose $x$ and reject $z$. Is this guaranteed by the Weak Axiom? The answer is: clearly yes.

To understand why this is so, imagine the contrary and suppose that he did choose $z$ instead of $x$. We could then offer him the choice over the set of three alternatives, $x$, $y$ and $z$. What could this man now choose? If he chose $x$, which would involve rejecting $z$, this would violate the Weak Axiom since he had earlier rejected $x$ and chosen $z$. If he chose $y$, which would imply that he would be rejecting $x$, this would also violate the Weak Axiom since he had rejected $y$ and chosen $x$ earlier. Finally, if he chose $z$, which would imply a rejection of $y$, he would again be running counter to the Weak Axiom since earlier he had chosen $y$ rejecting $z$. So no matter what he chose out of this set of three alternatives ($x$, $y$, $z$), he must violate the Weak Axiom. He is in this impasse only because he chose $z$ and rejected $x$ after having revealed a preference for $x$ over $y$ and for $y$ over $z$. To be able to choose in a manner consistent with the Weak Axiom of Revealed Preference, he would have to choose $x$ faced with a choice between the two.

Further, if he chose *both* $x$ and $z$ in a choice between the two, there must be inconsistency also. In a choice over ($x$, $y$, $z$), he could not choose $z$ since he had chosen $y$ rejecting $z$ in a choice between the two. For the same reason he could not choose $y$ since he had revealed a preference for $x$ over $y$. So he would have to choose only $x$ in the choice over $x$, $y$, $z$, rejecting $z$. But then he could not choose $z$ in the presence of $x$ in the choice over that pair in view of the Weak Axiom of Revealed Preference and this is a contradiction.

The Weak Axiom not only guarantees two-term consistency, it also prevents the violation of transitivity. The fact that the Axiom applies to two choices at a time does not rule out its repeated use to get the result of transitivity.

Why is it then that people have looked for stronger conditions than the Weak Axiom to get transitivity or similar properties? For example, Houthakker has proposed a condition, the so-called Strong Axiom of Revealed Preference, which demands more than the Weak Axiom of Samuelson to get us towards transitivity.[13] Similar conditions have been proposed by Ville, von Neumann and Morgenstern, and others.[14] Hicks, who noted that the Weak Axiom did make things fine for transitivity in a world of two goods only, proceeded to argue that 'three-term inconsistency is only ruled out in the two-goods case by the special properties of that case'.[15] But the simple argument we examined a few minutes ago assumed nothing about there being only two goods. What explains this mystery?

The clue lies in the fact that in the revealed preference literature, it has been customary to assume, usually implicitly, that the Weak Axiom holds only for those choices that can be observed in the market and not necessarily for other choices.[16] And given divisible commodities, the market can never offer the man under observation the choice, say, between $x$, $y$ and $z$ only. If these three baskets of goods were available then so should be an infinite number of other baskets that would cost no more at given market prices. This is how in the theory of consumer's behaviour, the man can get away satisfying the Weak Axiom over all the cases in which his behaviour can be observed in the market and nevertheless harbour an intransitive preference relation.

The moment this is recognized the question arises: why this distinction between those choices in which the person's behaviour can be observed in the market and other choices in which it cannot be? Presumably, the argument lies in the fact that if market choices are the only observable choices, then the Weak Axiom can be verified only for those choices and not for others that cannot be observed in the market. But as we saw earlier, the Weak Axiom cannot be verified anyway even for market choices and the case for its use

13. H. S. Houthakker, 'Revealed Preference and the Utility Function', *Economica*, 17 (1950). The Strong Axiom guarantees a property that Houthakker called semi-transitivity.

14. J. Ville, 'Sur les conditions d'existence d'une ophélimité totale et d'un indice du niveau des prix', *Annales de l'Université de Lyons*, 9 (1946); J. von Neumann and O. Morgenstern, *Theory of Games and Economic Behaviour* (Princeton, 1944).

15. Hicks, *op. cit.*, p. 110.

16. *Cf.* D. Gale, 'A Note on Revealed Preference', *Economica*, 27 (1960).

lies not in verification but in its intuitive plausibility given the preference-based interpretation of choice. And there is no reason whatsoever to expect that the Weak Axiom is more plausible for 'budget triangles' thrown up by market choice situations than for other choices that cannot be observed in the market; at any rate I have not seen any argument that has been put forward justifying such a dichotomy. The distinction lies only in the verification question and that, as we have seen, is really a red herring.

Treated as an *axiom* in the light of which consumer's choices are analysed and interpreted, rather than as a *hypothesis* which is up for verification, there is no case for restricting the scope of the Weak Axiom arbitrarily to budget sets only, and in the absence of this invidious distinction, transitivity follows directly from the Weak Axiom of Revealed Preference. If a consumer has chosen $x$ rejecting $y$ in one case, chosen $y$ rejecting $z$ in another, and chosen $z$ rejecting $x$ in a third case, then he has not only violated transitivity, he must violate the Weak Axiom of Revealed Preference as well. No matter what he chooses given the choice over $x$, $y$ and $z$, he must run counter to the Weak Axiom, as demonstrated. The fact that he cannot be observed in a choice over $(x, y, z)$ makes no real difference since *no matter what he chooses* he must logically violate the Weak Axiom.

In this sense, an observed violation of the Strong Axiom will logically imply a violation of the Weak Axiom as well. A number of other distinct axioms that have been proposed in the literature can also be shown to be equivalent once the arbitrary restrictions are removed.[17] (If the domain of the choice function includes all pairs and triples, then these apparently different axioms turn out to be logically equivalent.)

4

I would now like to turn to the fundamental assumption of the revealed preference approach, viz., that people do reveal their underlying preferences through their actual choices. Is this a reasonable presumption? If a person chose $x$ when $y$ was available, it would seem reasonable to argue that he did not really regard $y$ to be better than $x$. There is, of course, the problem that a person's choices may not be made after much thinking or after systematic comparisons of alternatives. I am inclined to believe that the chair on which you are currently sitting in this room was not chosen entirely thoughtlessly, but I am not totally persuaded that you in fact did choose the particular chair you have chosen through a careful calculation of the pros and cons of sitting in each possible chair that was vacant when you came in. Even some important

---

17. See K. J. Arrow, 'Rational Choice Functions and Orderings', *Economica,* **26** (1959); and A. K. Sen, 'Choice Functions and Revealed Preference', *Review of Economic Studies,* **38** (1971) [Essay 1 in this volume].

decisions in life seem to be taken on the basis of incomplete thinking about the possible courses of action, and the hypothesis of revealed preference, as a psychological generalization, may not be altogether convincing. These questions are well-known as also are the difficulties arising from open or hidden persuasion involved in advertisements and propaganda, which frequently mess up not only one's attitude towards the alternatives available but also towards the act of choice itself. These problems are important, but I shall not go into them any further, partly because they have been much discussed elsewhere, but also because I have no competence whatever to throw light on the psychological issues underlying these problems. Instead I shall try to discuss one and a half other issues which seem to me to be also important. The half issue should perhaps come first.

The logical property of connectedness (or completeness as it is sometimes called) of binary relations is an important characteristic to examine in the context of evaluating the fundamental assumption of revealed preference. Connectedness of preference requires that between any two alternatives $x$ and $y$, the person in question either prefers $x$ to $y$, or prefers $y$ to $x$, or is indifferent between $x$ and $y$. The approach of revealed preference makes considerable use of connectedness. If a person chooses $x$ rather than $y$, it is presumed that he regards $x$ to be at least as good as $y$, and not that maybe he has no clue about what to choose and has chosen $x$ because he had to choose something.

The point can be illustrated with a variation of the classic story of Buridan's ass. This ass, as we all know, could not make up its mind between two haystacks; it liked both very much but could not decide which one was better. Being unable to choose, this dithering animal died ultimately of starvation. The dilemma of the ass is easy to understand, but it is possible that the animal would have agreed that it would have been better off by choosing either of the haystacks rather than nothing at all. Not choosing anything is also a choice, and in this case this really meant the choice of starvation. On the other hand, had it chosen either of the haystacks, it would have been presumed that the ass regarded that haystack to be at least as good as the other, which in this version of the story was not the case. The ass was in a real dilemma *vis-à-vis* the revealed preference approach.

The traditional interpretation of the story is that the ass was indifferent between the two haystacks. That indifference may be a cause for dithering has often been stated. For example, Ian Little prefaced his closely reasoned attack on the concept of indifference by posing the rather thoughtful question: 'How long must a person dither before he is pronounced indifferent?'[18] But in fact there is hardly any real cause for dithering if one is *really* indifferent, since the loss from choosing one alternative rather than another is exactly zero. The person can choose either alternative and regret nothing in either

18. Little, *op. cit.*, p. 92.

case. This, however, is not the case if the preference relation is unconnected over this pair, i.e. if the chooser can neither say that he prefers x to y, nor y to x, nor that he is indifferent between the two.

If Buridan's ass was indifferent, choosing either haystack would have been quite legitimate and would not have misled the observer armed with revealed preference theory provided the observer chose a version of the theory that permitted indifference.[19] The real dilemma would arise if the ass had an unconnected preference. Choosing either haystack would have appeared to reveal a view that that haystack was no worse than the other, but this view the ass was unable to subscribe to since it could not decide what its preference should be. By choosing either haystack it would have given a wrong signal to the revealed preference theorist since this would have implied that he regarded the chosen haystack to be at least as good as the other. There is very little doubt that Buridan's ass died for the cause of revealed preference, though— alas—he was not entirely successful since non-choice leading to starvation would have looked like the chosen alternative, at any rate from the point of view of mechanical use of the fundamental assumption of revealed preference. There was no way the ass could have rescued that assumption given its unconnected preference.

But what if all these problems are ruled out? That is, if the person has a connected preference relation, takes his decisions deliberately after considering all alternatives, and is not swayed to and fro by the lure of advertisements. Obviously none of the problems discussed in the last few minutes will then arise. Will the life of the revealed preference theorist, then, be uncomplicated? I fear that it will not, and there is, it seems to me, a difficulty in some sense more fundamental than all the ones discussed so far. This problem I would like to go into now.

The difficulty is seen most easily in terms of a well-known game, viz., 'the Prisoners' Dilemma',[20] which has cropped up frequently in economics in other contexts. The story goes something like this. Two prisoners are known to be guilty of a very serious crime, but there is not enough evidence to convict them. There is, however, sufficient evidence to convict them of a minor crime. The District Attorney—it is an American story—separates the two and tells each that they will be given the option to confess if they wish to. If both of them do confess, they will be convicted of the major crime on each other's evidence, but in view of the good behaviour shown in squealing, the District Attorney will ask for a penalty of 10 years each rather than the full penalty of 20 years. If neither confesses, each will be convicted only of the minor crime and get 2 years. If one confesses and the other does not, then the one who does confess will go free and the other will go to prison for 20 years.

19. See Arrow, *op. cit.*; Sen, *op. cit.*; H. Herzberger, 'Ordinal Choice v. Rationality', *Econometrica,* **41** (1973); C. R. Plott, 'Path Independence, Rationality and Social Choice', *Econometrica,* **41** (1973).

20. See R. D. Luce and H. Raiffa, *Games and Decisions* (New York, 1958); also A. Rapoport, *Two Person Game Theory* (Michigan, 1966).

What should the prisoners do? It is not doubted by the game theorist that any self-respecting prisoner will begin by drawing a pay-off matrix to facilitate rational choice. The table of pay-offs will look something like that shown in Figure 1. (The first number in each slot is the sentence of prisoner 1 and the second of prisoner 2. The numbers are negative to remind us that the prisoners dislike going to prison.)

| | | Prisoner 2 | |
|---|---|---|---|
| | | Confess | Not Confess |
| Prisoner 1 | Confess | $-10, -10$ | $0, -20$ |
| | Not Confess | $-20, \quad 0$ | $-2, \quad -2$ |

FIGURE 1

Each prisoner sees that it is definitely in his interest to confess no matter what the other does. If the other confesses, then by confessing himself this prisoner reduces his own sentence from twenty years to ten. If the other does not confess, then by confessing he himself goes free rather than getting a two year sentence. So each prisoner feels that no matter what the other does it is always better for him to confess. So both of them do confess guided by rational self-interest, and each goes to prison for ten years. If, however, neither had confessed, both would have been in prison only for two years each. Rational choice would seem to cost each person eight additional years in prison.

This game has been much discussed in the literature of resource allocation as an illustration of the failure of individualistic decision taking and as a justification of a collective contract. It has an obvious bearing on the theory of optimum savings, on taxation theory, on allocation decisions involving externalities and public goods, and on a number of related issues.[21] Through a collective contract the group of individuals can do better than what they will do under individualistic action. The distinction has something to do with Rousseau's contrast between 'the general will' and 'the will of all', and with the necessity of a 'social contract' to achieve what the general will wills.[22] In

21. See W. J. Baumol, *Welfare Economics and the Theory of the State* (Cambridge, Mass., 1952); A. K. Sen, 'On Optimizing the Rate of Saving', *Economic Journal,* 71 (1961); S. A. Marglin, 'The Social Rate of Discount and the Optimal Rate of Investment', *Quarterly Journal of Economics,* 77 (1963); A. K. Sen, 'A Game Theoretic Analysis of Theories of Collectivism in Allocation', in T. Majumdar (ed.), *Growth and Choice* (Bombay, 1969).
22. W. G. Runciman and A. K. Sen, 'Games, Justice and the General Will', *Mind,* 74 (1965); J. Rawls, *A Theory of Justice* (Cambridge, Mass., 1971).

the particular story of the prisoners' dilemma, the general will can be interpreted to be the rule of non-confession which is beneficial for both, and the vehicle for achieving this will be a mutual non-confession treaty. If such a social contract can be accepted and enforced, both prisoners will be better off. So far so good. But what if no such contract can be arrived at? Are the prisoners doomed to suffer a heavy penalty constrained by their own rational choice calculus?

It is possible to argue that this is precisely the type of situation in which moral rules of behaviour have traditionally played an important part. Situations of the type of the prisoners' dilemma occur in many ways in our lives and some of the traditional rules of good behaviour take the form of demanding suspension of calculations geared to individual rationality. In different periods of history in different social situations in response to different types of problems particular rules of behaviour have been proposed which have in common the analytical property of trying to generate the results of a social contract without there being any such formal contract. Behavioural rules to handle problems of interdependence, arising in specific social and economic formations, can be seen in such diverse approaches as Christian or Buddhist ethics on the one hand and the philosophy of the Chinese 'cultural revolution' on the other. I shall have a bit more to say on this presently, but the implication of all this for the theory of revealed preference should be first spelt out.

Suppose each prisoner in the dilemma acts not on the basis of the rational calculations outlined earlier but proceeds to follow the dictum of not letting the other person down irrespective of the consequences for himself. Then neither person will confess and they will both get off lightly. Now, consider the job of the observer trying to guess the preferences that have been revealed by the choice of non-confession. There is, of course, an element of uncertainty in the exercise of choice that the prisoners face, for neither of them knows what the other is up to. It should be clear, however, that if there is anything in the assumption of revealed preference as it stands, it must be presumed that each prisoner prefers at least one of the possible outcomes resulting from his non-confession to what would have happened had he confessed, given other things. That is, either he prefers the consequence of his not confessing given the other prisoner's non-confession, or the consequence of his not confessing given the other prisoner's confession. But in fact neither happens to be true. The prisoner does not prefer to go to prison for twenty years rather than for ten; nor does he prefer a sentence of two years to being free. His choice has not revealed his preference in the manner postulated.

At this stage a couple of warnings may be worth stating since the point that is being made can be easily misunderstood. The prisoners' non-confession will be quite easy to put within the framework of revealed preference if it were the case that they had so much concern for the sufferings of each other that they would choose non-confession on grounds of joint welfare of the two. There is indeed nothing extraordinary in assuming that a person may prefer that both should go to prison for two years each rather than that the other should suffer twenty years while he himself goes free. The problem arises precisely because that is *not* being assumed. Each is assumed to be self-centred and interested basically only in his own prison term, and the choice of non-confession follows *not* from calculations based on this welfare function, but from following a moral code of behaviour suspending the rational calculus. The preference is no different in this case from that in the earlier example, but behaviour is. And it is this difference that is inimical to the revealed preference approach to the study of human behaviour.

A second point to note is that the entire problem under discussion can be easily translated into the case in which each person does worry about the other's welfare as well and is not concerned only with his own welfare. The numbers in the pay-off matrix can be interpreted simply as welfare indices of the two persons and each person's welfare index can incorporate concern for the other. The prisoners' dilemma type of problem can arise even where there is concern for each other.

Third, no special importance should be attached to the specific story of the prisoners in terms of which this particular analytical problem is expounded. The interest in the prisoners' dilemma lies not in the fiction which gives the problem its colour, but in the existence of a strictly dominant strategy for each person which together produce a strictly inferior outcome for all. One feature of the prisoners' dilemma is, in fact, particularly misleading. This concerns the complete symmetry of the positions of the two players. Some suggestions for the resolution of the dilemma within the framework of rational choice make considerable use of this particular feature,[23] but even with asymmetrical prison sentences as long as the orderings of the penalties are the same we can get exactly the same dilemma and the same implications for revealed preference theory.

5

The concentration on the contractual side of the prisoners' dilemma has perhaps tended to obscure the important implications of this type of situation for the relation between choice and preference. If the prisoners agree to a non-confession treaty and if that treaty can be enforced the prisoners will indeed get off the hook, but such a contract may be difficult to devise and conceivably impossible to enforce under certain circumstances. When it comes to the use of this type of model in economics in interpreting problems of resource allocation, one can distinguish between those situations in which

23. See Rapoport, *op. cit.*; and J. W. N. Watkins, 'Self-Interest and Morality in the Light of the Prisoners' Dilemma', paper read at the Bristol Conference on 'Practical Reason', September 1972. [Published later in S. Körner (ed.), *Practical Reason* (Oxford, 1974).]

a contract may be easy to operate and those cases in which it will be far from easy to do so.

I am concerned here with cases in which a contractual solution is not possible. This corresponds to the case in which the prisoners are not bound by any contract but nevertheless decide not to confess. The essence of the problem is that if both prisoners behave *as if* they are maximizing a different welfare function from the one that they actually have, they will both end up being better off even in terms of their *actual* welfare function. To take the extreme case, if both prisoners try to maximize the welfare of the other, neither will confess in the case outlined since non-confession will be a superior strategy no matter what is assumed about the other person's action. The result of each trying to maximize the welfare of the other will, therefore, lead to a better situation for each in terms of his own welfare as well. It is not necessary that the prisoners in fact have this much concern—or indeed any concern—for the other, but if they behave *as if* they have this concern, they will end up being better off in terms of their real preference. This is where the revealed preference approach goes off the rails altogether. The behaviour pattern that will make each better off in terms of their real preferences is not at all the behaviour pattern that will *reveal* those real preferences. Choices that reveal individual preferences may be quite inefficient for achieving welfare of the group.

I would argue that the philosophy of the revealed preference approach essentially underestimates the fact that man is a social animal and his choices are not rigidly bound to his own preferences only. I do not find it difficult to believe that birds and bees and dogs and cats do reveal their preferences by their choice; it is with human beings that the proposition is not particularly persuasive. An act of choice for this social animal is, in a fundamental sense, always a social act. He may be only dimly aware of the immense problems of interdependence that characterize a society, of which the problem under discussion is only one. But his behaviour is something more than a mere translation of his personal preferences.

6

In economic analysis individual preferences seem to enter in two different roles: preferences come in as determinants of behaviour and they also come in as the basis of welfare judgements. For example, in the theory of general equilibrium the behaviour of individuals is assumed to be determined by their respective preference orderings, and problems of existence, uniqueness and stability of an equilibrium are studied in the context of such a framework. At the same time, the optimality of an equilibrium, i.e., whether the market can lead to a position which yields maximal social welfare in some sense, is also examined in terms of preference with the convention that a preferred position involves a higher level of welfare of that individual.[24] This dual link between choice and preference on the one hand and preference and welfare on the other is crucial to the normative aspects of general equilibrium theory. All the important results in this field depend on this relationship between behaviour and welfare through the intermediary of preference.

The question that is relevant in this context is whether such heavy weight can be put on the slender shoulders of the concept of preference. Certainly, there is no remarkable difficulty in simply defining preference as the underlying relation in terms of which individual choices can be explained; provided choices satisfy certain elementary axioms, the underlying relation will be binary, and with some additional assumptions it will be an ordering with the property of transitivity.[25] In this mathematical operation preference will simply be the binary representation of individual choice. The difficulty arises in interpreting preference thus defined as preference in the usual sense with the property that if a person prefers $x$ to $y$ then he must regard himself to be better off with $x$ than with $y$. As illustrated with the example of the prisoners' dilemma, the behaviour of human beings may involve a great deal more than maximizing gains in terms of one's preferences and the complex interrelationships in a society may generate mores and rules of behaviour that will drive a wedge between behaviour and welfare. People's behaviour may still correspond to some consistent *as if* preference but a numerical presentation of the *as if* preference cannot be interpreted as individual welfare. In particular, basing normative criteria, e.g., Pareto optimality, on these *as if* preferences poses immense difficulties.

To look at the positive side of the issue, the possibilities of affecting human behaviour through means other than economic incentives may be a great deal more substantial than is typically assumed in the economic literature. The rigid correspondence between choice, preference and welfare assumed in traditional economic theory makes the analysis simpler but also rules out important avenues of social and economic change. An example may make the point clearer.

Suppose it is the case that there are strong environmental reasons for using glass bottles for distributing soft drinks (rather than single-use steel cans) and for persuading the customers to return the bottles to the shops from where they buy these drinks (rather than disposing of them in the dustbin). For a relatively rich country the financial incentives offered for returning the

24. See J. R. Hicks, *Value and Capital* (Oxford, 1939); P. A. Samuelson, *Foundations of Economic Analysis* (1947); G. Debreu, *Theory of Value* (New York, 1959); K. J. Arrow and F. H. Hahn, *General Competitive Analysis* (San Francisco and Edinburgh, 1971).

25. The respective conditions for binariness, transitivity of strict preference and full transitivity are presented in Sen (1971) [Essay 1 here]. For the conditions that guarantee a numerical representation of the individual welfare function based on their preference relation, see Debreu, *op. cit.*; M. K. Richter, 'Revealed Preference Theory', *Econometrica*, **34** (1966); Arrow and Hahn, *op. cit.*

bottles may not be adequate if the consumers neither worry about the environment nor are thrilled by receiving back small change. The environment affects the life of all, true enough, but from the point of view of any one individual the harm that he can do to the environment by adding his bottles to those of others will be exceedingly tiny. Being generally interested in the environment but also being lazy about returning bottles, this person may be best off if the others return bottles but not he, next best if all return bottles, next best if none does, and worst of all if he alone returns bottles while others do not. If others feel in a symmetrical way we shall then be in a prisoners' dilemma type situation in which people will not return bottles but at the same time all would have preferred that all of them should return bottles rather than none. To tackle this problem, suppose now that people are persuaded that non-return is a highly irresponsible behaviour, and while the individuals in question continue to have exactly the same view of their welfare, they fall prey to ethical persuasion, political propaganda, or moral rhetoric. The welfare functions and the preference relations are still exactly the same and all that changes is behaviour. The result is good for the environment but sad for the theory of revealed preference.

I am not, of course, arguing that a change in the sense of responsibility is the *only* way of solving this problem. Penalizing non-return and highly rewarding return of bottles are other methods of doing this, as indeed will occur to any economist. In this particular case, these methods can also be used quite easily (since the problem of checking is not serious with the return of bottles), even though any system of payments and rewards also involve other issues like income distribution. The real difficulty arises when the checking of people's actions is not easy. Examples of these cases vary from such simple acts as littering the streets to such complex behaviour as paying one's taxes.

7

To avoid a possible misunderstanding, I would like to distinguish clearly between four possible cases all of which involve the same choice (e.g., the use and reuse of glass bottles) but the underlying preferences have different interpretations:

(1) The person simply prefers using glass bottles rather than steel cans from a purely self-regarding point of view, e.g., because he likes glass, or (perhaps somewhat incredibly) he believes the impact on environment of his using single-use steel cans (*given* the choices of others) will hurt him significantly.

(2) The person is worried about the welfare of others as well and his own

welfare function includes concern for other people's welfare,[26] and he refuses glass bottles because he takes the hurt on others as hurt on himself.

(3) The person's concern for other people's welfare reflected in his notion of his own welfare would not be sufficient to prevent him from using single-use steel cans if he could do it on the sly, but he is afraid of the social stigma of being seen to do the 'wrong' thing, or afraid of others emulating him in doing the 'wrong' thing and thereby his getting hit indirectly.

(4) The person can do the 'wrong' thing on the sly without being noticed and he feels that if he did that he personally would be better off (even after taking note of whatever weight he might wish to put on the welfare of the others), but he feels that he would be acting socially irresponsibly if he did proceed to do it, and therefore does not do so.

I am primarily concerned with case (4), even though case (3) would also pose some problem for revealed preference theory (and the normative aspects of general equilibrium) since preferences are not usually defined on the space of stigmas and such things, and identical commodity choices will involve quite different welfare levels depending on the reaction of others. But case (3) can be, in principle, taken care of through a suitable redefinition of the domain of choice. Case (4) poses a more serious difficulty and it is with this case that I am concerned.

It is, of course, perfectly possible to argue that actions based on considerations of social responsibility as opposed to one's own welfare do reflect one's 'ultimate' preferences, and in a certain sense this is undoubtedly so. The question is whether the identification of welfare with preference (in the sense of the former being a numerical representation of the latter) will survive under this interpretation. The problem arises from the dual link-up between choice and preference on the one hand and preference and welfare on the other. Preference can be quite reasonably defined in such a way as to maintain one or the other, but the issue is whether *both* can be maintained through some definition of preference, and it is this dual role that I am trying to question here.[27]

With what frequency do problems of the kind of case (4) arise? I do not know the answer to this question. It seems clear, however, that they arise often enough to be worried about their implications for traditional economic

26. *Cf.* A. K. Sen, 'Labour Allocation in a Cooperative Enterprise', *Review of Economic Studies,* 33 (1966).

27. The problem discussed here should not be confused with the important but different problem of strategic reasons for 'not revealing preference' (see, for example, T. Majumdar, *The Measurement of Utility*, London, 1958; R. Farquharson, *Theory of Voting*, Oxford, 1970). The latter is a problem of establishing correspondence between rankings of the outcome space and those of the strategy space. Our problem arises in the ranking of the outcome space itself.

analysis. Moral considerations involving the question 'if I do not do it, how can I morally want others to do it?', do affect the behaviour of people. The 'others' involved may be members of narrowly defined groups or classes, or widely defined societies, but such considerations do have a role in influencing choice.[28]

What harm would there be, it might be asked, in identifying welfare with what is revealed by a person's choices, even if that is not what he would claim to be his welfare as he himself sees it? Apart from the danger of being misled by the confusing use of words, like 'preference' or 'welfare', which have some specific meanings as used in normal communication, there are also some difficulties for normative economics in basing optimality criteria (e.g., Pareto optimality) on *as if* preferences. There is a distinction from the point of view of social judgement between the relevance of a choice made under a moral sense of social responsibility and that made under a straightforward pursuit of one's welfare (including any pleasure one takes in the happiness of others). The identification of welfare with *as if* preferences blurs this distinction and withholds relevant information from the analysis of social welfare and collective choice.

8

An interesting illustration of the problem of the relation between preference, choice and social responsibility can be seen in the recent Chinese debates on the use of financial incentives in the allocation of labour in communal agriculture. During the so-called Great Leap Forward in 1958–60 the Chinese tried to reduce drastically the use of work rewards and raised very substantially the proportion of income distributed in the communes on other criteria such as the size of the family. In the absence of what the Chinese called 'socialist consciousness', a system of this kind produces precisely the prisoners' dilemma type of problem. Each may prefer that others should work hard, but given the actions of others may prefer to take it easy oneself, even though given the choice between all working hard and none doing so people may prefer the former. A social contract of sincere efforts by all is easy to think of but difficult to enforce, given the difficulties of supervision of the intensity of work.

At the end of the Leap Forward period this experiment was abandoned, or drastically cut, and it was generally thought that the experiment was premature. The use of financial incentives was again expanded. How much of the

---

28. I have tried to argue elsewhere that there are advantages in viewing moral judgements not as one other ordering of actions or outcomes but as an ordering (or a quasi-ordering) of orderings of actions or outcomes. 'Choice, Orderings and Morality', paper read at the Bristol Conference on 'Practical Reason', September 1972. [Published in S. Körner (ed.), *Practical Reason* (Oxford, 1974); Essay 3 in this volume.]

difficulties of the Leap Forward period arose from this attempt at dissociating work from material incentives is not known clearly, but it certainly did not make things any easier.

After the end of the Leap Forward period there have been several further attempts to move away from material incentives. Meanwhile the Chinese also tried out a programme of reorientation of behaviour patterns. The well-known 'cultural revolution' put particular emphasis (as the so-called 'Sixteen Points' explained) on 'an education to develop morally, intellectually and physically and to become labourers with socialist consciousness.'[29] The relation of all this to the problem of work motivation is, of course, very close, and I have tried to discuss it elsewhere.[30] Briefly, this can take one of two forms, viz., either (i) a reorientation of the individual welfare functions of the people involved, or (ii) a different basis of behaviour emphasizing social responsibility whether or not individual welfare functions are themselves revised. In practice it was probably a mixture of both.

How successful the Chinese experimentation has been in the reorientation of behaviour patterns, it is difficult to assess fully at this stage. What is, anyway, important for our purposes is to note the relevance of this experiment on work motivation in China to the problem of the relation between choice, preference and welfare.

9

I should perhaps end with a critical observation on what tends to count as hard information in economics. Much of the empirical work on preference patterns seems to be based on the conviction that behaviour is the only source of information on a person's preferences. That behaviour is a major source of information on preference can hardly be doubted, but the belief that it is the only basis of surmising about people's preferences seems extremely questionable. While this makes a great deal of sense for studying preferences of animals, since direct communication is ruled out (unless one is Dr Dolittle), for human beings surely information need not be restricted to distant observations of choices made. There is, of course, something of a problem in interpreting answers to questions as correct and in taking the stated preference to be the actual preference, and there are well-known limitations of the questionnaire method. But then there are problems, as we have seen, with the interpretation of behaviour as well. The idea that behaviour is the one real source of information is extremely limiting for empirical work and is not easy to justify in terms of the methodological requirements of our discipline.

29. For a penetrating analysis of work motivation in China, see C. Riskin, 'Maoism and Motivation: A Discussion of Work Motivation in China', *Bulletin of Concerned Asian Scholars*, 1973.

30. A. K. Sen, *On Economic Inequality* (Oxford, 1973), chapter 4.

There is an old story about one behaviourist meeting another, and the first behaviourist asks the second: 'I see you are very well. How am I?' The thrust of the revealed preference approach has been to undermine thinking as a method of self-knowledge and talking as a method of knowing about others. In this, I think, we have been prone, on the one hand, to overstate the difficulties of introspection and communication, and on the other, to underestimate the problems of studying preferences revealed by observed behaviour.

## 10

Perhaps I should now gather together the main themes that I have tried to develop in this lecture. First, I have tried to argue that the interest of revealed preference theory lies in the skilful use of the assumption that behaviour reveals preference and not, despite claims to the contrary, in explaining 'behaviour without reference to anything other than behaviour'.

Second, if revealed preference is interpreted in this light, some of the additional axioms of revealed preference theory can be seen to be redundant for the purpose for which they are used. For example, the Weak Axiom of Revealed Preference can be seen to be quite strong and certainly sufficient for transitivity without requiring a stronger axiom.

Third, the fundamental assumption about the revelation of preference can be critized from many points of view, including the possibility that behaviour may not be based on systematic comparison of alternatives. More interestingly, the person in question may not have a connected preference pattern and in terms of observation it is difficult to distinguish such incompleteness from indifference.

Fourth, even if all these problems are ruled out, there remains a fundamental question of the relation between preference and behaviour arising from a problem of interdependence of different people's choices which discredits individualistic rational calculus. The problem was illustrated in terms of the game of the prisoners' dilemma. The usual analysis of the prisoners' dilemma has tended to concentrate on the possibility of a collective contract, but in many problems such a contract cannot be devised or enforced. Even in the absence of a contract, the parties involved will be better off following rules of behaviour that require abstention from the rational calculus which is precisely the basis of the revealed preference theory. People may be induced by social codes of behaviour to act *as if* they have different preferences from what they really have. This type of departure may also be stable for those codes since such behaviour will justify itself in terms of results from the point of view of the group as a whole.

Finally, this problem has an important bearing on normative problems of resource allocation formulated in terms of the dual link between choice and preference and between preference and welfare. The type of behaviour in question drives a wedge between choice and welfare, and this is of relevance to general equilibrium theory as well as to other aspects of normative economics. Preference can be defined in such a way as to preserve its correspondence with choice, or defined so as to keep it in line with welfare as seen by the person in question, but it is not in general possible to guarantee both simultaneously. Something has to give at one place or the other.

# 3

# Choice, Orderings and Morality

## 1 *Introduction*

As my starting point I shall take David Gauthier's somewhat liberal rewording of a question of Plato: 'Do you really want to convince us that the dictates of morality are in all circumstances coincident with those of rational self-interest or not?'[1] Whether or not youthful Plato was being thus led up the garden path, a generation of the theory of games seems to have made it exceedingly difficult to respond to the question in the affirmative. Gauthier's own answer derives from a study of 'the Prisoners' Dilemma' in which individual rationality seems to lead to collective ill.[2] I think this game is interesting to examine in this context and I shall propose to do so, but first I wish to comment on a preliminary question.

Rationality, as a concept, would seem to belong to the relationship between choices and preferences, and a typical question will take the form: '*Given your preference, was it rational for you to choose the actions you have chosen?*'[3] There is no immediate reason why it should discriminate between

---

1. D. P. Gauthier, *Morality and Rational Self-Interest* (Prentice-Hall: Englewood Cliffs, NJ, 1970), p. 2. Plato's own question seems to have been somewhat less specific and more mysterious: 'Do you really want to convince us that right is in all circumstances better than wrong or not?' (quoted by Gauthier, p. 1, from the translation by H. D. P. Lee of *The Republic*, p. 357).

2. 'The Prisoners' Dilemma' is presented in R. D. Luce and H. Raiffa, *Games and Decisions* (Wiley: New York, 1958), ch. 5. An interpretation of Rousseau's distinction between 'the general will' and 'the will of all' in terms of the Prisoners' Dilemma can be found in W. G. Runciman and A. K. Sen, 'Games, Justice and the General Will', *Mind,* 74 (October 1965), and whether the idea of optimality breaks down in a Prisoners' Dilemma-type situation has been investigated by A. Rapoport, *Two-Person Game Theory* (Michigan, 1966), and J. Watkins, 'Imperfect Rationality', in R. Borger and F. Cioffi (eds.), *Explanation in the Behavioural Sciences* (CUP: Cambridge, 1970).

3. *Cf.* K. J. Arrow, 'Rational Choice Functions and Orderings', *Economica*, N.S., **28** (1959).

---

Presented at the Bristol Conference on Practical Reason, 1972, published in S. Körner (ed.), *Practical Reason* (Blackwell: Oxford, 1974). That volume also includes an exchange with J. W. N. Watkins on this paper.

one type of preference and another. On the other hand, it seems hardly perplexing to ask: 'While your actions follow rationally from your preferences, will you not agree that these are nasty preferences and your actions weren't morally justifiable?' Morality would seem to require a judgement among preferences whereas rationality would not. Thus viewed, the assertion that the dictates of morality need not coincide with those of rationality might appear to be trivial.

This straightforward disposal of the problem is, however, unjustified for two separate reasons. First, in a situation where the outcome depends on other people's actions in addition to one's own, there is no clear translation from one's preferences over outcomes to actions to be chosen by him. The choice of rational action depends then on the actions of others, and ultimately on the preferences of others. On the other hand, many models of morality would specify certain actions as immoral (or unfair or unjust) given the preferences of all the people involved. Thus rational action and moral action may both be defined on the set of preferences of all and in this context the question of the correspondence of rationality and morality has some substance to it.

Second, one of the interests in games like the Prisoners' Dilemma lies in the fact that the usual postulates of rational behaviour (even after taking into account the preferences of others) yields a situation that is inferior for all. Thus the concept of individual rationality becomes very difficult to define and an attempt to escape from this problem through the use of the notion of collective—as opposed to individual—rationality would involve ideas that relate to the concept of morality.

In the next section the Prisoners' Dilemma is examined in the light of these observations. In Section 3 two variants of the Prisoners' Dilemma are introduced and in this context the idea of a moral ranking of preference orderings is studied. Developing this idea further, in Section 4 a model of morality is proposed and some of its uses examined.


## 2  The Prisoners' Dilemma, Rationality and Morality

There are, so the story runs, two prisoners to be tried, each known to be guilty of a major crime (jointly committed), but the prosecution does not have enough evidence to prove this. What the prosecution does have is proof of a joint minor crime. So each prisoner is asked separately whether he will confess or not. If both do, then they will be tried for the major crime but get a reduced sentence, say 10 years. If neither does then they will be tried for the minor crime and will get 2 years each. If one does and the other does not, then the pillar of society goes free and the other gets the full penalty of 20 years. Given this choice, each argues that if the other does confess it is better for him to confess also and if the other does not then again it is better that he confesses. So each decides to confess and led by reason they go to prison for 10 years each whereas they would have got only 2 years each if they each refused to confess. That's the dilemma.

Notationally, let $a_1$ and $a_0$ stand respectively for prisoner A confessing and not doing it, and similarly $b_1$ and $b_0$ for prisoner B confessing and not doing it. The preference orderings of A and B (in descending order) are respectively:

A:　$a_1 b_0,\ a_0 b_0,\ a_1 b_1,\ a_0 b_1.$
B:　$a_0 b_1,\ a_0 b_0,\ a_1 b_1,\ a_1 b_0.$

For A and B respectively $a_1$ and $b_1$ are strictly dominant strategies and $a_1 b_1$ will be the outcome, but both prefer $a_0 b_0$ to $a_1 b_1$. They would be both better off with a mutual non-confession contract, but it would be in the interest of each to break it unless there is enforcement. Rousseau's much-researched-on statement on the necessity of being 'forced to be free' seems to be shockingly relevant.[4] But in the absence of enforcement, they are both worse off despite strictly 'rational' behaviour.

In what sense is confession rational? In the absence of a contract neither prisoner can influence the other prisoner's action and given the other prisoner's action—no matter what—it is better for each to confess. That individual rationality may produce a situation that is collectively worse is known in other contexts also, but this case brings out the conflict very sharply indeed.

What about morality? We would seem to get a lead from Kant's dictum: 'Act always on such a maxim as thou canst at the same time will to be a universal law'.[5] Certainly neither prisoner would like that confessing becomes a universal practice, and the only universal law that each prisoner would like is that everyone should refuse to confess, since $a_0 b_0$ is superior to $a_1 b_1$. Thus non-confessing would seem to satisfy Kant's 'moral law'.[6] It satisfies Sidgwick's 'principle of equity' as well which would require that 'whatever action any of us judges to be right for himself, he implicitly judges to be right for all similar persons in similar circumstances'.[7]

What about Rawls' concepts of fairness and justice?[8] In the primordial equality of the 'original position', each would have clearly preferred that neither should confess. It certainly improves the position of the worst-off

4. Runciman and Sen, p. 556.

5. I. Kant, *Fundamental Principles of the Metaphysics of Ethics*, translated by T. K. Abbott, 3rd edition (Longman: London, 1907), p. 66.

6. In this simple case, it also satisfies the somewhat more rustic 'golden rule' of the Gospel: 'Do unto others as ye would that others should do unto you'.

7. H. Sidgwick, *The Method of Ethics* (Macmillan: London, 1907), p. 379.

8. J. Rawls, 'Justice as Fairness', *Philosophical Review,* **67** (1958); also his *A Theory of Justice* (Harvard: Cambridge, Mass., 1972).

person since it improves the position of each.[9] Since $a_0b_0$ is the only outcome that is Pareto-superior[10] to the individualistic outcome, it is possible to derive a principle in favour of non-confession from the Pareto principle also.

And Hare?[11] His—as Hare takes a lot of pains to explain—is not a system of morality but one of the language of morals. But recommending non-confession would seem to satisfy Hare's two 'rules of moral reasoning': 'When we are trying, in a concrete case, to decide what we ought to do, what we are looking for (as I have already said) is an action to which we can commit ourselves (prescriptivity) but which we are at the same time prepared to accept as exemplifying a principle of action to be prescribed for others in like circumstances (universalizability)'.[12] Again the choice would seem to fall between $a_0b_0$ and $a_1b_1$, and each would prefer the rule of non-confession.

Suppes' 'grading principle' of justice will support this too and it is easily checked that non-confession is a 'justice-saturated strategy' for each.[13] Also Harsanyi's 'ethical preferences' must demand that each should prefer non-confession to confession though their actual preferences—Harsanyi calls them 'subjective preferences'—might go in favour of confession.[14]

We can discuss moral models (or principles of moral reasoning) put forward by others, but we have already covered a broad spectrum and it is indeed easy to see that it will be difficult to find a moral argument in favour of confession by the prisoners. The conflict between moral (or just) action in any of these models and rational behaviour in the usual sense is, therefore, obvious in this case. It is, however, significant that if all pursued dictates of morality rather than rationally pursuing their own self-interests, all would have been better off. This isn't really very surprising. Sacrificing some individual gain—given the action of others—for the sake of a rule of good behaviour by all which

9. In a critique of the Runciman–Sen paper referred to earlier, John Smyth argues that 'there is no reason to suppose that the general will does will the *just* resolution of conflicting interests' ('The Prisoners' Dilemma II', *Mind*, **81** (July 1972)). He points out that 'there is every reason for supposing that "just", like good in G. E. Moore's scheme of things, is a unique predicate that cannot be identified with any particular set of things—conduct, contracts, rules, or whatever' (p. 430). Even without entering into a debate as to whether this is the case or not, it should be explained that we were referring to the particular theory of justice of Rawls—as we did say and as Smyth quotes us saying—and in that framework it is clear that non-confession would correspond to a just solution.

10. V. Pareto, *Manuale di Economia Politica* (Societa Editrice Libraria: Milano, 1906).

11. R. M. Hare, *The Language of Morals* (Clarendon Press: Oxford, 1952); *Freedom and Reason* (Clarendon Press: Oxford, 1963); *Essays on the Moral Concepts* (Macmillan: London, 1972).

12. Hare, *Freedom and Reason*, pp. 89–90.

13. P. Suppes, 'Some Formal Models of Grading Principles', *Synthese,* **6** (1966); reprinted in his *Studies in the Methodology and Foundations of Science* (Dordrecht, 1969).

14. J. C. Harsanyi, 'Cardinal Welfare, Individualistic Ethics and Interpersonal Comparisons of Utility', *Journal of Political Economy,* **63** (1955). See also P. K. Pattanaik, 'Risk, Impersonability and the Social Welfare Functions', *Journal of Political Economy,* **76** (1968).

ultimately makes everyone better off is indeed one of the most talked-of aspects of morality. But it is interesting to enquire in this context whether morality can be expressed in the form of choice between preference patterns rather than between actions. We take up this question in the next section.

### 3 Preference Types, Morality and Welfare

Consider a variation of the preference orderings of the two prisoners:

A: $a_0b_0$, $a_1b_0$, $a_1b_1$, $a_0b_1$.
B: $a_0b_0$, $a_0b_1$, $a_1b_1$, $a_1b_0$.

In this case each prisoner would prefer to confess if he felt that the other would do that and let him down, but would not confess if he thought that the other would not. In this variant of the Prisoners' Dilemma there are two equilibrium points, viz., $a_0b_0$ and $a_1b_1$, and what the outcome would be would depend on how each prisoner expects the other to behave. The interesting difference between this game—I have called it the Assurance Game—and the Prisoners' Dilemma is that a contract of mutual non-confession does not need any enforcement in the Assurance Game whereas it is the crux of the matter in the Prisoners' Dilemma.[15] Each prisoner will do the right thing if it is simply assured that the other is doing it too and there is no constant temptation to break the contract.

The preferences in the Prisoners' Dilemma and in the Assurance Game will be called here PD-preferences and AG-preferences respectively for the sake of brevity. It is of interest to note that not only is it the case that acting according to the AG-preferences makes it possible to avoid social inoptimality in terms of AG-preferences, it makes it possible to avoid social inoptimality in terms of PD-preferences as well. That is if everyone behaved *as if* they had AG-preferences and had the assurance of similar good behaviour by others, they would be better off even if they actually had PD-preferences.

Even the requirement of assurance does not arise if the individual preferences were the following:

A: $a_0b_0$, $a_0b_1$, $a_1b_0$, $a_1b_1$.
B: $a_0b_0$, $a_1b_0$, $a_0b_1$, $a_1b_1$.

Here $a_0$ and $b_0$ are strictly dominant strategies for A and B respectively and each would appear to be adamant on not letting the other person down. Calling these preferences OR-preferences, meaning other-regarding preferences, it is clear that if both behaved *as if* they had OR-preferences they would definitely be better off even in terms of PD-preferences compared with what would happen under individually rational behaviour under PD-preferences.

15. A. K. Sen, 'Isolation, Assurance and the Social Rate of Discount', *Quarterly Journal of Economics,* **81** (1967), and 'A Game-Theoretic Analysis of Theories of Collectivism in Allocation', in T. Majumdar (ed.), *Growth and Choice* (Oxford University Press: London, 1969).

Under AG-preferences and OR-preferences $a_0 b_0$ is clearly the best outcome for all and under PD-preferences it is the only outcome better for both than the non-cooperative solution of the PD-game. AG-preferences guarantee that this optimum will be reached given 'assurance', OR-preferences guarantee the optimum unconditionally, while PD-preferences guarantee that this outcome will never be reached except through an enforceable contract. In so far as morality has got something to do with reaching social optimality, it is tempting to rank the three pairs of preferences in a moral order: OR-preferences, AG-preferences, PD-preferences, and society may evolve traditions by which preferences of the OR-type are praised most, AG-type preferences next, and PD-type preferences least of all. Since for each pair the two members are exactly symmetrical except for the substitution of 'you' for 'me' and vice versa (they are isomorphic to each other), we can treat this as a ranking of three orderings over the possible outcomes. Moral rankings of this kind would seem to correspond closely to the possibility of securing mutual benefits through individual rationality calculus.

The fact that by acting as if one's preferences were of the OR-type mutual benefits could be obtained in terms of PD-preferences or AG-preferences as well, raises the further question of the relation between welfare and preferences. It is common to identify individual preferences as reflection of individual welfare, and—from the end of observations—to treat welfare as a numerical representation of preferences revealed by individual choices.[16] If social pressures are generated to persuade people to act according to, say, OR-preferences, a dichotomy between revealed preferences and welfare would seem to be necessary.[17] Social inoptimality might be avoidable only by

16. This assumption is very widely used in welfare economics as well as in studies of consumers' behaviour. A critical evaluation of this approach in some detail is presented in 'Behaviour and the Concept of Preference', *Economica,* **40** (1973). [Essay 2 in this volume.]

17. While this is not the occasion to go into practical debates on modes of behaviour, the controversy in China on the possible use of non-material incentives for running the collectives and communes was closely related to the issue under discussion and even to the particular contrast between PD-preferences on the one hand and AG- and OR-preferences on the other. During the 'Great Leap Forward' period (1958–60), there was a strong attempt to move away from incentive payments towards distribution of a substantial part of the total income on some criterion of needs ('the supply portion')—sometimes as much as 80 to 90 per cent (see C. Hoffman, *Work Incentive Practices and Policies in the People's Republic of China, 1953–1965* (Albany, NY, 1967)). Interpreting $a_0$ as working hard oneself, $a_1$ as not working hard, $b_0$ as others working hard and $b_1$ as others not working hard, the PD-preferences may well be typical results of *individualistic* calculus in a system without material incentives (cf. my 'Labour Allocation in a Cooperative', *Review of Economic Studies,* **33** (1969)). There seems to have been a vigorous controversy in China on the subject and also moral argumentation relating to contrasts broadly corresponding to the dichotomy between PD-preferences and AG- or OR-preferences, and an aspect of the 'cultural revolution', which followed the 'Great Leap Forward' and the problems generated then, seems to have been closely connected with this type of issue. See C. Riskin, 'Maoism and Motivation: A Discussion of Work Motivation in China', *Bulletin of Concerned Asian Scholars,* 1973.

a moral code of behaviour that drives a wedge between preferences and welfare.

An analytical aspect of this whole question is the relevance of ordering the possible orderings of outcomes. Rather than expressing moral views in terms of one ordering of outcomes, it may be necessary to express them through a ranking of the possible *orderings* of outcomes. In the next section this question is examined.

## 4 Ordering the Orderings

Let $X$ be the set of all possible outcomes and $\pi$ be the set of all possible orderings of the elements of $X$. A moral view can be defined as a quasi-ordering $Q$ of the elements of $\pi$. (A quasi-ordering is a ranking relation that is reflective and transitive but not necessarily complete, as indeed a moral view need not be.)

What does a moral quasi-ordering $Q$ stand for? Various interpretations are possible. It might take the form of a moral desire to have one preference pattern over outcomes rather than another, i.e., for $R^1$, $R^2 \in \pi$, if $R^1 Q R^2$ but not $R^2 Q R^1$, the person concerned would have morally *preferred* to have $R^1$ preference ordering rather than $R^2$ over $X$. Or else $Q$ may correspond to one's ranking in terms of praiseworthiness, i.e., $R^1$ deserving more praise than $R^2$.

Are there any advantages in viewing the problem in this way rather than in terms of a more traditional framework? There would seem to be some. In some models a contrast between moral orderings and actual orderings is not permitted at all and the failure to pursue a moral course—a commonly recognized phenomenon—is quite firmly put on what seems to me to be the rather slender shoulders of *akrasia* ('the weakness of will'). In models that do permit such a distinction (e.g., Harsanyi's) there is a zero–one contrast between the actual ordering and one moral (or 'ethical') ordering. In the model prepared here there can be gradations of morality, e.g., one can say—if one wishes to—that AG-preferences are morally superior to PD-preferences and OR-preferences morally superior to AG-preferences. The 'moral-non-moral' zero—one distinction is frequently not robust enough to permit the expression of our thoughts.

Furthermore, the problem of *akrasia* itself, on which some ethical theories depend heavily,[18] becomes much easier to understand once the all-or-none distinction of moral and non-moral behaviour is dropped. There may be a sequence of preference orderings of outcomes ranked by this person in moral terms. He might wish to have a different preference ordering $R$ from the one

---

18. See, for example, R. M. Hare, *The Language of Morals*, pp. 169–70, and *Freedom and Reason*, pp. 77–80.

he does have and might try to move towards higher ranked members of $\pi$. But what preference one has is not entirely in one's control. There is nothing particularly schizophrenic in saying: 'I wish I had a vegetarian's tastes, for I disapprove of the killing oy animals, but I find vegetarian food so revolting that I can't bear to eat it, so I do eat meat'.[19] This person's attempt at shifting his preferences in the vegetarian direction is clearly a moral exercise given his disapproval of killing, but should he fail to make it, it might be a bit glib to describe it as a 'weakness of will'. But it is a case of a failure to do something which the man in question would regard as morally superior (on the grounds of its following from an ordering that he morally prefers).

This model may be of some relevance also in resolving the problem of the impossibility of the 'Paretian liberal' which I have tried to discuss elsewhere.[20] There are two persons $A$ and $B$, the latter a prude and the former anything but one. There is a book, say, *Lady Chatterley's Lover* (henceforth *LCL*) to which $A$ is pro and $B$ is anti. $A$ would like best that both read it, next best that $B$ alone reads it ('stuffy $B$'s horizon needs broadening more than mine'), next best that he himself reads it, and worst of all nobody reads it. For $B$, the best alternative is that nobody reads it, next best that he himself does so alone ('poor $A$ is more vulnerable than me'), next best that $A$ alone reads it and the worst of all that both read it. There is only one copy of the book. A liberal who believes in the Paretian criterion of social improvement ('if everybody prefers $x$ to $y$, then $x$ is socially better than $y$') faces the following dilemma:

If the choice is between $B$ alone reading *LCL* and nobody reading it, I should think that it is better that he doesn't, since he himself doesn't wish to and as a liberal I shouldn't let $A$'s desire that $B$ reads *LCL* interfere with this. If the choice is between nobody reading it and $A$ reading it, I think $A$ should read it, since $A$ wants to and I shouldn't let $B$'s desire to stop $A$ from doing it interfere with this. If the choice is between $A$ reading it and $B$ reading it, as a believer in the unanimity rule (the Pareto principle) I must support $B$'s reading it since both prefer that to $A$'s reading it. So—let's see—it is better that $B$ reads it rather than $A$, better still that nobody reads it (rather than $B$ does), even better that $A$ reads it (rather than none), still better that $B$ reads it (rather than $A$), ... $\infty$

In this triple every alternative seems worse than another; there is an intransitivity—in fact there is no best element, which is an even stronger result

19. In terms of the classification used in my paper 'The Nature and Classes of Prescriptive Judgements', *Philosophical Quarterly*, **17** (1967), this would be a 'non-compulsive' value judgement.

20. A. K. Sen, 'The Impossibility of a Paretian Liberal', *Journal of Political Economy*, **78** (1970) [Essay 13 in this volume], and *Collective Choice and Social Welfare* (Oliver & Boyd: London, 1971), chs. 6 and 6*.

than intransitivity for a finite set.[21] So there is a conflict in this and one must choose between the unanimity rule (the Pareto principle) and the liberal principle as interpreted here. Consider now a liberal who is ready to stick his neck out in favour of $A$ reading it (since he clearly wants to) and $B$ not (since he does not). If he is an outsider, then there is no immediate problem and he simply overrides some preferences on grounds of their 'nosiness'. But if he is $A$ or $B$, how can he justify his decision? He himself 'prefers' that $B$ reads it rather than $A$, so how can he say that $A$ 'should' read it rather than $B$? The answer lies in his evaluation of his own preference. Suppose we are concerned with $A$. He can now argue:

I do prefer that prude $B$ reads it; it will do him a lot of good. But he does not want to. And I am liberal enough to believe that if he does not want to then he should not. So given his preference, I should not really prefer that he should read the book. I must rank my preferences, and my preference that he reads it is of a lower moral order than what my preference would be if I took his views into account.

Similarly a liberal $B$ would be able to escape from depriving $A$ from reading $LCL$ and reading it himself by preferring a more moral preference ordering (incorporating liberal values) to the one he actually expressed. Both the arguments turn on a ranking of preference orderings.

It can be seen that in terms of the basic preference structure the Paretian Liberal paradox has the same ordering as the Prisoners' Dilemma.[22] Putting $a_1$ and $a_0$ respectively for $A$'s reading $LCL$ and his not reading it, and putting $b_0$ and $b_1$ respectively for $B$'s reading the book and his not reading it, we get exactly the PD-preferences. Left to themselves $a_1 b_1$ will happen, i.e., $A$ the non-prude will read it and $B$ the prude will not. This is Pareto inferior to $a_0 b_0$, i.e., $A$ the non-prude not reading it and $B$ the prude reading it. In the Prisoners' Dilemma the individualistic outcome $a_1 b_1$ was criticized on Paretian grounds (and related ones). Here the liberal accepts $a_1 b_1$ and criticizes the use of the Paretian criterion. Where does the difference lie? Undoubtedly in the differential moral status of the respective preference orderings in the two cases. In the original Prisoners' Dilemma example the preference for $a_0 b_0$ over $a_1 b_1$ (shared by PD-, AG- and OR-preferences) is not dominated by some other ordering on any obvious moral grounds, whereas in the liberal

21. This problem arises not only in this example, but completely generally; see Theorems 6*1 and 6*2 in my *Collective Choice and Social Welfare*, pp. 87–8. For some internal inconsistencies in liberalism itself, see A. Gibbard, 'Is the Libertarian Claim Consistent?' (mimeographed), Dept. of Philosophy, Chicago University, 1972. [Revised version published later in *Journal of Economic Theory*, 7 (1974).]

22. Pointed out in Ben Fine's 'Individual Liberalism in a Paretian Society' (mimeographed), London School of Economics, 1972. [Revised version published later in *Journal of Political Economy*, 83 (1975).]

paradox it clearly is ranked lower by a liberal than a preference ordering incorporating liberal values. The difference lies in the ordering of the preference orderings.

## 5    Concluding Remarks

Games of the type of the Prisoners' Dilemma bring out a conflict between individual rationality and social optimality. From this a contrast between rational behaviour and morality can be derived in terms of the usual models of moral reasoning.

It is, however, significant that some simple variations of the preference pattern in the Prisoners' Dilemma make morality and rational behaviour perfectly consistent. More interestingly, if people behave *as if* they have these modified preferences (AG- or OR-preferences in our example), they end up being better off even in terms of their unmodified preferences (PD-preferences). On the practical side this raises important questions about cultural orientation of behaviour (an illustration of this problem was given in terms of work motivation in rural China) and on the analytical side this causes difficulties for the usual treatment of individual welfare orderings as identical with revealed preferences (common, for example, in welfare economics).

In this context a broader question on the framework of moral judgements was also examined. It is possible to define a moral ordering not directly on the space of outcomes (or actions) but on that of the orderings of outcomes (or actions). I have tried to demonstrate that there are advantages in such a framework.

# 4

# Rational Fools: A Critique of the Behavioural Foundations of Economic Theory

1

In his *Mathematical Psychics,* published in 1881, Edgeworth asserted that 'the first principle of Economics is that every agent is actuated only by self-interest'.[1] This view of man has been a persistent one in economic models, and the nature of economic theory seems to have been much influenced by this basic premise. In this essay I would like to examine some of the problems that have arisen from this conception of human beings.

I should mention that Edgeworth himself was quite aware that this so-called first principle of Economics was not a particularly realistic one. Indeed, he felt that 'the concrete nineteenth century man is for the most part an impure egoist, a mixed utilitarian'.[2] This raises the interesting question as to why Edgeworth spent so much of his time and talent in developing a line of inquiry the first principle of which he believed to be false. The issue is not why abstractions should be employed in pursuing general economic questions—the

For helpful comments on an earlier version, I am grateful to the Editors [of *Philosophy and Public Affairs*] and to Åke Andersson, Isaiah Berlin, Frank Hahn, Martin Hollis, Janos Kornai, Derek Parfit, Christopher Peacocke, and Tibor Scitovsky.

1. F. Y. Edgeworth, *Mathematical Psychics: An Essay on the Application of Mathematics to the Moral Sciences* (London, 1881), p. 16.
2. Edgeworth, p. 104. In fact, he went on to make some interesting remarks on the results of 'impure' egoism, admitting an element of sympathy for each other. The remarks have been investigated and analysed by David Collard, 'Edgeworth's Propositions on Altruism', *Economic Journal,* 85 (1975).

Herbert Spencer Lecture, delivered at Oxford University in October 1976, published in *Philosophy and Public Affairs,* 6 (Summer 1977), 317−44 and also in H. Harris (ed.), *Scientific Models and Man* (Oxford, 1978).

nature of the inquiry makes this inevitable—but why would one choose an assumption which he himself believed to be not merely inaccurate in detail but fundamentally mistaken? As we shall see, this question is of continuing interest to modern economics as well.

Part of the answer, as far as Edgeworth was concerned, undoubtedly lay in the fact that he did not think the assumption to be fundamentally mistaken in the *particular* types of activities to which he applied what he called 'economical calculus': (i) war and (ii) contract. 'Admitting that there exists in the higher parts of human nature a tendency towards and feeling after utilitarian institutions', he asked the rhetorical question: 'could we seriously suppose that these moral considerations were relevant to war and trade; could eradicate the controlless core of human selfishness, or exercise an appreciable force in comparison with the impulse of self-interest'.[3] He interpreted Sidgwick to have dispelled the 'illusion' that 'the interest of all is the interest of each', noting that Sidgwick found the 'two supreme principles— Egoism and Utilitarianism' to be 'irreconcilable, unless indeed by religion'. 'It is far from the spirit of the philosophy of pleasure to deprecate the importance of religion', wrote Edgeworth, 'but in the present inquiry, and dealing with the lower elements of human nature, we should have to seek a more obvious transition, a more earthy passage, from the principle of self-interest to the principle, or at least the practice, of utilitarianism'.[4]

Notice that the context of the debate is important to this argument. Edgeworth felt that he had established the acceptability of 'egoism' as the fundamental behavioural assumption for his particular inquiry by demolishing the acceptability of 'utilitarianism' as a description of actual behaviour. Utilitarianism is, of course, far from being the only non-egoistic approach. Furthermore, between the claims of oneself and the claims of all lie the claims of a variety of groups—for example, families, friends, local communities, peer groups, and economic and social classes. The concepts of family responsibility, business ethics, class consciousness, and so on, relate to these intermediate areas of concern, and the dismissal of utilitarianism as a descriptive theory of behaviour does not leave us with egoism as the only alternative. The relevance of some of these considerations to the economics of negotiations and contracts would be difficult to deny.

It must be noted that Edgeworth's query about the outcome of economic contact between purely self-seeking individuals had the merit of being immediately relevant to an abstract inquiry that had gone on for more than a hundred years already, and which was much discussed in debates involving Herbert Spencer, Henry Sidgwick, and other leading thinkers of the period. Two years before Edgeworth's *Mathematical Psychics* appeared, Herbert Spencer had published his elaborate analysis of the relation between egoism

3. Edgeworth, p. 52.
4. *Ibid.*, pp. 52–3.

and altruism in *The Data of Ethics.* He had arrived at the comforting — if somewhat unclear — conclusion that 'general happiness is to be achieved mainly through the adequate pursuit of their own happinesses by individuals; while, reciprocally, the happiness of individuals are to be achieved in part by their pursuit of the general happiness'.[5] In the context of this relatively abstract inquiry, Edgeworth's tight economic analysis, based on a well-defined model of contracts between two self-seeking individuals, or between two types of (identical) self-seeking individuals, gave a clear answer to an old hypothetical question.

It appeared that in Edgeworth's model, based on egoistic behaviour, there was a remarkable correspondence between exchange equilibria in competitive markets and what in modern economic terms is called 'the core' of the economy. An outcome is said to be in 'the core' of the economy if and only if it fulfils a set of conditions of unimprovability. These conditions, roughly speaking, are that not only is it the case that no one could be made better off without making somebody else worse off (the situation is what is called a 'Pareto optimum'), but also that no one is worse off than he would be without trade, and that no coalition of individuals, by altering the trade among themselves, could on their own improve their own lot. Edgeworth showed that given certain general assumptions, any equilibrium that can emerge in a competitive market must satisfy these conditions and be in the 'core'. Thus, in Edgeworth's model the competitive market equilibria are, in this sense, undominated by any feasible alternative arrangement, given the initial distribution of endowments. More surprising in some ways was the converse result that if the number of individuals of each type were increased without limit, the core (representing such undominated outcomes) would shrink towards the set of competitive equilibria; that is, the core would not be much more extensive than the set of competitive equilibria. This pair of results has been much elaborated and extended in the recent literature on general equilibrium with similar models and with essentially the same behavioural assumptions.[6]

Being in the core, however, is not as such a momentous achievement from the point of view of social welfare. A person who starts off ill-endowed may stay poor and deprived even after the transactions, and if being in the core is all that competition offers, the propertyless person may be forgiven for not regarding this achievement as a 'big deal'. Edgeworth took some note of this by considering the problem of choice between different competitive equilibria. He observed that for the utilitarian good society, 'competition requires to be supplemented by arbitration, and the basis of arbitration between self-interested contractors is the greatest possible sum-total utility'.[7] Into the

---

5. H. Spencer, *The Data of Ethics* (London, 1879; extended edition, 1887), p. 238.

6. See, especially, K. J. Arrow and F. H. Hahn, *General Competitive Analysis* (San Francisco, 1971).

7. Edgeworth, p. 56.

institutional aspects of such arbitration and the far-reaching implications of it for the distribution of property ownership, Edgeworth did not really enter, despite superficial appearance to the contrary. On the basis of the achievement of competition, however limited, Edgeworth felt entitled to be 'biassed to a more conservative caution in reform'. In calculating 'the utility of pre-utilitarian institutions', Edgeworth felt impressed 'with a view of Nature, not, as in the picture left by Mill, all bad, but a first approximation to the best'.[8]

I am not concerned in this essay with examining whether the approximation is a rather remote one. (This I do believe to be the case even within the structure of assumptions used by Edgeworth, but it is not central to the subject of this paper.) I am concerned here with the view of man which forms part of Edgeworth's analysis and survives more or less intact in much of modern economic theory. The view is, of course, a stylized one and geared specifically to tackling a relatively abstract dispute with which Spencer, Sidgwick, and several other leading contemporary thinkers were much concerned—namely, in what sense and to what extent would egoistic behaviour achieve general good? Whether or not egoistic behaviour is an accurate assumption in reality does not, of course, have any bearing on the accuracy of Edgeworth's answer to the question posed. Within the structure of a limited economic model it provided a clear-cut response to the abstract query about egoism and general good.

This particular debate has gone on for a long time and continues to provide motivation for many recent exercises in economic theory today. The limited nature of the query has had a decisive influence on the choice of economic models and the conception of human beings in them. In their distinguished text on general equilibrium theory, Arrow and Hahn state (pp. vi–vii):

> There is by now a long and fairly imposing line of economists from Adam Smith to the present who have sought to show that a decentralized economy motivated by self-interest and guided by price signals would be compatible with a coherent disposition of economic resources that could be regarded, in a well-defined sense, as superior to a large class of possible alternative dispositions. Moreover, the price signals would operate in a way to establish this degree of coherence. It is important to understand how surprising this claim must be to anyone not exposed to the tradition. The immediate 'common sense' answer to the question 'What will an economy motivated by individual greed and controlled by a very large number of different agents look like?' is probably: There will be chaos. That quite a different answer has long been claimed true and has indeed permeated the economic thinking of a large number of people who are in no way economists is itself sufficient ground for

8. *Ibid.*, p. 82.

investigating it seriously. The proposition having been put forward and very seriously entertained, it is important to know not only whether it *is* true, but whether it *could* be true. A good deal of what follows is concerned with this last question, which seems to us to have considerable claims on the attention of economists.

The primary concern here is not with the relation of postulated models to the real economic world, but with the accuracy of answers to well-defined questions posed with preselected assumptions which severely constrain the nature of the models that can be admitted into the analysis. A specific concept of man is ingrained in the question itself, and there is no freedom to depart from this conception so long as one is engaged in answering this question. The nature of man in these current economic models continues, then, to reflect the particular formulation of certain general philosophical questions posed in the past. The realism of the chosen conception of man is simply not a part of this inquiry.

2

There is another non-empirical—and possibly simpler—reason why the conception of man in economic models tends to be that of a self-seeking egoist. It is possible to define a person's interests in such a way that no matter what he does he can be seen to be furthering his own interests in every isolated act of choice.[9] While formalized relatively recently in the context of the theory of revealed preference, this approach is of respectable antiquity, and Joseph Butler was already arguing against it in the Rolls Chapel two and a half centuries ago.[10] The reduction of man to a self-seeking animal depends in this approach on careful definition. If you are observed to choose $x$ rejecting $y$, you are declared to have 'revealed' a preference for $x$ over $y$. Your personal utility is then defined as simply a numerical representation of this 'preference', assigning a higher utility to a 'preferred' alternative. With this set of definitions you can hardly escape maximizing your own utility, except through inconsistency. Of course, if you choose $x$ and reject $y$ on one occasion and then promptly proceed to do the exact opposite, you can prevent the revealed preference theorist from assigning a preference ordering to you, thereby restraining him from stamping a utility function on you which you must be

9. If a person's actions today affect his well-being in the future, then under this approach his future interests must be defined in terms of the way they are *assessed today*. In general, there is no reason to presume that the future interests as assessed today will coincide with those interests as assessed in the future. This adds an additional dimension to the problem, and I am grateful to Derek Parfit for convincing me of the conceptual importance of this question.

10. J. Butler, *Fifteen Sermons Preached at the Rolls Chapel* (London, 1726); see also T. Nagel, *The Possibility of Altruism* (Oxford, 1970), p. 81.

seen to be maximizing. He will then have to conclude that either you are inconsistent or your preferences are changing. You can frustrate the revealed preference theorist through more sophisticated inconsistencies as well.[11] But if you are consistent, then no matter whether you are a single-minded egoist or a raving altruist or a class-conscious militant, you will appear to be maximizing your own utility in this enchanted world of definitions. Borrowing from the terminology used in connection with taxation, if the Arrow–Hahn justification of the assumption of egoism amounts to an *avoidance* of the issue, the revealed preference approach looks more like a robust piece of *evasion*.

This approach of definitional egoism sometimes goes under the name of rational choice, and it involves nothing other than internal consistency. A person's choices are considered 'rational' in this approach if and only if these choices can *all* be explained in terms of some preference relation consistent with the revealed preference definition, that is, if all his choices can be explained as the choosing of 'most preferred' alternatives with respect to a postulated preference relation.[12] The rationale of this approach seems to be based on the idea that the only way of understanding a person's real preference is to examine his actual choices, and there is no choice-independent way of understanding someone's attitude towards alternatives. (This view, by the way, is not confined to economists only. When, many years ago, I had to take my qualifying examination in English Literature at Calcutta University, one of the questions we had to answer concerning *A Midsummer Night's Dream* was: Compare the characters of Hermia and Helena. Whom would you choose?)

I have tried to demonstrate elsewhere that once we eschew the curious definitions of preference and welfare, this approach presumes both too little and too much: too little because there are non-choice sources of information on preference and welfare as these terms are usually understood, and too much because choice may reflect a compromise among a variety of considerations of which personal welfare may be just one.[13]

11. See H. S. Houthakker, 'Revealed Preference and the Utility Function', *Economica,* **17** (1950); P. A. Samuelson, 'The Problem of Integrability in Utility Theory', *Economica,* **17** (1950).

12. For the main analytical results, see M. K. Richter, 'Rational Choice', *Preference, Utility and Demand Theory*, ed. J. S. Chipman *et al.* (New York, 1971).

13. A. K. Sen, 'Behaviour and the Concept of Preference', *Economica,* **40** (1973) [Essay 2 in this volume]. See also S. Körner's important recent study, *Experience and Conduct* (Cambridge, 1971). Also T. Schwartz, 'Von Wright's Theory of Human Welfare: A Critique', forthcoming in P. A. Schlipp (ed.), *The Philosophy of Georg Henrik von Wright*; T. Majumdar, 'The Concept of Man in Political Economy and Economics', mimeographed (Jawaharlal Nehru University, New Delhi, 1976); and F. Schick, 'Rationality and Sociality', mimeographed (Rutgers University, Philosophy of Science Association, 1976) [revised version published in C. A. Hooker, J. J. Leach and E. F. McClennen (eds), *Foundations and Applications of Decision Theory* (Reidel, Dordrecht, 1978)].

The complex psychological issues underlying choice have recently been forcefully brought out by a number of penetrating studies dealing with consumer decisions[14] and production activities.[15] It is very much an open question as to whether these behavioural characteristics can be at all captured within the formal limits of consistent choice on which the welfare-maximization approach depends.[16]

3

Paul Samuelson has noted that many economists would 'separate economics from sociology upon the basis of rational or irrational behaviour, where these terms are defined in the penumbra of utility theory'.[17] This view might well be resented, for good reasons, by sociologists, but the cross that economists have to bear in this view of the dichotomy can be seen if we note that the approach of 'rational behaviour', as it is typically interpreted, leads to a remarkably mute theory. Behaviour, it appears, is to be 'explained in terms of preferences, which are in turn defined only by behaviour'. Not surprisingly, excursions into circularities have been frequent. Nevertheless, Samuelson is undoubtedly right in asserting that the theory 'is not in a technical sense *meaningless*'.[18] The reason is quite simple. As we have already discussed, the approach does impose the requirement of internal consistency of observed choice, and this might well be refuted by actual observations, making the theory 'meaningful' in the sense in which Samuelson's statement is intended.

14. See T. Scitovsky, *The Joyless Economy: An Inquiry into Human Satisfaction and Consumer Dissatisfaction* (London and New York, 1976). See also the general critique of the assumption of 'rational' consumer behaviour by J. Kornai, *Anti-Equilibrium* (Amsterdam and London, 1971), chap. 11; and the literature on 'psychological choice models', in particular, D. McFadden, 'Economic Applications of Psychological Choice Models' (presented at the Third World Econometric Congress, August 1975).

15. See H. Liebenstein, 'Allocative Efficiency vs. x-Efficiency', *American Economic Review,* **56** (1966). Also critiques of the traditional assumption of profit maximization in *business* behaviour, particularly W. J. Baumol, *Business Behavior, Value and Growth* (New York, 1959); R. Marris, *The Economic Theory of Managerial Capitalism* (London, 1964); O. Williamson, *The Economics of Discretionary Behavior* (Chicago, 1967); and A. Silberston, 'Price Behaviour of Firms', *Economic Journal,* **80** (1970), reprinted in Royal Economic Society, *Surveys of Applied Economics,* **1** (London, 1973).

16. On the required conditions of consistency for viewing choice in terms of a binary relation, see my 'Choice Functions and Revealed Preference', *Review of Economic Studies,* **38** (1971) [Essay 1 in this volume]; H. G. Herzberger, 'Ordinal Preference and Rational Choice', *Econometrica,* **41** (1973); K. Suzumura, 'Rational Choice and Revealed Preference', *Review of Economic Studies,* **43** (1976); S. Kanger, 'Choice Based on Preference', mimeographed (Uppsala University, 1976).

17. P. A. Samuelson, *The Foundation of Economics* (Cambridge, Mass., 1955), p. 90.
18. *Ibid.*, p. 91.

The requirement of consistency does have surprising cutting power. Various general characteristics of demand relations can be derived from it. But in the present context, the main issue is the possibility of using the consistency requirement for actual *testing*. Samuelson specifies the need for 'ideal observational conditions' for the implications of the approach to be 'refuted or verified'. This is not, however, easy to satisfy since, on the one hand, our love of variety makes it illegitimate to consider individual acts of choice as the proper units (rather than *sequences* of choices) while, on the other hand, lapse of time makes it difficult to distinguish between inconsistencies and changing tastes. There have, in fact, been very few systematic attempts at testing the consistency of people's day-to-day behaviour, even though there have been interesting and useful contrived experiments on people's reactions to uncertainty under laboratory conditions. What counts as admissible evidence remains unsettled. If today you were to poll economists of different schools, you would almost certainly find the coexistence of beliefs (i) that the rational behaviour theory is unfalsifiable, (ii) that it is falsifiable and so far unfalsified, and (ii) that it is falsifiable and indeed patently false.[19]

However, for my purposes here this is not the central issue. Even if the required consistency were seen to obtain, it would still leave the question of egoism unresolved except in the purely definitional sense, as I have already noted. A consistent chooser can have any degree of egoism that we care to specify. It is, of course, true that in the special case of pure consumer choice over private goods, the revealed preference theorist tries to relate the person's 'preference' or 'utility' to his *own* bundle of commodities. This restriction arises, however, not from any guarantee that he is concerned only with his own interests, but from the fact that his own consumption bundle—or that of his family—is the only bundle over which he has direct *control* in his acts of choice. The question of egoism remains completely open.

I believe the question also requires a clearer formulation than it tends to receive, and to this question I shall now turn.

4

As we consider departures from 'unsympathetic isolation abstractly assumed in Economics', to use Edgeworth's words, we must distinguish between two separate concepts: (i) sympathy and (ii) commitment. The former corresponds to the case in which the concern for others directly affects one's welfare. If

---

19. The recent philosophical critiques of rational behaviour theory include among others, M. Hollis and E. J. Nell, *Rational Economic Man* (Cambridge, 1975); S. Wong, 'On the Consistency and Completeness of Paul Samuelson's Programme in the Theory of Consumer Behaviour' (Ph.D. thesis, Cambridge University, 1975, forthcoming). [Later published as *Foundations of Paul Samuelson's Revealed Preference Theory* (Routledge, London, 1978).] See also the pragmatic criticisms of Kornai, *Anti-Equilibrium*, chap. 11.

the knowledge of torture of others makes you sick, it is a case of sympathy; if its does not make you feel personally worse off, but you think it is wrong and you are ready to do something to stop it, it is a case of commitment. I do not wish to claim that the words chosen have any very great merit, but the distinction is, I think, important. It can be argued that behaviour based on sympathy is in an important sense egoistic, for one is oneself pleased at others' pleasure and pained at others' pain, and the pursuit of one's own utility may thus be helped by sympathetic action. It is action based on commitment rather than sympathy which would be non-egoistic in this sense. (Note, however, that the *existence* of sympathy does not imply that the action helpful to others must be *based on* sympathy in the sense that the action would not take place had one got less or no comfort from others' welfare. This question of *causation* is to be taken up presently.)

Sympathy is, in some ways, an easier concept to analyse than commitment. When a person's sense of well-being is psychologically dependent on someone else's welfare, it is a case of sympathy; other things given, the awareness of the increase in the welfare of the other person then makes this person directly better off. (Of course, when the influence is negative, the relation is better named 'antipathy', but we can economize on terminology and stick to the term 'sympathy', just noting that the relation can be positive or negative.) While sympathy relates similar things to each other—namely, welfares of different persons—commitment relates choice to anticipated levels of welfare. One way of defining commitment is in terms of a person choosing an act that he believes will yield a lower level of personal welfare to him than an alternative that is also available to him. Notice that the comparison is between *anticipated* welfare levels, and therefore this definition of commitment excludes acts that go against self-interest resulting purely from a failure to foresee consequences.

A more difficult question arises when a person's choice happens to coincide with the maximization of his anticipated personal welfare, but that is not the *reason* for his choice. If we wish to make room for this, we can expand the definition of commitment to include cases in which the person's choice, while maximizing anticipated personal welfare, would be unaffected under at least one counterfactual condition in which the act chosen would cease to maximize personal welfare. Commitment in this more inclusive sense may be difficult to ascertain not only in the context of others' choices but also in that of one's own, since it is not always clear what one would have done had the circumstances been different. This broader sense may have particular relevance when one acts on the basis of a concern for duty which, if violated, could cause remorse, but the action is really chosen out of the sense of duty rather than just to avoid the illfare resulting from the remorse that would occur if one were to act otherwise. (Of course, even the narrower sense of commitment will cover the case in which the illfare resulting from the remorse, if any, is *outweighed* by the gain in welfare.)

I have not yet referred to uncertainty concerning anticipated welfare. When this is introduced, the concept of sympathy is unaffected, but commitment will require reformulation. The necessary modifications will depend on the person's reaction to uncertainty. The simplest case is probably the one in which the person's idea of what a 'lottery' offers to him in terms of personal gain is captured by the 'expected utility' of personal welfare (that is, adding personal welfares from different outcomes weighted by the probability of occurrence of each outcome). In this case, the entire discussion is reformulated simply replacing personal welfare by *expected* personal welfare; commitment then involves choosing an action that yields a lower expected welfare than an alternative available action. (The broader sense can also be correspondingly modified.)

In the terminology of modern economic theory, sympathy is a case of 'externality'. Many models rule out externalities, for example, the standard model to establish that each competitive equilibrium is a Pareto optimum and belongs to the core of the economy. If the existence of sympathy were to be permitted in these models, some of these standard results would be upset, though by no means all of them.[20] But this would not require a serious revision of the basic structure of these models. On the other hand, commitment does involve, in a very real sense, counterpreferential choice, destroying the crucial assumption that a chosen alternative must be better than (or at least as good as) the others for the person choosing it, and this would certainly require that models be formulated in an essentially different way.

The contrast between sympathy and commitment may be illustrated with the story of two boys who find two apples, one large, one small. Boy *A* tells boy *B*, 'You choose'. *B* immediately picks the larger apple. *A* is upset and permits himself the remark that this was grossly unfair. 'Why?' asks *B*. 'Which one would *you* have chosen, if you were to choose rather than me?' 'The smaller one, of course', *A* replies. *B* is now triumphant: 'Then what are you complaining about? That's the one you've got!' *B* certainly wins this round of the argument, but in fact *A* would have lost nothing from *B*'s choice had his own hypothetical choice of the smaller apple been based on sympathy as opposed to commitment. *A*'s anger indicates that this was probably not the case.

Commitment is, of course, closely connected with one's morals. But moral this question is in a very broad sense, covering a variety of influences from religious to political, from the ill-understood to the well-argued. When, in Bernard Shaw's *The Devil's Disciple*, Judith Anderson interprets Richard Dudgeon's willingness to be hanged in place of her husband as arising

20. See A. K. Sen, 'Labour Allocation in a Cooperative Enterprise', *Review of Economic Studies,* 33 (1966); S. G. Winter, Jr, 'A Simple Remark on the Second Optimality Theorem of Welfare Economics', *Journal of Economic Theory,* 1(1969); Collard, 'Edgeworth's Propositions'; G. C. Archibald and D. Donaldson, 'Non-paternalism and Basic Theorems of Welfare Economics', *Canadian Journal of Economics,* 9 (1976).

from sympathy for him or love for her, Richard is adamant in his denial: 'What I did last night, I did in cold blood, caring not half so much for your husband, or for you as I do for myself. I had no motive and no interest: all I can tell you is that when it came to the point whether I would take my neck out of the noose and put another man's into it. I could not do it.'[21]

The characteristic of commitment with which I am most concerned here is the fact that it drives a wedge between personal choice and personal welfare, and much of traditional economic theory relies on the identity of the two. This identity is sometimes obscured by the ambiguity of the term 'preference', since the normal use of the word permits the identification of preference with the concept of being better off, and at the same time it is not quite unnatural to define 'preferred' as 'chosen'. I have no strong views on the 'correct' use of the word 'preference', and I would be satisfied as long as both uses are not *simultaneously* made, attempting an empirical assertion by virtue of two definitions.[22] The basic link between choice behaviour and welfare achievements in the traditional models is severed as soon as commitment is admitted as an ingredient of choice.

5

'Fine,' you might say, 'but how relevant is all this to the kind of choices with which economists are concerned? Economics does not have much to do with Richard Dudgeon's march to the gallows.' I think one should immediately agree that for many types of behaviour, commitment is unlikely to be an important ingredient. In the private purchase of many consumer goods, the scope for the exercise of commitment may indeed be limited and may show up rather rarely in such exotic acts as the boycotting of South African avocados or the eschewing of Spanish holidays. Therefore, for many studies of consumer behaviour and interpretations thereof, commitment may pose no great problem. Even sympathy may not be extremely important, the sources of interpersonal interdependence lying elsewhere, for example, in the desire to keep up with the Joneses or in being influenced by other people's habits.[23]

But economics is not concerned only with consumer behaviour; nor is consumption confined to 'private goods'. One area in which the question of

---

21. G. B. Shaw, *Three Plays for Puritans* (Harmondsworth, 1966), p. 94.

22. See my 'Behaviour and the Concept of Preference', *Economica,* **40** (1973) [Essay 2 in this volume], and Shick, 'Rationality and Sociality'.

23. See J. S. Duesenberry, *Income, Saving and the Theory of Consumer Behavior* (Cambridge, Mass., 1949); S. J. Prais and H. S. Houthakker, *The Analysis of Family Budgets* (Cambridge, 1955); W. Gaertner, 'A Dynamic Model of Interdependent Consumer Behaviour', mimeographed (Bielefeld University, 1973); R. A. Pollak, 'Interdependent Preferences', *American Economic Review,* **66** (1976).

commitment is most important is that of the so-called public goods. These have to be contrasted with 'private goods' which have the characteristic that they cannot be used by more than one person: if you ate a piece of apple pie, I wouldn't consider devouring it too. Not so with 'public goods', for example, a road or a public park, which you and I may both be able to use. In many economic models private goods are the only ones around, and this is typically the case when the 'invisible hand' is given the task of doing visible good. But, in fact, public goods are important in most economies and cover a wide range of services from roads and street lighting to defence. There is much evidence that the share of public goods in national consumption has grown rather dramatically in most countries in the world.

The problem of optimal allocation of public goods has also been much discussed, especially in the recent economic literature.[24] A lot of attention, in particular, has been devoted to the problem of correct revelation of preferences. This arises most obviously in the case of subscription schemes where a person is charged according to benefits received. The main problem centres on the fact that it is in everybody's interest to understate the benefit he expects, but this understatement may lead to the rejection of a public project which would have been justified if true benefits were known. Analysis of this difficulty, sometimes referred to as the 'free rider' problem, has recently led to some extremely ingenious proposals for circumventing this inefficiency within the framework of egoistic action.[25] The reward mechanism is set up with such ungodly cunning that people have an incentive to reveal exactly their true willingness to pay for the public good in question. One difficulty in this solution arises from an assumed limitation of strategic possibilities open to the individual, the removal of which leads to an impossibility result.[26]

24. See E. Lindahl, *Die Gerechtigkeit der Besteuerung* (Lund, 1919), translated in R. A. Musgrave and A. Peacock, *Classics in the Theory of Public Finance* (London, 1967); P. A. Samuelson, 'The Pure Theory of Public Expenditure', *Review of Economic Studies,* 21 (1954); R. Musgrave, *The Theory of Public Finance* (New York, 1959); L. Johansen, *Public Economics* (Amsterdam, 1966); D. K. Foley, 'Lindahl's Solution and the Core of an Economy with Public Goods', *Econometrica,* 38 (1970); E. Malinvaud, 'Prices for Individual Consumption, Quantity Indicators for Collective Consumption', *Review of Economic Studies,* 39 (1972).

25. T. Groves and J. Ledyard, 'Optimal Allocation of Public Goods: A Solution to the "Free Rider" Problem', *Econometrica,* 45 (1977); J. Green and J. J. Laffont, 'Characterisation of Satisfactory Mechanisms for the Revelation of Preferences for Public Goods', *Econometrica,* 45 (1977). See also J. Drèze and D. de la Vallée Poussin, 'A Tatonnement Process for Public Goods', *Review of Economic Studies,* 38 (1971); E. Malinvaud, 'A Planning Approach to the Public Goods Problem', *Swedish Journal of Economics,* 73 (1971); V. L. Smith, 'Incentive Compatible Experimental Processes for the Provision of Public Goods', mimeographed (Econometric Society Summer Meeting, Madison, 1976) [See the paper later published, 'Experiments with a Decentralized Mechanism for Public Good Decisions', *American Economic Review,* 70 (1980)].

26. See J. Ledyard and D. J. Roberts, 'On the Incentive Problem for Public Goods', Discussion Paper No. 116 (CMSEMS, Northwestern University, 1974). See also L. Hurwicz, 'On Informationally Decentralized Systems', in R. Radner and B. McGuire, *Decisions and Organizations* (Amsterdam, 1972).

Another difficulty concerns the fact that in giving people the incentive to reveal the truth, money is handed out and the income distribution shifts in a way unguided by distributional considerations. This effect can, of course, be undone by a redistribution of initial endowments and profit shares,[27] but that action obviously raises difficulties of its own.

Central to this problem is the assumption that when asked a question, the individual gives that answer which will maximize his personal gain. How good is this assumption? I doubt that in general it is very good. ('Where is the railway station?' he asks me. 'There', I say, pointing at the post office, 'and would you please post this letter for me on the way?' 'Yes', he says, determined to open the envelope and check whether it contains something valuable.) Even in the particular context of revelation of preferences for public goods the gains-maximizing behaviour may not be the best assumption. Leif Johansen, one of the major contributors to public economies is, I think, right to question the assumption in this context:

> Economic theory in this, as well as in some other fields, tends to suggest that people are honest only to the extent that they have economic incentives for being so. This is a homo oeconomicus assumption which is far from being obviously true, and which needs confrontation with observed realities. In fact, a simple line of thought suggests that the assumption can hardly be true in its most extreme form. No society would be viable without some norms and rules of conduct. Such norms and rules are necessary for viability exactly in fields where strictly economic incentives are absent and cannot be created.[28]

What is at issue is not whether people invariably give an honest answer to every question, but whether they always give a gains-maximizing answer, or at any rate, whether they give gains-maximizing answers often enough to make that the appropriate general assumption for economic theory. The presence of non-gains-maximizing answers, including truthful ones, immediately brings in commitment as a part of behaviour.

The question is relevant also to the recent literature on strategic voting. A number of beautiful analytical results have recently been established showing the impossibility of any voting procedure satisfying certain elementary requirements and making honest voting the gains-maximizing strategy for

---

27. See Theorem 4.2 in Groves and Ledyard, 'Optimal Allocation of Public Goods'.

28. L. Johansen, 'The Theory of Public Goods: Misplaced Emphasis' (Institute of Economics, University of Oslo, 1976). See also J. J. Laffont, 'Macroeconomic Constraints, Economic Efficiency and Ethics', mimeographed (Harvard University, 1974); P. Bohm, 'Estimating Demand for Public Goods: An Experiment', *European Economic Review*, 3 (1972).

everyone.[29] The correctness of these results is not in dispute, but is it appropriate to assume that people always do try to maximize personal gains in their voting behaviour? Indeed, in large elections, it is difficult to show that any voter has any real prospect of affecting the outcome by his vote, and if voting involves some cost, the expected net gain from voting may typically be negative. Nevertheless, the proportion of turnout in large elections may still be quite high, and I have tried to argue elsewhere that in such elections people may often be 'guided not so much by maximization of expected utility, but something much simpler, viz., just a desire to record one's true preference'.[30] If this desire reflects a sense of commitment, then the behaviour in question would be at variance with the view of man in traditional economic theory.


6


The question of commitment is important in a number of other economic contexts.[31] It is central to the problem of work motivation, the importance of which for production performance can hardly be ignored.

It is certainly costly and may be impossible to devise a system of supervision with rewards and punishment such that everyone has the incentive to exert himself. Every economic system has, therefore, tended to rely on the existence of attitudes towards work which supersede the calculation of net gain from each unit of exertion. Social conditioning plays an extremely important part

---

29. A. Gibbard, 'Manipulation of Voting Schemes: A General Result', *Econometrica,* **41** (1973); M. A. Satterthwaite, 'Strategy-proofness and Arrow's Conditions', *Journal of Economic Theory,* **10** (1975); D. Schmeidler and H. Sonnenschein, 'The Possibility of Non-manipulable Social Choice Functions' (CMSEMS, Northwestern University, 1974) [revised version later published under different title in H. W. Gottinger and W. Leinfellner (eds), *Decision Theory and Social Ethics* (Reidel, Dordrecht, 1978)]; B. Dutta and P. K. Pattanaik, 'On Nicely Consistent Voting Systems' (Delhi School of Economics, 1975) [later published in *Econometrica,* **46** (1978)]; P. K. Pattanaik, 'Strategic Voting without Collusion under Binary and Democratic Group Decision Rules', *Review of Economic Studies,* **42** (1975); B. Peleg, 'Consistent Voting Systems' (Institute of Mathematics, Hebrew University, Jerusalem, 1976) [later published in *Econometrica,* **46** (1978)]; A. Gibbard, 'Social Decision, Strategic Behavior, and Best Outcomes: An Impossibility Result', Discussion Paper No. 224 (CMSEMS, Northwestern University, 1976) [Later published in Gottinger and Leinfellner, *Decision Theory and Social Ethics,* 1978].

30. See A. K. Sen, *Collective Choice and Social Welfare* (Edinburgh and San Francisco, 1970), p. 195.

31. See Ragnar Frisch's discussion of the need for 'a realistic theoretical foundation for social policy' in his 'Samarbeid mellom Politikere og Økonometrikere om Formuleringen av Politiske Preferenenser' (Sosialøkonomen, 1971). (I am grateful to Leif Johansen for translating the relevant portions of the paper for me.) See also J. A. Mirrlees, 'The Economics of Charitable Contributions', Econometric Society European meeting (Oslo, 1973).

here.[32] I am persuaded that Britain's present economic difficulties have a great deal to do with work motivation problems that lie outside the economics of rewards and punishments, and one reason why economists seem to have so little to contribute in this area is the neglect in traditional economic theory of this whole issue of commitment and the social relations surrounding it.[33]

These questions are connected, of course, with ethics, since moral reasoning influences one's actions, but in a broader sense these are matters of culture, of which morality is one part. Indeed, to take an extreme case, in the Chinese 'cultural revolution' one of the primary aims was the increase of the sense of commitment with an eye on economic results: 'the aim of the Great Proletarian Cultural Revolution is to revolutionize people's ideology and as a consequence to achieve greater, faster, better and more economical results in all fields of work'.[34] Of course, China was experimenting with reducing dramatically the role of material incentives in production, which would certainly have increased the part that commitment was meant to play, but even within the traditional systems of payments, much reliance is usually placed on rules of conduct and modes of behaviour that go beyond strictly economic incentives.[35] To run an organization *entirely* on incentives to personal gain is pretty much a hopeless task.

I will have a bit more to say presently on what might lie behind the sense of commitment, but I would like to emphasize at this stage that the morality or culture underlying it may well be of a limited kind—far removed from the grandeur of approaches such as utilitarianism. The 'implicit collusions' that have been observed in business behaviour in oligopolies seems to work on the basis of a system of mutual trust and sense of responsibility which has well-defined limits, and attempts at 'universalization' of the same kind of behaviour in other spheres of action may not go with it at all. There it is

32. See A. Fox, *Beyond Contract: Work, Power and Trust Relations* (London, 1974); H. G. Nutzinger, 'The Firm as a Social Institution: The Failure of a Contractarian Viewpoint', Working Paper No. 52 (Alfred Weber Institute, University of Heidelberg, 1976).

33. Cf. 'Nor ... should we forget the extent to which conventional theory ignores how and why work is organized within the firm and establishment in the way it is, what may be called the "social relations" of the production process', R. A. Gordon, 'Rigor and Relevance in a Changing Institutional Setting', Presidential Address, *American Economic Review,* 66 (1976). See also R. Dahrendorf, *Class and Class Conflict in Industrial Society* (Stanford, 1959); O. E. Williamson, 'The Evolution of Hierarchy: An Essay on the Organization of Work', Fels Discussion Paper No. 91 (University of Pennsylvania, 1976); and S. A. Marglin, 'What Do Bosses Do? The Origins and Functions of Hierarchy in Capitalist Production', *Review of Radical Political Economics,* 6 (1974).

34. 'The Decision of the Central Committee of the Chinese Communist Party Concerning the Great Proletarian Cultural Revolution', adopted on 8 August 1966, reproduced in Joan Robinson, *The Cultural Revolution in China* (Harmondsworth, 1969). See also A. K. Sen, *On Economic Inequality* (Oxford, 1973); and C. Riskin, 'Maoism and Motivation: A Discussion of Work Motivation in China', *Bulletin of Concerned Asian Scholars,* 1973.

35. See Williamson, 'The Evolution of Hierarchy', for a critical analysis of the recent literature in this area.

strictly a question of business ethics which is taken to apply within a fairly limited domain.

Similarly, in wage negotiations and in collective bargaining the sense of solidarity on either side may have well-defined limits, and may not fit in at all with an approach such as that of general utilitarianism. Edgeworth's implicit assumption, on which I commented earlier, that egoism and utilitarianism exhaust the possible alternative motivations, will be especially unhelpful in this context. While the field of commitment may be large, that of commitment based on utilitarianism and other universalized moral systems may well form a relatively small part of it.


7


The economic theory of utility, which relates to the theory of rational behaviour, is sometimes criticized for having too much structure; human beings are alleged to be 'simpler' in reality. If our argument so far has been correct, precisely the opposite seems to be the case: traditional theory has *too little* structure. A person is given *one* preference ordering, and as and when the need arises this is supposed to reflect his interests, represent his welfare, summarize his idea of what should be done, and describe his actual choices and behaviour. Can one preference ordering do all these things? A person thus described may be 'rational' in the limited sense of revealing no inconsistencies in his choice behaviour, but if he has no use for these distinctions between quite different concepts, he must be a bit of a fool. The *purely* economic man is indeed close to being a social moron. Economic theory has been much preoccupied with this rational fool decked in the glory of his *one* all-purpose preference ordering. To make room for the different concepts related to his behaviour we need a more elaborate structure.

What kind of a structure do we need? A bit more room up top is provided by John Harsanyi's important distinction between a person's 'ethical' preferences and his 'subjective' preferences: 'the former must express what this individual prefers (or, rather would prefer), on the basis of impersonal social considerations alone, and the latter must express what he actually prefers, whether on the basis of his personal interests or on any other basis'.[36] This dual structure permits us to distinguish between what a person thinks is good from the social point of view and what he regards as good from his own personal point of view. Presumably sympathy enters directly into the so-called subjective preference, but the role of commitment is left somewhat unclear. In so far as a person's 'subjective' preferences are taken to 'define his utility function', the intention seems to be to exclude commitment from

36. J. Harsanyi, 'Cardinal Welfare, Individualistic Ethics, and Interpersonal Comparisons of Utility', *Journal of Political Economy*, **63** (1955), p. 315.

it, but an ambiguity arises from the fact that these are defined to 'express his preferences in the full sense of the word as they actually are'. Is this in the sense of choice, or in the sense of his conception of his own welfare? Perhaps Harsanyi intended the latter, since 'ethical' preferences are by contrast given the role of expressing 'what he prefers only in those possibly rare moments when he forces a special impartial and impersonal attitude on himself'.[37] But what if he departs from his personal welfare maximization (including any sympathy), not through an impartial concern for all,[38] but through a sense of commitment to some particular group, say to the neighbourhood or to the social class to which he belongs? The fact is we are still short of structure.

Even in expressing moral judgements from an impersonal point of view, a *dual* structure is deficient. Surely a preference ordering can be *more* ethical than another but *less* so than a third. We need more structure in this respect also. I have proposed elsewhere—at the 1972 Bristol conference on 'practical reason'—that we need to consider *rankings of preference rankings* to express our moral judgements.[39] I would like to discuss this structure a bit more. A particular morality can be viewed, not just in terms of the 'most moral' ranking of the set of alternative actions, but as a moral ranking of the rankings of actions (going well beyond the identification merely of the 'most moral' ranking of actions). Let $X$ be the set of alternative and mutually exclusive combinations of actions under consideration, and let $Y$ be the set of rankings of the elements of $X$. A ranking of the set $Y$ (consisting of action-rankings) will be called a meta-ranking of action-set $X$. It is my claim that a particular ranking of the action-set $X$ is not articulate enough to express much about a given morality, and a more robust format is provided by choosing a meta-ranking of actions (that is, a ranking of $Y$ rather than $X$). Of course, such a meta-ranking may include *inter alia* the specification of a particular action-ranking as the 'most moral', but in so far as actual behaviour may be based on a compromise between claims of morality and the pursuit of various other objectives (including self-interest), one has to look also at the relative moral standings of those action-rankings that are *not* 'most moral'.

To illustrate, consider a set $X$ of alternative action combinations and the following three rankings of this action-set $X$: ranking $A$ representing my

37. *Ibid.*, pp. 315–16.

38. Note that for Harsanyi 'an individual's preferences satisfy this requirement of impersonality if they indicate what social situation he would choose if he did not know what his general position would be in the new situation chosen (and in any of its alternatives) but rather had an equal chance of obtaining any of the social positions existing in this situation, from the highest down to the lowest' (p. 316).

39. A. K. Sen, 'Choice, Orderings and Morality', in S. Körner (ed.), *Practical Reason* (Oxford, 1974) [Essay 3 in this volume]. See also J. Watkins' rejoinder and my reply in the same volume, and R. C. Jeffrey, 'Preferences among Preferences', *Journal of Philosophy*, 71 (1974); K. Binmore, 'An Example in Group Preference', *Journal of Economic Theory*, 10 (1975); and B. A. Weisbrod, 'Toward a State-Preference Model of Utility Function Preferences: A Conceptual Note', mimeographed (University of Wisconsin, 1976).

personal welfare ordering (thus, in some sense, representing my personal interests), ranking $B$ reflecting my 'isolated' personal interests ignoring sympathy (when such a separation is possible, which is not always so),[40] and ranking $C$ in terms of which actual choices are made by me (when such choices are representable by a ranking, which again is not always so).[41] The 'most moral' ranking $M$ can, conceivably, be any of these rankings $A$, $B$, or $C$. Or else it can be some other ranking quite distinct from all three. (This will be the case if the actual choices of actions are not the 'most moral' in terms of the moral system in question, and if, furthermore, the moral system requires sacrifice of some self-interest and also of 'isolated' self-interest.) But even when some ranking $M$ distinct from $A$, $B$, and $C$ is identified as being at the top of the moral table, that still leaves open the question as to how $A$, $B$, and $C$ may be ordered vis-à-vis each other. If, to take a particular example, it so happens that the pursuit of self-interest, including pleasure and pain from sympathy, is put morally above the pursuit of 'isolated' self-interest (thereby leading to a partial coincidence of self-interest with morality), and the actual choices reflect a morally superior position to the pursuit of self-interest (perhaps due to a compromise in the moral direction), then the morality in question precipitates the meta-ranking $M$, $C$, $A$, $B$, in descending order. This, of course, goes well beyond specifying that $M$ is 'morally best'.

The technique of meta-ranking permits a varying extent of moral articulation. It is not being claimed that a moral meta-ranking must be a *complete* ordering of the set $Y$, that is, must completely order all rankings of $X$. It can be a *partial* ordering, and I expect it often will be incomplete, but I should think that in most cases there will be no problem in going well beyond the limited expression permitted by the twofold specification of 'ethical' and 'subjective' preferences.

The rankings of action can, of course, be ordered also on grounds other than a particular system of morality: meta-ranking is a general technique usable under alternative interpretations of the meta-ranking relation. It can be used to describe a particular ideology or a set of political priorities or a system of class interests. In quite a different context, it can provide the format for expressing what preferences one would have preferred to have ('I wish I liked vegetarian foods more', or 'I wish I didn't enjoy smoking so much'). Or it can be used to analyse the conflicts involved in addiction ('Given my current tastes, I am better off with heroin, but having heroin leads me to addiction, and I would have preferred not to have these tastes'). The tool of meta-rankings can be used in many different ways in distinct contexts.

This is clearly not the occasion to go into a detailed analysis of how this

40. This presupposes some 'independence' among the different elements influencing the level of overall welfare, implying some 'separability'. See W. M. Gorman, 'Tricks with Utility Functions', in M. Artis and A. R. Nobay (eds), *Essays in Economic Analysis* (Cambridge, 1975).
41. See fn. 16 above.

broader structure permits a better understanding of preference and behaviour. A structure is not, of course, a theory, and alternative theories can be formulated using this structure. I should mention, however, that the structure demands much more information than is yielded by the observation of people's actual choices, which would at most reveal only the ranking C. It gives a role to introspection and to communication. To illustrate one use of the apparatus, I may refer to some technical results. Suppose I am trying to investigate your conception of your own welfare. You first specify the ranking A which represents your welfare ordering. But I want to go further and get an idea of your *cardinal* utility function, that is, roughly speaking, not only which ranking gives you more welfare but also by how much. I now ask you to order the different rankings in terms of their 'closeness' to your actual welfare ranking A, much as a policeman uses the technique of photofit: is this more like him, or is that? If your answers reflect the fact that reversing a stronger preference makes the result more distant than reversing a weaker intensity of preference, your replies will satisfy certain consistency properties, and the order of rankings will permit us to compare your welfare *differences* between pairs. In fact, by considering higher and higher order rankings, we can determine your cardinal welfare function as closely as you care to specify.[42] I am not saying that this type of dialogue is the best way of discovering your welfare function, but it does illustrate that once we give up the assumption that observing choices is the only source of data on welfare, a whole new world opens up, liberating us from the informational shackles of the traditional approach.

This broader structure has many other uses, for example, permitting a clearer analysis of *akrasia*—the weakness of will—and clarifying some conflicting considerations in the theory of liberty, which I have tried to discuss elsewhere.[43] It also helps in analysing the development of behaviour involving commitment in situations characterized by games such as the Prisoners' Dilemma.[44] This game is often treated, with some justice, as the classic case

42. This result and some related ones emerged in discussions with Ken Binmore in 1975, but a projected joint paper reporting them is still, alas, unwritten. More work on this is currently being done also by R. Nader-Isfahani. [Completed later his Ph.D. thesis for London School of Economics, 1978.]

43. See Sen, 'Choice, Orderings and Morality', and also Sen, 'Liberty, Unanimity and Rights', *Economica,* **43** (1976) [Essay 14 in this volume]. Note also the relevance of this structure in analysing the incompleteness of the conception of liberty in terms of the ability to do what one *actually wishes.* Cf. 'If I find that I am able to do little or nothing of what I wish, I need only contract or extinguish my wishes, and I am made free. If the tyrant (or "hidden persuader") manages to condition his subjects (or customers) into losing their original wishes and embrace ("internalize") the form of life he has invented for them, he will, on this definition, have succeeded in liberating them' (I. Berlin, 'Two Concepts of Liberty', in *Four Essays on Liberty* (Oxford, 1969), pp. 139–40).

44. See R. D. Luce and H. Raiffa, *Games and Decisions* (New York, 1958); A. Rapoport and A. M. Chammah, *Prisoner's Dilemma: A Study in Conflict and Cooperation* (Ann Arbor, 1965); W. G. Runciman and A. K. Sen, 'Games, Justice and the General Will', *Mind,* **74** (1965); N. Howard, *Paradoxes of Rationality* (Cambridge, Mass., 1971).

of failure of individualistic rationality. There are two players and each has two strategies, which we may call selfish and unselfish to make it easy to remember without my having to go into too much detail. Each player is better off personally by playing the selfish strategy *no* matter what the other does, but both are better off if both choose the unselfish rather than the selfish strategy. It is individually optimal to do the selfish thing: one can only affect one's own action and not that of the other, and given the other's strategy—no matter what—each player is better off being selfish. But this combination of selfish strategies, which results from self-seeking by both, produces an outcome that is worse for both than the result of both choosing the unselfish strategy. It can be shown that this conflict can exist even if the game is repeated many times.

Some people find it puzzling that individual self-seeking by each should produce an inferior outcome for all, but this, of course, is a well-known conflict, and has been discussed in general terms for a very long time. Indeed, it was the basis of Rousseau's famous distinction between the 'general will' and the 'will of all'.[45] But the puzzle from the point of view of rational behaviour lies in the fact that in actual situations people often do not follow the selfish strategy. Real life examples of this type of behaviour in complex circumstances are well known, but even in controlled experiments in laboratory conditions people playing the Prisoners' Dilemma frequently do the unselfish thing.[46]

In interpreting these experimental results, the game theorist is tempted to put it down to the lack of intelligence of the players: 'Evidently the run-of-the-mill players are not strategically sophisticated enough to have figured out that strategy DD [the selfish strategy] is the only rationally defensible strategy, and this intellectual short-coming saves them from losing'.[47] A more fruitful approach may lie in permitting the possibility that the person is *more* sophisticated than the theory allows and that he has asked himself what type of preference he would like the other player to have, and on somewhat Kantian grounds has considered the case for himself having those preferences, or behaving *as if* he had them. This line of reasoning requires him to consider the modifications of the game that would be brought about by acting through commitment (in terms of 'revealed preferences', this would look *as if* he had different preferences from the ones he actually had), and he has to assess alternative behaviour norms in that light. I have discussed these issues elsewhere;[48] thus I shall simply note here that the apparatus of *ranking of*

45. See Runciman and Sen.

46. See, for example, L. B. Lave, 'An Empirical Approach to the Prisoner's Dilemma Game', *Quarterly Journal of Economics,* 76 (1962), and Rapoport and Chammah, *Prisoner's Dilemma.*

47. Rapoport and Chammah, p. 29.

48. Sen, 'Choice, Orderings and Morality'. See also K. Baier, 'Rationality and Morality', *Erkenntnis,* 11 (1977) and A. K. Sen, 'Rationality and Morality: A Reply', *Erkenntnis,* 11 (1977); K. Baier, *The Moral Point of View* (Ithaca, 1958); and Fred Schick's analysis, 'Rationality and Sociality'.

*rankings* assists the reasoning which involves considering the merits of having different types of preferences (or of acting as if one had them).

8

Admitting behaviour based on commitment would, of course have far-reaching consequences on the nature of many economic models. I have tried to show why this change is necessary and why the consequences may well be serious. Many issues remain unresolved, including the empirical importance of commitment as a part of behaviour, which would vary, as I have argued, from field to field. I have also indicated why the empirical evidence for this cannot be sought in the mere observation of actual choices, and must involve other sources of information, including introspection and discussion.

There remains, however, the issue as to whether this view of man amounts to seeing him as an irrational creature. Much depends on the concept of rationality used, and many alternative characterizations exist. In the sense of *consistency* of choice, there is no reason to think that admitting commitment must imply any departure from rationality. This is, however, a weak sense of rationality.

The other concept of rationality prevalent in economics identifies it with the possibility of justifying each act in terms of self-interest: when act $x$ is chosen by person $i$ and act $y$ rejected, this implies that $i$'s personal interests are expected by $i$ to be better served by $x$ than by $y$. There are, it seems to me, three distinct elements in this approach. First, it is a consequentialist view: judging acts by consequences only.[49] Second, it is an approach of *act* evaluation rather than *rule* evaluation. And third, the only consequences considered in evaluating acts are those on one's own interests, everything else being at best an intermediate product. It is clearly possible to dispute the claims of each of these elements to being a necessary part of the conception of rationality in the dictionary sense of 'the power of being able to exercise one's reason'. Moreover, arguments for rejecting the straitjacket of each of these three principles are not hard to find. The case for actions based on commitment can arise from the violation of any of these three principles. Commitment sometimes relates to a sense of obligation going beyond the consequences. Sometimes the lack of personal gain in particular *acts* is accepted by considering the value of *rules* of behaviour. But even within a consequentialist act-evaluation framework, the exclusion of any consideration other than self-interest seems to impose a wholly arbitrary limitation on the notion of rationality.

49. On the nature of 'consequentialism' and problems engendered by it, see B. Williams, 'A Critique of Utilitarianism', in J. J. C. Smart and B. Williams, *Utilitarianism: For and Against* (Cambridge, 1973).

Henry Sidgwick noted the arbitrary nature of the assumption of egoism:

If the Utilitarian has to answer the question, 'Why should I sacrifice my own happiness for the greater happiness of another?' it must surely be admissible to ask the Egoist, 'Why should I sacrifice a present pleasure for one in the future? Why should I concern myself about my own future feelings any more than about the feelings of other persons?' It undoubtedly seems to Common Sense paradoxical to ask for a reason why one should seek one's own happiness on the whole; but I do not see how the demand can be repudiated as absurd by those who adopt views of the extreme empirical school of psychologists, although those views are commonly supposed to have a close affinity with Egoistic Hedonism. Grant that the Ego is merely a system of coherent phenomena, that the permanent identical 'I' is not a fact but a fiction, as Hume and his followers maintain; why, then, should one part of the series of feelings into which the Ego is resolved be concerned with another part of the same series, any more than with any other series?[50]

The view of rationality that identifies it with consequentialist act-evaluation using self-interest can be questioned from any of these three angles. Admitting commitment as a part of behaviour implies no denial of reasoned assessment as a basis for action.

There is not much merit in spending a lot of effort in debating the 'proper' definition of rationality. The term is used in many different senses, and none of the criticisms of the behavioural foundations of economic theory presented here stands or falls on the definition chosen. The main issue is the acceptability of the assumption of the invariable pursuit of self-interest in each act. Calling that type of behaviour rational, or departures from it irrational, does not change the relevance of these criticisms, though it does produce an arbitrarily narrow definition of rationality. This paper has not been concerned with the question as to whether human behaviour is better described as rational or irrational. The main thesis has been the need to accommodate commitment as a part of behaviour. Commitment does not presuppose reasoning, but it does not exclude it; in fact, in so far as consequences on others have to be more clearly understood and assessed in terms of one's values and instincts, the scope for reasoning may well expand. I have tried to analyse the structural extensions in the conception of preference made necessary by behaviour based on reasoned assessment of commitment. Preferences as rankings have to be replaced by a richer structure involving meta-rankings and related concepts.

50. H. Sidgwick, *The Method of Ethics* (London, 1874; 7th ed., 1907), pp. 418–19. See also Nagel's forceful exposition of the thesis that 'altruism itself depends on a recognition of the reality of other persons, and on the equivalent capacity to regard oneself as merely one individual among many'. *The Possibility of Altruism*, p. 1.

I have also argued against viewing behaviour in terms of the traditional dichotomy between egoism and universalized moral systems (such as utilitarianism). Groups intermediate between oneself and all, such as class and community, provide the focus of many actions involving commitment. The rejection of egoism as description of motivation does not, therefore, imply the acceptance of some universalized morality as the basis of actual behaviour. Nor does it make human beings excessively noble.

Nor, of course, does the use of reasoning imply remarkable wisdom.

> It is as true as Caesar's name was Kaiser,
> That no economist was ever wiser,

said Robert Frost in playful praise of the contemporary economist. Perhaps a similarly dubious tribute can be paid to the economic man in our modified conception. If he shines at all, he shines in comparison—in contrast—with the dominant image of the rational fool.

# PART II

## Preference Aggregation

# 5

# A Possibility Theorem on Majority Decisions

In this note we show the consistency of majority decisions under preference conditions that are more general than Single-Peaked Preferences (Arrow [1], Black [2]), Single-Caved Preferences (Inada [5]), Preferences Separable into Two Groups (Inada [5]), and Latin-Square-less Preferences (Ward [12]). In the first part of the note, the underlying concepts and approach are introduced; in the second part the theorem is stated and proved; and in the third part its relationship with other sufficiency conditions is discussed.

## 1

For any set of alternatives, the voters who are indifferent between all of them raise some peculiar problems for the consistency of majority decisions. So we first separate them out.

*Definition:* A *Concerned Individual* with respect to a set of alternatives is one who is not indifferent between all the alternatives. An individual who is indifferent between all alternatives is *Unconcerned*.

Each individual is assumed to have a weak ordering ranging over all alternatives. Notationally, $x R_i y$ stands for the $i$th individual regarding alternative $x$ to be at least as good as alternative $y$, and $x P_i y$ stands for the $i$th individual preferring $x$ to $y$, which is equivalent to $x R_i y$, and *not* $y R_i x$. We follow Arrow (rather than Black) in defining the method of majority decisions. Let $x R y$ stand for $x$ being socially regarded at least as good as $y$, and

From *Econometrica*, **34** (April 1966), 491–9.

$x P y$ stands for the corresponding social preference, i.e., for $x R y$, and *not* $y R x$.[1]

*Definitions:   The method of majority decisions means that $x R y$ if and only if the number of individuals such that $x R_i y$ is at least as great as the number of individuals such that $y R_i x$.*[2]

The consistency of the majority decisions for a set of two alternatives has been shown by Arrow, but inconsistency can arise when there are three or more alternatives. We shall find the following lemma useful.[3]

LEMMA 1:   *If among a set of alternatives there is no triple such that, given the set of individual preferences, the method of majority decision gives intransitive results between them, then the method will give consistent results for the entire set of alternatives.*

*Proof.*   Suppose, to the contrary, there is no such triple, but there is nevertheless an inconsistency involving more than three (say, $n$) alternatives. We have, let us say, the following inconsistent result:

$$A_1 RA_2, A_2 RA_3, \ldots, A_{m-1} RA_m, A_m PA_{m+1},$$
$$A_{m+1} RA_{m+2}, \ldots, A_{n-1} RA_n, A_n RA_1.$$

Take the triple $(A_m, A_{m+1}, A_{m+2})$, which like all other triples must yield consistent results. Hence, $A_m PA_{m+2}$. Proceeding this way, we get $A_m PA_1$. Now, take the triple $(A_{m-1}, A_m, A_1)$, which, giving consistent results, yields $A_{m-1} PA_1$. Proceeding this way, we have $A_3 PA_1$. But since we have $A_1 RA_2$ *and* $A_2 RA_3$, we also have $A_1 RA_3$. This is a contradiction.

Similar contradictions occur, *a fortiori,* when there is more than one $P$ (preference) relation in the series. This proves that if in a set of alternatives there is no triple with intransitivity, majority decisions for the whole set must be consistent.

An alternative, $x$, can be called 'best' (strictly, 'among the best') of three alternatives ($x, y,$ and $z$), for a given individual $i$, if and only if, $x R_i y$, and $x R_i z$. Similarly, $x$ is a 'worst' alternative for him, if and only if $y R_i x$, and

1. We shall be avoiding discussion of the important problems arising from 'strategic masking or distorting of preferences' (see Rothenberg [9]; see also Majumdar [7] and Luce and Raiffa [6]). Also the lack of a one-to-one correspondence between preferences and voting in a model of continuous utility maximization, no matter whether the utility from voting is taken to be zero, positive, or negative (see Sen [10]).

2. It is easy to check that the method of majority decisions satisfies the conditions of *reflexivity* ($x R x$), and *connectedness* (either $x R y$ or $y R x$). The only property of a weak social ordering that is in doubt is *transitivity.*

3. Ward [12] discusses this, and though he confines his attention to a strict social ordering corresponding to the $P$-relation, which does not have the property of reflexivity and connectedness, our proof is nevertheless very similar to his. [The result is, of course, true for any binary relation, and not just for the majority relation.]

$z\,R_i\,x$. A 'medium' alternative for him is defined by $x$ satisfying either the conditions that $z\,R_i\,x$ and $x\,R_i\,y$, or the conditions that $y\,R_i\,x$ and $x\,R_i\,z$.

*Definition:*   The *value* of an alternative in a triple for an individual preference ordering is its characteristic of being '*best*', '*worst*', or '*medium*'.

Of course, in orderings involving indifference, an alternative can have more than one value; in fact, if individuals are not 'concerned', then each alternative has each value.

We now introduce the crucial definition of a Value-Restricted preference pattern. One alternative in a triple is excluded from having any one of the three values.

*Assumption of Value-Restricted Preferences*:   A set of individual preferences over a triple of alternatives such that there exist one alternative and one value with the characteristic that the alternative never has that value in any individual's preference ordering, is called a Value-Restricted Preference pattern over that triple for those individuals.

Finally, we introduce some notation. The number of individuals for whom $x\,R_i\,y$ is referred to by $N(x \geqslant y)$; the number for whom $x\,P_i\,y$ is called $N(x > y)$. The number for whom $x\,P_i\,y$ and $z\,P_i\,y$ is referred to as $N(x > y, y < z)$. The number who hold $x\,R_i\,y$ and $y\,R_i\,z$ is referred to as $N(x \geqslant y \geqslant z)$. These examples illustrate the principles of the notation, and the same system is employed for corresponding concepts.

2

The theorem to be proved is stated in terms of Arrow's Social Welfare Function, which clarifies the relevance of our result.

THEOREM 1 (POSSIBILITY THEOREM FOR VALUE-RESTRICTED PREFERENCES).   *The method of majority decision is a social welfare function satisfying Arrow's Conditions 2–5 and the consistency condition for any number of alternatives, provided the preferences of concerned individuals over every triple of alternatives is Value-Restricted, and the number of concerned individuals for every triple is odd.*

All the stated conditions, except the requirement of transitivity, have been shown by Arrow [1] to hold for the method of majority decision.[4] So we need be concerned only with transitivity. Thanks to Lemma 1, we only have to make sure that transitivity holds for all triples of alternatives.

---

4. See also May [8] showing that for pair-wise choice, the simple majority rule is the only rule satisfying the properties of 'decisiveness', 'anonymity', 'neutrality', and 'positive responsiveness'.

It is easy to check that with three alternatives, $x$, $y$, and $z$, all intransitivities must imply one and exactly one of the following, which for convenience we give two (rather arbitrary) names:

> *Forward Circle:* $x\,R\,y$, $y\,R\,z$, and $z\,R\,x$.
> *Backward Circle:* $y\,R\,x$, $x\,R\,z$, and $z\,R\,y$.

The existence of one of these circles is *necessary* for intransitivity, but it is not sufficient, for which we need, in addition, the absence of the other.

First take the forward circle. Since $x\,R\,y$ and $y\,R\,z$,

$$N(x\geqslant y)\geqslant N(y\geqslant x),\text{ and }N(y\geqslant z)\geqslant N(z\geqslant y).$$

By adding the two inequalities, we have

$$N(x\geqslant y)+N(y\geqslant z)\geqslant N(z\geqslant y)+N(y\geqslant x). \tag{1}$$

Now the left-hand side equals

$$\begin{aligned}\text{LHS} &= N(x\geqslant y\geqslant z)+N(x\geqslant y<z)+N(y\geqslant z)\\ &= N(x\geqslant y\geqslant z)+[N-N(x<y<z)],\end{aligned}$$

where $N$ is the total number of individuals. Similarly, the right-hand side equals

$$\text{RHS} = N(z\geqslant y\geqslant x)+[N-N(z<y<x)].$$

After simplifying, the inequality (1) becomes:

$$N(x\geqslant y\geqslant z)+N(x>y>z)\geqslant N(z\geqslant y\geqslant x)+N(z>y>x). \tag{1.1}$$

Similarly, taking respectively the combination $y\,R\,z$ and $z\,R\,x$, and the combination $z\,R\,x$ and $x\,R\,y$, we obtain:

$$N(y\geqslant z\geqslant x)+N(y>z>x)\geqslant N(x\geqslant z\geqslant y)+N(x>z>y), \tag{1.2}$$
$$N(z\geqslant x\geqslant y)+N(z>x>y)\geqslant N(y\geqslant x\geqslant z)+N(y>x>z). \tag{1.3}$$

The fulfilment of (1.1), (1.2), and (1.3) simultaneously is a necessary condition for the forward circle (though not a sufficient condition).

Consider now the special case when the only people who hold both $x\,R_i\,y$ and $y\,R_i\,z$ are the ones who are indifferent between all three (i.e., are not 'concerned' about these three). We then have:

> $N(x\geqslant y\geqslant z)=N(x=y=z)$ and $N(x>y>z) = 0$, so that the left-hand side of (1.1) becomes
> $\text{LHS} = N(x\geqslant y\geqslant z)+N(x>y>z)=N(x=y=z).$

Since $N(z\geqslant y\geqslant x)$ must be at least as great as $N(x=y=z)$, the RHS too must equal the latter so that (if intransitivity is to take place), no 'concerned individual' should hold $z\,R_i\,y$ and $y\,R_i\,x$ together.

Under these conditions, all 'concerned individuals' can only have strict preference between $x$ and $y$, and $y$ and $z$, and these two preferences must run in opposite directions. So the total number of individuals, $N$, can be strictly partitioned into three groups:

$$N = N(x = y = z) + N(x > y, y < z) + N(x < y, y > z).$$

Now since we have $x \, R \, y$ and $y \, R \, z$, we require, respectively, the following two conditions:

$$N(x > y, y < z) \geqslant N(x < y, y > z),$$
$$N(x < y, y > z) \geqslant N(x > y, y < z),$$

This means that the two sides are exactly equal. But since the two sides add up to the total number of concerned individuals, this can happen only if the number of such individuals is even. But by assumption of the theorem, this number is odd. Thus, there is a contradiction.

It is thus established that a forward circle is impossible if:

$$N(x \geqslant y \geqslant z) = N(x = y = z). \tag{i}$$

Identically, it can be shown that such a circle is impossible, if either of the two following conditions hold:

$$N(y \geqslant z \geqslant x) = N(x = y = z), \tag{ii}$$
$$N(z \geqslant x \geqslant y) = N(x = y = z). \tag{iii}$$

An exactly similar procedure establishes that a backward circle is impossible if any one of the following three conditions hold:

$$N(y \geqslant x \geqslant z) = N(x = y = z), \tag{iv}$$
$$N(x \geqslant z \geqslant y) = N(x = y = z), \tag{v}$$
$$N(z \geqslant y \geqslant x) = N(x = y = z). \tag{vi}$$

We can glorify this result into a lemma which we use for the proof of our theorem.

LEMMA 2.    *If for any triple of alternatives (x, y, z), at least one of the conditions* (i)–(iii) *and at least one of the conditions* (iv)–(vi) *hold and if the number of concerned individuals for the triple is odd, then the triple must yield transitive majority decisions.*

*Proof of Theorem 1:*    Since the preference ordering of every concerned individual is Value-Restricted for every triple, in each triple we can identify an alternative (say, $x$) such that it cannot have a given value (say, 'best'). If $x$ cannot be best for concerned individuals, then people satisfying respectively $(x \, R_i y, \, y \, R_i z)$ or $(x \, R_i z, \, z \, R_i y)$ must be unconcerned. Hence conditions (i) and (v) hold. Similarly if $y$ or $z$ cannot be best in any concerned individual's preferences, we have, respectively (ii) and (iv), and (iii) and (vi).

When $x$, $y$, or $z$ cannot be 'worst' for any concerned individual, we have respectively, (ii) and (vi), (iii) and (v), and (i) and (iv). When $x$, $y$, or $z$ cannot be 'medium' for any concerned individual, we have respectively, (iii) and (iv), (i) and (vi), and (ii) and (v).

Thus, in every case of Value-Restricted Preferences, at least one of the conditions (i)–(iii) and at least one of the conditions (iv)–(vi) are satisfied. Since the number of concerned individuals is odd for every triple, it follows from Lemma 2 that majority decisions are transitive for every triple.

The theorem now follows from Lemma 1.                *Q.E.D.*

### 3

We can now compare the theorem proved here with some of the ones that have preceded it. The most well-known sufficiency condition is Black's [2] and Arrow's [1] assumption of Single-Peaked Preferences.[5] Inada [5] has pointed out recently that Arrow assumes Single-Peaked Preferences for *all* alternatives, but in his proof uses that only for *all* triples, which is a weaker condition. The assumption of single-peakedness means that there is a strong ordering $S$ for arranging the alternatives such that if $y$ is 'between' $x$ and $z$, $x R_i y \to y P_i z$. This means that Single-Peaked Preferences over a triple imply: $Not(x R_i y, $ and $z R_i y)$, i.e., $y$ cannot be given the value 'worst'. The other two cases of Single-Peakedness imply that $x$ is not a 'worst' alternative, and that $z$ is not a 'worst' alternative. The theorem proved in this note covers all the cases.[6]

Inada's Possibility Theorem for Single-Caved Preferences [5] uses a concept opposite to that of Arrow's Single-Peakedness.[7] If $y$ is 'between' $x$ and $z$, then $y R_i x \to z P_i y$. This means: $Not(y R_i x, $ and $y R_i z)$. This only requires that $y$ not have the value 'best'. The other cases of Single-Caved Preferences

---

5. There are slight differences between the two versions, and indeed between Black's original presentation [2], which rules out indifference, and his later presentation [3], which even allows individuals to be indifferent between all alternatives, not allowed by Arrow. Since, however, Black assumes that the number of all individuals is odd and not (as we do) that the number of *concerned individuals* is odd, his theorem is, strictly speaking, incorrect. See the example on the top of page 39 of Dummet and Farquharson [4], which is Single-Peaked in Black's sense [3], but shows intransitivity.

6. The extension proposed by Dummet and Farquharson [4] is, however, not covered. But they solve a different problem from ours, viz., when will a set of alternatives 'have a top,' i.e., 'there should be at least one outcome $x$ such that for every other outcome $y$ some majority regards $x$ as at least as good as $y$' (p. 40). Dummet and Farquharson show that for this it is sufficient to assume that 'of every three outcomes there is one which no voter thinks *worse* than *both* the other two' (p. 40). It is easily checked, however, that this is not sufficient for the requirement of transitivity of majority decisions. Take, for example, the following three orderings: (1) $x P_1 y P_1 z;$ (2) $y P_2 x I_2 z;$ (3) $z P_3 x P_3 y$. This satisfies Dummet and Farquharson's restriction ($x$ is not strictly worse than $y$ and $z$ for any one), and the alternatives 'have a top', viz., $x$. But there is intransitivity, since $x P y, y P z$, but $z I x$.

7. Cf. Vickrey [11, pp. 514–15]. Vickrey calls it 'single-troughed preferences' and confines his attention to strong orderings only.

rule out, respectively, $x$ being 'best', and $z$ being 'best'. All these cases are, therefore, subsumed in the theorem proved in the last section.

We can now consider Inada's theorem for preferences such that the 'set of alternatives [are] *separable into two groups*' A and B, with any alternative in A being always preferred to any alternative in B, or vice versa. Such separability for *all* alternatives is equivalent to the separability for all triples.[8] Suppose A consists of $x$ and B of $(y, z)$. Now, we have: (1) $x P_i y$ if and only if $x P_i z$, (2) $y P_i x$ if and only if $z P_i x$, and (3) either $x P_i y$ or $y P_i x$. This excludes all possibilities where $x$ can be 'medium'. The other cases of separability into two groups exclude respectively $y$ and $z$ being 'medium'. All these cases are, therefore, also covered by our theorem.

Ward's [12] Latin-Square-lessness applies to cases with strong ordering, but in those cases they are exactly equivalent to Value-Restricted Preferences. Under these special conditions, Ward shows that if among the preference orderings of all individuals for any triple, there are not three that form a latin square, then majority decisions (in the sense of strict orderings, $P$-relation) will be transitive.[9] Assuming strong ordering with our Value-Restricted preferences, it is easy to check that a latin square cannot be formed of the permitted preferences of the concerned individuals.[10] Thus Ward's cases are subsumed in the cases covered here, and hold for majority decisions interpreted both as the $R$-relation and the $P$-relation.

It should be added that the theorems which are shown to be subsumed by the one developed here all assume that (a) the number of *all* individuals is odd, and (b) there are *no* individuals who are indifferent between all three alternatives in any triple. We have not assumed (b), and have assumed instead of (a) that the number of *concerned* individuals is odd. When (a) and (b) are fulfilled, our condition is also fulfilled, but there are cases when our condition is fulfilled but (a) and (b) are not. For example, when there are an even number of individuals, an odd number of whom are not concerned in any triple; this violates both (a) and (b). Thus, in this respect also, there is a slight generalization.

When this question of unconcerned individuals is ignored, however, and $N (x = y = z)$ is taken to be zero, the set of our cases partitions exactly into three proper subsets of cases: (I) When one alternative cannot be 'best', equivalent to Single-Caved Preferences; (II) When one alternative cannot be 'worst', equivalent to Single-Peaked Preferences, and (III) when one alternative cannot be 'medium', equivalent to the case of alternatives Separable into Two Groups.

---

8. See Inada [5, pp. 530–1].

9. See also Vickrey [11, pp. 513–16], who discusses cases similar to Ward's [12].

10. Value-Restricted Preferences can be viewed as a weak-ordering generalization of Latin-Squarelessness. We can define Value-Restricted Preferences as preferences such that a latin square cannot be formed out of them by *any permutation of its indifferent alternatives*.

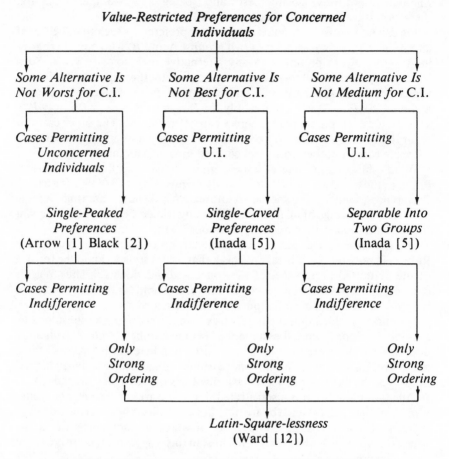

FIGURE 1   RESTRICTION ON PREFERENCES FOR EACH TRIPLE

Since mine is only an attempt to extend the pioneering work of Arrow, Black, Inada, Vickrey, and Ward, I end with a chart explaining the relationship between the assumptions made in the theorem proved here and the assumptions made in their respective theorems (see figure 1).

It is important to note, however, that we need not assume that the same 'restriction' holds for one triple that holds for another. If it is possible for one triple to have, say, Single-Peaked Preferences, and another triple to have, say, Single-Caved Preferences, and so on, the Theorem will still be valid, though such cases will not be covered by either of the three separate theorems involving Single-Peakedness, Single-Cavedness, and Separability. Consider, for example, the following set of five preference orderings over four alternatives (*w, x, y, z*):

(1) $w \, I_1 \, x \, P_1 \, y \, P_1 \, z$,
(2) $x \, I_2 \, w \, P_2 \, z \, P_2 \, y$,
(3) $z \, I_3 \, x \, P_3 \, y \, P_3 \, w$,
(4) $z \, P_4 \, y \, I_4 \, x \, P_4 \, w$,
(5) $z \, P_5 \, y \, P_5 \, x \, P_5 \, w$.

All the four possible triples are Value-Restricted: $(w, x, y)$ is Single-Peaked ($x$ is not worst); $(x, y, z)$ is Single-Caved ($y$ is not best); $(w, x, z)$ is Single-Peaked ($x$ is not worst); $(w, y, z)$ is both Separable into Two Groups ($w$ is not medium) and Single-Caved ($y$ is not best). The majority decisions are all transitive, yielding the social ordering: $x \, I \, z \, P \, y \, P \, w$. This consistency is covered by Theorem 1, though it is not covered by any of the individual theorems of Single-Peakedness (Arrow [1]), Single-Cavedness (Inada [5]), Separation into Two Groups (Inada [5]), and Latin-Square-lessness (Ward [12]).

It would seem that Value-Restricted Preferences will cover a variety of practical cases. A comparatively limited measure of agreement seems to be sufficient to guarantee consistent majority decisions, and to get from it a Social Welfare Function with the other properties specified by Arrow.

## References

[1]   Arrow, K. J.: *Social Choice and Individual Values* (New York: Wiley, 1951), chapter VII.

[2]   Black, D.: 'On the Rationale of Group Decision-Making', *Journal of Political Economy,* **56** (February 1948).

[3]   ____ *The Theory of Committees and Elections* (Cambridge: Cambridge University Press, 1958).

[4]   Dummet, M. and R. Farquharson: 'Stability in Voting', *Econometrica,* **29** (January 1961).

[5]   Inada, K.: 'A Note on the Simple Majority Decision Rule', *Econometrica,* **32** (October 1964).

[6]   Luce, R. D. and H. Raiffa: *Games and Decisions* (New York: Wiley, 1958), chapter 14.

[7]   Majumdar, T.: 'Choice and Revealed Preference', *Econometrica,* **26** (1956).

[8]   May, K. O.: 'A Set of Independent, Necessary and Sufficient Conditions for Simple Majority Decision', *Econometrica,* **20** (1952).

[9]   Rothenberg, J.: *The Measurement of Social Welfare* (Englewood Cliffs, NJ : Prentice-Hall, 1961), chapter 11.

[10]  Sen, A. K.: 'Preferences, Votes and the Transitivity of Majority Decisions', *Review of Economic Studies,* **31** (April 1964).

[11]  Vickrey, W.: 'Utility, Strategy, and Social Decision Rules', *Quarterly Journal of Economics,* **74** (November 1960).

[12]  Ward, B.: 'Majority Voting and Alternative Forms of Public Enterprises', in J. Margolis (ed.), *The Public Economy of Urban Communities* (Baltimore: Johns Hopkins Press, 1965).

# 6

# Quasi-transitivity, Rational Choice and Collective Decisions

This paper has three objectives. First, we investigate certain logical properties of the binary relations of preference and of choice functions generated by them. While these properties are elementary, they do not seem to have been systematically investigated in the literature perhaps because of an overwhelming concern with transitivity and continuity, neither of which will be necessarily assumed in what follows. Second, we apply some of these results to the general possibility theorem of Arrow [1], and show that the Arrow theorem does not hold when reformulated in the context of social preference relations that yield a choice function as opposed to an ordering with transitivity. We also indicate the rationality requirements that may be imposed on social choice as additional conditions to revive the impossibility result of Arrow. Third, our results on preference relations without transitivity also permit an extension of an earlier theorem of Sen [17] on majority decisions, which was itself an extension of earlier results of Black [3], Arrow [1], Vickrey [22], Inada [7], and Ward [23]. This extension is closely related to a theorem of Pattanaik [12], and one of the by-products of this section of the paper is a considerable shortening of the proof of Pattanaik's theorem. Sections 1, 2 and 3 are devoted respectively to the three sets of exercises, while Section 4 contains some concluding remarks.

## 1  Preference and Choice

Consider the binary relation of weak preference $R$, where $xRy$ stands for $x$ being regarded as at least as good as $y$. We shall define $xPy$ as $xRy$ and *not*

My greatest debt is to Prasanta Pattanaik for numerous helpful suggestions. I have also benefited greatly from the comments of Hans Herzberger, Tjalling Koopmans, and Tapas Majumdar.

From *Review of Economic Studies*, **36** (July 1969), 381–93.

$yRx$, and $xIy$ as $xRy$ and $yRx$; they stand respectively for 'strict preference' and 'indifference'.

We now define a choice set $C(S, R)$ of a set of alternatives $S$ with respect to the preference relation $R$, the choice set being the set of 'best' alternatives.[1]

*Definition* 1.          $C(S, R) = [x \mid (x \in S) \, \& \, \forall y \in S{:}xRy]$.

Next a choice function. We define it such that a best set of alternatives exists for every subset $S$ of alternatives in $X$, when $X$ is the set of all alternatives.

*Definition* 2.    A *choice function* $C(S, R)$ defined over $X$ is a functional relationship such that the choice set $C(S, R)$ is non-empty for every non-empty subset $S$ of $X$.

We shall now investigate the existence and nature of choice functions generated by preference relations that are not necessarily transitive. We assume throughout that $R$ is reflexive and complete, i.e., $xRy \lor yRx$ for all $x$, $y$ in $X$. It is elementary that in the absence of reflexivity and completeness a choice function will not exist.

As a preliminary we may note the following well-known result. If $R$ is transitive, i.e., if for all $x, y, z$ in $X$ we have $xRy \, \& \, yRz \rightarrow xRz$, then for all $x$, $y, z$ in $X$:

(i)    $xPy \, \& \, yPz \rightarrow xPz$,
(ii)   $xPy \, \& \, yIz \rightarrow xPz$,
(iii)  $xIy \, \& \, yPz \rightarrow xPz$,
(iv)   $xIy \, \& \, yIz \rightarrow xIz$.

We shall refer to these properties as *PP*, *PI*, *IP* and *II* respectively. The interdependence between these various conditions is an important aspect of the theory of rational choice. Denoting transitivity by $T$, the following seems to be a complete picture of the interdependence between $T$, *PP*, *PI*, *IP* and *II*.[2]

THEOREM I.    $T \rightarrow PP, PI, IP, II.$                                                        (I.1)

                *PP is independent of PI, IP, II, severally and collectively.* (I.2)

                $PI \leftrightarrow IP.$                                                        (I.3)

                $PI \rightarrow II.$                                                        (I.4)

                $PP \, \& \, II \rightarrow PI.$                                                        (I.5)

                $PP \, \& \, PI \rightarrow T.$                                                        (I.6)

*Proof.*    (I.1) is well-known; see Arrow [1], Chapter 2.

(I.2) is proved by considering two examples. Consider $xPy$, $yPz$ and $zPx$.

---

1. We use the following notation of mathematical logic: $\forall$ the universal quantifier, $\exists$ the existential quantifier, $\sim$ negation, & conjunction, $\rightarrow$ conditional 'if-then', $\leftrightarrow$ conditional 'if-and-only-if', $\lor$ logical 'or', $\in$ element of, $\subset$ subset of, and $\cap$ intersection of the two sets.

2. When we say that this is a 'complete' statement we include the simple implications of the relations stated. For example, since we state $PI \leftrightarrow IP$, and also $PI \rightarrow II$, clearly $IP \rightarrow II$. Similarly, $PP \, \& \, II \rightarrow T$, since $PP \, \& \, II \rightarrow PI$ and $PI \, \& \, PP \rightarrow T$. See figure 1.

This violates *PP*, but not *PI, IP, II*. Next consider *xPy, yIz* and *xIz*. This violates *PI, IP, II*, but not *PP*.

(I.3) has been noted and proved by Sonnenschein [19]; see his Theorem 3, and also Lorimer [8], Theorem 1.

(I.4) can be proved thus. Suppose, to the contrary, *PI* but not *II*. Then there is a triple *x, y, z* such that *xIy, yIz*, and [*xPz* v *zPx*], in view of reflexivity and completeness. By *PI, xPz* & *yIz*→*xPy*; but *xPy* is false. Further, by *PI*, *zPx* & *xIy*→*zPy*; but *zPy* is also false. Hence *PI* cannot hold, which contradiction proves the result.[3]

(I.5) is established by assuming, on the contrary, *PP* and *II* but not *PI*. Obviously, then, for some triple *x, y, z*, we have *xPy, yIz*, and [*zPx* v *zIx*]. Now *zPx* & *xPy*→*zPy* by *PP*; but this is false. Similarly by *II, zIx* & *yIz*→*yIx*; this is also false. Hence the contrary supposition leads to contradiction.

(I.6) is proved by making the contrary supposition that *PI* and *PP* but not *T*. For some triple *x, y, z*, we must then have *xRy, yRz*, and *zPx*. Now, *xRy* implies *xPy* v *xIy*. Suppose *xPy*. Then from *zPx* and by virtue of *PP* we must have *zPy*. But this is false. Therefore *xIy*. Then from *zPx* and by virtue of *PI* we must have *zPy*, which is the same false statement. This contradiction establishes the result, and this completes the proof of the theorem.

The content of Theorem I is represented below in terms of a diagram where the direction of the arrow indicates the direction of implication. If we cannot move from some property to another through a series of directional arrows, then the latter does not follow from the former, and if this does not work either way then the two properties are independent of each other, e.g., *PP* and *PI*.

From Theorem I it is clear that we can think of transitivity *T* consisting of two independent parts, viz., *PP* and *PI*. In the later sections of this paper we shall be much concerned with *PP*, and it will be convenient to give it a more usable name.

*Definition* 3.    A binary relation *R* is defined as *quasi-transitive* if and only if it satisfies condition *PP*.

It is obvious from Theorem I that if *R* is quasi-transitive then any one of the remaining three conditions *PI, IP*, and *II*, will imply full transitivity, and in this sense there cannot be any intermediate position between quasi-transitivity and full transitivity.

It is obvious that a binary relation even if complete and reflexive might not generate a choice function. Consider, for example, a relation *R* such that *xPy, yPz* and *zPx*, which is the case with social preference in the famous case of

---

3. Note that the converse does not hold. Take *xPy, yIz*, and *zPx*. This violates *PI*, but not *II*, so that *II* does not imply *PI*.

the 'paradox of voting' (see Arrow [1], Chapter 1). Here $C([x, y, z], R)$ is empty. When the number of alternatives is finite, transitivity is a sufficient condition for the existence of a choice function. But it is not a necessary condition. In fact, quasi-transitivity is sufficient.

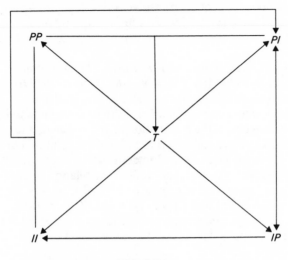

FIGURE 1

THEOREM II. *If $R$ is reflexive, complete and quasi-transitive, then a choice function $C(S, R)$ defined over any finite set $X$ exists, i.e., there is a best alternative in every subset $S$ of $X$, provided $X$ has a finite number of elements.*[4]

*Proof.* Let there be $n$ alternatives, viz., $x_1, x_2, \ldots, x_n$, in $S$. First consider the pair $x_1, x_2$. By reflexivity and completeness of $R$, the choice set of $[x_1, x_2]$ is non-empty. Let $a_1 = x_1$ or $x_2$ belong to this choice set, i.e., $a_1 R x_i$, for $i = 1, 2$. Consider now the pair $a_1, x_3$. If $a_1 R x_3$, then $a_1 R x_i$, $i = 1, 2, 3$, and $a_1$ then belongs to the choice set of $[x_1, x_2, x_3]$. If, on the other hand, $x_3 P a_1$, then $x_3$ can fail to belong to the choice set of $[x_1, x_2, x_3]$ only if $x_1 P x_3$ or $x_2 P x_3$. If $a_1 = x_1$, the former is impossible. But the latter is also impossible since $x_2 P x_3$ and $x_3 P a_1$ must imply $x_2 P a_1$, which contradicts $a_1 R x_2$. A similar argument holds if $a_1 = x_2$. Hence $x_3 \in C([x_1, x_2, x_3], R)$. In either case, $C([x_1, x_2, x_3], R)$ is non-empty, and let $a_2$ be an element of it. Proceeding this way, $a_{n-1}$ is an element of $C(S, R)$ which must thus be non-empty.

4. In case the assumption of the finiteness of the set $X$ appears as unduly restrictive, it may be recalled that even full transitivity $T$ does not guarantee the existence of a choice set for an infinite set. Incidentally, a slight generalization of Theorem II is immediate, viz., $R$ being quasi-transitive, reflexive and complete implies that $C(S, R)$ is non-empty for every finite subset $S$ of a set $X$ (not necessarily finite). The proof is substantially the same.

The condition of quasi-transitivity may be compared with a condition that has been discussed by Pattanaik [12], viz., $xPy$ & $yRz{\rightarrow}xRz$.

LEMMA 1.   *R is quasi-transitive if and only if $\forall x, y, z \in X:xPy$ & $yRz{\rightarrow}xRz$.*

*Proof.*   Suppose $R$ is quasi-transitive, but the latter condition does not hold. Then because of reflexivity and completeness we must have $zPx$, given $xPy$ and $yRz$. But $zPx$ and $xPy$ imply, given quasi-transitivity, $zPy$. But this is false.

Similarly, suppose $R$ is not quasi-transitive. Then for some $x, y, z$ in $X$, we have $xPy, yPz$, and $zRx$. If $yPz$ & $zRx{\rightarrow}yRx$, then $xPy$ will be contradicted. Thus this implication cannot be true. This proves the lemma.

Note that the equivalence of quasi-transitivity with Pattanaik's condition is crucially dependent on the assumption of completeness and reflexivity.

We now introduce two conditions of rationality of choice. For this purpose we define $C(S)$ as any choice function defined over some $X$, not necessarily derived with respect to some binary preference relation. Indeed it is easy to think of choice functions that cannot be derived from any binary relation, e.g., $C([x, y, z]) = [x]$ and $C([x, y]) = [y]$. To guarantee that not only can we choose, but we can choose rationally, certain properties of the choice function may have to be specified. We consider two.

*Property $\alpha$.*   $x \in S_1 \subset S_2 \rightarrow [x \in C(S_2) \rightarrow x \in C(S_1)]$.
*Property $\beta$.*   $[x, y \in C(S_1)$ & $S_1 \subset S_2] \rightarrow [x \in C(S_2) \leftrightarrow y \in C(S_2)]$.

Property $\alpha$ states that if some element of subset $S_1$ of $S_2$ is best in $S_2$, then it is best in $S_1$. This is a very basic requirement of rational choice, and in a different context has been called the condition of 'the independence of irrelevant alternatives'.[5]

Property $\beta$ is also appealing, though is perhaps somewhat less intuitive than Property $\alpha$. It requires that if $x$ and $y$ are both best in $S_1$, a subset of $S_2$, then one of them cannot be best in $S_2$ without the other being also best in $S_2$. To give an example, Property $\alpha$ states that if the world champion in some game is a Pakistani, then he must also be the champion in Pakistan, while Property $\beta$ states that if some Pakistani is a world champion, then *all* champions of Pakistan must be champions of the world.†

The following Lemma is immediate.

---

5. See Nash [11], Chernoff [4], Radner and Marschak [14], and Luce and Raiffa [9]. This condition should not, however, be confused with Arrow's [1] condition of the same name, which is a condition on the functional relationship between social preference and individual preferences.

† [Georges Bordes has pointed out that this description fits exactly a more demanding condition than $\beta$, and that condition he calls $\beta +$, which turns out to be an important consistency condition on its own right (see G. Bordes, 'Consistency, Rationality and Collective Choice', *Review of Economic Studies,* **43** (1976)); see also Essay 8 in this volume. To fit $\beta$ exactly the description needs the following emendation: if some Pakistani *champion* is a world champion, then *all* champions of Pakistan must be champions of the world.]

LEMMA 2.    *Every choice function C(S, R) generated by a binary relation R satisfies Property α but not necessarily Property β.*

*Proof.*  If $x$ belongs to $C(S, R)$, clearly $xRy$ for all $y$ in $S$, and therefore $xRy$ for all $y$ in any subset of $S$. Hence Property α is satisfied.

Next consider a triple $x$, $y$, $z$, such that $xIy$, $xPz$, and $zPy$. It is clear that

$$[x, y] = C([x, y], R), \text{ and } [x] = C([x, y, z], R).$$

This violates Property β.

There seems to be a close relationship between a choice function fulfilling Property β and the underlying preference relation satisfying condition *PI*.

THEOREM III.    *A choice function C(S, R) generated by a binary relation R satisfies Property β if and only if R fulfils condition PI.*

*Proof.*    It is trivial that a binary relation must be complete and reflexive to generate a choice function. Now suppose that *PI* is violated. Then there is a triple $x$, $y$, $z$ such that $xPy$, $yIz$, and $zRx$. Obviously $[y, z] = C([y, z], R)$. Further, $z \in C([x, y, z], R)$, but $y \notin C([x, y, z], R)$. Thus Property β is violated.

Conversely, suppose that Property β is violated. Then we have a pair $x$, $y$ such that $x, y \in C(S_1, R)$, $x \in C(S_2, R)$, and $y \notin C(S_2, R)$, when $S_1 \subset S_2$. Clearly, there exists some $z$ in $S_2$ such that $zPy$ & $xRz$. We known that $xIy$, since $x, y \in C(S_1, R)$. Now,

$$zPy \& yIx \rightarrow zPx,$$

by condition *PI*. But we know that $xRz$. Hence $R$ cannot possibly satisfy condition *PI*. This completes the proof of the theorem.

We can now extend this result by noting that when a choice function exists, condition *PI* implies condition *PP*, so that, by Theorem (I.6), it also implies transitivity in full and $R$ is an ordering. While a number of Theorems have been presented in the literature on the conditions under which *PI* implies an ordering (see, for example, Rader [13], Sonnenschein [19], [20], and Lorimer [8]),[6] this extremely simple result seems to have been overlooked.

THEOREM IV.    *If a binary relation R generates a choice function, then condition PI implies that R is an ordering.*

*Proof.*    Reflexivity and completeness of $R$ are trivial. By Theorem (I.6) we need only show that *PI* implies *PP*.

Suppose *PP* is violated. Then there is a triple $x$, $y$, $z$ such that $xPy$, $yPz$, and $zRx$. If $zPx$, then $C([x, y, z], R)$ will be empty. Hence $zIx$ holds. But $yPz$ & $zIx \rightarrow yPx$, by condition *PI*. We know, however, that $xPy$. Thus condition

6. On related questions, see also Eilenberg [6], Samuelson [16], Arrow [2], Uzawa [21], and Richter [15].

*PI* must also be violated. Thus *PI* implies *PP*, so that *PI* also implies that *R* is an ordering, in view of Theorem (I.6).

Theorem IV might appear to be somewhat counter-intuitive since it seems to elevate one of the four aspects of transitivity, viz., condition *PI*, to a very special position. However, it may be recalled that by Theorem I, *PI* is equivalent to *IP*, and furthermore *PI* implies *II*. What remains is *PP*. We have seen earlier that *PP* implies the existence of a choice function, but the converse is not the case. For example, *xPy, yPz*, and *xIz*, yields a *C(S, R)* that generates non-empty choice sets for every subset of [*x, y, z*], but it violates *PP*. What Theorem IV asserts is that if a choice function is generated by a binary relation that violates *PP*, then it will also violate *PI*. (That this is the case in the example in question is readily checked.) It is possible to have a choice function generated by a relation *R* that satisfies *PP* and violates *PI*, but not vice versa.

As a corollary to Theorem III we get the following result, in view of Theorem IV.

COROLLARY 1. A choice function *C(S, R)* derived from a binary relation *R* satisfies Property *β* if and only if *R* is an ordering.
The proof is immediate.[7]

The relation between conditions *PP, PI,* and transitivity of *R* and the existence of *C(S, R)* and the Properties *α* and *β*, as reflected in the above results, can be summarized in the form of Figure 2, with the direction of implication being represented by the direction of the arrow. In the box on the right hand side, the implications are subject to the condition that the choice function *C(S, R)* exists.

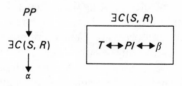

FIGURE 2

## 2. *Possibility Theorems on Social Choice*

In his classic treatment of the problem of collective decisions, Arrow [1] has

---

7. For a direct proof, see Arrow [2]. Arrow combines Properties *α* and *β* in his C. 4. Arrow's combined condition is the following: If $S_1 \subset S_2$, and $C(S_2) \cap S_1$ is non-empty, then $C(S_1)$ is identical with $C(S_2) \cap S_1$. It is easy to check that this is equivalent to a combination of Properties *α* and *β*. However, we do not really need to bring in Property *α*, since it is satisfied anyway (Lemma 2).

been concerned with obtaining a complete social ordering. His 'impossibility' result is crucially dependent on this requirement. We might now investigate whether we gain anything by redefining the problem in terms of choice functions rather than orderings.

Let $R_i$ be the preference relation of individual $i$, and $R$ that for the society. It is assumed that each $R_i$ is a complete ordering. Arrow assumes the same for $R$, and here we shall deviate a little, and redefine Arrow's problem of obtaining a rule for social choice more generally than he did.

*Definition* 4.　A *Rule* is a functional relation $f$ that specifies one and only one social binary relation $R$ for each set of individual orderings $R_i$ with one $R_i$ for each $i$.

A Rule takes the form: $R = f(R_1, \ldots, R_n)$.

If we require $R$ to be a complete ordering then a Rule is a Social Welfare Function as defined by Arrow.

*Definition* 5.　A *Social Welfare Function* (henceforth SWF) is a Rule $f$ the range of which is restricted to the set of orderings.

In contrast we can consider a class of Rules that are not necessarily social welfare functions, but which nevertheless indicate unambiguously the 'best' alternatives in every choice situation. In the case of the 'paradox of voting' referred to earlier there is *neither* transitivity, *nor* a best alternative. We now wish to dissociate the two problems. Earlier discussions relating to this dissociation can be found in Dummet and Farquharson [5], Sen [18], and Pattanaik [12], though all these papers have been concerned with the existence of a choice set for the universal set and not with the existence of a choice function.

*Definition* 6.　A *Social Decision Function* (henceforth SDF) is a Rule $f$ the range of which is restricted to only those binary relations $R$ each of which generates a choice function $C(S, R)$ over the entire $X$.

Arrow's 'General Possibility Theorem' consists of imposing certain restrictions on the Rule, and these conditions are shown to be mutually incompatible. We state these conditions below,[8] with one difference on which we shall comment presently.

---

8. We have used different labelling of the conditions from Arrow's own and used the first letter of the crucial word to facilitate recollection.

| *Arrow's* | *Ours* |
|---|---|
| Condition 1′ | Condition *U* (Unrestricted Domain) |
| Condition *P* (Pareto Principle) | Condition *P* (Pareto Principle) |
| Condition 3 (Independence of Irrelevant Alternatives) | Condition *I* (Independence of Irrelevant Alternatives) |
| Condition 5 (Non-dictatorship) | Condition *D* (Non-dictatorship) |

*Condition U* (Unrestricted Domain).   The domain of the Rule $f$ must include all logically possible combinations of individual orderings.

*Condition P* (Pareto Principle).    For any pair $x$, $y$ in $X$, $[\forall i{:}xP_iy] \to xPy$.

*Condition I* (Independence of Irrelevant Alternatives).   Let $R$ and $R'$ be the social binary relations corresponding respectively to two sets of individual preferences $(R_1, \ldots, R_n)$ and $(R'_1, \ldots, R'_n)$. If for all pairs of alternatives $x$, $y$ in a subset $S$ of $X$, $xR_iy \leftrightarrow xR'_iy$, for all $i$, then $C(S, R)$ and $C(S, R')$ are the same.

*Condition D* (Non-dictatorship).    There exists no individual $i$ such that for every element in the domain of Rule $f$, $\forall x, y \in X$: $xP_iy \to xPy$.

We have stated the non-dictatorship condition somewhat differently from Arrow by specifying a universal quantifier over the elements in the domain of rule $f$. This is to prevent a possible ambiguity in Arrow's somewhat rough definition. If someone is indifferent between every pair of alternatives, then trivially $xP_iy \to xPy$ or all $x$, $y$, since the antecedent is false. This is clearly not Arrow's intention. The ambiguity arises from the fact that the condition of non-dictatorship is a *denial* of an implication, unlike, say, the condition of Pareto Rule which *asserts* an implication. The SWF has to consider the possibility $xP_iy$ whether or not individual $i$ will in fact ever entertain such a view.[9]

Arrow's 'impossibility' theorem states the following:

*General Possibility Theorem*: There is no SWF satisfying Conditions $U$, $P$, $I$ and $D$.[10]

The question we now ask is the following: Does the General Possibility Theorem extend to Social Decision Functions as well? Or does the expansion of the range of $f$ consequent on shifting attention from SWFs to SDFs make it possible for $f$ to satisfy Conditions $U$, $P$, $I$ and $D$, simultaneously? Fortunately the last is precisely what happens when we consider a finite number of alternatives. (In the case of an infinite set even an ordering might not yield a choice function so that that case raises other problems, which we discuss later.)

THEOREM V.    *There is a SDF satisfying Conditions U, P, I and D, for any finite set X.*

*Proof.*   An example will suffice. Define:

$$xRy \leftrightarrow \sim [(\forall i{:}yR_ix) \ \& \ (\exists i{:}yP_ix)].$$

---

9. Condition $D$ now operates in conjunction with Condition $U$, which requires an unrestricted domain of $f$.

10. Arrow [1], pp. 97–100.

Clearly $R$ is reflexive and complete.[11] Further, the SDF satisfies Conditions $P$, $I$ and $D$. We show now that $R$ is quasi-transitive for every logically possible combination of individual orderings.

$$xPy \ \& \ yPz \rightarrow [\forall i{:}xR_iy \ \& \ \exists i{:}xP_iy] \ \& \ \forall i{:}yR_iz$$
$$\rightarrow \forall i{:}xR_iz \ \& \ \exists i{:}xP_iz$$
$$\rightarrow xPz.$$

Thus, $R$ is quasi-transitive, and by Theorem II, no restriction need be put on the domain of the SDF defined, i.e., Condition $U$ is also satisfied. This completes the proof.

Two comments may be worth making in the context of Theorem V. First, the social preference relation $R$ generated by the SDF defined above is merely quasi-transitive, and is not fully transitive. Suppose there are two individuals 1 and 2 and three alternatives $x$, $y$, $z$ such that: $xP_1y \ \& \ yP_1z$, and $zP_2x \ \& \ xP_2y$. We have then $xPy$, $yIz$, and $xIz$. This is clearly intransitive.[12] All that is guaranteed is that a 'best' alternative will be present in every subset, i.e., a choice function will exist, no matter what the individual preferences are.

Second, we can strengthen Theorem V by strengthening the Pareto Rule and the Non-dictatorship Condition. Define:

*Condition $P^*$ (Strong Pareto Rule).* For any pair $x$, $y$ in $X$,

$$[\forall i{:}xR_iy \ \& \ \exists i{:}xP_iy] \rightarrow xPy.$$

*Condition $D^*$ (Strong Non-dictatorship).* There exists no individual $i$ such that for all $(R_1, \ldots, R_n)$ in the domain of $f$ either of the following conditions holds:

$$\exists x, y \in X{:} \ xP_iy \rightarrow xPy; \tag{1}$$
$$\exists x, y \in X{:} \ xR_iy \rightarrow xRy. \tag{2}$$

Clearly, Condition $P^*$ implies Condition $P$, and Condition $D^*$ implies Condition $D$, but not vice versa in either case. The following theorem does, however, hold.

THEOREM V*.   *There is a SDF satisfying Conditions U, $P^*$, I and $D^*$ for any finite set X.*

The proof is provided by the same example as in the proof of Theorem V.[13]

We can also relax the condition that the set be finite. With infinite sets Conditions $U$ and $P$ are inconsistent for a SDF, as is readily checked by assuming that all the individuals share the same antisymmetric ordering with no greatest element. But if we require that at least one person's preference

11. Essentially this converts the 'incompleteness' of the Pareto relation into 'indifference'.

12. Thus the SDF quoted is not a SWF with unrestricted domain, and this is not a counter-example to Arrow's General Possibility Theorem.

13. Note, however, that for every individual $i$, $xP_iy \rightarrow xRy$, in this example. [This property has since been called a veto, and it has been extensively explored in the recent literature; see Essay 8, Section 5.]

relation $R_i$ generates a choice function, then we can find a SDF for the society satisfying $U$, $P$, $I$ and $D^*$.

THEOREM V**.    *There is a SDF satisfying Conditions U, P, I and D\*, if at least one of the individual orderings generates a choice function over X.*

*Proof.*    We can use the insight of Theorem V to suggest a very short proof. Define $xRy \leftrightarrow \sim (\forall i{:}yP_ix)$. Then it can be shown that any element in the choice set of any individual must be in the choice set of the society. Hence the choice function of the society exists. There is no need to restrict the domain of the SDF except in so far as it is involved already in assuming that at least one individual has a choice function. Conditions $P$, $I$ and $D^*$ are also fulfilled.[14]

Theorems V, V* and V**, should dispel a small part of the gloom surrounding Arrow's 'impossibility' result. We can satisfy all the conditions of Arrow (viz., $U$, $I$, $P$, $D$) and still get rules for social choice such that in every choice situation an unambiguous best alternative exists. Arrow's result hinges crucially on the requirement of full transitivity, whereas for the existence of a social choice function quasi-transitivity is quite sufficient.

Lest we jubilate too much at the disappearance of Arrow's impossibility result for social decision functions, two notes of caution are due. First, Conditions $U$, $I$, $P$ and $D$ were thought by Arrow to be *necessary* for a reasonable social choice mechanism; he did not claim this set to be *sufficient* for it. And indeed the insufficiency of these Conditions (and of $P^*$ and $D^*$) is transparent from the examples in terms of which we have proved Theorems V, V* and V**. The SDFs used satisfy these conditions of Arrow (in fact, somewhat stronger ones), and still the SDFs would appear to be unattractive to most of us, except perhaps to the high priests of 'Pareto optimality and no more'. Interestingly enough we can add some other conditions proposed in the literature without upsetting the applecart, viz., May's [10] conditions of 'anonymity', 'neutrality', and pair-wise 'decisiveness'. Our previous examples of SDFs, unattractive as they are, pass all these tests perfectly. May [10] showed that only one pair-wise 'decisive' rule of group decision passes 'anonymity', 'neutrality', and 'positive responsiveness' to individual preferences, viz., the method of majority decision. The examples in the proof of Theorems V−V** fail to satisfy only 'positive responsiveness', though they do pass Arrow's [1] weaker condition of 'positive association', which demands non-negative rather than positive association. If we demand that 'positive responsiveness' be satisfied too, then we get the majority rule, which will not generate even a social choice function for some configurations of individual preferences. We discuss this question further in Section 3.

---

14. We can use Theorem V** for an indirect proof of Theorem V, since an individual ordering over a finite set must imply the existence of an individual choice function.

Second, we might wish to impose certain rationality conditions on the choice functions generated by the SDF. In Section 1 we have discussed two such conditions extensively, viz., Properties $\alpha$ and $\beta$. There is no difficulty in this case in satisfying Property $\alpha$. We know from Lemma 2 that the social choice functions with which we are concerned in the context of SDFs will necessarily satisfy Property $\alpha$, since these choice functions are derived from binary relations. We know, however, from Corollary 1 to Theorem III that a binary relation generating a choice function satisfying Property $\beta$ will necessarily be an ordering. Condition $PP$ (quasi-transitivity) is not sufficient for Property $\beta$, which seems to be equivalent to Condition $PI$ (Theorem III). The following theorems follow immediately.

THEOREM VI. *There is a SDF satisfying Conditions U, P, I and D, for any finite set X, and fulfilling the requirement that each social choice function should satisfy Property α.*

THEOREM VII. *There is no SDF satisfying Conditions U, P, I and D, and fulfilling the requirement that each social choice function must satisfy Property β.*

Theorem VI follows from Theorem V and Lemma 2, while Theorem VII follows from Arrow's General Possibility Theorem and Corollary 1 to Theorem III. The problem, thus, really boils down to the importance we attach respectively to Properties $\alpha$ and $\beta$.

## 3  A Theorem on Majority Decisions

As an escape route from the General Possibility Theorem, Arrow proposes that we relax the condition of unrestricted domain (our Condition $U$) and try to get reasonably wide domains within which actual preference patterns may usually lie and on which a SWF satisfying the other conditions can be defined. This lead has been followed, and more and more general conditions have been found in Black's [3] and Arrow's [1] condition of 'single peaked preferences', Inada's [7] condition of 'single-caved preferences' and 'preferences separable into two groups', Ward's [23] condition of 'latin-square-less preferences', and Sen's [17] condition of 'value restricted preferences'. But all these require that the number of voters (or non-indifferent voters) be odd. This is a somewhat peculiar requirement, but the method of majority decisions might lead to intransitivities even when these conditions hold *if* the number of individuals is even.

The restrictive nature of this assumption has been forcefully brought out by Professors Williamson and Sargent:

... the requirement that the number of non-indifferent individuals expressing themselves with respect to *every* triple be odd is rather severe. Indeed, we should expect that on the average, the number of individuals expressing such preferences would, for any triple selected at random, be even 50 per cent of the time. In the absence of additional restrictions the probability that an even number of individuals will be involved in the voting in at least one out of the total of all such triples can obviously approach unity very rapidly. Thus, since it is easy to construct examples in which social intransitivities result from an even number of voters where no Latin-square exists within the set of individual preferences, the condition that the number of voters expressing non-indifferent preferences be odd seriously limits the operational significance of those possibility theorems of which Sen's is the general case.[15]

Fortunately, once the problem is redefined in terms of a choice function rather than a social ordering, the restriction on the number of individuals can be dispensed with. We proceed to the theorem via two definitions contained in Sen [17]. If $xR_iy$ and $xR_iz$, then $x$ is said to have the value 'best' in individual $i$'s preference ordering over the triple $x, y, z$. Similarly, the values 'worst' and 'medium'.

*Definition* 6.    A set of individual preferences over a triple such that there exist one alternative and one value ('best', 'medium', 'worst') with the characteristic that the alternative never has that value in any individual's preference ordering, is called a *value restricted* preference pattern over that triple for those individuals.

For example, if $yR_ix$ and $zR_ix$ do not simultaneously hold in any individual's preference pattern then $x$ does not have the value 'worst' in anyone's preference ordering. Similarly, if $xR_iy$ and $xR_iz$ does not hold for anyone, then $x$ does not have the value 'best'. If neither $[yR_ix \& xR_iz]$, nor $[zR_ix \& xR_iy]$, for anyone, then $x$ does not have the value 'medium'.

*Definition* 7.    A *concerned individual* with respect to a set of alternatives is one who is not indifferent between all the alternatives.

Now the theorem. It is to be noted that it imposes no condition on the number of individuals being odd.

THEOREM VIII.    *The method of majority decisions is a SDF satisfying Conditions P, I and D, with a domain that includes all logically possible combinations of individual preferences that are value restricted over every triple for concerned individuals.*

---

15. Williamson and Sargent [24]. We do not discuss here the other points made by Williamson and Sargent in their important paper.

*Proof.*    Conditions *I, P* and *D* are not in dispute. Nor are the properties of reflexivity and completeness generated by the majority rule.

By Theorem II, all we need to prove is the quasi-transitivity of *R*.

Suppose, to the contrary, *R* is not quasi-transitive. Then clearly for some set of three alternatives *x, y, z*, we have $xPy$, $yPz$ and $zRx$. It will be now shown that this must violate value restriction for that triple.

We use the notation used in Sen [17], viz. $N(x > y)$ represents the number of people who prefer *x* to *y*, $N(x \geqslant y)$ the number who regard *x* as at least as good as *y*, $N(x \geqslant y > z)$ the number who regard *x* as at least as good as *y* and *y* as better than *z*, and so on. First take $yPz$ and $zRx$.

$$yPz \rightarrow N(y > z) > N(z > y),$$
$$zRx \rightarrow N(z > x) \geqslant N(x > z).$$

We have thus: $[N(y > z) - N(x > z)] + [N(z > x) - N(z > y)] > 0$.

This implies that: $N(y > z \geqslant x) + N(y \geqslant z > x) > 0$. Thus there is a concerned individual for whom *y* has the value 'best', *z* the value 'medium', and *x* the value 'worst'.

Similarly, by taking $xPy$ and $yPz$, and $zRx$ and $xPy$, respectively, we can show that *x* and *z* have the value 'best', *y* and *x* the value 'medium', and *z* and *y* the value 'worst', in the respective preference patterns of some concerned individual or other. Hence the value restriction is violated, which contradicts our assumption.

This proves that *R* must be quasi-transitive over every triple, and now from Theorem II, Theorem VIII follows.

This theorem can also be derived with the help of Pattanaik's [12] theorem on the existence of a choice set under majority rule. Pattanaik is not concerned with the existence of a choice *function* but with the particular choice set for the *whole* set of alternatives. But by a repeated application of his result, Theorem VIII can be derived. However, the proof here is direct and shorter. Incidentally, our proof also contains a much shorter alternative proof of Pattanaik's crucial Lemma 2 since quasi-transitivity implies that $xPy$ & $yRz \rightarrow xRz$, given reflexivity and completeness, as shown in Lemma 1 above.

## 4    *Concluding Remarks*

In Section 1 of this paper we derived certain elementary results on preference relations and choice functions. These results (Theorems I–IV) are derived without any assumption of continuity and related conditions as these conditions might not be very realistic for certain problems of rational choice, especially in dealing with social decisions. In particular it is noted that quasi-transitivity, i.e., the transitivity of the strict relation ($xPy$ & $yPz \rightarrow xPz$), guarantees the existence of a choice function (Theorem II). Further every choice function derived from a binary relation satisfies Property $\alpha$. which is a rationality condition that has been discussed a great deal in the literature and has sometimes been called the 'condition of the independence of irrelevant alternatives' (a condition that should not be confused with Arrow's condition of the same name). It is also shown (Theorem III) that another rationality condition, viz., Property $\beta$, imposed on the choice function is satisfied if and only if the preference relation satisfies the condition (we call it *PI*) that $xPy$ & $yIz \rightarrow xPz$. Further, it is demonstrated that when a choice function exists, *PI* implies that $R$ is transitive (Theorem IV). A corollary of these results is that if the choice function has to satisfy Property $\beta$, then the underlying preference relation must be an ordering. Thus, much depends on how we view this additional rationality restriction in the form of Property $\beta$. While Property $\alpha$ states that if the best alternative $x$ of a set $S_2$ lies in some subset $S_1$ of it, then $x$ must also be the best alternative in that subset $S_1$. Property $\beta$ requires, on the other hand, that if two alternatives $x$ and $y$ are best in some subset $S_1$, then one of them can be best in a set $S_2$ containing this subset $S_1$ if and only if the other is best in that set as well.

In Section 2 we reinterpreted Arrow's problem on social choice in terms of obtaining a social *choice function* rather than a social *ordering*. A Social Decision Function was defined as a rule that specifies a social choice function for every permitted combination of individual orderings. This is to be contrasted with Arrow's Social Welfare Function which specifies a complete social ordering for every permitted combination of individual orderings. It was shown (Theorem V) that the 'impossibility' theorem about Social Welfare Functions does not carry over to Social Decision Functions, and we can indeed find a SDF satisfying all the conditions of Arrow (unrestricted domain, Pareto principle, independence of irrelevant alternatives, and non-dictatorship). Making our analysis choice-oriented does, therefore, dispel some of the gloom generated by Arrow's General Possibility Theorem.

The crucial difference turns out to be related to the property of transitivity. Quasi-transitivity is sufficient for the existence of a choice function, and Arrow's General Possibility Theorem rests squarely on the requirement of full transitivity of the social preference relation $R$.

However, even with this emphasis on choice rather than on obtaining an ordering, an impossibility result very close to Arrow's can be constructed. If we demand that Property $\beta$ must also be satisfied by the choice function generated by the social binary relation derived from the SDF, then the 'impossibility' result of Arrow comes back (Theorem VII).

This raises a fundamental question regarding our values concerning group choice. On top of the four conditions of Arrow as applied to a social decision function and on top of Property $\alpha$, do we also wish to impose some further restriction on group choice, such as Property $\beta$? In the theory of group choice much seems to depend on this particular question on the precise meaning of rationality of choice.

An alternative route back to the 'impossibility' result will be to introduce some additional restrictions on $f$, e.g., the restrictions of May [10], in particular his condition of 'positive responsiveness', i.e., a strict association of individual and social preferences. This condition is violated by the example used in the proof of Theorem V, though the example passes May's other three conditions (anonymity, decisiveness, and neutrality), and also passes Arrow's [1] weaker version of the condition of association of individual and social preferences. May has shown that the only pair-wise-decisive group decision rule that satisfies anonymity, neutrality and positive responsiveness is the method of majority decision.

Finally, if we are concerned with social decision functions as opposed to social welfare functions, the conditions necessary for the successful use of the method of majority decision becomes weaker. In particular in the conditions involving Arrow's 'single-peaked preferences', Inada's 'single-caved preferences', and 'preferences separable into two groups', Ward's 'latin-squareless preferences', and Sen's 'value restricted preferences', the somewhat arbitrary requirement that the number of concerned voters be odd can be totally dispensed with in the generation of a choice function as opposed to an ordering. This is proved (Theorems VIII) only for 'value restricted preferences', since this subsumes all the other cases.[16]

## References

[1] Arrow, K. J.: *Social Choice and Individual Values* (Wiley, New York, 1951. Second edition, 1963).

[2] Arrow, K. J.: 'Rational Choice Functions and Orderings', *Economica,* **26** (1959).

[3] Black, D.: *The Theory of Committees and Elections* (Cambridge University Press, Cambridge, 1958).

[4] Chernoff, H.: 'Rational Selection of Decision Functions', *Econometrica,* **22** (1954).

[5] Dummet, M., and Farquharson, R.: 'Stability in Voting', *Econometrica,* **29** (1961).

[6] Eilenberg, S.: 'Ordered Topological Spaces', *American Journal of Mathematics,* **63** (1941).

[7] Inada, K.-I.: 'A Note on the Simple Majority Decision Rule', *Econometrica,* **32** (1964).

[8] Lorimer, P.: 'A Note on Orderings', *Econometrica,* **35** (1967).

[9] Luce, R. D., and Raiffa, H.: *Games and Decisions* (Wiley, New York, 1958).

[10] May, K. O.: 'A Set of Independent Necessary and Sufficient Conditions for Majority Decisions', *Econometrica,* **20** (1952).

[11] Nash, J. F.: 'The Bargaining Problem', *Econometrica,* **18** (1950).

[12] Pattanaik, P. K.: 'A Note on Democratic Decisions and the Existence of Choice Sets', *Review of Economic Studies,* **35** (1968).

16. Sen [17].

[13] Rader, T.: 'The Existence of a Utility Function to Represent Preferences', *Review of Economic Studies,* **31** (1963).

[14] Radner, R. and Marschak, J.: 'Note on Some Proposed Decision Criteria', in Thrall, Coombs and Davis (eds), *Decision Processes* (Wiley, New York, 1954).

[15] Richter, M. K.: 'Revealed Preference Theory', *Econometrica,* **34** (1966).

[16] Samuelson, P. A.: *Foundations of Economic Analysis* (Harvard University Press, Cambridge, 1947).

[17] Sen, A. K.: 'A Possibility Theorem on Majority Decisions', *Econometrica,* **34** (1966). [Essay 5 in this volume.]

[18] ____ 'Planners' Preferences: Optimality, Distribution and Social Welfare', presented at the International Economic Association Round-table conference on the Economics of the Public Sector, Biarritz, 1966. [Published later in J. Margolis and H. Guitton (eds), *Public Economics* (Macmillan, London, 1969).]

[19] Sonnenschein, H.: 'The Relationship between Transitive Preference and the Structure of the Choice Space', *Econometrica,* **33** (1965).

[20] ____ 'Reply to "A Note on Orderings" ', *Econometrica,* **35** (1967).

[21] Uzawa, H.: 'Preference and Rational Choice in the Theory of Consumption', in Arrow, K. J. *et al.* (eds), *Mathematical Methods in Social Sciences* 1959 (Stanford University Press, Stanford, 1960).

[22] Vickrey, W.: 'Utility, Strategy and Social Decision Rules', *Quarterly Journal of Economics,* **74** (1960).

[23] Ward, B.: 'Majority Voting and Alternative Forms of Public Enterprises', in Margolis, J. (ed.), *Public Economy of Urban Communities* (Johns Hopkins Press, Baltimore, 1965).

[24] Williamson, O. E. and Sargent, T. J.: 'Social Choice: A Probabilistic Approach', *Economic Journal,* **77** (1967).

# 7

# Necessary and Sufficient Conditions
# for Rational Choice
# under Majority Decision

## 1 Introduction

Interest in the analytical problems of the method of majority decision goes back at least two centuries to Borda (1770), Condorcet (1785), and Laplace (1814). Since then there have been various attempts to identify precisely the conditions under which the method of majority decision may be free from inconsistencies and can serve as a basis for rational choice. This question is of importance for the theory of social choice in general and for welfare economics in particular (see, for example, Arrow, 1951, Chapter VII), and it is useful to enquire what are the necessary and sufficient conditions that the pattern of individual preferences must satisfy for the method of majority decision to serve as a basis for consistent choice. One of the objects of this paper is to present a solution to this problem.

A restriction that is sufficient for the transitivity of majority decisions was proposed by Black (1948, 1958) and more formally by Arrow (1951), and this condition has been extended by Vickrey (1960), Inada (1964, 1969), Ward (1965), Sen (1966), and Majumdar (1969). The type of conditions considered in these papers has the following general form: if anyone has an ordering of type $p$, then no one should have an ordering of type $q$. This paper is concerned with restrictions of this class.

Recently, in a remarkable paper, Inada (1969) has identified the necessary and sufficient conditions for the transitivity of majority decisions. However, the problem of rational choice is not the same as that of transitivity of the preference relation, even though all the contributions quoted above have been concerned exclusively with transitivity in the shape of *orderings* for the society.[1] The difference between the existence of a best alternative and the

---

1. An ordering is defined to mean a preference relation that is reflexive, complete, and transitive. Reflexivity and completeness are, however, never in doubt with majority decisions.

From *Journal of Economic Theory,* 1 (August 1969), written jointly with Prasanta K. Pattanaik.

existence of an ordering has been noted and analysed by Dummet and Farquharson (1961), Sen (1966a, 1969), and Pattanaik (1966, 1968). Indeed, the basic question, as Condorcet (1785) was aware, is the existence of an alternative that receives a majority over every other alternative. This does not imply transitivity. If such a majority candidate existed, argued Condorcet, we should choose that one on the basis of 'straightforward reasoning' (*simple raisonnement*), without considering the complicated exercises that Condorcet recommended in other cases. The crucial consideration, thus, is the existence of a choice set.

Basing ourselves on two alternative interpretations of the requirement of rationality in social choice, we identify in this paper the respective sets of necessary and sufficient conditions on the pattern of individual preferences for rational choice through majority decisions.[2]

Our second objective relates to a line of enquiry initiated by May (1952) and extensively studied by Murakami (1966, 1968). May demonstrated that the method of majority decision satisfies four characteristics that he called 'decisiveness', 'anonymity', 'neutrality', and 'positive responsiveness', and further that it is the only pair-wise group decision function that satisfies all four of these characteristics. It is interesting to enquire whether the conditions on individual preferences that are sufficient for rational choice under the method of majority decision are also sufficient for group decision processes that satisfy some but not all of these four characteristics (and some others intermediate between them). We show that many of these conditions on individual preferences are sufficient for more general decision rules than the method of majority decision, but that there is at least one condition that is sufficient for transitivity and rational choice under majority decision but not for group decision functions lying indefinitely close to the method of majority decision.

## 2   *Notation, Definitions and Concepts*

We shall refer to the relation of weak preference ('at least as good as') of individual $i$ as $R_i$, with $P_i$ and $I_i$ standing for the corresponding strict preference and indifference, that is, $xP_iy \leftrightarrow [xR_iy \& \sim (yR_ix)]$, and $xI_iy \leftrightarrow [xR_iy \& yR_ix]$. Similarly, $R$, $P$, and $I$, will refer to the relations of weak preference, strict preference, and indifference for the society as a whole. A social welfare function (hereafter, SWF) as defined by Arrow (1951) is a functional relation that specifies one and only one social ordering $R$ for any set of individual orderings $R_i$ (one ordering $R_i$ for each individual $i$):

$$R = f(R_1, \ldots, R_n).$$

2. In the process we also provide a simplification of some of the theorems in Inada (1969) and give more economic proofs, even though our focus of attention is social choice functions and not social orderings.

The method of majority decision is such a SWF, and it postulates that for all $x$ and $y$, $xRy$ if and only if the number of individuals for whom $xR_iy$ is at least as large as the number for whom $yR_ix$. But its domain is limited, since certain configurations of individual orderings will not yield a social ordering $R$, but merely a preference relation that violates transitivity. However, as we noted before, transitivity is an over-demanding requirement for social choice. Condorcet's (1785) problem of some alternative getting a majority over all others is formally the problem of the existence of a non-null choice set generated by the majority preference relation.

*Definition 1.* A *choice set* of a set of alternatives $S$ is that subset $C(S)$ of $S$ of which every element $x$ is socially at least as good as every element in $S$, i.e.:

$$C(S) = [x \mid (x \in X) \& \forall y \in S: xRy].$$

*Definition 2.* A *choice function* $C(S)$ defined over $X$ is a functional relation such that the choice set $C(S)$ is non-empty for every non-empty subset $S$ of $X$.

The fulfilment of the 'Condorcet criterion'[3] presents no problem if a choice function is generated by the method of majority decision, i.e., if in every subset of alternatives $S$ in $X$ we can find at least one alternative that will receive a majority over every other alternative in $S$.

In this line we weaken the requirement of a social welfare function, requiring no longer that $R$ be transitive.

*Definition 3.* A *social decision function* (hereafter, SDF) is a functional relation that for any set of individual preference orderings $R_i$ (one $R_i$ for each individual $i$) specifies one and only one social preference relation $R$ that will generate a choice function.

Note that any SWF is also a SDF as long as the number of alternatives is finite. However, in the case of an infinite set even an ordering does not guarantee a choice function. In this paper we shall be concerned only with finite sets of alternatives.

The method of majority decision is also a SDF, and as a SDF its domain is larger than that as a SWF, since some configurations of individual preferences may yield a choice function for the society but no social ordering, e.g., a social preference relation $R$ such that $xPy$, $yIz$, and $xIz$. However, the domain of SDF is also limited since some configurations of individual preferences will yield no choice function either, e.g., $xPy$, $yPz$, and $zPx$, as in the famous case of 'paradox of voting', popularized by Nanson (1882).[4] In this paper we shall be mainly concerned with the domain of majority decisions viewed as a SDF but in Section 7 we shall also examine majority decisions as a

3. See Arrow (1963), p. 94. See also Black (1958), pp. 57–9.

4. Three persons and three alternatives are assumed in this classic case, with person 1 preferring $x$ to $y$ and $y$ to $z$, person 2 preferring $y$ to $z$ and $z$ to $x$, and person 3 preferring $z$ to $x$ and $x$ to $y$.

SWF. We shall refer to these respectively as majority-decision-SDF and majority-decision-SWF.

We now have to clarify the precise meaning of necessary and sufficient conditions on the pattern of individual preferences. Since these definitions will be applied to both SWF and SDF we shall refer to the domain of $f$, which would be interpreted appropriately in the respective cases.

*Definition* 4.  A condition on the set of individual preferences is *sufficient* if every set of individual preferences satisfying this condition must be in the domain of $f$.

*Definition* 5.  A condition on the set of individual preferences is *necessary* if every violation of the condition yields a list of individual orderings such that some assignment of these orderings over some number of individuals[5] will make the individual preference pattern lie outside the domain of $f$.

The definition of sufficiency was used by Arrow (1951), and that of necessity first proposed by Inada (1969). These are not the only possible definitions of necessary and sufficient conditions, but they do make sense if restrictions have to be about the list of permissible orderings for individuals and not about the distribution of the number of individuals over possible orderings. If more than 50 per cent of the electors share the same [strict] ordering, then no matter what orderings the others hold, majority decision will yield a social ordering. However, the restrictions that we consider are those that apply only to types of permissible preference orderings and not on numbers holding them.

Before we specify some restrictions it will be convenient to separate out those persons who are indifferent between all the alternatives, for they introduce peculiar logical problems.

*Definition* 6.  A *concerned individual* for a set of alternatives is one who is not indifferent between every pair of elements in the set.

We now define three specific restrictions. The first is the assumption of value-restricted preferences proposed in Sen (1966).[6]

*Definition* 7.  *Value Restriction* (VR). In a triple $(x, y, z)$ there is some alternative, say $x$, such that all the concerned individuals agree that it is not worst, or agree that it is not best, or agree that it is not medium, i.e., for

---

5. Each individual must have one and only one ordering, but any given ordering can, of course, be assigned to as many individuals as we like, or to none at all.

6. In Sen (1966) 'value restriction' was defined as a condition on the preferences of *all* individuals, concerned or unconcerned, but in the Possibility Theorem on Value Restricted Preferences it was shown that it was sufficient to apply the restriction only to the concerned individuals. Here we define value restriction in such a manner that only concerned individuals are involved. There is in this no gain in generality, only in brevity.

concerned individuals:

$$[\forall i: xP_iy \underline{\vee} xP_iz] \underline{\vee} [\forall i: yP_ix \underline{\vee} zP_ix]$$
$$\underline{\vee} [\forall i: (xP_iy \& xP_iz) \underline{\vee} (yP_ix \& zP_ix)].$$

The next restriction we shall call 'extremal restriction'. This has not been so far proposed in the literature, but it can be shown to subsume three restrictions of Inada (1969), viz., 'dichotomous preferences', 'echoic preferences', and 'antagonistic preferences', and can be further shown to be equivalent to the union of these three restrictions.

*Definition 8.* *Extremal Restriction* (ER): If for an ordered triple $(x, y, z)$, there is someone who prefers $x$ to $y$ and $y$ to $z$, then anyone who prefers $z$ to $x$ also prefers $z$ to $y$ and $y$ to $x$ i.e.,

$$[\exists i: xP_iy \& yP_iz] \rightarrow [\forall j: zP_jx \rightarrow zP_jy \& yP_jx].$$

It can be checked that this is equivalent to saying that if there is someone who prefers $x$ to $y$ and $y$ to $z$, then anyone regards $z$ to be uniquely best if and only if he regards $x$ to be uniquely worst.

Lastly, we shall use a weaker version of the restriction of 'Taboo Preference' of Inada (1969), and call it Limited Agreement.

*Definition 9.* *Limited Agreement* (LA): In a triple there is an ordered pair $(x,y)$ of distinct alternatives such that everyone regards $x$ to be at least as good as $y$, i.e., $\forall i: xR_iy$.

Inada rules out the individuals who are indifferent between all three of the alternatives in the triple, and requires that no individual holds $xI_iyI_iz$, nor $yP_ix$. We shall not need the former restriction.

We shall refer to the number of individuals for whom $xP_iy$ as $N(xPy)$, the number for whom $xR_iy$ as $N(xRy)$, the number for whom $xP_iy \& yR_iz$ as $N(xPyRz)$, and so on.

We now define certain possible properties of group decision rules. Since our concern is with pair-wise choice we define a group decision rule as a functional relation between the binary relation of social preference and the set of binary relations of individual preference holding *for each pair of alternatives, x, y.*

*Definition 10.* A *binary group decision rule* specifies for each pair $x, y \in X$, one and only one binary relation of social preference over the pair given the set of individual preferences over that pair. The domain of this functional relation is assumed to include all logically possible combinations of individual preferences.

Note that neither is a binary group decision rule necessarily a SWF or SDF (since the social binary relation may be neither transitive nor generate a choice function), nor is a SWF or a SDF necessarily a binary group decision rule (since the relation between individual and social preference may not hold pair-wise).[7] In particular, the method of majority decision is a binary group decision rule with unrestricted domain, whereas as a SWF or a SDF certain configurations of individual preferences would have to be ruled out for ensuring transitivity or a choice function. On the other hand, the rank-order method of voting is always a SWF and a SDF, whereas it is not in general a binary group decision rule.

We now define the properties of 'anonymity', 'neutrality', 'positive responsiveness', 'non-negative responsiveness', 'weak Pareto Criterion', and 'strict Pareto Criterion'. The first three are May's conditions (his fourth, viz., 'decisiveness' has already been built into our definition of a binary group decision rule).

*Definition* 11.  Let $(R_i)$ and $(R_i')$ be any two sets of individual orderings, and let a group decision rule map these two respectively into social preference relations $R$ and $R'$.

(11.1) *Anonymity.* If for any pair of individuals $j$, $k$, $R_j = R_k'$, and $R_k = R_j'$, and for all $i$ other than $j$ and $k$, $R_i = R_i'$, then $R = R'$.

(11.2) *Neutrality.* For all $x$, $y$, $z$ and $w$ belonging to $X$, if for all $i$, $(xR_iy \leftrightarrow wR_i'z)$ and $(yR_ix \leftrightarrow zR_i'w)$, then $(xRy \leftrightarrow wR'z)$ and $(yRx \leftrightarrow zRw)$.

(11.3) *Positive Responsiveness.* For all $x$ and $y$ belonging to $X$, if $xP_iy \rightarrow xP_i'y$ and $xI_iy \rightarrow xR_i'y$ for all $i$, and for some $k$ either $(xI_ky$ & $xP_k'y)$ or $(yP_kx$ & $xR_k'y)$, then $xRy \rightarrow xP'y$.

(11.4) *Non-negative Responsiveness.* For all $x$, $y$, if $xP_iy \rightarrow xP_i'y$ and $xI_iy \rightarrow xR_i'y$ for all $i$, then $xPy \rightarrow xP'y$ and $xIy \rightarrow xR'y$.

(11.5) *Weak Pareto Criterion.* For all $x$ and $y$ belonging to $X$, if $xP_iy$ for all $i$, then $xPy$.

(11.6) *Strong Pareto Criterion.* For all $x$ and $y$ belonging to $X$, if $xR_iy$ for all $i$, and $xP_ky$ for some $k$, then $xPy$, and if $xI_iy$ for all $i$, then $xIy$.

Anonymity requires that a permutation of individual preferences between individuals should not alter social preference. Neutrality requires that a permutation of the alternatives in everyone's preference should produce the same permutation in social preference. Positive responsiveness requires that if one alternative, say $x$, goes up in some one's preference vis-à-vis $y$ without going down in anyone's view, then if it was previously socially at least as good as $y$, now $x$ must be socially *better* than $y$. Non-negative responsiveness merely requires that if $x$ rises or remains still in everyone's preference vis-à-vis $y$, then $x$ should not fall in the social preference vis-à-vis $y$. The weak Pareto Criterion requires that if everyone unanimously prefers one alternative to another, then so does society. The strong Pareto Criterion requires that if everyone unanimously regards one alternative as at least as good as another

---

7. This definition of a binary group decision rule encompasses the essence of Arrow's (1951) 'Condition of the Independence of Irrelevant Alternatives'.

and at least one strictly prefers it, society must strictly prefer it. If everyone is indifferent, then so is society.

The following results are immediate, and are noted here without proof.[8]

LEMMA 1.    (1.1) *Neutrality and positive responsiveness together imply the strong Pareto Criterion.*

(1.2) *Neutrality and non-negative responsiveness together imply that either the weak Pareto Criterion holds, or social indifference always holds for all pairs of alternatives.*

(1.3) *The strong Pareto Criterion implies the weak Pareto Criterion.*

(1.4) *For a binary group decision rule, positive responsiveness implies non-negative responsiveness.*

## 3    Preliminary Results

In this section we derive certain preliminary results which we shall use in the later sections. We first note without proof a result on the complete independence of the three proposed conditions.

LEMMA 2.    ER, VR, *and* LA *are completely independent of each other, i.e., any pair of these three could be satisfied without the third, and anyone of these could be satisfied without the remaining pair.*

Our next result concerns the joint denial of the three, i.e., a simultaneous violation of VR, ER, and LA.†

LEMMA 3.    *If a set of orderings over a triple violates* VR, ER, *and* LA, *then there is a subset of three orderings in that set which itself violates* VR, ER, *and* LA.

*Proof.*    Over a triple $x$, $y$, $z$, there are thirteen logically possible orderings, and there are 8192 ($= 2^{13}$) different subsets of the set of these thirteen orderings. We label these orderings in a special manner for convenience. (We dispense with the subscript $i$ in the preference relation, e.g., write $P$ for $P_i$)

| | | |
|---|---|---|
| (1.1) $xPyPz$ | (1.2) $xPyIz$ | (1.3) $xIyPz$ |
| (2.1) $yPzPx$ | (2.2) $yPzIx$ | (2.3) $yIzPx$ |
| (3.1) $zPxPy$ | (3.2) $zPxIy$ | (3.3) $zIxPy$ |
| (4) $xPzPy$ | (5) $zPyPx$    (6) $yPxPz$ | (7) $xIyIz$. |

If ER is to be violated, at least one of these orderings must be linear, i.e., satisfy anti-symmetry. Without loss of generality, let us choose ordering 1.1

---

8. See Murakami (1968) for a discussion of (1.1) and (1.2) and other interesting properties of group decision.

† [The Proof has been partially revised to take care of a difficulty pointed out by Maurice Salles.]

i.e., *xPyPz*. We may first note that there is no other ordering which combined with 1.1 will form a pair that violates VR and LA. Hence the smallest set of orderings that violates VR, ER, and LA, must have at least three elements.

It is easy to check that the only three-ordering-sets inclusive of 1.1 that violate VR are given by : [1.1, 2.1 *or* 2.2 *or* 2.3, 3.1 *or* 3.2 *or* 3.3]. There are nine such sets. Each of these violates ER as well as LA [1.1, 2.2, 3.3]. There are, thus, eight three-ordering-sets that violate VR, ER, and LA, and this class of eight sets we call $\Omega$.

Consider next sets inclusive of 1.1 but having more than three orderings that violate VR, ER, and LA. If these sets include any member of $\Omega$, then the result follows immediately. It is easily checked by simple but laborious accounting that there is no set containing four or more orderings which violates VR, ER and LA, but does not contain any member of $\Omega$ as a subset. For example, in order to violate VR without containing any of the nine sets of three-orderings mentioned in the last paragraph, a set of orderings must include at least one of the following four-ordering sets:[9]

(I)  1.1, 1.2, 1.3, 2.3;     (III) 1.1, 1.2, 2.2, 2.3;
(II) 1.1., 1.2, 1.3, 3.2;     (IV) 1.1, 1.3, 3.2, 3.3.

Do these four-ordering sets violate LA? None of them do. For example, *yRz* holds in every ordering in (I). To include an ordering with *zPy*, either (a) we must include 3.1, or 3.2, or 3.3, in which case the set will then include some member of $\Omega$, or (b) we must include ordering 4 or 5, in which case again the set can be seen to include some member of $\Omega$ except for formal interchange of *y* and *z*, and of *x* and *z*, respectively. Similarly II lacks *yPz*, III lacks *zPy*, and IV lacks *yPx*, and in each case the inclusion of any ordering filling this gap brings in some member of $\Omega$. The proof is completed by applying the same method to the case in which the set of orderings includes [1.1, 2.2, 3.3], the only set of the initial nine not included in $\Omega$.

We now state, without proof, a result that was proved in Sen (1969). This was labelled Theorem II in that paper.

LEMMA 4.   *If R is reflexive, complete and quasi-transitive over a finite set of alternatives X, then a choice function defined over X exists.*

It may be recalled that quasi-transitivity is defined as follows: *R* is quasi-transitive over *X* if and only if $\forall x, y, z \in X$: (*xPy* & *yPz*) → *xPz*.

### 4   VR, LA, and ER: Sufficiency under Majority Decision and More General Conditions

From a theorem of May (1952) we know that the method of majority deci-

---

9. This might appear to be not so if we include ordering 4 or 5 or 6, e.g., [1.1, 4, 5 *or* 3.2 *or* 2.3, 6 *or* 2.2 *or* 1.3]. But the last three elements of each of these possibilities do form a member of $\Omega$ except for the substitution of *x* and *y*, or *y* and *z*, or *z* and *x*.

sion satisfies 'anonymity', 'neutrality', and 'positive responsiveness', and is the only possible binary group decision rule that satisfies these characteristics. It has been shown in Pattanaik (1968) and Sen (1968) that Value Restriction is sufficient for quasi-transitivity of the majority preference relation $R$, and by Lemma 4 is thus sufficient for generating a choice function over a finite set of alternatives. We can also show that Limited Agreement too is sufficient for quasi-transitivity of the majority preference relation. We can, however, obtain a more general result that VR and LA are sufficient for other types of group decision rules as well.[10] So we relate the sufficiency of these conditions directly to certain properties of the group decision rule, and since these properties are valid for majority decision among other rules, the sufficiency of VR and LA follows as a corollary to the results proved below.

THEOREM I.    *If a binary group decision rule is neutral and non-negatively responsive then it must yield a quasi-transitive preference relation if individual preferences are value restricted for every triple.*

*Proof.* A necessary and sufficient condition for $R$ to violate quasi-transitivity is that for some triple $u$, $v$, $w$, we have $uPv$, $vPw$, and $wRu$. We treat $u$, $v$, $w$ as variables and $x$, $y$, $z$ as constants in a given triple. It was shown in Sen (1966) that if individual preferences are value restricted over a triple $x$, $y$, $z$, then the following condition holds: at least one of the implication (1), (2), (3), and at least one of the implications (4), (5), (6), must be true.

$$(1)\ N(yRzRx) = N(xIyIz) \qquad (2)\ N(xRyRz) = N(xIyIz)$$
$$(3)\ N(zRxRy) = N(xIyIz).$$
$$(4)\ N(xRzRy) = N(xIyIz) \qquad (5)\ N(yRxRz) = N(xIyIz)$$
$$(6)\ N(zRyRx) = N(xIyIz).$$

First consider (1). We can check that:

$(1) \rightarrow \forall i: \{\ \sim(xI_iyI_iz) \rightarrow \sim(yR_iz\ \&\ zR_ix)\}$
$\quad \rightarrow \forall i: \{\ \sim(xI_iyI_iz) \rightarrow [(yR_iz \rightarrow xP_iz)\ \&\ (zR_ix \rightarrow zP_iy)]\ \}$
$\quad \rightarrow \forall i: \{\ [(yP_iz \rightarrow xP_iz)\ \&\ (yI_iz \rightarrow xR_iz)]\ \&\ [(zP_ix \rightarrow zP_iy)\ \&\ (zI_ix \rightarrow zR_iy)]\ \}$
$\quad \rightarrow\ [(yRz \rightarrow xRz)\ \&\ (zRx \rightarrow zRy)]$, by neutrality and non-negative responsiveness[11]
$\quad \rightarrow\ [(xRy\ \&\ yRz\ \&\ zRx) \rightarrow (xRy\ \&\ yIz\ \&\ zIx)]$.

---

10. Arrow's 'single-peakedness' being a special case of VR is covered by this. When the number of voters is odd, the sufficiency of VR to generate full transitivity is shown in Sen (1966). In the present paper we do not impose any restriction on the numbers.

11. This is easily checked. If $(yP_iz \leftrightarrow xP_iz)\ \&\ (yI_iz \leftrightarrow xI_iz)$, then by neutrality, $(yPz \rightarrow xPz)\ \&\ (yIz \rightarrow xIz)$. Therefore, if $(yP_iz \rightarrow xP_iz)\ \&\ (yI_iz \rightarrow xR_iz)$, then by non-negative responsiveness, $(yPz \rightarrow xPz)\ \&\ (yIz \rightarrow xRz)$, so that $yRz \rightarrow xRz$. Similarly, $zRx \rightarrow xRy$. On this line of reasoning, see Murakami (1968).

Similarly:

(2) $\to [(xRy \ \& \ yRx \ \& \ zRx) \to (zRx \ \& \ xIy \ \& \ yIz)]$.
(3) $\to [(xRy \ \& \ yRz \ \& \ zRx) \to (yRz \ \& \ zIx \ \& \ xIy)]$.

Thus if at least one of the three implications (1), (2) or (3) holds, then it is impossible to have $uPv, uPw,$ and $wRu$, assigning $(u, v, w)$ as $(x, y, z)$, or as $(y, z, x)$, or as $(z, x, y)$. Similarly if one of (4), (5) or (6) holds, then $uPv, vPw,$ and $wRu$ is impossible for the assignments of $(u, v, w)$ as $(y, x, z)$, or $(x, z, y)$, or $(z, y, x)$. But there is no other possible assignment. Hence if value restriction is satisfied by individual preferences over every triple, then the social preference relation must be quasi-transitive for every triple.

THEOREM II.    *If a binary group decision rule is neutral, non-negatively responsive, and satisfies the strong Pareto Criterion, then it must yield a quasi-transitive preference relation if individual preferences satisfy Limited Agreement over every triple.*

*Proof.*    Let $x, y, z$ be any triple. Without loss of generality, let $\forall i: xR_iy$. Hence $\forall i: (yP_iz \to xP_iz) \ \& \ (yI_iz \to xR_iz)$, so that by neutrality and non-negative responsiveness,[12] we have $yRz \to xRz$. Similarly, $zRx \to zRy$. Thus $(xRy \ \& \ yRz \ \& \ zRx) \to (xRy \ \& \ yIz \ \& \ xIz)$. Consider now the hypothesis $yRx$. Since $\forall i: xR_iy$, clearly the strong Pareto Criterion implies that $\forall i: xI_iy$. Hence

$$yRx \to \forall i: \{ [(xP_iz \to yP_iz) \ \& \ (xI_iz \to yI_iz)] \ \& \ [(zP_iy \to zP_ix) \ \& \ (zI_iy$$
$$\to zI_ix)] \} \to [(xRz \to yRz) \ \& \ (zRy \to zRx)].$$

Thus

$$(yRx \ \& \ xRz \ \& \ zRy) \to (yRx \ \& \ xIz \ \& \ zIy).$$

$R$ cannot violate quasi-transitivity without at least one of the two 'circles' $(xRy \ \& \ yRz \ \& \ zRx)$ and $(yRx \ \& \ xRz \ \& \ zRy)$ holding, and if either of them holds then at least two indifferences must rule in this set of three relations. This of course means that violation of quasi-transitivity is impossible, which establishes the theorem.

We next turn to the Extremal Restriction. We shall show later that it is sufficient for transitivity under majority decision, but it is easily checked that ER for every triple is not necessarily sufficient even for quasi-transitivity for group decision functions that satisfy any or all of the conditions of neutrality, non-negative responsiveness, anonymity, and the strong Pareto Criterion, i.e., all the properties listed under Definition 10 except positive responsiveness. But if we impose positive responsiveness also, then from May's (1952) theorem, the group decision rule must be the method of majority decision. Can we move in the direction of majority decision without going all the way?

---

12. The reasoning is given in the preceding footnote.

An example of a decision rule that is neutral, anonymous, and non-negatively responsive, is the following.

*Definition* 12.    *The Strict Majority Rule.* $\forall x, y \in X: N(xPy)/N > \frac{1}{2} \leftrightarrow xPy$, where $N$ is the total number of individuals. Further, $xRy \leftrightarrow \sim (yPx)$.[13]

The following lemma is immediate.

LEMMA 5.    *If $xPy$ according to the strict majority rule, then $xPy$ according to the method of majority decision.*

In fact, it may be noted that $xPy$ under majority decision requires that $N(xPy)$ be larger than $\frac{1}{2}N^*$, is the number of non-indifferent individuals in the relation between $x$ and $y$. Lemma 5 follows simply from the fact that $N^* \leqslant N$.

We know that the strong Pareto Criterion will be implied by positive responsiveness in the presence of neutrality (Lemma 1), but the converse does not hold. Since positive responsiveness will also usher in majority decision given the other conditions, one way of moving toward majority decision without getting there is to incorporate the strong Pareto Criterion as well. Consider a Pareto-inclusive version of the strict majority rule.

*Definition* 13.    *The Pareto-inclusive Strict Majority Rule.* $\forall x, y \in X: xPy$ if and only if $N(xPy)/N > \frac{1}{2}$, or $\forall i: xR_iy$ & $\exists i: xP_iy$. Further $xRy \leftrightarrow \sim (yPx)$.

We can now define a continuum of group decision rules that will lie intermediate between the Strict Majority Rule (in either the Pareto-inclusive form or not) and the method of majority decision. $N(xPy)$ can be required to be greater than some convex combination of $N$ and $N^*$.

*Definition* 14.    *Semi-strict Majority Rule.* $\forall x, y \in X: N(xPy)/[pN + (1-p)N^*] > \frac{1}{2} \leftrightarrow xPy$, for some given $p$ chosen from the open interval $]0, 1[$. Further $xRy \leftrightarrow \sim (yPx)$.

Clearly, if $p = 0$, then this is majority rule, and if $p = 1$ then this is the strict majority rule. However, since we confine $p$ to the *open* interval $]0, 1[$, these possibilities are ruled out though we can come indefinitely near either the majority rule, or the strict majority rule.

Since within the class of semi-strict majority rule we can come indefinitely close to the method of majority decision, the question arises as to whether Extremal Restriction may be sufficient for some cases of semi-strict majority rule. However, we show that it is not sufficient for semi-strict majority rule no matter how close we are to the method of majority decision.

---

13. $R$ under the strict majority rule corresponds to $R_{maj}$ in Dummet and Farquharson (1961); this is called 'non-minority rule' in Pattanaik (1968).

THEOREM III.   *Extremal Restriction is not a sufficient condition for the quasi-transitivity of the semi-strict majority rule over any triple no matter which p we select.*

*Proof.*   Since we are interested in the strong Pareto Criterion also, we prove this theorem with a line of reasoning that will not be disturbed if we were to impose additionally Pareto-inclusiveness. Consider a triple $x$, $y$, $z$, and the following four individual preference orderings, which is a set that satisfies ER.

$$(1)\ xP_iyP_iz;\quad (2)\ zP_iyP_ix;\quad (3)\ yP_izI_ix;\quad (4)\ xI_izP_iy.$$

Let $N_j$ be the number of individuals holding ordering $j$, for $j = 1, 2, 3, 4$. Take $N_1 = 2$, $N_2 = 1$, and $N_3 = N_4 = q$ where $q$ is a positive integer such that $0 < 1/q < p$. It is easy to check that such a $q$ always exists no matter how small $p > 0$ is. By construction, $xPy$, $yPz$, and $xIz$, which violates quasi-transitivity.

We can, thus, get as close as we like to the majority rule by taking $p$ indefinitely close to 0, but ER remains insufficient. It is also clear that the Pareto Criterion (weak or strict) will make no difference since both are satisfied (trivially) by the group decisions specified above.

However, as soon as $p$ instead of being close to 0 becomes 0, i.e., as soon as we have the method of majority decision, ER becomes a sufficient condition for not merely quasi-transitivity but also for full transitivity. There is an abrupt change in this case.

THEOREM IV.   *All logically possible sets of individual preferences satisfying extremal restrictions for every triple are in the domain of the majority-decision-SWF.*

*Proof.*   If every individual is indifferent between at least two alternatives in a triple then ER will be fulfilled for that triple trivially, and the transitivity of majority decisions in this case follows from Theorem 2′ in the first paper of Inada (1964). We need be concerned, therefore, only with non-trivial fulfilment of ER. Without loss of generality, let $xP_iy$ & $yP_iz$, for some triple $x$, $y$, $z$, and some $i$.

Suppose that contrary to the theorem ER holds over this triple, but majority decisions are still intransitive. We know then that *exactly* one of the following must be true: $[xRy,\ yRz,\ zRx]$, 'the forward circle', and $[yRx,\ xRz,\ zRy]$, 'the backward circle'.[14] Suppose the former holds. Since there is an individual such that $xP_iyP_iz$, we have:

$$zRx \rightarrow [N(zPx) \geqslant N(xPz)] \rightarrow [N(zPx) \geqslant 1] \rightarrow \exists i:\ zP_iy\ \&\ yP_ix,$$

by ER. The last is a strict ordering over this triple, and applying ER once

14. See Sen (1966).

again, we are left with a set of four orderings that satisfy ER, which are:

(1) $xP_iyP_iz$;   (2) $zP_iyP_ix$;   (3) $yP_izI_ix$;   and   (4) $xI_izP_iy$.

Referring to the number of persons holding each of these orderings as $N_1$, $N_2$, $N_3$, and $N_4$, respectively, we obtain:

$$xRy \And yRz \And zRx \rightarrow [N_1 + N_4 \geqslant N_2 + N_3] \And [N_1 + N_3 \geqslant N_2 + N_4]$$
$$\And [N_2 \geqslant N_1].$$
$$\rightarrow [N_1 = N_2] \And [N_3 = N_4]$$
$$\rightarrow yRx \And xRz \And zRy.$$

Thus the forward circle implies the backward circle, and intransitivity is impossible.

The only remaining possibility is that the backward circle holds alone.

$$zRy \And yRx \rightarrow [N(zPy) - N(xPy)] + [NyPx) - N(yPz)] \geqslant 0$$
$$\rightarrow N(zPyRx) + N(zRyPx) \geqslant 0.$$

If $\exists i$: $zP_iyP_ix$, then we proceed as in the last paragraph, and show the impossibility of intransitivity. If not, then thanks to ER, we must have:

$$N(zPyRx) = N(zRyPx) = 0.$$

In that case $[N(zPy) - N(xPy)] + [N(yPx) - N(yPz)] = 0$. Therefore $(zRy \And yRx)$ will imply $(zIy \And yIx)$.

Now,          $\forall i$: $zP_iy \rightarrow xR_iy$, since $\sim \exists i$: $zP_iyP_ix$
                  $\rightarrow xP_iy$, since $N(zPyRx) = 0$.

Hence $N(xPy) \geqslant N(zPy)$. Exactly similarly we can show that $N(yPz) \geqslant N(yPx)$. Since we also have $xIy \And yIz$, we must have: $N(yPx) = N(xPy) \geqslant N(zPy) = N(yPz) \geqslant N(yPx)$, so that $N(xPy) = N(zPy)$. But we also know from the fact that $\forall_i$: $zP_iy \pm xP_iy$, and $\exists i$: $xP_iyP_iz$, that $N(xPy) > N(zPy)$. This contradiction completes the proof of the theorem.


## 5   Necessary and Sufficient Conditions for a Choice Function under Majority Decision

We now derive the necessary and sufficient conditions for deriving a social choice function through the method of majority decision for a finite set of alternatives.

THEOREM V.   *The necessary and sufficient condition for a set of individual orderings to be in the domain of the majority-decision-SDF is that every triple of alternatives must satisfy at least one of the conditions, VR, ER, and LA.*

*Proof.*   It is clear from the proofs of Theorems I, II, and IV that if each triple satisifes VR, LA or ER, then the social weak preference relation must be quasi-transitive over every triple. Hence from Lemma 4 the sufficiency of VR, LA, and ER is immediate. We need concern ourselves only with necessity.

We know from Lemma 3 that if a set of individual orderings violates VR, ER, and LA, then that set must include a three-ordering-subset which also vilates those three restrictions. Further, from the proof we know that there are eight three-orderings-subsets[15] that violate VR, ER, and LA, viz., [1.1, 2.1 *or* 2.2 *or* 2.3, 3.1 *or* 3.2 *or* 3.3], excluding [1.1, 2.2, 3.3], where:

$$(1.1)\ xPyPz$$

| | | |
|---|---|---|
| (2.1) *yPzPx* | (2.2) *yPzIx* | (2.3) *yIzPx* |
| (3.1) *zPxPy* | (3.2) *zPxIy* | (3.3) *zIxPy.* |

We have to show that in each of these eight cases some assignment of these orderings over some number of individuals will produce a majority preference relation that does not yield a choice function.

First consider the cases represented by [1.1, 2.1 *or* 2.3, 3.1 *or* 3.2]. Let $N_1$ be the number of persons holding 1.1, $N_2$ the number holding 2.1 or 2.3, and $N_3$ the number holding 3.1 or 3.2. If we assume $N_1 > N_2$, $N_1 > N_3$, and $(N_2 + N_3) > N_1$, then we must have $xPy$, $yPz$, and $zPx$. A simple example is $N_1 = 3$, $N_2 = N_3 = 2$.

This leaves four cases. Consider next the following two sets, viz., [1.1, 2.1 *or* 2.3, 3.3]. With the same convention on numbering, if we take $N_2 > N_1 > N_3$, and $N_1 + N_3 > N_2$, we have again $xPy$, $yPz$, and $zPx$. A simple example is $N_1 = 3$, $N_2 = 4$, and $N_3 = 2$. Finally, we take the cases given by [1.1, 2.2, 3.1 *or* 3.2]. Taking $N_3 > N_1 > N_2$, and $N_1 + N_2 > N_3$, we get $xPy$, $yPz$, and $zPx$, as for example with $N_1 = 3$, $N_2 = 2$, and $N_3 = 4$. This completes the proof of necessity, which estabishes the theorem.

It is thus clear that whenever VR, ER, or LA, is satisfied by each triple,[16] there must be in every subset of alternatives a majority winner satisfying the 'Condorcet Criterion', irrespective of the number of individuals and their distribution over the possible orderings. On the other hand, whenever VR, ER, and LA, are violated for any triple, then a majority winner will fail to exist for some subset (in particular, for that triple) for some number of individuals distributed in some manner over the orderings.

## 6  *Existence of a Best Alternative for the Entire Set*

It may be noted that even when there is no best alternative for some subset,

---

15. There are in fact forty-eight such subsets if we treat *x*, *y*, and *z*, as constants. But the remaining ones are all exactly like the one described below but for the substitution of *x* for *y*; or *y* for *z*; or *z* for *x*; or *y* for *x* and *z* for *y* and *x* for *z*; or *z* for *x* and *x* for *y* and *y* for *z*. Exactly the same analysis applies in each case.

16. It need not of course be the same restriction in each triple.

e.g., a triple, there may still be a best alternative for the entire set. The motivation behind demanding a choice function is that no matter which set of alternatives are offered for choice, there should be a clear decision. In some real situations, however, we may be fairly confident that choice will be confined to some particular set, and in such a case we may not be too depressed if there is no clear decision for some proper subset of alternatives which we may feel will never be offered as the set to choose from. This raises the question of investigating the necessary and sufficient conditions for the existence of a non-null choice set for a given set of alternatives, as opposed to the existence of a choice function, i.e., as opposed to the existence of a non-null choice set for every non-null subset of that given set. It would be fair to expect that the restrictions can be relaxed for this more limited demand on the method of majority decision, and it is to this question that we now turn.

We first prove a preliminary result.

LEMMA 6.    *Under the method of majority decision, a set of alternatives has a non-empty choice set if and only if the subset of Pareto-optimal alternatives in that set has a non-empty choice set.*

*Proof.*    That the existence of a non-empty choice set for the set of Pareto-optimal alternatives in a given set of alternatives is sufficient for the existence of a non-empty choice set for the entire set has been proved in Pattanaik (1968), Lemma 1. All that we have to prove is, therefore , the necessity of the condition.

Let $S^*$ be the set of Pareto-optimal alternatives in S, and let $C(S^*)$ be empty.

Then $\qquad\qquad\qquad \forall x \in S^*: [\exists y \in S^*: \sim (xRy)]$

Hence $\qquad\qquad\qquad \forall x \in S^*: [\exists y \in S: \sim (xRy)]$ $\qquad$ (1)

By definition of $S^*$,

$$\forall x \in S: \sim (x \in S^*) \rightarrow [\exists y \in S: (\forall i: yR_i x) \,\&\, (\exists i: yP_i x)]$$

Hence

$$\forall x \in S: \sim (x \in S^*) \rightarrow [\exists y \in S: \sim (xRy)]. \qquad (2)$$

From (1) and (2) it follows that $C(S)$ is empty, which completes the proof of necessity.

Now the theorem.

THEOREM VI.    *A sufficient condition for a given set of alternatives to have a non-empty choice set under the method of majority decision is that every triple of Pareto-optimal alternatives in the set satisfies ER or VR.*

*Proof.*    If every triple of Pareto-optimal alternatives satisfies ER or VR, then, by Theorem V, the set of Pareto-optimal alternatives will have a non-empty choice set under the method of majority decision. Hence, by Lemma 6, it will follow that the entire set of alternatives under consideration will have a non-empty choice set.

Two points should be noted about Theorem VI. Firstly, the condition LA does not figure in the theorem. This is because fulfilment of LA over a triple of Pareto-optimal alternatives implies that there are at least two alternatives in the triple between which everybody is indifferent. But in this case ER is trivially satisfied. Secondly, Theorem VI gives only a sufficient condition and not a necessary and sufficient condition. In fact, it is clear that fulfilment of ER or VR over every triple of Pareto-optimal alternatives cannot be a necessary condition for a given set of alternatives to have a non-empty choice set. For, if ER and VR are both violated over a triple of Pareto-optimal alternatives, then for some configuration of individual orderings the choice set for that triple will be empty. But this does not prevent the entire set of Pareto-optimal alternatives from having a non-empty choice set. Consider the following example when all four alternatives in the given set $\{x, y, z, w\}$ are Pareto-optimal alternatives:

$$xP_1yP_1zP_1w$$
$$wP_2yP_2zP_2x$$
$$wP_3zP_3xP_3y$$

ER and VR are both violated over the triple $(x, y, z)$. But

$$C(\{x, y, z, w\}) = \{w\}.$$

The difficulty arises from the fact that a given set of alternatives can have a non-empty choice set though a proper subset of the given set has none. This difficulty does not arise in the context of a choice function since if the choice function is not defined over a proper subset of any set of alternatives, then it is not also defined over the entire set of alternatives. Indeed, no necessary condition could be defined in terms of restriction over every triple of Pareto-optimal alternatives, for any given set of alternatives to have a non-empty choice set. This can be proved as follows. Take again the set $\{x, y, z, w\}$ of four Pareto-optimal alternatives. Individual orderings over $(x, y, z)$ can be allowed to vary so as to violate any restriction, but we can have a non-empty $C(\{x, y, z, w\})$ by assuming that all the individuals excepting one strictly prefer $w$ to $x$, $y$, and $z$, and one individual strictly prefers $x$, $y$ and $z$ to $w$ so that $x$, $y$ and $z$ are not rendered Pareto-inoptimal.

If, however, the number of Pareto-optimal alternatives is assumed to be not more than three, then we can formulate a necessary and sufficient condition.

THEOREM VII.  *Provided that a given set of alternatives has at most three Pareto-optimal alternatives, a necessary and sufficient condition for the given set to have a non-empty choice set under the method of majority decision is that every triple of Pareto-optimal alternatives in the set satisfies* ER *or* VR.

*Proof.*  The sufficiency of the condition for the existence of a non-empty choice set for the given set of alternatives follows from Theorem VI. We have only to prove the necessity of the condition. If the condition that every triple of Pareto-optimal alternatives satisfies ER and VR is violated for a given set of alternatives that has at most three Pareto-optimal alternatives, then it follows that the set has only one triple of Pareto-optimal alternatives and that both ER and VR are violated over this triple. In such a case, we can have a configuration of individual orderings such that the choice set for the triple of Pareto-optimal alternatives will be empty. By Lemma 6, this implies that we can have a configuration of orderings such that the choice set for the entire set of alternatives will be empty.

## 7 The Case of Antisymmetric Individual Preferences

Borda (1770) and Condorcet (1785) were mainly concerned with strict orderings, i.e., with anti-symmetric preference relations. This is true of quite a bit of modern work as well. In this special case in which individuals are never indifferent between any pair of alternatives, the necessary and sufficient conditions for the existence of a choice set and of a choice function become somewhat simpler. This is mainly because ER and LA both imply VR when individual orderings are antisymmetric.

LEMMA 7. *If individual orderings are antisymmetric, then* ER $\rightarrow$ VR, *and* LA $\rightarrow$ VR.

*Proof.* Suppose ER is satisfied over some triple. Since indifference is impossible the case of trivial fulfilment of ER does not arise. Let us assume $xP_iyP_iz$ for some $i$. We know from ER that

$$\forall i: zP_ix \rightarrow zP_iy \ \& \ yP_ix.$$

If there is no individual such that $zP_ix$, then $z$ is not best in anyone's ordering, since $\sim(zP_ix) \rightarrow xP_iz$, in the case of antisymmetric ordering. In this case VR holds. If, on the other hand, there is someone who holds $zP_ix$ therefore $zP_iyP_ix$, then anyone holding $xP_iz$ must hold $xP_iyP_iz$ by ER. Since $\forall i:xP_iz \ \underline{v} \ zP_ix$, it follows that in this case $\forall i: xP_iyP_iz \ \underline{v} \ zP_iyP_ix$. Once again VR is satisfied since $y$ is not best (nor indeed worst) in anyone's ordering. Hence ER $\rightarrow$ VR.

Suppose LA is satisfied over some triple. Without loss of generality, let $xR_iy$ hold for all $i$, which in this case means $\forall i: xP_iy$. Hence $x$ is not worst (nor indeed is $y$ best) in anyone's ordering. Thus VR holds.

It may be noted that the converse does not hold. VR does not imply either ER or LA. This is readily checked by looking at the following configuration: $xP_1yP_1z$, $zP_2yP_2x$, and $yP_3zP_3x$. ER and LA are both violated, but $y$ is not worst in anyone's ordering, and hence VR holds.

We can now state the theorems for strict orderings.

THEOREM VIII. *The necessary and sufficient condition for a set of in-dividual orderings to be in the domain of the majority-decision SDF is that every triple must satisfy value restriction.*[17]

*Proof.* Since ER, VR, and LA are sufficient for all individual orderings, strict or not, VR is clearly sufficient in the case of strict orderings. By Theorem V, VR or ER or LA must hold for every triple as a necessary con-dition for the existence of a social choice function, and by Lemma 7, if ER or LA holds, then so must VR, in the case of linear orderings. Hence VR is both sufficient *and* necessary.

Similarly we can derive the following theorems.

THEOREM IX. *A sufficient condition for a given set of alternatives to have a non-empty choice set under the method of majority decision, when all individual preferences are strict, is that every triple of Pareto-optimal alter-natives in the set satisfies value restriction.*

THEOREM X. *Provided that a given set of alternatives has at most three Pareto-optimal alternatives and all individual preferences are strict, a necessary and sufficient condition for the given set to have a non-empty choice set under the method of majority decision is that every triple of Pareto-optimal alternatives in the set satisfies value restriction.*

Given Lemma 7, Theorems IX and X follow from Theorems VI and VII, respectively.

## 8 Rational Choice and Social Ordering

The existence of a socially best alternative in the sense that it will get a majority over every other alternative in the set does solve the basic problem of rational choice under majority decisions. But we might wish that our choice function should satisfy certain additional conditions of rationality. Two such condi-tions were discussed in Sen (1968).

*Property α.* $x \in S_1 \subset S_2 \rightarrow [x \in C(S_2) \rightarrow x \in C(S_1)]$.
*Property β.* $[x, y \in C(S_1) \,\&\, S_1 \subset S_2] \rightarrow [x \in C(S_2) \leftrightarrow y \in C(S_2)]$.

Property $\alpha$ requires that if $x$ is a best alternative in a given set and belongs to a certain subset of it, then $x$ must also be best in that subset, e.g., a world champion must also be champion in his country. Property $\beta$ requires that if two alternatives are both best in a certain subset, then one can be best for the whole set if and only if so is the other, e.g., if there are two champions in a nation, then either both or neither must be world champion. Property $\beta$ is

---

17. This theorem holds even with the original definition of value restriction in Sen (1966), as opposed to Definition 7 above (see footnote 6 on the difference), since with strict orderings all individuals must be 'concerned'.

perhaps intuitively less basic than Property $\alpha$, though it would undoubtedly appeal to some. The following result holds.[18]

LEMMA 8. *Every choice function generated by a binary relation R satisfies Property $\alpha$, and it satisfies Property $\beta$ if and only if R is an ordering.*

Therefore, if someone wishes to adhere also to Property $\beta$ for social choice, then he has no alternative but to demand a social ordering with full transitivity. This brings us back to the question of transitivity of majority decision — the form of the problem as posed in Black (1948, 1958), Arrow (1951), Vickrey (1960), Inada (1964, 1969), Ward (1965), and Sen (1966).

We obtain now the necessary and sufficient conditions for the transitivity of majority decision. This precise question has been studied earlier by Inada (1969), and our work derives much from his pioneering work.

THEOREM XI. *The necessary and sufficient condition for a set of individual orderings to be in the domain of majority-decision-SWF is that every triple of alternatives must satisfy extremal restriction.*

*Proof.* Consider the necessity of ER. Suppose ER is violated. This means that there is (say) some individual $i$ such that $xP_iyP_iz$, while there is another whose preference satisfies either (1) $zP_jx$, $zP_jy$, and $xR_jy$, or (2) $zP_jx$, $yP_jx$. and $yR_jz$. Let there be one individual $i$ and one individual $j$. If $j$ holds (1), then majority decision will yield $xPy$, $yIz$, and $xIz$, which implies a choice function but is not an ordering. Similarly, if $j$ holds (2) then $xIy$, $yPz$, and $xIz$, which is also not an ordering. Hence the necessity of ER is proved. The sufficiency of ER has already been proved in Theorem IV, and the proof is now complete.

The above theorem subsumes the following theorems of Inada (1969), viz., Theorem 1 (sufficiency of dichotomous preferences), Theorems 2 and 2' (sufficiency of echoic preferences), Theorem 3 (sufficiency of antagonistic preferences), and Theorem 4 (necessity of satisfying one of the three). While there is some gain in economy, there is, however, in this case, no gain in generality, since Theorem XI can also be derived from Inada's Theorems 1, 2, 3, and 4. It can be shown that ER is exactly equivalent to the union of Inada's three conditions.

We may note that in the case of strict orderings value restriction becomes a necessary condition but not sufficient since by Lemma 7, ER $\rightarrow$ VR, but not vice versa.

THEOREM XII. *A necessary condition for a set of individual strict orderings to be in the domain of a majority-decision-SWF is that every triple of alternatives must satisfy value restriction, but it is not a sufficient condition.*

18. See Sen (1969) for a proof and discussion of significance. Arrow (1959) had proposed a rationality condition that can be shown to be equivalent to the union of Properties $\alpha$ and $\beta$. One of his theorems proved that a choice function satisfies Properties $\alpha$ and $\beta$ if and only if it is based on an ordering, which is almost equivalent to Lemma 8.

The proof of necessity is obvious from Theorem XI and Lemma 7. The following example shows the insufficiency of VR. Let there be two individuals such that $xP_1yP_1z$, and $zP_2xP_2y$, which yields $xPy$, $yIz$, and $xIz$. VR is satisfied but there is an intransitivity. Incidentally, the necessary and sufficient condition is still given by extremal restriction, as in Theorem XI.

## 9  Concluding Remarks

While possibility theorems on majority decisions (e.g., Black, 1948, 1958; Arrow, 1951; Vickrey, 1960; Inada, 1964, 1969; Ward, 1965; Sen, 1966; Majumdar, 1969) have been mostly concerned with finding sufficient or necessary conditions for the transitivity of major decisions, transitivity is an unnecessarily strict requirement for the existence of a choice function. A choice function implies that no matter which subset of alternatives we choose there is some alternative in it that receives a majority over every other alternative in that subset, so that majority decisions yield a rational outcome satisfying the so-called 'Condorcet decisions'.[19] In this paper we have presented a set of necessary and sufficient conditions for the existence of a choice function.

The restrictions with which we have been concerned rule out certain configurations of individual orderings but do not in any way restrict the number of persons holding any ordering in a permitted configuration. This lack of restriction on numbers makes the concept of sufficiency very strict though that of necessity somewhat weak. This concept of sufficiency was first used by Black (1948) and Arrow (1951) in the context of 'single-peaked preferences' and that of necessity is due to Inada (1969). Though they used the concepts for conditions on transitivity of majority decisions, we have used them for the problem of the choice function.

One interesting result of this paper is that the necessary and sufficient conditions turn out to be conditions on *triples* of alternatives. For transitivity this must obviously be so, but for choice functions it is a result of some interest. The point may be explained in terms of two conditions on triples, viz., for all $x, y, z$:

(1)   $xPy \ \& \ yPz \rightarrow xPz$.
(2)   $xPy \ \& \ yPz \rightarrow xRz$.

The former, which we called quasi-transitivity,[20] is sufficient for a choice function irrespective of the number of a finite set of alternatives (Lemma 3). But it is not necessary, since the latter — a weaker condition — is sufficient for a choice function defined over one triple. However, the latter, i.e., (2), is

---

19. See Arrow (1963), pp. 94–5.
20. It is weaker than transitivity as it does not imply that $xRy \ \& \ yRz \rightarrow xRz$.

*not* sufficient for a choice function over four alternatives. For example, [*xPy, yPz, zPw, wPx, xIz, yIw*] satisfies (2) but has an empty choice set. It is, therefore, of some interest that the necessary and sufficient conditions on individual preferences for a choice function turns out to be a condition on triples, irrespective of the total number of alternatives, in the special case of majority decisions. It seems that if a configuration of individual preferences violates (1), then it will also violate (2) for some number-distribution of individuals, so that (1) emerges as not merely sufficient but also necessary even for a triple to have a choice function. Take, for example, a weaker form of the 'paradox of voting' with three individuals: $xP_1yP_1z$, $yP_2zP_2x$, and $zP_3xI_3y$. This yields *yPz, zPx,* and *yIx,* which violates (1) but not (2). However, if we take a 5-member community with two individuals each holding first, two holding the last, and one holding the second ordering, we obtain: *xPy, yPz, zPx,* which violates (2) as well.

The main results are presented below in table 1. In addition to the general case, we have also investigated the case when the choice function is required to satisfy a strong condition of rationality (Property $\beta$), which makes it

TABLE 1    Necessary and sufficient conditions for majority decisions
to yield a choice function

|  | General case | Special case: individual orderings are all linear |
|---|---|---|
| General case | VR,ER,LA | VR |
| Special case: must satisfy property $\beta$ | ER | ER [VR necessary, not sufficient] |

necessary that the choice function be generated by a social ordering. The problem of a social ordering has been discussed and solved earlier by Inada (1969), and in this particular case, our results, though somewhat simpler in statement and proof, can be shown to be exactly equivalent to his results. The conditions noted below are to apply to each triple.

We also noted a sufficient condition for the existence of a non-empty choice set for a given set of alternatives (and not necessarily for the existence of a non-empty choice set for each of its subsets). If VR or ER is fulfilled for every triple consisting exclusively of Pareto-optimal alternatives, then the choice set for the entire set will be non-empty. While it is demonstrated that no necessary and sufficient conditions on triples exist for this problem, the noted condition *is* necessary and sufficient when the number of Pareto-optimal alternatives is at most three.

Finally, we related the sufficiency of various restrictions on individual preferences for rational choice under majority decision to specific characteristics of the method of majority decision. Since some of these characteristics are shared by other group decision mechanisms as well, the sufficiency of the relevant restrictions for these mechanisms could be simultaneously proved. In particular, Value Restriction[21] is shown to be sufficient for the existence of a choice function under any binary group decision mechanism that is neutral and non-negatively responsive, and the additional characteristics of majority decision (viz., anonymity and positive responsiveness) are not relevant for this result. Similarly, Limited Agreement is sufficient for all binary group decision rules that are neutral, non-negatively responsive, and satisfy the strong Pareto Criterion, which includes the method of majority decision but also others. Our third category of restriction, viz., Extremal Restriction is, however, rather different in its properties. It is sufficient for transitivity of majority decision but not sufficient even for quasi-transitivity for group decision rules that could be made to lie indefinitely close to the method of majority decision, e.g., semi-strict majority rule. In this the relevance of Extremal Restriction is peculiar to majority decision, unlike Value Restriction and Limited Agreement.

## References

Arrow, K. J. (1951): *Social Choice and Individual Values*, (John Wiley and Sons, Inc., New York); second edition, 1963.

Black, D. (1948): 'On the rationale of group decision-making', *Journal of Political Economy*, **56**.

_____ (1958): *The Theory of Committees and Elections*, (Cambridge University Press, Cambridge).

De Borda, J.-C. (1781): 'Mémoire sur les élections au scrutin', read to the French Academy of Sciences in 1770, printed in *Histoire de l'Académie Royal des Sciences*, 1781, and published in 1784.

De Condorcet, M. (1785): Essai sur l'application de l'analyse à la probabilité des décisions rendues à la pluralité des voix (Paris).

Dummet, M. and R. Farquharson (1961): 'Stability in voting', *Econometrica*, **29**.

Inada, K. (1964): 'A note on the simple majority decision rule', *Econometrica*, **32**.

_____ (1969): 'On the simple majority decision rule', *Econometrica*, **37**.

Laplace, P.-S. (1814): *Théorie Analytique des Probabilités,* 2nd edition.

Majumdar, T. (1969): 'Sen's theorem on transitivity of majority decisions: an alternative proof', *in* T. Majumdar (ed.), *Growth and Choice*. (Oxford University Press, Bombay).

21. Black's (1948) and Arrow's (1951) category of 'single-peaked preferences' being a special case of Value Restriction (see Sen, 1966) is also sufficient for rational choice under conditions more general than majority decision. In this context, see also Murakami (1968).

May, K.O. (1952): 'A set of independent necessary and sufficient conditions for simple majority decision', *Econometrica,* **20.**

Murakami, Y. (1966): 'Formal structure of majority decision', *Econometrica,* **34.**

_____ (1968): *Logic and Social Choice* (Dover Publications, Inc., New York).

Nanson, E. J. (1882): 'Methods of election', *Transactions and Proceedings of the Royal Society of Victoria,* **19** (1882). Reprinted in British Government blue book, Misc. No. 3 (1907), Cd. 3501.

Pattanaik, P. K. (1962): 'A note on democratic decision and the existence of choice sets', *Review of Economic Studies,* **35.**

_____ (1966): 'Sufficient conditions for the existence of a choice set under majority voting', Working Paper No. 14, Department of Economics, Delhi School of Economics, University of Delhi, 1966. [Published later in *Econometrica,* **38** (1970).]

Sen, A. K. (1966): 'A possibility theorem on majority decisions', *Econometrica,* **34.** [Essay 5 in this volume.]

_____ (1966a): 'Planners' preferences: optimality, distribution and social welfare', presented at the International Economic Association Round-Table on the Economics of the Public Sector, at Biarritz, 1966. [Later published in J. Margolis and H. Guitton (eds), *Public Economics* (Macmillan, London, 1969).]

_____ (1969): 'Quasi-transitivity, rational choice and collective decisions', *Review of Economic Studies,* **36** (1969). [Essay 6 in this volume.]

Vickrey, W. (1960): 'Utility, strategy and social decision rules', *Quarterly Journal of Economics,* **74.**

Ward, B. (1965): 'Majority voting and alternative forms of public enterprises', *in* J. Margolis (ed.), *Public Economy of Urban Communities.* (Johns Hopkins Press, Baltimore).

# 8

# Social Choice Theory:
# A Re-examination

Social choice theory is 'concerned with relationships between individuals' preferences and social choice' (Fishburn, 1973, p. 3). But a great many problems fit this general description and they can be classified into types that are fundamentally different from each other. It can be argued that some of the difficulties in the general theory of social choice arise from a desire to fit essentially different classes of group aggregation problems into one uniform framework and from seeking excessive generality. An alternative is to classify these problems into a number of categories and to investigate the appropriate structure for each category. In a small way, this is what will be done in this paper, and some of the recent developments in the theory of social choice will be examined in that light.

## 1 Aggregation Types

To illustrate varieties of exercises coming under the broad heading of interpersonal aggregation, consider the three following problems:

(i)   *Committee decision*: A committee has to choose among alternative proposals for action on the relative merits of which the members hold different views.[1]
(ii)  *Social welfare judgement*: A person wants to make a judgement whether a certain change will be better for the society, some members of which will gain from the change while others will lose.[2]

For helpful comments I am most grateful to Julian Blau, Peter Fishburn, Geoff Heal, Hans Herzberger, Michael Intriligator, Jerry Kramer, Charles Plott, and Kotaro Suzumura.

1. Among the classic statements of this problem are Borda (1781) and Condorcet (1785). See Black (1958) for a good overview of the subject.
2. This involves a judgement *about* society *by* an individual. Cf. 'Of course, when I speak of preference "from a social standpoint", often abbreviated to social preferences and the like, I

Based on an invited paper presented at the Third World Congress of the Econometric Society at Toronto, 1975, published in *Econometrica*, **45** (January 1977), 53–89.

(iii) *Normative indication*: Measurement of 'national income', 'inequality', 'poverty', and other 'indicators' defined with normative motivation incorporating interpersonal weighting in some easily tractable way.[3]

These exercises differ from each other in many ways. For example, the typical committee decision problem is concerned with aggregating the *views* of its members on what should be done rather than with aggregating the *personal* welfare levels of members with which social welfare judgements are frequently concerned. Also, a social welfare judgement is typically interpreted in terms of 'optimality', usually involving binary concepts like 'better', whereas the focus of committee decisions is on arriving at actual choices in a fair manner whether or not such choices could be described as being 'best' or 'optimal'. In committee decisions, the format for expression of views is typically rather limited, e.g., voting for one alternative among many, or ranking all alternatives. In social welfare judgements the magnitudes of welfare gains and losses are frequently invoked as well as interpersonal rankings of welfare (e.g., 'the poor will gain more from this policy'), which are typically not applied to members in committee decision procedures. On the other hand, the individual preferences are expressed by the persons themselves in committee meetings whereas the rankings of personal welfare in social welfare judgements are frequently made by some kind of guesswork rather than direct inquiry. That is, social welfare judgements frequently involve a *wider* class of information but are based on *less firm* evidence than committee decision mechanisms.[4]

The use of normative indicators usually involves compromises of different peoples' 'interests' rather than of their 'views'. The focus is not on reaching actual decisions as such, but on making systematic judgements according to certain well-defined criteria. In these respects there is closer similarity with

always mean preferences based on a given individual's value judgement concerning "social welfare"' (Harsanyi, 1955, p. 310). See also Bergson (1938), Samuelson (1947), Little (1950), Arrow (1951), Graaff (1957), Rawls (1958 and 1972), Hicks (1958), Vickrey (1960), Rothenberg (1961), Kolm (1969), Gintis (1961), Pattanaik (1971).

3. The literature on normative indication has been growing fast in recent years. See, for example, Atkinson (1970 and 1975), Newbery (1970), Bentzel (1970), Nordhaus and Tobin (1972), Sheshinski (1972), Shinohara *et al.* (1973), Dasgupta, Sen, and Starrett (1973), Rothschild and Stiglitz (1973), Hamada (1973), Sen (1973, 1976, and 1976a), Muellbauer (1974 and 1974a), Champernowne (1974), Wolfson (1974), Chipman (1974), Lindbeck (1975), Hansson (1975), Mehran (1976), and Pyatt (1976).

4. However, the possibility of 'strategic' voting (see Farquharson, 1969) makes the evidence of individual preference in committee votings not very firm, either. A remarkable theorem, established by Gibbard (1973) and Satterthwaite (1975), and also by Schmeidler and Sonnenschein (1975), indicates that if choice sets are singleton (i.e., from any set available for choice, precisely one social state is chosen), and if at least three different states are chosen from different available sets, then any non-dictatorial social choice function must be 'manipulable', i.e., at least one person in some choice situation will gain by voting differently from his true preference. For somewhat different formulations of the problem, see Pattanaik (1973, 1974, and 1975), Gibbard (1975), Kelly (1975), and Barbera (1975).

social welfare judgements than with committee decisions. On the other hand, the exercise is limited by using only that information which can be rather mechanically collected, and usually also by keeping the exercise confined to welfare judgements of a limited nature rather than presenting a total judgement about overall social welfare.

Many other exercises also fit the general description of 'social choice' and have other differences. In what follows I shall focus on only two criteria of classification:

(i)   Is the aggregation that of individual *interests*, or that of individual *judgements*? The first type of exercise will be marked *I* and the second *J*.

(ii)  Is the intention to arrive at *decisions* or at *welfare* judgements? The first type will be called *D* and the second *W*.

These yield four categories, viz., *ID*, *JD*, *IW*, and *JW*.

## 2   The Majority Method

The method of majority decisions (henceforth MMD) has been much discussed in the context of social choice theory. How does it fare in the four exercises—*ID*, *JD*, *IW*, and *JW*? The focus of the recent attention that MMD has received has been mostly on the consistency of majority decisions. It is reasonable to argue that the consistency requirements are rather stronger for a procedure yielding welfare judgements than for a decision mechanism. For a welfare judgement the binary concept of being 'at least as good as'—call it *R*—has an obvious meaning, and it is also clear that this relation can be expected to be transitive. This is, however, an unduly strong requirement if choice is what we are concerned with, since a binary relation *R* can generate a choice function without being transitive.

Let *R* be reflexive and complete over the set *X* of alternative states; it clearly must be under MMD if individual preferences are reflexive and complete.[5] Denote indifference and strict preference as *I* and *P*; these are, respectively, the symmetric and asymmetric factors of *R*. (We shall use *R*, *I*, and *P*, respectively, for social weak preference, indifference, and strict preference without these necessarily standing for the majority preference relations unless otherwise stated.) Define the choice set generated by *R* for any non-empty subset *S* of *X* as (cf. Condorcet, 1785):

$$\hat{C}(S, R) = [x \mid x \text{ is in } S \text{ and for all } y \text{ in } S: xRy]. \tag{1}$$

5. Let $N(a, b)$ be the number of people who strictly prefer $a$ to $b$. MMD says: $xRy$ if and only if $N(x, y) \geqslant N(y, x)$. Reflexivity ($xRx$) is trivial. Completeness, i.e., $xRy$ or $yRx$ for all $x$, $y$, also verges on triviality since $N(x, y) \geqslant N(y, x)$ can be false only if $N(y, x) > N(x, y)$, both being real numbers (in fact, integers).

Transitivity is obviously not sufficient for $\hat{C}(S, R)$ to be non-empty for any non-empty $S$, since $S$ may be infinite (and MMD might generate an infinitely ascending chain). It is, however, sufficient for all finite subsets $S$. But it is not necessary, e.g., $xPy, yIz, xIz$. 'Quasi-transitivity', i.e., transitivity of $P$, is sufficient but, again, not necessary. The necessary and sufficient conditions for $R$ to generate a choice function over a finite $X$ are 'acyclicity', reflexivity, and completeness of $R$.[6] Acyclicity is defined as: if there is a finite sequence $x_1Px_2, x_2Px_3, \ldots, x_{n-1}Px_n$, then not $x_nPx_1$.

MMD as a basis for binary decision (requiring a choice function) might seem to be much more promising than MMD as a basis for social welfare judgements (requiring transitivity), since acyclicity is weaker than quasi-transitivity which is weaker than transitivity. The mileage thus gained, however, is not necessarily enormous. It turns out that, if individual preferences are orderings, the conditions on individual preferences that are necessary and sufficient[7] for acyclicity are identical to conditions that are necessary and sufficient for quasi-transitivity. (See Sen and Pattanaik, 1969 and Inada, 1970.) If a list of preferences guarantees acyclicity (no matter how many individuals have each of these preferences), then that list guarantees quasi-transitivity as well (no matter how many persons have each of these preferences). The converse is, of course, obviously true, since quasi-transitivity implies acyclicity. Further, the conditions that guarantee quasi-transitivity are the same as the conditions that guarantee full transitivity if the number of individuals is odd. (See Sen, 1969; Fishburn, 1972 and Pattanaik and Sengupta, 1974.) Thus, in terms of relaxation of conditions that are necessary and sufficient for transitivity through the two-stage weakening of the consistency condition to acyclicity, the gain is entirely related to the removal of the restriction of oddness of the number of voters.[8]

This is not to say that there is no real gain for MMD in relaxing the transitivity requirement to acyclicity. Even the removal of the requirement of odd-

---

6. See Sen (1970, Lemma 1*1). For generalizations of this result for infinite sets with additional restrictions, and some related theorems, see Bergstrom (1975), Brown (1973), Mukherji (1975), and Suzumura (1973). For consistency conditions on binary relations in general, see Richter (1966), Hansson (1968), Fishburn (1970, 1974a, and 1974b), Parks (1971), Sen (1971), Chipman et al. (1971), Schwartz (1972), Majumdar (1969 and 1970), Plott (1973), Jamison and Lau (1973), and Deb (1974).

7. Sufficiency is more naturally defined than necessity, which can be given several alternative interpretations (see Inada, 1969, Sen and Pattanaik, 1969, and Kelly, 1974a). The one used here is that 'a condition on the set of individual preferences is necessary if every violation of the condition yields a list of individual orderings such that some assignment of these orderings over some number of individuals will make the individual preference pattern lie outside the domain of $f$, i.e., would lead to the violation of the consistency condition in question' (Sen and Pattanaik, 1969, p. 181) [Essay 7 in this volume].

8. This is, however, not so when the individual preferences themselves can be intransitive (see Inada, 1970; Pattanaik, 1970 and 1971; Fishburn, 1970a, 1972, and 1973; Batra and Pattanaik, 1972 and Pattanaik and Sengupta, 1974).

ness is important, since 'the requirement that the number of non-indifferent individuals expressing themselves with respect to *every* triple be odd is rather severe' (Williamson and Sargent, 1967, p. 798). Further, for the class of restrictions that are number-dependent,[9] these coincidence results do not hold. Under the assumption of 'equi-probability' of all preference patterns, the probability of acyclicity holding will be clearly higher than that of transitivity holding. But even the probability of acyclicity seems rather low when the number of alternatives is large.[10] There is obviously some gain in moving to the choice set approach from the transitivity line, but this is far from doing away with the basic problem of majority inconsistency.

There remains, of course, the possibility of generating a choice function out of the majority decision relation without using (1), the so-called Condorcet condition. One possibility that has been explored in several different ways is that of taking the transitive closure $R^*$ of the majority decision relation $R$ over the set from which choice is to be made, i.e.,

$$xR^*y \text{ if and only if there exist } x_1, x_2, \ldots, x_n \in S: \qquad (2)$$
$$xRx_1, x_1Rx_2, \ldots, x_nRy,$$

and then choosing $\hat{C}(S, R^*)$ using definition (1) (see Schwartz, 1970; Bloomfield, 1971; Campbell, 1972; Deb, 1974 and Bordes, 1975a). This eliminates the strict preference cycles, e.g., $xPy, yPz,$ and $zPx$ yields $xI^*y, yI^*z, zI^*x.$ Some have seen in this a way of escaping the Arrow impossibility result with only a little relaxation of the conditions, and the procedure has been given several alternative axiomatizations which look appealing as a 'second best' way of solving the problem given the 'impossibility' theorems in general and majority cycles in particular.[11]

We shall have the occasion to go into this question a bit more in the next three sections in the context of a general discussion of 'collective rationality', but it should be remarked here that the way of solving the problem of intransitivity of $R$ by taking its transitive closure $R^*$ is particularly problematic for welfare judgements, i.e., for $IW$ and $JW$. In the example discussed above, while $y$ is regarded as strictly 'worse' than $x$, it is also regarded as among the 'best' in $(x, y, z)$. To use this approach for welfare comparisons is an invitation to boggle the mind. However, if the intention is to use the procedure for

---

9. See, for example, Nicholson (1965), Tullock (1967), Plott (1967), Hinich, Ledyard, and Ordeshook (1972), Saposnik (1975), Kuga and Nagatani (1974), Slutsky (1975 and 1975a), and Rosenthal (1975). These, however, do involve quite severe numerical restrictions.

10. The probability calculus has typically been done for the existence of majority winners (see Guilbaud, 1952; Riker, 1961; Campbell and Tullock, 1965; Garman and Kamien, 1968; Niemi and Weisberg, 1968; and De Meyer and Plott, 1970), and for large numbers of alternatives the probability of there being no majority winner is indeed very large. See also Jamison and Luce (1973).

11. The axiom systems have also thrown much light on precisely what causes the impossibility results.

decision making (*ID* and *JD*), where nothing else seems to promise salvation, the case for it may be thought to be rather stronger.

Turning now to the other half of the classification, viz., interest aggregation as opposed to judgement aggregation, I would like to argue that MMD has extremely little to offer for the former exercise. And this is essentially because MMD bases itself on individual *orderings* only, taking note neither of magnitudes of gains and losses, nor of rankings of well-being of different individuals. To see this, take the problem of a division of a cake among $n$ individuals ($n > 2$). Pick the worst off person and take away half his share, throw away half of that, and then divide the remainder among the rest. We have just made a majority improvement. To raise 'social welfare' still further, repeat the exercise. I doubt that this will do.

The cake division problem is rather an interesting one to consider in the context of MMD, partly because it is simple, but also because it invariably displays intransitivity[12]—the traditional reason for rejecting the majority rule. But the difficulty we are concerned with has nothing to do with intransitivity. Making the poor much poorer and passing on half the plunder to the rest would seem to be both wasteful and inequitous, but MMD strongly supports such a change. Intransitivity is not the source of our trouble here; in fact it may well be a partial saviour if the rule of using $R^*$, the transitive closure of $R$, is used. It is easily checked that, thanks to universal $P$-cycles, we get $xI^*y$ for every pair of distributions $[x, y]$ of the cake, and universal social indifference may be regarded as being less objectionable than perverse preference, even though it is not particularly attractive itself.[13]

The use of MMD for interest aggregation would seem to be, therefore, inappropriate. That leaves us with $JW$ and $JD$. But as was argued earlier, MMD is very problematic for social welfare judgements because of inconsistencies of the binary relation generated by it. The way out of taking the transitive closure $R^*$ was seen to be of little help for welfare judgements. That really leaves $JD$ only, viz., the exercise of aggregating individual judgements

---

12. For $n > 2$, with each preferring more cake to less.

13. The certainty of intransitivity (in fact, of cyclicity) in the cake division problem raises the question as to whether MMD will turn out to guarantee intransitivity in a wider class of problems. The most impressive theorem on this is that of Kramer (1973), who shows that MMD cyclicity is guaranteed by 'a very modest degree of heterogeneity of tastes' when the voters have quasi-concave differentiable utility functions over a multi-dimensional space. See also Heal (1973, Chapter 2) and Kramer and Klevorick (1974). Kramer notes that the pessimistic conclusions may be somewhat unwarranted when the problem is one of choosing 'from among a relatively small set of discrete proposals or candidates'. This is relevant for committee decisions. One can also argue that if the problem is one of aggregation of *interests* over a real space (e.g., a commodity space), which will very likely lead to intransitivity (as is clear from Kramer's elegant theorem), that fact is still not very disturbing, since, as argued here, MMD is inappropriate anyway for such problems. Indeed, preference cycles can soften the blow by forcing us to move from $R$ to its transitive closure $R^*$ with lots of indifferences replacing perverse preferences. See also Schofield (1975) and McKelvey (1976).

(rather than interests) to arrive at decisions (rather than social welfare judgements), e.g., in some types of committee decisions. Even there, MMD may lead to problems because of the violation of elementary properties of collective rationality, and much depends on which of these properties we regard as basic. In the next three sections this question is discussed in more general terms.

## 3  *Impossibility Results for Binary Social Relations*

In this section we discuss a class of impossibility results on collective choice rules, beginning with Arrow's (1951) general possibility theorem. Let $X$ be the set of alternative social states; it is assumed that there are at least three such states. There are at least two persons, and let them be numbered $i = 1$, ..., $n$. (Arrow's theorem does not hold for an infinite set of individuals without substantial modification (see Fishburn, 1970b; Kirman and Sondermann, 1972; Hansson, 1972 and Brown, 1974).) Each person $i$ has a preference ordering $R_i$. Any $n$-tuple of preference orderings—one ordering per person—is to be called a preference profile, or simply profile. $R$ stands for the binary relation of social preference.[14] Its symmetric and asymmetric factors are denoted $I$ (indifference) and $P$ (strict preference), respectively. $I_i$ and $P_i$ are the indifference and strict preference relations of persons $i$.

A 'collective choice rule' (CCR) specifies one social preference relation $R$ for each profile $[R_i]$,

$$R = f([R_i]).\tag{3}$$

Arrow was concerned with the case in which $R$ is required to be an ordering, and restricted his attention to such $f$ functions, which he called 'social welfare functions' (SWF). His general possibility theorem, in one version, uses four conditions imposed on the SWF:[15]

*Condition U* (Unrestricted Domain).    The domain of $f$ includes all logically possible $n$-tuples of individual preference orderings on $X$.

*Condition P* (Weak Pareto Principle).    For any $x$, $y$ in $X$, if everyone strictly prefers $x$ to $y$, then $xPy$.

*Condition D* (Non-dictatorship).    There is no person whose strict preference over any pair $[x, y]$ is invariably reflected in social strict preference,

---

14. Cases of stochastic individual or social choices, which will not be discussed in this paper, have been analysed by Zeckhauser (1969), Shepsle (1970 and 1972), Fishburn (1972a, 1972b, and 1975), and Intriligator (1973).

15. Arrow (1963) and Blau (1957). See also Arrow (1951), Murakami (1968), Hansson (1969 and 1973), Pattanaik (1971), Blau (1972), Fishburn (1973 and 1974), Wilson (1972 and 1975), and Binmore (1974, 1974a and 1975).

i.e., there is no $i$ such that for all profiles in the domain of $f$ and for all pairs $[x, y]$ in $X$, if $xP_iy$, then $xPy$.

*Condition I* (Independence of Irrelevant Alternatives). If for any subset $S$ of $X$, everyone's preference remains the same for every pair of alternatives from $S$, then the choice set of $S$ should remain the same too, i.e., $xR_iy$ if and only if $xR_i'y$ for all $x, y$ in $S$, for all $i$, implies that $C(S) = C'(S)$, when $C(S)$ and $C'(S)$ are the chosen elements of $S$ under the two profiles $[R_i]$ and $[R_i']$, respectively.[16]

Note that Condition $I$ has been stated in choice-theoretic terms, though all the other conditions are relation-theoretic. This contrast will prove to be of some significance when extensions of Arrow's theorem are considered. However, for Arrow's own case Condition $I$ corresponds exactly to the following relation-theoretic statement, denoting $R = f([R_i])$, bearing in mind Arrow's definition (Arrow, 1951, p. 15) of choice functions—the same as (1) above—and the fact that $R$ is required to be an ordering for a SWF.

*Condition I\** (Relation Independence). If for any pair $x, y$ in $S$, for all $i$: $xR_iy$ if and only if $xR_i'y$, and $yR_ix$ if and only if $yR_i'x$, then $f([R_i])$ and $f([R_i'])$ rank $x$ and $y$ in exactly the same way.

GPT (Arrow's General Possibility Theorem): *There exists no SWF satisfying Conditions U, I, P, and D.*

Escape routes from this result (and related ones) have been sought in many different ways,[17] and in this section and in the next two our concern will be with the condition of collective rationality only, i.e., with the requirement that social choice be guided by an ordering $R$. Two types of weakening have been considered. One line—pursued by, among others, Sen (1966, 1969, 1970, and 1970b), Pattanaik (1968 and 1971), Schick (1969), Gibbard (1969), Inada (1970), Mas-Colell and Sonnenschein (1972), Guha (1972), Ferejohn and Grether (1974), Deb (1974), and Blau and Deb (1975)—has been concerned with exploring the results of weakening the rationality requirements of $R$ (in particular, its transitivity). Another—pursued by, among others, Hansson (1969), Schwartz (1970 and 1972), Fishburn (1970, 1973, 1974 and 1974b), Plott (1971a and 1973), Batra and Pattanaik (1972a), Campbell (1972 and 1976), Parks (1971), Brown (1974 and 1975), Kelly (1974), Suzumura (1974

---

16. See Blau (1971), Hansson (1972), and Binmore (1974a) for illuminating discussions of the role of independence in Arrow's theorem. For impossibility theorems that do not make use of the inter-profile condition of independence of irrelevant alternatives (in fact, use no inter-profile condition at all), see Sen (1970b), Parks (1973), Kelly (1976), and Kemp and Ng (1976); see also Blau (1975).

17. Relaxing Condition $I$—an old favourite among Arrow-dodgers—has been utilized recently in a novel way by McManus (1975), who also provides a reformulation of the problem of social choice by introducing direct welfare comparisons across taste regimes for each individual and then making social welfare a function of the set of individual welfares.

and 1976a), Blair (1974 and 1975), Bordes (1975 and 1975a)—has investigated the consequences of studying social choice directly in terms of a choice function without involving a binary preference relation $R$. This can be done by making the value of the collective choice rule $f$ to be a choice function $C(\cdot)$. We may distinguish between:[18]

Relational collective choice rule:   $R = f([R_i])$;                     (4)

Functional collective choice rule:   $C(\cdot) = f([R_i])$.             (5)

It may look as if the distinction corresponds to our contrast between welfare judgement ($W$) problems and decision ($D$) problems. This is so only in a very limited way, and it will be argued later (Section 5) that the contrast between the two types of formulation has been overdrawn, which has been responsible for a certain amount of confusion in interpreting these results.

Arrow's GPT is dependent on the social preference relation $R$ being transitive. Within the framework of relational collective choice rules, it was shown that the impossibility result does not hold if $R$ is required to be only *quasi-transitive*, i.e., if $xPy$ and $yPz$ is taken to imply $xPz$, without demanding transitivity of indifference as well (Sen, 1969, Theorem V; see also Schick, 1969). A 'social decision function' (SDF) was defined by Sen (1969) to be a relational collective choice rule that always generates an $R$ such that $\hat{C}(S, R)$ is non-empty for all non-empty $S$. From the discussion in Section 2, we know that this requires $R$ to be acyclic, complete, and reflexive.

PROPOSITION 1.   *For a finite X, there is an SDF satisfying Conditions U, I, P, and D.*

This is established by an example, e.g., let $xRy$ unless $y$ is Pareto preferred to $x$. This collective choice rule is an SDF and satisfies all the conditions. In interpreting this impossibility-disappearance result, it must be remembered 'lest we jubilate too much' that 'Conditions $U, I, P$, and $D$ were thought by Arrow to be *necessary* for a reasonable social choice mechanism; he did not claim this set to be *sufficient* for it' (Sen, 1969, p. 388).[19]

Allan Gibbard showed, in a regrettably unpublished paper, in 1969 that

18. Fishburn (1973) defines a 'social choice function' as a functional relation of the form $F(S, [R_i])$ which specifies for any non-empty subset $S$ of $X$ and any $n$-tuple of individual preference orderings, a non-empty (choice) subset of $S$. This is essentially equivalent to (5). Collective choice procedures can also be seen as voting games, e.g., in Wilson (1971 and 1972a), Bloomfield (1971), Brown (1973), Kramer and Klevorick (1974), Salles (1975 and 1975a), Schofield (1975), and McKelvey (1976).

19. 'Does this mean that the Arrow problem is not really serious for social choice? I am afraid it does not. What all this really shows is how *economic* Arrow's impossibility theorem is. Release any of his restrictions and his result collapses ... In fact, it may be noted that Lemma 3*a, which says that any person who is decisive over a pair must be a dictator, still holds, for the proof does not use anything more than quasi-transitivity' (Sen, 1970, p. 49).

the class of SDF's generating quasi-transitive $R$ was restricted to 'oligarchies', viz., there is a unique group of persons in the community such that if anyone of them strictly prefers any $x$ to any $y$ $(xP_iy)$, society must regard $x$ to be at least as good as $y$ $(xRy)$, and if all members of the group strictly prefer $x$ to $y$ $(xP_iy$ for all $i)$, then society must strictly prefer $x$ to $y$ $(xPy)$.[20] Each person in the oligarchy has a veto.

PROPOSITION 2.    *Any SDF generating a quasi-transitive R and satisfying Conditions U, I, and P must be oligarchic.*[21]

A related result was proved by Mas-Colell and Sonnenschein (1972) by using the additional condition of 'positive responsiveness' $(PR)$, which permits the reinstatement of dictatorship. Let $R = f([R_i])$ and $R' = f([R_i'])$.

*Condition PR* (Positive Responsiveness).    If $R_i = R_i'$ for all $i$ except $j$, and either $(yP_jx$ and $xR_j'y)$ or $(xI_jy$ and $xP_j'y)$, then $xRy$ implies $xP'y$.

Social preference is required to move in the same direction as individual preferences.

PROPOSITION 3.    *Any SDF generating a quasi-transitive R and satisfying Conditions U, I, P, and PR, must be dictatorial, if there are at least three individuals.*

Remembering, however, that quasi-transitivity of $R$ is sufficient but not necessary to generate a choice function $\hat{C}(S, R)$ over a finite $X$, the question arises as to whether any *SDF* without a quasi-transitive $R$ may be free from these problems. Mas-Colell and Sonnenschein have proved the following important theorem. (A person $i$ has a veto if $xP_iy$ for him implies $xRy$.)

PROPOSITION 4.    *For any SDF satisfying Conditions U, I, P, and PR, if there are at least four individuals, then someone has a veto.*

As an alternative to using positive responsiveness the weaker property of 'non-negative responsiveness' ('monotonicity') coupled with a weak form of 'neutrality' provides another veto result.

*Condition NIM* (Weak Neutrality, Independence, and Monotonicity).    If

20. This important result was independently obtained also by Tom Schwartz, Andren Mas-Colell and Hugo Sonnenschein, and Ashok Guha. Guha also proved—using a stricter version of the Pareto principle—that there is an oligarchy for *every subset* of the set $N$ of individuals (Guha, 1972). If, for example, all members of the oligarchy $H$ were silenced, there will emerge a new oligarchy among the rest $(N - H)$.

21. For proof, see Sen (1970, pp. 76–7). (Note that the 'Anonymity' condition is not used until after the step related to Proposition 2 has been completed.) See also Mas-Colell and Sonnenschein (1972, Theorem 1).

for any $a, b, x, y$ in $X$, for all $i$:$aP_ib$ implies $xP_i' y$, and $yP_i' x$ implies $bP_ia$, then $aPb$ implies $xP' y$.

Blau and Deb (1975) have proved the following result:[22]

PROPOSITION 5. *For any SDF satisfying Conditions U and NIM, if the number of alternatives is at least as large as the number of individuals, then someone has a veto.*

The proof of Proposition 5 is sufficiently simple and illuminating to be presented here. If someone $i$ does not have a veto, then for some pair $[x, y]$, while he holds $xP_iy$, the social preference is $yPx$. Given non-negative responsiveness, if this is ever the case, it must be so when the person is unanimously opposed. Thus $xP_iy$ and $yP_jx$ for all $j \neq i$ must yield $yPx$. By Condition *NIM*, this must be so for all $[x, y]$ for any person $i$. Consider now the profile:

$$x_1P_1x_2, x_2P_1x_3, \ldots, x_{n-1}P_1x_n;$$
$$x_2P_2x_3, x_3P_2x_4, \ldots, x_nP_2x_1; \tag{6}$$
$$\cdot$$
$$\cdot$$
$$\cdot$$
$$x_nP_nx_1, x_1P_nx_2, \ldots, x_{n-2}P_nx_{n-1}.$$

From the hypothesis it follows that $x_1Px_2, \ldots, x_{n-1}Px_n, x_nPx_1$. Hence, if no person has a veto, acyclicity is violated and this is no SDF. So someone must have a veto.[23]

Blair (1974), Suzumura (1974), and Bordes (1975) have considered variations of Proposition 4 by dropping the 'acyclicity' requirement implicit in an SDF by requiring, respectively, the fulfilment of Property $\alpha$ (to be discussed in the next section), quasi-transitivity over triples, and acyclicity over triples. The last is the weakest condition of the three and is much weaker than acyclicity in general (see Sen, 1970, p. 16).

*Triple Acyclicity*: There is no triple $[x, y, z]$ such that $xPy$, $yPz$, and $zPx$.

PROPOSITION 6. *For any relational collective choice rule, generating only*

22. See also Hansson (1972), Brown (1973a, 1974, 1975, and 1975a), Ferejohn and Grether (1974), and Gauthier (1975) for related results. Brown (1963a) demonstrates that with individual acyclic preferences over an infinite set of bocial states, a collective choipe rule generating acyclic social preferences and satisfying Arrow's conditions will fail to produce an oligarchy only if there is a subset of individuals ('the collegium') who must all prefer $x$ to $y$ for social preference for $x$ against $y$; their unanimous assent is, thus, a necessary condition, though not sufficient.

23. Blau and Deb go on to prove that under the conditions postulated in Proposition 4 there is a 'veto hierarchy', i.e., a sequence $V_1, V_2, \ldots, V_n$ which is a partition of the set $N$ of all individuals, such that each $V_i$ is non-empty, and (i) each member of $V_n$ has a veto, (ii) each member of $V_t$ has a veto when all in $\cup_{i=1, \ldots, t-1} V_i$ are indifferent.

*reflexive, complete and triple-acyclic R, satisfying Conditions U, I, P, and PR, if there are at least four individuals, then someone has a veto.*

The proof is rather similar to that of Proposition 4.

Triple acyclicity is the weakest rationality condition on $R$ that will still permit choice sets over all triples, i.e., over the smallest subsets larger than pairs. Propositions 2 through 6 make the Arrovian gloom extend to one of the weakest requirements of collective rationality. If triple acyclicity is violated, there will be no guarantee that social preference relation $R$ will provide a binary basis for choice for any sets larger than pairs. So the violation of triple acyclicity would make it quite untenable to interpret $R$ as a welfare relation guiding optimal choice. This is very damaging for exercises of the $J$ type. What about decision problems ($D$ type)? The next section explores the connections between choice functions and preference relations, permitting us to examine in Section 5 the relevance of the impossibility results to $D$ type problems.

## 4   Choice Functions and Consistency Conditions

In the last section no attempt was made to break away from the relational collective choice rules. It has occasionally been supposed that that is the source of the problem. In general, functional collective choice rules are thought to provide greater freedom in choosing social decision procedures than relational collective choice rules. It will be argued that this is the case only in a very limited sense. A choice function has to satisfy some consistency conditions as well and there are obviously some correspondences between restrictions on $R$ for relational collective choice rules and those on $C(\cdot)$ for functional collective choice rules.[24]

Let $C(S)$ be the 'choice set' (the chosen elements) of a subset $S$ of $X$. A 'choice function' is a functional relation that specifies a non-empty choice set $C(S)$ for any non-empty subset $S$ of $X$.[25] Given a binary relation $R$ defined

24. The correspondences between choice functions and preference relations were traditionally studied in economics under the assumption of availability sets being 'budget sets' (e.g., Samuelson, 1938). There has, however, been much research recently on choice functions without that particular domain restriction. See Uzawa (1956), Houthakker (1956), Arrow (1959), Richter (1966), Sen (1966, 1969, 1970, and 1971), Hansson (1968), Pattanaik (1968 and 1971), Majumdar (1969 and 1970), Fishburn (1970, 1974a, and 1974b), Wilson (1970), Parks (1971), Chipman, *et al.* (1972), Rader (1972), Schwartz (1972), Campbell (1972), Herzberger (1973), Plott (1973), Brown (1973 and 1975), Suzumura (1973, 1974, and 1976), Smith (1974), Deb (1974), Blair (1974 and 1974a), Kelly (1974), Bergstrom (1975), Mukherji (1975), Bordes (1975 and 1975a), among others.

25. The effects of domain restrictions are of interest, though in this note we impose no restrictions. The results are easy to accommodate in a more general framework as long as all pairs and triples are included.

over $X$, a choice set $\hat{C}(S, R)$ can be defined by pairwise comparison, as expressed in (1), following a procedure discussed by Condorcet. Similarly, a binary relation $R_C$ can be obtained from any choice function $C(\cdot)$, such that for any $x$, $y$ in $X$:

$$xR_Cy \text{ if and only if for some subset } S \text{ of } X, x \text{ is in } C(S) \text{ and } y \text{ in } S. \qquad (7)$$

A choice function is 'normal' if and only if the binary relation $R_C$ generated by a choice function through (7) regenerates that choice function through (1) (Sen, 1971). Normality holds if and only if for all non-empty $S$ in $X$:

$$C(S) = \hat{C}(S, R_C). \qquad (8)$$

It is obvious that if a choice function is normal, then the information content of the choice function $C(\cdot)$ is the same as that of the binary relation $R_C$. In this sense, a normal choice function is essentially binary (see Sen, 1971 and Herzberger, 1973).[26]

There is, however, another sense of binariness, which may be thought to be more elementary. Take the relation obtained by looking at choices over pairs only:

$$x\bar{R}_Cy \text{ if and only if } x \text{ is in } C([x, y]). \qquad (9)$$

Herzberger (1973) has called $\bar{R}_C$ the 'base relation' of the choice function. 'Binariness' may also be defined as (see Bordes, 1975) holding if and only if for all non-empty $S$ in $X$:

$$C(S) = \hat{C}(S, \bar{R}_C). \qquad (10)$$

A choice function satisfying (10) may be called 'basic binary'.

It is easily checked that the following proposition is true:

PROPOSITION 7. *A choice function is normal if and only if it is basic binary.*[27]

This gives a crucial role to the base relation $\bar{R}_C$ in the analysis of choice functions. This is of relevance in analysing impossibility theorems of the class pioneered by Arrow (1951).

Normality and basic binariness can be seen to be equivalent to the fulfilment of two consistency conditions of choice, viz., Properties $\alpha$ and $\gamma$.

*Property $\alpha$.* For all $S$ and $T$, with $S$ a subset of $T$, any $x$ that belongs to $S$ and to $C(T)$, belongs to $C(S)$.

---

26. This corresponds to Richter's (1966) concept of 'rationalizability'. See also Plott (1973).

27. Indeed, $R_C = \bar{R}_C$ if (8) or (10) holds. See Sen (1971, T.5 and T.7), Herzberger (1973, Theorem 1), and Bordes (1975a, Theorem 1).

*Property γ.* For any class $M$ of sets, if $x$ belongs to $C(S)$ for all $S$ in $M$, then $x$ belongs to $C(\cup M)$.

PROPOSITION 8. *A choice function is normal if and only if it satisfies Properties α and γ* (Sen, 1971, p. 314).

Two weakened versions of $α$ and $γ$ in line with concentrating on pairwise choice only are, in fact, also adequate for normality.[28]

*Property α2.* For any $S$, if $x$ belongs to $C(S)$, then it belongs to $C([x, y])$ for all $y$ in $S$.

*Property γ2.* For any $S$, if $x$ belongs to $C([x, y])$ for all $y$ in $S$, then $x$ belongs to $C(S)$.

PROPOSITION 9. *A choice function is normal if and only if it satisfies α2 and γ2.*

In view of Propositions 8 and 9:

PROPOSITION 10. *In the presence of α2, γ2 is equivalent to γ, and in the presence of γ2, α2 is equivalent to α.*

Since $α$ implies $α2$ and $γ$ implies $γ2$, it follows that in the presence of $α$ (resp. $γ$), $γ$ (resp. $α$) is equivalent to $γ2$ (resp. $α2$).

Note that $α$ is concerned with keeping a chosen alternative $x$ choosable as the set is *contracted* (by dropping other alternatives), while $γ$ is concerned with keeping a chosen alternative $x$ choosable as it is *expanded* (by adding other alternatives dominated by $x$ in other choices). Essentially, therefore, we can see $α$ and $γ$ to be concerned, respectively, with consistency of inclusion under set-contraction and set-expansion—a distinction that will prove to be of importance in dealing with impossibility theorems in social choice theory.

Consistency under set-expansion can be viewed from another point of view also. If $x$ is chosen from $S$ from which $y$ is also chosen, then in an expanded set $T$, $x$ must also be chosen if $y$ is.

*Property β.* If $x$ and $y$ both belong to $C(S)$, and $S$ is a subset of $T$, then $x$ must belong to $C(T)$, if $y$ does.

The following Proposition can be established (Sen, 1970):

PROPOSITION 11. *A choice function $C(\cdot)$ is normal and generates an ordering $R_C$ if and only if it satisfies α and β.*

---

28. Herzberger (1973, pp. 204–5). Property $γ2$ has been called by Plott (1973) 'Extension' $(E)$ and by Blair (1974) 'Generalized Condorcet Property' $(GC)$.

Note that $\beta$ is concerned with a consistency property under set expansion that is somewhat different in spirit from $\gamma$. $\gamma$ requires that an element that beats (or draws with) every other element in smaller contests should be a winner in the large contest as well, whereas $\beta$ requires that if two elements 'draw' in a smaller contest (in the sense of both winning) then they must not be separated in a larger contest (in the sense that if one wins, so should the other).[29] It is, however, clear from Propositions 8 and 11 that in the presence of $\alpha$, $\beta$ must imply $\gamma$.

Is there a strengthened version of $\beta$ that incorporates $\gamma$ whether or not $\alpha$ holds? The following strengthened version of $\beta$ does exactly that.[30]

*Property $\beta(+)$.*   If $x$ belongs to $C(S)$ and $y$ belongs to $S$ which is a subset of $T$, then $x$ must belong to $C(T)$ if $y$ does.

PROPOSITION 12.   *If a choice function satisifes $\beta(+)$, it satisfies both $\beta$ and $\gamma$, but the converse does not hold.*

That $\beta(+)$ implies $\beta$ is immediate. To show that $\beta(+)$ implies $\gamma$, let there be an $x$ such that it belongs to both $C(S)$ and $C(T)$, but not to $C(S \cup T)$. Since $C(S \cup T)$ is not empty, let $y$ belong to it. Clearly $y$ must belong to $S$ or to $T$. Whichever it is (or both), by $\beta(+)$, $x$ must belong to $C(S \cup T)$ after all. Which contradiction shows that $\gamma$ is implied by $\beta(+)$. Regarding the converse, the following counterexample is adequate: $[x] = ([x, y])$, $[y] = C([y, z])$, $[x] = C([x, z])$, and $[x, z] = C([x, y, z])$, which satisfies $\beta$ and $\gamma$ but not $\beta(+)$.

Property $\beta(+)$ is, therefore, a fairly strong requirement incorporating both types of consistency of inclusion under expansion, viz., $\gamma$ and $\beta$, but is somewhat stronger than the union of the two. We shall call $\beta(+)$ the 'strongest expansion-consistency' to be contrasted with the 'weakest contraction-consistency'—a much weakened version of $\alpha$—to bring out their contrasting roles in precipitating impossibility results in social choice theory.[31]

29. To show the independence of the two types of expansion consistency, consider the two following examples. Example 1: $[x] = C([x, y])$, $[y] = C([y, z])$, $[x] = C([x, z])$, and $[y] = C([x, y, z])$. This satisfies $\beta$ but not $\gamma$. Example 2: $[x] = C([x, y])$, $[y] = C([y, z])$, $[x, z] = C([x, z])$, and $[x] = C([x, y, z])$. This satisfies $\gamma$ but not $\beta$.

30. Proposed by Bordes (1975a) in a somewhat different context to be discussed in Section 5. Bordes has pointed out to me that the informal example given in Sen (1970) in explaining $\beta$ is, in fact, exactly an explanation of $\beta(+)$: 'if some Pakistani is a world champion, then *all* champions of Pakistan must be champions of the world' (p. 17).

31. Note that 'expansion' and 'contraction' consistency refer to the property of *inclusion*. Indeed, the roles can be reversed for *exclusion*. $\beta(+)$ can be formulated as: if $y$ belongs to $C(T)$ and $x$ does not, and if $y$ belongs to a subset $S$ of $T$, then $x$ should not belong to $C(S)$. This looks superficially like contraction consistency, but note that the consistency demanded is of *exclusion* and not of inclusion. Similarly, $\alpha$ can superficially look like a condition of expansion consistency if the focus is exclusion: if $x$ does not belong to $C(S)$, then it does not belong to $C(T)$ if $S$ is a subset of $T$. It is important to recognize, therefore, that both expansion and contraction consistency refer to *inclusion* conditions.

Before we move to the weakening of $\alpha$, one important aspect of $\beta(+)$ is worth checking. Does $\beta(+)$ imply anything about the regularity properties of the preference relations $R_C$ and $\bar{R}_C$ generated by the choice function? Bordes (1975a) has shown that $\beta(+)$ guarantees that $R_C$ must be transitive.

PROPOSITION 13.    *If $C(\cdot)$ satisfies $\beta(+)$, then $R_C$ is transitive.*

Let $xR_Cy$ and $yR_Cz$. Then there are $S$ and $T$ such that $x$ is in $C(S)$, $y$ in both $S$ and $C(T)$, and $z$ in $T$. Consider now $C(S \cup T)$. If some element (say, $w$) in $T$ is in $C(S \cup T)$, then by $\beta(+)$ $y$ is in $C(S \cup T)$. But since $y$ belongs to $S$, by $\beta(+)$ again, $x$ is in $C(S \cup T)$. Hence, $xR_Cz$. This leaves the case in which no element of $T$ is in $C(S \cup T)$. Then clearly some element of $S$ is in $C(S \cup T)$, which by $\beta(+)$ must also include $x$. Hence, $xR_Cz$ in this case also.

But note that $\beta(+)$ does not guarantee the transitivity—not even acyclicity or triple acyclicity—of the base relation $\bar{R}_C$—a fact which will prove to be of significance for the impossibility theorems (Section 5).

PROPOSITION 14.    *A choice function satisfying $\beta(+)$ does not imply that its base relation $\bar{R}_C$ must be triple acyclic.*

Consider the example $[x] = C([x, y])$, $[y] = C([y, z])$, $[z] = C([z, x])$, $[x, y, z] = C([x, y, z])$.

This example also makes clear that in the fulfilment of transitivity of $R_C$, there can be an element of pulling oneself up by one's bootstraps. It is $[x, y, z] = C([x, y, z])$ which leads to transitivity being satisfied all around. What it violates robustly is any vestige of contraction-consistency. Which brings us to $\alpha$.

Does $\alpha$ guarantee transitivity? No, but as Fishburn, Blair, and Suzumura have noted, it guarantees the acyclicity of the base relation $\bar{R}_C$.

PROPOSITION 15.    *If a choice function $C(\cdot)$ satisfies $\alpha$, then $\bar{R}_C$ is acyclic.*

Suppose $\bar{R}_C$ is not acyclic. Then there is a finite sequence $x_1\bar{P}_Cx_2$, $x_2\bar{P}_Cx_3$, ..., $x_n\bar{P}_Cx_1$. Consider $C([x_1, \ldots, x_n])$. Whatever is chosen must now contradict Property $\alpha$.

Since $\alpha$ also implies that $R_C = \bar{R}_C$ (Sen, 1971, T.7), clearly it guarantees the acyclicity of $R_C$ as well.

Property $\alpha$ has been widely used as a fundamental consistency requirement of choice (see, for example, Nash, 1950; Arrow, 1951, p. 27; Radner and Marschak, 1954; Chernoff, 1954; and Luce and Raiffa, 1957), and it has been known by various names.[32] As noted before, it is essentially a condition of contraction-consistency. Is it possible to weaken it without losing this

32. Including being called 'independence of irrelevant alternatives', causing not a little confusion. On this, see Ray (1973).

characteristic? Fishburn (1974b) has proposed various weakenings of this condition; the weakest version he considers, viz., his A5, which he describes as 'just about the weakest imaginable vestige' of $\alpha$ (his A1), is the following.

*Fishburn's Condition A5.* If $S$ contains more than two alternatives and if $x$ is in $C(S)$, then $x$ is in $C([x, y])$ for some $y \neq x$ in $S$.

For our purpose this is unsuitable, since this permits no chosen element $x$ to get any guarantee of being chosen vis-à-vis other alternatives in $S$ (except one) through contraction-consistency. The binary version of $\alpha$, viz., $\alpha 2$, discussed earlier in this note, requires $x$ to be in $C([x, y])$ for all $y$ in $S$, and contrasts with Fishburn's Condition A5 in this respect.

It is, however, possible to argue that contraction-consistency need not be demanded for more than one of the elements in the choice set $C(S)$, since we need choose only one element, and this is a weakening of $\alpha 2$ in a direction different from Fishburn's.

*Property $\alpha(-)$.* For each non-empty $S$, for *some* $x$ in $C(S)$, $x$ is in $C([x, y])$ for all $y$ in $S$.

Note that this is a minimal condition of contraction-consistency in the sense of retaining it for at least one chosen element.[33]

Property $\alpha(-)$ may be weakened even further if we demand its fulfilment only for the smallest subsets larger than a pair (for pairs, of course, the problem of contraction-consistency does not arise), viz., for triples. This we call the 'weakest contraction-consistency' property.[34]

*Property $\alpha(--)$.* For each triple $S$, for some $x$ is $C(S)$, $x$ is in $C([x, y])$ for all $y$ in $S$.

PROPOSITION 16. *A choice function satisfying Property $\alpha(--)$ must have its base relation $\bar{R}_C$ triple acyclic.*

Consider any triple $[x, y, z]$, and let $\alpha(--)$ hold with $x$ being the element in the choice set of the triple referred to in the statement of $\alpha(--)$. Then clearly $x\bar{R}_C y$ and $x\bar{R}_C z$, which rules out a $\bar{P}_C$-cycle.

Note that the converse does not hold, as seen from this example: $[x] = C([x, y])$, $[y] = C([y, z])$, $[x] = C([x, z])$, and $[y] = C([x, y, z])$, which does not satisfy $\alpha(--)$, but $\bar{R}_C$ is triple acyclic.[35]

33. Note that neither does $\alpha(-)$ imply Fishburn's A5, nor does the latter imply $\alpha(-)$. The former is seen by considering the example: $[x] = C([x, y])$, $[y] = C([y, z])$, $[x] = C([x, z])$, and $[x, z] = C([x, y, z])$ which satisfies $\alpha(-)$ but not Fishburn's A5. The latter is seen in the example: $[x] = C([x, y])$, $[y] = C([y, z])$, $[z] = C([x, z])$, and $[x] = C([x, y, z])$, which satisfies Fishburn's A5 but not $\alpha(-)$.

34. It is 'weakest' subject to the condition that some element in the choice set of a triple retains contracting-consistency.

35. Note that in the example considered, $\gamma$ is also violated. Given $\gamma$ or $\gamma 2$, a triple-acyclic $\bar{R}_C$ must lead to $\alpha(--)$ being satisfied.

Finally, a class of consistency properties has been referred to in the literature as 'path independence', which has been illuminatingly analysed by Plott (1973). Plott's version of path independence can be stated in several different ways, one of which is the following:

*PI* (Path independence): For any pair of sets *S* and *T*:

$$C(S \cup T) = C(C(S) \cup C(T)).\qquad(13)$$

Of the two motivations for path independence discussed by Plott, the one that seems to be more persuasive is based on making the process of selection independent of the way the alternatives are split up. To quote Plott:

> the process of choosing, from a dynamic point of view, frequently pro-
> ceeds in a type of 'divide and conquer' manner. The alternatives are
> 'split up' into smaller sets, a choice is made over each of these sets, the
> chosen elements are collected, and then a choice is made from them.
> Path independence, in this case, would mean that the final result would
> be independent of the way the alternatives were initially divided up for
> consideration (1973, pp. 1079–80).[36]

It is easily checked that *PI* implies $\alpha$. In fact, an important result was established by Parks (1971) (reported by Plott, 1973, p. 1088) showing $\alpha$ to be equivalent to a part of path independence.

PROPOSITION 17. *A choice function satisfies Property $\alpha$ if and only if for all pairs of sets S and T:*

$$C(S \cup T) \subseteq C(C(S) \cup C(T)).\qquad(14)$$

Let (14) be true. Consider now an *x* in a subset *A* of *B* belonging also to the choice set *C(B)*. By (14), *x* belongs to $C(C(A) \cup C(B - A))$. This is impossible unless *x* belongs to *C(A)*. Hence, $\alpha$ holds. To prove the converse, consider any *x* which belongs to $C(S \cup T)$. If *x* belongs to *S*, then by $\alpha$, it belongs to *C(S)*. If it does not belong to *S*, then it must belong to *T*, and by $\alpha$, it belongs to *C(T)*. In either case it belongs to $C(S) \cup C(T)$. This is a subset of $S \cup T$, and by $\alpha$, *x* must belong to $C(C(S) \cup C(T))$, which establishes (14).

Stringing Propositions 15 and 17 together we know that the preference relation $R_C$ and the base relation $\bar{R}_C$ generated by a path independent choice function must be acyclic. Blair (1974), Kelly (1974), and Suzumura (1974) have noted that a stronger result is true:

PROPOSITION 18. *A path independent choice function generates a quasi-transitive $\bar{R}_C$.*

36. This is, strictly speaking, a justification of what Suzumura (1974) calls 'weak path independence', which requires that *S* and *T* referred to in (13) be disjoint, but the rationale can be extended
to the case in which we do not start from a partition ('split up') of the set of alternatives.

Consider $x\bar{P}_C y$ and $y\bar{P}_C z$, which means that $[x] = C([x, y])$ and $[y] = C([y, z])$. By $PI$, $[x] = C([x, y, z])$. If $not\ x\bar{P}_C z$, then $z$ is in $C([x, z])$. Then $C([x, y, z]) = C(C([x, y] \cup C([z])) = C([x, z])$, which must contain $z$, and that is a contradiction.

An axiomatization of path independence has been established by Blair (1974), by coupling $\alpha$ with a condition he calls $\varepsilon$.

*Property $\varepsilon$.* If $A$ is a subset of $B$, then $C(B)$ should not be a proper subset of $C(A)$.

PROPOSITION 19. *A choice function is path independent if and only if it satisfies $\alpha$ and $\varepsilon$.*

From Proposition 17 we know that $PI$ implies $\alpha$. To check that it satisfies $\varepsilon$, consider $A \subseteq B$, and note that $B = A \cup B$. By $PI$:

$$C(B) = C(C(A) \cup C(B)).$$

If $\varepsilon$ does not hold, then $C(B)$ is a proper subset of $C(A)$, and $C(C(A) \cup C(B))$ $= C(C(A))$, which equals $C(A)$, by $\alpha$. So $C(A) = C(B)$ after all, which is a contradiction. To prove the converse, note that $C(S) \cup C(T)$ is a subset of $S \cup T$, and hence by $\varepsilon$:

$$C(S \cup T) \not\subset C(C(S) \cup C(T)). \tag{15}$$

But by $\alpha$, (14) holds, and (14) and (15) together imply (13), guaranteeing path independence.

Note that $\varepsilon$ is an expansion-consistency condition like $\gamma$, $\beta$, and $\beta(+)$. It demands that as we move from choosing from a subset $A$ of $B$ to choosing from $B$ itself, we should not drop off some elements of $C(A)$ retaining others, unless we include in $C(B)$ some outside elements not in $C(A)$. It is a strengthening of a condition called $\delta$ used in Sen (1971): 'if $x$ and $y$ are both best in $S$, a subset of $T$, then neither of them can be uniquely best in $T$' (p. 315). Under $\delta$ some elements of $C(A)$ can be dropped as long as more than one is retained (without any element from outside $C(A)$ being included in $C(B)$—a condition shared by both $\delta$ and $\varepsilon$).[37]

It is easily checked that $\gamma$ and $\varepsilon$ are independent, and in fact normality (i.e., the conjunction of $\alpha$ and $\gamma$) is also independent of path independence (i.e.,

---

37. Plott (1973) shows that $PI$ and $\gamma 2$ (his $E$) together are equivalent to normality (rationalizability) with a quasi-transitive base relation. To appreciate the result, note that $PI$ implies $\alpha$ and $\varepsilon$, and while $\alpha$ and $\gamma 2$ guarantees normality, $\varepsilon$ implies $\delta$. A normal choice function satisfying $\delta$ has a quasi-transitive $R_C (= \bar{R}_C)$ relation (Sen, 1971, T.10). The fact that the converse also holds indicates that the difference between $\varepsilon$ and $\delta$ is wiped out in the presence of $\alpha$ and $\gamma$ (or $\gamma 2$).

the conjunction of $\alpha$ and $\varepsilon$.[38] But all these different expansion-consistency properties are subsumed by $\beta(+)$.

PROPOSITION 20.    *A choice function satisfying $\beta(+)$ satisfies $\beta$, $\gamma$, $\delta$, and $\varepsilon$.*

That $\beta(+)$ subsumes $\beta$ and $\gamma$, we know from Proposition 12. We can check that $\beta$ subsumes $\varepsilon$ by noting that a violation of $\varepsilon$ implies that some elements of $C(A)$ are included without others being included in $C(B)$ for some $A \subseteq B$, and this implies a violation of $\beta$. That $\varepsilon$ implies $\delta$ has already been noted.

It would appear that $\beta(+)$ does deserve its somewhat pretentious informal description as 'the strongest expansion-consistency property'.

Finally, just as one part of path independence, viz., (14), is equivalent to $\alpha$, the other part follows from $\beta(+)$ without, however, implying $\beta(+)$ or even $\beta$. (Hardly surprising that, since if it had implied $\beta$, then *PI* would have implied normality, which we have seen it does not.) The part of *PI* in question is the complement to (14):

$$C(C(S) \cup C(T)) \subseteq C(S \cup T). \tag{16}$$

Following Ferejohn and Grether (1975) we denote this *PI*, corresponding to (14) being called *PI**, the two together making up *PI*. They interpret, with some justice, Arrow's justification for 'path independence' in terms of avoiding 'decisions that are clearly unsatisfactory' (1963, p. 120) as a justification for *PI*, and argue that 'a satisfactory choice procedure is one that ensures that if the problem of choosing over $V$ is broken up into choosing over $V_1$ and $V_2$ [with $V_1 \cup V_2 = V$] and then choosing over the remaining elements [chosen elements from $V_1$ and $V_2$], the final choice from this procedure should still be in the choice set from $V$' (p. 3).

Bordes has noted a result that is of some interest in this context:

PROPOSITION 21.    *A choice function satisfying $\beta(+)$ must satisfy *PI*.*

Let $x$ be in $C(S \cup T)$. Without loss of generality, let $x$ be in $S$. Then by $\beta(+)$, $C(S) \subseteq C(S \cup T)$. Since $C(S) \cup C(T)$ is a subset of $S \cup T$, and some element of the former is in the choice set $C(S \cup T)$, by $\beta(+)$ again: $C(C(S) \cup C(T)) \subseteq C(S \cup T)$.

So some kind of path independence is guaranteed by $\beta(+)$, but not full path independence in Plott's sense.

_____

38. From Proposition 18 it is clear that any normal choice function with a non-quasi-transitive $\bar{R}_C$ will be an example of normality without path independence, e.g., $[x] = C([x, y])$, $[y] = C([y, z])$, $[x, z] = C([x, z])$, and $[x] = C([x, y, z])$. The converse case was discussed by Plott (1973), i.e., path independent but not normal, e.g., $[x, y] = C([x, y])$, $[y, z] = C([y, z])$, $[x, z] = C([x, z])$, and $[x] = C([x, y, z])$.

To conclude this section on consistency conditions on choice, a few of the more important conclusions may be briefly stated:

(i) There are two basic types of consistency conditions, viz., those that are concerned with *contraction-consistency* (e.g., $\alpha$), and those that deal with *expansion-consistency* (e.g., $\beta$, $\gamma$, $\delta$, $\varepsilon$, and $\beta(+)$).

(ii) $\beta(+)$ subsumes all the expansion-consistency properties proposed. In fact, $\beta(+)$ implies $\beta$, which implies $\varepsilon$, which implies $\delta$. It also implies $\gamma$. In the presence of $\alpha$, $\beta$ and $\beta(+)$ are equivalent, and $\beta$ implies $\gamma$.

(iii) Normality, which is equivalent to basic binariness, corresponds exactly to $\alpha$ and $\gamma$ together. Normality with a transitive base relation $\bar{R}_C$ is equivalent to $\alpha$ and $\beta$ together.

(iv) Path independence is equivalent to $\alpha$ and $\varepsilon$. One part of path independence, $PI^*$, guarantees that all elements of $C(S)$ are choosable through every path (through any subdivision of $S$); this is equivalent to $\alpha$. The other part, $^*PI$, guaranteeing that all choosable points through each path are in $C(S)$, is implied by $\beta(+)$.

(v) Acyclicity of the base relation ($\bar{R}_C$) and of the preference relation generated ($R_C$) are guaranteed by $\alpha$, and therefore by $PI^*$. Quasi-transitivity of each is guaranteed by path independence. Transitivity of the preference relation follows from $\beta(+)$, which does not, however, imply the transitivity (or even acyclicity or triple acyclicity) of the base relation. The 'weakest contraction-consistency property', viz., $\alpha(--)$, ensures triple acyclicity.

## 5    *Impossibility Results for Choice Functions*

In Section 3, a class of impossibility results was presented within the framework of *relational* collective choice rules. In view of Proposition 8, these results will apply to *functional* collective choice rules as well if the choice function for society is taken to be normal, i.e., if social choice satisfies $\alpha$ and $\gamma$. There is, obviously, nothing to be gained in terms of avoiding impossibility by moving from relational to functional collective choice rules if normality of social choice is to be insisted on.

This much is obvious. What does not seem to have been quite so obvious is that even if normality of social choice is not insisted on, impossibility results for the relation collective choice rules translate immediately to functional CCR's. This recognition is impeded by Arrow's formulation of the condition of independence of irrelevant alternatives (Condition *I* above) in terms of a choice function which, by virtue of its binary construction, given by (1), must be normal or basic binary. In fact, in proving the theorem (GPT), normality has no part whatsoever, and the impossibility is precipitated by non-transitivity of the base relation $\bar{R}_C$ without going into choice sets $C(S)$ for $S$ larger than pairs. In this sense, the relational collective choice rules provide a *less* and not *more* demanding framework than functional collective choice rules satisfying the same restriction for choices over pairs.

All the impossibility results discussed in Section 3 are in fact about base relations $\bar{R}_C$ only, as is clear from the proofs. All references to the 'social preference relation' $R$ can be replaced by references to $\bar{R}_C$, and then these theorems can be seen to be about *functional* collective choice rules as well without any assumption of normality or basic binariness of the choice function for society in general. Arrow's independence condition (Condition *I*) obscures this by carrying a lot of excess baggage, and the alternative version (Condition *I\**), which is equivalent to it under Arrow's assumption of normality and transitivity, is in fact much weaker in general. It is, however, adequate for the entire class of relational impossibility results Propositions 2 through 6, and related ones, under the general interpretation of taking $R$ as the base relation $\bar{R}_C$.[39] Essentially, a relational collective choice rule for this purpose can be viewed as a functional relation:

$$\bar{R}_C = f([R_i]).\tag{3*}$$

Under this interpretation, Propositions 2 through 6 immediately imply a host of impossibility results for functional collective choice rules, taking into account the correspondences between consistency properties of choice functions and the regularity conditions of the base relation $\bar{R}_C$ analysed in the last section. While many of these important results have been proved independently by Blair (1974), Kelly (1974), Suzumura (1974), and Bordes (1975), to be published jointly in Blair, *et al.* (1976), they can in fact be derived from impossibility theorems on relational CCR's under the interpretation given by (3*).

PROPOSITION 22.   *Any functional CCR generating choice functions with quasi-transitive $\bar{R}_C$, and satisfying Conditions U, I\*, and P, must be oligarchic.*[40].

This is, in fact, the same as Proposition 2 under the interpretation $R = \bar{R}_C$. This and the following theorems exploit the fact that in Propositions 2 through 6 the use of Condition *I* is confined to *I\** only.

---

39. Fishburn (1974) and Binmore (1975) have recently translated some of the binary impossibility results into corresponding *m*-ary impossibility theorems. For example, Fishburn (1974) proves a 'generalized impossibility theorem' showing the inconsistency of *m*-ary versions of independence, Pareto principle, nonweak-dictatorship, positive responsiveness, for a collective rationality condition he calls $(R_m)$, which amounts to an *m*-ary version of contraction-consistency. Similar *m*-ary translations should be possible with the other theorems focusing on the base relation $\bar{R}_C$.

40. Suzumura (1974, Theorem 1 and Remark 2) established directly the existence of a person with veto. The full oligarchic structure also follows from Proposition 2. See also Fishburn (1973, Theorem 16.2), Blair (1974), and Kelly (1974).

In view of Proposition 18, which shows that path-independent choice functions must generate quasi-transitive base relations, it follows immediately from Proposition 22 that:

PROPOSITION 23.   *Any functional CCR generating path independent choice functions, and satisfying Conditions U, I\*, and P, must be oligarchic.*[41]

Similarly, by Propositions 3 and 18:

PROPOSITION 24.   *If the number of individuals is 3 or more, any functional CCR generating path independent choice functions, and satisfying Conditions U, I\*, P, and PR, must be dictatorial.* (Cf. Blair, 1974; Kelly, 1974; and Suzumura, 1974.)

Again, by Proposition 15 a choice function satisfying Property $\alpha$ must generate an acyclic $\bar{R}_C$. Combining this result with Proposition 5 we get:

PROPOSITION 25.   *If the number of alternatives in X is at least as large as the number of individuals, then any functional CCR satisfying Conditions U and NIM, and generating choice functions satisfying Property $\alpha$, must give someone a veto.*

Similarly, stringing together Proposition 16, using the weakest contraction-consistency property $\alpha(--)$, and Proposition 6, it is seen that:

PROPOSITION 26.   *If the number of individuals is four or more, then any functional CCR satisfying Conditions U, I, P\*, and PR (positive responsiveness), and generating choice functions satisfying Property $\alpha(--)$, must give someone a veto.*

Note, however, that $\beta(+)$, which implies that the preference relation $R_C$ must be transitive, does not imply any such thing—not even triple acyclicity—for the base relation $\bar{R}_C$. It is this contrast, which makes it impossible to translate the impossibility results of relational CCR's (with $R$ or $\bar{R}_C$) to functional CCR's generating choice functions satisfying the 'strongest expansion-consistency property' $\beta(+)$ without any of the contraction-consistency properties. Bordes (1975a) shows:

PROPOSITION 27.   *There exists a functional CCR satisfying Conditions U, I, P, pair positive responsiveness, N (neutrality), and A (anonymity), and generating choice functions satisfying $\beta(+)$.*

41. Blair (1974), Kelly (1974), and Suzumura (1974) have proved the existence of veto ('weak dictatorship') directly.

The proof, which is essentially an adaptation of the example involving the transitive closure $R^*$ of the weak majority relation $R$, is in the same spirit as Schwartz (1970 and 1972) and Campbell (1972).[42] We may call the rule of choosing through the transitive closure of the majority rule the majority closure method (MCM). It is clear that making social choices through $\hat{C}(S, R^*)$ satisfies $U, P, N$, and $A$. One might, however, wonder about the fulfilment of the condition of independence of irrelevant alternatives, which calls for some discussion. Consider the classic paradox of voting with Person 1 preferring $x$ to $y$ to $z$, Person 2 preferring $y$ to $z$ to $x$, and Person 3 preferring $z$ to $x$ to $y$, leading to $xPy$, $yPz$, and $zPx$, in terms of the majority rule. In terms of $R^*$ over the triple $[x, y, z]$, clearly $xI^*y$, $yI^*z$, and $zI^*x$. If now Person 3 should give up preferring $z$ to $x$ to $y$, and relocate $z$ vis-à-vis $x$ by preferring $x$ to $z$ to $y$, we shall get $xPy$, $yPz$, and $xPz$. In terms of $R^*$ over the triple: $xP^*y$, $yP^*z$, $xP^*z$. It might look as if Condition $I$ is violated since $xI^*y$ gets converted to $xP^*y$ through a change of Person 3's preference over $x$ and $z$, an 'irrelevant' pair. But this is not so, since the choice over the pair $[x, y]$ is not to be guided by $R^*$ generated over the triple $[x, y, z]$, but by $R^*$ over that set $[x, y]$ itself, and this means that $R^*$ for the purpose of the choice over $[x, y]$ remains the same, viz., $xP^*y$, in either case. So Condition $I$ is kept satisfied by using $R^*$ generated by $R$ over $S$ for choosing from $S$ through $\hat{C}(S, R^*)$.

The point at issue is, therefore, simply the adequacy of $\beta(+)$ as a consistency condition. As seen before, in Proposition 20, $\beta(+)$ is a very inclusive criterion of expansion-consistency, justifying our calling it the 'strongest expansion-consistency property', but it does not include any guarantee of contraction-consistency.[43] So the basic question relating to this class of impossibility results is: Do we want any contraction-consistency property? If so, we are in trouble. If not, we can sail through easily, no matter how much expansion-consistency we want to incorporate in our social choices.

Turning now to our classification of social choice problems into $D$ exercises focusing on decisions and $W$ exercises focusing on social welfare judgements, it is clear that, for the latter, Proposition 27 gives little relief. As was noted before, Property $\alpha$ is quite basic to optimality, and it does not make much sense to pose questions of the kind: 'Sartre is the best living philosopher in the world, but is he the best living philosopher in France?' Some amount of

---

42. Schwartz's rationality conditions is GOCHA (General Optimal Choice Axiom) whereby the choice set of $S$ is identified as the union of minimum $\bar{P}_C$-undominated subsets of $S$. He shows that GOCHA is equivalent to the conjunction of three axioms, which he calls 'External Stability', 'Narrowness', and 'Reducibility'. See also Bloomfield (1971) and Deb (1974).

43. It satisfies Fishburn's (1974b) A5, but that—as we saw before—is such a severe weakening of $\alpha$ that the contraction-consistency property is not preserved for even one element in the choice set. Incidentally, the example also satisfies Batra and Pattanaik's (1972a) B.3, which can be written as: if $x$ is in $C(S)$ and $y$ is not in $C(S)$, then it must not be the case that $[y] = C([x, y])$. This does not give any contraction-consistency to $x$ or $y$ if $both$ belong to $C(S)$.

contraction-consistency seems ingrained in welfare judgements and optimality. But in $D$ exercises, the question is more open.

The concept of path independence is specifically cut out for decision problems without an obvious welfare interpretation. But as we saw, this provides no respite, since $PI$ implies $\alpha$, and indeed makes $\bar{R}_C$ quasi-transitive. Accepting path independence is, therefore, a good ground for pessimism even for decision problems. The position changes if path independence is weakened to $*PI$, eliminating $PI*$ which is equivalent to $\alpha$. If $*PI$ is accepted as sufficient, there is hope, since as we saw in Proposition 21, $\beta(+)$ guarantees $*PI$.

But an exclusive reliance on $\beta(+)$ for consistency is problematic. When there are cyclical choices involving the Pareto relation—as in the presence of Condition $L*$ ('minimal liberalism') discussed by Sen (1970b)—a choice function satisfying $\beta(+)$, but no contraction-consistency, can exist only by putting Pareto-inferior states in the choice set for the alternatives over which the cycle holds.[44] Batra and Pattanaik (1972a) have shown how conflicts between the Pareto principle and a weak condition of 'minimal federalism'— a weakening of Sen's 'minimal liberalism'—are endemic in choice rules of the 'Schwartz type'. Ferejohn and Grether (1975) show a similar conflict between the Pareto principle and the majority closure method (MCM) by considering the following example of preferences of three persons over four alternatives (in strict descending order)

1:  $x, y, z, w$

2:  $y, z, w, x$

3:  $z, w, x, y.$

By simple majority rule, $xPy$, $yPz$, $zPw$, and $wPx$. This leads to $xI*y$, $yI*z$, $zI*w$, and $wI*x$, and all available elements are chosen in the choice over the four-element set: $C([x, y, z, w]) = [x, y, z, w]$; and the choice function using $R*$ satisfies $\beta(+)$.[45] It is also consistent with $*PI$. But note that everyone prefers $z$ to $w$, which is strictly Pareto inoptimal, and a strictly Pareto-inferior social state is in the choice set for the four alternatives. There exists a 'path' that takes us to $w$, viz.,

$$[w] = C(C[w] \cup C(C[x] \cup C([y, z]))).$$

Thus a Pareto inferior alternative gets selected through a legitimate path even though the basic rule is an extension of the method of majority decision.[46]

---

44. For nonbinary versions of the 'impossibility of the Paretian liberal', see Sen (1970, pp. 81–2); Batra and Pattanaik (1972a), and Ramachandra (1972). See also Gibbard (1974), Nozick (1974, pp. 165–6), Blau (1975), Seidl (1975), Farrell (1976), Kelly (1976), Suzumura (1976a), Campbell (1976), and Sen (1976b).

45. Schwartz's (1970 and 1974) GOCHA axiom would have also led to the selection of all the elements of $[x, y, z, w]$ given the $P_C$-cycle over them. See also Fishburn (1973, pp. 89 and 93).

46. This example leads Ferejohn and Grether (1975) to an impossibility result using $*PI$ and a version of the Pareto principle $P$. See also Batra and Pattanaik (1972a) and Deb (1974).

The choice of $w$ for this group every member of which prefers $z$ to $w$ is not easy to defend, and this has been possible only because of the enormous freedom introduced into the system by the dropping of all vestiges of contraction-consistency $\alpha$, including consistency with $z\bar{P}_Cw$ arising from strict Pareto preference. The total abandonment of contracting-consistency is achieved at some significant cost even for decision problems. Thus while $D$ type exercises are more accommodating than $W$-type exercises, the former also do throw up many serious consistency problems in group aggregation.

## 6 Aggregation of Interests and of Judgements

It was argued in Section 2 that the method of majority decision was an inadequate basis for aggregating interests even if transitivity or consistency problems were never to arise. The source of the difficulty is the inadequacy of individual orderings as an informational basis for the interest-aggregation exercise (extensively discussed in Sen, 1973 and 1974). The difficulty is not specific to majority rule, though the cake division exercise discussed there shows why MMD is a nonstarter.

Consider the two following exercises of interest aggregation involving dividing a cake (100 units) among three identical people. Cake is the only good they have—there is no bread (as Marie Antoinette had shrewdly noticed).

*Exercise 1.* Choose between $x_1 = (98, 1, 1)$ and $x_2 = (96, 2, 2)$.

*Exercise 2.* Choose between $y_1 = (4, 48, 48)$ and $y_2 = (2, 49, 49)$.

The two problems are not similar since Person 1 is very well off with both alternatives in Exercise 1, whereas he is very poorly off in general in Exercise 2. In terms of individual rankings, however, Exercises 1 and 2 are exactly the same in the choice over $(x_1, x_2)$ and that over $(y_1, y_2)$. The method of majority decision implies that $x_2$ is preferred to $x_1$ and $y_2$ to $y_1$. (So does, obviously, the majority closure method, MCM.) But the problem is much more general. In fact, armed only with individual rankings, it is not very easy to discriminate between the choice over $x_1$ and $x_2$ and that over $y_1$ and $y_2$ (in both cases Person 1 prefers the former alternative to the latter and the other two do the opposite). Furthermore, the widely used condition of neutrality (May, 1952) will make it obligatory to follow the rule: choose $x_1$ over $x_2$ if and only if $y_1$ is chosen over $y_2$. Neutrality as a condition is easily derived from a strict version of the Pareto principle and independence of irrelevant alternatives over a wide domain. (See Blau, 1974 and Guha, 1972; in fact the use of the Pareto principle can be weakened, demanding reflection of unanimous *indifference* only.)

There are two main ways of bringing in a difference between the two choice problems $[x_1, x_2]$ and $[y_1, y_2]$. One is to drop the requirement that only individual preference rankings of alternative social states are to be included as admissible evidence, i.e., not to define the collective choice rules as functions of $[R_i]$. The intention will be to bring in some interpersonal welfare comparisons, e.g., that Person 1 is much better off than Person 2 and Person 3 in $x$, but not in $y$, or that Person 1's welfare loss in moving from $x_1$ to $x_2$ is rather small compared with Person 2's and Person 3's gains but not so in moving from $y_1$ to $y_2$. The other is to discriminate between different alternatives in terms of income distributions, e.g., Person 1's preference for $x_1$ over $x_2$ is that for being very rich rather than a bit less rich (but still very rich), while his preference for $y_1$ over $y_2$ is to avoid penury. The latter method, while often used at least in informal discussions, is rather ad hoc, and there is little doubt that if we are concerned about this type of issue, then the appropriate solution is to widen the informational basis of welfare aggregation by directly bringing in interpersonal comparisons of welfare as arguments of the social welfare function, or of collective choice rules in general.[47]

Once interpersonal comparisons are brought in, various possibilities of social aggregation open up which cannot be translated into 'collective choice rules' of the type of Arrow's social welfare functions defined as they are on the space of $n$-tuples of orderings.[48] The two rules that have been most discussed are the utilitarian rule ($W = \Sigma_i W_i$), and the Rawlsian maximin rule ($W = \text{Min}_i W_i$), usually in its lexicographic version.[49] The two use rather different types of welfare information, with utilitarianism being concerned only with interpersonal comparisons of welfare *gains and losses* (the level comparisons do not matter) and the Rawlsian rules being concerned with interpersonal comparisons of *levels* only (the gain-loss comparisons do not matter).[50] Axiomatic derivation of normative indicators of real national

---

47. The recent investigation of 'fairness' in terms of 'non-envy' (see Foley, 1967; and also Schmeidler and Vind, 1972; Feldman and Kirman, 1974; Feldman and Weiman, 1974; and Varian, 1974) widens the information framework from the set of $n$-tuples $[R_i]$ of individual orderings of $X$ (the environment), even though no genuine interpersonal comparisons are involved, since each person is assumed to be judging the other persons' commodity bundles *in terms of his own tas es*. This characteristic, incidentally, is also the source of a possible conflict of this concept of fairness with the Pareto principle (see Sen, 1970, pp. 149–50, 154–6; and Pazner and Schmeidler, 1974).

48. The literature on this has been growing fast. See Sen (1970, chapters 7 and 9, 1973, 1974, and 1975), Waldner (1972), Mueller (1974), Blackorby (1975), Fine (1975), Hammond (1975 and 1976), d'Aspremont and Gevers (1975), Strasnick (1976), Blackorby and Donaldson (1975), Rae (1975), Gaertner (1975), Maskin (1975), Saposnik (1975a). See also the excellent collections of Phelps (1973), and the classic contributions of Harsanyi (1955), Rawls (1958 and 1971), Vickrey (1960), Suppes (1966), and Kolm (1966).

49. See Rawls (1971) and Sen (1970). Hammond (1976) has established an axiomatization of the lexicographic version of the maximin rule involving a more primitive equity axiom; see also d'Aspremont and Gevers (1975) and Strasnick (1975). On related issues, see Arrow (1973), Dasgupta (1974), Harsanyi (1975 and 1975a), Maskin (1975), and Sen (1976c).

50. See Sen (1970a and 1973), Phelps (1973), Hammond (1975 and 1976), Strasnick (1976), d'Aspremont and Gevers (1975), and Maskin (1976).

income, poverty and inequality in a social welfare framework can also be based on different *types* of interpersonal comparisons.[51]

These alternative methods of aggregating conflicting interests all generate complete social orderings given the appropriate types of information, and the choice between them is not essentially dependent on the consistency conditions of the type discussed in the earlier parts of this paper.[52] The focus of impossibility theorems of the class pioneered by Arrow cannot, in my judgement, be on interest aggregation.

But cannot one say the same thing about aggregation of judgements? Are interpersonal comparisons not relevant to combining judgements? People feel 'strongly' about some rankings and not so strongly about others. Indeed, the concept of welfare difference seems quite easily translatable to judgements as well, e.g., '$x$ is really much better for society than $y$, but $y$ is only just marginally better than $z$'. Interpersonal comparisons of intensity of preference make a lot of sense for judgements as well. What is not so easy to translate is the notion of level comparability (used in weighing interests) to the problem of aggregating judgements of different people.[53] Thus a basic class of information relevant for $I$ type exercises do not have a clear counterpart in $J$ type exercises.

Even for comparisons of 'differences', however, there is probably more arbitrariness in making interpersonal comparisons of preference intensity in judgements than in comparisons of welfare gains and losses. It seems easier

51. The approaches of real national income comparisons and to the measurement of poverty proposed in Sen (1976 and 1976a) use only *ordinal* interpersonal comparisons to motivate the axioms used. I take this opportunity of noting two small corrections in Sen (1976a). First, in equation (2) the normalizing coefficient $A$ should be made to depend on the poverty line and the numbers of people above and below the line, i.e., it should read $A(z, q, n)$, and *not* $A(z, y)$. This is implicit in deriving equation (14). Second, Mr. MacLeod has drawn my attention to the fact that the remark in parentheses on page 220, lines 7–8, is inaccurate, and the poverty measure $P$ need not invariably satisfy the 'transfer axiom' unless it is modified to read: 'Given other things, a pure transfer of income from a person below the poverty line to anyone richer must strictly increase the poverty measure unless the number of people below the poverty line is strictly reduced by the transfer'. The transfer axiom was not used to derive any results in the paper but only for motivation, and all the motivational remarks remain unaffected by the modified formulation of the axiom. In particular, both the 'head-count ratio' and the 'poverty gap' still violate the transfer axiom, while the measure $P$ satisfies it.

52. In the literature on normative indication, sometimes ranking relations are taken to be incomplete (e.g., the use of the Lorenz ranking in, say, Atkinson, 1970), but its transitivity has not been typically much questioned. See also Muellbauer (1974).

53. There is some ambiguity as to what 'level comparability' may mean in the context of judgements. For two alternative interpretations, contrast the two following statements: (i) 'Let's listen to George. He gets so little chance to speak in this gathering of bullies.' (ii) 'George has very few views. Let's listen to him carefully.' The concept of equity in interests (e.g., income distribution) is rather easier to discuss than equity in holding or expressing judgements, or in being effective.

to agree on certain clear formulae for comparisons of welfare differences (e.g., 'a richer man gains less from a dollar of income') than possible formulae of comparisons of preference intensity in welfare judgements. Not surprisingly therefore aggregation of judgements are frequently based only on orderings of alternatives, i.e., within the Arrow framework. And in these cases, the issues of collective rationality—discussed in earlier sections—come into their own.

One indirect method of judging preference intensity from orderings is to attach importance to positions of alternatives in a person's orderings. E.g., if I rank $x_1$, $x_2$, $x_3$, $x_4$, and $x_5$ in that order, it may be said that my preference for $x_1$ over $x_3$ is 'stronger' than my preference for $x_4$ over $x_5$, and—perhaps less controversially—my preference for $x_1$ over $x_3$ is 'stronger' than my preference for $x_1$ over $x_2$. A rule to derive social preference relations—assumed to be quasi-orderings—from only the positions occupied by alternatives in individuals' orderings has been called a 'positional rule', and Gärdenfors (1973), and Fine and Fine (1974) have studied the class of such rules very extensively. (See also Fishburn, 1973; Hansson, 1973; Smith, 1973; and Young, 1974.)

One of the simpler positional rules is the 'Borda rule', or the rank order method, in which an alternative ranked $j$th in a set of $m$ alternatives by a person gets a weight of $(m + 1 - j)$ from that person and its total score is the sum of the weights from all voters. While this is a widely used procedure, two common arguments against this rule are that it violates Arrow's 'independence of irrelevant alternatives' and that it violates the consistency condition given by Property $\alpha$ (e.g., Arrow, 1951, p. 27). Is this so?

Consider two variants of the Borda rule. The first—call it the broad Borda rule (BBR)—checks the rank of all alternatives in the set $X$ in a person's ordering and the scores are given as $(m + 1 - j)$, where $m$ is the number of alternatives in the set $X$. Then in the choice over any subset $S$ of $X$, $C(S)$ is selected by using the Borda scores for $X$. The second—christen it the narrow Borda rule (NBR)—gives the Borda scores according to rankings of the set $S$ for a choice over $S$, i.e., $m$ then stands for the number of alternatives in $S$.[54]

NBR clearly satisfies Condition $I$. If everyone's preference ordering over $S$ is the same, then so is every alternative's narrow Borda score. The choice set cannot change. On the other hand, the choice functions generated by NBR can lead to the violation of Property $\alpha$. In the classic paradox of voting (1: $x$, $y$, $z$; 2: $y$, $z$, $x$; 3: $z$, $x$, $y$), each alternative scores six, and all belong to the choice set of $[x, y, z]$. Then if $z$ is dropped and choice over $[x, y]$ is considered, $x$'s narrow Borda score is five, while $y$'s is four, so $y$ is not in $C([x, y])$.

On the other hand, choice functions yielded by BBR clearly satisfy Property

---

54. Arrow's (1951, p. 27) example is of the narrow Borda rule, while Ray's (1973) is of the broad Borda rule.

$\alpha$. In fact, it generates a normal choice function with a transitive preference relation. The Borda scores of all alternatives in $X$ remain the same as long as individual preferences do, and alternatives can be ordered according to their Borda scores. The choice sets $C(S)$ of all subsets $S$ of $X$ are simply the elements of $S$ with the highest Borda score. But BBR can violate Arrow's independence of irrelevant alternatives. Even if individual preferences remain the same over subset $S$ of $X$, the Borda scores of alternatives in $S$ may change if the individual preferences over $(X - S)$ change.

Hence, NBR satisfies Condition $I$ but has problems with $\alpha$ in choice, while BBR is fine on $\alpha$, but violates Condition $I$. It is easily checked that no rule of this form can be on the right side of *both* $\alpha$ and $I$. In this respect the Borda rule is similar to the example of choice according to the transitive closure $R^*$ of the weak majority relation $R$, i.e., MCM. If $R^*$ is derived from the restriction of $R$ on $S$, as discussed in Section 5, Condition $I$ is satisfied, but choices can violate $\alpha$. On the other hand, if we derive $R^*$ from the closure of $R$ on the entire $X$, then clearly choice over any subset $S$ of $X$ is guided by the same $R^*$, and so choice consistency is no problem. This form, however, runs afoul of Condition $I$, since $\hat{C}(S, R^*)$ can change without any change of any $R_i$ on $S$ if it changes over $X - S$.

Despite this similarity between the two respective versions of the Borda rule and the majority closure rule, the two are rather different approaches. The latter tends to be better from the view of consistency of choice. The choice functions generated by the majority closure rule (MCM) satisfy $\beta(+)$ and have no problem with expansion-consistency; it also satisfies the weaker version of the path independence condition, viz., $*PI$. This is not the case with the narrow Borda rule. Consider Person 1 preferring $x$ to $y$ to $z$, and Person 2 preferring $y$ to $z$ to $x$. The Borda scores rank the three in the descending order: $y$, $x$, $z$. So $y$ is chosen over this triple. But in the choice over the pair $[x, y]$, the narrow Borda scores are the same for $x$ and $y$. Hence, they tie, and $x$ too is chosen along with $y$. This means that the addition of $z$ makes $x$ drop out without dropping $y$ in the choice over the triple. This is a violation of $\beta$, $\gamma$, and $\delta$—all.

On the other hand, the Borda rule always satisfies Pareto optimality of all chosen elements, unlike the majority closure rule. In the example (p. 182) with failure of Pareto optimality of the majority closure rule, the rankings of the four alternatives in descending order according to the Borda scores are $z$, $y$, $x$, $w$. The choice set will contain only $z$. The Borda rule always respects Pareto since Pareto superiority means a higher Borda score from each person. The Borda rule, as is illustrated in this example, leads to more discrimination than MCM, which incorporates *all* elements belonging to a dominant $\bar{P}_C$-cycle into the choice set. It also takes note of some indirect information on intensity of preference. The majority closure rule achieves its expansion-consistency at some real cost.

## 7  Concluding Remarks

Different categories of social choice problems seem to require very different treatments. The relevance of the central results in the general theory of social choice varies a lot with the aggregation type. Four types were considered in this paper, viz., *IW* (aggregation of individual interests into social welfare judgements), *ID* (aggregation of individual interests for social decisions), *JW* (aggregation of individual welfare judgements into social welfare judgements), and *JD* (aggregation of individual welfare judgements for social decision).

One of the by-products of this paper is an investigation of the interrelations among consistency properties of choice functions and their links with binary relations and path independence, leading to consolidation and some extension of results in this area (see Propositions 7 through 21). The more important results are summed up with an eye to social choice theory at the end of Section 4.

As far as social choice theory itself is concerned, the main conclusions to emerge are the following.

(i) The classic framework, pioneered by Arrow, seems to be quite inappropriate for interest aggregation, i.e., for *IW* and *ID*. The *n*-tuples of individual orderings are informationally inadequate for representing conflicts of interests. The problem of intransitivity of social preference, or of inconsistency of social choice, seems to be secondary in comparison with the inability of the classic framework to distinguish systematically between essentially different choice situations. It is not surprising, therefore, that the focus of work on interest aggregation has moved towards a wider informational basis, especially in making room for systematic interpersonal comparisons. The classic impossibility results are of little interest for *IW* and *ID*.

(ii) The classic framework comes into its own with judgement aggregation, and the impossibility theorems take a heavy toll on *JW*. For welfare judgement, the binary relation of social preference seems basic, and even if the requirement of transitivity is weakened to quasi-transitivity, or to acyclicity, or even to acyclicity over triples only, new impossibility results crop up.

(iii) With *JD*, the situation is less gloomy in some sense, but the advantage that is gained in moving away from welfare relations to choice functions has been overestimated. Even very weak conditions of consistency of choice bring us to the regularity properties of the base relation of the choice function, and the impossibility theorems proved for *relational* collective choice rules applied to its 'base relation' (involving choices from pairs only).

(iv) While Arrow defines the choice function in binary terms, viz., '*C(S)* is the set of all alternatives $x$ in $S$ such that for every $y$ in $S$, $xRy$' (Arrow, 1963, p. 15, Definition 3), no use whatsoever is made of this property. He also remarks: 'If, then, we know $C([x, y])$ for all two-element sets, we have completely defined the relation $P$ and $I$ and therefore the relation $R$; *but, by Definition 3, knowing the relation R completely determines the choice function C(S) for all sets of alternatives*' (Arrow, 1963, p. 16, italics added). But, in fact, the property referred to in the italicized statement plays no part in the General Possibility Theorem. While Arrow can certainly hold that 'one of the consequences of the assumptions of rational choice is that choice in any environment can be determined by a knowledge of the choices in two-element environments' (Arrow, 1963, p. 16), the validity of GPT—and indeed of Arrow's own proof of it—is completely independent of rational choice in this sense. (Nor does it depend on whether the much discussed 'Condorcet criterion' holds.) Impossibility theorems for *relational* collective choice rules, $R = f([R_i])$, involving transitivity of $R$ (as in Arrow), or weaker properties than transitivity (e.g., quasi-transitivity, acyclicity, triple-acyclicity), are best interpreted by taking $R$ as the 'base relation' $\bar{R}_C$ of a choice function (involving choices over pairs only). In this sense, the relational framework for social choice pioneered by Arrow is more—not less—general than that of *functional* collective choice rules involving choice functions for society over the entire environment $X$.

(v) There is a fundamental asymmetry in the ability of social decision procedures to cope with choice consistency conditions of two types. The 'contraction-consistency properties' (e.g., $\alpha$) cause problems even in the weakest form, while the 'expansion-consistency properties' (e.g., $\beta$, $\gamma$, $\delta$, $\varepsilon$) are easily accommodated even in their strongest form. The weakest contraction-consistency property ($\alpha(--)$) implies triple-acyclicity of the base relation, but is not implied by it.

(vi) Regarding 'path independence', impossibility theorems emerge easily within the framework of path independent choice functions. Factorizing path independence into two parts, the one ($PI^*$) which corresponds to contraction-consistency ($\alpha$) is seen to be the source of the problem, while the other part ($^*PI$), which is implied by expansion-consistency ($\beta(+)$), is easily met. However, relying exclusively on expansion-consistency permits questionable social choices to be made, e.g., the choice of a Pareto inferior alternative through a legitimate path.

On the impact of Arrow-type impossibility results, the score card seems to look something like this: $ID$: not disturbing; $IW$: not disturbing; $JD$: quite disturbing (depends much on the importance we attach to contraction-consistency); $JW$: dismal.

How relevant are these respective exercises? Contrast the types of questions in each category: $IW$: 'These are the interests of the different people involved. How should I rank alternative policies in terms of social good (or a specified aspect of social good)?' $ID$: 'These are the interests of the different people involved. What should be done?' $JD$: 'These are the judgement rankings of alternative policies in terms of social good as seen by each of us. What should be done?' *JW*: 'These are the judgement rankings of alternative policies in terms of social good as seen by each of us. How do we arrive at a combined judgement giving one ranking in terms of social good aggregating all our rankings?'

*JD* is a practical exercise and is frequently faced (e.g., in committee decisions). *ID* is also a common enough exercise (e.g., in arbitration awards). *IW* is basic to our thinking on policy (e.g., in the formation of personal political judgements), and in a somewhat arbitrary form appears in normative indication as well (e.g., in the 'measurement' of national income, inequality, poverty, or the so-called 'net national welfare'). In contrast *JW* is, in some sense, a bit of a luxury. Do we need a *combined* judgement giving one ranking for society in addition to facing the social *decision* problem? There is little doubt that *JW* is of considerable philosophical interest; but in view of the fact that there is greater cause for pessimism for *JW* compared with the other exercises, it is somewhat comforting that *JW* seems to have less practical interest than the three other exercises.

It is important to distinguish between different types of aggregation exercises covered by social choice theory since they involve quite different problems. To use one general framework for all of them leads to a loss of structure which has been a source of much trouble in this field.[55]

## References

Arrow, K. J. (1951): *Social Choice and Individual Values* (New York: Wiley).

____ (1959): 'Rational Choice Functions and Orderings', *Economica,* **26,** 121–7.

____ (1963): *Social Choice and Individual Values,* second edition (New York: Wiley).

____ (1973): 'Some Ordinalist-Utilitarian Notes on Rawls' Theory of Justice', *Journal of Philosophy,* **70,** 245–80.

Atkinson, A. B. (1970): 'On the Measurement of Inequality', *Journal of Economic Theory,* **2,** 244–63.

____ (1975): *Economics of Inequality* (Oxford: Clarendon Press).

Barbera, S. (1975): 'The Manipulability of Social Choice Mechanisms That Do Not Leave Too Much To Chance', mimeographed, Northwestern University.

Batra, R. N. and P. K. Pattanaik (1972): 'Transitive Multi-Stage Majority Decisions with Quasi-transitive Individual Preferences', *Econometrica,* **40,** 1121–35.

____ (1972a): 'On Some Suggestions for Having Non-binary Social Choice Functions', *Theory and Decisions,* **3,** 1–11.

Bentzel, R. (1970): 'The Social Significance of Income Distribution Statistics', *Review of Income and Wealth,* Series 16, 253–64.

---

55. Arrow was undoubtedly right in saying that 'one of the great advantages of abstract postulational methods is the fact that the same system may be given several different interpretations, permitting a considerable saving of time' (Arrow, 1951, p. 87). But *that* probably is *also* one of the great disadvantages of these methods.

Bergson, A. (1938): 'A Reformulation of Certain Aspects of Welfare Economics', *Quarterly Journal of Economics,* **52,** 310–34.

Bergstrom, E. (1975): 'Maximal Elements of Acyclic Relations on Compact Sets', *Journal of Economic Theory,* **10,** 403–4.

Bergstrom, E. and T. Rader (1975): 'An Economic Approach to Social Choice II', mimeographed, Washington University, St. Louis, Missouri.

Binmore, K. (1974): 'Social Choice and Parties', mimeographed, London School of Economics. [Published later in *Review of Economic Studies,* **43** (1976), 459–64.]

—— (1974a): 'Arrow's Theorem with Coalitions', mimeographed.

—— (1975): 'An Example in Group Preference', *Journal of Economic Theory,* **10,** 377–85.

Black, R. D. (1958): *The Theory of Committees and Elections* (Cambridge: Cambridge University Press).

Blackorby, C. (1975): 'Degrees of Cardinality and Aggregate Partial Ordering', *Econometrica,* 845–52.

Blackorby, C. and D. Donaldson (1975): 'Utility vs. Equity: Some Plausible Quasi-orderings', Discussion Paper No. 75-05, Department of Economics, University of British Columbia. [Revision version published later in *Journal of Public Economics,* **7** (1977), 365–81.]

Blair, D. H. (1974): 'Possibility Theorems for Non-binary Social Choice Functions', mimeographed, Yale University.

—— (1973): 'Path Independent Social Choice Functions: A Further Result', *Econometrica,* **43,** 173–4.

Blair, D. H., G. Bordes, J. S. Kelly, and K. Suzumura (1976): 'Impossibility Theorems without Collective Rationality', *Journal of Economic Theory,* **13,** 361–79.

Blau, J. H. (1957): 'The Existence of a S~cial Welfare Function', *Econometrica,* **25,** 302–13.

—— (1971): 'Arrow's Theorem with Weak Independence', *Economica,* **40,** 413–20.

—— (1972): 'A Direct Proof of Arrow's Theorem, *Econometrica,* **40,** 61–7.

—— (1975): 'Liberal Values and Independence', *Review of Economic Studies,* **42,** 395–401.

—— (1976): 'Neutrality, Monotonicity and the Right of Veto', *Econometrica,* **44,** 603.

Blau, J. H. and R. Deb (1977): 'Social Decision Functions and the Veto', mimeographed, 1975. [Revised version published later in *Econometrica,* **45,** 871–9.]

Bloomfield, S. (1971): 'An Axiomatic Formulation of Constitutional Games', Technical Report No. 71-18, Stanford University.

Borda, J. C. (1781): 'Memoire sur les Elections au Scrutin', *Memoires des l'Academie Royale des Sciences,* English translation by A. de Grazia, *Isis,* **44** (1953).

Bordes, G. (1975): 'Alpha Rationality and Social Choice: A General Possibility Theory', mimeographed, Laboratoire d'Analyse et de Recherche Economiques, Université de Bordeaux I.

—— (1975a): 'Consistency, Rationality, and Collective Choice', mimeographed. [Revised version published later in *Review of Economic Studies,* **43** (1976), 447–57.]

Brown, D. J. (1973): 'Acyclic Choice', Cowles Foundation Discussion Paper, Yale University.

—— (1973a): 'Aggregation of Preferences', Cowles Foundation Discussion Paper, Yale University. [Revised version published in *Quarterly Journal of Economics,* **89** (1975), 459–69.]

____ (1974): 'An Approximate Solution to Arrow's Problem', *Journal of Economic Theory,* **9,** 375–83.

____ (1975): 'Acyclic Aggregation over a Finite Set of Alternatives', Cowles Foundation Discussion Paper No. 391, Yale University.

____ (1975a): 'Collective Rationality', Cowles Foundation Discussion Paper No. 393, Yale University.

Campbell, C. D. and G. Tullock (1965): 'A Measure of the Importance of Cyclical Majorities', *Economic Journal,* **75,** 853–7.

Campbell, D. E. (1972): 'A Collective Choice Rule Satisfying Arrow's Five Conditions in Practice', in *Theory and Application of Collective Choice Rule,* Institute for Quantitative Analysis of Social and Economic Policy, Working Paper No. 7206, University of Toronto.

____ (1973): 'Social Choice and Intensity of Preference', *Journal of Political Economy,* **81,** 211–18.

____ (1973a): 'Democratic Choice Rules', mimeographed, Scarborough College, University of Toronto.

____ (1976): 'Democratic Preference Functions', *Journal of Economic Theory,* **12,** 259–72.

Champernowne, D. C. (1974): 'A Comparison of Measures of Inequality of Income Distribution', *Economic Journal,* **84,** 787–816.

Chernoff, H. (1954): 'Rational Selection of Decision Functions', *Econometrica,* **22,** 423–43.

Chipman, J. S. (1974): 'The Welfare Ranking of Pareto Distributions', *Journal of Economic Theory,* **9,** 275–82.

Chipman, J. S., L. Hurwicz, M. K. Richter, and H. F. Sonnenschein (1971): *Preference, Utility and Demand* (New York: Harcourt).

Condorcet, Marquis de (1785): *Essai sur l'Application de l'Analyse à la Probabilité des Decisions Rendues à le Pluralité des Voix* (Paris).

Dasgupta, P. (1974): 'On Some Problems Arising from Professor Rawls' Conception of Distributive Justice', *Theory and Decision,* **4,** 325–44.

Dasgupta, P., A. Sen, and D. Starrett (1973): 'Notes on the Measurement of Inequality', *Journal of Economic Theory,* **6,** 180–7.

D'Aspremont, C. and L. Gevers (1975): 'Equity and the Informational Basis of Collective Choice', mimeographed, presented at the Third World Econometric Congress, Toronto. [Revised version published in *Review of Economic Studies,* **44** (1977), 199–210.]

Deb, R. (1974): 'Rational Choice and Cyclic Preferences', Ph.D. dissertation, London University.

De Meyer, F. and C. R. Plott (1970): 'The Probability of a Cyclical Majority', *Econometrica,* **38,** 345–54.

Farquharson, R. (1969): *Theory of Voting* (New Haven, Conn.: Yale University Press).

Farrell, M. J. (1976): 'Liberalism in the Theory of Social Choice', *Review of Economic Studies,* **43,** 3–10.

Feldman, A. and A. Kirman (1974): 'Fairness and Envy', *American Economic Review,* **64,** 995–1005.

Feldman, A. and D. Weiman (1974): 'Class Structures and Envy', mimeographed, Brown University.

Ferejohn, J. A. and D. M. Grether (1974): 'On a Class of Rational Social Decision

Procedures', *Journal of Economic Theory*, **8**, 471–82.

____ (1974): 'On Normative Problems of Social Choice', Social Science Working Paper No. 80, California Institute of Technology.

____ (1975): 'Weak Path Independence', Social Science Working Paper No. 124, California Institute of Technology. [Revised version published in *Journal of Economic Theory*, **14** (1977), 19–31.]

Fine, B. (1974): 'Individual Decisions and Social Choice', Ph.D. dissertation, London School of Economics.

____ (1975): 'A Note on "Interpersonal Comparison and Partial Comparability"', *Econometrica*, **43**, 169–72.

Fine, B. and K. Fine (1974): 'Social Choice and Individual Ranking', *Review of Economic Studies*, **42**, 303–22 and 459–75.

Fishburn, P. C. (1970): *Utility Theory for Decision Making* (New York: Wiley).

____ (1970a): 'Conditions for Simple Majority Decision with Intransitive Individual Indifference', *Journal of Economic Theory*, **2**, 354–67.

____ (1970b): 'Arrow's Impossibility Theorem: Concise Proof and Infinite Voters', *Journal of Economic Theory*, **2**, 103–6.

____ (1972): 'Conditions on Preferences that Guarantee a Simple Majority Winner', *Journal of Mathematical Sociology*, **2**, 105–12.

____ (1972a): 'Lotteries and Social Choice', *Journal of Economic Theory*, **5**, 189–207.

____ (1972b): 'Even-Chance Lotteries in Social Choice Theory', *Theory and Decision*, **3**, 18–40.

____ (1973): *The Theory of Social Choice* (Princeton, N.J.: Princeton University Press).

____ (1974): 'On Collective Rationality and a Generalized Impossibility Theorem', *Review of Economic Studies*, **41**, 445–57.

____ (1974a): 'Choice Functions on Finite Sets', *International Economic Review*, **15**, 729–49.

____ (1974b): 'Subset Choice Conditions and the Computation of Social Choice Sets', *Quarterly Journal of Economics*, **88**, 320–9.

____ (1975): 'A Probabilistic Model of Social Choice: Comment', *Review of Economic Studies*, **42**, 297–301.

Foley, D. K. (1967): 'Resource Allocation and the Public Sector', *Yale Economic Essays*, **7**, 45–98.

Gaertner, W. (1975): 'On Rawls's Two Principles of Justice', Discussion Paper, Department of Economics, Bielefeld University.

Gärdenfors, P. (1973): 'Positionalist Voting Functions', *Theory and Decision*, **4**, 1–24.

Garman, M. and M. Kamien (1968): 'The Paradox of Voting: Probability Calculations', *Behavioral Science*, **13**, 306–16.

Gauthier, D. (1975): 'Acyclicity, Neutrality and Collective Choice', mimeographed, Department of Philosophy, Toronto University.

Gibbard, A. (1969): 'Intransitive Social Indifference and the Arrow Dilemma', unpublished manuscript.

____ (1973): 'Manipulation of Voting Schemes: A General Result', *Econometrica*, **41**, 587–601.

____ (1974): 'A Pareto-Consistent Libertarian Claim', *Journal of Economic Theory*, **7**, 388–410.

____ (1975): 'Manipulation of Schemes that Combine Voting with Chance', duplicated,

Philosophy Department, University of Pittsburgh.

Gintis, H. (1969): 'Alienation and Power: Towards a Radical Welfare Economics', Ph.D. Dissertation, Harvard University.

Graaff, J. de V. (1957): *Theoretical Welfare Economics* (Cambridge: Cambridge University Press).

Guha, A. S. (1972): 'Neutrality, Monotonicity, and the Right of Veto', *Econometrica*, **40**, 821–6.

Guilbaud, G. T. (1966): 'The Theories of the General Interest and the Logical Problem of Aggregation', in *Readings in Mathematical Social Science*, ed. by Lazarfeld and Henry (Chicago: Science Research Associates Inc. (English translation)).

Hamada, K. (1973): 'A Simple Majority Rule on the Distribution of Income', *Journal of Economic Theory*, **6**, 243–64.

Hammond, P. J. (1975): 'Dual Interpersonal Comparisons of Utility and the Welfare Economics of Income Distribution', mimeographed, 1975. [Revised version published in the *Journal of Public Economics*, **6** (1977), 51–71.]

____ (1976): 'Equity, Arrow's Conditions, and Rawls' Difference Principle', *Econometrica*, **44**, 793–804.

Hansson, B. (1968): 'Choice Structures and Preference Relations', *Synthese*, **18**, 443–58.

____ (1969): 'Voting and Group Decision Functions', *Synthese*, **10**, 526–37.

____ (1969a): 'Group Preferences', *Econometrica*, **37**, 50–4.

____ (1972): 'The Existence of Group Preferences', Working Paper No. 3, The Mattias Fremling Society, Lund, Sweden.

____ (1973): 'The Independence Condition in the Theory of Social Choice', *Theory and Decision*, **4**, 25–49.

____ (1975): 'The Measurement of Social Inequality', invited address at the International Congress of Logic, Methodology and Philosophy of Science, London, Ontario. [Published later in R. Butts and J. Hintikka (eds), *Foundational Problems in the Special Sciences* (Boston: Reidel, 1977).]

Harsanyi, J. C. (1955): 'Cardinal Welfare, Individualistic Ethics, and Interpersonal Comparisons of Utility', *Journal of Political Economy*, **63**, 309–21.

____ (1975): 'Can the Maximin Principle Serve as a Basis for Morality: A Critique of John Rawls's Theory', *American Political Science Review*, **69**, 594–606.

____ (1975a): 'Non-linear Social Welfare Functions, or Do Welfare Economists Have a Special Exemption from Bayesian Rationality', *Theory and Decision*, **6**, 311–32.

Heal, G. M. (1973): *The Theory of Economic Planning* (Amsterdam: North-Holland).

Herzberger, H. G. (1973): 'Ordinal Preference and Rational Choice', *Econometrica*, **41**, 187–237.

Hicks, J. R. (1958): 'The Measurement of Income', *Oxford Economic Papers*, **10**, 125–62.

Hinich, M., J. Ledyard, and P. Ordeshook (1972): 'Non-Voting and the Existence of Equilibrium under Majority Rule', *Journal of Economic Theory*, **4**, 144–53.

Houthakker, H. S. (1956): 'On the Logic of Preference and Choice', in *Contributions to Logic and Methodology in Honour of J. M. Bochenski* (Amsterdam: North-Holland).

Inada, K. (1969): 'The Simple Majority Decision Rule', *Econometrica*, **29**, 490–506.

____ (1970): 'Majority Rule and Rationality', *Journal of Economic Theory*, **29**, 27–40.

Intriligator, M. (1973): 'A Probabilistic Model of Social Choice', *Review of Economic Studies*, **40**, 553–60.

Jamison, D. T. and L. J. Lau (1973): 'Semi-Orders and the Theory of Choice', *Econometrica,* **41,** 901–12.

Jamison, D. T. and E. Luce (1972): 'Social Homogeneity and the Probability of Intransitive Majority Rule', *Journal of Economic Theory,* **5,** 79–87.

Kelly, J. S. (1974): 'Two Impossibility Theorems on Independence of Path', mimeographed, Syracuse University.

_____ (1974a): 'Necessity Conditions in Voting Theory', *Journal of Economic Theory,* **8,** 149–60.

_____ (1974b): 'Voting Anomalies, the Number of Voters and the Number of Alternatives', *Econometrica,* **42,** 239–52.

_____ (1975): 'Strategy-proofness and Social Choice Functions with a Large Image Set', mimeographed.

_____ (1976): 'The Impossibility of a Just Liberal', *Economica,* **43,** 67–76.

Kemp, M. C. and K. Ng (1976): 'On the Existence of Social Welfare Functions, Social Orderings, and Social Decision Functions', *Economica,* **43,** 59–66.

Kirman, A. P. and D. Sondermann (1972): 'Arrow's Theorem, Many Agents and Invisible Dictators', *Journal of Economic Theory,* **5,** 267–78.

Kolm, S. Ch. (1969): 'The Optimum Production of Social Justice', paper presented in the Biarritz conference on Public Economics; published in *Public Economics,* ed. by J. Margolis (London: Macmillan).

_____ (1972): *Justice et Equité* (Paris: Editions de Centre National de la Recherche Scientifique).

Kramer, G. H. (1973): 'On a Class of Equilibrium Conditions for Majority Rule', *Econometrica,* **41,** 285–98.

Kramer, G. H. and A. K. Klevorick (1974): 'Existence of a "Local" Cooperative Equilibrium in a Voting Game', *Review of Economic Studies,* **41,** 539–48.

Kuga, K. and H. Nagatani (1974): 'Voter Antagonism and the Paradox of Voting', *Econometrica,* **42,** 1045–68.

Lindbeck, A. (1975): 'Inequality and Redistribution Policy Issues. Principles and Swedish Experience', mimeographed, Institute for International Economic Studies, University of Stockholm.

Little, I. M. D. (1957): *A Critique of Welfare Economics* (Oxford: Clarendon Press, 1950; 2nd edition, 1957).

Luce, R. D. and H. Raiffa (1957): *Games and Decisions* (New York: Wiley).

Majumdar, T. (1969): 'Revealed Preference and the Demand Theorem in a Not-Necessarily Competitive Market', *Quarterly Journal of Economics,* **83,** 167–70.

_____ (1969): 'A Note on Arrow's Postulates for a Social Welfare Function: A Comment', *Journal of Political Economy,* **77,** 528–31.

_____ (1970): 'Revealed Preference According to Notions of Consistency and Types of Choice Situations', *Indian Economic Review,* **5,** 137–46.

_____ (1973): 'Amartya Sen's Algebra of Collective Choice', *Sankhya,* **35,** Series B, Part 4, 533–42.

Mas-Colell, A. and H. Sonnenschein (1972): 'General Possibility Theorem for Group Decisions', *Review of Economic Studies,* **39,** 185–92.

Maskin, E. (1976): 'Decision-Making under Ignorance with Implications for Social Choice', mimeographed, Jesus College, Cambridge, 1976. [Revised version published in *Theory and Decision,* **19** (1979), 319–37.]

May, K. O. (1952): 'A Set of Independent, Necessary and Sufficient Conditions for Simple Majority Decision', *Econometrica,* **20,** 680–4.

McKelvey, R. D. (1976): 'Intransitivities in Multi-dimensional Voting Models and Some Implications for Agenda Control', *Journal of Economic Theory*, **12**.

McManus, M. (1975): 'Inter-Tastes Consistency in Social Welfare Functions', in M. Parkin and A. R. Nobay, *Current Economic Problems* (Cambridge: Cambridge University Press).

Mehran, F. (1976): 'Linear Measures of Economic Inequality', *Econometrica*, **44**, 805–9.

Mukherji, A. (1975): 'On Choice, Demand and Preference', mimeographed, J. Nehru University, New Delhi. [Revised version, 'The Existence of Choice Functions', *Econometrica*, **45** (1977), 889–94.]

Muellbauer, J. (1974): 'Inequality Measures, Prices and Household Composition', *Review of Economic Studies*, **41**, 493–504.

_____ (1974a): 'The Political Economy of Price Indices', mimeographed.

Mueller, D. C. (1974): 'Intergenerational Justice and the Social Discount Rate', *Theory and Decision*, **5**, 263–73.

Murakami, Y. (1968): *Logic and Social Choice* (London: Macmillan).

Nash, J. F. (1950); 'The Bargaining Problem', *Econometrica*, **18**, 155–62.

Newbery, D. M. G. (1970): 'A Theorem on the Measurement of Inequality', *Journal of Economic Theory*, **2**, 264–6.

Ng, Y. K. (1971): 'The Possibility of a Paretian Liberal: Impossibility Theorems and Cardinal Utility', *Journal of Political Economy*, **79**, 1397–1402.

Nicholson, M. B. (1965): 'Conditions for the "Voting Paradox" in Committee Decisions', *Metroeconomica*, **42**, 29–44.

Niemi, R. and H. Weisberg (1968): 'A Mathematical Solution for the Probability of Paradox of Voting', *Behavioral Sciences*, **13**, 317–23.

Nordhaus, W. and J. Tobin (1972): 'Is Growth Obsolete?', in *Economic Growth*, Fifth Anniversary Colloquium (New York: NBER).

Nozick, R. (1974): *Anarchy, State and Utopia* (Oxford: Blackwell).

Parks, R. R. (1971): 'Rationalizations, Extensions and Social Choice Paths', Washington University, St Louis (cited by Plott (1973)).

_____ (1973): 'The Bergson-Samuelson Welfare Function: An Impossibility', mimeographed, Washington University, St Louis. [Revised version, 'An Impossibility Theorem for Fixed Preferences: A Dictatorial Bergson-Samuelson Social Welfare Function', published in *Review of Economic Studies*, **43** (1976), 447–50.]

Pattanaik, P. K. (1968): 'A Note on Democratic Decision and the Existence of Choice Sets', *Review of Economic Studies*, **35**, 1–9.

_____ (1970): 'On Social Choice with Quasi-transitive Individual Preferences', *Journal of Economic Theory*, **2**, 267–75.

_____ (1971): *Voting and Collective Choice* (Cambridge: Cambridge University Press).

_____ (1973): 'On the Stability of Sincere Voting Situations', *Journal of Economic Theory*, **6**, 558–74.

_____ (1974): 'Stability of Sincere Voting under Some Classes of Non-Binary Group Decision Procedures', *Journal of Economic Theory*, **8**, 206–24.

_____ (1975): 'Strategic Voting without Collusion under Binary and Democratic Group Decision Rules', *Review of Economic Studies*, **42**, 93–104.

Pattanaik, P. K. and M. Sengupta (1974): 'Conditions for Transitive and Quasi-transitive Majority Decisions', *Economica*, **41**, 414–23.

Pazner, E. A. and D. Schmeidler (1974): 'A Difficulty in the Concept of Fairness',

*Review of Economic Studies,* **41,** 441–3.

Phelps, E. S. (1973) (ed.): *Economic Justice* (Harmondsworth: Penguin).

Plott, C. R. (1967): 'A Notion of Equilibrium and Its Possibility under Majority Rule', *American Economic Review,* **57,** 787–806.

_____ (1971): 'Recent Results in the Theory of Voting', in *Frontiers of Quantitative Economics,* ed. by M. Intriligator (Amsterdam: North-Holland).

_____ (1971a): 'Social Choice and Social Rationality', Social Science Working Paper No. 2, California Institute of Technology.

_____ (1972): 'Ethics, Social Choice Theory and the Theory of Economic Policy', *Journal of Mathematical Sociology,* **2,** 181–208.

_____ (1973): 'Path Independence, Rationality and Social Choice', *Econometrica,* **41,** 1075–91.

Pyatt, G. (1976): 'On the Interpretation and Disaggregation of Gini Coefficients', *Economic Journal,* **86,** 243–55.

Rader, T. (1972): *Theory of Microeconomics* (New York: Academic Press).

_____ (1973): 'An Economic Approach to Social Choice', *Public Choice,* **15,** 49–75.

Radner, R. and J. Marschak (1954): 'Note on Some Proposed Decision Criteria', in *Decision Processes,* ed. by R. M. Thrall, D. H. Coombs, and R. L. Davis (New York: Wiley).

Rae, D. (1975): 'Maximin Justice and an Alternative Principle of General Advantage', *American Political Science Review,* **69,** 630–47.

Ramachandra, V. S. (1972): 'Liberalism, Non-binary Choice and the Pareto Principle', *Theory and Decision,* **3,** 49–75.

Rawls, J. (1958): 'Justice as Fairness', *Philosophical Review,* **67,** 164–94.

_____ (1971): *A Theory of Justice* (Oxford: Clarendon Press).

Ray, P. (1973): 'Independence of Irrelevant Alternatives', *Econometrica,* **41,** 987–91.

Richter, M. R. (1966): 'Revealed Preference Theory', *Econometrica,* **34,** 635–45.

Riker, W. (1961): 'Voting and the Summation of Preferences', *American Political Science Review,* **55,** 900–11.

Rosenthal, R. W. (1975): 'Voting Majority Sizes', *Econometrica,* **43,** 293–300.

Rothenberg, J. (1961): *The Measurement of Social Welfare* (Englewood Cliffs, NJ: Prentice-Hall).

Rothschild, M. and J. E. Stiglitz (1973): 'Some Further Results on the Measurement of Inequality', *Journal of Economic Theory,* **6,** 188–204.

Salles, M. (1975): 'A General Possibility Theorem on Group Decision Rules with Pareto-Transitivity', *Journal of Economic Theory,* **11,** 110–18.

_____ (1975a): 'Characterization of Transitive Individual Preferences for Quasi-transitive Collective Preferences under Simple Games', Fascicule No. 12, Centre d'Etudes et de Recherches d'Economie Mathématique, Université de Caen. [Revised version published in *International Economic Review,* **17** (1976), 308–18.]

Samuelson, P. A. (1938): 'A Note on the Pure Theory of Consumers Behaviour', *Economica,* **5,** 61–71.

_____ (1950): 'Evaluation of Real National Income', *Oxford Economic Papers,* **2,** 1–29.

_____ (1967): 'Arrow's Mathematical Politics', in *Human Values and Economic Policy,* ed. by S. Hook (New York: New York University Press).

Saposnik, R. (1975): 'On Transitivity of the Social Preference Relation under Simple Majority Rule', *Journal of Economic Theory,* **10,** 1–7.

_____ (1975a): 'Social Choice with Continuous Expression of Individual Preferences',

*Econometrica,* **43,** 683–90.

Satterthwaite, M. A. (1975): 'Strategy-Proofness and Arrow's Conditions', *Journal of Economic Theory,* **10,** 187–217.

Schick, F. (1969): 'Arrow's Proof and the Logic of Preferences', *Philosophy of Science,* **38,** 127–44.

Schmeidler, D. and H. Sonnenschein (1975): 'The Possibility of Non-manipulable Social Choice Function', mimeographed, Northwestern University.

Schmeidler, D. and K. Vind (1972): 'Fair Net Trades', *Econometrica,* **40,** 637–42.

Schofield, N. (1975): 'Transitivity of Preferences on a Smooth Manifold of Alternatives', mimeographed, University of Essex. [Revised version published in *Journal of Economic Theory,* **14** (1977), 149–72.]

Schwartz, T. (1970): 'On the Possibility of Rational Policy Evaluation', *Theory and Decision,* **1,** 89–106.

_____ (1972): 'Rationality and the Myth of the Maximum', *Nous,* **7,** 97–117.

_____ (1974): 'Notes on the Abstract Theory of Collective Choice', mimeographed, Carnegie-Mellon University.

Seidl, C. (1975): 'On Liberal Values', *Zeitschrift für Nationalökonomie,* **35,** 257–92.

Sen, A. K. (1969): 'Planners' Preferences: Optimality, Distribution and Social Welfare', presented at the Biarritz Conference on Public Economics, 1966; published in *Public Economics,* ed. by J. Margolis (New York: Harcourt).

_____ (1969): 'Quasi-transitivity, Rational Choice and Collective Decision', *Review of Economic Studies,* **36,** 381–94.

_____ (1970): *Collective Choice and Social Welfare* (San Francisco: Holden-Day).

_____ (1970a): 'Interpersonal Aggregation and Partial Comparability', *Econometrica,* **38,** 393–409. [Essay 9 in this volume.] 'A Correction', *Econometrica,* **40** (1972), 959.

_____ (1970b): 'The Impossibility of a Paretian Liberal', *Journal of Political Economy,* **78,** 152–7. [Essay 13 in this volume.]

_____ (1971): 'Choice Functions and Revealed Preference', *Review of Economic Studies,* **38,** 307–17. [Essay 1 in this volume.]

_____ (1973): *On Economic Inequality* (Oxford: Clarendon Press).

_____ (1974): 'Informational Bases of Alternative Welfare Approaches: Aggregation and Income Distribution', *Journal of Public Economics,* **3,** 387–403.

_____ (1976): 'Real National Income', *Review of Economic Studies,* **43,** 19–39. [Essay 18 in this volume.]

_____ (1976a): 'Poverty: An Ordinal Approach to Measurement', *Econometrica,* **44** (1976a), 219–31. [Essay 17 in this volume.]

_____ (1976b): 'Liberty, Unanimity and Rights', *Economica,* **43,** 217–45. [Essay 14 in this volume.]

_____ (1976c): 'Welfare Inequalities and Rawlsian Axiomatics', invited address, International Congress of Logic, Methodology and Philosophy of Science, London, Ontario. *Theory and Decision,* **7** (1976), 243–62.

Sen, A. K. and P. K. Pattanaik (1969): 'Necessary and Sufficient Conditions for Rational Choice under Majority Decision', *Journal of Economic Theory,* **1,** 178–202.

Sengupta, M. (1974): 'On a Concept of Representative Democracy', *Theory and Decision,* **5,** 249–62.

Shepsle, K. A. (1970): 'A Note on Zeckhauser's "Majority Rule with Lotteries on

Alternatives": the Case of the Paradox of Voting', *Quarterly Journal of Economics,* **84**, 705–9.

_____ (1972): 'The Paradox of Voting and Uncertainty', in *Probability Models in Collective Decision Making*, ed. by R. G. Niemi and H. F. Weisberg (Columbus, Ohio: Merrill).

Sheshinski, E. (1972): 'Relation between Social Welfare Function and the Gini Index of Inequality', *Journal of Economic Theory*, **4**, 98–100.

Shinohara, M. *et al.* (1973): *Measuring Net National Welfare of Japan* (Tokyo: Economic Council of Japan).

Slutsky, S. (1975): 'Abstentions and Majority Equilibrium', *Journal of Economic Theory*, **11**, 292–304.

_____ (1975a): 'A Characterization of Societies with Consistent Majority Decision', mimeographed, Cornell University. [Revised version published in *Review of Economic Studies*, **44** (1977), 211–26.]

Smith, J. H. (1973): 'Aggregation of Preferences and Variable Electorate', *Econometrica*, **41**, 1027–43.

Smith, T. E. (1974): 'On the Existence of Most Preferred Alternatives', *International Economic Review*, **15**, 184–94.

Strasnick, S. (1976): 'Social Choice and the Derivation of Rawls' Difference Principle', *Journal of Philosophy*, **73**, 85–99.

Suppes, P. (1966): 'Some Formal Models of Grading Principles', *Synthese*, **6** (1966), 284–306; reprinted in Suppes, P.: *Studies in the Methodology and Foundations of Science* (Reidel, Dordrecht, 1969).

Suzumura, K. (1973): 'Acyclic Preference and the Existence of Choice Function', Discussion Paper No. 068, Kyoto Institute of Economic Research.

_____ (1974): 'General Possibility Theorems for Path-Independent Social Choice', mimeographed, London School of Economics.

_____ (1976): 'Rational Choice and Revealed Preference', *Review of Economic Studies*, **43**, 149–58.

_____ (1976a): 'Remarks on the Theory of Collective Choice', *Economica*, **43**, 381–90.

Taylor, M. (1971): 'Mathematical Political Theory', *British Journal of Political Science*, **1**, 339–82.

Tullock, G. (1967): *Towards a Mathematics of Politics* (Ann Arbor: University of Michigan Press).

Uzawa, H. (1956): 'A Note on Preference and Axioms of Choice', *Annals of the Institute of Statistical Mathematics*, **8**, 35–40.

Varian, H. (1974): 'Equity, Envy and Efficiency', *Journal of Economic Theory*, **9**, 63–91.

Vickrey, W. (1960): 'Utility, Strategy and Social Decision Rules', *Quarterly Journal of Economics*, **74**, 507–35.

Waldner, I. (1972): 'The Empirical Meaningfulness of Interpersonal Utility Comparisons', *Journal of Philosophy*, **69**, 87–103.

Williamson, O. E. and J. G. Sargent (1967): 'Social Choice: A Probabilistic Approach', *Economic Journal*, **77**, 797–813.

Wilson, R. B. (1970): 'The Finer Structure of Revealed Preferences', *Journal of Economic Theory*, **2**, 348–53.

_____ (1971): 'Stable Coalition Proposals in Majority Rule Voting', *Journal of Economic Theory*, **3**, 254–71.

—— (1972): 'Social Choice Theory without the Pareto Principle', *Journal of Economic Theory*, **5**, 478–86.

—— (1972a): 'The Game-Theoretic Structure of Arrow's General Possibility Theorem', *Journal of Economic Theory*, **5**, 14–20.

—— (1975): 'On the Theory of Aggregation', *Journal of Economic Theory*, **10**, 89–99.

Wolfson, M. C. (1974): 'Strength of Transfers, Stochastic Dominance, and the Measure of Economic Inequality', mimeographed, Statistics Canada.

Young, H. P. (1974): 'An Axiomatization of Borda's Rule', *Journal of Economic Theory*, **9**, 43–52.

Zeckhauser, R. (1969): 'Majority Rule with Lotteries on Alternatives', *Review of Economic Studies*, **42**, 696–703.

# PART III

# Welfare Comparisons and

# Social Choice

# 9

# Interpersonal Aggregation and
# Partial Comparability

The object of this paper is to provide a systematic treatment of aggregation of individual welfare as a basis for social preference. Two polar cases of inter-personal comparability seem to have received all the attention in the literature so far. Either it is assumed that individual welfare measures are fully comparable, e.g., in Marshall [12], or that they are not comparable at all, e.g., in Robbins [15].[1] It is clear, however, that we frequently make judgements that are not consistent with non-comparability but which do not require full comparability. Part of the object of this paper is to examine the formal basis of such judgements and to develop a continuum of intermediate assumptions.

## 1  *Motivation*

Judgements about social welfare are intimately connected with possibilities of interpersonal comparability of individual welfare in the usual form that such judgements take. The type of interpersonal comparability needed for various types of judgements, however, varies a great deal. For example, in

For helpful comments I am extremely grateful to Kenneth Arrow, Peter Diamond, Franklin Fisher, Tjalling Koopmans, James Mirrlees, and Jerome Rothenberg.

1. The literature on optimality also reveals this polarization. The discussions on the 'optimality' of general equilibrium (e.g. Arrow [1], Debreu [4]) are consistent with non-comparability, since they do not go beyond Pareto optimality, whereas the literature on 'optimal' accumulation would seem to assume complete comparability (see *Review of Economic Studies* [21]). Similarly, Arrow's [2] formulation of the social welfare function assumes complete non-comparability since it is defined on the space of individual orderings, and the social ordering is not permitted to change with comparisons of welfare (marginal or total) of different individuals. On the other hand, Pigou's [13] formulation of it requires complete comparability of units.

From *Econometrica*, **38** (May 1970), 393−409. A correction made in *Econometrica*, **40** (September 1972) is incorporated.

comparing the *sums* of individual welfare levels for distinct alternatives, as under 'utilitarianism', what we take as 'origins' of the respective individual welfare functions of different persons makes no difference to the ordering of the alternatives, because the origins get subtracted out in pairwise comparisons. Origins thus need not be comparable for rankings of aggregate welfare, but comparability of 'units' of individual welfare obviously is required. In contrast if we take some criteria of 'justice' such as that of Rawls [14], where the social ordering is based on comparing the welfare levels of the 'worst off' individual in the respective social states, 'origins' are clearly important. On the other hand, we do not need at all a cardinal measure of individual welfare levels for the Rawls ordering, thus comparability of welfare 'units' is irrelevant, and all we need compare are absolute levels of welfare.[2]

Another illustration could help to clarify the point. Recently Diamond [5] has criticized the use of 'the sure thing principle' in social choice, in the context of rejecting Harsanyi's [10] model of social aggregation. The example that Diamond considers is the following. Let $U_A$ and $U_B$ stand respectively for welfare levels of individuals $A$ and $B$, and let $L^1$ and $L^2$ be two lotteries with a fifty-fifty probability of two social alternatives specified thus:

|  | Prize 1 | Prize 2 |
|---|---|---|
| Lottery $L^1$ | $U_A = 1, U_B = 0,$ | $U_A = 0, U_B = 1,$ |
| Lottery $L^2$ | $U_A = 1, U_B = 0,$ | $U_A = 1, U_B = 0,$ |

It seems reasonable to be indifferent between the second prize of $L^1$ and that of $L^2$ because they seem very much the same except for the substitution of name tags $A$ and $B$. But the first prize of both the lotteries is the same, so that 'the sure thing principle' (or 'the strong independence assumption'[3]) would make us indifferent between $L^1$ and $L^2$. But lottery $L^2$ seems so unfair to individual $B$, while lottery $L^1$ 'gives $B$ a fair shake'. Hence Diamond's rejection of 'the sure thing principle' as applied to social choice.

It should, however, be noted that the Diamond argument depends crucially on the individual welfare levels (and thus also 'origins') being comparable—an assumption that is not needed for Harsanyi's model of aggregate welfare, or for that matter in any model that is based on ordering the *sum* of welfare. Suppose we add 1 to individual $B$'s welfare function, keeping $A$'s welfare function unchanged. In the utility space the two lotteries get transformed to the following:

---

2. Strictly speaking it does not make sense to talk of 'origins' in the case of purely ordinal utility, so that it is somewhat misleading to speak of 'origins' being relevant for the Rawls ordering. But if individual welfare *is* cardinally measured, *then* origins in addition to units are relevant for Rawls, while only units are relevant for the strict 'utilitarian'.

3. See Samuelson [18]. It should be added that Samuelson was not advocating the use of this axiom for social choice.

|  | Prize 1 | Prize 2 |
|---|---|---|
| Lottery $L^1$ | $U_A = 1, U_B = 1,$ | $U_A = 0, U_B = 2,$ |
| Lottery $L^2$ | $U_A = 1, U_B = 1,$ | $U_A = 1, U_B = 1,$ |

It will now be easy to build an argument in favour of $L^2$ against $L^1$ on much the same grounds ('a fair shake') as Diamond's reason for preferring $L^1$ to $L^2$. And this is brought about by a mere change in the origin of one individual's welfare function, which leaves the ordering of aggregate welfare completely unchanged. Clearly the type of comparability that Harsanyi needs is in this respect less demanding than that which Diamond needs for criticizing Harsanyi, even though Diamond might argue that Harsanyi did not specify his assumptions.

The Harsanyi–Diamond argument is exceedingly important for theories of social choice,[4] and while we have just seen that the controversy really turns on the type of interpersonal comparability we are assuming, neither Harsanyi nor Diamond state explicitly what precise assumptions they are making. This is one of many illustrations that can be found in the literature of welfare economics where the vagueness of the framework of interpersonal comparability conceals important features of controversies. Part of the object of this paper is to provide a fairly rigorous presentation of a possible framework of interpersonal comparability. While in this paper we shall be exclusively concerned with *adding* individual welfare levels, the framework itself is more general. However, our focus of attention will be those variations of comparability that are relevant for comparing the sums of individual welfare. As such our major concern will be the comparability of units, and we shall try to develop a continuum of intermediate assumptions between full comparability of 'units' of individual welfare of different persons and no comparability at all. The precise motivation of this particular exercise may also need some spelling out.

Suppose we are debating the consequence on the aggregate welfare of Romans of the burning of Rome while Nero played the fiddle. We recognize that Nero was delighted while the other Romans suffered, but suppose we still say the sum total of welfare went down as a consequence. What type of interpersonal comparability are we assuming? Clearly not the extreme case of non-comparability, for then the statement makes no sense whatever.[5] But are we assuming that every Roman's welfare units can be put into one-to-one correspondence with the welfare units of every other Roman? Not necessarily.

---

4. See also the controversy between Strotz [19, 20], and Fisher and Rothenberg [7, 8], which was concerned with related issues.

5. We shall show later that comparisons of welfare sums do make sense even under non-comparability if one alternative is Pareto superior to another (Theorem 1.3). In the present case this does not make any difference because Nero preferred the burning, which made it Pareto optimal in this two alternative set.

We might not be sure what precise correspondence to take, and we might admit some possible variability, but we could still assert that no matter which of the various possible combinations we take, the sum total of welfare went down in any case. This is a case intermediate between non-comparability and full comparability of units.

To take another example, suppose we are found complaining bitterly about the existing inequality in the distribution of money income, and assert that this amounts to a lower aggregate of individual welfare. Are we assuming that we can put everyone's welfare units into one-to-one correspondence? We don't have to. We might be somewhat uncertain about the precise welfare functions of the different individuals and the precise correspondence between the respective welfare units, but we could quite reasonably still assert that in every possible case within permitted variations the sum total is less than what could happen with a more equal distribution. The attack of Robbins [15] and others on interpersonal comparability, so blithely assumed by Marshall [12], has not distinguished between *some* comparability and *total* comparability of units, and the consequence has been the virtual elimination of certain types of questions from the formal literature on welfare economics.[6]

A third example may clarify another aspect of our motivation. In discussing the method of assigning the values 0 and 1 to the worst and the best alternatives of every individual 'to make individual utilities interpersonally comparable', Arrow [2] shows that the assignment is 'extremely unsatisfactory' by a suitably chosen example. One can recommend other methods of normalization, e.g. assigning 0 to the worst alternative and 1 to the *sum* of the utilities of all the alternatives taken together, or alternatively using some hypothetical alternatives for scaling, but each of these can be shown to be 'unsatisfactory' for some particular choices, not necessarily the same for each case. Therefore, we might list a number of such alternative methods of interpersonal normalization, and then follow the rule that if the sum of individual welfare is as great for $x$ as for $y$ under *all* the methods, then and only then would we say that $x$ has at least as much aggregate welfare as $y$. This would be another possible use of a notion of comparability of individual welfare units that is not quite total but it is not a case of non-comparability. We wish to catch this type of motivation as well.[7]

---

6. This is one reason for the remarkable concentration on Pareto optimality in modern welfare economics. One of the few attempts at analysing distributional value judgements and their consequences is to be found in Fisher [6], and Kenen and Fisher [11], under the general approach of treating social welfare as a function of individual utilities.

7. We concentrate on partial comparability of 'units', because our object of study is the aggregate of individual welfare. A framework of partial comparability for absolute levels of welfare can be similarly developed to deal with problems of fairness or justice, where absolute levels are important.

## 2 The Aggregation Quasi-ordering

Let $X$ be the set of alternative social states, $x$. Every individual $i$ has a set $L_i$ of real-valued welfare functions, $W_i$, each defined over $X$. If individual welfare is 'ordinally measurable', then every element of $L_i$ is a positive monotonic transformation of every other element, and furthermore every positive monotonic transformation of any element of $L_i$ belongs to $L_i$. If, on the other hand, individual welfare is 'cardinally measurable', then every element of $L_i$ is a positive linear transformation of every other element, and every positive linear transformation of any element of $L_i$ belongs to $L_i$.[8] We shall assume cardinal measurability of individual welfare, but it can be shown to be an unnecessarily strict requirement for the approach to partial comparability outlined in this paper.

To sum the levels of individual welfare, we have to choose one element from every $L_i$. Any such $n$-tuple of individual welfare functions we shall call a functional combination.

*Definition* 1: *A functional combination, $W$, is any element of the* Cartesian product $\Pi_{i=1}^{n} L_i$, denoted $L$.

For the purpose of comparison of aggregate welfare of alternative social states in $X$, we define a subset $\bar{L}$ of $L$, and sum the individual welfare differences between any pair, $x$, $y$, in $X$ for every element of $\bar{L}$. The specification of $\bar{L}$ reflects our assumptions of interpersonal comparability. We denote $xR^a y$ for $x$ having at least as much aggregate welfare as $y$.

*Definition* 2: *A comparison set $\bar{L}$ is any specified subset of $L$ such that* we declare that $x$ has at least as much aggregate welfare as $y$, for any pair $x$, $y$, if and only if the sum of the individual welfare differences between $x$ and $y$ is non-negative for every element $W$ of $\bar{L}$, i.e.,

$$\forall x, y \in X : [xR^a y \leftrightarrow \forall W \in \bar{L} : \sum_i [W_i(x) - W_i(y)] \geq 0].$$

We define $xP^a y$ as $xR^a y$ and $\sim (yR^a x)$, and $xI^a y$ as $xR^a y$ and $yR^a x$.

---

8. Chipman [3] points out that the terms 'ordinal' and 'cardinal' as used in economics 'bear scant if any relation to the mathematicians' concept of ordinal and cardinal numbers; rather they are euphemisms for the concepts of order-homomorphism to the real numbers and group-homomorphism to the real numbers' (p. 216). Further, by convention 'cardinality' has been associated with the *additive* group of real numbers (i.e., a cardinal utility function is assumed to be group invariant under affine transformations), rather than with the *multiplicative* group, even though Frisch's pioneering paper [9] revealed a preference for the multiplicative representation. We shall stick to the conventional usage of the terms, after sounding this note of warning. It may also be noted that in this branch of the literature, an affine transformation, such as $U^1 = a + bU^2$, is called a linear transformation, which algebraists would reserve for homogeneous transformations of the type $U^1 = bU^2$.

Certain distinguished cases of interpersonal comparability deserve special mention, and should help to illustrate the relation between interpersonal comparability and the comparison set.

*Definition* 3.   (3.1) *Non-comparability* holds if and only if $\bar{L} = L$.

(3.2) *Full comparability* holds if and only if $\bar{W}$ being any element of $\bar{L}$ implies that $\bar{L}$ includes only and all functional combinations $W$ such that for all $i$

$$W_i = a + b\bar{W}_i,$$

where $a$ and $b$ can be any two real numbers with $b > 0$.

(3.3) *Unit comparability* holds if and only if $\bar{W}$ being any element of $\bar{L}$ implies that $\bar{L}$ includes only and all functional combinations $W$ such that for all $i$

$$W_i = a_i + b\bar{W}_i,$$

where $a_i$ can vary with $i$ but $b > 0$ must be invariant with respect to $i$.

In the case of noncomparability the set $L$ of functional combinations is not restricted in any way to arrive at the comparison set $\bar{L}$. In the case of 'full comparability' a one-to-one correspondence is established between the welfare functions of different individuals. In the case of 'unit comparability' if the welfare function of one individual is specified, it specifies a one parameter family of welfare functions for every other individual, each member of the family differing from any other by a constant (positive or negative). It may be noted that with unit comparability the absolute levels of individual welfare are not comparable (e.g., it makes no sense to say that person $A$ is better off than person $B$), but welfare differences are comparable (e.g., it does make sense to say that person $A$ gains more than $B$ in the choice of social state $x$ rather than $y$). In this case, welfare units are comparable (there is a one-to-one correspondence of welfare units), though the origins are arbitrary.

*Definition* 4 (*Pareto Criterion*).    For any pair $x, y \in X : xR^p y \leftrightarrow \forall i : xR_i y$.

$R^p$ is, of course, a quasi-ordering (see Arrow [2]), i.e., reflexive and transitive, but not necessarily complete.

We define $xP^p y$ as $xR^p y$ and $\sim (yR^p x)$, and it stands for the *strict* Pareto preference relation, which generates a strict partial ordering.

The following results concerning the binary relation of aggregation, $R^a$, are important.

THEOREM 1:    (1.1) *For any $\bar{L}$, i.e. for every possible assumption of interpersonal comparability, $R^a$ is a quasi-ordering.*

(1.2) *For any $\bar{L}$, i.e., for every possible assumption of interpersonal comparability, $R^p$ is a subrelation of $R^a$, i.e.,*

$$\forall x, y \in X : [xR^p y \rightarrow xR^a y] \text{ and } [xP^p y \rightarrow xP^a y].$$

(1.3) *With non-comparability, $R^a = R^p$.*

(1.4) *With unit comparability, or with full comparability, $R^a$ is a complete ordering.*

*Proof.* (1.1) Reflexivity of $R^a$ follows directly from each $W_i$ being an order preserving transformation of $R_i$ for every element of $L$. Transitivity of $R^a$ is also immediate. For any $x$, $y$, $z \in X$:

$$xR^a y \text{ and } yR^a z \to \sum_i [W_i(x) - W_i(y)] \geqslant 0 \text{ and } \sum_i [W_i(y) - W_i(z)] \geqslant 0,$$
$$\text{for all } W \in \bar{L},$$

$$\to \sum_i [W_i(x) - W_i(z)] \geqslant 0 \quad \text{for all } W \in \bar{L},$$

$$\to xR^a z.$$

(1.2) For any $x$, $y \in X$:

$$xR^p y \to \forall i [W_i(x) - W_i(y)] \geqslant 0 \quad \text{for every } W \in L,$$
$$\to xR^a y, \quad \text{since } \bar{L} \subset L.$$

Further,

$$xP^p y \to \exists i: xP_i y \text{ and } \forall i: xR_i y,$$
$$\to \exists i: [W_i(x) - W_i(y)] > 0 \quad \text{and } \forall i [W_i(x) - W_i(y)] \geqslant 0,$$
$$\text{for every } W \in L,$$
$$\to xP^a y, \text{ since } \bar{L} \subset L.$$

(1.3) In view of (1.2) all we need show is: $xR^a y \to xR^p y$. For any $x$, $y$ in $X$: $\sim (xR^p y) \to \exists j: yP_j x \to \exists j: [W_j(y) - W_j(x)] > 0$ for every $W \in L$. For each $W$, define $\alpha_1(W) = W_j(y) - W_j(x)$, and $\alpha_2(W) = \sum_{i \neq j}[W_i(x) - W_i(y)]$. Take any arbitrary $W^* \in \bar{L}$. If $\alpha_1(W^*) > \alpha_2(W^*)$, then clearly $\sim (xR^a y)$. Suppose, however, that $\alpha_1(W^*) \leqslant \alpha_2(W^*)$. Consider now $W^{**} \in L$ such that $W_i^{**} = W_i^*$ for all $i \neq j$, and $W_j^{**} = nW_j^*$, where $n$ is any real number greater than $\alpha_2(W^*)/\alpha_1(W^*)$. Clearly, $\alpha_1(W^{**}) > \alpha_2(W^{**})$, and $W^{**} \in L$. Since $\bar{L} = L$, given non-comparability, we have $\sim (xR^a y)$, which completes the proof.

(1.4) In view of (1.1) all we need show is the completeness of $R^a$. First assume unit comparability. Take any $W^* \in \bar{L}$, and any $x$, $y \in X$. Obviously, $\sum_i [W_i^*(x) - W_i^*(y)] \geqslant 0$, or $\leqslant 0$. Since for every $W \in \bar{L}$, for each $i$, $W_i = a_i + bW_i^*$, for some $b > 0$, we must have $\sum_i [W_i(x) - W_i(y)]$ either non-negative for each $W \in \bar{L}$, or non-positive for each $W \in \bar{L}$. Hence $R^a$ must be complete. Since full comparability implies that $\bar{L}$ is even more restricted, clearly $R^a$ must be complete also in this case.

## 3  *Partial Comparability*

Partial comparability is the generic term to be used for every case of interpersonal comparability lying in between unit comparability and non-comparability. Let $\bar{L}(0)$ and $\bar{L}(1)$ stand respectively for $\bar{L}$ under non-comparability and unit comparability.

*Definition* 5:    Partial comparability implies that $\bar{L}$ is a subset of $\bar{L}(0)$ and a superset of $\bar{L}(1)$. We shall refer to $\bar{L}$ under partial comparability as $\bar{L}(p)$.

We know from Theorem 1.1 that the aggregation relation $R^a$ is a quasi-ordering under every case of partial comparability. Since for the purpose of aggregation we are really interested in the welfare *units* and not in the respective *origins*, it is convenient to specify the set of vectors $b$ of coefficients of individual welfare measures with respect to any comparison set $\bar{L}(p)$. The set of $b$ must obviously be defined with respect to some particular $W^* \in L$ chosen for normalization.

*Definition* 6:    The coefficient set of $\bar{L}$ with respect to $W^*$, denoted $B(W^*, \bar{L})$, consists exactly of all vectors $b$ such that some $W \in \bar{L}$ can be expressed as:

$$W_i = a_i + b_i W_i^*$$

where $W_i$ is the $i$th element of $W$, and $a_i$ any real number.[9] When there is no possibility of ambiguity $B(W^*, \bar{L})$ may be called $B$.

A representation of $B$ may be helpful. Consider the $n$-dimensional Euclidean space $E^n$, when there are $n$ individuals. With unit comparability $B$ is an open half line with origin 0, but excluding 0.[10]. If some element $b$ of the coefficient set $B$ is revealed, the rest can be obtained simply by scalar multiplication by $t > 0$. The precise specification of the half line from origin 0 will depend on the element $W^*$ chosen for the representation; the important point is that in this case $B$ will simply be one ray from the origin. If $W^* \in \bar{L}$, then for all $i,j$: $b_i = b_j$, e.g., $B$ will be the forty-five degree line in the two person case. (There are some advantages in choosing $W^* \in \bar{L}$, but this may not always be possible since different $\bar{L}$ sets that may have to be compared under uniform normalization may have no $W$ in common.)

On the other hand with non-comparability $B$ will equal the positive orthant of $E^n$, i.e., the entire non-negative orthant except the boundary.[11] Any strictly positive vector can be chosen as $b$.

Before we go deeper into the properties of $B$, it is important to note that the exact content of $B$ is, of course, very much dependent on the precise choice of $W^*$, and the choice of $W^*$ is quite arbitrary. A shift from one $W^*$ to another will mean that the $i$th element of each $b$ will have to be multiplied by a positive constant $\beta_i$, for $i = 1, \ldots, n$. Thus the properties of $B$ that are invariant with respect to such linear transformations are the ones that are independent of the choice of $W^*$. While we shall not go on repeating this for all the properties that are discussed below, it can be checked that these properties are, in fact, independent of the choice of $W^*$. There is one exception, viz., the case of 'strong symmetry', where the choice of $W^*$ is relevant but this still

9. Note that $b_i$ is the $i$th component of $b$.
10. It is necessary to exclude 0 since only *positive* linear transformations are permitted.
11. The boundary is excluded since only *positive* linear transformations are allowed.

does not make it really arbitrary since the relevant axiom is defined in an existential form to be discussed later.

We have so far defined partial comparability very generally. Any $B$ from a half line to the entire positive orthant falls in this category. It would be reasonable to expect, however, that $B$ under partial comparability will satisfy certain regularity conditions. First, the coefficients should be scale independent. If $b \in B$, then for all $\lambda > 0$, $(\lambda b) \in B$, i.e., $B$ should include all points on the half line 0, $b$, except 0 itself. For example, if $(1, 2, 3)$ is a possible $b$, then so should be, say, $(2, 4, 6)$, for nothing essential depends on the scale of representation. This implies that $B$ will be a cone with vertex 0 but excluding 0 itself, i.e., it is the complement of 0 in a cone with vertex 0.

Second, it seems reasonable to assume the convexity of $B$. For example, given a coefficient of 1 for individual 1, if we are ready to apply both the coefficients 1 and 2 to individual 2's welfare units, then we should be ready to apply 1.5 as well. More generally, if $b^1$ and $b^2$ are two elements of $B$, then so is $tb^1 + (1 - t)b^2$ for any $t: 0 < t < 1$. Since with the exception of 0, $B$ is a cone, this is equivalent to the convexity of the cone defined as $b^1$, $b^2 \in B \rightarrow (t^1 b^1 + t^2 b^2) \in B$, for all $t_1, t_2 \geqslant 0$, except for $t_1 = t_2 = 0$.

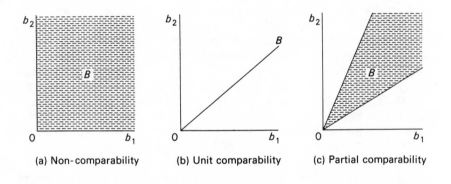

(a) Non-comparability        (b) Unit comparability        (c) Partial comparability

FIGURE 1    COEFFICIENT SETS IN $E^2$

In Figure 1 we represent the cases of non-comparability, unit comparability, and partial comparability with the assumptions of scale independence and convexity in the special case of two individuals.

Given the set of social states $X$ and the set of individual utility functions defined over $X$, we might wonder what the relation would be between the size of $B$ and the aggregation quasi-ordering generated in each case. We first obtain the following elementary result. Let $R^1$ and $R^2$ be two aggregation quasi-orderings with respect to $B^1$ and $B^2$ respectively.

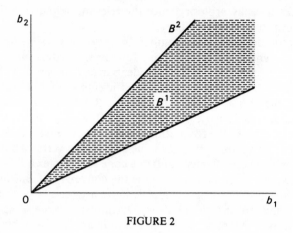

FIGURE 2

LEMMA 1.    *If $B^2 \subset B^1$, then for all $x, y \in X: xR^1y \rightarrow xR^2y$.*

The proof is obvious.

What does not follow, however, is that $xP^1y \rightarrow xP^2y$, so that we cannot say that $R^1$ must be a subrelation of $R^2$. An illustration will prove this point. Consider, in a two-person world, $B^2$ consisting of the half line 0, (1, 1), and $B^1$ as the convex polyhedral cone formed by the sum of the half lines 0, (1, 1) and 0, (1, $\frac{1}{2}$) as illustrated in Figure 2. Clearly $B^2 \subset B^1$. Assume further that $W^*_1(y) - W^*_1(x) = W^*_1(x) - W^*_1(y) > 0$. Clearly $xI^2y$, but $xP^1y$, since for any $(b^1_2/b^1_1) < 1$, $\Sigma_i[W^*_1(x) - W^*_1(y)]b^1_i > 0$. Hence $xP^1y$ cannot possibly imply $xP^2y$, and $R^1$ is not a subrelation of $R^2$ in this case.

If we assume an additional regularity condition, we can be sure that if $B^2 \subset B^1$, then $R^1$ will be a subrelation of $R^2$.

REGULARITY AXIOM.    *For every possible partition of the set of individuals into subsets $J$ and $K$:*

$$B^2 \subset B^1 \text{ and } (B^1 \not\subset B^2) \rightarrow \exists(b^1 \in B^1 \text{ and } b^2 \in B^2): [\forall i \in J: b^2_i < b^1_i]$$
*and $[\forall i \in K: b^2_i > b^1_i]$.*

We shall discuss this axiom after using it in the following theorem.

THEOREM 2.    *If the Regularity Axiom holds, then $B^2 \subset B^1$ implies that $R^1$ is a subrelation of $R^2$.*

*Proof.*    If $B^1 = B^2$, then clearly $R^1 = R^2$, so that we can concentrate on the case when $B^2$ is a proper subset of $B^1$. In view of Lemma 1 all that need be proved is that $xP^1y \rightarrow xP^2y$, for all $x, y \in X$. Suppose, to the contrary, that for some $x$, $y \in X$, we have $xP^1y$ but *not* $xP^2y$. In view of Lemma 1 this implies that $xP^1y$, $xR^2y$ and $yR^2x$. Since $xI^2y$, we must have $\forall b^2 \in B^2$: $\Sigma_i[W_i^*(x) - W_i^*(y)]b_i^2 = 0$. Partition the individuals into two groups $J$ and $K$ such that $i \in J$ if and only if $xP_iy$, and $i \in K$ otherwise. By the Regularity Axiom, we can assert that $\exists b^1 \in B^1$:$\Sigma_i[W_i^*(x) - W_i^*(y)]b_i^1 < 0$, or $\forall_i$:$xI_iy$. But neither of the alternatives could be true since $xP^1y$, and this contradiction establishes the theorem.

It may be noted that the assumption of convexity and scale independence are not necessary for Theorem 2. This fact may not be very important from a practical point of view, however, since convexity and scale independence appear to make the Regularity Axiom less objectionable.

How demanding a condition is the Regularity Axiom? Consider $B^1$ and $B^2$ as two convex cones (excluding the vertex). What the Regularity Axiom asserts is that if $B^2$ is a proper subset of $B^1$, then there is at least one half line in $B^2$ that is an *interior ray*[12] of $B^1$. All this excludes is the possibility that the relaxation of comparability is so biased that all permitted cases in the smaller set are simply boundary positions in the larger set. This is, in any case, impossible if the linear dimension of the cone representing $B^2$ is $n$, where $n$ is the number of individuals. Further, even if the linear dimension of $B^2$ is less than $n$, the Regularity Axiom will hold unless the move from $B^2$ to $B^1$ is severely biased. The object is to leave out cases like the one represented in Figure 2 (for the two-person situation). Note that in Figure 2 the linear dimension of $B^2$ is less than 2, as $B^2$ consists only of one half line, and further the shift from $B^2$ to $B^1$ is entirely one sided, so that the ray that makes up $B^2$ is a boundary ray of $B^1$. A change from $B^2$ to $B^1$ permits the raising of the measures of welfare differences for person one vis-à-vis the measures for person two, but not vice versa. The Regularity Axiom rules out this type of bias in the relative coverage of the different comparison sets.

## 4 *Symmetry: Weak and Strong*

The Regularity Axiom can be viewed as a condition of symmetry but of a very mild kind. A somewhat more demanding condition is the following.†

12. An interior ray of a cone $C$ is a ray ($r$) such that $C$ contains an $\varepsilon$ neighbourhood of ($r$), for some $\varepsilon > 0$. For this we have to define a metric on rays related to the usual topology of $E^n$. This can be done in many ways which are essentially similar, and we might chose, for the purpose of specification, the chord distance between two points $x/|x|$ and $y/|y|$ on the unit sphere $|z| = 1$, where $|u|$ represents the norm of vector $u$, defined as the inner product $(u \cdot u)$.

† [Corrected as in my 'Interpersonal Comparison and Partial Comparability: A Correction', *Econometrica*, **40** (September 1972), which went on to note the following: 'While the intuitive rationale of restricting the coefficient sets to a class of such convex polyhedral cones seems to be satisfactory, it remains an open question as to whether it may be better to permit the coeffi-

WEAK SYMMETRY AXIOM. *Each B is a convex polyhedral cone defined by $B = [b \mid \forall i, j: (b_i/b_j) \leqslant \beta_{ij} \geqslant 1]$, except the origin, and for any pair $B^1$ and $B^2$, $[\exists i,j: \beta^1_{ij} > \beta^2_{ij}] \rightarrow [\forall i,j: \beta^1_{ij} > \beta^2_{ij}]$.*

This is a much stronger requirement than the Regularity Axiom. (See Figure 3 in Section 5 where the contrasts are made.) With the latter it is sufficient that one ray in $B^2 \subset B^1$ be an interior ray of $B^1$, whereas with weak symmetry every ray in $B^2$ has to be interior in $B^1$, if $B^2$ is a proper subset of $B^1$. When the extent of comparability is relaxed for any pair of individuals, it has to be relaxed for every pair of individuals, in the case of weak symmetry. However, the precise extent of the relaxation may vary from pair to pair (hence it is 'weak', to be contrasted with 'strong symmetry' later). It also imposes a directional symmetry between each individual in a pair. If the least upper bound of the ratio of coefficients goes up between $i$ and $j$, then the greatest lower bound of the ratio must go down (i.e., the least upper bound of the ratio between $j$ and $i$ must go up). The ethical acceptability of the axiom depends on the appeal of such directional symmetry between pairs and between each individual in a pair.

LEMMA 2. *Given scale independence, convexity, and weak symmetry, the binary relation of set inclusion defines a complete ordering over the class of all admissible coefficient sets.*

*Proof.* Clearly, $B \subset B$, and $[B^3 \subset B^2$ and $B^2 \subset B^1] \rightarrow B^3 \subset B^1$, so that $\subset$ is reflexive and transitive. All we need prove, therefore, is the property of completeness. If $B^1 \neq B^2$, then given convexity, for some $i, j$, $\sup_{b^1 \in B^1} (b^1_i/b^1_j)$ is either strictly greater or strictly less than $\sup_{b^2 \in B^2} (b^2_i/b^2_j)$. Without loss of generality let it be strictly greater. Then by the Weak Symmetry Axiom, i.e., for admissible $B$ sets, we have for all $i, j$, $\sup_{b^1 \in B^1} (b^1_i/b^1_j) > \sup_{b^2 \in B^2} (b^2_i/b^2_j)$. Since $B^1$ and $B^2$ are convex cones (excluding the vertex), this implies that $B^2 \subset B^1$.

LEMMA 3. *If $R^1$ and $R^2$ are two quasi-orderings generated by two cases of partial comparability, then given scale independence, convexity, and weak symmetry, either $R^1$ is a subrelation of $R^2$, or $R^2$ is a subrelation of $R^1$, and the binary relation between quasi-orderings of 'being a subrelation of' defines a complete ordering over all possible aggregation quasi-orderings under partial comparability.*

cient sets to be any closed convex cone and to impose restrictions only on the relations between different cones. To obtain the result presented in Lemma 2, one could then impose the requirement that in any pair of coefficient sets there is one set such that for all hyperplanes through the origin if that set lies on one side of it, the other lies strictly on that side. It is easy to devise a partial comparability index from 0 to 1 in this case also' (p. 959).]

The proof follows directly from Lemma 2 and Theorem 2, noting the fact that weak symmetry implies regularity (though not vice versa).

We have thus a sequence of aggregation quasi-orderings, each a subrelation of the next, starting from the Pareto quasi-ordering, which is yielded by non-comparability, and ending up with a complete ordering, which is yielded by unit comparability. In between lie all cases of partial comparability, and as the extent of partial comparability is raised, i.e., as $B$ is shrunk, the aggregation quasi-ordering gets extended (if it changes at all), without ever contradicting an earlier quasi-ordering obtained for a lower extent of partial comparability.

A measure of the degree of partial comparability may be useful in this case. Define for every ordered pair of individuals $i$, $j$, the following ratio, which we shall call the comparability ratio:

$$c_{ij} = \inf_{b \in B} \left( \frac{b_i}{b_j} \right) \bigg/ \sup_{b \in B} \left( \frac{b_i}{b_j} \right).$$

We can define the degree of partial comparability as the arithmetic mean of the comparability ratios for every ordered pair of individuals.

*Definition 7.* In the presence of convexity, scale independence, and weak symmetry, the degree of partial comparability $d(B)$ will be measured by the arithmetic mean of $c_{ij}$ for all ordered pairs $i$, $j$.

Since each $c_{ij}$ must lie within the closed interval $[0,1]$, the degree of partial comparability is also defined over this interval. Further the following theorem holds.

THEOREM 3.   *Given convexity, scale independence, and weak symmetry, $d(B) = 0$ implies that the aggregation quasi-ordering will be the same as the Pareto quasi-ordering, and $d(B) = 1$ implies that it will be a complete ordering. Further, if $d(B^2) > d(B^1)$, the aggregation quasi-ordering $R^1$ will be a subrelation of the aggregation quasi-ordering $R^2$.*

*Proof:* If $d(B) = 1$, clearly $c_{ij} = 1$ for each ordered pair $i$, $j$. In this case $B$ will consist of only one ray through the origin, and unit comparability will hold. We know from Theorem 1 that in this case $R^a$ will be a complete ordering. If, on the other hand, $d(B) = 0$, each $c_{ij}$ must equal zero, so that the ratio $b_i/b_j$ can be varied without bound (except those already implied in each $b_i$ being positive) for every $i$, $j$. This implies that non-comparability holds, and from Theorem 1 we know that $R^a$ will equal the Pareto quasi-ordering $R^p$.

If $d(B^2) > d(B^1)$, then for some $i$, $j$, $c^1_{ij} < c^2_{ij}$. This implies that for some pair $i$, $j$, either $\sup (b^1_i/b^1_j) > \sup (b^2_i/b^2_j)$, or $\inf (b^1_i/b^1_j) < \inf (b^2_i/b^2_j)$. If the former, then it follows from the Weak Symmetry Axiom that $B^2$ is a proper subset of $B^1$. If the latter, then $\sup (b^1_j/b^1_i) > \sup (b^2_j/b^2_i)$, and once again $B^2$ must be a proper subset of $B^1$. Since the Weak Symmetry Axiom implies the Regularity Axiom, it now follows from Theorem 2 that $R^1$ must be a subrelation of $R^2$.

From Theorem 3 it is clear that if the Axiom of Weak Symmetry holds, in addition to the relatively harmless assumptions of convexity and scale independence, then all cases of partial comparability can be measured by a precise degree, $d(B) = q$, of partial comparability with interesting properties. It is a real number lying in the closed interval $[0,1]$, and the corresponding quasi-ordering $R^q$ is a subrelation of all quasi-orderings obtained with higher degrees of partial comparability, i.e., for $d(B) > q$, while all quasi-orderings with lower degrees of partial comparability, i.e., $d(B) < q$, are subrelations of $R^q$. This monotonicity property in the relation between the continuum of degrees of comparability in the interval $[0,1]$ and the sequence of aggregation quasi-orderings from the Pareto quasi-ordering to a complete ordering is a phenomenon of some importance.

It should also be noted that it is not *necessary* to assume $d(B) = 1$ for a complete ordering to be generated, though it is sufficient. Even with $d(B) < 1$, completeness may be achieved; we shall presently discuss this further. The necessary degree will depend on the precise configuration of individual welfare functions.

If we are ready to make a stronger assumption than weak symmetry, we can get an even neater picture.

STRONG SYMMETRY AXIOM. *There exists some functional combinations* $W^* \in \bar{L}(p)$ *such that for each* $B(W^*, \bar{L})$, $\sup_{b \in B}(b_i/b_j)$ *is exactly the same for all ordered pairs i, j.*

Obviously strong symmetry implies weak symmetry,[13] but not vice versa. Further, under strong symmetry $c_{ij}$ is the same for all $i, j$. We can express the degree of partial comparability simply as any $c_{ij}$. It is to be noted that the property of having the same upper bound is one that depends on which $W^*$ we choose as the reference point; $W^*$ is thus no longer inconsequential. The Strong Symmetry Axiom asserts that for *some* $W^*$ this set of equalities holds, but not of course for every arbitrary choice of $W^*$.

Cases of strong symmetry take the following form. Consider the restriction (with respect to some $W^*$) that for some real number $p : 0 \leq p \leq 1$, for all $i, j$, we must have $p \leq (b_i/b_j) \leq 1/p$. The degree of partial comparability according to Definition 7 will be given by $p^2$, which will itself lie in the closed interval $[0,1]$, and as $p$ would be raised from 0 to 1, we would move monotonically from non-comparability to unit comparability.

With strong symmetry a sufficient degree of partial comparability that will

---

13. If the antecedent of the implication in weak symmetry is true, then strong symmetry implies that the conclusion must also be true, since $\sup_{b \in B}(b_i/b_j)$ is invariant with respect to the choice of $i$ and $j$ under strong symmetry.

guarantee the completeness of the aggregation quasi-ordering is easy to specify. For any pair of alternatives $x$, $y$ in $X$, partition the individuals into two classes, viz., $J$ consisting of all those who prefer $x$ to $y$, and $K$ consisting of all those who regard $y$ to be at least as good as $x$. Define:

$$m(x,y) = \sum_{i \in J} [W_i^*(x) - W_i^*(y)],$$

and

$$m(y,x) = \sum_{i \in K} [W_i^*(y) - W_i^*(x)].$$

Now define $a(x, y)$ as

$$a(x, y) = \frac{\min [m(x, y), m(y, x)]}{\max [m(x, y), m(y, x)]}.$$

THEOREM 4. *With convexity, scale independence, and strong symmetry, the aggregation quasi-ordering will be complete if the degree of partial comparability is greater than or equal to $(a^*)^2$, where $a^* = \sup_{x,y \in X} a(x, y)$.*

*Proof.* For any pair $x$, $y$, completeness will fail to be fulfilled if and only if $[W_i(x) - W_i(y)] > 0$ for some $W \in \bar{L}$ and $< 0$ for some other $W \in \bar{L}$. First consider $W^*$. Without loss of generality, let $\sum_i [W_i^*(x) - W_i^*(y)] > 0$, i.e., $m(x, y) > m(y, x)$. We have to show that the sum of welfare differences between $x$ and $y$ is non-negative for all $W \in \bar{L}$. Assume the degree of partial comparability to be $d$, so that the ratio of the welfare units of any two individuals can be reduced at most by a factor $p = d^{\frac{1}{2}}$. If, contrary to the Lemma, the sum of welfare differences between $x$ and $y$ is negative for any $W \in \bar{L}$, then $[pm(x, y) - m(y, x)] < 0$. Hence $p < [m(y, x)/m(x, y)]$. But this is impossible, since $d = p^2 \geq (a^*)^2$, and $a^* = \sup_{x,y \in X} a(x, y)$. This contradiction proves that the aggregation quasi-ordering must be complete.†

It is clear that unit comparability is an unnecessarily demanding assumption unless it so happens that $\sum_i W_i^*(x)$ is exactly equal to $\sum_i W_i^*(y)$ for some $x$ and $y$,[14] and some degree of strict partial comparability, i.e., $d < 1$, will yield a complete ordering—precisely the same ordering as one would get under unit comparability (or full comparability).[15]

---

14. Strictly this is not necessary, since with an infinite set $X$ it is possible that $\sup_{x, y \in X} a(x, y) = 1$, even though for no $x$, $y$, it is the case that $\sum_i W_i^*(x) = \sum_i W_i^*(y)$. However, the former also is a very special assumption.

† [A minor error in the statement of the theorem and the proof has been corrected.]

15. The estimation of sufficient degrees of strict partial comparability is not easy when the assumption of strong symmetry is dropped. This is because the range of variation $[p, 1/p]$ will then vary from individual to individual. However, since $d$, which is an arithmetic mean of $c_{ij}$, cannot fall below the minimum $c_{ij}$ or rise above the maximum $c_{ij}$, we can find a corresponding value of $d$ which will be sufficient for completeness in this case also.

## 5  *Concluding Remarks*

We have studied in this paper a framework for interpersonal comparability in the context of aggregating the welfare measures of individuals. We began by defining an aggregation relation $R^a$ between any pair of social states and showed it to be always a quasi-ordering (irrespective of the comparability assumption) subsuming the Pareto quasi-ordering, and also showed that $R^a$ is identical with the Pareto quasi-ordering under non-comparability, and is a complete ordering under unit comparability, and of course under full comparability (Theorem 1). We also obtained a set of results about the relative completeness of aggregation quasi-orderings under different comparability assumptions, and obtained a sufficient condition for one aggregation quasi-ordering being a subrelation of another (Lemma 1 and Theorem 2). Some axioms on the relationship between different assumptions of partial comparability have been studied in this context. We moved from a mild assumption of 'regularity' to one of 'weak symmetry', which permitted some new results to be obtained. In particular under the latter assumption we showed the completeness of the relation of 'being a subrelation of' defined over the set of aggregation quasi-orderings (Lemma 2). Further we proposed a measure of partial comparability by a real number lying in the closed interval [0, 1], such that as the degree of comparability is raised the aggregation quasi-ordering gets monotonically extended. Here the two extremes of 0 and 1 stand respectively for non-comparability and unit comparability, yielding

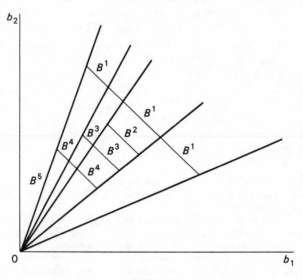

FIGURE 3

respectively the most limited quasi-ordering, viz., the Pareto quasi-ordering, and the most extensive quasi-ordering, viz., a complete ordering (Theorem 3). With a stronger assumption of 'strong symmetry' we showed that the picture is even simpler. Except in special situations it appears that unit comparability is an unnecessarily demanding assumption and some degree of partial comparability $d < 1$ seems sufficient to generate a complete ordering through the aggregation relation.

In one respect the analysis of this paper can be easily extended. The assumption of cardinality of individual welfare is too strong, and aggregation can be based on non-cardinal utility as well. Theorems 1.1, 1.2, and 1.3 can be easily extended to ordinal individual welfare functions for the proofs make no use of cardinality. While the other results do use cardinality, a weakening of that assumption is possible. Suppose we have a welfare measure such that an individual can compare welfare differences between two pairs of alternatives, but not in a manner such that the ratio of these differences must be constant for every permitted transformation, i.e., it need not be linear.[16] We can consider alternative values of this ratio and proceed to use them just as well as we have been using alternative ratios of units. Variability of interpersonal correspondences can be combined with a weakening of the measures of welfare functions of individuals. We do not pursue this here, especially since it raises problems that are essentially similar to the ones discussed in this paper.[17]

Finally, we may comment on the variety of axioms introduced in this paper on sets of partial comparability. Scale independence and convexity seem very proper restrictions. Regularity is mildest, then comes weak symmetry, and finally strong symmetry. These conditions were defined precisely, but since their differences might conceivably appear to be somewhat opaque we give in Figure 3 a comparison of the different cases in the special context of a two individual world. If the only two coefficient sets are $B^1$ and $B^2$, then regularity, weak symmetry, and strong symmetry are all satisfied. If we take $B^1$ and $B^3$, then regularity and weak symmetry are satisfied but not strong symmetry. If $B^1$ and $B^4$ are taken, then regularity is satisfied but no symmetry, strong or weak. If we take $B^1$ and $B^5$ (which is one half line on the boundary), then not even regularity is satisfied.

This hierarchy of stronger and stronger assumptions is worth noting since some of the precise results depend on where we are in the hierarchy from the

16. For a more general framework, see Chipman [3]. Incidentally, if individual welfare functions are group homomorphic with respect to multiplicative reals and not with respect to the additive reals, then adding may not be the most sensible way of proceeding to combine individual welfare functions into a social welfare measure. We have abstracted from these broader questions in this paper.

17. This is pursued in my *Collective Choice and Social Welfare*, Holden Day-Oliver and Boyd Series in Mathematical Economics and Econometrics, 1970 [reprinted by North-Holland, Amsterdam 1980].

most limited case of strong symmetry to the most general case where not even regularity is necessarily satisfied.

These axioms are concerned with sets of partial comparability. Unit comparability and non-comparability represent two polar cases of partial comparability. Since much of welfare economics has been concerned with these polar cases, the extremely limited nature of the conventional framework is striking. This paper has been written as a small attempt to broaden this framework.

## References

[1] Arrow, K.J.: 'An Extension of the Basic Theorems of Classical Welfare Economics', in J. Neyman (ed.), *Proceedings of the Second Berkeley Symposium on Mathematical Statistics and Probability* (Berkeley: California University Press, 1951).

[2] ____ *Individual Values and Social Choice* (New York: Wiley, 1951; second edition, 1963).

[3] Chipman, J.S.: 'The Foundations of Utility', *Econometrica*, **28** (April 1960).

[4] Debreu, G.: *Theory of Value* (New York: Wiley, 1959).

[5] Diamond, P.: 'Cardinal Welfare, Individualistic Ethics and Interpersonal Comparisons of Utility', *Journal of Political Economy*, **75** (October 1967).

[6] Fisher, F.M.: 'Income Distributions, Value Judgements, and Welfare', *Quarterly Journal of Economics*, **70** (August 1956).

[7] Fisher, F.M. and J. Rothenberg: 'How Income Ought to be Distributed: Paradox Lost,' *Journal of Political Economy*, **69** (April 1961).

[8] ____ 'How Income Ought to be Distributed: Paradox Enow', *Journal of Political Economy*, **70** (1962).

[9] Frisch, R.: 'Sur un Probleme d'Economie Pure', *Norsk Matematisk Forenings Skrifter*, Series 1, **16** (1926).

[10] Harsanyi, J.: 'Cardinal Welfare, Individualistic Ethics, and Interpersonal Comparisons of Utility', *Journal of Political Economy*, **63** (August 1955).

[11] Kenen, P.B. and F.M. Fisher: 'Income Distributions, Value Judgements and Welfare: A Correction', *Quarterly Journal of Economics*, **70** (August 1956).

[12] Marshall, A.: *Principles of Economics* (9th (Variorum) edition, London: Macmillan, 1961).

[13] Pigou, A.C.: *Economics of Welfare* (4th edition, London: Macmillan, 1932).

[14] Rawls, J.: 'Distributive Justice', in P. Laslett and W.G. Runciman (eds.), *Philosophy, Politics and Society*, Series III (London, 1967).

[15] Robbins, L.: *An Essay on the Nature and Significance of Economic Science* (London: Macmillan, 1935).

[16] Rothenberg, J.: *The Measurement of Social Welfare* (Englewood Cliffs, NJ: Prentice-Hall, 1961).

[17] Samuelson, P.A.: *Foundations of Economics* (Cambridge, Mass.: Harvard University Press, 1947).

[18] ____ 'Probability, Utility and the Independence Axiom', *Econometrica*, **20** (October 1952).

[19] Strotz, R.: 'How Income Ought to be Distributed: A Paradox in Distributive Ethics', *Journal of Political Economy*, **66** (June 1958).

[20] ___ 'How Income Ought to be Distributed: Paradox Regained', *Journal of Political Economy*, **69** (June 1961).

[21] 'Symposium on Optimal Infinite Programmes', *Review of Economic Studies*, **34** (January 1967).

# 10

# On Ignorance and Equal Distribution

There has recently been a revival of interest in Abba Lerner's proposition on maximization of probable aggregate welfare through a policy of equal distribution in a situation of Bayesian ignorance as to who has which utility function. Maurice McManus, Gary Walton, and Richard Coffman (1972) and Roger McCain (1972) have presented in the June 1972 issue of this *Review* formal versions of Lerner's (1944) theorem based on explicit formulation of probability distributions of utility functions for different individuals. Further, McManus *et al*. have shown that the optimality of equal distribution holds also under the 'maximin' strategy of maximizing the lowest value of aggregate welfare for any distribution, and this result does not, naturally, depend on the exact assumptions about probability distributions. As it happens, these two theorems were stated and proved in my paper presented to the International Economic Association Round-Table Conference on Public Economics in Biarritz in 1966 and were published in Sen (1969) as Theorems II ('Probabilistic Egalitarianism') and III ('Maximin Egalitarianism').

This fact in itself is scarcely interesting, except conceivably to the authors and editors, but what may interest the readers of this journal is the fact that both these theorems can be substantially generalized by dropping the framework of *additive* social welfare functions and only requiring social welfare to be a concave (or quasi-concave) function of individual utilities, which need not even be separable.

This generalization is of particular relevance in the context of Milton Friedman's (1966) penetrating criticism of Lerner's approach:

> Eliminate the assumption of ignorance, and the same analysis immediately yields a justification of inequality if individuals do differ in capacity to enjoy satisfaction ... Suppose, further, that it is discovered by this technique that a hundred persons in the United States are enormously more efficient pleasure machines than any others, so that each of these would have to be given an income ten thousand times as large as the

---

From *American Economic Review*, **63** (December 1973), 1022–4.

income of the next most efficient pleasure machine in order to maximize aggregate utility. Would Lerner be willing to accept the resulting division of income as optimum ...? (pp. 310–11)

The theorems presented below indicate that Lerner does not have to do any such thing since the maximizing property of the equal distribution holds for probable social welfare even if it is not of the additive form. A concave social welfare function $W$ need not necessarily award a higher income to a more efficient pleasure machine.[1] The 'maximin' result presented in Sen (1969) and McManus *et al.* can also be similarly generalized.

1

The results are proved for the case in which there are $n$ individuals and $n$ utility functions, when it is not known who has which utility function.[2] The following notation is used:

$y$ = any income vector $(y_1, \ldots, y_n)$, in which $y_i$ is the income of person $i$
$z$ = vector of equal incomes, i.e., $z_i = z_j$ for all $i, j$
$U^j$ = individual welfare function $j$
$W$ = social welfare
$u_i$ = individual welfare of person $i$
$p_i^j$ = probability of person $i$ having $U^j$

*Assumption 1 (Total Income Fixity).* The total income to be distributed is constant $(y^*)$:

$$y_1 + \ldots + y_n = y^* \tag{1}$$

*Assumption 2 (Concavity of the Group Welfare Function).* Social Welfare $W$, an increasing and symmetric function of individual welfare levels: $W = W(u_1, \ldots, u_n)$, is concave.

*Assumption 3 (Concavity of Individual Welfare Functions).* Each individual welfare function $U_j(y)$ is concave.

*Assumption 4 (Equi-probability).* For each $j$, $p_i^j = p_m^j$, for every pair of individuals $i, m$.

---

1. This is an important issue for the measurement of income distribution, on which see Partha Dasgupta, Sen, and David Starrett (1973), and Michael Rothschild and Joseph Stiglitz (1973). I have discussed the underlying normative framework in my book, Sen (1973). The 'Weak Equity Axiom' used there would guarantee that the more efficient pleasure machine would get, in fact, *less* income, and this is consistent with a concave social welfare function. See also Sen (1970), ch. 9.

2. We can take a wider set $V$ of individual welfare functions and extend the proofs. On this see Sen (1969).

THEOREM 1.   *Given Assumptions 1, 2, 3 and 4, the mathematical expectation of social welfare is maximized by an equal division of income.*

*Proof.*   Thanks to the symmetry property of $W$, we can take the social welfare function to be $W(u^1, \ldots, u^n)$, where $u^j$ is the utility of the person with the $j$th utility function; nothing depends on precisely which numbered individual enjoys $U^j$. Corresponding to any income distribution vector $y$, let $\tilde{y}$ be a permutation of it such that $\tilde{y}^j$ is the income going to the person with the $j$th utility function. There are $n!$ different ways of assigning $n$ individual welfare functions to $n$ persons, and corresponding to each such assignment $k$, we have a permuted vector $\tilde{y}(k)$, for any income vector $y$. Therefore for any distribution $y$, there are $n!$ values of social welfare given by $F(\tilde{y}(k))$, for $k = 1, \ldots, n!$, and given Assumption 4, the expected value of social welfare from $y$ is given by:

$$E(y) = \frac{1}{n!} \sum_k F(\tilde{y}(k)) \qquad (2)$$

Of course, since all permutations $z$ of the equi-distribution vector $z$ are the same:

$$E(z) = F(z) \qquad (3)$$

By Assumptions 2 and 3, $F$ is a concave function, and by Assumption 1, we have:

$$z = \frac{1}{n!} \sum_k \tilde{y}(k) \qquad (4)$$

Since $F$ is concave, it is clear that:

$$E(y) \leqslant E(z) \qquad (5)$$

Since this is true of all $y$, Theorem 1 holds.

## 2

For the 'maximin' result, Assumption 4 is weakened to:

*Assumption 4\* (Shared Set of Welfare Functions).*   For any individual $i$ and any welfare function $j$, it is possible that $i$ has $j$. Nothing is said on relative probabilities.

For the existence of minimal individual welfare levels, something has to be assumed about the lower bounds of these functions. The following simple assumption is sufficient.[3]

*Assumption 5 (Bounded Individual Welfare Functions).*   Each individual welfare function $U^j$ is bounded from below.

3. It can, however, be easily weakened.

THEOREM 2. *Given Assumptions 1, 2, 3, 4\*, and 5, the maximin strategy for social welfare is to distribute income equally.*

*Proof.* Since $z$ is an average of $\bar{y}(k)$ for all $k$, for any quasi-concave welfare function $F$, we must have:

$$F(z) \geqslant \underset{k}{\text{Min}}\, F(\bar{y}(k)) \tag{6}$$

Furthermore, $z$ being an equal division, the value of $\bar{z}$ is invariant with respect to interpersonal permutations of individual welfare functions. Hence Theorem 2.[4]

Friedman's criticism of Lerner, quoted above, treats him as a prisoner of utilitarianism, but Lerner is free to leave the Benthamite jail.

## References

Dasgupta, P., A. K. Sen and D. Starrett (1973): 'Notes on the Measurement of Inequality', *J. Econ. Theor.*, **6**, 180–7.

Friedman, M. (1947): 'Lerner on the Economics of Control', *J. Polit. Econ.*, **55**, 405–16; reprinted in M. Friedman, *Essays in Positive Economics* (Chicago, 1966).

Lerner, A. P. (1944): *The Economics of Control* (New York).

McCain, R. A. (1972): 'Distributional Equality and Aggregate Utility: Further Comment', *Amer. Econ. Rev.*, **62**, 497–500.

McManus, M., G. M. Walton and R. B. Coffman (1972): 'Distributional Equality and Aggregate Utility: Further Comment', *Amer. Econ. Rev.*, **62**, 489–96.

Rothschild, M. and J. E. Stiglitz (1973): 'Some Further Results on the Measurement of Inequality', *J. Econ. Theor.*, **6**, 188–204.

Sen, A. K. (1969): 'Planners' Preferences: Optimality, Distribution and Social Welfare', in J. Margolis and H. Guitton (eds), *Public Economics* (London/New York).

\_\_\_\_ (1970): *Collective Choice and Social Welfare* (San Francisco 1970).

\_\_\_\_ (1973): *On Economic Inequality* (Oxford/New York).

4. Note that for this result even Assumption 2 is much too strong and the quasi concavity of $W$ is sufficient.

# 11

# On Weights and Measures: Informational Constraints in Social Welfare Analysis

## 1 *Introduction*

The formal theory of collective choice is by now nearly two centuries old, dating from Borda [16]. In this long period applications of this theory have been sought in such diverse fields as examination of electoral rules, study of committee decisions, investigation of voting strategies, analysis of political judgement, evaluation of arbitration rules, exploration of moral concepts (such as fairness, justice, liberty, egality and rights), use of social welfare criteria, formulation of planning objectives, and the construction of evaluative economic statistics (such as national income, inequality or poverty). While all these exercises involve aggregation over groups of people—thereby coming within the broad domain of collective choice theory—they differ from each other in many important respects.

One basis of distinction lies in the nature of the end product of aggregation. In some of these exercises the aggregation has to lead to judgements of 'social welfare', while in others the focus is on arriving merely at 'acceptable decisions'. In an earlier paper (Sen [96]), I have tried to analyse the different requirements of the two types of exercises (along with exploring some other ways of partitioning collective choice problems). In this lecture my focus will be on exercises where the notion of 'social welfare' is involved. As such the

In revising the text for publication [in *Econometrica*] I had benefited a great deal from comments of, or helpful discussions with, George Bordes, Louis Gevers, Frank Hahn, Peter Hammond, Leif Johansen, Eric Maskin, Robert Pollak, Kevin Roberts, Kotaro Suzumura, and Lars-Gunnar Svensson.

Walras–Bowley Lecture, presented at the North American meeting of the Econometric Society, at Madison, Wisconsin, on 24 June 1976, and published in *Econometrica,* **45** (October 1977), 1539–72.

results presented may be of more direct relevance to welfare economics, normative planning theory, evaluative statistics, and political or moral judgements, than to, say, committee decisions, voting strategy, or electoral rules.[1]

Alternative approaches to social welfare evaluation can be subjected to informational analysis: examining each approach in terms of the types of information that it admits and the types it 'excludes' (in the sense of making the evaluation invariant with respect to that information). The analysis begins with the general class of 'social welfare *functionals*' SWFL (see Sen [86]), from which more restrictive structures (such as 'social welfare functions' in the sense of Arrow) can be obtained by suitable 'invariance' restrictions narrowing the informational base.

In Section 2, SWFLs are first defined and then discussed from the point of view of informational admissibility, examining certain distinguished cases, found in the literature, of restrictions on personal welfare information. In Section 3, Arrow's impossibility theorem is examined from the informational point of view (see also Sections 6 and 8). In Section 4 axiomatizations of utilitarianism and Rawlsian lexicographic maximin rules are presented with a focus on axioms that impose informational constraints directly or indirectly.

Sections 5, 6, and 7 are much concerned with the condition of independence of irrelevant alternatives. In Section 5 a class of rules is investigated each of which violates independence but uses interpersonal comparisons (an interpersonal extension of the Borda Rule being an interesting special case). Section 6 identifies some of the far-reaching implications of independence with unrestricted domain in rendering a variety of information inadmissible. The Rawlsian lexicographic maximin rule is derived in Section 7 from its acceptance in the special case where there are only two non-indifferent persons. Unrestricted independence plays the crucial part in this extension.

Section 8 goes into the consequences of basing social welfare judgements exclusively on individual *welfare* information and into the inability of such 'welfarism' to accommodate values like liberty as well as 'historical' theories of 'rights' (e.g., Marxian conception of 'exploitation', Nozick's system of 'entitlements'). In Section 9, the relevance of Arrow-type impossibility results for the Bergson—Samuelson approach to welfare economics is investigated, and it is shown that the crucial issue is again an informational one. Some general remarks on the informational analysis of alternative approaches to social welfare are briefly made in Section 10.

---

1. A corresponding analysis can, of course, be undertaken for decision-oriented exercises as well. For some formal results linking possibility theorems in the context of generating *choice functions* to possibility theorems generating *binary relations* of social welfare, see Sen [96, Sections 4 and 5]. See also Plott [72].

## 2 Social Welfare Functionals

For the set $X$ of alternative social states and the set $H$ of persons involved, the class of social welfare functionals SWFL are considered first.[2] A SWFL specifies exactly one social ordering $R$ over the set $X$ of social states for any given $n$-tuple of real-valued personal welfare functions $W_i(\cdot)$ each defined over $X$, for each person $i = 1, \ldots, n$, in $H$:

$$R = F(\{ W_i \}). \tag{1}$$

Depending on the type of welfare measurability (e.g., 'ordinal', 'cardinal', etc.), to each person $i$ can be attributed a *family* $L_i$ of personal welfare functions, and depending on the assumption of interpersonal comparability, the admissible $n$-tuples of personal welfare functions $\{ W_i \}$ are chosen from the Cartesian product $L$ of these $n$ families (Sen [86, p. 105]). The specification of a SWFL is supplemented by an *invariance* requirement over the set of $n$-tuples that reflect the *same* welfare situation given the measurability and comparability assumptions. For example, given cardinality of personal welfare functions and full interpersonal comparability, two welfare $n$-tuples $\{ W_i \}$ and $\{ W_i' \}$ give the same welfare signals if one can be obtained from the other by subjecting each personal welfare function to some positive, affine transformation—the same for all persons. Given cardinality and full comparability, it would be legitimate to require that such $\{ W_i \}$ and $\{ W_i' \}$ should yield the same social ordering $R$ through the SWFL.

If $L$ is the Cartesian product of the $n$ families of personal welfare functions (one family for each person), the invariance property is required to be satisfied for a subset $\bar{L}$ of $L$. $\bar{L}$ is the 'comparability set' of welfare $n$-tuples which give the *same* welfare signals interpreted in terms of the chosen assumptions of measurability and interpersonal comparability.

*Invariance Requirement*: If any two personal welfare $n$-tuples $\{ W_i \}$ and $\{ W_i' \}$ belong to the same comparability set $\bar{L}$ for the chosen assumptions of measurability and interpersonal comparability, then $F(\{ W_i \}) = F(\{ W_i' \})$.[3]

---

2. Sen [86, p. 129, and Ch. 7−9]. See also Sen [89, 90], Blackorby [9], Fine [26], Hammond [38, 39, 40], d'Aspremont and Gevers [20], Deschamps and Gevers [21, 22], Gevers [33], Maskin [57, 58], and Roberts [78, 79, 80].

3. There are two alternative ways of imposing an invariance requirement. One is to require that the invariance must hold for the ranking of every pair of social states (Sen [86, pp. 129−30], Roberts [79]). The second is not to demand that it holds everywhere, but to *accept only those* parts of the social preference relation that are, in fact, thus invariant; this will in general lead to a social *quasi*-ordering (Sen [86, pp. 106−8], Blackorby [9], Fine [26]). The invariance requirement imposed here uses the first approach. Note that in those cases in which the second approach yields an *incomplete* quasi-ordering, the first approach yields no social preference relation at all over any pair whatsoever. In this sense the second approach is less restrictive. [See Essay 9 in this volume.]

This invariance requirement will be used parametrically by varying the measurability-comparability assumptions.

It is obvious that $\bar{L}$ depends both on the measurability-comparability assumptions as well as on the actual welfare situation. For a given welfare situation, a particular $\bar{L}$ contains all the alternative descriptions that are equivalent for the chosen measurability-comparability framework. It should also be clear that the *stronger* the measurability-comparability assumptions, the *narrower* will be each $\bar{L}$ and the *weaker* will be the invariance requirement. There is, in this sense, a negative relation between the 'strength' of the welfare information and the 'strength' of the invariance restriction. This is, of course, as is to be expected, since the *less* the information, the *wider* is the range of values over which no discrimination is possible.

Some distinguished cases of measurability-comparability assumptions are characterized below.

*Alternative Measurability-Comparability Frameworks*: For any welfare $n$-tuple { $W_i^*$ } belonging to $\bar{L}$, $\bar{L}$ consists of exactly all welfare $n$-tuples { $W_i$ } such that: (1) CFC (*cardinal full comparability*): there exists some positive affine transformation $\Psi$ for which $W_i = \Psi(W_i^*)$, for all $i$; (2) OLC (*ordinal level comparability*): there exists some positive monotonic transformation $\Psi$ for which $W_i = \Psi(W_i^*)$, for all $i$; (3) CUC (*cardinal unit comparability*): there exists a positive real number $b$ and an $n$-vector $a$ for which $W_i = a_i + bW_i^*$ for all $i$; (4) CNC (*cardinal non-comparability*): there exists an $n$-tuple of positive affine transformations { $\Psi_i$ } for which $W_i = \Psi_i(W_i^*)$ for all $i$; (5) ONC (*ordinal non-comparability*): there exists an $n$-tuple of positive monotonic transformations { $\Psi_i$ } for which $W_i = \Psi_i(W_i^*)$ for all $i$.

These cases are discussed more fully and other cases considered (including cases of *partial* comparability and *partial* cardinality) in Sen [86, 89].[4]

The invariance requirements corresponding to CFC, OLC, CUC, CNC and ONC will be denoted *CF, OL, CU, CN*, and *ON* respectively (e.g., *CF* is the invariance requirement under cardinal full comparability when the comparability set $\bar{L}$ is defined as in CFC).

Of the distinguished cases of measurability-comparability frameworks characterized above, the *most* demanding informational set up (implying the *least* demanding invariance requirement) is given by cardinal full comparability CFC. Note, however, that the informational structure can be *further* strengthened in at least two respects. First, the measurability of personal welfare can be extended *beyond* cardinality by making the 'origin' non-arbitrary through the use of, say, a 'ratio scale' (see Sen [89, p. 4]). This has an obvious relevance for the welfare analysis of poverty, and is particularly crucial in normative population theory (see Dasgupta [19]). If full compara-

---

4. See also Blackorby [9], Fine [26], Hammond [38, 39], d'Aspremont and Gevers [20], Deschamps and Gevers [21], Gevers [33], Maskin [57, 58], Roberts [78, 79], and Basu [5].

bility is combined with this more demanding kind of measurability of personal welfare, additional types of aggregation rules can be considered (see Roberts [79]).

Second, even with cardinal full comparability (indeed even with ratio-scale full comparability), the invariance property is unable to distinguish between (i) everyone having *more* welfare (better off) in some real sense and (ii) a reduction in the *unit* of measurement of personal welfares. Invariance in all the cases considered here, including cardinal full comparability (or ratio-scale full comparability), requires that the social ordering should not change at all if everyone's welfare function is, say, doubled. But while this requirement is reasonable enough if interpreted as a halving of the unit of measurement, it is quite a restriction if the interpretation is that of a general increase in personal welfare, since the social welfare ordering need not be accepted to be a mean-independent function of individual welfares. But in all cases of measurability-comparability frameworks discussed here (and in other works), the invariance requirement covers both interpretations since there is no natural 'unit' of measurement of personal welfare.

Making each comparability set $\bar{L}$ consist of exactly one personal welfare $n$-tuple $\{W_i\}$ will, of course, avoid this characteristic of mean-independence. But this *most* demanding structure of welfare information (and the *least* demanding invariance condition, which will be vacuous) is not usable without first independently specifying a *unit* of personal welfare. The difficulties in doing this are obvious enough. Nevertheless, I would argue that there is much scope for fruitful analysis in considering stronger informational set-ups than ratio-scale full comparability; but in this paper this idea will not be pursued further.

The next section will be concerned with the *least* demanding informational set-up in our list, viz., ordinal non-comparability. This yields the *most* demanding invariance condition, viz., *ON*, and this, of course, narrows a SWFL into a social welfare function in the sense of Arrow.

## 3   Arrow's Theorem and Informational Extensions

The conditions used for Arrow's General Possibility Theorem (Arrow [1, pp. 96–7]) for social welfare functions correspond to the following applied to social welfare *functionals* (Sen [86, pp. 129–30]). Denote the symmetric and asymmetric factors of the social ranking relation $R$ as $I$ (indifference) and $P$ (strict preference). Also, for brevity, denote $F(\{R_i'\})$ as $R'$, just as $F(\{R_i\})$ is denoted $R$.

*Condition U* (Unrestricted Domain).   The domain of $F$ includes all logically possible welfare $n$-tuples.

*Condition I* (Independence of Irrelevant Alternatives).   For any two welfare *n*-tuples { $W_i$ } and { $W_i'$ }, if for any pair *x*, *y*, it so happens that $W_i(x)$ = $W_i'(x)$, and $W_i(y)$ = $W_i'(y)$, for all *i*, then *xRy* if and only if *xR'y*.

*Condition P* (Weak Pareto Principle).   For any pair *x*, *y*, if $W_i(x) > W_i(y)$ for all *i*, then *xPy*.

*Condition D* (Non-Dictatorship).   *F* must not be dictatorial, i.e., there must not be any person *i* such that for all welfare *n*-tuples in the domain of *F*, for all *x*, *y*, whenever $W_i(x) > W_i(y)$, the result is *xPy*.

Throughout this paper it is assumed that there are at least two persons and three social states, and that the set *H* of persons and the set *X* of social states are finite (though the finiteness of *X* can be easily dispensed without upsetting the results). Arrow's General Possibility Theorem [1, p. 97, Theorem 2] may now be restated in this framework.

THEOREM 1.   *There is no SWFL satisfying Conditions ON, U, I, P and D.*

In this wider informational context, is the Arrow theorem as tight as it can be? There is, in fact, some redundancy. Ordinal non-comparability can be replaced by the weaker requirement of cardinal non-comparability without affecting the result. Theorem 8*2 in Sen [86, pp. 129–30] can be stated thus.

THEOREM 2.   *There is no SWFL satisfying Conditions CN, U, I, P, and D.*

The loss of information induced by ruling out interpersonal comparisons is sufficient to precipitate the impossibility result (given the other conditions), even without ruling out cardinal welfare information. The result is not surprising when one considers that cardinal representations offer two degrees of freedom and by using Condition *I* pair by pair the informational gain from cardinality (without interpersonal comparisons) can be wiped out (see Sen [86, pp. 124–5]).[5]

However, the remaining conditions are necessary for the impossibility, in the sense that the removal of any of them makes it possible to obtain a SWFL satisfying the rest of the conditions. Indeed, in each case we can also postulate ordinality in addition to the rest of the conditions, i.e., it is possible to eschew the use of cardinal welfare information. We can demand *ordinal* non-comparability in each case, except of course where comparability is intro-

---

5. Cardinal non-comparability constrained by unrestricted domain and independence of irrelevant alternatives can be shown to be equivalent to ordinal non-comparability in this context.

duced within an ordinal framework, when we get ordinal level comparability (Case 5 below). A possibility example in each case is given below.

*Case 1.*   Satisfying *ON, U, I, P* (dropping *D*): Dictatorship of a given person *i*.

*Case 2.*   Satisfying *ON, U, I, D* (dropping *P*): Reverse dictatorship of a given person *i*.[6]

*Case 3.*   Satisfying *ON, U, P, D* (dropping *I*): The Borda Rule.[7]

*Case 4.*   Satisfying *ON, I, P, D* (dropping *U*): Majority decision with 'extremal restriction'.[8]

*Case 5.*   Satisfying *OL, U, I, P, D* (dropping the 'non-comparability' part of *ON*): Rawls's 'maximin' rule.

Note that each of the above cases can be seen in terms of relaxation of informational constraints, and in Cases 3 and 5 this interpretation is immediate. In Case 5, information on interpersonal comparisons is made usable.[9] In Case 3, the relaxation applies to the constraint that individual rankings of all pairs other than $\{x, y\}$ be ignored in socially ranking $x$ vis-à-vis $y$; in Sections 5, 6, and 7 the far-reaching implications of this constraint will be examined.

Conditions *U, P,* and *D* are not primarily focused on information, so that informational interpretations of Cases 1, 2, and 4 are not immediate. However, relaxation of *U, P,* or *D* does permit reasoning involving information of other types, which are ruled out in the Arrow framework. Suppose we know that in social state $x$ each person happens to be richer in every good than in $y$, and that free disposal is possible. Then we may not feel too disturbed by an impossibility proof some step of which builds on the supposition that everyone prefers $y$ to $x$ (by invoking 'unrestricted domain'). If we know nothing about the social states and the persons involved, obviously 'unrestricted domain' is

---

6. See Wilson [105] and Binmore [8].

7. Borda [16]. This class of conditions has been extensively analysed by Hansson [41], Gärdenfors [31], Smith [98], Fine and Fine [27], and Young [106]. Note that the Borda rule is an appropriate example for this case only if the Borda scores are derived for the environment $X$ and then applied for ranking all pairs drawn from $X$. In contrast with this '*broad* Borda rule', the '*narrow* Borda rule' reassigns scores depending on the set $S \subseteq X$ from which choice is being made (possibly a pair); and this satisfies Condition *I* but does not guarantee transitivity of social preference (see Sen [96], on the contrast between the two interpretations of the Borda rule).

8. See Sen and Pattanaik [97], also Inada [45], and Fishburn [28]. Note that Arrow's condition of 'single-peakedness' is *not* an appropriate example since it does not guarantee transitivity of social preference unless the number of individuals is odd.

9. While ordinal level comparability is *sufficient* to break the Arrow impasse, that is of course no reason why one should assume no more. Indeed, some of the most interesting recent contributions to the theory of social welfare and evaluative statistics have used a welfare informational base that is much richer (see, for example, Kolm [52], Atkinson [3], Chipman [17], Muellbauer [63]).

a sensible assumption, but not necessarily so if we do know something and wish to use that information. Relaxation of Condition $U$ leads to Case 4. Just leaving out Condition $U$ is, of course, patently inadequate, and to pursue the analysis further systematic domain restriction appropriate to the context will have to be considered.[10] But it is worth noting at this stage that the rationale of this exercise relates to the use of information made usable by Condition $U$.

Consider, now, a case where it so happens that the social states in $X$ differ from each other in only one respect, viz., a particular person $i$ watches BBC1, BBC2 or ITV, with nothing else differing. Armed with this information, many people making social judgements may not object to making person $i$ a 'dictator' in this particular choice problem, even though this will formally involve a violation of Condition $D$. Case 1 permits this type of use of information about the set $X$ of social states and the persons $H$. While this case is relevant for a libertarian social judgement, Case 2 permits the use of information about $X$ and $H$ relevant to a paternalistic approach (e.g., an outsider judging *against* the unanimous preference of a group of heroin addicts in a case where the alternative states in $X$ differ only in heroin consumption of this group $H$).

It is far from my intention to suggest that the additional information made 'admissible' by the relaxation of each of these conditions is always useful, or even typically so. Obviously the relevance will depend on the context, including the nature of the sets $X$ and $H$ in the case in question, as well as on the particular moral systems invoked. What is being commented on here is the blanket prohibition on the use of all types of information other than of some very limited kinds, irrespective of the nature of $X, H$, and the approach towards social welfare. Arrow's theorem and related ones can be fruitfully viewed in terms of these implicit informational constraints; I shall return to this question again in Sections 6 and 8.

### 4   Utilitarianism and Rawls: Axiomatic Derivations

If the Arrow framework is informationally enriched by admitting cardinal full comparability, then many aggregation rules will satisfy the Arrow conditions. Two distinguished ones are the utilitarian rule of maximizing the sum of personal welfares and the Rawlsian rule ('Difference Principle') of maximizing the welfare level of the worst off person.[11] However, if the 'weak

10. Domain restrictions that are necessary and sufficient for the class of social welfare functions satisfying the other Arrow conditions have been derived recently by Maskin [59].

11. The 'Difference Principle' is only a part of Rawls's moral framework, and while I shall be concentrating on this aspect of the Rawlsian system in this paper, it should be borne in mind that this is only one part of his 'theory of justice' and is, arguably, secondary to his conception of 'fairness' (see Sen [86, pp. 135–41]). For a penetrating discussion of many of the more general issues, see Phelps [71]. See also Kolm [52], Barry [4], Phelps [70], Daniels [18], Gaertner [30], Gärdenfors [32], Blackorby and Donaldson [10], Svensson [103], and Arrow [2].

Pareto principle' used by Arrow is strengthened to the more demanding strong Pareto principle, then the Rawlsian rule would have to be modified to its lexicographic form (see Sen [86, p. 138]).

*Condition $P^*$* (Strong Pareto Principle).   For any pair $x$, $y$, if for all $i$: $W_i(x) \geqslant W_i(y)$, then $xRy$; and if, in addition for some $i$: $W_i(x) > W_i(y)$, then $xPy$.

Let $i(x)$ be called the $i$th 'position' in $x$, being defined as the $i$th worst off person in social state $x$ identified by comparing the values of $W_i(x)$ for all $i$. (In case of 'ties', the tied persons may be ranked in any arbitrary strong order for doing the numbering $i(x)$.) Each position $i$ in each social state $x$ is called a 'station' $(x, i)$. The lexicographic maximum rule—leximin for short—is now defined.

*Leximin.*   For any pair of social states $x$, $y$, we have $xPy$ if and only if there is some $r$: $1 \leqslant r \leqslant n$, such that

$$W_{r(x)}(x) > W_{r(y)}(y), \quad \text{and} \tag{I}$$
$$W_{i(x)}(x) = W_{i(y)}(y), \text{ for all } i < r. \tag{II}$$

If, on the other hand, $W_{i(x)}(x) = W_{i(y)}(y)$, for all $i \leqslant n$, then $xIy$.

*Utilitarianism.*   For any pair of social states $x$, $y$, we have $xRy$ if and only if

$$\sum_{i=1}^{n} W_i(x) \geqslant \sum_{i-1}^{n} W_i(y).$$

It is easily checked that both leximin and utilitarianism generate complete social orderings for each personal welfare $n$-tuple $\{W_i\}$, fulfilling the invariance requirement of $CF$, and satisfy conditions $U$, $I$, $P^*$, and $D$.

Indeed, the non-dictatorship condition can be readily strengthened to anonymity (see May [60], Sen [86, p. 72], and Pattanaik [69]).

*Condition A* (Anonymity).   If $\{W_i'\}$ is a reordering of the personal welfare $n$-tuple $\{W_i\}$, then $F(\{W_i\}) = F(\{W_i'\})$.

Anonymity is an informational constraint ensuring that in generating social orderings no use is made of information as to *who* has which welfare function. Both leximin and utilitarianism are SWFLs satisfying $CF$, $U$, $I$, $P^*$, and $A$.

So far no conflict between Bentham and Rawls. To discriminate between the two approaches, the informational constraints can be tightened in different directions. If cardinality is dropped and the invariance requirement is strengthened from $CF$ to $OL$, then utilitarianism will be eliminated but not leximin, and if comparability is confined to units of welfare (and not extended to levels), then leximin will fail but not utilitarianism (see Sen [86, p. 146; 89, pp. 44–5]). This informational contrast turns out to be important in the elegant axiomatizations of leximin and utilitarianism achieved recently by Hammond [38], Strasnick [99], d'Aspremont and Gevers [20], Deschamps and Gevers [21], Maskin [57, 58], and Roberts [78, 79].

The informational contrast has a clear ethical connection. Comparisons of *units* play a crucial part in calculating 'net advantages' in an aggregative framework, and this is the focus of utilitarianism; comparisons of levels of welfare are irrelevant to this (Sen [89, p. 18]). On the other hand, the notion of equity involves special considerations being given to the badly off, and this does bring in comparisons of welfare *levels*. The idea of giving priority to the interests of a person who is going to be worse off anyway compared with another was used in a limited context in the 'weak equity axiom' proposed by Sen [89, pp. 18–20], but captured much more generally in an equity axiom suggested by Hammond [38].

*Condition HE* (Hammond's Equity Axiom).  If for any pair of social states $x$, $y$, for some personal welfare $n$-tuple $\{W_i\}$, it is the case that for two persons $g$ and $h$: $W_g(y) < W_g(x) < W_h(x) < W_h(y)$, and for all $i \neq g, h$: $W_i(x) = W_i(y)$, then $xRy$.

Person $g$ is worse off than person $h$ no matter whether $x$ or $y$ is chosen (while all others are indifferent), and $g$'s preference for $x$ over $y$ is thus given weak priority over $h$'s for $y$ over $x$. Since Condition *HE* is based on comparisons of levels only, with no attention being paid to the 'magnitudes' of the gains and losses of the two persons involved, use of Condition *HE* tends to convert the informational framework of cardinal full comparability *effectively* into one of ordinal level comparability.

THEOREM 3.  *Any SWFL satisfying CF, U, P\*, I, A and HE must be leximin.*[12]

THEOREM 4.  *Any SWFL satisfying CU, U, P\*, I and A must be utilitarian.*[13]

The Arrow axioms strengthened to the extent of using the strong Pareto principle (rather than the weak Pareto principle) and anonymity (rather than non-dictatorship) yield (i) utilitarianism for the informational framework of

---

12. See Hammond [38], Strasnick [99], d'Aspremont and Gevers [20]. While OL rather than CF is used in the first two contributions, the theorem goes through with CF since Condition *HE* itself leads to the exclusive focus on welfare levels only. See also Maskin [58], Sen [94], Deschamps and Gevers [21], Gevers [33], Roberts [78, 79], and Arrow [2].

13. See d'Aspremont and Gevers [20]. Also Deschamps and Gevers [21], Maskin [57, 58], and Roberts [79].

cardinal unit comparability, and (ii) Rawlsian leximin if combined with the equity condition *HE* concentrating on comparisons of welfare levels.[14]

It must, however, be noted that the strengthened Arrow conditions (viz., *U, P\*, I*, and *A*) do not themselves lead to a two-alternative choice between utilitarianism and leximin in the general informational framework of cardinal full comparability.[15] To get that two-alternative choice, eliminating other possibilities, some additional axioms are needed. The following, proposed by Deschamps and Gevers [21], suffice.

*Condition ME* (Minimal Equity).   For some welfare $n$-tuple $\{ W_i \}$, for some person $g$, and some pair of social states $x, y$: $W_i(y) < W_i(x) < W_g(x) < W_g(y)$ for all $i \neq g$, and $xRy$.

*Condition SE* (Separability with Respect to Unconcerned Individuals).   If for two welfare $n$-tuples $\{ W_i \}$ and $\{ W_i' \}$, for all persons $i$ in some subset $H^*$ of $H$: $W_i(x) = W_i'(x)$ for all $x$ in $X$, and for all persons $i$ in $(H - H^*)$: $W_i(x) = W_i(y)$ and $W_i'(x) = W_i'(y)$ for all $x, y$ in $X$, then $R = R'$.

*ME* is a very weak condition of equity in the presence of unrestricted domain, requiring only that a person who is going to be best off anyway does not *always* strictly have his way. *SE* is more debatable, but seemingly innocuous. *SE* demands that if two welfare $n$-tuples coincide for some persons, and the rest of the people are indifferent among *all* alternative social states, then the two should lead to the same social ordering.[16]

Consider now a weakening of utilitarianism, leaving out the case in which the utility sums for the two social states being compared are exactly equal.

*Utilitarian-type SWFL.*   A SWFL is of the utilitarian type if and only if $xPy$ whenever

$$\sum_{i=1}^{n} W_i(x) > \sum_{i=1}^{n} W_i(y).$$

Deschamps and Gevers [21] have established the following neat result.

14. Axiomatizing moral principles through informational constraints might appear as a confusion of ethical and epistemological considerations. But informational contrasts do have a profound influence on the acceptability of particular moral approaches, e.g., 'utilitarianism may be accepted with enthusiasm if we can compare differences of welfare for different persons, but not levels', while 'if we *cannot* compare units, or if we *can* compare levels, the enthusiasm may be limited' (Sen [86, p. 146, italics added]). On some underlying philosophical issues, see Sen [85].

15. For an example of a rule other than leximin and utilitarianism satisfying these axioms, consider 'leximax', which gives priority to the ranking of better off stations just in the same way as leximin gives priority to the ranking of worse off stations (see d'Aspremont and Gevers [20] and Deschamps and Gevers [21]).

16. Separability is a powerful restriction especially in conjunction with the condition of independence of irrelevant alternatives. For pros and cons of such separability restrictions in this context, see Sen [94] and Deschamps and Gevers [22]. In a more general context, see Gorman [35].

THEOREM 5. *Any SWFL satisfying CF, U, I, P\*, A, ME, and SE must either be leximin or of the utilitarian type.*

Any additional axiom that eliminates one of these permitted approaches without the other will lead to an axiomatic derivation of that approach.

Ordinal level comparability will suffice to eliminate utilitarian type SWFLs, leading to axiomatization of leximin (see d'Aspremont and Gevers [20]). In this informational framework the derivation of leximin can be explained in the following way (at the risk of some oversimplification). With $OL, U, I, P$, and $A$, the only SWFLs involve the 'dictatorship' of a particular 'position' (the Rawlsian 'dictatorship' of the 'worst off' position being only a distinguished case of this). With separability $SE$ added to this, the Pareto principle strengthened to $P^*$, the dictatorship must be of the best off or the worst off, leading to a lexicographic hierarchy: either leximin or leximax. Minimal equity $ME$ eliminates leximax.[17]

Hammond's equity axiom, which is used in the alternative axiomatization of leximin in Theorem 3, serves three distinct purposes for SWFLs satisfying $U, I, P^*$, and $A$. First, by using only level comparisons without any regard for the magnitudes of gains and losses, it brings in effectively a restriction much like $OL$. (Hammond [36], in fact, assumed $OL$ also, but he need not have.) Second, since it is formulated with an implicit element of separability by ignoring the influence of indifferent individuals in the particular context specified, it incorporates the element of separability that is used to focus attention on leximin and leximax. Third, as a strong principle of equity, it does, of course, subsume minimal equity $ME$, thereby knocking out leximax.

Turning now to the derivation of utilitarianism from Theorem 5, cardinal unit comparability (with welfare levels non-comparable) does exclude leximin (and leximax too, without invoking $ME$). The necessary element of separability follows from the other axioms given $CU$; they also bridge the gap between SWFLs of the utilitarian-type and utilitarianism as such.

An alternative route to the axiomatization of utilitarianism established by Maskin [57] lies in imposing a condition of continuity on the SWFL, which also excludes leximin (and leximax).[18] Maskin shows that a SWFL satisfying continuity, $CF, U, I, P^*, A$, and $SE$ must be utilitarian.[19]

17. For these and some related results, see Gevers [33] and Roberts [78].

18. Note that none of these alternative axiomatizations of utilitarianism begin with the requirement that social preference must be cardinally representable satisfying the axioms necessary for such representation (e.g., von Neumann–Morgenstern axioms). Contrast this with the classic axiomatization of utilitarianism by Harsanyi [42]. On disputes regarding the merits of beginning with the von Neumann–Morgenstern framework for social preferences and related issues, see Diamond. [23], Harsanyi [43, 44], Sen [94, 95], and Deschamps and Gevers [22].

19. See also Roberts [79] for some related results. The replacement of CF by full comparability with 'ratio scale measurability' of personal welfare permits a wider class of aggregation formulae, including the addition of suitably chosen strictly concave transforms of personal welfares, as proposed by Mirrlees [61], with considerable gain in versatility in handling issues of 'equity'.

Elimination of utilitarianism by the use of ordinal level comparability—explicitly or by implication—is somewhat overdemanding. Similarly, unit comparability has something of the subtlety of a sledgehammer in smashing leximin. (The alternative route through continuity is demanding too.) The same eliminating effects can be achieved by much weaker axioms. Indeed, making the invariance condition apply to comparability sets lying *in between* those given by cardinal full comparability and ordinal level comparability will also exclude utilitarianism, given the other axioms; we do not have to strengthen the invariance requirement all the way to *OL*. If comparability sets for cardinal full comparability and ordinal level comparability are denoted respectively as $\bar{L}$(CFC) and $\bar{L}$(OLC), the *intermediate* possibilities are given by $\bar{L}$ such that $\bar{L}$(CFC) $\subset \bar{L} \subset \bar{L}$(OLC). By exploiting the condition of unrestricted domain utilitarianism can be shown to violate the invariance restriction for such 'intermediate' sets $\bar{L}$. This violation can be established even for some $\bar{L}$ containing only one more *n*-tuple than $\bar{L}$(CFC). Similarly making the invariance condition relate to comparability sets *in between* those given by cardinal full comparability and cardinal unit comparability, 'intermediate' sets $\bar{L}$ can be used to eliminate leximin, without going all the way to *CU*. It is possible to axiomatize leximin and utilitarianism in terms of the weaker requirements of such 'partial' information sets, but I won't pause to pursue the formalities here.[20]

## 5     Interpersonal Positional Rules

In the literature of collective choice theory there has been much exploration of rules that incorporate *both* independence and interpersonal comparisons (e.g., utilitarianism, leximin) as well as of rules using only independence (e.g., in the Arrow problem). The possibility of having *neither* independence *nor* interpersonal comparisons has also been used beginning with Borda [16], and recently this class of rules has received very thorough exploration in contributions by Fishburn [28], Hansson [41], Gärdenfors [31], Smith [98], Fine and Fine [27], Young [106], and Plott [72]. But the possibility of using interpersonal comparisons *without* independence does not seem to have been explored at all.

This possibility is particularly worth exploring in the case in which the personal welfare information come in somewhat limited form, such as with ordinal level comparability. As was seen in Section 4, independence when

---

20. The case for using 'partial' comparability frameworks and the formal characterizations of certain types of partial comparability are presented in Sen [86, 87, 88], Blackorby [9], and Fine [26]. While the focus of those works is on generating *partial* orderings by using the invariance condition pair by pair without demanding that it holds for every pair (see footnote 3 above), the requirement of completeness built into the axioms being used here will eliminate a partial ordering that is, in fact, strictly incomplete.

combined with ordinal level comparability, unrestricted domain, the Pareto principle and anonymity does produce dictatorship of some 'position' (the Rawlsian 'dictatorship' of the worst off being only a special case). Independence plays a crucial part in this derivation.

Dropping independence, but retaining ordinal level comparability, unrestricted domain, the strict Pareto principle, and anonymity, we can consider a class of 'interpersonal positionalist' rules. For any station $(x, i)$, define $S(x, i)$ as the set of non-superior stations to $(x, i)$:

$$S(x, i) = [(y, j) \mid (y, j) \in X \times H \& W_i(x) \geqslant W_j(y)].$$

Let the cardinality of $S(x, i)$ be called the interpersonal positional value of $(x, i)$, denoted $v(x, i)$. The 'interpersonal positional information' $\Omega = (\{v(x, i)\})$ is an $mn$-tuple giving the cardinal numbers for each $(x, i)$. It is clear that $\Omega$ contains no more and no less information than personal welfare comparisons under ordinal level comparability, since either set of information can be constructed from the other.

The class of interpersonal positionalist rules may be defined as methods of ranking social states according to the sum of some specified transformation $\rho(\cdot)$ of the interpersonal positional values $v(x, i)$ associated with $x$.

*Interpersonal Positional Rules (IPR).*    For some real-valued function $\rho(\cdot)$, $xRy$ if and only if $\Sigma_i \rho(v(x, i)) \geqslant \Sigma_i \rho(v(y, i))$.

To prevent negative association between personal and social welfares, this function $\rho(\cdot)$ may legitimately be required to be non-decreasing, and quite reasonably even strictly increasing.

A special case of IPR is given by interpersonal extension of the Borda rule (the 'rank order method of voting'), when $\rho(\cdot)$ is the identity mapping: $\rho(r) = r$.

*Interpersonal Rank Order Rule (IROR).*    $xRy$ if and only if $\Sigma_i v(x, i) \geqslant \Sigma_i v(y, i)$.

This can be given a 'broad' or a 'narrow' interpretation as the Borda rule itself, depending on whether the $S(x, i)$ used for numbering $v(x, i)$ in a choice over $\{x, y\}$ is taken from the entire $X \times H$ (as above), or from $\{x, y\} \times H$. The former will tend to violate Condition $I$ but satisfy transitivity, while the latter will tend to violate transitivity but satisfy independence (as with the Borda rule, on which see Sen [96] [pp. 186–7 in this volume]. IROR also satisfies the invariance requirement under full comparability as well as under ordinal level comparability.

To bring out the contrasting features of IROR vis-à-vis other well-known criteria, consider the strict descending welfare order of stations: $(x, 1)$, $(y, 2)$, $(z, 3)$, $(x, 2)$, $(y, 3)$, $(z, 1)$, $(x, 3)$, $(y, 1)$, $(z, 2)$. The method of majority decision implies: $zPy$, $yPx$, and $xPz$ (a robust cycle). The Borda rule yields: $xIy$, $yIz$, and $xIz$ (universal indifference). But note that in an interpersonal context $x$

has a dominance over $y$, and $y$ over $z$ (cf. Suppes [100]). The interpersonal rank order rule IROR does reflect this in declaring: $xPy$, $yPz$, $xPz$.

The Rawlsian maximin or leximin will also generate the same ordering as IROR in this case.[21] But a different can be brought about by just reversing the ordering of the last three stations only: $(z, 2), (y, 1), (x, 3)$. This yields under maximin or leximin: $zPy$, $yPx$, $zPx$. But the IROR ranking is unchanged.

The equi-ordering of gaps between positions in IROR is somewhat in the same spirit as utilitarianism, and it can be interpreted as doing with rank differences as 'surrogates' for welfare differences. This feature with the formula of simple addition may go against 'equity' considerations of the type incorporated in the 'weak equity axiom' (Sen [89]), or Hammond's [38] equity axiom ($HE$ used in Section 4). To reflect equity considerations the increasing function $\rho(.)$ may be taken to be *strictly concave*, and the more severely concave this function is for the lowest values of $c(x, i)$, the closer to Rawlsian leximin one would expect IPR to be.

## 6 Unrestricted Independence and Non-welfare Information

The independence of irrelevant alternatives applied to a SWFL with unrestricted domain is a powerful restriction, and it plays an important part both in precipitating impossibility results (Section 3) as well as in the axiomatic derivations of special aggregation procedures like utilitarianism and leximin (Section 4). Some of the information that has to be rendered inadmissible in arriving at the impossibilities, or in being confined to special procedures (like utilitarianism or leximin, with their narrow informational focus) are, in fact, ruled out through crucial use of the independence of irrelevant alternatives.

What is quite transparent is that in socially ordering a pair $x$, $y$, Condition $I$ rules out the use of all *welfare* information other than those relating to the pair $x$, $y$. What may be less clear is that in the presence of other conditions, especially unrestricted domain, Condition $I$ rules out a great deal of *non-welfare* information as well. Indeed, Condition $I$ is a great *generalizer* of informational parsimony. If some type of information is ignored in a particular class of choice for some special reason, Condition $I$ can be relied upon to exploit unrestricted domain to rule out that type of information in all other circumstances as well.

Consider the characteristic of 'neutrality' of the aggregation procedures with respect to non-welfare features, i.e., making no use of descriptions of social states $x$, $y$, etc. (other than that of personal welfares in $x$, $y$, etc.). In a

---

21. Note also that unlike the Borda rule or the method of majority decision, which throw away a lot of information used by IROR, the Rawlsian rules have an informational base similar to that of IROR, viz., the welfare ordering of 'stations' $(x, i)$. This was called an 'extended ordering' $R$ in Sen [86].

very limited way this feature of neutrality is present in the Pareto conditions. Consider the part of the Pareto principle dealing with unanimous indifference.

*Condition $P^0$* (Pareto Indifference Rule). For any $x$, $y$, if $W_i(x) = W_i(y)$ for all $i$, then $xIy$.

This rules out the use of any information regarding the *description* of $x$ and $y$ as social states in the *special case* when everyone happens to be indifferent between the two.

Condition $I$ with unrestricted domain converts this into a *general* condition of 'neutrality among alternatives'—in its strictest form—for SWFLs with unrestricted domain.

*Strong Neutrality (SN).* For any two pairs of social states $\{x, y\}$ and $\{a, b\}$, and any two welfare $n$-tuples $\{W_i\}$ and $\{W_i'\}$, if for all $i$: $W_i(x) = W_i'(a)$, and $W_i(y) = W_i'(b)$, then $xRy$ if and only if $aR'b$.[23]

Strong neutrality has been obtained from independence with the strong Pareto principle for social decision functions by Guha [37] and Blau [14], and for social welfare functionals by d'Aspremont and Gevers [20]. The following theorem, which uses the *weaker* Pareto condition $P^0$, capitalizes on these earlier demonstrations.

THEOREM 6. *For any SWFL satisfying Condition U and $P^0$, Condition I holds if and only if strong neutrality does.*

*Proof.* Putting $\{x, y\} = \{a, b\}$, it is obvious that Condition $I$ is implied by strong neutrality. Regarding the converse, a lemma involving three alternatives $p$, $q$, $r$ with $q \neq r$ is proved first: if for any two welfare $n$-tuples $\{W_i\}$ and $\{W_i'\}$: $W_i(p) = W_i'(p)$ and $W_i(q) = W_i'(r)$, then $pRq$ implies $pR'r$, and $qRp$ implies $rR'p$. This is denoted $\{p, q\} N \{p, r\}$. The proof proceeds by assuming a welfare $n$-tuple $\{W_i^*\}$ such that $W_i(p) = W_i^*(p)$ and $W_i(q) = W_i^*(q) = W_i^*(r)$. By Condition $P^0$, $qI^*r$. If now, $pRq$, then by Condition $I$, $pR^*q$, and thus $pR^*r$. By Condition $I$, $pR'r$. Similarly $qRp$ implies $rR'p$. Hence $\{p, q\} N \{p, r\}$.

Note now that for any four alternatives $x$, $y$, $a$, $b$, unless $x = b$ and $y = a$, strong neutrality is easily established by considering: *either $\{x, y\} N \{a, y\}$ and $\{a, y\} N \{a, b\}$, or $\{x, y\} N \{x, b\}$ and $\{x, b\} N \{a, b\}$.* If $x = b$ and $y = a$, take a third alternative $z$, and prove strong neutrality by the sequence: $\{x, y\} N \{x, z\}$, $\{x, z\} N \{y, z\}$, $\{y, z\} N \{y, x\}$, completing the proof.

---

22. This requires neutrality to hold pair by pair and was called 'neutrality' in Sen [86]. A weaker requirement of neutrality for the set of social states as a whole was used by Arrow [1, p. 101]. On the distinction between the two ways of defining neutrality, see Blair [11], who calls SN 'neutrality and independence'; see also Pollak [73]. Needless to say a theorem that establishes strong neutrality must lead to neutrality in the weaker sense as well.

Note that the Arrow conditions don't quite imply neutrality or strong neutrality, since the Pareto principle used there (Condition $P$) deals only with strict preferences. But even that has the important feature of neutrality that if any group of individuals is decisive over some pair of social states, that group must be decisive over *every* pair of social states (see Blau [12], and Arrow [1, pp. 98–100]).[23]

While strong neutrality eschews information about social states in reflecting $R$ over $\{x, y\}$ to $R'$ over $\{a, b\}$, Condition $A$ (anonymity) discussed earlier rules out the use of information on *who* holds which preference. In the context of SWFLs, this condition of anonymity can be strengthened to a condition in which individuals' stations may be permuted for *some* particular social state $x$ *without* permuting them for any other social state, still demanding that there be no change in the resulting social ordering. It is a strong condition of 'symmetry' with respect to individuals.

*Strong Anonymity* (*SA*).   If for any pair of welfare $n$-tuples $\{W_i\}$ and $\{W_i'\}$, there is a permutation function $\rho$ over the set $H$ of persons such that for some $x$, for all $i$: $W_i(x) = W_{\rho(i)}'(x)$, and if $W_i(y) = W_i'(y)$ for all $i$, for all $y \neq x$, then $R = R'$.

Note that anonymity is easily derived from strong anonymity by repeated use over a finite $X$, but the converse does not hold. Note also that the permutation referred to in the definition of strong anonymity may *reverse* the actual individual preferences, and still the same social preference is demanded. Strong anonymity is, thus, indeed much stronger than anonymity as such. Many collective choice procedures satisfy anonymity but not strong anonymity, e.g., majority rule.

Strong anonymity can be obtained by a generalization (through unrestricted independence) of the acceptance of such interpersonal permutation in a special case. The weak version of Suppes' [100] 'grading principle' is adequate for this; it is in fact an interpersonal extension of the Pareto indifference rule $P^0$.

*Condition $S^0$* (Suppes Indifference).   For any given welfare $n$-tuple $\{W_i\}$, for some $x, y$, if there is a permutation function $\rho$ over the set of persons such that for all $i$: $W_i(x) = W_{\rho(i)}(y)$, then $xIy$.

Hammond [38] has established that SWFLs that satisfy $U$, $I$, and $S^0$ must also satisfy anonymity (Theorem 5.2). In fact, strong anonymity is also implied. Unrestricted independence plays its usual role of generalizing the irrelevance of information as to who has how much welfare from the special case referred to in $S^0$ to every case whatsoever.

---

23. To get neutrality (or strong neutrality) fully with Arrow's Pareto principle $P$ (dealing with strict individual preferences), Conditions $I$ and $U$ have to be supplemented by some suitable continuity condition (see Roberts [79]).

THEOREM 7. *For any SWFL satisfying Conditions U and $S^0$, Condition I holds only if strong anonymity also does.*

*Proof.* Consider the antecedent in the condition of strong anonymity. Since for all $i$: $W_i(y) = W_i'(y)$ for all $y \neq x$, the coincidence of $R$ and $R'$ follows immediately from Condition $I$ for pairs not including $x$. Consider now $\{x, y\}$. Take two other welfare $n$-tuples $\{W_i^*\}$ and $\{W'^*_i\}$, such that for $x$, $y$ and for some third alternative $z$, for all $i$:

$$W_i(x) = W_i^*(x) = W_i^*(z) = W_i'^*(z); \tag{2}$$
$$W_i'(x) = W_i'^*(x); \tag{3}$$
$$W_i(y) = W_i^*(y) = W_i'(y) = W_i'^*(y). \tag{4}$$

Let $xRy$. By Condition $I$: $xR^*y$, from (2) and (4). By Condition $S^0$: $xI^*z$, from (2). Hence $zR^*y$ by transitivity of $R^*$. Therefore, from (2) and (4) by Condition $I$: $zR'^*y$. If now the antecedent of the strong anonymity condition is assumed, we have $W_i(x) = W'_{\rho(i)}(x) = W'^*_{\rho(i)}(x)$, by (3). This combined with $W_i'^*(z) = W_i(x)$ from (2), yields by $S^0$: $xI'^*z$. Combined with $zR'^*y$, this implies $xR'^*y$ by transitivity of $R'^*$. Finally, by Condition $I$: $xR'y$ from (3) and (4).

Similarly, it is shown that $xR'y$ implies $xRy$ and also that $yRx$ if and only if $yR'x$, completing the proof.

Since $S^0$ implies $P^0$, the effect of Theorems 6 and 7 is that for SWFLs satisfying unrestricted domain and $S^0$, Condition $I$ implies both strong neutrality and strong anonymity. This results in having to rule out the use of all non-welfare information about the social states and the individuals involved in the choice problem. All that is considered is the set of (unordered) personal welfare numbers for each state; nothing else can be allowed to matter. The information that is ignored in special circumstances postulated in the antecedent of $S^0$ is axed from use in *every* circumstance by Condition $I$ given unrestricted domain. The far-reaching implications of these restrictions from the ethical point of view are discussed in Section 8.

## 7  Rawls from Inch to Ell: An Alternative Axiomatic Derivation

Another examination of the role of independence of irrelevant alternatives in *generalizing* informational parsimony can be provided by an alternative axiomatization of the Rawlsian leximin rule. It can be argued that in a two-person conflict, the Rawlsian rule of giving priority to the interests of the worse off is appealing. One *or* the other has to win in a two-person situation, so why not give priority to saving someone from the *very worst* station? The appeal of the Rawlsian rule may be thought to be much weaker in $n$-person conflicts where the interests of one may go against the interests of everyone else (perhaps a billion of them!). But such is the generalizing power of independence with unrestricted domain that if we want leximin in two-person conflicts, we must have leximin in $m$-person conflicts as well, no matter how large $m$ is!

Before stating and proving the theorem, leximin is defined first for $m$-person conflict situations with $m \leqslant n$.

*Leximin-m.*  If leximin holds over every pair $x$, $y$, whenever exactly $m$ persons are non-indifferent between $x$ and $y$ and the rest indifferent between them, then leximin-$m$ is said to hold.

THEOREM 8.  *For a SWFL satisfying Conditions U and I, if leximin-2 holds, then leximin-m must for all m*: $1 \leqslant m \leqslant n$.

*Proof.*  It is first shown that leximin-2 implies leximin-1. It is clear that the only content of leximin-1 is simply the part of the strong Pareto principle which says that if for some $\{ W_i \}$ everyone other than one person (say, $r$) is indifferent between $x$ and $y$ and $r$ is strictly better off with $x$ than with $y$, then $xPy$.

Since there are at least two persons, pick a person $k$ other than $r$, and consider the following welfare $n$-tuple $\{ W_i^* \}$ defined over $x$ and $y$ and some other state, say $z$:

$$W_r(x) = W_r^*(x) > W_r^*(z) > W_r^*(y) = W_r(y); \qquad (5)$$
$$W_k(x) = W_k^*(x) = W_k^*(z) = W_k^*(y) = W_k(y); \qquad (6)$$
$$W_i(x) = W_i^*(x) = W_i^*(z) = W_i^*(y) = W_i(y) \text{ for all } i \neq r, k. \quad (7)$$

By leximin-2: $xP^*z$ and $zP^*y$. By transitivity of $P^*$: $xP^*y$. By Condition $I$: $xPy$. This establishes leximin-1.

Now it is shown that for any $m$: $2 \leqslant m < n$, if leximin-1, leximin-2, $\ldots$, leximin-$m$ hold, then so does leximin-$m + 1$. Consider a welfare $n$-tuple $\{ W_i \}$. Of the set $H$ of individuals, let a subset $H^*$ of $m + 1$ persons be non-indifferent between $x$ and $y$, everyone else being indifferent. Let $p(x)$ and $p(y)$ be the persons occupying the $p$-worst off position among $H^*$ in $x$ and $y$ respectively for the given welfare $n$-tuple $\{ W_i \}$.

To establish leximin-$m + 1$, we have to consider two types of cases.

*Case* 1.  For all $p = 1, \ldots, m + 1$: $W_{p(x)}(x) = W_{p(y)}(y)$.

*Case* 2.  There exists an $r \leqslant m + 1$ such that $W_{r(x)}(x) > W_{r(y)}(y)$, and for all $p < r$: $W_{p(x)}(x) = W_{p(y)}(y)$.

It has to be shown that in case 1, $xIy$ holds, and in case 2, $xPy$. (The case leading to $yPx$ is exactly similar to case 2, and need not be covered separately.)

*Case* 1.  Take a third social state, say $z$, and consider another welfare $n$-tuple $\{ W_i^* \}$ such that for $x$ and $y$ it specifies the same social welfare for everyone as $\{ W_i \}$, and furthermore everyone not in $H^*$ is indifferent between $x$, $y$ and $z$.

$$\text{for all } i \text{ in } H: \quad W_i^*(a) = W_i(a) \text{ with } a = x, y; \tag{8}$$

$$\text{for all } i \text{ in } H - H^*: \quad W_i^*(x) = W_i^*(y) = W_i^*(z). \tag{9}$$

In addition require that in $\{W_i^*\}$ for the set $H^*$ of non-indifferent individuals, the $p$th worst off persons are equally well off in $x$, $y$, and $z$ for all $p$, and furthermore that the $s$th worst persons in $x$ and $z$ are the same, and the $t$th worst persons in $y$ and $z$ are also identical. Defining $p^*(a)$ as the $p$th worst off person among $H^*$ in $a = x, y, z$ respectively, for $\{W_i^*\}$:

$$\text{for all } p = 1, \ldots, m+1: \quad W_{p^*(x)}^*(x) = W_{p^*(y)}^*(y) = W_{p^*(z)}^*(z); \tag{10}$$

$$\text{for some } s, t \leqslant m+1: \quad s^*(x) = s^*(z), \text{ and } t^*(y) = t^*(z). \tag{11}$$

It is easily checked that for $m+1 \geqslant 3$ (i.e., for $m \geqslant 2$), there is no inconsistency among these conditions (given the specification of case 1).

It is clear from restrictions (9), (10), and (11) that there are at most $m$ non-indifferent persons between $x$ and $z$ and also between $y$ and $z$ for $\{W_i^*\}$. Since leximin-$k$ for $k = 1, \ldots, m$, hold by assumption, it follows from (9) and (10) that $xI^*z$ and $yI^*z$. By transitivity of $I^*$: $xI^*y$. It follows from (8) by virtue of Condition $I$ that $xIy$.

*Case* 2. The strategy in this case also is to convert a leximin-$m+1$ judgement between $x$ and $y$ into two leximin-$m$ judgements between $x$ and $z$, and $z$ and $y$, respectively, by making an additional person indifferent between $x$ and $z$, and another between $y$ and $z$.

Consider the following restrictions on a welfare $n$-tuple $\{W_i^*\}$.

$$\text{the equalities specified in (10) hold for all } p < r; \tag{10*}$$

$$\text{for } s, t \neq r, \text{ and satisfying } W_{s^*(x)}^*(x) = W_{s^*(z)}^*(z), \text{ and} \tag{11*}$$
$$W_{t^*(y)}^*(y) = W_{t^*(z)}^*(z):^{24}$$

$$s^*(x) = s^*(z), \text{ and} \tag{11*.1}$$

$$t^*(y) = t^*(z); \tag{11*.2}$$

$$W_{r^*(x)}^*(x) > W_{r^*(z)}^*(z) > W_{r^*(y)}^*(y). \tag{12}$$

When it is possible to satisfy restrictions (8), (9), (10*), (11*), and (12) simultaneously—whether it is or not is yet to be investigated—the proof can be completed very similarly to Case 1. We proceed tentatively on that assumption. From (9) and (11*) it follows that there are at most $m$ non-indifferent persons between $x$ and $z$ and between $y$ and $z$ for $\{W_i^*\}$. Since leximin-$k$ holds by assumption for $k = 1, \ldots, m$, it follows from (9), (10*), and (12) that $xP^*z$ and $zP^*y$. By transitivity of $P^*$: $xP^*y$. It follows from (8) by the use of Condition $I$ that $xPy$.

This leaves us with the remaining question as to whether conditions (8), (9), (10*), (11*), and (12) can always be satisfied simultaneously; if not, when will it be impossible? It is obvious that in the absence of (11*) there can be no

---

24. Note that for $s, t < r$, these additional requirements are satisfied automatically by virtue of (10*), but not necessarily if $s, t > r$.

inconsistency between the remaining conditions (given the specification of $\{W_i\}$ as in Case 2). It is also clear that if $m > 2$, i.e., if there are more than three persons $(m+1)$ in $H^*$, there is no difficulty in satisfying (11*) also (assigning the two persons in $z$ as specified). Since we are concerned only with $m \geq 2$, we need therefore concentrate only on $m = 2$, i.e., with exactly three persons in $H^*$ (who are not indifferent between all three $x$, $y$ and $z$).

There is obviously never any inconsistency problem in requiring only that *one* of the two conditions (11*.1) and (11*.2) be satisfied. But both may not be satisfiable simultaneously if it so happens that $s^*(x)$ and $t^*(y)$ are the same person:

$$s^*(x) = t^*(y). \tag{13.1}$$

Note that $s$ and $t$ are variables, and of the three possible positional values $p = 1, 2, 3$, while one is taken by the arbitrarily given $r$, there are still two different ways in which the values of the pair $\{s, t\}$ can be chosen. If we treat $s$ and $t$ as *constants*, viz., two *particular* positional values other than the given $r$, then the program of rendering one additional person indifferent between $x$ and $z$ and another between $y$ and $z$, which is implicit in (11*), can be met also by doctoring (11*) in the form: $t^*(x) = t^*(z)$, and $s^*(y) = s^*(z)$. But this, in its turn, may be impossible to satisfy if $t^*(x)$ and $s^*(y)$ are the same person:

$$t^*(x) = s^*(y). \tag{13.2}$$

The real problem arises, therefore, only when (13.1) and (13.2) *both* hold. This is precisely the case in which the earlier proof based on the fulfilment of (11*)—interpreting $s$ and $t$ as variables—does not work.

The proof is now extended to the case in which (13.1) and (13.2) both hold. Bearing in mind the fact that the ranking of persons both for $x$ and $y$ are the same in $\{W_i\}$ as in the constructed $\{W_i^*\}$ (see (8)), we economize on notation by christening the three persons in terms of their relative welfare position in $y$:

$$s(x) = t(y) = t; \tag{14.1}$$
$$t(x) = s(y) = s; \tag{14.2}$$
$$r(x) = r(y) = r. \tag{14.3}$$

There are three alternative possibilities satisfying (13.1) and (13.2): (A) $r > s, t$; (B) $s, t > r$; and (C) $t > r > s$. (The case of $s > r > t$ is exactly like (C) and need not be separately covered.) Different welfare $n$-tuples $\{W_i^*\}$ would have to be considered for the three subcases. It has to be borne in mind in what follows that by the assumption of Case 2, persons occupying the *same* welfare rank in $x$ and $y$ *below* the rank $r$ must enjoy the same level of welfare in $\{W_i\}$ (and therefore also in $\{W_i^*\}$ by (8)). Further since the numbering of the persons corresponds to the welfare ranks in $y$, while the $r$th ranked person in $x$ is $r$, the $t$th ranked person in $x$ happens to be $s$, and the $s$th ranked person in $x$ is, in fact, $t$, as specified in (14.1) to (14.3).

In subcase (A), with $r$ being a higher welfare position than $s$ and $t$, let $\{ W_i^* \}$ satisfy in addition to (8) and (9):

$$W_r^*(x) = W_r^*(z) > W_r^*(y); \tag{15.1}$$
$$W_t^*(x) = W_s^*(y) = W_s^*(z); \tag{15.2}$$
$$W_s^*(x) = W_t^*(y) = W_t^*(z). \tag{15.3}$$

By leximin-2: $xI^*z$. By leximin-1: $zP^*y$. Hence $xP^*y$. By Condition $I$: $xPy$.

In subcase (B), with $r$ being a lower welfare position than $s$ and $t$, let $\{ W_i^* \}$ satisfy in addition to (8) and (9):

$$W_r^*(x) > W_r^*(z) > W_r^*(y); \tag{16.1}$$
$$W_s^*(x) = W_s^*(z); \tag{16.2}$$
$$W_t^*(y) = W_t^*(z). \tag{16.3}$$

By leximin-2: $xP^*z$ and $zP^*y$. Hence $xP^*y$. By Condition $I$: $xPy$.

In subcase (C), with $t$ being a higher welfare position than $r$ and $r$ than $s$, let $\{ W_i^* \}$ satisfy in addition to (8) and (9):

$$W_r^*(x) = W_r^*(z) > W_r^*(y); \tag{17.1}$$
$$W_t^*(x) = W_s^*(y) = W_s^*(z); \tag{17.2}$$
$$W_s^*(x) \geqslant W_t^*(z). \tag{17.3}$$

By leximin-2: $xR^*z$. By leximin-2 or leximin-1: $zP^*y$. Hence $xP^*y$. By Condition $I$: $xPy$.

This completes the demonstration that if leximin-1, leximin-2, ..., leximin-$m$ are satisfied, then leximin-$m+1$ must also hold. Since it was shown earlier that leximin-2 implies leximin-1, the proof that leximin-2 implies leximin-$m$ for all $m$ is now complete.[25]

The acceptance of Rawlsian leximin for two-person conflicts implies its acceptance for $m$-person conflicts, no matter how large is $m$. While the social ranking can go against the interest of at most one person among the two in the former case, it can go against the interests of $m - 1$ persons among $m$ in the latter case, no matter how large $m$ happens to be. The ban on using any welfare information other than that relating to the least well off non-indifferent station, which may not be very objectionable in two-person conflicts is generalized by unrestricted independence to apply to *all* conflicts, no matter how many persons are involved.

25. Commenting on this paper, Peter Hammond has suggested an alternative proof of this theorem by first establishing the lemma that Suppes indifference for two-person permutations $(S^0 - 2)$ must imply Suppes indifference in general $(S^0)$, in the presence of Conditions $U$ and $I$. That lemma is also of some considerable interest on its own. [Hammond has published his results later in 'Equity in Two Person Situations: Some Consequences', *Econometrica*, **47** (1979), 1127–36.]

## 8   *Neutrality and Welfarism*

Leximin and utilitarianism are two examples of a 'neutral' approach: they have no use for any information about the social states other than the personal welfares generated in each state. As was seen earlier (Section 6), any SWFL satisfying independence with unrestricted domain and the Pareto indifference rule must be strongly neutral. The general approach of making no use of any information about the social states other than that of personal welfares generated in them may be called 'welfarism'. I would like to argue that (i) welfarism as an approach to social decisions is very restrictive, and (ii) when the information on personal welfare is itself limited, it can be positively obnoxious.

One way of viewing the question of 'welfarism' is in terms of its ability to accommodate some of the general social principles or values that have been widely acclaimed. Take, first, the question of liberty. It can be argued that any 'neutral' framework cannot properly accommodate the principles of liberty (see Sen [86, pp. 78–9]). Liberty involves the assignment of rights to persons not on grounds of comparisons of welfare, but on the acknowledgement of a special relation between a person and certain choices that are thought to be, in some ways, in his 'personal' domain. Since this priority applies to choices over *particular* pairs of states, the result is clearly nonneutral. I have tried to discuss elsewhere the fact that libertarian principles (assertively non-neutral as they are) tend to conflict with neutral principles— even with the weakest of them all, viz., the weak Pareto principle.[26]

It can, of course, be argued that the justification of libertarian rights may *ultimately* be traced to some kind of 'welfaristic' argument, e.g., the view that assigning personal rights of liberty is a rule that leads to the maximization of 'long run' welfare aggregates. But other routes to the justification of libertarian rights also exist, e.g., in terms of contractual notions of justice, or of theories of 'entitlements'.[27] (Indeed some find liberty to be a 'primitive' value not requiring justification in terms of 'prior' values.) It is also worth noting that even if the rule of assigning libertarian rights is justified on welfaristic grounds, that would not in general provide an argument for applying welfarism *act by act*. Judgements of choices over social states have the characteristics of 'act evaluation' rather than of 'rule evaluation'; and a 'rule utilitarian'

26. Sen [86, Chapters 6 and 6*]. There has been quite vigorous controversy on the scope and interpretation of this result, on which see, among others, Ng [65], Batra and Pattanaik [6], Nozick [66,67], Gibbard [34], Bernholz [7], Blau [13], Seidl [84], Kelly [47,48], Suzumura [101, 102], Farrell [24], and Ferejohn [25]. [See Essay 14 in this volume.]

27. See Rawls [76] and Nozick [67] for two alternative approaches to the issue of liberty. For critiques of these approaches, see Daniels [18]—including (among others) the contributions by Dworkin, Hart, Nagel, and Scanlon—and Nagel [64], respectively.

justification of libertarian rights need not lead to a 'neutral' framework for *choices over social states.*

The conception of rights can, of course, extend beyond the sphere of personal liberty. Nozick [67] has recently proposed an 'entitlement system' with a very wide scope, incorporating a variety of rights, including those relating to private property. While Marx's [56] conception of 'exploitation' belongs to the other end of the political spectrum, both systems share a rejection of welfarism, and relate social evaluation to historical information (e.g., dated labour in the case of Marx, and past savings and inheritance in the case of Nozick).

That these 'historical' approaches militate against 'neutrality' is clear enough. What is less clear is whether they also require a rejection of the entire framework of social welfare functionals (including, of course, the special case of social welfare functions). Can the historical information be captured in the data base of social welfare functionals *even if* neutrality is not imposed (i.e., even if welfarism is avoided)?

A SWFL can admit three types of information for use in making judgements of social welfare: (i) $n$-tuples of personal welfare functions without identification of who has which function; (ii) non-welfare data about each social state; (iii) identification of persons related to personal welfare functions and non-welfare data about each person.

Neutrality rules out the use of (ii). Strong neutrality restricts, in addition, the use of (i) by ignoring the welfare information except over the pair of social states that are currently being socially ranked. Anonymity rules out the use of (iii). Strong anonymity goes further. Anonymity as such does not rule out the use of information of the type that the same person (whoever he may be) who will enjoy welfare level $u$ in the state $x$ will also enjoy welfare level $v$ in the state $y$; the anonymity of the personal welfare *functions* still permits such correspondences to be identified and used. Strong anonymity bans this, treating welfare *numbers* in each state anonymously, thereby severely constraining the use of (i). The usable data base is, therefore, very limited for social welfare approaches that are both strongly neutral and strongly anonymous. Both utilitarianism and leximin are confined to this narrow box.[28]

But even when (i), (ii), and (iii) are all admitted, *historical* information need not still be covered except in so far as such information is incorporated in the description of the social states or of the persons themselves. It can, of course, be argued that to be relevant to decisions today, historical data must be present in some extant record (or in memory), and it is possible to treat these data to be parts of the 'description' of the states involved in today's

---

28. Both are also 'end-state principles', as has been pointed out by Nozick [67]. Note, however, that being an 'end-state principle' is less restrictive than being 'welfaristic' since description of end-states can admit information other than those relating to personal welfares.

choices. This requires non-trivial extension of the meaning of 'social state' from conventional usage, incorporating the information about its past to which the evaluator has access. It is only with such re-interpretation that social welfare functionals remain versatile enough to cover historical approaches by eschewing neutrality and anonymity.

I turn now to the principle of egality. Of the major social principles, egality is the one that is probably best captured under welfarism. At least one common conception of egality is based on equating welfare levels of different persons. While such considerations are unusable under an informational framework involving non-comparability or unit comparability (see Section 2), they are not ruled out by welfarism as such. Of course utilitarian social evaluation cannot give any role to egality in this sense (see Sen [89, pp. 15–18]), but other approaches under welfarism (including Rawlsian leximin) can capture a concern for egality.[29]

If, however, egality is defined not in terms of welfare but some other characteristics, e.g., income, wealth, education, or treatment before the law, then welfarism may, in fact, be unable to accommodate even egality. (This problem is present even if egality is conceived 'ultimately' in terms of welfare, but in the absence of detailed welfare information, other characteristics are chosen as 'surrogates'.) Similarly, the principle of 'equal pay for equal work' violates welfarism, but it is, of course, central to an important conception of egality in the context of sexual or racial discrimination.

It can be argued that the limitation of welfarism is not entirely independent of the amount of welfare information we can use. The need for surrogates is strong when the welfare information is very limited or vague. For example, when welfare information is taken to be of the ordinal level comparison type on grounds that our cardinal welfare information is too imprecise, we may still wish to make some distinctions based on the observed non-welfare characteristics.[30] To illustrate: 'person $i$ is better off in $x$ than in $y$' may not be treated in the same way irrespective of whether $i$ gains a dollar in moving from $y$ to $x$, or a million dollars. The possibility of combining incomplete welfare information with non-welfare characteristics is particularly great in evaluative statistics, such as national income evaluation, or the measurement of poverty (for illustrations of such 'mixed' frameworks, see Sen [91, 92][31]).

Welfarism is restrictive even with the richest welfare information, but when the welfare information is poor, it is particularly limiting. A fairly extreme case arises when strong neutrality (leading to welfarism) is combined with welfare information involving ordinal non-comparability. In fact,

29. Even Marx took a needs-based, welfare-oriented egalitarian approach in his analysis of the 'ultimate stage' of communism (see Marx [55], pp. 21–3]).

30. An alternative is, of course, to use 'partial' cardinality, or 'partial' unit comparability, on which see Sen [86, 87], Blackorby [9], Fine [26]. Blackorby, in fact, combines a *non-neutral* extension of utilitarianism with partial unit comparability, thereby expanding the informational base very substantially.

31. See also Fisher [29] and Kenen and Fisher [51].

Arrow's axioms for his impossibility theorem take us very close to such a combination. Ordinal non-comparability *is* assumed by virtue of beginning with social welfare functions rather than SWFLs. While Arrow holds that 'the principle of neutrality is not intuitively basic' [1, p. 101], the effect of using unrestricted domain, independence of irrelevant alternatives and the weak Pareto principle is to get very close to a strongly neutral framework. Indeed, if instead of the *weak* Pareto principle either the *strong* Pareto principle or the Pareto indifference principle were chosen, then the framework would have been strongly neutral (see Theorem 6 above). Since the weak Pareto principle deals only with *strict* personal preferences, the neutrality element in the Arrow system is confined to neutrality of 'winning' sets of persons: if a set of persons wins over the rest in a choice over one pair, it wins in choices over all pairs (see Arrow [1, pp. 98–100]). The scope for non-neutrality lies only for pairs over which the winning set has not precipitated a strict ranking. 'Near neutrality' in this sense, bringing us close to 'welfarism', is thus combined in the Arrow framework with poor welfare information, viz., ordinal non-comparability. Arrow's impossibility theorem has much to do with this informational famine.

## 9  *Bergson–Samuelson Impossibilities*

In disputing the applicability of Arrow's impossibility theorem to the Bergson–Samuelson social welfare function, Little [54] and Samuelson [82] have both emphasized that the Bergson–Samuelson function does not impose any *inter-profile* condition.[32] It admits only one 'profile', i.e., only one $n$-tuple of individual preference orderings. The Bergson–Samuelson exercise is based on the 'individual tastes being given' (Little [54, p. 423]). 'For Bergson, one and only one of the . . . possible patterns of individuals' orderings is needed' (Samuelson [82, pp. 48–9]). Since an Arrovian social welfare function does use inter-profile conditions, it is alleged that 'Arrow's work has no relevance to the traditional theory of welfare economics, which culminates in the Bergson–Samuelson formulation' (Little [54, p. 425]), and that 'it is not true, as many used to believe, that Professor Kenneth Arrow of Stanford has proved "the impossibility of a social welfare function"' (Samuelson in his 'Foreword' to Graaff [36, p. vii]).

Where exactly does the Bergson–Samuelson framework differ from that of Arrow? The Bergson–Samuelson function like Arrow's seems to be rooted in ordinal non-comparability as far as welfare information is concerned and also requires the social preference relation to be an ordering (Samuelson [82, p. 45]). Furthermore, both have an unrestricted domain: while the Bergson–Samuelson function is concerned with only one $n$-tuple of individual orderings,

---

32. For the distinction between 'inter-profile' and 'intra-profile' conditions, see Fishburn [28, pp. 178–83].

'it could be *any* one' (Samuelson [82, p. 49]). Both functions respect the weak Pareto principle; indeed the Bergson–Samuelson function also incorporates the strong Pareto principle (Samuelson [82, p. 49]). While the Bergson–Samuelson formulation does not invoke a non-dictatorship condition, there is nothing to indicate that Bergson or Samuelson will seek a solution in terms of reflecting a given person's strict preferences over *every* pair of social states in the social ordering (even for a *given* $n$-tuple of individual orderings). This leaves us with Arrow's condition of independence of irrelevant alternatives, which Arrow requires but presumably the Bergson–Samuelson framework does not since independence *is* an inter-profile condition.

This interpretation of the distinction runs into difficulty with Samuelson's [82, p. 47] firm statement: 'Many people think that the Independence of Irrelevant Alternatives is one that must go. I cannot agree. My formulation builds it *from the beginning* into Axiom 1'. Thus, while Condition *I* is not a part of the Bergson–Samuelson function, it does not look as if escape is being sought from the Arrow impossibility by dropping Condition *I*. But then is the escape possible, since Arrow's other conditions are not being dropped either?

The fact is that it *is* independence of irrelevant alternatives that is being eschewed, though Samuelson does not notice this because of a formal misunderstanding. In fact, Samuelson seems to be under the impression that 'if the ordering is transitive, it *automatically* satisfies the condition called "independence of irrelevant alternatives"' (Samuelson [82, p. 43]). It isn't so much that this statement is false, but that it incorporates what Gilbert Ryle calls a 'category mistake', since Arrow's independence of irrelevant alternatives is not a property of a *binary relation* (of which an ordering will be a special case), but of the *functional relation* between the social preference relation and the $n$-tuple of individual preference relations. (The mistake may have arisen from concentrating on Arrow's informal illustration, which was misleading, rather than on his formal statement of Condition *I*; see Arrow [1, p. 27].)[33] Given the fact that Samuelson [82] is admitting only one preference $n$-tuple, but not restricting that one in any way ('it could be *any* one, but it is *only* one', p. 49), Samuelson is in fact combining unrestricted domain with the absence of any inter-profile condition. This eliminates Condition *I*, which is an inter-profile condition, from the list (except in a trivial sense, viz., an inter-profile condition when only one $n$-tuple of preferences is admitted is vacuous and is thus unviolated).[34]

33. This is, in fact, a confusion between the 'independence of irrelevant alternatives' as defined by Arrow and the condition with the same name as defined by Radner and Marschak [74]. On the distinction, see Sen [86, p. 17], and Ray [77].

34. Since Samuelson wishes to admit *any* preference ordering, unrestricted domain cannot be generally dropped, and therefore the domain restriction for Condition *I* has to be a part of the formulation of that condition itself. There is, obviously, not much merit in defining an inter-profile condition with a domain (viz., just one preference $n$-tuple) such that it is always vacuous.

That the Arrow result does not survive when one of the conditions, viz., Condition *I*, is dropped is clear enough. (In fact the theorem would have been a pretty flabby one if that were not the case.) The question is whether impossibilities of the Arrow 'type' can arise for Bergson—Samuelson social welfare functions as well *when* the conditions have been reformulated in a way that makes sense for a single-profile approach. As Johansen [46] notes in his elegant and helpful examination of the relevance of Arrow's theorem for economic planning, 'a Bergson welfare function is essentially nothing but such a social preference ordering which is positively associated with the individual preference orderings in the . . . Paretian sense' (p. 19). Until some other consistency conditions have been imposed, 'the impossibility of the traditional Bergson welfare function of economics', which Samuelson [82] rightly holds to be false (p. 42), is hardly worth investigating. A Pareto partial ordering can, of course, be completed into an ordering (as all partial orderings can be).[35]

We have seen before that in the Arrow framework with unrestricted domain and independence, the Pareto indifference rule (and *a fortiori* the strong Pareto principle) will imply strong neutrality (Theorem 6). Strong neutrality is, of course, an inter-profile condition, but it also has intra-profile implications. If individual preferences over $\{x, y\}$ are all exactly the same as those over $\{a, b\}$ for a *given* preference profile, then the corresponding *social* ordering must be the same over $\{x, y\}$ as over $\{a, b\}$.

*Condition SPN* (Single-Profile Neutrality). For any given $n$-tuple of individual preference orderings $\{R_i\}$, if there is a permutation function $\mu$ over the set $X$ of social states such that for some $x$ and $y$ in $X$ and for all $i$:

$$xR_iy \text{ if and only if } \mu(x)R_i\mu(y),$$

and

$$yR_ix \text{ if and only if } \mu(y)R_i\mu(x),$$

then $xRy$ if and only if $\mu(x)R\mu(y)$, and $yRx$ if and only if $\mu(y)R\mu(x)$.

If this intra-profile part of the condition of strong neutrality is accepted, then impossibility results can be precipitated in the Bergson—Samuelson framework in ways that are very similar to the Arrow impossibility theorem. This was first established by Parks in 1973 (see Parks [68]), and this and several other related results have been independently established also by Kemp and Ng [49] and Pollak [73], and further theorems have been obtained also by Hammond [40] and Roberts [80]. As a result of these important contributions it is now clear that the standard inter-profile collective choice results have exact intra-profile counterparts, and this applies to impossibility results as well as to axiomatic derivations of particular social choice procedures (see particularly Pollak [73] and Roberts [80]).

35. This general analytical result was first established by Szpilrajn [104].

What this single-profile approach does is to replace the problem of inter-profile consistency by that of inter-pair consistency *within* a given profile. This translation makes a fair amount of sense since inter-profile consistency also includes *inter alia* some consistency requirements for a given profile, obtainable as a special case. Since the condition of independence of irrelevant alternatives works pair by pair, inter-pair consistency for a given profile comes quite close to a part of it.

I illustrate below the nature of this inter-pair consistency problem for a given profile with a very simple example, choosing my conditions not for economy but with an eye to the transparency of the inconsistency that is precipitated. Strengthen condition *SN* by demanding intra-profile anonymity as well.

*Condition SPNA* (Single-Profile Neutrality and Anonymity).  For any given *n*-tuple of individual preference orderings $\{R_i\}$, if there is a permutation function $\mu$ over the set $X$ of social states and a permutation function $\rho$ over the set $H$ of individuals such that for some $x$ and $y$ in $X$, for all $i$ in $H$:

$$xR_iy \text{ if and only if } \mu(x)R_{\rho(i)}\mu(y),$$

and

$$yR_ix \text{ if and only if } \mu(y)R_{\rho(i)}\mu(x),$$

then $xRy$ if and only if $\mu(x)R\mu(y)$, and $yRx$ if and only if $\mu(y)R\mu(x)$.

If for a given preference profile, the rankings of $\{x, y\}$ and $\{a, b\}$ are the same ignoring the name tags, the social ordering of $\{x, y\}$ must be the same as that of $\{a, b\}$.

Consider the above consistency condition with that part of the strong Pareto principle that demands monotonicity.

*Condition P\*\*.*   For any pair $x$, $y$, if for all $i$: $xR_iy$, and for some $i$: $xP_iy$, then $xPy$.

THEOREM 9.   *There exists an n-tuple of personal preference orderings such that conditions SPNA and P\*\* rule out all conceivable social orderings.*

*Proof.*   Let person 1 have the strict descending order: $x$, $y$, $z$, and person 2: $z$, $x$, $y$, while all others are indifferent between $x$, $y$, and $z$. Take $\rho$ and $\mu$ such that: $\rho(1) = 2$, $\rho(2) = 1$, and $\rho(i) = i$ for all $i \neq 1, 2$, and $\mu(x) = z$, and $\mu(z) = x$. By SPNA $xRz$ holds if and only if $zRx$ does. Thus $xIz$. Similarly $yIz$. Hence $xIy$ by transitivity. But $xPy$ by the Pareto relation $P\*\*$.

It is consistency problems of this kind that are exploited in precipitating impossibility results *within* a given profile. Anonymity is not needed in extending Arrow's theorem to the single-profile context. Indeed, by virtue of the single-profile neutrality assumption SPN, it is easily established that a person who is almost decisive over *some* pair is decisive over *every* pair for the given profile. This when combined with the demonstration that for some *n*-tuple of individual preferences someone is indeed almost decisive over some pair (for which Arrow too had used a single-profile argument), leads to the impossibility result by violating the single-profile version of the non-dictatorship condition.

These impossibility results depend crucially on neutrality applied in the intra-profile context. The debates on Bergson–Samuelson impossibilities have been characterized by some ambiguity on this point. When Kemp and Ng [50] reassert that 'a (Bergson–Samuelson) individualistic SWF cannot be constructed without introducing elements of cardinality',[36] they eliminate a counter-example on the ground that in that example 'social preference is based not just on individual orderings but also on the objective amounts of the first commodity consumed' (p. 89). This counter-example would indeed be non-admissible if an 'individualistic' social welfare function is interpreted to include what we have been calling 'welfarism'. Welfarism may appear to be implied by the form in which the Bergson–Samuelson function is sometimes written: $W = f(U_1, \ldots, U_n)$ (see Samuelson [81, pp. 228–9⅛, Graaff [36, pp. 48|54]). There is an ambiguity here: if $W$ and $U_i$ are taken not to be welfare *numbers* but *functions* defined over $X$, then welfarism is not, in fact, implied. (Indeed then $f(.)$ will be very like a social welfare *functional* SWFL defined by (1), with $W$ being a real-valued representation of the social $R$ determined by a SWFL.) However, it appears that this 'functional' interpretation of $f(.)$ was not intended in the formulations in question (see the operations of Samuelson [81, p. 246, equation (31)], and Graaff [36, p. 51, figure 7(b)]). And if $(U_1, \ldots, U_n)$ is simply a vector of individual utilities, then welfarism will follow, and impossibilities will be round the corner given unrestricted domain and the absence of interpersonal comparisons.

The objections to neutrality in the inter-profile setting (see last section) apply in the intra-profile context also, since it rules out the use of a lot of relevant information. Intra-profile welfarism combined with non-comparable personal utilities leaves us with very little information to use (see Hammond [40] and Pollak [73]). If we are inclined to reject neutrality both in the inter-profile and intra-profile context, these impossibility results may not be thought to be particularly upsetting.

But does this question of neutrality, then, provide a real dividing line between single-profile and multiple-profile impossibility results? This is so only in a very limited sense. The Arrow framework for multiple profiles also *implies* a strong element of neutrality both in the inter-profile and intra-profile

---

36. The focus on cardinality in Kemp–Ng's statement seems a bit misplaced since impossibility results depend really on the absence of interpersonal comparability rather than cardinality. There is little difficulty in extending Theorem 2 to the intra-profile framework.

context (see Sections 6 and 8 above), and would imply strong neutrality fully if the weak Pareto condition is strengthened to the strong Pareto condition (or even replaced by the Pareto indifference rule: see Theorem 6). The impossibility results of the Arrow type whether precipitated in a multiple-profile or in a single-profile context do make essential use of elements of neutrality, which may be assumed directly (as in the single-profile transla-tions of the Arrow theorem), or precipitated by other restrictions (as in the multiple-profile Arrow theorem). If we object to the characteristic of neutrality and the axioms that lead to it, then we question the applicability not merely of single-profile impossibility results, but also of multiple-profile impossibility theorems. There isn't much of a line to draw between them from this particular point of view.

Finally, it should be observed that there do exist a class of single-profile impossibility theorems that do not use the condition of neutrality, viz., 'the impossibility of the Paretian liberal' and related results (Sen [86, 93], Batra and Pattanaik [6], Nozick [66, 67], Gibbard [34], Blau [13], Kelly [47, 48], Suzumura [101, 102], Farrell [24], and Ferejohn [25], among others). No inter-profile condition is used, and no condition of intra-profile neutrality as such is invoked. But—as was remarked earlier—a limited element of neutrality is implicit in the Pareto principle itself, while the consideration of liberty imposes strictly non-neutral (and non-anonymous) restrictions (see Section 8 above).[37] This class of single-profile impossibility results do apply to the Bergson–Samuelson framework, despite no use of neutrality other than what is involved in the weak Pareto principle itself. There isn't, of course, a line to draw in this case between the Bergson–Samuelson and the Arrow frameworks, since single-profile impossibilities hold *a fortiori* to the corresponding multiple-profile frameworks as well.

## 10    Concluding Remarks

There will be no attempt here to summarize the discussion presented in this paper, but a few general remarks will be made.

(1) Each social welfare rule makes certain types of information 'inadmis-sible' in the sense of making social judgements *invariant* with respect to information of those types. For example, utilitarianism makes the following types of information inadmissible (among others): (i) information about social states other than individual welfares generated by them, (ii) information about persons other than their welfares, (iii) information as to whether a given set of welfare numbers in different states relate to the same person (no matter who), (iv) information on individual welfares other than those relating

---

37. For a weakening of the Pareto principle in a non-neutral form avoiding conflicts with any consistent assignment of personal rights, see Sen [93, pp. 235–7, 243–4].

to the two social states that are being ranked in a pairwise comparison, and (v) information about individual welfare *levels* as opposed to welfare *units* ('origins' of individual welfare functions mattering not at all). Similarly, regularity conditions and 'principles' used in social welfare analysis also serve as informational constraints. These constraints are often implicit rather than explicit, and informational analyses of social welfare approaches, thus, have to undertake investigations of informational implications of axiom sets.

(2) Alternative restrictions on the use of personal welfare information can take various forms, both explicit (Section 2) and implicit (Sections 3 and 4). The same is true of restrictions on the use of non-welfare information, e.g., about the social states and the persons (Sections 6, 8, and 9). These informational constraints play important roles both in precipitating impossibility results as well as in axiomatic derivation of specific social welfare rules. The Arrow impossibility theorem follows exclusion of sets of possible rules by ensuring the inadmissibility of the information needed to use them (Sections 2, 6, and 8). Similarly, axiomatic derivations of specific social welfare rules such as utilitarianism or Rawlsian lexicographic maximin use informational constraints, often implicitly, to eliminate rival rules (Sections 4–7).

(3) The use of independence of irrelevant alternatives rules out aggregation rules that are 'positionalist'. While such rules have been much investigated recently in an informational framework with no interpersonal comparability, combining the positional approach with ordinal interpersonal comparisons opens up a new class of aggregation rules; the interpersonal modification of the Borda Rule is a distinguished member of this class (Section 5).

(4) Independence of irrelevant alternatives acts as a great *generalizer* of informational parsimony in the presence of unrestricted domain (Section 6). When combined with the strict Pareto principle (or even just the Pareto indifference rule, which makes it possible to declare two social states as equally good without knowing anything about these states in the special case in which everyone is indifferent between them), independence with unrestricted domain precipitates full-fledged 'neutrality' (outlawing the use of any non-welfare information about *any* social state in *any* choice). When combined with the Suppes indifference rule, which permits social indifference to be declared between $x$ and $y$ without checking *who* has which welfare number in one special case (viz., one in which everyone in $x$ has the same welfare level as the corresponding person in $y$, for some one-to-one correspondence), unrestricted independence implies 'strong anonymity', ruling out the use of *any* personal information in *any* choice. (This is a considerable strengthening of the usual 'anonymity' condition, proposed by May [60].)

(5) Independence with unrestricted domain also has the effect of generalizing the use of Rawlsian lexicographic maximin from two-person conflicts (where at most one person's interests can be violated to cater to the worse off) to conflicts involving any finite number of persons (where the interests of all

except one person can be violated) (Section 7). This provides an alternative axiomatization of lexicographic maximin (compare Section 4).

(6) To accommodate values such as liberty, it is necessary to reject the informational constraints of neutrality and anonymity. The same applies to systems of entitlements and rights envisaged in 'historical' theories as different as those of Marx and Nozick (Section 8). Indeed, in addition, the descriptions of social states have to be enriched beyond the conventional ones to accommodate these historical approaches.

(7) Welfarism, i.e., treating social welfare to be functions only of the individual welfare vectors (without admitting any non-welfare description of social states), is restrictive even with all possible welfare information, but when the welfare information itself is poor, it can be extraordinarily limited. This question has considerable bearing on social welfare analysis for evaluative statistics (e.g., national income, inequality, poverty), where poor welfare information may have to be supplemented systematically by other information (Section 8). For social decision rules, 'welfarism' is much more restrictive than being an 'end-state principle', in the sense of Nozick [67], since descriptions of end-states can admit non-welfare information.

(8) The much-debated issue as to whether the Arrow-type impossibility results apply to the Bergson–Samuelson welfare framework is also closely related to the information question (Section 9). The informational inadmissibility implied by the Arrow conditions is somvwhat relaxed automatically in  he single-profile Bergson–Samuelson context because of the non-usability of the inter-profile condition of independence or irrelevant alternatives. To compensate for this, in the single-profile 'translations' of the Arrow theorem, informational inadmissibility is tightened in another direction, viz., requiring *intra*-profile neutrality (leading to welfarism in the single-profile context). The new restriction is not, however, *entirely* additional since in the Arrow framework independence, unrestricted domain and the weak Pareto principle together imply a substantial part of neutrality (both intra-profile and inter-profile), and will imply all of it if the Pareto indifference rule (or the strong Pareto principle) is accepted instead of the weak Pareto principle (Section 6). Finally, the impossibility of the Paretian liberal and related theorems apply to both single-profile (Bergson–Samuelson) structures as well as to multiple-profile (Arrow) structures, and involve no 'neutrality' condition other than what is implicit in the weak Pareto principle itself (Section 9).

## References

[1] Arrow, K. J. *Social Choice and Individual Values*, second edition (New York: Wiley, 1963).

[2] _____ 'Extended Sympathy and the Possibility of Social Choice', *American Economic Review*, **67** (1977), 219–25.

[3] Atkinson, A. B. 'On the Measurement of Inequality', *Journal of Economic Theory,* **2** (1970), 244–63.

[4] Barry, B. *The Liberal Theory of Justice* (Oxford: Clarendon Press, 1973).

[5] Basu, K. 'Revealed Preference of Governments: Concepts, Analysis and Evaluation', Ph.D. dissertation, London University, 1976. [Published later by Cambridge University Press, 1979.]

[6] Batra, R. N. and P. K. Pattanaik 'On Some Suggestions for Having Non-Binary Social Choice Functions', *Theory and Decision,* **3** (1972), 1–11.

[7] Bernholz, P. 'Is a Paretian Liberal Really Impossible?' *Public Choice,* **19** (1974), 99–107.

[8] Binmore, K. G. 'Social Choice and Parties', *Review of Economic Studies,* **43** (1976), 449–64.

[9] Blackorby, C. 'Degrees of Cardinality and Aggregate Partial Ordering', *Econometrica,* **43** (1975), 845–52.

[10] Blackorby, C. and D. Donaldson 'Utility vs. Equity: Some Plausible Quasi-orderings', *Journal of Public Economics,* **4** (1975).

[11] Blair, D. H. 'Neutrality and Independence Conditions in Social Choice Theory', mimeographed, Rutgers University, 1976.

[12] Blau, J. H. 'The Existence of a Social Welfare Function', *Econometrica,* **25** (1957), 302–13.

[13] ____ 'Liberal Values and Independence', *Review of Economic Studies,* **42** (1975), 395–402.

[14] ____ 'Neutrality, Monotonicity and the Right of Veto: A Comment', *Econometrica,* **44** (1976), 603.

[15] Blau, J. H. and R. Deb. 'Social Decision Functions and the Veto', *Econometrica,* **45** (1977), 871–9.

[16] Borda, J. C. 'Mémoire sur les Élections au Scrutin', *Mémoires de l'Académie Royale des Sciences*; English translation by A. de Grazia, *Isis,* **44** (1953).

[17] Chipman, J. S. 'The Welfare Ranking of Pareto Distributions', *Journal of Economic Theory,* **9** (1974), 275–82.

[18] Daniels, N. (ed.) *Reading Rawls* (Oxford: Basil Blackwell, 1975).

[19] Dasgupta, P. S. 'On Optimum Population Size', in A. Mitra (ed.), *Economic Theory and Planning: Essays in Honor of A. K. Dasgupta* (London: Oxford University Press, 1974).

[20] d'Aspremont, C. and L. Gevers. 'Equity and the Informational Basis of Collective Choice', *Review of Economic Studies,* **46** (1977), 199–210.

[21] Deschamps, R. and L. Gevers. 'Leximin and Utilitarian Rules: A Joint Characterization', *Journal of Economic Theory*, forthcoming. [Published in **17** (1978), 143–63.]

[22] ____ 'Separability, Risk-bearing and Social Welfare Judgements', mimeographed, 1976. [Revised version published later in J.-J. Laffont (ed.), *Aggregation and Revelation of Preferences* (Amsterdam: North-Holland, 1979).]

[23] Diamond, P. 'Cardinal Welfare, Individualistic Ethics and Interpersonal Comparisons of Utility: A Comment', *Journal of Political Economy,* **61** (1967), 765–6.

[24] Farrell, M. J. 'Liberalism in the Theory of Social Choice', *Review of Economic Studies,* **43** (1976), 3–10.

[25] Ferejohn, J. 'The Distribution of Rights in Society', presented at the Reisenburg Symposium on Decision Theory and Social Ethics, mimeographed, 1976. [Revised version published in H. Gottinger and W. Leinfellner (eds), *Decision Theory and Social Ethics* (Dordrecht: Reidel. 1978).]

[26] Fine, B. 'A Note on "Interpersonal Comparisons and Partial Comparability"', *Econometrica,* **43** (1975), 169–72.

[27] Fine, B. and K. Fine. 'Social Choice and Individual Ranking', *Review of Economic Studies,* **42** (1974), 303–32, 459–75.

[28] Fishburn, P. C. *The Theory of Social Choice* (Princeton, NJ: Princeton University Press, 1973).

[29] Fisher, F. M. 'Income Distribution, Value Judgements and Welfare', *Quarterly Journal of Economics,* **70** (1956), 380–424.

[30] Gaertner, W. 'On Rawls' Two Principles of Justice', Discussion Paper, Department of Economics, University of Bielefeld, 1975.

[31] Gärdenfors, P. 'Positional Voting Functions', *Theory and Decision,* **4** (1973), 1–24.

[32] ____ 'Fairness without Interpersonal Comparisons', Working Paper No. 15, Mattias Fremling Society, Lund, 1975.

[33] Gevers, L. 'On Interpersonal Comparability and Social Welfare Orderings', mimeographed, Faculté des Sciences Économiques et Sociales, Namur, 1976. [Revised version published in *Econometrica,* **47** (1979), 75–90.]

[34] Gibbard, A. 'A Pareto-Consistent Libertarian Claim', *Journal of Economic Theory,* **7** (1974), 338–410.

[35] Gorman, W. M. 'Tricks with Utility Functions', in *Essays in Economic Analysis,* ed. by M. Artis and A. R. Nobay (Cambridge: Cambridge University Press, 1975).

[36] Graaff, J. de V. *Theoretical Welfare Economics,* with a foreword by Paul A. Samuelson (Cambridge: Cambridge University Press, 1967).

[37] Guha, A. S. 'Neutrality, Monotonicity and the Right of Veto', *Econometrica,* **40** (1972), 821–6.

[38] Hammond, P. J. 'Equity, Arrow's Conditions and Rawls' Difference Principle', *Econometrica,* **44** (1976), 793–804.

[39] ____ 'Dual Interpersonal Comparisons of Utility and the Welfare Economics of Income Distribution', *Journal of Public Economics,* **6** (1977), 51–61.

[40] ____ 'Why Ethical Measures of Inequality Need Interpersonal Comparisons', *Theory and Decision,* **7** (1976), 263–74.

[41] Hansson, B. 'The Independence Condition in the Theory of Social Choice', *Theory and Decision,* **4** (1973), 25–49.

[42] Harsanyi, J. C. 'Cardinal Welfare, Individualistic Ethics and Interpersonal Comparisons of Utility', *Journal of Political Economy,* **63** (1955), 309–21.

[43] ____ 'Non-linear Social Welfare Functions, or Do Welfare Economists have a Special Exemption from Bayesian Rationality', *Theory and Decision,* **6** (1975), 311–32.

[44] ____ 'Non-linear Social Welfare Functions: A Rejoinder to Professor Sen', in *Logic, Methodology and Philosophy of Science,* ed. by R. Butts and J. Hintikka (Dordrecht: Reidel, 1977).

[45] Inada, K.-J. 'The Simple Majority Decision Rule', *Econometrica,* **37** (1969), 490–506.

[46] Johansen, L. 'An Examination of the Relevance of Kenneth Arrow's General Possibility Theorem for Economic Planning', in *Optimation et Simulation de Macro-décisions*, Économie Mathématique et Économétrie, No. 3 (Namur: Gembloux, 1970).

[47] Kelly, J. S. 'The Impossibility of a Just Liberal', *Economica*, **43** (1976), 67–76.

[48] ____ 'Rights-Exercising and a Pareto Consistent Libertarian Claim', *Journal of Economic Theory*, **13** (1976), 138–53.

[49] Kemp, M. C. and Y.-K. Ng. 'On the Existence of Social Welfare Functions, Social Orderings and Social Decision Functions', *Economica*, **43** (1976), 59–66.

[50] ____ 'More on Social Welfare Functions: The Incompatibility of Individualism and Ordinalism', *Economica*, **44** (1977), 89–90.

[51] Kenen, P. B. and F. M. Fisher. 'Income Distribution, Value Judgements and Welfare: A Correction', *Quarterly Journal of Economics*, **71** (1957), 322–4.

[52] Kolm, S. Ch. 'The Optimum Production of Social Justice', in *Public Economics*, ed. by J. Margolis and H. Guitton (London: Macmillan, 1969).

[53] Little, I. M. D. *A Critique of Welfare Economics* (Oxford: Clarendon Press, 1950; 2nd edition, 1957).

[54] ____ 'Social Choice and Individual Values', *Journal of Political Economy*, **60** (1952), 422–32.

[55] Marx, K. *Critique of the Gotha Programme*. English translation in K. Marx and F. Engels, *Selected Works*, vol. II (Moscow: Foreign Languages Publishing House, 1958).

[56] ____ *Capital: A Critical Analysis of Capitalist Production*, vol. I (London: Sonnenschein. Republished London: Allen & Unwin, 1938).

[57] Maskin, E. 'A Theorem on Utilitarianism', *Review of Economic Studies*, forthcoming. [Published in **45** (1978), 93–6.]

[58] ____ Decision-Making under Ignorance with Implications for Social Choice', mimeographed, Jesus College, Cambridge, 1976. [Revised version published in *Theory and Decision*, **11** (1979), 319–37.

[59] ____ 'Social Welfare Functions on Restricted Domain', mimeographed, Jesus College, Cambridge, 1976.

[60] May, K. O. 'A Set of Independent Necessary and Sufficient Conditions for Simple Majority Decision', *Econometrica*, **20** (1952), 680–4.

[61] Mirrlees, J. A. 'An Exploration in the Theory of Optimal Income Taxation', *Review of Economic Studies*, **38** (1971), 1975–2008.

[62] Moon, J. W. 'A Problem on Rankings by Committees', *Econometrica*, **44** (1976), 241–6.

[63] Muellbauer, J. 'Inequality Measures, Prices and Household Composition', *Review of Economic Studies*, **41** (1974), 403–504.

[64] Nagel, T. 'Libertarianism without Foundations', *Yale Law Journal*, **85** (1975), 136–49.

[65] Ng, Y.-K. 'The Possibility of a Paretian Liberal: Impossibility Theorems and Cardinal Utility', *Journal of Political Economy*, **79** (1971), 1397–1402.

[66] Nozick, R. 'Distributive Justice', *Philosophy and Public Affairs*, **3** (1973), 45–126.

[67] ____ *Anarchy, State and Utopia* (Oxford: Blackwell, 1974).

[68] Parks, R. P. 'An Impossibility Theorem for Fixed Preferences: A Dictatorial Bergson–Samuelson Welfare Function', *Review of Economic Studies,* **43** (1976), 447–50.

[69] Pattanaik, P. K. *Voting and Collective Choice* (Cambridge: Cambridge University Press, 1971).

[70] Phelps, E. S. *Economic Justice* (Harmondsworth: Penguin, 1973).

[71] ____ 'Recent Development in Welfare Economics: Justice et Equité', Discussion Paper 75-7617, The Economics Workshop, Columbia University, 1976. [Revised version published in M. Intriligator (ed.), *Frontiers of Quantitative Economics*, vol. III (Amsterdam: North-Holland, 1977).]

[72] Plott, C. R. 'Axiomatic Social Choice Theory: An Overview and Interpretation', *American Journal of Political Science,* **20** (1976), 511–96.

[73] Pollak, R. A. 'Bergson–Samuelson Social Welfare Functions and the Theory of Social Choice', Discussion Paper 350, Department of Economics, University of Pennsylvania, 1976. [Revised version published in *Quarterly Journal of Economics,* **93** (1979), 73–90.]

[74] Radner, R. and J. Marschak. 'Notes on Some Proposed Decision Criteria,' in *Decision Processes*, ed. by R. M. Thrall, D. H. Coombs, and R. L. Davis (New York: Wiley, 1954).

[75] Rawls, J. 'Justice as Fairness', *Philosophical Review,* **67** (1958).

[76] ____ *A Theory of Justice* (Cambridge, Mass.: Harvard University Press, and Oxford: Clarendon Press, 1971).

[77] Ray, P. 'Independence of Irrelevant Alternatives', *Econometrica,* **32** (1973), 987–91.

[78] Roberts, K. W. S. 'Possibility Theorems with Interpersonally Comparable Welfare Levels', *Review of Economic Studies*, forthcoming. [Published in **47** (1980), 409–20.]

[79] ____ 'Interpersonal Comparability and Social Choice Theory', *Review of Economic Studies*, forthcoming. [Published in **47** (1980), 421–39.]

[80] ____ 'Social Choice Theory: The Single- and Multi-Profile Approaches', mimeographed, St John's College, Oxford, 1976. [Published later in *Review of Economic Studies,* **47** (1980), 441–50.]

[81] Samuelson, P. A. *Foundations of Economic Analysis* (Cambridge, Mass.: Harvard University Press, 1947).

[82] ____ 'Arrow's Mathematical Politics', in *Human Values and Economic Policy*, ed. by S. Hook (New York: New York University Press, 1967), pp. 41–52.

[83] ____ 'Reaffirming the Existence of Reasonable Bergson–Samuelson Social Welfare Functions', *Economica,* **44** (1977), 81–8.

[84] Seidl, C. 'On Liberal Values', *Zeitschrift fur Nationalokonomie,* **35** (1975), 257–92.

[85] Sen, A. K. 'The Nature and Classes of Prescriptive Judgements', *Philosophical Quarterly,* **17** (1967), 46–62.

[86] ____ *Collective Choice and Social Welfare* (San Francisco: Holden Day, and Edinburgh: Oliver & Boyd, 1970).

[87] ____ 'Interpersonal Aggregation and Partial Comparability', *Econometrica,* **38** (1970), 393–409. [Essay 9 in this volume.]

[88] ____ 'Interpersonal Aggregation and Partial Comparability: A Correction', *Econometrica,* **40** (1972), 959.

[89] ____ *On Economic Inequality* (Oxford: Clarendon Press, and New York: Norton, 1973).

[90] ____ 'Informational Bases of Alternative Welfare Approaches', *Journal of Public Economics,* **3** (1974), 387–403.

[91] ____ 'Poverty: An Ordinal Approach to Measurement', *Econometrica,* **44** (1976), 219–31. [Essay 17 in this volume.]

[92] ____ 'Real National Income', *Review of Economic Studies,* **43** (1976), 19–39. [Essay 18 in this volume.]

[93] ____ 'Liberty, Unanimity and Rights', *Economica,* **43** (1976), 217–35. [Essay 14 in this volume.]

[94] ____ 'Welfare Inequalities and Rawlsian Axiomatics', *Theory and Decision,* **7** (1976), 243–62; also in *Logic, Methodology and Philosophy of Science,* ed. by R. Butts and J. Hintikka (Dordrecht: Reidel, 1976).

[95] ____ 'Non-Linear Social Welfare Functions: A Reply to Professor Harsanyi', in *Logic, Methodology and Philosophy of Science,* ed. by R. Butts and J. Hintikka (Dordrecht: Reidel, 1977).

[96] ____ 'Social Choice Theory: A Re-examination', *Econometrica,* **45** (1977), 53–90. [Essay 8 in this volume.]

[97] Sen, A. K. and P. K. Pattanaik. 'Necessary and Sufficient Conditions for Rational Choice under Majority Decision', *Journal of Economic Theory,* **1** (1969), 178–202. [Essay 7 in this volume.]

[98] Smith, J. H. 'Aggregation of Preferences and Variable Electorate', *Econometrica,* **41** (1973), 1027–43.

[99] Strasnick, S. 'Social Choice Theory and the Derivation of Rawls' Difference Principle', *Journal of Philosophy,* **73** (1976), 85–99.

[100] Suppes, P. 'Some Formal Models of Grading Principles', *Synthese,* **6** (1966), 284–306; reprinted in P. Suppes, *Studies in the Methodology and Foundations of Science* (Dordrecht: Reidel, 1969).

[101] Suzumura, K. 'Remarks on the Theory of Collective Choice', *Economica,* **43** (1976), 381–90.

[102] ____ 'On the Consistency of Libertarian Claims', Discussion Paper 101, Kyoto Institute of Economic Research, 1976. [Revised version published in *Review of Economic Studies,* **45** (1978), 329–42.]

[103] Svensson, L.-G. 'Social Justice and the Fairness Criterion', mimeographed, Department of Economics, University of Lund, 1976. [Revised version published in *Social Justice and Fair Distributions,* Lund Economic Studies, Lund, 1977.]

[104] Szpilrajn, E. 'Sur l'Extension de l'Ordre Partiel', *Fundamenta Mathematicae,* **16** (1930).

[105] Wilson, R. B. 'Social Choice Theory without the Pareto Principle', *Journal of Economic Theory,* **5** (1972), 478–86.

[106] Young, H. P. 'An Axiomatization of Borda's Rule', *Journal of Economic Theory,* **9** (1974), 43–52.

# 12

# Interpersonal Comparisons
# of Welfare

## 1 *Introduction*

In his insightful survey of welfare economics Scitovsky's (1951) main theme
was the limitations imposed by the two assumptions that had become
'axioms generally accepted by most people who were concerned with such
matters', viz., 'the ordinal nature of utility and the impossibility of interpersonal utility comparisons' (p. 175). He noted that even the most 'obvious'
recommendations of policy (e.g., measures based on preferring 'prosperity'
to 'depression') involved interpersonal comparisons:

> The overwhelming majority of people may be better off in times of
> prosperity; but there are some, however few, who live on fixed incomes
> or accumulated savings, and who in depression, can 'pick up bargains',
> as one economist has put it, that are not available to them in times of
> prosperity. The economist, therefore, who favours prosperity and
> advocates a policy of full employment makes an implicit value judge-
> ment. He implies that the gain of those millions who benefit by pros-
> perity is in some sense greater or more important than the loss of real
> income suffered by those few whose money incomes are fixed. (pp.
> 177–8)

Things have changed a great deal since those bleak days when Scitovsky
had rather little company in questioning the rejection of interpersonal comparisons. There have been many recent attempts to make systematic use of
interpersonal comparisons of welfare. This paper is concerned primarily
with interpersonal comparisons, and with cardinality only in that context.

I have benefited much from discussions with Ken Binmore, Peter Hammond, Richard Layard,
and Eric Maskin, and from the comments of an anonymous 'quasi-referee'.

From M. Boskin (ed.), *Economics and Human Welfare: Essays in Honor of Tibor Scitovsky*
(New York: Academic Press, 1979).

The chief intention is to clarify alternative *interpretations* of interpersonal comparisons as well as alternative formal structures of the *type* of comparability.

Statements on interpersonal comparisons can be broadly classified into *descriptive* and *prescriptive* types. Robbins's well-known attack on interpersonal comparisons as treated by utilitarians was essentially based on denying that there was any descriptive meaning of such comparisons, and not, as often supposed, based on asserting that such comparisons should not be made.[1] Robbins (1935) could see no way of settling differences of views on interpersonal comparisons 'in a purely scientific manner' (p. 129)', 'Introspection does not enable A to measure what is going on in B's mind, nor B to measure what is going on in A's' (p. 140). Thus Robbins saw 'no way of comparing the satisfactions of different people' (p. 140) and took interpersonal comparisons to be 'essentially normative' (p. 139).

I would like to argue that *both* descriptive and normative interpretations of interpersonal comparisons are possible, but it is important that they be clearly distinguished from each other.[2] I would also argue that *several* descriptive interpretations are possible and these different interpretations must also be distinguished from each other. And there are several distinct normative interpretations as well. The problem is not one of poverty, but of an embarrassment of riches.

In Section 2 alternative descriptive interpretations are considered, while Section 3 is devoted to normative interpretations. Sections 4 and 5 are concerned with alternative formal structures dealing with different types of interpersonal comparisons (e.g., of 'levels', of 'gains and losses').

## 2  Descriptive Interpretations

At least three distinct descriptive interpretations can be distinguished, based respectively on (i) behaviourism, (ii) introspective welfare comparison, and (iii) introspective *as if* choice.[3]

The behaviourist approach has been explored by Little and more recently by Waldner and others, using comparative behaviour as the basis for making comparative statements on mental states. Obviously, the behaviour observed

1. Scitovsky (1951) too possibly misinterprets Robbins on this: 'Considering that practically every economic change favours some and hurts others, Professor Robbins was in effect barring himself and his colleagues from any policy recommendation whatever' (p. 176). I believe I have been guilty of the same misinterpretation (Sen, 1973a, pp. 81–3), as has been pointed out by Baumol (1975) in his review of Sen (1973a).

2. See Sen (1970, Chapters 7 and 9), Jeffrey (1971), Waldner (1972, 1974), and Hammond (1977).

3. On methodological issues involved in the distinction between 'introspective' and 'behaviourist' interpretations of personal welfare statements, see Majumdar (1962).

in this case is not choice based in the sense of 'revealed preference', since we do not in fact have the option of becoming someone else. But there are other kinds of observation, e.g., 'we generally associate certain facial expression with frustration', and the focus is on developing 'theories connecting desires to observables other than choices' (Waldner, 1972, p. 96).[4] Little (1957) explains the rationale of the behaviourist approach for interpersonal comparisons in persuasive terms:

> We can say of a man that he is habitually miserable, or that he has a disposition to be miserable. Obviously we cannot be meaning that he has a disposition to be more miserable than he usually is. We mean that he has a disposition to be more miserable than men usually are. . . . if we say of a man that he is always miserable, basing our judgement on how he looks and behaves, and how we know we would feel if we looked and behaved like that, and on a wide knowledge of his character gathered by observing his behaviour and words in a variety of situations, and on the opinions of all his friends who similarly knew him well, then we would think it just nonsense to say that he might really be deceiving everyone all the time and be the happiest of men. (pp. 54–5)

It has been noted that Little's approach was influenced by 'the concept of mind' as developed by Ryle (1949).[5] This might have been the case, but Little's view is a good deal less extreme than Ryle's, especially in the treatment of introspection in interpreting behaviour.[6] For Ryle (1949), mental states are not essentially different from behaviour as such: 'overt intelligent performances are not clues to the workings of minds: they are those workings'. 'Boswell described Johnson's mind when he described how he wrote, talked, etc., fidgeted and fumed' (p. 57).[7] Contrast this with Little's view that 'we *use* different men's behaviour, in a wide sense of the word, to compare their mental states' (Little, 1957, p. 54, italics added).

---

4. Some choices must, however, be relevant for interpersonal comparisons under the behaviourist approach, e.g., the purchase of mourning dresses, not to mention tear-wiping tissues. For a more ambitious attempt at making interpersonal comparisons based on consumption behaviour, see Muellbauer (1975).

5. See, e.g., Banerji (1964). See also Little's (1957), Preface, p. vii.

6. Compare Little (1957, pp. 54–7) with Ryle (1949, I.(1)).

7. The concept of the mind as a separate entity from behaviour, Ryle (1949) argued, was a 'category mistake'. Of the same kind as made 'by a foreigner visiting Oxford or Cambridge for the first time', who 'is shown a number of colleges, libraries, playing fields, museums, scientific departments and administrative offices', and who then proceeds to ask: 'But where is the University?' (pp. 17–18). Or as made by 'a foreigner watching his first game of cricket', learning 'what are the functions of the bowlers, the batsmen, the fielders, the umpires and the scorers', who goes on to observe that 'there is no one left on the field to contribute the famous element of team-spirit' (p. 18). (I must confess to being more persuaded that a foreigner has a tough time in Oxbridge, than that mind cannot be distinguished from behaviour.)

There are several variants of the behaviourist approach, and Little's concentration on behaviour as giving evidence on mind is, in this sense, a weak version. It contrasts, however, quite sharply with making interpersonal comparisons based essentially on introspection. The usability of the behaviourist approach even in this weak sense depends on the existence of *agreed* criteria firmly linking comparative behaviour to comparative mental states, and this is no slight issue (on this see Waldner (1972)).

The approach of *introspective welfare comparison* interprets interpersonal comparisons as personal statements, each reflecting a particular person's thoughts in answering a question of the kind: 'Do I feel I would be better off as person $i$ in social state $x$ rather than as person $j$ in social state $y$?' They are descriptive statements, but they describe a particular person's thoughts on the subject, e.g., 'I would hate to be in your position'. The thought experiment involves placing oneself in the position of another, including considering that person's mental characteristics. Needless to say, in placing oneself in the position of another, note may be taken of that person's behaviour and the light it throws on his mind, but the immediate reference in a statement of interpersonal comparison in this approach is to the author's own thoughts (no matter how they are derived). As a prelude to a moral exercise, the description of the results of such a thought experiment is frequently invited,[8] and the use of introspective comparison is certainly one of the oldest approaches to interpersonal contrasts.[9]

The approach of introspective choice is similar to this, except that the exercise of placing oneself in the position of another is not followed by the question, 'In which position do I feel I would be better off?' but by the query, 'Which position would I *choose*?' The two questions are not identical, even though identifying welfare with choice is an established tradition in economics, especially in the context of 'revealed preference'.[10] There are two different issues involved in this identification, viz., legitimacy and convenience. While considering person $i$ in $x$ to be better off then person $j$ in $y$ is an argument for choosing to be $i$ in $x$ rather than $j$ in $y$ in this *as if* choice, other considerations may well enter the arena of choice, e.g., pride or ethics. For example, 'Of course, I believe I would be better off as a rich Brahmin rather than the poor untouchable I am, but I would not dream of wishing to be one of *them*'. Thus, interpersonal comparisons of welfare based on *as if choices* do raise some problems of legitimacy of interpretation.

8. 'Take physic, pomp,
   Expose thyself to feel what wretches feel,
   That thou mayst shake the superflux to them,
   And show the heavens more just' (*King Lear*, III, iv. 33–6).
   9. For examples of ethical treatises based on such introspective comparisons, see Kant (1785) and Sidgwick (1874), and more recently Hare (1952), Harsanyi (1955), Rawls (1958, 1971), Suppes (1966), and Pattanaik (1971), among many others.
   10. For critical appraisal of different aspects of the foundations of the revealed preference approach, see Hicks (1958, 1974), Sen (1973b), Scitovsky (1976), Wong (1978).

Even if rankings revealed by choice and welfare rankings are identified, there is the important issue of *which* to take as the 'primitive' concept. A preference for the so-called 'operational' quality of choice seems to be a conspicuous characteristic of the economist's taste, and this is extended to introspective choice as well (Arrow, 1963):

> The ordinalist would ask what possible meaning the comparison could have to anyone; a comparison should represent at least a conceivable choice among alternative actions. Interpersonal comparisons of the extended sympathy type can be put in the operational form; the judge-ment takes the form: It is better (in my judgement) to be myself in state $x$ than to be you in state $y$. (p. 115)

The existence of a 'conceivable choice', which does certainly help to contem-plate the contrast, does not, however, oblige us to identify the alternative chosen as being necessarily better. Furthermore, the use of operationalism in this particular context raises some intricate questions of relevance. While there may be an obvious advantage in dealing with choice-based statements when the choices are of other people and are also observable, it is not obvious that a similar advantage exists in the case of one's own introspection over *as if* choices. It does not seem to make much less sense to say 'I feel I would be better off as $i$ than as person $j$, so I would choose to be $i$ and not $j$', than to say 'I would choose to be $i$ and not $j$, and so I must be better off as $i$ than as $j$'. The advantage of operational meaningfulness in taking choice as the primitive in this case is not really convincing.

Each of the three descriptive approaches considered here have some advan-tages and some problems. The contrast among them is of relevance to the formal structures for interpersonal comparisons to be proposed in Section 4, as will be discussed there. Meanwhile, before discussing the normative inter-pretations, it is worth examining how these various descriptive approaches cope with Robbins's query about how to 'settle our differences in a purely scientific manner' when we differ on interpersonal comparisons of welfare of person $i$ and person $j$.[11] In the behaviourist approach the answer is clear enough. The test has to take the form of contrasting observed behaviour,

---

11. It is interesting to note, in the context of the history of economic thought, that Robbins's denial of the fruitfulness of 'scientific' arguments on interpersonal comparisons, while derived from his particular interpretation of such comparative statements, was related to his concentra-tion on market behaviour as the predominant source of information on preference and welfare, anticipating the approach of 'revealed preference' to be developed later by Paul Samuelson. Robbins (1935) concluded 'It [interpersonal comparison] is a comparison which is never needed in the theory of equilibrium and which is never implied by the assumptions of that theory. It is a comparison which necessarily falls outside the scope of any positive science' (p. 139). Robbins contrasted interpersonal comparisons with an individual's *personal* comparison of welfare levels in two situations as revealed by market behaviour (p. 138).

e.g., whether we agree that person $i$ is laughing away while $j$ is weeping pitiably. In the weaker interpretation of behaviourism (e.g., as given by Little), there could be further arguments as to whether these behaviour characteristics do give us legitimate clues as to their respective mental states, though in this we have been given rather little guidance as to how to conduct the argument beyond going through the more obvious questions, e.g., are they play acting?

In the stronger version of behaviourism, the comparison of mental states is not essentially different from the comparison of behaviours. Given a set of criteria relating behaviour to mental states, the disputes can indeed take a scientific form of whether or not a certain behaviour was observed. It is worth remarking here that the fact that different people may be thought to have different ways of 'expression' may weaken the appeal of moral rules based on welfare comparisons on behavioural lines, e.g., giving a unit of income to the person whose face *lights up* most (under Benthamism), or to the person who *looks* in general unhappiest (under 'maximin'). But this weak appeal of moral rules based on behaviourist interpersonal comparisons does not render statements on interpersonal comparisons of welfare in this approach any less scientific. The statements in question are simply those of comparative behaviour.

The picture is quite different with the two introspective approaches. If person 1 thinks that $i$ is happier than $j$ and person 2 holds the opposite, there is nothing to 'resolve', since each is a personal statement of the respective author on the results of placing himself in the positions of $i$ and $j$.[12] For descriptive statements on our feelings and thoughts on the subject, there is no need to 'settle our differences', even though we could well discuss whether we have taken all the relevant aspects into account. If you say that given the choice you would have preferred to live in Pompeii of AD 79 rather than in London of 1979, and I boringly express a preference for London of 1979, we can discuss whether we have considered the relevant facts (e.g., whether you have heard of Vesuvius), but there is no need to 'settle our differences'. But note that the statements themselves are not moral ones, nor normative in the usual sense; they *describe* our preferences.

The moral relevance of interpersonal comparisons based on introspective comparison or introspective choice arises from moral rules that may be formulated *using* these comparisons, e.g., Bentham's rule of maximizing the welfare sum, or Rawls's rule of making the worst-off individual as well off as possible. But the comparisons themselves are descriptive.

The contrast can be brought out with a specific example, e.g., the 'Weak Equity Axiom' (WEA) (Sen, 1973a):

12. There is an analogy here with Ramsey's (1931) complaint about the nature of many arguments: 'I think we realize too little how often our arguments are of the form:—$A$: "I went to Grantchester this afternoon". $B$: "No, I didn't!"' (p. 289). It will be a pity to conclude from the conversation that the subject of going to Grantchester is, in Robbins's phrase, 'essentially normative'.

Let person $i$ have a lower level of welfare than person $j$ for each level of individual income. Then in distributing a given total of income among $n$ individuals including $i$ and $j$, the optimal solution must give $i$ a higher level of income than $j$. (p. 18)

On the interpretation of 'introspective choice', 'WEA amounts to saying that if I feel that for any given level of income I would prefer to be in the position of person $j$ [with his tastes and his non-income characteristics] than in that of person $i$, then [in distributing a given total of income] I would recommend that $i$ should get a higher income level than $j$' (p. 19). In this if— then statement, the antecedent which involves interpersonal comparison is purely descriptive, and the moral element comes in only in the requirement that the antecedent must lead to the recommendation specified. A similar picture holds for using WEA with interpreting interpersonal comparisons in terms of behaviourism, or of introspective welfare comparison.

## 3   Normative Interpretations

We turn now to normative interpretations. Robbins (1935) had argued for interpreting interpersonal comparisons in this way. 'To state that $A$'s preference [for $n$ over $m$] stands above $B$'s [for $m$ over $n$] in order of importance ... is essentially normative' (p. 139).

It should be noted, however, that any normative interpretation is entirely relative to the maximand chosen. For example, if the maximand is taken to be the utilitarian one of welfare *sum*, then the consequent interpersonal comparisons are of welfare *differences*. With the utilitarian normative form, the statement just quoted amounts to identifying $A$'s welfare difference between $n$ and $m$ as greater than $B$'s welfare difference between $m$ and $n$.

On the other hand, if we take the Rawlsian maximand, viz., the welfare of the worst-off individual, then the interpersonal comparison is of welfare *levels*.[13] The statement quoted then amounts to stating that $B$ in social state $n$ is better off than $A$ in social state $m$. Interpretation of $A$'s preference for $n$ over $m$ and $B$'s for $m$ over $n$ as their respective personal welfare rankings permits us to identify the following interpersonal partial ordering, represented in the form of a Hasse diagram (with a downward line indicating superiority)[14] (Figure 1).

---

13. This is, strictly speaking, an apocryphal version of Rawls (1971), whose 'Difference principle' judges advantage not in terms of *welfare levels*, but in terms of access to 'primary social goods' (pp. 90–5). In this paper, however, we shall stick to the interpretation of the Rawlsian criteria popular among economists.

14. The position of $A$ in social state $n$ is not ranked vis-à-vis those of $B$ in $m$ and $n$.

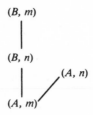

FIGURE 1

Similarly, with other normative maximands, interpersonal comparisons will take different forms, and there is no unique normative interpretation of interpersonal comparisons.[15]

It must also be noted that on a normative interpretation of interpersonal comparisons, 'basing' two-person social welfare judgements on these comparisons will be purely tautologous, since these comparisons merely reflect those two-person social welfare judgements. However, to base $n$-person social welfare judgements on these interpersonal values is non-tautologous, since this would imply a particular class of restrictions relating two-person judgements to $n$-person judgements.

For example, consider the Rawlsian maximin rule, which implies that if person $i$, who prefers $n$ to $m$, is worse off in social state $m$ than everyone in social state $n$, then socially $n$ is better than $m$. On the corresponding normative interpretation of interpersonal comparisons, this amounts to saying that if person $i$'s preference for $n$ over $m$ should prevail in the two-person social welfare judgement for each pair $(i, j)$ of persons including $i$ and everyone else $j$ one by one, then it must do so for the community as a whole. This is, of course, far from tautologous, and indeed it is easily checked that this relation does not hold for utilitarianism.[16] The utilitarian rule implies, on the normative interpretation of interpersonal comparisons, a different class of restrictions relating $n$-person judgements to two-person judgements, and the contrast between the different classes of restrictions implied by different normative rules throws much light on the respective ethical approaches (d'Aspremont and Gevers, 1977; Deschamps and Gevers, 1976, 1978; Hammond, 1977; Maskin, 1976, 1978; Roberts, 1978).

15. The definiteness of Robbins's (1935, 1938) own normative interpretation arises from his taking the utilitarian form for granted; an example, I fear, of what he himself identifies so perceptively, in a different context, as 'the accidental deposit of the historical association of English Economics with Utilitarianism' (1935, p. 141).

16. Cf. the axioms of binary build-up $B$ and single-focus equity for $n$-member communities SFE($n$), which hold for the Rawlsian maximin and lexicographic maximin rules but not for the utilitarian rule (Sen, 1976).

## 4   Comparability Types: Formal Structures

The dichotomy between interpersonal comparability of *levels* of welfare—relevant for Rawlsian maximin rules (and more generally for criteria of equity)—and that of *units* of welfare—relevant for utilitarianism—was discussed elsewhere (Sen, 1970, 1973a).[17] The formal structures developed there is now presented with some extensions.

Let $W_i(\cdot)$ be any welfare function, defined over the set $X$ of social states, attributable to person $i$. Denote the set of all positive monotonic transformations of $W_i(\cdot)$ as $M(W_i)$, and the set of all positive 'linear' (strictly, affine) transformations of $W_i(\cdot)$ as $A(W_i)$. Let $L_i$ be the set of all welfare functions attributable to person $i$. If welfare is 'ordinal', then $L_i = M(W_i)$; if 'cardinal', then $L_i = A(W_i)$; if 'ordinal-type' (Sen, 1970, p. 116), then $A(W_i) \subseteq L_i \subseteq M(W_i)$.

We define welfare being 'transcardinal' as $L_i \subset A(W_i)$. This is more restrictive than cardinality in not permitting all positive 'linear' transformations. A special case of this—we call it 'homocardinal'—is $L_i$ being the set of all *homogeneous*, positive 'linear' transformations of $W_i$, denoted $H(W_i) \subset A(W_i)$. With homocardinality, the 'origin' of a person's welfare function is not arbitrary and is invariant with respect to the permitted transformations, viz., multiplication of $W_i(\cdot)$ by any positive real number. (The interpretation may be to identify a distinguished point below which misery dominates—a concept of possible relevance for population policy; other interpretations are also possible.) This is sometimes called a 'ratio scale'.

The Cartesian product $L = \Pi_{i=1}^n L_i$ specifies all the possible $n$-tuples of individual welfare functions—one for each person—admissible *with respect to the measurability assumptions*. Interpersonal comparability assumptions may restrict the admissible set of $n$-tuples further, e.g., not being allowed to admit an $n$-tuple that 'blows up' the welfare function of one person arbitrarily keeping those of others unchanged. The set of admissible $n$-tuples of individual welfare functions with respect to measurability *and* comparability assumptions together is given by specifying some $\bar{L} \subseteq L$.

Some distinguished cases of comparability types are clear enough.[18]

*Non-comparability.*   $\bar{L} = L$: Comparability imposes no additional restriction in this case, and each person's welfare function can be varied freely—within the restrictions imposed by the measurability assumptions—without

17. See also Fine (1975), Blackorby (1975), Hammond (1976, 1977), Kelly (1976), d'Aspremont and Gevers (1977), Maskin (1976, 1978), Deschamps and Gevers (1978), Gevers (1979), and Roberts (1976, 1978). Hammond's (1977) analysis of 'dual comparability' differs from the framework presented here in one essential respect, to be discussed in the next section.

18. All the distinguished cases covered here except the last two have been discussed in Sen (1970, 1973a). 'Partial unit comparability' was called 'partial comparability'.

reference to the welfare function of the others. $\bar{L}$ under non-comparability is denoted $\bar{L}(0)$.

*Full comparability.*   For any $\bar{W}$ in $\bar{L}$, $\bar{L}$ includes exactly all $W$ in $L$ such that for all $i$: $W_i(\cdot) = g(\bar{W}_i(\cdot))$, for some increasing function $g$ (invariant with $i$), permitted by the measurability assumption. $\bar{L}$ under full comparability is denoted $\bar{L}(F)$.

*Unit comparability.*   For any $\bar{W}$ in $\bar{L}$, $\bar{L}$ includes exactly all $W$ in $L$ such that for all $i$: $W_i = a_i + b\bar{W}_i$, for some $a_i$ and some $b > 0$ invariant with $i$. $\bar{L}$ under unit comparability is denoted $\bar{L}(1)$.

*Level comparability.*   For any $\bar{W}$ in $\bar{L}$, $\bar{L}$ includes exactly all $W$ in $L$ such that for any $i, j$, and any $x, y \in X$: $\bar{W}_i(x) \geq \bar{W}_j(y)$ if and only if $W_i(x) \geq W_j(y)$. $L$ under level comparability is denoted $\bar{L}(L)$.

*Partial unit comparability.*   $\bar{L}$ such that $\bar{L}(1) \subseteq \bar{L} \subseteq \bar{L}(0)$.

*Partial level comparability.*   $\bar{L}$ such that $\bar{L}(L) \subseteq \bar{L} \subseteq \bar{L}(0)$.

*Partial full comparability.*   $\bar{L}$ such that $\bar{L}(F) \subseteq \bar{L} \subseteq \bar{L}(0)$.

It may be remarked that full comparability makes interpersonal comparability just as 'full' as the measurability of individual welfares will allow. With 'ordinal' individual welfare functions, the comparability will not, thus, extend beyond level comparability, but with individual 'cardinality', the units will be comparable also.[19] In fact, with 'homocardinal' individual welfare functions, even interpersonal welfare *ratios* will be invariant under full comparability. Intermediate cases of measurability (e.g., 'ordinal-type' or 'transcardinal' individual welfare functions) will be similarly reflected in the interpersonal framework by full comparability.

The use of comparability assumptions is in terms of *invariance* with respect to the choice of a particular $W$ from $\bar{L}$. The restriction is imposed on a 'social welfare functional' (SWFL) (see Sen, 1970, p. 129).

*SWFL.*   A social welfare functional is a functional relation $F$ that specifies exactly one social ordering $R$ for any $W$ (an $n$-tuple of individual welfare functions): $R = F(W)$.[20]

---

19. The case of full comparability discussed in Sen (1970, Chapter 7) corresponds to this, viz., to one with individual 'cardinal' welfare functions. See also d'Aspremont and Gevers (1977), Maskin (1978), and Roberts (1978).

20. In some cases the need for real-valued representability implicit in a $W_i$ can be dropped, dealing directly with an extended ordering $\bar{R}$ defined over the Cartesian product of $X$ (the set of social states) and $H$ (the set of individuals) (Sen, 1970, Chapters 9 and 9*). Such a function $R = f(R)$—Hammond calls it a generalized social welfare function GSWF—is very close to a SWFL under the comparability restriction of level comparability, or of full comparability with *ordinal* individual welfare (see also Strasnick, 1976; Kelly, 1976; Hammond, 1976; Gevers, 1979; Roberts, 1976a).

*Comparability restriction.*    For any $\bar{L}$, the social ordering $R$ yielded by the SWFL for each $W \in \bar{L}$ must be the same.[21]

This type of framework can be used to examine analytically the links between comparability-cum-measurability assumptions and ethical structures for social welfare judgements (Sen, 1970, 1973a, 1976, 1977a; Fine, 1975; Blackorby, 1975; Hammond, 1976; d'Aspremont and Gevers, 1977; Deschamps and Gevers, 1976, 1978; Maskin, 1976, 1978; Gevers, 1979; Roberts, 1976, 1978).

How are the alternative *interpretations* of interpersonal comparability related to the choice of comparability types? As was discussed in Section 3, on the purely normative interpretation of interpersonal comparisons, the comparability type to emerge will depend on the normative maximand chosen. In particular, utilitarianism will yield partial unit comparability, and Rawlsian maximin, or the lexicographic maximin, will lead to partial level comparability.

As far as the descriptive interpretations are concerned, the picture is more complicated. The approach of 'behaviourism' can be used to compare levels as well as differences, but the usual criteria linking behaviour to welfare are not very exact (on this, see Waldner (1972)). Partial full comparability seems to be the appropriate category, but precisely *how* partial the comparability will be must vary from case to case.

'Introspective choice' would seem to promise comparability of *levels* only. However, by considering lotteries, or generally by invoking (assumed) additive separability properties of these choices, a 'cardinalization' can be achieved, which in this case will lead to full comparability. But the relevance of such cardinalization for social welfare judgements remains problematic since it incorporates the person's attitude to gambling or similar arbitrary characteristics reflected in the separable choices (Arrow, 1963, p. 10; Hammond, 1977). However, in the specific case of Harsanyi's model of 'ethical judgements' with *as if* equiprobability of being anyone in the community (as part of the ethical requirement of 'impersonality'), the attitudes to gambling may be thought to be relevant (Harsanyi, 1955, 1975). But full interpersonal comparability achieved this way is interpretable only in the context of choices over lotteries, and the temptation to interpret these utility differences as reflecting relative 'urgency' of needs (Harsanyi, 1975, p. 319) may have to be resisted.[22]

'Introspective welfare comparison' can be applied to both levels and units. The comparison of levels is probably more easily made, but units can also be compared through ranking differences (Krantz *et al.*, 1971; Fishburn, 1970), or through higher-order rankings (i.e., rankings of alternatives, rankings of

21. The measurability and comparability assumptions *restrict* the class of admissible ethical rules in terms of the 'informational framework' (Sen, 1974a,b).

22. See Sen (1976), and also Harsanyi (1977) and Sen (1977c).

rankings, rankings of rankings of rankings, etc.).[23] Inability to go beyond a few stages in comparing higher-order differences, or higher-order rankings, will typically lead to partial full comparability, possibly with levels fully comparable and units only partially so.

## 5   Dual Comparability

For utilitarianism, concerned as it is with maximizing the sum of individual welfares, comparison of *units* is crucial and that of *levels* irrelevant. On the other hand, criteria of 'equity' (e.g., the Difference Principle (Rawls, 1971), the Weak Equity Axiom (Sen, 1973a)), tend to use comparisons of levels of welfare, and sometimes ignore comparison of units. This contrast between maximizing the sum of welfare and having a more equal distribution of welfare, which has some characteristics of an 'efficiency–equity' contrast, relates closely to the dichotomy between comparability of units and that of levels, and the conflict can surface when *both* units and levels are comparable (Sen, 1973a).[24]

Hammond (1977) has recently explored the possibility of avoiding this conflict by using one set (*n*-tuple) of individual welfare functions { $W_i$ } for comparing levels of welfare and another set { $V_i$ } for comparing welfare units. As a criterion of equity, Hammond uses an axiom E which is a strengthened and generalized version of the Weak Equity Axiom. There are various versions of the Equity Axiom. The following is the most quoted (see Hammond, 1976).

E (EQUITY AXIOM).    *If person i is worse off than person j both in x and in y, and if i is better off himself in x than in y, while j is better off in y than in x, and if furthermore all others are just as well off in x as in y, then x is socially at least as good as y.*[25]

Hammond considers the problem of ranking alternative distributions of a

23. See Sen (1977b). Cardinalization through higher-order rankings was jointly investigated with Ken Binmore, and is currently being further explored by R. Nader-Isfahani at LSE. For some related results, see Basu (1976).

24. Under every assumption of comparability with ordinal or cardinal individual welfares, the utilitarian rule generates a quasi-ordering $R_u$ and the Rawlsian lexicographic maximin rule another quasi-ordering $R_m$, and both subsume the Pareto quasi-ordering $R_p$. Under non-comparability, $R_u = R_m = R_p$. Under unit comparability, $R_u$ is a complete ordering but $R_m = R_p$. Under level comparability, $R_m$ is a complete ordering, while $R_u$ is not, but it coincides with the quasi-ordering $R_s$ proposed by Suppes based on dominance which is also subsumed by $R_m$. See also Sen (1970, Chapter 9*) and Blackorby and Donaldson (1977) for related results.

25. This can also be seen to arise from a preference for reducing inequality of welfare distribution in the relatively uncontroversial sense of 'ordinal intensity', viz., if $a > b > c > d$, then $(a, d)$ has more inequality than $(b, c)$; on this class of criteria, see Sen (1976).

given total income where each person $i$ is better off whenever he has more income $y_i$. He calls a ranking procedure 'equity-regarding' if it satisfies E. If the Equity Axiom is applied to $\{W_i\}$ and the utilitarian rule of ranking is used through $\{V_i\}$, then utilitarianism will be equity-regarding if and only if a higher welfare $W_i$ goes with a lower marginal utility $V_i'$ for all $y_i$ and all $i$.[26]

Problems of interpretation raised by Hammond's analytical results are not easy to handle. In what sense are $\{W_i\}$ and $\{V_i\}$ alternative representations of the same reality? Hammond imposes no restrictions on their relationship except that for each $i$, $V_i$ must be a positive monotonic transformation of $W_i$, because 'each represents consumer $i$'s preferences'. But this leaves the correspondence of the interpersonal comparisons of levels and units in $\{W_i\}$ and $\{V_i\}$ quite unrestricted. I shall call this case that of dual non-comparability (DN).

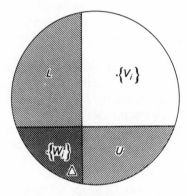

FIGURE 2

In the framework of interpersonal comparability presented in Section 4, based on Sen (1970), the comparability set $\bar{L}$ does typically include more than one $n$-tuple $\{W_i\}$, but all these admissible $n$-tuples are then used for comparing *both* levels and units (asserting only those rankings that hold for *every* $n$-tuple in $\bar{L}$). In Fig. 2, the set $L$ of $n$-tuples permitted by the measurability assumptions is represented by the (circular) area, with the shaded region $U$ representing its unit comparable subset $\bar{L}(1)$ and the shaded region $L$ representing the level comparable subset $\bar{L}(L)$. The intersection $\Delta$ of $U$ and $L$ permits comparability of both units and levels. Consider any $\{W_i\}$ from $\Delta$. Hammond's DN combines with it a $\{V_i\}$ that may come from anywhere in $L$.

26. See Hammond (1977, Theorem 3.2). Hammond also considers the case of 'intermediate' dual comparability with $V_i$ obtained from $W_i$ through multiplication by a positive number $y_i$, and obtains the necessary and sufficient conditions for utilitarianism to be equity-regarding in this more restricted case (Theorem 3.3).

How is such a $\{V_i\}$ chosen? What characteristics make both $\{W_i\}$ and $\{V_i\}$ admissible but no other $n$-tuple? And why use one for comparing levels only and the other for comparing units only?

I would argue that dual non-comparability in this form can be interpreted both within the descriptive framework and within the normative framework, and each interpretation raises some problems. The descriptive approach first. Evidently, both $\{W_i\}$ and $\{V_i\}$ cannot reflect interpersonal comparisons under the *same* descriptive interpretation. Clearly then, under the descriptive approach, $\{W_i\}$ must be obtained from one descriptive interpretation and $\{V_i\}$ from another. To use them in the particular way proposed by Hammond, the descriptive interpretation underlying $\{W_i\}$ must be thought to be the relevant one for the equity criterion and that underlying $\{V_i\}$ the right one for utilitarianism. Such a contrast is certainly possible and need not imply schizophrenia, since the attractions of utilitarianism and equity criteria are not independent of the chosen descriptive interpretations of personal welfare comparisons, and these can differ.

As an example, consider basing utilitarianism on behaviourist interpersonal comparisons and the equity criterion on introspective choice. Let the problem be one of giving a small gift to one of two persons. The question is, To whom? The rules now are the following.

*Behaviourist utilitarianism.*   Give it to the person whose behaviour would indicate a greater gain (e.g., whose face would light up more).

*Introspective choice equity.*   Give it to the person in whose position you would rather not choose to be with or without the gift.

The different descriptive interpretations of interpersonal comparisons are now woven into the respective ethical imperatives.

Note that this approach to the interpretation of dual non-comparability goes beyond the freedom introduced in Hammond's analytical requirements: there is now no need even to presume that $V_i$ is an increasing transformation of $W_i$, since comparison of levels of welfare of a given person $i$ under one interpretation (e.g., behaviourism) may differ from that under another (e.g., introspective choice).

While this type of interpretation makes DN quite legitimate within the descriptive approach to interpersonal comparisons, it is not at all clear that this will help in avoiding a conflict between utilitarianism and equity. For avoiding such a conflict, what is needed is not the independence of $\{V_i\}$ from $\{W_i\}$, but a *very special kind of dependence* (though not a coincidence of the two). If, according to $\{W_i\}$, person $i$ is better off in $x$ than in $y$, $j$ is better off in $y$ than in $x$, and $j$ is better off than $i$ both in $x$ as well as in $y$, then the sum of individual welfares according to $\{V_i\}$ *must* be no less in $x$ than in $y$. There is, of course, no reason whatsoever why such a thing must happen under two different descriptive interpretations. Thus while DN may be legitimately interpretable under the descriptive approach, it need not help much in resolving the conflict between utilitarianism and equity.

Consider now the normative approach. As discussed earlier, the normative values depend on the maximand chosen. A given set of ethical judgements can be used for normative comparison of individual welfare *units* with respect to utilitarianism and also for normative comparison of individual welfare *levels* with respect of some level-oriented rule (e.g., lexicographic maximin, the Weak Equity Axiom, or Axiom E). If $\{V_i\}$ is chosen consistently with the former and $\{W_i\}$ consistently with the latter, then the two $n$-tuples can be used respectively for unit-comparing operations and level-comparing operations, reflecting alternative readings of the same set of judgements. This would certainly reduce the possibility of a conflict between utilitarian rankings based on $\{W_i\}$ and equity-regarding rankings based on $\{V_i\}$. Indeed, the judgement of giving the *small* gift to person $i$ rather than $j$ in the two-person world would be interpreted under utilitarianism as $V_i' > V_j'$, and under Rawlsianism (or the Equity Axiom) as $W_i < W_j$. This would certainly help in making utilitarianism (based on $\{V_i\}$) consistent with the pursuit of equity (based on $\{W_i\}$).

It should be mentioned, however, that this happy outcome is largely tautologous. The *same* judgement is being interpreted here in Benthamite and Rawlsian terms, respectively, and the coincidence reflects not a congruence of Bentham and Rawls but of the same judgement expressed in two different languages.[27] However, the approach in general is not entirely tautologous. First, a set of normative judgements may not fully specify two $n$-tuples $\{W_i\}$ and $\{V_i\}$, but only impose some constraints on the choices of $\{W_i\}$ and $\{V_i\}$ respectively (see Section 3), and in using specific $n$-tuples $\{W_i\}$ and $\{V_i\}$ satisfying these constraints to derive other judgements, problems of consistency can certainly still arise.[28] Second, even if $\{W_i\}$ and $\{V_i\}$ were fully specified on the basis of judgements dealing with two-person choice situations, the use of these $n$-tuples in $n$-person choice situations raises problems of correspondence and consistency.

In making utilitarianism consistent with the usual criteria of equity, dual non-comparability under the normative approach is, therefore, a help but not a guarantee. The help is, however, more nominal than real. In contrast, DN under the descriptive approach is a real possibility and involves no circularity, but it does not seem to be of a great deal of help in resolving the conflict

---

27. The possibility of taking one descriptive interpretation and one normative interpretation also opens up the possibility of tautologous reconciliation, e.g., judgements based on level comparisons derived from a descriptive interpretation being *translated* into unit comparison under a normative interpretation.

28. Note also that level comparisons can be derived with respect to several alternative maximands, e.g., lexicographic maximin and lexicographic maximax, and equity regard may or may not be reflected in these valuations. Similarly, unit comparison can arise from non-utilitarian maximands as well.

in question. Hammond's proposal of dual non-comparability would, therefore, appear to be of greater intrinsic worth—it draws attention to a real possibility—than of applied value in avoiding 'efficiency—equity' conflicts of welfare distribution, for which it was, in fact, devised.

## 6  Concluding Remarks

The central problem in the theory of interpersonal comparisons of welfare seems to be an embarrassment of riches—there are many reasonable ways of making such comparisons and they need not coincide. Starting from the dichotomy of normative and descriptive approaches to interpersonal comparisons, several distinct interpretations have been presented, examined, and contrasted (Sections 2 and 3).

In addition to this problem of interpretation and procedure, there is also the question of the *type* of comparability to be used, e.g., whether of units only, of levels only, of both, of none, or partially of one or the other or both. Section 4 has been concerned with contrasting different types of comparability within a formal structure.

Finally, the possibility of basing level comparisons on one set of welfare functions and unit comparisons on another set ('dual non-comparability') proposed by Hammond (1977) has been examined in Section 5, both in terms of intrinsic merit as well as likely usefulness in serving the purpose for which the possibility was proposed. The former seems more satisfying than the latter.

## References

Arrow, K. J. (1963): *Social Choice and Individual Values*, 3rd ed. (New York: Wiley).

Banerji, D. (1964): Choice and Order: Or First Things First. *Economica,* 31.

Basu, K. (1976): Revealed Preference of Government: Concepts, Analysis and Evaluation, Ph.D. dissertation, London School of Economics. [Later published, (London and New York: Cambridge University Press, 1979).]

Baumol, W. J. (1973): Review of A. K. Sen's *On Economic Inequality. Economica,* 42.

Butts, R. E. and Hintikka, J. (eds) (1977): *Foundational Problems in the Special Sciences* (Dordrecht and Boston: Reidel).

Blackorby, C. (1975): Degrees of Cardinality and Aggregate Partial Ordering. *Econometrica,* 43.

Blackorby, C. and Donaldson, D. (1977): Utility vs. Equity: Some Plausible Quasi-orderings. *Journal of Public Economics.* 7.

d'Aspremont, C. and Gevers, L. (1977): Equity and the Informational Basis of Collective Choice. *Review of Economic Studies,* 46.

Deschamps, R. and Gevers, L. (1976): Separability, Risk-Bearing and Social Welfare Judgements (mimeographed), Namur. [Revised version published in J.-J. Laffont (ed.), *Aggregation and Revelation of Preferences* (Amsterdam: North-Holland, 1979).]

Deschamps, R. and Gevers, L. (1978): Leximin and Utilitarian Rules: A Joint Characterization. *Journal of Economic Theory,* **17.**

Fine, B. (1975): A Note on 'Interpersonal Comparisons and Partial Comparability'. *Econometrica,* **43.**

Fishburn, P. C. (1970): *Utility Theory for Decision Making* (New York: Wiley).

Gevers, L. (1979): On Interpersonal Comparability and Social Welfare Orderings. *Econometrica,* **47.**

Hammond, P. J. (1976): Equity, Arrow's Conditions and Rawls' Difference Principle. *Econometrica,* **44.**

____ (1977): Dual Interpersonal Comparisons of Utility and the Welfare Economics of Income Distribution. *Journal of Public Economics,* **6.**

Hare, R. M. (1952): *The Language of Morals* (London and New York: Oxford University (Clarendon) Press).

Harsanyi, J. C. (1955): Cardinal Welfare, Individualistic Ethics, and Interpersonal Comparisons of Utility. *Journal of Political Economy,* **63.**

____ (1975): Nonlinear Social Welfare Functions. *Theory and Decision,* **6.**

____ (1977): Nonlinear Social Welfare Functions: A Rejoinder to Prof. Sen, in Butts and Hintikka (1977).

Hicks, J. R. (1958): The Measurement of Income. *Oxford Economic Papers,* **10.**

____ (1974): Preference and Welfare. In *Economic Theory and Planning: Essays in Honour of A. K. Dasgupta* (A. Mitra, ed.) (London and New Delhi: Oxford University Press).

Jeffrey, R. C. (1971): On Interpersonal Utility Theory. *Journal of Philosophy,* **68.**

Kant, I. (1785): *Fundamental Principles of Metaphysics of Ethics* (transl. by T. K. Abbott) (London: Longman, 1907).

Kelly, J. (1976): The Impossibility of a Just Liberal. *Economica,* **43.**

Krantz, D. H., Luce, R. D., Suppes, P. and Tversky, A. (1971): *Foundations of Measurement,* Vol. I (New York: Academic Press).

Little, I. M. D. (1957): *A Critique of Welfare Economics,* 2nd ed. (London and New York: Oxford University (Clarendon) Press).

Majumdar, T. (1962): *The Measurement of Utility,* 2nd ed. (London: Macmillan).

Maskin, E. (1976): Decision-making under Ignorance with Implications for Social Choice (mimeographed), Jesus College, Cambridge (1976). [Revised version published in *Theory and Decisions,* **11.**]

____ (1978): A Theorem on Utilitarianism, *Review of Economic Studies,* **45.**

Muellbauer, J. (1975): Can We Base Comparisons of Welfare between Households on Behaviour? (mimeographed), Birkbeck College, London University.

Pattanaik, P. K. (1971): *Voting and Collective Choice* (New York and London: Cambridge University Press).

Ramsey, F. P. (1931): *Foundations of Mathematics and Other Logical Essays* London–New York: Kegan Paul-Harcourt).

Rawls, J. (1958): Justice as Fairness. *Philosophical Review,* **67.**

____ (1971): *A Theory of Justice* (Cambridge, Massachusetts–London and New York: Harvard University Press–Oxford University (Clarendon) Press).

Roberts, K. W. S. (1976): Possibility Theorems with Interpersonally Comparable

Welfare Levels, mimeographed. [Revised version later published in *Review of Economic Studies,* **47** (1980).]

_____ (1978): Interpersonal Comparability and Social Choice Theory, mimeographed (1978). [Revised version later published in *Review of Economic Studies,* **47** (1980).]

Robbins, L. (1935): *An Essay on the Nature and Significance of Economic Science,* 2nd ed. (London: Macmillan).

_____ (1938): Interpersonal Comparisons of Utility, *Economic Journal,* **48**.

Ryle, G. (1949): *The Concept of Mind* (Harmondsworth: Penguin, 1963).

Scitovsky, T. (1951): The State of Welfare Economics. *American Economic Review,* **41**.

_____ (1976): *The Joyless Economy* (London and New York: Oxford University Press).

Sen, A. K. (1970): *Collective Choice and Social Welfare* (San Francisco–Edinburgh: Holden-Day–Oliver & Boyd; distribution taken over by North-Holland).

_____ (1973a): *On Economic Inequality* (London–New York: Oxford University (Clarendon) Press–Norton).

_____ (1973b): Behaviour and the Concept of Preference, *Economica,* **40**. [Essay 2 in this volume.]

_____ (1974a): Informational Bases of Welfare Approaches, *Journal of Public Economics,* **3**.

_____ (1974b): Rawls versus Bentham: An Axiomatic Examination of the Pure Distribution Problem, *Theory and Decision,* **4**. (Reprinted in N. Daniels (ed.), *Reading Rawls* (Oxford: Blackwell, 1975)).

_____ (1976): Welfare Inequalities and Rawlsian Axiomatics, *Theory and Decision,* **7**. (Reprinted in R. E. Butts and J. Hintikka, 1977.)

_____ (1977a): On Weights and Measures: Informational Constraints in Social Welfare Analysis, *Econometrica,* **45**. [Essay 11 in this volume.]

_____ (1977b): Rational Fools: A Critique of the Behavioural Foundations of Economic Theory, *Philosophy and Public Affairs,* **6**; also in H. Harris (ed.), *Scientific Models and Man* (London and New York: Oxford University Press, 1979). [Essay 4 in this volume.]

_____ (1977c): Nonlinear Social Welfare Functions: A Reply to Prof. Harsanyi, in Butts and Hintikka (1977).

Sidgwick, H. (1874): *The Method of Ethics* (London: Macmillan, 1907).

Strasnick, S. (1976): Social Choice Theory and the Derivation of Rawls' Difference Principle, *Journal of Philosophy,* **73**.

Suppes, P. (1966): Some Formal Models of Grading Principles, *Synthese,* **6**. (Reprinted in P. Suppes, *Studies in the Methodology and Foundations of Science* (Dordrecht: Reidel, 1969).

Waldner, I. (1972): The Empirical Meaningfulness of Interpersonal Utility Comparisons, *Journal of Philosophy,* **69**.

_____ (1974): Bare Preferences and Interpersonal Utility Comparisons, *Theory and Decision,* **5**.

Wong, S. (1978): *The Foundations of Paul Samuelson's Revealed Preference Theory: A Study by the Method of Rational Reconstruction* (London: Routledge).

# Part IV

# Non-utility Information

# 13

# The Impossibility of a Paretian Liberal

## 1  *Introduction*

The purpose of this paper is to present an impossibility result that seems to have some disturbing consequences for principles of social choice. A common objection to the method of majority decision is that it is illiberal. The argument takes the following form: Given other things in the society, if you prefer to have pink walls rather than white, then society should permit you to have this, even if a majority of the community would like to see your walls white. Similarly, whether you should sleep on your back or on your belly is a matter in which the society should permit you absolute freedom, even if a majority of the community is nosy enough to feel that you must sleep on your back. We formalize this concept of individual liberty in an extremely weak form and examine its consequences.

## 2  *The Theorem*

Let $R_i$ be the ordering of the $i$th individual over the set $X$ of all possible social states, each social state being a complete description of society including every individual's position in it. There are $n$ individuals. Let $R$ be the social preference relation that is to be determined.

*Definition 1.  A collective choice rule* is a functional relationship that specifies one and only one social preference relation $R$ for any set of $n$ individual orderings (one ordering for each individual).

A special case of a collective choice rule is one that Arrow (1951) calls a social welfare function, namely, a rule such that $R$ must be an ordering.

*Definition 2.  A social welfare function* is a collective choice rule, the range of which is restricted to orderings.

For comments and criticisms I am grateful to Kenneth Arrow, Peter Diamond, Milton Friedman, Tapas Majumdar, Stephen Marglin, and Thomas Schelling.

From *Journal of Political Economy*, **78** (January/February 1970), 152–7.

A weaker requirement is that each $R$ should generate a 'choice function', that is, in every subset of alternatives there must be a 'best' alternative, or, in other words, there must be some (but not necessarily only one) alternative that is at least as good as all the other alternatives in that subset. This may be called a 'social decision function'.

*Definition 3. A social decision function* is a collective choice rule, the range of which is restricted to social preference relations that generate a choice function.

It was shown in Sen (1969) that the conditions that were proven to be inconsistent by Arrow (1951, 1963) in his justly famous 'impossibility theorem' in the context of a social welfare function are in fact perfectly consistent if imposed on a social decision function. The impossibility theorem to be presented here holds, however, for social decision functions as well.

Arrow's condition of collective rationality (Condition 1') can be seen to be merely a requirement that the domain of the collective choice rule should not be arbitrarily restricted.

*Condition U* (Unrestricted Domain).    Every logically possible set of individual orderings is included in the domain of the collective choice rule.

Arrow used a weak version of the Pareto principle.

*Condition P.*    If every individual prefers any alternative $x$ to another alternative $y$, then society must prefer $x$ to $y$.

Finally, we introduce the condition of individual liberty in a very weak form.

*Condition L* (Liberalism).    For each individual $i$, there is at least one pair of alternatives, say $(x, y)$, such that if this individual prefers $x$ to $y$, then society should prefer $x$ to $y$, and if this individual prefers $y$ to $x$, then society should prefer $y$ to $x$.[1]

The intention is to permit each individual the freedom to determine at least one social choice, for example, having his own walls pink rather than white, other things remaining the same for him and the rest of the society.[2]

---

1. The term 'liberalism' is elusive and is open to alternative interpretations. Some uses of the term may not embrace the condition defined here, while many uses will. I do not wish to engage in a debate on the right use of the term. What is relevant is that Condition $L$ represents a value involving individual liberty that many people would subscribe to. Whether such people are best described as liberals is a question that is not crucial to the point of this paper.

2. Even this informal statement, which sounds mild, is much more demanding than Condition $L$. If the individual's preference over a personal choice (like choosing the colour of his wall) is to be accepted by the society, other things remaining the same, then this gives the individual rights not only over one pair, which is all that is required by Condition $L$, but over many pairs (possibly an infinite number of pairs) varying with the 'other things'. If it is socially all right for me to

The following impossibility theorem holds.

THEOREM I.    *There is no social decision function that can simultaneously satisfy Conditions U, P, and L.*

In fact, we can weaken the condition of liberalism further. Such freedom may not be given to all, but to a proper subset of individuals. However, to make sense the subset must have more than one member, since if it includes only one then we might have a dictatorship. Hence, we demand such freedom for at least two individuals.

*Condition L\** (Minimal Liberalism).    There are at least two individuals such that for each of them there is at least one pair of alternatives over which he is decisive, that is, there is a pair of $x$, $y$, such that if he prefers $x$ (respectively $y$) to $y$ (respectively $x$), then society should prefer $x$ (respectively $y$) to $y$ (respectively $x$).

The following theorem is stronger than Theorem I and subsumes it.

THEOREM II.    *There is no social decision function that can simultaneously satisfy Conditions U, P, and L\*.*

*Proof.*    Let the two individuals referred to in Condition $L^*$ be 1 and 2, respectively, and the two pairs of alternatives referred to be $(x, y)$ and $(z, w)$, respectively. If $(x, y)$ and $(z, w)$ are the same pair of alternatives, then there is a contradiction. They have, therefore, at most one alternative in common, say $x = z$. Assume now that person 1 prefers $x$ to $y$, and person 2 prefers $w$ to $z\,(=x)$. And let everyone in the community including 1 and 2 prefer $y$ to $w$. There is in this no inconsistency for anyone, not even for 1 and 2, and their respective orderings are: 1 prefers $x$ to $y$ and $y$ to $w$, while 2 prefers $y$ to $w$ and $w$ to $x$. By Condition $U$ this should be in the domain of the social decision mechanism. But by Condition $L^*$, $x$ must be preferred to $y$, and $w$ must be preferred to $x\,(=z)$, while by the Pareto principle, $y$ must be preferred to $w$. Thus, there is no best element in the set $(x = z, y, w)$ in terms of social preference, and every alternative is worse than some other. A choice function for the society does not therefore exist.

Next, let $x$, $y$, $z$, and $w$, be all distinct. Let 1 prefer $x$ to $y$, and 2 prefer $z$ to $w$. And let everyone in the community including 1 and 2 prefer $w$ to $x$ and $y$ to $z$. There is no contradiction for 1 or 2, for 1 simply prefers $w$ to $x$, $x$ to $y$, and $y$ to $z$, while 2 prefers $y$ to $z$, $z$ to $w$, and $w$ to $x$. By Condition $U$ this configuration of individual preferences must yield a social choice function. But by Condition $L^*$ society should prefer $x$ to $y$ and $z$ to $w$, while by the

---

have my walls either pink or white as I like in a social state where you smoke cigars, it should be socially all right for me to do the same where you indulge yourself in ways other than smoking cigars. Even this is not required by Condition $L$, which seems to demand very little.

Pareto principle society must prefer $w$ to $x$, and $y$ to $z$. This means that there is no best alternative for this set, and a choice function does not exist for any set that includes these four alternatives. Thus, there is no social decision function satisfying Conditions $U$, $P$, and $L^*$, and the proof is complete.[3]

## 3   An Example

We give now a simple example of the type of impossibility that is involved in Theorem II by taking a special case of two individuals and three alternatives. There is one copy of a certain book, say *Lady Chatterley's Lover*, which is viewed differently by 1 and 2. The three alternatives are: that individual 1 reads it ($x$), that individual 2 reads it ($y$), and that no one reads it ($z$). Person 1, who is a prude, prefers most that no one reads it, but given the choice between either of the two reading it, he would prefer that he read it himself rather than exposing gullible Mr 2 to the influences of Lawrence. (Prudes, I am told, tend to prefer to be censors rather than being censored.) In decreasing order of preference, his ranking is $z$, $x$, $y$. Person 2, however, prefers that either of them should read it rather than neither. Furthermore, he takes delight in the thought that prudish Mr 1 may have to read Lawrence, and his first preference is that person 1 should read it, next best that he himself should read it, and worst that neither should. His ranking is, therefore, $x$, $y$, $z$.

Now if the choice is precisely between the pair ($x$, $z$), i.e., between person 1 reading the book and no one reading it, someone with liberal values may argue that it is person 1's preference that should count; since the prude would not like to read it, he should not be forced to. Thus, the society should prefer $z$ to $x$. Similarly, in the choice exactly between person 2 reading the book ($y$) and no one reading it ($z$), liberal values require that person 2's preference should be decisive, and since he is clearly anxious to read the book he should be permitted to do this. Hence $y$ should be judged socially better than $z$. Thus, in terms of liberal values it is better that no one reads it rather than person 1 being forced to read it, and it is still better that person 2 is permitted to read the book rather than no one reading it. That is, the society should prefer $y$ to $z$, and $z$ to $x$. This discourse could end happily with the book being handed over to person 2 but for the fact that it is a Pareto inferior alternative, being worse than person 1 reading it, in the view of both persons, i.e., $x$ is Pareto superior to $y$.

Every solution that we can think of is bettered by some other solution, given the Pareto principle and the principle of liberalism, and we seem to

---

3. We can strengthen this theorem further by weakening Condition $L^*$ by demanding only that 1 be decisive for $x$ against $y$, but not vice versa, and 2 be decisive for $z$ against $w$, but not vice versa, and require that $x \neq z$, and $y \neq w$. This condition, too, can be shown to be inconsistent with Condition $U$ and $P$, but the logical gain involved in this extension does not, alas, seem to be associated with any significant increase of relevance that I can think of.

have an inconsistency of choice. This is an example of the type of problem that is involved in Theorems I and II.


## 4  *Relevance*

The dilemma posed here may appear to be somewhat disturbing. It is, of course, not necessarily disturbing for every conceivable society, since the conflict arises with only particular configurations of individual preferences. The ultimate guarantee for individual liberty may rest not on rules for social choice but on developing individual values that respect each other's personal choices. The conflict posed here is concerned with societies where such a condition does not hold and where pairwise choice based on liberal values may conflict with those based on the Pareto principle. Like Arrow's 'General Possibility Theorem', here also the Condition of Unrestricted Domain is used.

However, unlike in the theorem of Arrow, we have not required transitivity of social preference. We have required neither transitivity of strict preference, nor transitivity of indifference, but merely the existence of a best alternative in each choice situation.[4] Suppose society prefers $x$ to $y$, and $y$ to $z$, and is indifferent between $z$ and $x$. Arrow would rule this out, since there is an intransitivity; but we do not, for here alternative $x$ is 'best' in the sense of being at least as good as both the other alternatives. Our requirements are, in this respect, very mild, and we still have an impossibility.

Second, we have not imposed Arrow's much debated condition of 'the independence of irrelevant alternatives'.[5] Many people find the relaxation of

---

4. It may appear that one way of solving the dilemma is to dispense with the social choice function based on a binary relation, that is, to relax not merely transitivity but also *acyclicity*. A choice function that need not correspond to any binary relation has undoubtedly a wider scope. But then Condition $P$ and Condition $L$ would have to be redefined, for example, (1) $x$ should not be chosen when $y$ is available, if everyone prefers $y$ to $x$, and (2) for each individual there is a pair $(x_i, y_i)$ such that if he prefers $x_i$ (respectively $y_i$) to $y_i$ (respectively $x_i$), then $y_i$ (respectively $x_i$) should not be chosen if $x_i$ (respectively $y_i$) is available. Thus redefined, the choice set for the set of alternatives may be rendered empty even without bringing in acyclicity, and the contradiction will reappear. This and other possible 'ways out' are discussed more fully in my forthcoming book (Sen, 1970, chap. 6).

5. Using the condition of the independence of irrelevant alternatives, A. Gibbard, in an unpublished paper, has recently proved the following important theorem: Any social decision function that must generate social preferences that are all transitive in the strict relation (quasi-transitive) and which must satisfy Conditions $U$, $P$, non-dictatorship, and the independence of irrelevant alternatives, must be an oligarchy in the sense that there is a unique group of individuals each of whom, by preferring $x$ to $y$, can make the society regard $x$ to be at least as good as $y$, and by all preferring $x$ to $y$ can make the society prefer $x$ to $y$, irrespective of the preferences of those who are not in this group. Gibbard's Theorem is disturbing, for the conditions look appealing but the resultant oligarchy seems revolting, and it is a major extension of the problem posed by Arrow (1951, 1963). Gibbard argues against the simultaneous insistence on a binary relation of social preference generating a choice function and on the condition of the independence of irrelevant alternatives. We have not imposed the latter.

this condition to be an appealing way of escaping the Arrow dilemma. This way out is not open here, for the theorem holds without imposing this condition.

The Pareto principle is used here in a very weak version, as in Arrow. We do not necessarily require that if someone prefers $x$ to $y$ and everyone regards $x$ to be at least as good as $y$, then $x$ is socially better. We permit the possibility of having collective choice rules that will violate this provided everyone strictly preferring $x$ to $y$ must make $x$ socially better than $y$.

Nevertheless it turns out that a principle reflecting liberal values even in a very mild form cannot possibly be combined with the weak Pareto principle, given an unrestricted domain. If we do believe in these other conditions, then the society cannot permit even minimal liberalism. Society cannot then let more than one individual be free to read what they like, sleep the way they prefer, dress as they care to, etc., *irrespective* of the preferences of others in the community.

What is the moral? It is that in a very basic sense liberal values conflict with the Pareto principle. If someone takes the Pareto principle seriously, as economists seem to do, then he has to face problems of consistency in cherishing liberal values, even very mild ones.[6] Or, to look at it in another way, if someone does have certain liberal values, then he may have to eschew his adherence to Pareto optimality. While the Pareto criterion has been thought to be an expression of individual liberty, it appears that in choices involving more than two alternatives it can have consequences that are, in fact, deeply illiberal.†

## References

Arrow, K. J. (1951): *Individual Values and Social Choice* (New York: Wiley; 2d ed., 1963).

Sen, A. K. (1969): 'Quasi-transitivity, Rational Choice and Collective Decisions', Discussion paper no. 45, Harvard Institute of Economic Research. *Rev. Economic Studies,* 36, no. 3 (July 1969): 381–93. [Essay 6 in this volume.]

_____ (1970): *Collective Choice and Social Welfare* (San Francisco: Holden-Day; and Edinburgh: Oliver & Boyd. [Reprinted, Amsterdam: North-Holland, 1980.])

6. The difficulties of *achieving* Pareto optimality in the presence of externalities are well known. What is at issue here is the *acceptability* of Pareto optimality as an objective in the context of liberal values, given certain types of externalities.

†[The proper characterization of liberty and rights is a matter of some moral philosophical dispute. The characterizations used in Essays 13 and 14 (and in the social-choice-theoretic contributions that followed) have been variously disputed by Nozick, Bernholz, Buchanan, Gärdenfors, Barry, Sugden and others. These philosophical issues, among others, are discussed in three of my recent papers dealing with rights in general and liberty in particular: 'Rights and Agency', *Philosophy and Public Affairs,* 11 (1982); 'Liberty as Control: An Appraisal', *Midwest Studies in Philosophy,* 8 (1982); 'Liberty and Social Choice', *Journal of Philosophy,* forthcoming, January 1983.]

# 14

# Liberty, Unanimity and Rights

Two of the more widely used principles in evaluating social states are:

(a) The Pareto principle: if everyone in the society prefers a certain social state to another, then the choice of the former must be taken to be better for the society as a whole.

(b) Acceptance of personal liberty: there are certain personal matters in which each person should be free to decide what should happen, and in choices over these things whatever he or she thinks is better must be taken to be better for the society as a whole, no matter what others think.

It was argued in Sen (1970a, b) that these two principles conflict with each other in a significant sense—a sense that was precisely described (see (T.1) and (T.7) in the Appendix). The Pareto principle implies that if more than one person is given the guarantee of having his preference reflected in social preference even over one pair each (no matter how 'personal' to him the choice over that pair is), then contradictory cycles may result (e.g., $x$ socially preferred to $y$, $y$ to $z$ and $z$ to $x$) for some set of individual preferences.

This thesis of the 'impossibility of the Paretian liberal' has received searching examinations in a number of recent contributions, e.g., Batra and Pattanaik (1972), Bernholz (1974, 1975), Blau (1975), Blau and Deb (1976), Campbell (1975), Deb (1974), Farrell (1976), Fine (1975), Gibbard (1974), Hammond (1974), Hillinger and Lapham (1971), Karni (1974a, b), Kelly (1976a, b), Ng (1971), Nozick (1973, 1974), Peacock and Rowley (1972), Ramachandra (1972), Rowley and Peacock (1975), Seidl (1975) and Suzumura (1976). While some authors have disputed the existence of the conflict, others have investi-

For comments and criticisms on an earlier draft of this paper and for fruitful general discussions on this subject over a long period, I am most grateful to Kenneth Arrow, Peter Bauer, Julian Blau, Donald Campbell, John Broome, Ralf Dahrendorf, Rajat Deb, Ben Fine, Allan Gibbard, Frank Hahn, Peter Hammond, Jerry Kelly, Steve Marglin, Jim Mirrlees, Robert Nozick, Prasanta Pattanaik, Morris Perlman, John Rawls, Ray Richardson and Kotaro Suzumura, and to the anonymous referees of [*Economica*].

From *Economica*, **43** (August 1976), 217–45.

gated ways of escaping the difficulty, while still others have been concerned with extending this impossibility result to a wider class of social choice problems. Part of the object of this note is to reappraise the question in the light of these contributions, but partly it is also aimed at presenting some additional results which may help to clarify the nature of the conflict and its implications for social choice theory.

The formal statements of conditions and theorems and the proofs have been banished to the Appendix, permitting the text of the paper to be almost completely informal. The underlying issues are, I believe, general enough to be of interest to a wide class of readership in addition to social choice enthusiasts. Also, the discussion is self-contained and a familiarity with the earlier literature on the subject has not been presupposed.

## 1  *Recall*

Some choices between alternative social states may involve differences that are personal to someone; e.g., *with everything else the same* Jack sleeps on his back ($x$) or on his belly ($y$). Choices of this type—though formally between alternative social states—may be taken to be the 'concern' only of the relevant person. Even if persons other than Jack entertain preferences as to how Jack should sleep, it seems reasonable to argue that the choice between $x$ and $y$ should be settled by Jack's preference only. Choices of this kind lie in what is sometimes referred to as a person's 'protected sphere' (see Hayek, 1960). Such spheres may be taken to be very wide or rather narrow depending on, among other things, our political philosophy, but the existence of some personal protected sphere seems to be widely acknowledged; see, for example, Mill (1859), Hayek (1960) and Gramsci (1971), whose conceptions of liberty differ sharply in other respects.

The existence of such 'protected spheres' for all persons was demanded in a weak condition (Condition $L$), which we may call 'weak libertarianism'—an expression that I prefer to my earlier use (Sen, 1970a) of the more ambiguous term 'liberalism'. Condition $L$ demands that for each person there is *at least* one pair of social states, say, $x$ and $y$, such that his preference over that pair must be decisive for social judgement; i.e., if he prefers $x$ to $y$, then $x$ must be acknowledged to be socially better than $y$ and correspondingly if he prefers $y$ to $x$. The acceptability of Condition $L$ will 'depend on the nature of the alternatives that are offered for choice', and 'if the choices are all non-personal, e.g., to outlaw untouchability or not, to declare war against another country or not', this condition 'should not have much appeal' (Sen, 1970a, p. 83). But in choices involving personal variations of the kind discussed earlier, $L$ would seem to be appealing. Indeed, the terms 'liberalism' and 'libertarianism' may make the condition look too narrow, since 'support for $L$' may also 'come from people who are not "liberals" in the usual sense' (p. 83). Indeed, such mild endorsement of libertarian values is a common feature of most modern cultures, and of many ancient ones.

The 'impossibility of the Paretian liberal' asserts that this Condition $L$ conflicts with the Pareto principle if contradictory cycles of social preference must not arise for any set of individual preferences. Formally, the theorem establishes a conflict between three conditions for social choice, viz., Condition $L$, Condition $P$ (the Pareto principle) and Condition $U$ ('unrestricted domain', which essentially requires that for no set of individual preferences should the social strict preference involve a cycle). For a rigorous statement of the result and proof of it, the reader should turn to the Appendix (see T.1), but the nature of the conflict can be brought out by an example used earlier (in Sen, 1970a). There is a book (e.g., *Lady Chatterley's Lover*) which may be read by Mr A ('the prude') or Mr B ('the lascivious') or by neither. Given other things, these three alternatives define three social states, $a$, $b$ and $o$ respectively. Consider now the following possibility. The prude A most prefers $o$ (no one reading it), then $a$ ('I'll take the hurt on myself'), and lastly $b$ ('imagine that lascivious lapping it up'). The lascivious prefers most $a$ ('it will give that lilywhite baby a nice shock'), then $b$ ('it will be fun'), and last $o$ ('what a waste of a good book'). On grounds of individual freedom, since B wants to read the book rather than no one reading it, $b$ is socially better than $o$; note that *in either case* A does not read the book here. Similarly, since A does not want to read it, $o$ is socially better than $a$. But $a$ is Pareto superior to $b$, yielding a preference cycle.

In establishing the 'impossibility of the Paretian liberal', Condition $L$ can be further weakened, demanding only that at least two persons (not necessarily everyone) should have a protected sphere, i.e., an assigned pair each, over which the person's preference will be reflected in social judgement. This condition was called Condition $L^*$ in Sen (1970a), in which it was given the name 'minimal liberalism', but is possibly better called 'minimal libertarianism'.

In the context of those social choice problems in which there are personal issues, for which Condition $L$ (or $L^*$) makes sense, this impossibility result points towards a serious questioning of the Pareto principle. This was one of the main lessons drawn from (T.1) in Sen (1970a), suggesting that the 'sense of ethical invulnerability' of the Pareto principle in traditional welfare economics 'does not seem to survive a close scrutiny' (p. 200). This may appear puzzling since 'unanimity' is a powerful enough reason for a policy to be pursued, but the argument was that it is important 'not merely ... to know who prefers what, but also *why* he has this preference' (p. 83). People may agree on a particular ranking for quite different reasons (as in preferring $a$ to $b$ in the 'Lady Chatterley' illustration), and a mechanical use of the Pareto rule irrespective of context seems questionable. One of the issues that will be examined in this note in the light of subsequent contributions is whether this questioning of the Pareto principle stands, since many of these contributions (e.g., Blau, 1975; Gibbard, 1974; Hillinger and Lapham, 1971;

Karni, 1974a; Kelly, 1976b) have revealed a preference for resolving the conflict by weakening Condition $L$ rather than by weakening the Pareto principle.

A more general issue in social choice theory is also related to this question. In traditional theory, social choice has been taken to be a function of individual preferences (e.g., formalized as an Arrow-type 'social welfare function'). But the argument questioning the Pareto principle can be also used to establish the need to consider other information (e.g., the *motivation* behind those preferences). In this approach, judgements on social choices 'would then no longer be a function of individual preferences only' (Sen, 1970a, p. 83). This line of argument is quite distinct from the important radical critique of basing social judgements on individual preferences because of the individual's 'alienation from himself' (see particularly Gintis, 1972) and also from the argument for subjecting individual preferences to 'rational assessment' (Broome, 1974), but it shares with these approaches a rejection of the refusal to look beyond the set of individual preferences in making a critical assessment of social choices.

Finally, one other aspect of (T.1) relates to the possible argument that 'the eventual guarantee for individual freedom cannot be found in mechanisms of collective choice, but in developing values and preferences that respect each other's privacy and personal choices' (Sen, 1970a, p. 85). Formally, this points the finger at Condition $U$ (unrestricted domain) on the weakening of which one may base the possibility of realizing libertarian rights without running afoul of the Pareto principle, but more substantially it points to difficulties of taking individual preferences as *given* in pursuing demanding social objectives.

The theorem of 'the impossibility of the Paretian liberal' was presented with the intention of raising these questions, and in this note the recent contributions will be examined and some new results presented with a focus on these issues.


## 2   The Paretian Epidemic

The Pareto principle is sometimes referred to as the 'unanimity rule', requiring that preferences unanimously held must be fully reflected in social judgement. This description is somewhat misleading, since the unanimity in question is not of the whole preference but only over a pair. A less demanding formulation which may be called 'unanimity rule' is the following: if everyone has the same preference over the entire set of social states, then social judgement should reflect this preference fully. This unanimity rule—let us call it UR— will yield the Pareto principle if something is required additionally; viz., social preference over any pair must depend only on individual preferences over that pair. This last condition is called, following Arrow (1951), 'the independence of irrelevant alternatives' (Condition $I$). The Pareto principle has this 'independence' property, and this takes us beyond the unanimity rule UR.

This 'independence' property of the Pareto principle can be used to obtain a rather peculiar result, which will be called the 'Paretian epidemic'. Define a person as being 'decisive' over a pair $x$ and $y$ if and only if, whenever he prefers $x$ to $y$, $x$ is judged to be socially better than $y$. He is 'decisive both ways' if in addition it is the case that, whenever he prefers $y$ to $x$, $y$ is judged to be socially better than $x$. Note that the condition of 'weak libertarianism', $L$, makes each person decisive both ways over one pair of alternatives each, and that of 'minimal libertarianism', $L^*$, makes at least two persons thus decisive.

A weaker form of decisiveness is 'semidecisiveness'. This requires that, if this person prefers $x$ to $y$, then $x$ is judged to be socially *at least as good as* $y$. A still weaker requirement is 'potential semidecisiveness', which requires that, given certain configurations of individual preferences over *other* pairs, if this person prefers $x$ to $y$, then $x$ is judged socially at least as good as $y$, no matter how the others rank $x$ *vis-à-vis* $y$. Now, it can be proved—see (T.2) in the Appendix—that, if social preference cycles are to be avoided no matter what the individual preferences are, then the Pareto principle, even in its weakest form, implies that a person who is decisive both ways over *any* pair of social states whatsoever must be potentially semidecisive both ways for *all* pairs of social states. The Pareto principle converts any limited outbreak of decisiveness into a veritable 'epidemic' of decisiveness, even though in the weaker form of potential semidecisiveness. In the presence of the Pareto principle, no one, it seems, can be given an inch without being given an ell.

The impossibility of the Paretian liberal is an immediate corollary of this more general result of the 'Paretian epidemic'. If one person is made decisive over one pair, representing a tiny protected sphere of personal choice, then by virtue of the 'Paretian epidemic' he is potentially semidecisive over *every* pair of social states. So no one else can be decisive over any pair whatsoever, thereby ruling out the possibility of guaranteeing the libertarian rights of anyone else.

This epidemic property takes stronger shapes if additional conditions such as Arrow's 'independence of irrelevant alternatives' and transitivity of strict preference (and not merely the absence of strict preference cycles) are imposed (see (T.3), (T.4), (T.5) in the Appendix). But the pure Paretian epidemic (T.2) gets a remarkable amount of mileage from the Pareto principle itself. The limited element of 'independence' implicit in the Pareto principle, combined with the inter-pair consistency requirement of always avoiding preference cycles, is sufficient to spread decisiveness of a person from one pair to every pair, albeit in a weakened form.

## 3   *Preference Intensity and Dependent Liberalism*

The impossibility of the Paretian liberal (T.1) is based on the assumption that social preference be dependent on individual *preference orderings only* without bringing in *intensity* of preference. In this respect (T.1) is similar to Arrow's impossibility theorem. Ng (1971) has proposed getting round the problem through admitting intensity of preference as part of the informational setup; a person's right over his 'protected sphere' may be thought to be dependent on the strength of his preference. I am, however, inclined to argue that the notion of a person's 'protected sphere' is somewhat at variance with the notion that his right depends on his preferences being sharp. Even if Jack prefers *mildly* that he sleeps on his belly rather than on his back, and busybodies feel *strongly* that he should do the opposite, one can defend on libertarian grounds Jack's right to sleep as he pleases. Ng's way out—logically perfectly feasible—seems to contain the danger of throwing the baby out with the bath water.

Blau (1975) explores an avenue that is also based on bringing in 'intensity of preference' but in a way that involves nothing more than individual *orderings*, and it works by comparing the intensity of a person's preference for choices on his own assigned pair *vis-à-vis* the same person's intensity of preferences for choices on someone else's assigned pair:

> *Ordinal intensity*: If a person prefers $x$ to $a$, $a$ to $b$ and $b$ to $y$, then his preference for $x$ over $y$ is stronger than his preference for $a$ over $b$. Furthermore, this is so even if he is indifferent between $x$ and $a$, *or* between $b$ and $y$, but not both.

A person is 'meddlesome' according to Blau if and only if his preference over the two alternatives in his own assigned pair is weaker than his opposition to someone else's preference over that person's assigned pair.

Blau shows that, if at least one person is not meddlesome in each configuration of individual preferences, then in a two-member community the Pareto principle and Condition $L$ (or $L^*$) cannot lead to a social preference cycle. (Note that in the *Lady Chatterley's Lover* illustration both persons are meddlesome.)

Is this a way out of the problem of the Paretian liberal? Blau notes that it isn't so for an $n$-person community, since cycles can still arise based on Paretian and libertarian rankings if there are three or more persons; but for a two-person community it works. Blau proposes a 'modified liberalism', which makes the libertarian rights conditional on preferences being non-meddlesome. Under various alternative versions of his 'modified liberalism', the liberal privileges are withheld (a) for all if everyone's preference is meddlesome ($SL'$), (b) for all if someone's preference is meddlesome ($WL'$), and (c) for those whose preferences are meddlesome ($L'$). In the two-person case conflicts occur—as noted before—only if both are meddlesome, and thus all the versions of modified liberalism lead to the same conclusion, viz., withhold libertarian privileges from both. We are left with only the Pareto principle and there is no consistency problem for social decision.

But is this an acceptable solution? Since libertarian values come into their own in defending personal liberty against meddling, one can argue that the presence of meddling makes libertarian values more (*not* less) important. If everyone meddles in the sense of Blau, surely libertarian values should demand that the meddling part of each person's preferences be ignored but the non-meddling parts dealing with one's own affairs be defended against other people's meddling. Indeed, the ingenious consideration of meddlesomeness, so well discussed by Blau, seems to lead naturally to a critique of the part of the individual preferences incorporated in the Pareto relation rather than of the part incorporated in the personal rights, i.e., precisely the opposite of what Blau proposes.

Consider four alternative social states $\{x_1, y_1, x_2, y_2\}$ with $\{x_1, y_1\}$ being person 1's assigned pair and $\{x_2, y_2\}$ being person 2's pair. Let person 1 prefer $x_1$ to $y_1$, and person 2 be meddlesome by ordering the four alternatives in the strict descending order: $y_1, x_2, y_2, x_1$. No one denies 2's right to rank $x_2$ and $y_2$ as he likes. If we are upset about his being meddlesome, surely the object of our wrath should be his preference for $y_1$ over $x_2$, or for $y_2$ over $x_1$, or both. And these are precisely the pairs over which 2's preferences give muscle to the Pareto relation. The same applies to 1; he can be meddlesome by ordering: $y_2, x_1, y_1, x_2$. No one denies his right to prefer $x_1$ to $y_1$, but since he also prefers $y_2$ to $x_1$ and $y_1$ to $x_2$, he is meddlesome. Once again the finger points towards precisely the same two pairs on which person 1's preference—like person 2's—gives the Pareto relations their content.

We can divide person 2's rankings in the ordering $\{y_1, x_2, y_2, x_1\}$ into three ordered pairs, viz., a 'self-regarding' ordered pair $\{x_2, y_2\}$ and two 'non-self-regarding' ordered pairs $\{y_1, x_2\}$ and $\{y_2, x_1\}$. If person 1 happens to prefer $x_1$ to $y_1$ then this overall order of person 2 is meddlesome. Given that, we might decide to follow one of the following three alternative ways of discounting meddlesome 2's preference ordering:

(a) ignore his entire ordering;
(b) ignore his ordering of non-self-regarding pairs;
(c) ignore his ordering of the self-regarding pair.

It would seem rather natural to follow (a) or (b), whereas Blau follows (c), whereby the preference is ignored precisely over the pair on which the person in question can be hardly accused of being meddlesome.

The dispute can be illustrated in terms of the following example, which will be called the *work choice case*. Let persons 1 and 2 each have a part-time job, and suppose the possibility arises of a full-time job being available. Each prefers more of a job to less (i.e., 1 to $\frac{1}{2}$ to 0) given the job situation of the other, but prefers that the other should be jobless (i.e., 0 to $\frac{1}{2}$ to 1 for the other), spoilt as they are by the competitive society in which they live. In fact, they are each 'meddlesome' enough to attach greater importance to the other being jobless than to their own job situation. Consider now four alternative possibilities with the first number standing for person 1's job state, while the second for person 2's: $(1, \frac{1}{2})$, $(0, \frac{1}{2})$, $(\frac{1}{2}, 1)$ and $(\frac{1}{2}, 0)$. On grounds of one having the right to work if one wishes to, no matter what others want, the choice over $(1, \frac{1}{2})$ and $(0, \frac{1}{2})$ may be assigned to person 1 and that over $(\frac{1}{2}, 1)$ and $(\frac{1}{2}, 0)$ to person 2, since the job of the other person in each case is unaffected. This will lead to either $(1, \frac{1}{2})$ or $(\frac{1}{2}, 1)$ as the solution, eliminating $(0, \frac{1}{2})$ and $(\frac{1}{2}, 0)$ on libertarian grounds.

Let the two persons have the following strict orders, for reasons mentioned above:

| Person 1 | Person 2 |
|----------|----------|
| $(\frac{1}{2}, 0)$ | $(0, \frac{1}{2})$ |
| $(1, \frac{1}{2})$ | $(\frac{1}{2}, 1)$ |
| $(0, \frac{1}{2})$ | $(\frac{1}{2}, 0)$ |
| $(\frac{1}{2}, 1)$ | $(1, \frac{1}{2})$ |

Both are 'meddlesome' in the sense of Blau. On grounds of each of the alternative versions of Blau's 'modified liberalism' ($WL'$, $SL'$ and $L'$), the liberal privilege will be withheld from each. On grounds of the Pareto principle, the choice of $(1, \frac{1}{2})$ or $(\frac{1}{2}, 1)$ should be avoided since both are Pareto-inferior, and the choice should be confined to $(0, \frac{1}{2})$ and $(\frac{1}{2}, 0)$. But this amounts precisely to permitting the meddlesome parts of the two persons' preferences to hold sway. Left to himself, person 1 will prefer to work more, i.e., will choose $(1, \frac{1}{2})$ over $(0, \frac{1}{2})$, and left to himself person 2 will prefer to work more also, i.e., will choose $(\frac{1}{2}, 1)$ over $(\frac{1}{2}, 0)$, despite meddling by the other in each case, and Blau's solution amounts to eliminating the non-meddlesome part of one's preference and retaining the influence of meddling.

A more appropriate solution would seem to be to respect the self-regarding or the non-meddling parts, viz., 1's preference for $(1, \frac{1}{2})$ over $(0, \frac{1}{2})$ and 2's for $(\frac{1}{2}, 1)$ over $(\frac{1}{2}, 0)$, and to ignore the non-self-regarding parts and the Pareto relations based on them.

Blau is, of course, both right and illuminating in asserting the role of 'independence' in these impossibility theorems, which is 'the main thesis' of his paper. He has also taken me to task for claiming that in (T.1) I had not 'imposed Arrow's condition of "the independence of irrelevant alternatives"' (Blau, 1975, p. 395). He points out that the impossibility result makes substantial use of independence properties. This is indeed so, but the fact is that these independence properties were used only *in so far as* they were already incorporated in the Pareto condition and in the liberal condition in determining social choices over a pair on the basis of individual preferences over that pair under special circumstances. There was no need to impose Arrow's condition of 'independence of irrelevant alternatives' as such—a much more demanding condition, about the pervasive implications of which Blau (1957, 1971) himself has made us so aware. Incidentally, the Paretian epidemic discussed in the last section also exploits the *implicit* independence element in the Pareto principle.

Our difference does not lie in our respective recognitions of the role of independence, but on precisely *how* to bring in 'non-independent' considerations into the decision. Blau would like to sacrifice personal right (based on independence), retaining Pareto (also based on independence), whereas it appears that in many circumstances (as illustrated above) being prepared to go against the Pareto principle is at least as reasonable. An alternative will be to follow approach (a) above, which will remove the sanctity of both the Pareto principle as well as of liberal privileges when preferences are 'meddlesome' in the sense of Blau.

## 4   Alienability of Rights

Blau's 'modified liberalism' gives each person a right that is conditional on non-meddlesome preferences. This is an example of libertarian rights being treated as alienable. Gibbard (1974) has developed a rights system that makes libertarian rights alienable if it conflicts with other people's libertarian rights or the Pareto principle. A rights system is a set of ordered triples $\{x, y, i\}$ where $\{x, y\}$ is assigned to person $i$. *Under ordinary circumstances* person $i$ has his way over $\{x, y\}$ in the sense that, if he prefers $x$ to $y$, then $x$ is judged socially better than $y$. But this right can be waived if others beside $i$ 'claim their rights' to $z$ over $x$, and person $i$ himself regards $y$ at least as good as $z$. Others can claim their rights to $z$ over $x$ if and only if there is a sequence of strict preferences: $z$ over $a_1$, $a_1$ over $a_2$, ..., $a_{m-1}$ over $a_m$ and $a_m$ over $x$, such that the ranking over each pair is derived either from Pareto preference or from the preference of someone other than $i$ to whom the relevant pair has been assigned under the rights system. This weakening of the libertarian requirements makes it consistent with the Pareto principle for a social decision function with unrestricted domain. Gibbard proceeds to show that these alienable rights are rights in a very stringent sense—waived only under very special circumstances. (For formal statements, see Gibbard, 1974. He has also provided a deep and penetrating analysis of formulations of the libertarian principle identifying some formulations which may turn out to be self-contradictory; on this see Section 10 below.)

There are, it seems to me, two ways of viewing Gibbard's system of alienable rights. One takes off from his observation that under certain circumstances a right may be 'useless' to a person (Gibbard, 1974, p. 398) when by exercising it the person may end up at no better a position than by not exercising it, and this leads to a dichotomy between the *existence* of rights and the *exercise* of these rights. This I shall call the 'pragmatic interpretation'. The other starts off from Gibbard's concern with 'how the conflict *ought* to be resolved' (p. 398, italics added) and basing a system of rights on that consideration. This may be called the 'ethical interpretation'.

The pragmatic interpretation has been penetratingly explored recently by Kelly (1976b), who seems to take that to be the only interpretation. He identifies a number of difficulties with Gibbard's system, on this interpretation, essentially arising from problems in deciding *when* a right is useful for a person. (Kelly also discusses the 'very heavy demands on the information structure', viz., 'not only must each individual know all his rights as well as his preference ordering, he must know the preference orderings of all other individuals and must know all right assignments' (Kelly, 1976b, pp. 5–6 of manuscript).) Some of these difficulties are eliminated by modifications of the Gibbard system proposed by Kelly, but a basic problem of 'correctable miscalculation' remains. The difficulty arises from each person deciding what right is 'useless' for him on the basis of some presumption as to what rights the others would exercise, but one person's decision not to exercise his right (on the supposed ground of its being 'useless' when others exercise their rights) renders erroneous another person's conviction that his right is 'useless' (based on that person's assumption that others will exercise their rights). This problem of interdependence and of 'correctable miscalculation' proves to be a deep one for the 'pragmatic interpretation' of the Gibbard system (see especially Kelly, 1976b, Theorem 3). I shall not go into this interpretation anymore, since it is the 'ethical interpretation' of the Gibbard system that seems to me to be the relevant one for analysing libertarian ethics in general and 'the Pareto-consistent libertarian claim' in particular.

The ethical interpretation of the Gibbard system of alienable rights appears to be open to the same type of criticism as Blau's 'modified liberalism'. When meddling in each other's affairs causes a cycle involving the Pareto principle and personal rights, the axe in the Gibbard system falls invariably on personal rights (based on the 'self-regarding' part of a person's preference), leaving intact the effectiveness of the Pareto rule (based on the 'non-self-regarding' parts of people's preferences). Consider, for example, the 'work choice case' discussed in the last section. Each person prefers full-time work to being unemployed (given the other person's half-time job), and let this be the assigned pair of each over which the Gibbard system gives him an alienable right. Does person 1, in fact, end up getting the society to respect his rights of choosing $(1, \frac{1}{2})$ over $(0, \frac{1}{2})$? The answer is no, since this right is 'waived' in the Gibbard system because of the fact that person 1 prefers $(0, \frac{1}{2})$ to $(\frac{1}{2}, 1)$, person 2 has an alienable right to choose $(\frac{1}{2}, 1)$ over $(\frac{1}{2}, 0)$, and $(\frac{1}{2}, 0)$ is Pareto-preferred to $(1, \frac{1}{2})$ thanks to their jealousy of each other. Similarly, person 2's right to full-time work is 'waived'. Given the Pareto rule—respected in the Gibbard system—social choice is confined to $(0, \frac{1}{2})$ and $(\frac{1}{2}, 0)$, and the conflict with individual rights is eliminated by 'waiving' these rights.

It is not my intention to argue that, even if people have meddlesome preferences, as both these people seem to have, their preferences should continue to be fully respected, but to suggest that in some cases the 'waiving' should deal not with the unmeddlesome 'self-regarding' part of the preference, but with the 'non-self-regarding' parts. The right to be counted in to give the Pareto relation its muscle is a right too, and in situations such as this at least as strong a case can be made for 'waiving' that right as for the Gibbard solution of waiving the right to choose over one's 'assigned pair' unaffected by the other person's meddling. In this alternative system of 'alienation', the mechanical use of the Pareto principle must go, leading in this case to the choice of $(1, \frac{1}{2})$ or $(\frac{1}{2}, 1)$, rather than $(0, \frac{1}{2})$ or $(\frac{1}{2}, 0)$.

Gibbard gives relatively little space to the justification of his ingenious system of rights, though he does establish, in my judgement convincingly, that the 'extreme fears' that 'a person's right on an issue would usually be waived' are 'groundless' (Gibbard, 1974, p. 403). But that still leaves us with cases of waiving that are not easy to justify. Motivationally, Gibbard seems to proceed from a particular case (his 'Angelina–Edwin case') in which to him 'it is plain ... how the conflict ought to be resolved', and then in his system 'to generalize the moral of the example' (p. 398). But what is 'plain' in one case need not be in another, as is apparent from the 'work choice case', which also arises—as does the 'Angelina–Edwin case'—from 'one person's taking a perverse interest in the affairs of another' (p. 398).

Consider, now, Gibbard's own case. 'Angelina wants to marry Edwin but will settle for the judge, who wants whatever she wants. Edwin wants to remain single, but would rather wed Angelina than see her wed the judge'. Denoting 'Edwin weds Angelina' as $e$, 'the judge weds Angelina and Edwin remains single' as $j$ and 'both Edwin and Angelina remain single' as $o$, we have the following preference orders (in strict descending order):

Angelina: $e, j, o$
Edwin: $o, e, j$.

Gibbard takes $(j, o)$ to be Angelina's assigned pair ('Angelina has a right to marry the willing judge instead of remaining single') and $(o, e)$ to be Edwin's assigned pair ('Edwin has the right to remain single rather than wed Angelina'). Edwin's right is 'waived' in the Gibbard system of alienable rights since Edwin prefers $e$ to $j$ (he is ready to marry Angelina to prevent her from marrying the judge), and Angelina 'claims her right' to marry the judge rather than remaining single, preferring $j$ to $o$. With Edwin's right to remain single 'waived', Edwin and Angelina would seem to be heading towards a conjugal life since both prefer $e$ to $j$. 'Left freely to bargain away their rights ... Edwin and Angelina would agree to the outcome: wedding each other' (p. 398).

The appeal of this solution in this particular example lies, I would argue, not merely in the preferences specified, but also on what we presume to be the motivation underlying the preferences as described by Gibbard. Let us consider a different interpretation of the orderings. Angelina loves the judge—truly—and would have preferred most to marry him but for her fury at being scorned by the unwillingness of Edwin ('oh, I hate him!') to marry her ('I *will*, Edwin, just you see!'), and hence her strict order: *e, j, o*. Edwin hates Angelina's guts ('in so far as she has any'), and knowing that she will be very happy married to the judge, he would do anything to stop her, even—if need be—himself marrying her ('that will teach her all right'), and hence his strict order: *o, e, j*. While Gibbard makes arrangements for the wedding of Edwin and Angelina, Edwin can do worse than recite: 'I don't want to wed Angelina and have a right not to—I won't let Gibbard "waive" it; and to stop Angelina from getting happiness married to the judge is none of my bloody business, and my perverse preference on this should not really affect whether they marry or not'. One can, indeed, in such a situation make a case for respecting Edwin's right not to wed Angelina, but not attach great social importance to his views on whether Angelina should marry the judge.

My point is not that the above reflects a more natural interpretation of the preferences of Angelina and Edwin, but that these preference orderings are consistent with quite different interpretations, and without going into the motivations it may *not* be 'plain in this case how the conflict ought to be resolved'. (Fine (1975) has pointed out that, judged purely as orderings, the configuration of preferences assumed in proving (T.1) is very similar to that of the 'Prisoner's Dilemma', though the lessons drawn are quite different.)

The fundamental issue really is whether individual preference orderings alone provide enough of a basis for a social judgement without going into the causation of and the motivation behind these preferences (see Section 1). While there undoubtedly do *exist* cases where the optimal solution may involve waiving a person's libertarian rights—Gibbard is convincing on this existential proposition though not, in my judgement, in its generalization in the form of his system of rights—there also exist cases where the optimal solution involves waiving the Pareto principle. Principles that take account of nothing other than what individual preferences happen to be, however superficially appealing (and the Pareto principle is certainly appealing) are essentially 'non-basic' (see Sen, 1967; 1970a, Chapter 5). To axe invariably personal rights over assigned pairs and never the Pareto principle, when they conflict, as Gibbard's system does, seems to me to be hard to justify.

## 5 Other Weakenings of Condition L

While Blau's and Gibbard's methods consist of accepting the basic idea behind Condition *L* but qualifying its scope in terms of preferences over other pairs, some other authors have proposed ways of avoiding the dilemma by declaring

Condition $L$ to be essentially inappropriate. Hillinger and Lapham (1971) argue that Condition $L$ has got very little to do with liberalism as they see it, and claim that 'whenever the choices of one individual impinge on the welfare of others there is no general presumption in favour of freedom of individual choice' (pp. 1403–4). This makes 'liberalism' immediately consistent with the Pareto principle, since person $i$'s right to having his way over any pair depends on non-opposition by others over that pair itself. Everyone's right to do anything whatsoever is made conditional on non-opposition by others, and one does not see much trace of liberal values in Hillinger and Lapham's modified liberalism, consistent though it is with the Pareto principle.

Hillinger and Lapham (1971, p. 1405) argue: 'In conditions of interdependence, we cannot conceive of any 'principle of liberalism' which would govern what actions are to be left to individuals independently of the majority preference of the individuals concerned'. Rowley and Peacock (1975), writing on the same subject, 'cannot endorse such a judgement', but agree that 'Sen has grossly misinterpreted the liberalist philosophy in his Condition $L^*$ as was noted by Hillinger and Lapham' (pp. 82–3). They view liberalism as 'concerned essentially though not exclusively, with the maintenance and extension of individual freedom, defined as that condition of mankind in which coercion of some individuals by others is reduced to the minimum possible degree' (p. 78). Despite lengthy (and otherwise interesting) discussion, they never seem to take note of the fact that, in the type of situations considered, a denial of Condition $L^*$ would involve precisely the loss of the guarantee of even a *minimal* element of 'individual freedom'.

It is worth examining Karni's (1974a, b) interesting reformulation of liberalism. Essentially, he proposes that the libertarian right be weakened to being semi-decisive over a pair rather than decisive; i.e., if the pair containing $x$ and $y$ is assigned to a person, then whenever he strictly prefers $x$ to $y$, $x$ is judged to be socially at least as good as $y$. This makes person $i$ semi-decisive over this pair $x$, $y$. This weakened libertarianism is consistent with the Pareto principle in the sense of not producing strict preference cycles, even though the social preference thus generated will involve intransitive indifference. Social *strict* preference may be transitive, but if so, all Pareto non-comparable states may have to be declared socially indifferent (a direct corollary of Lemma 5*f in Sen, 1970), which will be a very peculiar system indeed.

An even more serious difficulty with Karni's method of resolution lies in the fact that $i$ being semi-decisive for $x$ against $y$ guarantees only that $x$ *is chosen from that pair* (though not necessarily uniquely), but it does not prevent $y$ from being chosen with $x$ rejected from *larger* sets containing both $x$ and $y$. In the *Lady Chatterley's Lover* illustration, under Karni's rule Mr B will be able to read the book if the choice is between his reading it and no one reading it (both alternatives will be judged equally acceptable), but not if the possibility of Mr A reading it is also included. Indeed, thanks to the Pareto principle, kept intact by Karni, Mr B will definitely not be able to read the book when the choice is over the three alternatives. Thus semi-decisiveness over a pair is a very limited right indeed, and it will be a very tame libertarian who will settle for it.

Kelly (1976a) has explored the possibility of introducing information on interpersonal comparisons of welfare into the framework and has used Suppes' (1966) 'grading principle of justice' in restricting the scope of Condition $L$. Under his 'weak just liberalism', at least two persons have the right to be decisive both ways over one pair each *provided* no one else believes that the opposite preference over that pair will reflect justice in the sense of Suppes. Kelly demonstrates that, even with this restriction, Condition $L$ conflicts with the Pareto principle (and with Suppes' grading principle of justice, applied over other pairs) for a possible set of extended orderings incorporating views on interpersonal comparisons (see Theorem 3). Kelly's 'impossibility of a just liberal' is an important extension of the problem of the Paretian liberal, and as he points out the result demonstrates that, for this class of impossibility results, introducing interpersonal comparisons is not much of a cure (in contrast with the impossibility results of the Arrow type).

Condition $L$ has been subjected to serious scrutiny also by Seidl (1975). He criticizes the existential form in which Condition $L$ is defined, and points out that 'it is perfectly consistent with Sen liberalism, if individual $j$ is socially decisive on the regime of the society (say, whether monarchy or republic should obtain), whereas individual $k$ is socially decisive with respect to his sleeping on back or belly' (p. 279). This is certainly so, but the result of defining liberalism in the existential form is that, if it is denied, then $j$ loses his right to decide singlehanded on the 'regime' (this loss will not be regretted) *as well as* his right to sleep as he likes (this loss will be regretted). Wanting decisiveness over 'some' pair is, of course, weaker than demanding it over a *specified* pair, and since the object was to show an inconsistency, there was something to be said for choosing as weak a condition as possible. But Seidl (1975) is clearly right that a constructive study of liberalism requires us to go more into the nature of the alternatives involved, and here his investigation of 'technological separability' clarifies what kind of choices can be reasonably put under a person's 'protected sphere'. Bernholz (1974, 1975) discusses a similar issue. However, Bernholz's (1974) assertion that 'the rule of liberalism generally gives only the right to decide among certain alternative measures or actions belonging to certain issues' and not 'among social states' (p. 101) would seem to be based on a misunderstanding of the type of space on which these preferences are formulated. Given the rest of the world $\Omega$, Jack's choice over the 'measure' of sleeping on his back and that of sleeping on his belly *is* a choice over two 'social states'. Seidl's and Bernholz's discussions do not affect the impossibility result, but are helpful in clarifying the types of choices over which such a conflict can occur.

Osborne (1975) also objects to the existential form and argues that Condition $L$ permits 'a person to govern on a pair belonging to another person's protected sphere' (p. 1286). 'Sen's Condition $L$ is as consistent with universal busy-bodiedness as with liberalism'. True enough, in the sense that both imply Condition $L$. The consequence of this, however, is not that the impossibility of the Paretian liberal does not hold, but that, for a social decision function with unrestricted domain, more than one person cannot be permitted to determine the choices irrespective of others' preferences *even* in their *own* 'protected spheres' (and not on others'—a consequence that also holds but is hardly disturbing). 'The impossibility of the Paretian busy-body' to which Osborne refers does not in any way reduce 'the impossibility of the Paretian liberal', given the *existential* form of Condition $L$.

Osborne's rebuttal of the inconsistency result is based on an unadulterated piece of logical error:

> The weak Pareto principle operates only in case of unanimity; . . . in that case the liberal principle is empty. On the other hand the liberal principle is forceful only in cases of certain kinds of disagreement; and in those cases the Pareto principle is silent. Thus when the one is binding, the other is empty or silent. *If that is true they cannot possibly be inconsistent.* (Osborne, 1975, p. 1286, italics added)

The Pareto principle can operate over one or more pairs (without conflicting with the liberal principle over *those* pairs) and the liberal principle can operate over two or more other pairs (without conflicting with the Pareto principle over *those* pairs), and these choices *together* can be inconsistent. The theorem of the impossibility of the Paretian liberal is based on such interpair inconsistency (as indeed are other 'impossibility' theorems in this field, including Arrow's famous one).

## 6  Rights as Constraints

In contrast with the weakenings of Condition $L$ discussed in the preceding sections, Nozick (1973, 1974) suggests a way out of the dilemma that gives liberal rights priority by making social choice constrained by the exercise of these rights.

> The trouble stems from treating an individual's right to choose among alternatives as the right to determine the relative ordering of these alternatives within a social ordering . . . A more appropriate view of individual rights is as follows. Individual rights are co-possible; each person may exercise his rights as he chooses. The exercise of these rights fixes some features of the world. Within the constraints of these fixed features, a choice can be made by a social choice mechanism based upon a social ordering, if there are any choices left to make! Rights do not determine

a social ordering but instead set the constraints within which a social choice is to be made, by excluding certain alternatives, fixing others, and so on ... If entitlements to holdings are rights to dispose of them, then social choice must take place within the constraints of how people choose to exercise these rights. If any patterning is legitimate, it falls *within* the domain of social choice, and hence is constrained by people's rights. *How else can one cope with Sen's result?* (Nozick, 1973, pp. 60-1; 1974, pp. 165-6)

This neat solution of the problem is indeed attractive, since the conflict between the Pareto rule and the liberal principle is resolved by giving them two quite different roles; viz., the former determines a strict partial ordering with which the social ordering has to be consistent, and the latter restricts the choice situations over which the social ordering is to be applied. In the 'work choice case' discussed in Section 3, Nozick's solution—unlike Blau's, Gibbard's, Hillinger and Lapham's, Karni's, etc.—would amount to social choice of $(1, \frac{1}{2})$ or $(\frac{1}{2}, 1)$, and our criticism will not apply. The same would be true in the *Lady Chatterley's Lover* case.

There is, however, a problem of interpretation of a social ordering. It can be taken either to be purely a mechanism for choice, or as reflecting a view of social welfare. In the latter interpretation to say $xPy$ ($x$ is 'socially preferred' to $y$) is to assert that in one's judgement society is better off with $x$ than with $y$, and vice versa. In the 'work choice case', if someone—an outsider *or* even one of the persons involved in taking an 'ethical' view—tries to decide what is the best solution, does he eliminate $(0, \frac{1}{2})$ and $(\frac{1}{2}, 0)$ by saying that, while these are socially better than $(\frac{1}{2}, 1)$ and $(1, \frac{1}{2})$ respectively (thanks to Pareto), they *cannot* be chosen since 1 and 2 have exercised their rights by eliminating them from social choice (as one would do under Nozick's solution)? Or should he assert that the choice of $(\frac{1}{2}, 1)$ or $(1, \frac{1}{2})$ would in fact be socially better, despite the Pareto preference to the contrary, since the Pareto preference is based on preference rankings that deserve to be ignored (on some grounds, e.g., meddlesomeness)? Like the other authors, Nozick does not seem to dispute the acceptability of the Pareto ranking as a sufficient condition for higher social welfare, but eliminates its impact by excluding the Pareto-superior alternatives from social choice on grounds of rights.

The difference can be brought out in terms of Nozick's example: 'If I have a right to choose to live in New York or in Massachusetts, and I choose Massachusetts, then alternatives involving my living in New York are not appropriate objects to be entered in a social ordering' (Nozick, 1973, p. 62). But one can also argue that, if I believe that it is a better society which—given other things—lets Nozick decide where he wishes to live, then I must *assert* that it is socially *better* that Nozick should be permitted to live in Massachusetts as desired by him. If Nozick is forced out of Massachusetts, then one would wish to say not only that Nozick's rights have been violated, but that society is worse off—given other things—by stopping Nozick from living where he wishes.

I do not wish to enter here into a more general discussion of Nozick's ingenious theory of rights as such, or of his analysis of the role of the state. Nozick's (1974) system of rights does, of course, have an exceptionally wide coverage, while Conditions $L$ and $L^*$ demand very little; but in either case acknowledging certain rights would seem to have consequences on our judgements on what is socially good. It is not a matter of unconcern, in making pronouncements on what is socially good and what not, to examine whether the rights acknowledged can be exercised freely. There is a clear sense in which Nozick's ability to choose to live where he pleases *is* in 'the domain of social choice'.

Thus the dichotomy with the help of which Nozick solves the conflict, permitting support for personal rights without conflict with the Pareto principle, can lead to fresh problems. It is certainly possible to follow Nozick in defining a 'social ordering' without taking note of acknowledged rights, but if a social ordering is supposed to reflect a judgement of social welfare taking everything into account, then the ability to exercise these rights must enter the 'social ordering' after all. One can use the approach of having a 'ranking of rankings', as discussed in Sen (1974) (see also Nozick, 1968, and Jeffrey, 1974), in which a 'higher' ranking incorporates these rights while a 'lower' ranking does not. But at some stage, i.e., with a 'higher' ranking, the conflict with the Pareto principle will surface again, and in the latter ordering we shall have to go against some Pareto relations in the cases discussed if it is accepted that it is a better social state which incorporates the exercise of these personal rights.

In order to avoid an ambiguity, I should make it clear that it is not my contention that Condition $L$, or some strengthening of it in that general line, can catch whatever there is to catch in our conception of rights in general, and of liberty in particular. Condition $L$ does focus on the end-state, and it may be important from a libertarian point of view to ensure not merely that the consequences corresponding to the desires of the persons in question take place, but also that these consequences are brought about in the right way. For example, from a libertarian point of view it may not be sufficient to distinguish only between Nozick's remaining in Massachusetts ($x$) and his not going to New York ($y$). Even though it may be known by everyone that Nozick would prefer to live in Massachusetts, it can be argued that an order served on him to stay in Massachusetts will be an infringement of his liberty. A distinction may be made between there being such an order and Nozick living in Massachusetts ($x_1$), and there being no such order and Nozick living in Massachusetts ($x_2$). A libertarian may well prefer $x_2$ to $x_1$, even though the order does not have any consequence on where Nozick lives, and the libertarian position would seem to include 'non-consequentialist' features (on the structure of 'consequentialism', see Williams, 1973, pp. 82–93). This does not, however, contradict that a libertarian would find $y$, i.e., Nozick's living in New York (and in the case described, this can happen only if he is forced) to be worse than *both* $x_1$ and $x_2$. If $y$ is the outcome, then it is sufficient ground for concluding that the libertarian principle has been violated, and that is all that is needed for the 'impossibility of the Paretian liberal'. There is no need to deny that libertarian ethics might also involve other elements as long as it incorporates, *inter alia*, Condition $L$ or $L^*$. (This is so independently of the fact that in this case $x_1$ and $x_2$ can also be treated as two separate states, and there is no obligation to treat them as socially equivalent in our formulation.)

## 7 Preference Amendment and the Liberal Partition

Farrell (1976) has explored two rather different avenues of ensuring consistency in social choices involving the exercise of liberal rights. The first takes the form of 'amending' a person's preference so that 'he is deemed indifferent between any pair of states for which some other individual is to be decisive' (p. 12), which amounts 'in spirit' to ignoring a person's strict preference on choices that are 'none of his business'. This way of avoiding a conflict raises interesting problems of consistency, which have been thoroughly investigated by Farrell, and he outlines a method of moving from true preferences $\{R_i\}$ of the individuals to 'amended' preferences $\{R_i'\}$ such that each $R_i'$ is also an ordering, and each individual can be assigned (many) decisive pairs without running into social preference cycles (taking the Pareto relation as defined by the *amended* preferences).

Farrell points out several objections to this procedure, including the basic objections to 'deeming' a person's preference to be different from what it is, and the particular result that the Pareto relation on the 'amended preferences' may be the exact opposite of the Pareto relation on the true preferences. While Farrell finds these objections 'overwhelming', I am not so sure that they are. 'Amending' preferences in the Farrell system is essentially like ignoring a person's 'meddlesome' preferences (defined more widely than Blau's) and spelling out the consequences of this for the rest of the preference ranking to preserve its ordering character. As we argued in Sections 3 and 4, there exist situations in which the case for violating the Pareto principle is strong. Indeed, we criticized Blau's 'modified liberalism' and Gibbard's system of 'alienable rights' for making the axe fall invariably on personal rights, ignoring a person's non-meddlesome 'self-regarding' parts of the preference ranking and keeping intact 'non-self-regarding' parts (reflected in the Pareto preferences). In effect, Farrell does the exact opposite, and for the type of cases we discussed in Sections 3 and 4, e.g., the 'work choice case', the Farrell system will lead to 'amended' preferences such that the pernicious consequences of the mechanical use of the Pareto rule will be eliminated, keeping the personal rights untouched. While I shall argue in Section 11 below that there is a better way of achieving this than 'amending' preferences, Farrell's approach seems to have much merit in it.

One problem with Farrell's ingenious system of 'amendments' lies in the fact that it too—like Blau's 'modified liberalism' and Gibbard's 'alienable rights'—tries to make social judgements based on what individual preferences happen to be, without going into the motivation that lies behind these preferences. And as we saw, there are situations in which, with appropriate individual motivation, the Gibbard system or the Blau system will be appealing (e.g., in Gibbard's version of the 'Angelina—Edwin case'), and here Farrell's solution would be unattractive, while there are other cases with the *same* individual rankings but different motivations underlying them in which the Gibbard solution or the Blau solution will be unattractive (e.g., in the perverse interpretation of the 'Angelina—Edwin case' discussed in Section 4, or in the 'work choice case', under the given interpretation), and here Farrell's solution seems perfectly legitimate. While Farrell's approach is in some ways the exact opposite of those of Gibbard and Blau, and is immune to the difficulties discussed in Sections 3 and 4, it shares with those approaches the attempt to make do with rather inadequate information.

Farrell's second approach involves a significant departure from the usual format of social choice theory. The set $X$ of social states is first partitioned into 'socially equivalent' subsets, the motivation for which arises from his observation that a liberal is likely to hold that 'there is no social choice to be made between $x$ and $y$ [when] they differ in a matter private to individual $j$' (Farrell, 1976, p. 9). Social choice is then seen as a choice over elements of a partition $P$ of $X$. The choice among alternatives within such a 'socially equivalent' subset 'will be determined by private decisions' (p. 9)

Farrell notes that this radical solution 'generates a number of questions'. One that worries me is similar to my difficulty with Nozick's approach. If the choice among 'socially equivalent' partitions are 'removed from social choice theory', are we asserting that from the social point of view it *does not matter* which element of such a subset is chosen? Does it then make no difference to our idea of social welfare whether the choice between $x$ and $y$ differing 'in a matter private to individual $j$' (and thus declared 'socially equivalent' and left to be 'determined by private decisions') is, in fact, decided the way $j$ wants it, rather than in some other way, e.g., as strong-armed $k$ wants it? If it does not make a difference, then in what sense is this a 'liberal' approach? If it does, then in a significant sense $x$ and $y$ are *not* 'socially equivalent'; if $j$ prefers $x$ to $y$, then in a non-trivial sense there is a social preference in favour of $x$ against $y$, and the choice between $x$ and $y$ is not 'removed from social choice theory' after all. A 'liberal partition' is indeed a useful way of looking at the issue of personal rights, but in so far as such a partition is combined with recommending social support for ensuring that person $j$ decides over alternatives that 'concern' $j$ only, the approach is not altogether different from a social choice system incorporation Condition $L$.

## 8  *Domain Restriction*

As mentioned in Section 1, one way of resolving the conflict is the weakening of Condition *U*, the 'unrestricted domain' (see Sen, 1970a, pp. 85–6; Fine, 1975, and Blau, 1975). However, the interpretation of a relaxation of Condition *U* may not be obvious.

If a particular configuration of individual preferences is 'outside the domain' of a social decision procedure, then nothing can be deduced from that procedure if such a configuration were to arise. When we 'rule out' a preference configuration, that is only a refusal to open our mouth in that case, and obviously has no bearing on whether that configuration will, *in fact*, arise or not. If such a preference configuration does, in fact, occur, then to say that it is outside the domain of a procedure is merely an admission of defeat as far as that procedure is concerned. The relevance of the investigation of 'domain restriction' lies in the light it throws on the type of configurations that would have to be absent. The investigation comes into its own when we move away from the assumption of *given* individual preferences, and consider the changes that will help to eliminate the conflict. It is in *this* context that one can remark that 'the eventual guarantee for individual freedom' may have to be found 'in developing values and preferences that respect each other's privacy and personal choices' (Sen, 1970a, p. 85). This is a 'way out' of the dilemma only in this rather limited sense.

The belief that 'unrestricted domain' is the condition to axe is not uncommon, though the argument on this is rarely spelt out clearly. Perhaps the most persuasive comments on this come from Blau (1975), who does not, however, himself base his solution of the problem on this—at any rate not on this exclusively. He points out that, in the two-person case, the conflict between the Pareto principle and Condition *L* arises only if *both* persons are meddlesome in the sense of having stronger preferences *against* the other on the other's assigned pair than on his own assigned pair. 'That one of them might exhibit such a preference is remarkable enough, but that both should do so seems to border on the socially pathological' (Blau, 1975, p. 396). Whether pathological is an appropriate description of this type of occurrence I find difficult to decide, but as we saw with several examples (e.g., the *Lady Chatterley's Lover* case, the 'work choice case', the 'Angelina–Edwin case'), such preference configurations may not be unplausible even over pairs the choices over which are regarded as 'purely personal' from the common libertarian point of view. If meddlesomeness is a disease, it is certainly not a rare disease.

Blau shows that the conflict between the Pareto principle and Condition *L* will not arise in the case of two individuals and four alternatives, if only four of the possible $75^2$ configurations of individual preferences were to be ruled out (Blau, 1975, p. 398). If any preference pattern were as likely as any other, this would give it a very low probability of occurrence, even though for a large community there will be a fair number of cases of conflict even under this assumption. Equi-probability is, however, not a very good assumption (on which see Sen, 1970a, pp. 163–6), so that the interpretation of Blau's striking result remains a little problematic. Blau is, therefore, quite right in not basing his 'way out' of the inconsistency on the relaxation of the condition of 'unrestricted domain', but on weakening the other conditions, specifying what 'should' be done if such a meddlesome preference configuration were to arise. It was argued earlier that Blau's solution is not quite adequate (see Section 3, above), but our differences there do not lie in the role of the condition of unrestricted domain.

## 9  Non-binary Frameworks of Choice

The conflict between the Pareto principle and libertarian requirements has been discussed so far in terms of cycles of strict preference. While a preference cycle makes it impossible to choose an alternative that is not judged strictly worse than any other, it can be argued that choice from a set of alternatives need not be based on such pair-wise non-defeat. Is there much hope of avoiding the conflicts of Paretian liberalism by moving away from this 'binary' framework? This question is particularly important, since escape from Arrow's Impossibility Theorem has recently been sought by many authors in the eschewing of the binary structure and reformulation of the problem in terms of 'choice functions' (see Schwartz, 1970; Campbell, 1972; Fishburn, 1973; Plott, 1973; Deb, 1974; Bordes, 1976; and Blair et al., 1976).

I don't believe there is much mileage in this. As was noted in Sen (1970a, pp. 81–2), the Pareto principle and Conditions $L$ and $L^*$ can be easily reformulated in non-binary terms, without losing their rationale. The Pareto principle can then be read as: if everyone prefers $x$ to $y$, then $y$ should not be socially chosen from any set if $x$ is available in that set. Similarly, Condition $L$ will be transformed into requiring that if any person $i$ prefers $x$ to $y$ when $\{x, y\}$ is his assigned pair, then $y$ should not be socially chosen from any set that contains $x$. For some configuration of individual preferences, these two conditions will leave nothing to choose (see (T.7) in the Appendix). Alternatively, Condition $L$ can be made less demanding; viz., if any person $i$ prefers $x$ to $y$ when $\{x, y\}$ is his assigned pair, then $y$ should not be socially chosen from that pair. Combined with a relatively mild requirement of consistency of choice proposed by Batra and Pattanaik (1972), this too makes social choice impossible from some sets for particular individual preferences when combined with the non-binary Pareto principle (see (T.8) in Appendix).

## 10 *Motivation and the Internal Consistency of Rights*

The problem of consistency of libertarian and Paretian principles has recently been supplemented by Gibbard's (1974) pointer to *internal* inconsistency of the libertarian principle itself 'under one natural interpretation' (see also Farrell, 1976). If more than one person is given the right to make a class of personal decisions without outside interference, this itself can give rise to a strict preference cycle.

An example may bring out the nature of the difficulty envisaged. Let Zubeida be keen on dressing in the same colour as Rehana, while Rehana wishes to differentiate from Zubeida. Consider four alternatives with $R$ standing for red, $G$ for green, with the first letter denoting the colour of Zubeida's dress and the second Rehana's: $RR$, $GG$, $RG$ and $GR$. If it is accepted that the way one dresses is a person's own business and whatever she decides about her own dressing must be judged to be socially better, then there is now a problem of consistency. Zubeida's preference for matching Rehana leads to $RR$ being superior to $GR$ and $GG$ being superior to $RG$ (in these decisions only Zubeida's dress varies), while Rehana's preference for differentiating leads to $RG$ being superior to $RR$, and $GR$ being superior to $GG$ (in these choices only Rehana's dress varies). There is now a cycle of strict preference order: $RR$, $GR$, $GG$, $RG$, $RR$.

Cycles of this kind cannot be caused by Condition $L$ or $L^*$ alone, since for this we need at least two assigned pairs per person related to each other in this 'closed circle' way. But Gibbard argues, with some force, that the rationale for Condition $L$ or $L^*$ should extend to giving each person rights over *all* choices that differ only in a feature of the world that is exclusively his or her 'business'. And then the problem of internal consistency can arise, as illustrated above.

But can we decide that some choice is a person's concern alone totally independently of the *motivation* that lies behind his or her preferences? Zubeida's desire to match Rehana, and Rehana's desire to differentiate from Zubeida, are not particularly inward-looking, and what either does is clearly of real consequence to the other if their respective desires to match or differentiate are taken seriously. So while the personal right to choose the colour of one's dress may well be conceded in general, the presence of the types of motivations discussed would tend to question the coverage of this right. We may be upset about an order prohibiting the wearing of red dresses (because this *is* a private business in general), without being prepared to weep too much about Zubeida's failure to secure the right to match Rehana, should Rehana be cunning enough to frustrate Zubeida's matching programme. The problem of *internal* consistency of the kind with which Gibbard is concerned arises only with preference configurations requiring rather other-oriented motivations, and the weakening of these 'rights' in the presence of other-oriented motivations would not seem to involve any great violations of libertarianism. This is so irrespective of whether or not problems of internal consistency do *in fact* arise. But, of course, the issue has an additional interest when problems of internal consistency are present, as in Gibbard's example; and more generally when the condition of 'consistent rights assignment' discussed in the Appendix (section A5) is violated.

The question of motivation seems central to the force of *both* the Pareto principle (as discussed earlier) and the libertarian principles (especially in Gibbard's extension). Both types of judgements seem to be 'non-basic' (in the sense discussed in Sen, 1967), and it seems difficult to assert or deny either type of judgement *irrespective* of the motivations underlying the personal preferences.

## 11 *Restraining the Pareto Principle*

One of the main preoccupations of this paper has been the unacceptability of the Pareto principle as a universal rule. The 'Paretian epidemic', that is (T.2), shows how powerful the Pareto principle is in spreading decisiveness from one pair to all. The 'impossibility of the Paretian liberal' (T.1) is just a corollary of the 'Paretian epidemic'. The power of a principle is not itself an argument against it—in fact, it may even be treated as an argument in favour—but some of the consequences that follow from this power seem to be unacceptable, thereby indicating the unacceptability of the Pareto principle. The fact that even a minimal guarantee of individual liberty may have to be revoked is viewed as one such consequence.

The suggestion that the Pareto principle be rejected meets with resistance, which is perfectly understandable, since there is something very central in the idea that preferences unanimously held by members of a community cannot be rejected by that community. As Blau (1975, p. 401) puts it, 'I can see no case for an outside observer denying a unanimous choice. This leads inevitably to modifying [Condition] *L*.'

But is an outsider necessarily involved in denying a unanimous preference? An important distinction exists, it seems to me, between person *i preferring x* to *y*, and person *i* wanting his preference for *x* over *y* to *count* in determining social choice. I can easily take the view that, while I would prefer you to read what I consider to be good literature as opposed to what appears to me to be muck, I do not want my preference to count in the social evaluation as to whether it is better that you read good literature or bury yourself in muck. I might accept taste differences as legitimate and accept the greater relevance of your taste in matters that I agree are essentially your 'concern'.

Extending this reasoning, I may decide, for the sake of consistency, not to insist that my preferences be taken into account even in choices over some pairs that are not exclusively your concern. Let me be the 'prude' (Mr A) in the example of *Lady Chatterley's Lover* (see Section 1), while you are 'lascivious' (Mr B). I would rather not read the stuff myself (i.e., I prefer *o* to *a*), and I would rather you would not (i.e., I prefer *o* to *b*), but I decide to 'respect' your tastes on what I agree is your benighted business (while wondering whether 'respect' is quite the word), conceding that my preference for *o* over *b* be ignored. My dislike of your gloating over 'muck' was so strong that I would have preferred to read the work myself to stop you from falling into this (i.e., I preferred *a* to *b*), but being a consistent kind of man, I notice that, if I insist that my preference for *o* over *a* should count as well as my preference for *a* over *b*, then there is not much point in my 'renouncing' my preference for *o* over *b*. So I may decide not to want my preference for *a* over *b* to count, even though the choice over the pair {*a, b*} is not exclusively your business.

On a similar ground, you might not want your preference for *a* over *b* to count, since you do wish your preference for *b* over *o* to count and decide not to want that your preference for *a* over *o* should count (since it is my business). But the Pareto preference for *a* over *b* is built on counting my preference and yours for *a* over *b*, and if neither of us wants our respective preferences over this pair to count, there can hardly be much force in the Pareto ranking in this case. If on these grounds the Pareto preference is overridden, this is not done by virtue of any 'outside observer denying a unanimous choice', but on the basis of our own denial that our preferences for *a* over *b* should 'count' in deciding what is socially better.

This notion of counting suggests a *conditional* version of the Pareto principle. If everyone in a community prefers *x* to *y* and wants that preference to count, then *x* must be socially preferred to *y* (conditional weak Pareto principle, denoted PC). A person can be described as respecting the rights of others if and only if he wants only a part of his total preference to count such that it can be combined with everyone's preferences over *their* respective 'protected spheres'. (There may be many more than one pair in any person's protected sphere, but the rights of different people are required to be consistent with each other, avoiding Gibbard's problem.) The conditions involved are stated more rigorously in the Appendix, and it is shown there—see (T.9)— that, if *at least one* person respects the rights of others, then there can be no conflict between the conditional Pareto principle (even in a strengthened form) and the weak libertarian principle (even after considerable strengthening), no matter what the individual preferences are. But it does mean that some Pareto preferences in the traditional sense may have to be violated.

In this procedure, no one pretends that his preference is, in fact, different from what it actually is, and there is no question of 'amending' preferences (contrast Farrell, 1976). A person wants a part of his preference to count, thereby asserting 'the truth' and 'nothing but the truth', but does not demand that 'the whole truth' of his preference be brought to bear on every choice for the society.

Note also that, while the conditional Pareto principle as defined here (and its strengthened version in the Appendix) do not bring in any outsiders, it is possible to consider 'arbitration problems' in which the job of restricting is not left only to the persons involved. Some outsider may try to judge what should be done and may decide that certain parts of a person's preferences *should not* count in the choice in question. For example, a person judging what should be done in the *Lady Chatterley's Lover* case may decide that, while the prude Mr A prefers *o* to *a*, and *a* to *b*, and wants every ounce of it to count, there is nevertheless a case for discounting his preference for *o* over *b* since B should himself decide whether to read the book or not, and therefore A's preference for *a* over *b* should not count either since his preference for *o* over *a* must. Thus arguments may be constructed that suggest the violation of not merely the Pareto principles, but also of the *conditional* versions of these principles proposed here.

It is difficult to decide where exactly to draw the line when such judgements are concerned, and indeed, as I have tried to argue earlier in this paper, the set of individual orderings in general provides too little information for deciding what to do. To discuss whether a person's preference should count or not we may need to know more than what the preferences happen to be, e.g., the *reasons* for holding these preferences. As argued before, the same set of individual orderings under one interpretation of the motivations underlying the preferences might suggest the dropping of the Pareto principle, while under another interpretation of the motivations it might point the finger at Condition $L$.

## 12   Concluding Remarks

No attempt will be made here to summarize the discussion in the earlier sections, but a few general remarks will be made.

(1) While most of the attempts at avoiding the conflict that may arise between the Pareto principle and Condition $L$ (or $L^*$) has taken the form of weakening the latter, a strong case can be made for weakening the former as well. This may appear superficially puzzling since 'unanimity' is a strong argument, but the 'unanimity' used in the Pareto principle is of a rather limited kind (*contrast* the 'unanimity rule' UR in Section 2), and it leaves many issues open.

(2) To reject the Pareto principle as a universal rule does not amount to an outsider overriding the wishes of members of the community. The difference between 'preferring $x$ to $y$' and wanting one's preference to 'count in favour of $x$ against $y$' is relevant to this. Indeed, the guarantee of a minimal amount of personal liberty may require that certain parts of individual rankings should not count in some specific social choices, and in some cases even the persons in question may agree with this.

(3) The Pareto principle (as opposed to the unanimity rule UR) has some 'epidemic' properties for a social decision function with unrestricted domain. If a person is decisive over any pair, he turns out to have a weak form of decisiveness ('potentially semidecisive') over *every* ordered pair. It is this result, viz., (T.2), that does not permit even two persons to decide on certain personal things on their own, because if one is decisive over a single pair, he is potentially semidecisive over every ordered pair, and thus the other cannot be decisive over any pair at all, no matter how 'personal' the choice might be to him. This leads to the impossibility of the Paretian liberal (T.1).

(4) The same reason applies to two or more groups of people with no members in common, who cannot be decisive over one pair each (see (T.6) in the Appendix), ruling out even the most minimal forms of local autonomy, or a federal structure. The Paretian epidemic threatens not merely individual liberty but also group autonomy.

(5) Relaxing the 'binary' framework of social choice is no way out of these conflicts, since weak consistency conditions on the choice function generate the 'impossibility', as is shown in the Appendix (see also Batra and Pattanaik, 1972).

(6) Condition $L$ reflects only a very small part of what a 'liberal', or a 'libertarian', is typically concerned with. Support for Condition $L$ in specific classes of choices will come even from those who would not be described as 'liberals'. (Even Joseph Stalin (1913), not especially known for his libertarian sympathies, wrote eloquently about group autonomy which involves similar problems of consistency *vis-à-vis* the Pareto principle.) While there are enormous differences in the conception of freedom in different philosophies, most social philosophies accept certain personal or group rights. The fact that unqualified use of the Pareto principle potentially threatens all such rights gives the conflict an extraordinary wide scope. This applies also to the so-called positive (as opposed to negative) freedoms, e.g., freedom from hunger, or right to work.

(7) While Blau's partial solution of the problem through weakening Condition $L$ to versions of 'modified liberalism' in the presence of 'meddlesome' preferences is illuminating, it seems to have the remarkable property of responding to meddlesomeness by ignoring the self-regarding, non-meddlesome part of the preference and making effective the non-self-regarding parts. The problem arises from Blau's determination not to weaken the Pareto principle. The same difficulty applies to Gibbard's interesting solution through weakening Condition $L$ by making the libertarian rights 'alienable', while keeping the Pareto principle unaffected. If everyone other than myself prefers $x$ to $y$, then the Pareto principle gives me the right to ensure the social choice of $x$ over $y$ by my preferring $x$ to $y$, and there exist situations in which the case for the 'alienation' of this right is at least as strong as that of the libertarian right. And this does require a violation of the Pareto principle.

(8) Nozick's ingenious solution of the conflict in terms of the domain of

social choice being constrained by considerations of individual rights (including Condition $L$), while the choice over that domain is made through a social ordering incorporating the Pareto principle, avoids the Paretian epidemic by systematic domain restrictions. There remains, however, the problem of making judgements about changes that lie outside that constraint, e.g., when a person's recognized rights are violated. These judgements re-introduce the conflict. The difficulty seems to arise, once again, from the reluctance to go against the Pareto relation in the social ordering itself.

(9) Farrell's first approach involves 'amendment' of individual preferences, so that if person $i$ prefers $x$ to $y$ over his assigned pair, then everyone else is 'deemed' to regard $x$ to be at least as good as $y$, and other changes are made that follow from consistency requirements. With the 'amended' preferences, there is no conflict between the Pareto principle and Condition $L$. Farrell is critical of this first approach, arising partly from his disapproval of the result that an actual Pareto preference for $x$ over $y$ may be changed to the opposite Pareto preference, with the amended preferences. (The procedure explored in Section 11 and in Appendix A5 avoids this and involves no *amendment* of the actual preferences, only taking a sub-relation of it, and I prefer it to Farrell's, but it must be pointed out that the two approaches are motivationally similar.) Farrell's second approach partitions the set of social states into 'socially equivalent' subsets on liberal grounds and then confines social choice theory to choosing between these subsets. If violation of personal rights (involving two points in a 'socially equivalent' subset) is, thereby, not to be described as socially inferior, this limits the scope of social choice theory rather arbitrarily.

(10) The attempted solutions seems to have been severely constrained by the unwillingness to drop the Pareto principle. I have tried to argue here that the Pareto principle, in the form in which it is used, is a prime candidate for rejection. A more general question concerns whether the set of individual preferences irrespective of the motivation underlying them is an adequate basis for social judgement involving issues such as liberty. I have tried to argue that it is not. I have argued elsewhere that, for social judgements involving issues of equity and justice, the informational framework of concentrating only on preference orderings is also inadequate (Sen, 1970a, Chapter 9; 1973). While those issues indicate the need for *interpersonal comparisons of welfare*, the discussion of liberty puts us in the direction of *motivations* that underlie the preferences. This question of the relevance of motivation underlying preferences has implications for the analytical framework used in the current social choice theory, and needless to say for welfare economics.

## APPENDIX   SOME FORMAL STATEMENTS AND PROOFS

### A1   *Introduction*

$X$ is the set of alternative social states, and each person $i$ has a complete preference ordering (reflexive, complete and transitive) $R_i$ over $X$, with $i = 1$, ..., $n$. It is assumed that there are at least two persons and at least three distinct social states in $X$. A collective choice rule $f$ specifies a reflexive ('weak') social preference relation $R$ for every $n$-tuple of individual orderings $\{R_i\}$—one ordering for each person in the community:

$$R = f(\{R_i\}). \tag{A1}$$

If $R$ must be an ordering, then $f$ is a 'social welfare function', SWF, in the sense of Arrow (1951). A weaker requirement is that $R$ must be reflexive, complete and *acyclic* (not necessarily transitive). This is necessary and sufficient for $R$ to generate a choice function defined over the class of all finite subsets of the set $X$, i.e., in each finite subset $S$ of $X$, the set $C(S)$ of $R$-greatest elements is non-empty (see Sen, 1970a, p. 16). A collective choice rule satisfying this requirement is called a 'social decision function', SDF, which is a slight broadening of SDF as defined in Sen (1970a, p. 52). Since the set of SWFs is a proper subset of the set of SDFs, the non-existence of any SDF satisfying a set of conditions will imply the non-existence of any SWF satisfying those conditions. (The converse is, of course, not true; e.g., there are SDFs satisfying the Arrow (1951) conditions but no such SWF.)

$P$ and $I$ stand respectively for the asymmetric and symmetric factors of $R$, i.e., for social 'strict preference' and 'indifference' respectively. Similarly, $P_i$ and $I_i$ are the asymmetric and symmetric factors of $R_i$.

The 'impossibility of the Paretian liberal' uses the following conditions.

*Condition U (unrestricted domain).*   The domain of $f$ includes all logically possible $n$-tuples $\{R_i\}$ of individual preference orderings over $X$.

*Condition P (weak Pareto principle).*   For any $x, y$ from $X$, if $x P_i y$ for all $i$, then $x P y$.

*Condition L\* (minimal libertarianism).*   There is at least one pair of persons decisive both ways over at least one pair of alternatives each; i.e., for each of them $i$, there is a pair of alternatives in $X$, which we may rechristen $(x_i, y_i)$, such that $x_i P_i y_i$ implies $x_i P y_i$, and $y_i P_i x_i$ implies $y_i P x_i$.

(T.1)   *There is no SDF satisfying Conditions U, P and L\*.*

For proof, see Sen (1970a, pp. 87–8) [see pp. 287–8 in this volume].

*Condition L (weak libertarianism).*   Everyone is decisive both ways over at least one pair of alternatives each.

(T.1.1)   *There is no SDF satisfying Conditions U, P and L.*

An immediate corollary of (T.1).

## A2   *The Paretian Epidemic and Related Results*

*Semidecisiveness.*   Person $J$ is semidecisive over an ordered pair $\{x, y\}$ if and only if for any $\{R_i\}$ in the domain of $f$, if $xP_Jy$, then $xRy$.

Decisiveness and semidecisiveness can be respectively weakened by making the effectiveness of person $J$ over $\{x, y\}$ conditional on some specified individual rankings over pairs *other than* $\{x, y\}$ without however restricting the ranking of anyone over $\{x, y\}$.

*Potential decisiveness and semidecisiveness.*   Person $J$ is potentially decisive (resp. potentially semidecisive) over an ordered pair $\{x, y\}$ if and only if for any $\{R_i\}$ in the domain of $f$ satisfying some specified restrictions on the rankings of pairs other than $\{x, y\}$, which leaves the rankings of $\{x, y\}$ by all $i \neq J$ completely free, if $xP_Jy$, then $xPy$ (resp. $xRy$).

Note that in the above definition $xPy$ (resp. $xRy$) is required to follow from $xP_Jy$ irrespective of the nature of the ranking of anyone else over $\{x, y\}$.

The 'Paretian epidemic' shows that, for an SDF with an unrestricted domain, the weak Pareto principle is sufficient to spread decisiveness over one pair of alternatives to all in the weaker form of potential semidecisiveness.

(T.2)   *For any social decision function satisfying U, the weak Pareto principle P implies that if any person J is decisive both ways over any one pair in X, then J is potentially semidecisive over every ordered pair in X.*

*Proof.*   Let $J$ be decisive both ways over $\{x, y\}$. Take any other pair $\{z, w\}$. There are three possibilities: (I) $x, y, z$ and $w$ are all distinct; (II) $\{z, w\}$ and $\{x, y\}$ have one element in common, and (III) $\{x, y\} = \{z, w\}$. The three cases are considered in turn.

*Case I.*   Let $J$ rank the four distinct states in the strict descending order: $z, x, y, w$. Let everyone else strictly prefer $z$ to $x$ and $y$ to $w$, leaving the ranking of all other pairs completely free. By the weak Pareto principle, $zPx$ and $yPw$. By $J$'s decisiveness over $\{x, y\}$, $xPy$. If now $wPz$, then there is a preference cycle, which is impossible since $f$ is an SDF with an unrestricted domain. Hence $zRw$, since $R$ must be complete. But only $J$'s preference over $\{z, w\}$ has been specified here, and since $zRw$ follows no matter how everyone else ranks $z$ vis-à-vis $w$, clearly $J$ is potentially semidecisive over $\{z, w\}$.

*Case II.*   There are four sub-cases. Consider first the case in which $x = z$. Let $J$ have a strict descending order, $x, y, w$, and let everyone else strictly prefer $y$ to $w$, leaving the ranking of $y$ and $w$ vis-à-vis $x$ open. Then, by the decisiveness of $J$ over $\{x, y\}$, $xPy$, and by the weak Pareto principle, $yPw$.

To prevent a preference cycle, $xRw$, i.e., $zRw$. This makes $J$ potentially semi-decisive over $\{z, w\}$. The sub-case of $y = z$ is identically covered since $J$'s decisiveness applies to both the ordered pairs $\{x, y\}$ and $\{y, x\}$. Next, let $y = w$. Consider now $J$'s strict descending order, $z, x, y$, and let everyone else prefer $z$ to $x$. By the decisiveness of $J$ over $\{x, y\}$, $xPy$, and by the weak Pareto principle, $zPx$. To prevent a preference cycle, $zRy$, i.e., $zRw$. Hence $J$ is potentially semidecisive over $\{z, w\}$. The remaining sub-case of $x = w$ is covered similarly.

*Case III.* Finally, if $\{x, y\}$ and $\{z, w\}$ are the same pairs, then the implication is trivial since decisiveness over $\{x, y\}$ both ways must imply potential semidecisiveness over the ordered pair $\{z, w\}$, which completes the proof.

A corollary of the Paretian epidemic (T.2) is immediate.

(T.2.1)    *For any social decision function satisfying U, the weak Pareto principle implies that if anyone J is decisive both ways over a pair of alternatives, then no subset of individuals which does not include J can be decisive over any ordered pair whatsoever.*

Note that (T.2.1) rules out, *inter alia*, any person other than $J$ being decisive anywhere at all. Thus (T.1) follows from (T.2.1) and, therefore, from (T.2).

If quasi-transitivity of social preference (i.e., transitivity of strict $P$) is required, the spread of decisiveness of $J$ is more exacting.

(T.3)    *For any social decision function satisfying U and yielding quasi-transitive P, the weak Pareto principle P implies that, if any person J is decisive both ways over any one pair in X, then J is potentially decisive over every ordered pair of alternatives from X.*

The proof is omitted here, since it is very similar to that of (T.2); with quasi-transitivity $zPx$, $xPy$ and $yPw$ together imply $zPw$, and $zPy$ and $yPw$ together imply $zPw$.

None of the results so far invokes Arrow's much-debated condition of 'independence of irrelevant alternatives'.

*Condition I (independence of irrelevant alternatives).*    The restriction $R^{x,y}$ of social preference $R$ over any pair $\{x, y\}$ is a function only of the $n$-tuple of restrictions $R_i^{x,y}$ of $R_i$ over $\{x, y\}$: $R^{x,y} = f^{x,y}(\{R_i^{x,y}\})$.

If this condition is imposed additionally, (T.2) and (T.3) transform into the following theorems (cf. Arrow, 1963, Theorem 2, pp. 97–100; Sen, 1970a, Lemma 3*a; Blau and Deb, 1976, Section VII). Decisiveness over an *ordered* pair is sufficient for (T.5) but not for (T.4).

(T.4)    *For any social decision function satisfying U, the weak Pareto principle P and the independence of irrelevant alternatives I together imply that if any person J is decisive both ways over any pair in X, then J is semidecisive over every ordered pair of alternatives from X.*

(T.5)   *For any social decision function satisfying U and yielding quasi-transitive R, the weak Pareto principle P and the independence of irrelevant alternatives I together imply that if any person J is decisive over any ordered pair of alternatives from X, then J is decisive over every ordered pair from X.*

To summarize, for a social decision function with unrestricted domain, if $J$ is decisive (both ways in the first three cases) over some pair, then:

(T.2)   $P$ (weak Pareto principle) $\Rightarrow$ $J$ potentially semidecisive everywhere

(T.3)   $P$ + social quasi-transitivity $\Rightarrow$ $J$ potentially decisive everywhere

(T.4)   $P$ + independence of irrelevant alternatives $\Rightarrow$ $J$ semidecisive everywhere

(T.5)   $P$ + both $\Rightarrow$ $J$ a dictator.

(T.2) is our *pure* 'Paretian epidemic', while (T.5) is the central lemma for Arrow's General Possibility Theorem (see Lemma 3*a in Sen, 1970a), and the others are intermediate cases.


### A3   *Libertarianism and Federalism*

While (T.3), (T.4) and (T.5) involve strengthening of the conditions imposed in the pure 'Paretian epidemic' (T.2), the 'impossibility of the Paretian liberal' (T.1) follows immediately from (T.2) itself. Another direct consequence of (T.2) is the impossibility of combining Paretianism with what Batra and Pattanaik (1972) have called 'minimal federalism'.

*Condition F\** (*minimal federalism*).   There are at least two disjoint subsets of the community which are each decisive both ways over at least one pair of distinct alternatives each; i.e., if everyone in such a subset $J$ prefers $x$ to $y$ (resp. $y$ to $x$) when $\{x, y\}$ is the assigned pair of $J$, then $xPy$ (resp. $yPx$).

(T.6)   *There is no social decision function satisfying Conditions U, P and F\*.*

This follows from (T.2) by reinterpreting $xP_Jy$ to mean that everyone in the subset $J$ strictly prefers $x$ to $y$. (It may be worth remarking that not only (T.2) but also (T.3), (T.4) and (T.5) hold under this reinterpretation of $J$.)


### A4   *Non-Binary Social Choice*

The focus is now shifted from SDFs (with social choices being expressed in the form of a binary relation of social preference $R$) to 'functional collective choice rules' FCCR (see Sen, 1976). An FCCR specifies for each $n$-tuple of individual preference orderings $\{R_i\}$ a choice function $C(.)$ for the society yielding a non-empty subset $C(S)$ of $S$ for any non-empty subset $S$ of $X$:

$$C(\cdot) = \phi(\{R_i\}). \tag{A2}$$

Conditions $U$, $P$, $L$, $L^*$ and $F^*$ may now be reformulated for an FCCR. The wording of $U$ may be kept unchanged replacing $f$ by $\phi$ and denoting the condition thus reformulated as $\hat{U}$. The other conditions may be redefined by interpreting $xPy$ as $y$ is not socially chosen when $x$ is available, i.e., for any $S$, if $x \in S$, then $y \notin C(S)$. These 'non-binary' conditions are respectively denoted as $\hat{P}$, $\hat{L}$, $\hat{L}^*$ and $\hat{F}^*$. The 'impossibility of the Paretian liberal', (T.1), now readily translates to the non-binary framework (see Sen, 1970a, pp. 81–2), and so does the impossibility of the Paretian federalism, (T.6) (see Batra and Pattanaik, 1972).

(T.7)  *There is no functional collective choice rule satisfying Conditions $\hat{U}$, $\hat{P}$ and $\hat{L}^*$ (or $\hat{F}^*$).*

*Proof.* Let 1 and 2 be two persons (resp. two disjoint subsets of individuals) with assigned pairs $\{x, y\}$ and $\{z, w\}$ respectively. If the four alternatives are all distinct, consider the following preferences of persons 1 and 2 (resp. unanimous preferences of groups 1 and 2) respectively in strict descending order: (1) $w, x, y, z$; and (2) $y, z, w, x$. Let everyone else prefer $w$ to $x$ and also $y$ to $z$. By $L^*$, neither $y$ nor $w$ should belong to $C(\{x, y, z, w\})$. By $P$, neither $x$ nor $z$ should belong to it. Since $(C\{x, y, z, w\})$ must then be empty, the FCCR violates $U$. The cases of one alternative in common between $\{x, y\}$ and $\{z, w\}$ are handled similarly.

The proof makes it clear that the impossibility results will hold even if the definition of an FCCR were weakened to demand non-empty choice sets for only 3-element and 4-element subsets of $X$, without demanding anything about choices from subsets of other cardinality.

Batra and Pattanaik (1972) have pointed out an alternative way of deriving these impossibility results with weaker requirements of libertarianism and federalism, but with an additional condition of consistency of social choice, viz.:

*BP (Batra–Pattanaik condition of choice consistency).*  If $\{x\} = C(\{x, y\})$, then for any $S$, if $x \in S$, then $y \in C(S)$ implies that $x \in C(S)$.

With this weak consistency condition, $\hat{L}^*$ and $\hat{F}^*$ can be weakened by redefining $L^*$ and $F^*$ through interpreting $xPy$ as $x$ being uniquely chosen over the *pair* $\{x, y\}$. These conditions may be called $\hat{\hat{L}}^*$ and $\hat{\hat{F}}^*$ respectively.

(T.8)  *There is no functional collective choice rule satisfying Conditions $\hat{U}$, $\hat{P}$, BP and $\hat{\hat{L}}^*$ (or $\hat{\hat{F}}^*$).*

The proof of (T.7) translates readily for (T.8). With the postulated preferences $x$ and $z$ do not belong to $C(\{x, y, z, w\})$ in view of $\hat{P}$. By $\hat{\hat{L}}^*$ (or $\hat{\hat{F}}^*$), $\{x\} = C(\{x, y\})$ and $\{z\} = C(\{z, w\})$. By $BP$, $y$ or $w$ can belong to $C(\{x, y, z, w\})$

only if $x$ or $z$ respectively does. But neither does. Hence $C(\{x, y, z, w\})$ is empty.

## A5    Conditional Pareto Principles

A weakening of the weak Pareto principle is now examined. Let $\bar{R}_i$ be a sub-relation of individual preference $R_i$ reflecting the parts of his preference ordering $R_i$ that person $i$ wants to count in social choice. $\bar{P}_i$ and $\bar{I}_i$ are the asymmetric and symmetric factors of $\bar{R}_i$ respectively.

*Condition PC (conditional weak Pareto principle).*    For any $x$, $y$ in $X$, if $x\bar{P}_i y$ for all $i$, then $xPy$.

*Condition PC\* (conditional strong Pareto principle).*    For any $x$, $y$ in $X$, if $x\bar{R}_i y$ for all $i$, then $xRy$, and if furthermore, for some person $i$, $x\bar{P}_i y$, then $xPy$.

Next the problem of a consistent assignment of rights to avoid problems of internal consistency discussed by Gibbard (1974).

*Consistent rights assignment.*    Each person $i$ is assigned a non-empty set $D_i$ of pairs such that no matter how they order them, there is an ordering $T$ of $X$ of which each $i$'s preference over each $\{x, y\}$ in his $D_i$ is a sub-relation.

*Condition $L+$.*    For any consistent assignment of rights, if $\{x, y\}$ is in $D_i$, then $xP_i y$ implies $xPy$.

The concept of 'respecting' other people's rights is defined in the framework of a consistent assignment.

*Respecting rights.*    For any consistent rights assignment a person $j$ respects the rights of others if and only if for each $n$-tuple of individual preference orderings $\{R_i\}$, person $j$ wants a sub-relation $\bar{R}_j$ of his preference ordering $R_j$ to count such that there exists an ordering $T_j$ of which $\bar{R}_j$ is a sub-relation and so is each $i$'s preference over each $\{x, y\}$ in $D_i$.

(T.9)    *There exists a social decision function satisfying Conditions U, $L+$ and PC\* if at least one person in the community respects the rights of others.*

*Proof.*    Suppose to the contrary person $j$ respects the rights of others but still the SDF generates a strict social preference cycle over some subset $S$ with $xP\mu(x)$ for all $x$ in $S$ for some one-to-one correspondence from $S$ to $S$. Let the subset $M$ of $S$ represent those $x$ for which $xP\mu(x)$ follows from the conditional strong Pareto principle $PC\*$. Given consistent rights assignment implied in $L+$, $M$ is non-empty. Since the Pareto relation is acyclic, $M$ must be a *proper* subset of $S$. And $xP\mu(x)$ for all $x$ in $(S-M)$ must be due to $L+$. Consider now

$\bar{R}_j$. By the definition of $PC^*$, $x\bar{R}_j\mu(x)$ for all $x$ in $M$. Since $j$ respects the rights of others, there is an ordering $T_j$ which incorporates $\bar{R}_j$ as well as $xP\mu(x)$ for all $x$ in $(S-M)$. This is a contradiction; the strict cyclicity of $P$ over $S$ must imply the intransitivity of such a $T_j$.

Note that (T.9) can be proved also constructively by showing that, from any ordering $T_j$ (incorporating $\bar{R}_j$ and the strict preference $P_i$ for each $\{x, y\}$ in $D_i$ for each $i$), an acyclic, complete and reflexive relation $P$ can be constructed by strengthening to $P$ those $\bar{I}_j$ which go with a strict Pareto preference according to $PC^*$.

Note also that this method of accommodating libertarian rights by restricting the Pareto principle can also be used for the non-binary framework discussed in Section A4.

## References

Arrow, K. J. (1951): *Social Choice and Individual Values* (2nd edn 1963) (New York: Wiley).

Batra, R. N. and Pattanaik, P. K. (1972): On some suggestions for having non-binary social choice functions. *Theory and Decision*, 3, 1–11.

Bernholz, P. (1974): Is a Paretian liberal really impossible? *Public Choice*, 19, 99–107.

_____ (1975): Is a Paretian liberal really impossible: a rejoinder. *Public Choice*, 23, 69–73.

Binmore, K. (1974): Social choice and parties (mimeographed). London School of Economics. [Revised version published later in *Review of Economic Studies*, 43 (1976), 459–464.]

Blair, D. H., Bordes, G., Kelly, J. S. and Suzumura, K. (1976): Impossibility theorems without collective rationality. *Journal of Economic Theory*, 13, 361–79.

Blau, J. H. (1957): The existence of a social welfare function. *Econometrica*, 25, 302–13.

_____ (1971): Arrow's theorem with weak independence. *Economica*, 38, 413–20.

_____ (1975): Liberal values and independence. *Review of Economic Studies*, 42, 395–402.

Blau, J. H. and Deb, R. (1976): Social decision functions and the veto, mimeographed. [Revised version published later in *Econometrica*, 45 (1977), 871–9.]

Bordes, G. (1976): Consistency, rationality and collective choice. *Review of Economic Studies*, 43, 447–57.

Broome, J. (1974): Consumer sovereignty. Birkbeck College Discussion Paper No. 32. [Revised version, 'Choice and Value in Economics', published later in *Oxford Economic Papers*, 30 (1978).]

Campbell, D. E. (1972): A collective choice rule satisfying Arrow's five conditions in practice. In *Theory and Application of Collective Choice Rule*, Institute for Quantitative Analysis of Social and Economic Policy, Working Paper No. 7206, University of Toronto.

_____ (1975): Freedom of choice and social choice (mimeographed).

Deb, R. (1974): *Rational Choice and Cyclical Preferences*. Ph.D. dissertation, London University.

Farrell, M. J. (1976): Liberalism in the theory of social choice. *Review of Economic Studies,* **43**, 3–10.

Fine, B. J. (1975): Individual liberalism in a Paretian society. *Journal of Political Economy,* **83**, 1277–82.

Fishburn, P. C. (1973): *The Theory of Social Choice* (Princeton: University Press).

Gibbard, A. (1974): A Pareto-consistent libertarian claim. *Journal of Economic Theory,* **7**, 388–410.

Gintis, H. (1972): Alienation and power. *Review of Radical Political Economics,* **4**, 1–34.

Gramsci, A. (1971): *Selections from the Prison Notebooks* (London: Lawrence & Wishart).

Hammond, P. (1974): On dynamic liberalism (mimeographed). Australian National University and the University of Essex.

Hansson, B. (1969): Group preferences. *Econometrica,* **37**, 50–4.

Hayek, F. A. (1960): *The Constitution of Liberty* (London: Routledge & Kegan Paul).

Hicks, J. R. (1956): *A Revision of Demand Theory* (Oxford: Clarendon Press).

Hillinger, C. and Lapham, V. (1971): The impossibility of a Paretian liberal: comment by two who are unreconstructed. *Journal of Political Economy,* **79**, 1403–5.

Jeffrey, R. C. (1974): Preferences among preferences. *Journal of Philosophy,* **71**, 377–91.

Karni, E. (1974a): Individual liberty, the Pareto principle and the possibility of social choice function. Working Paper No. 2, The Foerder Institute for Economic Research, Tel-Aviv University.

⎯⎯⎯ (1974b): Collective rationality, unanimity and liberal ethics (mimeographed), Tel-Aviv University. [Revised version published later in *Review of Economic Studies,* **45** (1978), 571–4.]

Kelly, J. S. (1976a): The impossibility of a just liberal. *Economica,* **43**, 67–76.

⎯⎯⎯ (1976b): Rights exercising and a Pareto-consistent libertarian claim. *Journal of Economic Theory,* **13**, 138–53.

Mill, J. S. (1859): *On Liberty.* Reprinted in M. Warnock (ed.) *Utilitarianism* (London: Fontana).

Ng, Y. K. (1971): The possibility of a Paretian liberal: impossibility theorems and cardinal utility. *Journal of Political Economy,* **79**, 1397–1402.

Nozick, R. (1968): Moral complications and moral structures. *Natural Law Forum,* **13**, 1–50.

⎯⎯⎯ (1973): Distributive justice. *Philosophy and Public Affairs,* **3**, 45–126.

⎯⎯⎯ (1974): *Anarchy, State and Utopia* (Oxford: Blackwell).

Osborne, D. K. (1975): On liberalism and the Pareto principle. *Journal of Political Economy,* **83**, 1283–8.

Peacock, A. T. and Rowley, C. K. (1972): Welfare economics and the public regulation of natural monopoly. *Journal of Political Economy,* **80**, 476–90.

Plott, C. R. (1973): Path independence, rationality, and social choice. *Econometrica,* **41**, 1075–91.

Ramachandra, V. S. (1972): Liberalism, non-binary choice and Pareto principle. *Theory and Decision,* **3**, 49–54.

Rowley, C. K. and Peacock, A. T. (1975): *Welfare Economics: A Liberal Restatement* (London: Martin Robertson).

Schwartz, T. (1970): On the possibility of rational policy evaluation. *Theory and Decision,* **1**, 89–106.

Seidl, C. (1975): On liberal values. *Zeitschrift für Nationalökonomie,* **35,** 257–92.

Sen, A. K. (1967): The nature and classes of prescriptive judgements. *Philosophical Quarterly,* **17,** 46–62.

____ (1970a): *Collective Choice and Social Welfare.* San Francisco: Holden-Day, and Edinburgh: Oliver and Boyd. [Reprinted Amsterdam: North-Holland.]

____ (1970b): The impossibility of a Paretian liberal. *Journal of Political Economy,* **78,** 152–7. [Essay 13 in this volume.]

____ (1973): *On Economic Inequality* (Oxford: Clarendon Press and New York: Norton).

____ (1974): Choice, orderings and morality. In *Practical Reason* (Proceedings of the Bristol Conference on Practical Reason, 1972) (S. Körner, ed.) (Oxford: Blackwell). [Essay 3 in this volume.]

____ (1975): Is a Paretian liberal really impossible: a reply. *Public Choice,* **21,** 111–13.

____ (1976): Social choice theory: a re-examination. *Econometrica,* **45,** 53–89. [Essay 8 in this volume.]

Stalin, J. (1913): Marxism and the national question. English translation in *The Essential Stalin* (B. Franklin, ed.) (London: Croom Helm).

Suppes, P. (1966): Some formal models of grading principles, *Synthèse,* **6,** 284–306. Reprinted in his *Studies in the Methodology and Foundations of Science* (Dordrecht: Reidel).

Suzumura, K. (1976): Remarks on the theory of collective choice. *Economica,* **43,** 381–90.

Williams, B. (1973): A critique of utilitarianism. In *Utilitarianism: For and Against* (J. J. C. Smart and B. Williams), pp. 77–150 (Cambridge: University Press).

# 15

# Personal Utilities and Public Judgements: or What's Wrong with Welfare Economics?

Wassily Leontief has succinctly summarized the normative properties 'on which something like a general consensus of opinion seems to exist' in the formal discussion of public economic policies:

> In the discussion of public economic policies—in contrast to the analysis of individual choice—the normative character of the problem has been clearly and generally recognized. Here the mathematical approach has crystallized the analysis around the axiomatic formulation of the (desirable or conventional) properties of the 'social welfare function'. Social utility is usually postulated as a function of the ordinally described personal utility levels attained by each of the individual members of the society in question.
>
> The only other property on which something like a general consensus opinion seems to exist is that 'the social welfare is increased whenever at least one of the individual utilities on which it depends is raised while none is reduced'. (Leontief, 1966, p. 27)

A critical examination of these properties is undertaken in this paper, and it is argued that they have played remarkably restrictive roles in traditional welfare economics by imposing—directly or indirectly—severe constraints

For useful comments on the earlier draft I would like to thank A. M. Ahsan, Sudhir Anand, Chuck Blackorby, James Buchanan, David Donaldson, F. Forte, Peter Hammond, Julius Margolis, Dennis Mueller, Mancur Olson and Gordon Tullock, among others. I also take this opportunity of expressing my debt to Kenneth Arrow, Maurice Dobb, and John Rawls, for stimulating discussions over a great many years on the subject-matter of this paper.

From *Economic Journal*, **89** (September 1979), 537–58. Based on an invited paper presented at the 34th Congress of the International Institute of Public Finance, 1978.

on the types of information that may be used in making social welfare judgements. In the process, Arrow's impossibility theorem and related results are reinterpreted in the informational perspective. While a good many technical issues are covered, the presentation is entirely informal, and no special familiarity with the technical literature has been presupposed.

## 1   The Favoured Properties

The first property identified by Leontief is made up of three distinct parts, and it is best to present it in a factorized way.

*Welfarism.*   Social welfare is a function of personal utility levels, so that any two social states must be ranked entirely on the basis of personal utilities in the respective states (irrespective of the non-utility features of the states).

*Ordinalism.*   Only the ordinal properties of the individual utility functions are to be used in social welfare judgements.

*Non-comparable utilities.*   The social welfare ranking must be independent of the way the utilities of different individuals compare with each other.[1]

The second property referred to by Leontief is simply the more demanding version of the principle of Pareto preference. For all pairs of states $x$, $y$, the following is required to hold:

*Pareto Preference Rule.*   If everyone has at least as much utility in $x$ as in $y$, and if someone has more utility in $x$ than in $y$, then $x$ is socially better than $y$.

Welfarism is a strong version of the condition of 'neutrality' used in the collective choice literature (see Sen, 1970; 1977b), and demands that the social ranking of any pair of states be *neutral* to the non-utility features of the states, i.e., the concentration must be exclusively on the utility information about the states. Combining welfarism with the Pareto preference rule would be natural, since social welfare—if a function of individual utilities only— should be expected to be an *increasing* function of these utilities.

*Pareto-inclusive Welfarism.*   Social welfare is an increasing function of personal utility levels, thus satisfying both welfarism and the Pareto preference rule.[2]

---

1. For more formal statements of these conditions and related ones, see Sen (1970; 1977b).

2. Note that Paretianism and welfarism are independent of each other in the sense that either can be satisfied without the other. However, there are analytical links between the two *in the presence of* other conditions (see Section 2 below). Also the two properties are closely allied in spirit, and it is difficult to justify demanding welfarism to be satisfied (making social welfare a function of individual utilities only) without requiring that social welfare should respond positively to individual utilities. See also Section 7 of this paper.

Utilitarianism—the classic approach to welfare economics—satisfies Pareto-inclusive welfarism, and in the usual applications is combined with the use of interpersonally comparable and cardinal individual utilities. It was the disquiet about interpersonal comparability and cardinality of utilities (expressed in such works as Robbins's (1932) methodological critique) that led to the addition of ordinalism and non-comparable utilities as further features to be satisfied. The so-called 'new welfare economics' accepted all these properties as legitimate. Social choice theory, pioneered by Arrow (1951), also accepted these conditions (though it used somewhat weaker versions of the Pareto principle and welfarism). The welfare economic propositions in standard general equilibrium theory (see Debreu, 1959; Arrow and Hahn, 1971), concentrating on Pareto optimality and related criteria, have also no need to go beyond a Pareto-inclusive welfarist framework with ordinal and non-comparable utilities. The choice of problems and frameworks reflects the 'general consensus of opinion' on the normative properties that Wassily Leontief has identified.[3]

## 2   *Arrow's Impossibility Theorem: an Informational Interpretation*

Arrow's impossibility theorem can be shown to be closely related to the nature of the informational restrictions implicit in these conditions. In this section this relationship will be brought out and the proof of the theorem will be set up in a way that makes the informational constraints transparent.

Arrow defined a social welfare function (SWF) as a function that determines one social welfare ordering $R$ of the set of social states for every combination of individual utility orderings of that set—one ordering for each person. In confining attention to the combination of individual orderings taken on their own, both ordinalism and non-comparable utilities are incorporated in the very conception of a SWF. In addition another general structural condition was used, namely *unrestricted domain*, so that the domain of the SWF was required to include every logically possible combination of individual orderings. Also the set of individuals is taken to be finite and the number of distinct social states at least three.

Arrow invoked a weak version of the Pareto principle.

*Weak Pareto Principle.*   If everyone has more utility in $x$ than in $y$, then $x$ is socially better than $y$.

In addition, he imposed two other conditions. The condition of *non-dictatorship* demands that there should be no one such that whenever he strictly prefers any $x$ to any $y$, then invariably $x$ is regarded as socially better than $y$. And finally, there was the much-debated condition of independence.

---

3. See also Graaff (1957) and Little (1957) for excellent critical accounts of the traditional approaches to welfare economics.

*Independence of Irrelevant Alternatives.* The social ranking of any pair of states must be the same as long as the individual utility information about the pair remains the same, which, in the special case of ordinal non-comparable utilities, amounts to individual orderings over the pair remaining the same.[4]

Arrow's 'impossibility theorem' establishes that there is no SWF satisfying all these four conditions.[5] I would like to argue that the impossibility can be seen as resulting from combining a version of welfarism ruling out the use of non-utility information with making the utility information remarkably poor (particularly in ruling out interpersonal utility comparisons). While the poverty of the utility information is part of the basic framework explicitly invoked, ruling out the use of non-utility information is the result of the combination of conditions used. Welfarism implies independence of irrelevant alternatives, but is not implied by it. However, the conditions of independence, weak Pareto principle and unrestricted domain put together imply a weak version of welfarism. Any SWF satisfying these three conditions may be called an 'Arrovian' social welfare function.

*Strict-ranking Welfarism.* If individual utility rankings are strict, then any two social states must be ranked entirely on the basis of personal utilities in the respective states.[6]

In fact, if the weak Pareto principle is replaced by the 'Pareto indifference rule' (demanding that personal indifference by all must together imply social indifference), then the three conditions (i.e., unrestricted domain, indepen-

---

4. I have defined here the condition of independence rather less demandingly than Arrow both (i) in permitting the use of cardinality and interpersonal comparability if such information is available, and (ii) in making no demands on choices over sets larger than pairs. This permits the use of this condition in frameworks other than Arrow's (e.g., to derive utilitarianism), which have a richer informational base, and also in cases where binariness of social choice is not required; see Sen (1977a, b). With Arrow's conditions (in particular, ordinalism, non-comparable utilities, unrestricted domain, and binariness of social choice) imposed additionally, this weaker version ends up delivering as much as Arrow's version in the special case of Arrow's framework. Binariness of social choice is not, however, needed for Arrow's impossibility theorem, see Sen (1977a), pp. 71–5, 81 [pages 178–83, 188–9, in this volume; see also pages 16–18].

5. This version of the theorem is to be found in Arrow (1963). The earlier version presented in Arrow (1951) had a formal error, detected by Blau (1957). The treatment of the Arrow impossibility result outlined here derives much also from Blau (1972). For critical surveys of various versions of the Arrow theorem, see Murakami (1968), Fishburn (1973), Pattanaik (1979), Plott (1976), and Kelly (1978).

6. This may appear to be substantially more demanding than the 'neutrality' condition used by Blau (1972) as an intermediate product in establishing the impossibility result, especially since Blau confined his attention not merely to strict individual preferences but also to *strict social preferences*—a constraint not used in the definition of 'strict-ranking welfarism'. However, as the proof of (T.1) makes clear, the case of social indifference is covered as a consequence of the case with strict social preference.

dence and the Pareto indifference rule) will imply welfarism fully.[7] But even the weak Pareto principle is adequate to imply strict-ranking welfarism, when combined with unrestricted domain and independence (as in the Arrow framework). This is established below for 'Arrovian' social welfare functions with individual utilities ordinal and non-comparable. In this framework strict-ranking welfarism demands that if everyone's ranking of $x$ vis-à-vis $y$ in one case is the same as his or her ranking of $a$ vis-à-vis $b$ in another, then the social ranking of $x$ vis-à-vis $y$ in the first case must be the same as the social ranking of $a$ vis-à-vis $b$ respectively in the second. Let the community be partitioned into two groups $M$ and $N$, with everyone in $M$ preferring $x$ to $y$ in case $\alpha$ and $a$ to $b$ in case $\beta$, while everyone in $N$ prefers $y$ to $x$ in case $\alpha$ and $b$ to $a$ in case $\beta$.[8] (Cases $\alpha$ and $\beta$ may or may not represent the same set of utility orderings over the whole set of social states in the two cases.) Strict-ranking welfarism demands that if $x$ is socially preferred to $y$ in case $\alpha$, then $a$ is socially preferred to $b$ in case $\beta$; similarly if $y$ is socially preferred to $x$ in the first case then $b$ is socially preferred to $a$ in the second. Furthermore, strict-ranking welfarism also demands that if $x$ is socially indifferent to $y$ in case $\alpha$, then $a$ is socially indifferent to $b$ in case $\beta$. The nature of the social states and their non-utility features should not make any difference to social preference as long as the utility information about them (in this case, the personal strict utility rankings) is the same.

In demonstrating this we do not need the full force of transitivity of social preference. Transitivity of social *strict* preference (but not necessarily of indifference) is enough; this is called quasi-transitivity.

(T.1) *Establishing Strict-ranking Welfarism.    For all 'Arrovian' social welfare functions (even with transitivity of social preference relaxed to quasi-transitivity), strict-ranking welfarism must hold.*

Consider the postulated preference patterns $\alpha$ and $\beta$, outlined above. First, the case of strict social preference is taken up, postulating—without loss of generality—that $x$ is socially preferred to $y$ in case $\alpha$. It has to be shown that $a$ is socially preferred to $b$ in case $\beta$. The proof proceeds by considering a third

7. See Guha (1972) and d'Aspremont and Gevers (1977), dealing respectively with the informational framework of individual non-comparable orderings and a more general framework covering richer informational availability as well. Guha's axioms were, however, too weak since he took the Pareto principle in the 'weak' form which did not cover the case of individual indifference (see Blau (1976)), while d'Aspremont and Gevers took axioms that were a bit too strong since they assumed the 'strong' Pareto principle whereas the Pareto indifference rule is sufficient for their result—and indeed for their own proof (see Sen, 1977b, and also Roberts, 1978).

8. The word 'preference' has some ambiguity since it can be defined in different ways which are not necessarily equivalent (see Sen, 1977c). Here the interpretation intended is that of personal utility, in the sense of a person's conception of his own well-being (see also Sections 3 and 7 below). The theorems, however, apply to other interpretations as well if the conditions are correspondingly redefined.

set of inaividual preferences $\gamma$—admissible thanks to unrestricted domain—as follows (in descending order of preference):

| Group M | Group N |
|:---:|:---:|
| a | y |
| x | b |
| y | a |
| b | x |

Since everyone's utility ranking of $x$ vis-à-vis $y$ in this regime is the same as in the $\alpha$ regime, by independence of irrelevant alternatives $x$ must be judged to be socially better than $y$ in the $\gamma$ regime, as in the $\alpha$ regime. By the weak Pareto principle, in the $\gamma$ regime, $a$ is socially better than $x$, and also $y$ is socially better than $b$. Thus, by quasi-transitivity of social preference (i.e., transitivity of strict social preference), $a$ is socially better than $b$ in the $\gamma$ regime. Since the utility information regarding $a$ vis-à-vis $b$ in the $\gamma$ and $\beta$ regimes is identical, by independence it follows that in the $\beta$ regime too $a$ must be preferred to $b$. This covers the case of *strict* social preference,[9] leaving us only with the case in which $x$ is socially indifferent to $y$ in the $\alpha$ regime.

In the indifference case, it would have to be established that $a$ is indifferent to $b$ in the $\beta$ regime. Suppose not. Then $a$ is preferred to $b$, or vice versa, and let it be the former, without loss of generality. If $a$ is preferred to $b$ in the $\beta$ regime, then by the above proof of strict-ranking welfarism in the case of *strict* social preference, it follows that $x$ must be socially preferred to $y$ in the $\alpha$ regime, since the utility information regarding $x$ vis-à-vis $y$ is the same in the $\alpha$ regime as that regarding $a$ vis-à-vis $b$, respectively, in the $\beta$ regime. But this contradicts the postulation that $x$ and $y$ are socially indifferent in the $\alpha$ regime. And that establishes strict-ranking welfarism in the case of social indifference as well.

The effect of (T.1) is to combine the poverty of the utility information with an embargo on the use of non-utility information. This restricts the class of social welfare rules to a very narrow group. The requirement of completeness rules out such partial procedures as the Pareto ranking being the only method of social judgement. The requirement of consistency in the form of transitivity of social preference rules out such procedures as the method of

9. This is not strictly correct, since we have not covered the case in which $x$, $y$, $a$ and $b$ are *not* all distinct. The same strategy of proof, however, applies in this case too. Take, for example, the case in which $x$ and $a$ are the same. Assume $\gamma$ regime preferences as the following. For all members of $M$: $a(= x)$ preferred to $y$ and that preferred to $b$; for all members of $N$: $y$ preferred to $b$ and that to $a(= x)$. Hence in the $\gamma$ regime: $a$ is socially preferred to $y$ (by independence) and $y$ to $b$ (by weak Pareto principle), and thus $a$ socially preferred to $b$ (by quasi-transitivity). By independence, $a$ is preferred to $b$ in the $\beta$ regime also. The basic strategy is the combination of such arguments; see Arrow (1963), Blau (1972), or Sen (1970, chapter 3*).

majority ranking. We would be left with nothing other than dictatorial rules. This is demonstrated now.

Define a group $M$ of persons as 'almost decisive' over some ordered pair $x$, $y$, if and only if $x$ is socially preferred to $y$ whenever everyone in group $M$ strictly prefers $x$ to $y$ while everyone not in group $M$ strictly prefers $y$ to $x$. The group $M$ is called 'decisive' over $x$, $y$, if and only if $x$ is socially preferred to $y$ whenever everyone in $M$ strictly prefers $x$ to $y$, *no matter what others prefer.*[10]

(T.2) *Irrelevance of Opposition. For all 'Arrovian' social welfare functions (even with transitivity of social preference relaxed to quasi-transitivity), if any group is almost decisive over some ordered pair of states, it is decisive over that ordered pair of states, i.e., it does not need to be opposed to win.*

Let group $M$ be almost decisive over $x$, $y$. To show that it is fully decisive over the pair $x$, $y$, postulate the following preference combination: everyone in $M$ prefers $x$ to some third alternative $z$ and that to $y$, while everyone not in $M$ prefers $z$ to both $x$ and $y$, which can be ranked in any way whatsoever vis-à-vis each other. By (T.1) $M$ is almost decisive over $x$, $z$, and hence $x$ is socially preferred to $z$. By the weak Pareto principle, $z$ is socially preferred to $y$. By quasi-transitivity of social preference, $x$ is socially preferred to $y$, and that is so irrespective of how those who are not in $M$ rank $x$ vis-à-vis $y$. Thus (T.2).

By virtue of (T.1) and (T.2), there is no difference between a group being almost decisive over some pair and being fully decisive over all pairs. Call such a group a decisive group.

(T.3) *Irrelevance of Support. For all 'Arrovian' social welfare functions, in any decisive group containing more than one person there is a subgroup that is decisive without the support of the rest.*

Let $M$ be a decisive group containing more than one person. Partition $M$ into two subgroups $M^1$ and $M^2$. Let the combination of preferences be the following.

| Subgroup $M^1$ | Subgroup $M^2$ | Rest (if any) |
|:---:|:---:|:---:|
| $x$ | $y$ | $z$ |
| $y$ | $z$ | $x$ |
| $z$ | $x$ | $y$ |

10. The simple point that being 'decisive' is stronger than (i.e., implies but is not implied by) being 'almost decisive' seems occasionally to pose difficulty for intuitive understanding, since winning against opposition might appear to be stronger than winning whether or not opposed. But obviously this is not so since the case of winning whether or not opposed includes, *inter alia*, the case of winning when opposed.

By the decisiveness of $M$ (that is, of $M^1$ and $M^2$ taken together), $y$ is socially preferred to $z$. Hence by the completeness and the transitivity of social preference, *either $y$ is socially preferred to $x$, or $x$ is at least as good as $y$* which is preferred to $z$, hence $x$ is socially preferred to $z$. If the former, the subgroup $M^2$ is almost decisive over $y$, $x$. If the latter, then subgroup $M^1$ is almost decisive over $x$, $z$. In either case, by (T.1) and (T.2) some proper subset of group $M$ must be fully decisive over every pair—winning without the need of the support of the rest of group $M$.

*Arrow's Impossibility Theorem.*    There is no non-dictatorial 'Arrovian' social welfare function, i.e., there is no SWF satisfying unrestricted domain, weak Pareto principle, independence of irrelevant alternatives and non-dictatorship.

*Proof.*    By the weak Pareto principle, the group of all persons is decisive. By virtue of (T.3) it is possible to go on reducing the decisive group as long as it contains more than one person. Since the set of individuals is finite, we must in this way arrive at one person being decisive over all pairs, i.e., being a dictator. And that contradicts the non-dictatorship condition. (*QED.*)

To take an over-all view of the proof, (T.1) eliminates any essential use of non-utility information (such as the nature of the social states), adding to the informational penury incorporated in the conditions, explicitly, in the form of poor utility information (non-comparable individual utility orderings). (T.2) and (T.3) capitalize on the fact that we are—by virtue of this total informational poverty—confined to social welfare rules of very simple kinds, e.g., majority rule, dictatorship, etc. Given that, the requirements of completeness and transitivity of social preference force us to go relentlessly in the direction of recognizing more and more information as unusable until we have the consistency of a dictatorial procedure, concentrating on the information in just one person's preference ordering.[11]

It is often asserted that the Arrow impossibility theorem is some kind of a generalization of the old 'paradox of voting'. This is so in the rather limited

---

11. In fact, the consistency requirements for social preference can be weakened without upsetting the impossibility result. See Blau (1979) and Blair and Pollak (1979), for proofs involving a sequence of consistency conditions weaker than full transitivity, e.g., semi-orderings, even though the result does not follow merely from quasi-transitivity; see also Blau (1959), Hansson (1972), Schwartz (1974), Brown (1975), Wilson (1975), for related results and Sen (1979c). In fact, the strategy of proof used above can be easily extended to apply to such weaker consistency conditions. Take, for example, the case of semi-transitivity, which requires that if $x$ is strictly preferred to $y$, and that to $z$, then for any other state $s$, either $x$ is preferred to $s$, or $s$ is preferred to $z$ (or both). Since semi-transitivity implies quasi-transitivity, (T.1) and (T.2) remain unaffected. But to clinch (T.3), four distinct states $x, y, z, s$ are taken and the following preference combinations are postulated, in descending order of strict preference. Subgroup $M^1$: $x, y, z, s$; subgroup $M^2$: $y, z, s, x$; the rest $z, s, x, y$. By the decisiveness of $M$, we have $y$ preferred to $z$, and also $z$ preferred to $s$. Thus by semi-transitivity, either $x$ is preferred to $s$, or $y$ is preferred to $x$. The former makes $M^1$ decisive, the latter $M^2$. The rest of the proof is unaffected.

sense that the informational exclusions do ultimately confine us to simple welfarist rules (ignoring non-utility information) with utility reflected by the set of individual orderings only (ignoring interpersonal comparisons and cardinality), and all *these* rules—with the exception of dictatorship—run into consistency problems as the majority rule does in the 'paradox of voting'. But we need not have found ourselves confined to such a limited field had there not been such informational exclusions forcing us to make social welfare judgements in an informational famine. It is only *after* the informational constraints have bitten in that the analogy with the paradox of voting becomes relevant.

## 3 Inequality, Welfarism and Utility Information

The severity of the information restrictions in the Arrovian framework can be illustrated by taking up a problem of income distributional judgement. Consider the principle of giving priority to the interests of the poor over the interests of the rich. Do we have the information necessary for the use of this principle in the Arrovian framework?

I have tried to argue elsewhere that the aggregation exercise in the collective choice literature can be split into several distinct types—one of the distinctions being based on whether the exercise is one of aggregating the conflicting *interests* of different people, *or* one of aggregating the conflicting *judgements* of different people as to what should be done.[12] The informational limitation is restrictive for both, but a good deal more disturbing for the former than for the latter. When judgements are being aggregated, e.g., views of supporters of different political parties, there may be no practical possibility of having a mechanism that can actually use anything other than the set of individual preferences or votes. On the other hand, in aggregating conflicting interests of different persons, groups or classes, e.g., in planning decisions, or in comparisons of national welfare in alternative or successive situations,[13] the informational limitations of the Arrovian framework are exceptionally telling. Indeed, many acts of political and social judgements, e.g., the personal decision as to what kind of a government or a society one should want, are themselves based on aggregating conflicting interests,[14] and in making these

12. See Sen (1977a). The exercise can also be of a mixed kind, aggregating both interests and judgements; see Graaff (1977).

13. See Lerner (1944), Dobb (1955), Fisher (1956), Little (1957), Kolm (1969), Atkinson (1970), Mirrlees (1971), Pattanaik (1971), Phelps (1973), Chipman (1974), Muellbauer (1974), Meade (1976), Hammond (1976b), Graaff (1977) and Blackorby and Donaldson (1977), for illustrations of various types of exercises in which such interest conflicts have to be explicitly considered. I have tried to examine the assessment of interest conflicts in the economic analyses of inequality, poverty and real national income in Sen (1973; 1976b, c; 1979a).

14. See Harsanyi (1955), particularly his contrast between a person's 'ethical preferences' vis-à-vis his 'subjective preferences'.

judgements, to be constrained by the informational base of non-comparable individual orderings would be peculiarly limiting. The same applies to welfare economic criteria which are typically geared to the exercise of interest aggregation.

Returning to the income distributional conflict, it can be seen as a classic case of aggregation of conflicting interests. In terms of individual orderings of utility, it might be the case that each person is better off with the unit of additional income coming to him rather than to anyone else. And this can hold no matter whether the person is rich or poor. The question then is, on what basis do we discriminate in favour of the poor vis-à-vis the rich in the Arrovian framework applied to the case of interest aggregation?

Can we identify the rich through the observation that they have more utility than the poor? Not in the Arrow framework, since interpersonal comparisons are not admitted. Perhaps as those with a lower marginal utility of income? No, of course not, since that will go against *both* non-comparability and ordinalism. Can we then distinguish the rich as those who happen to have more income, or more consumer goods (nothing about utility need be said), and bring this recognition to bear in social judgements? No, not that either, since this will go against welfarism (and against strict-ranking-welfarism), since this discrimination has to based on non-utility information.

'Social utility', in Leontief's characterization, as 'a function of the ordinally described personal utility levels' without interpersonal comparisons robs us of our ability to 'tell' effectively the rich from the poor. It is this peculiarity of traditional welfare economics in insisting on both that social judgements be based on utility information only *and* that the utility information be used in a particularly poor form, that can be seen as paving the way to inconsistency or incompleteness—and thus to impossibilities.

## 4  Bergson–Samuelson Impossibilities

Much the same can be said about impossibility results geared to Bergson–Samuelson social welfare functions as opposed to Arrow social welfare functions (Bergson, 1938; Samuelson, 1947), despite assertions of the freedom of the Bergson–Samuelson framework from Arrow-type impossibility (e.g., by Samuelson, 1967). The difference between the two frameworks rests primarily in the fact that Bergson and Samuelson did not impose any 'interprofile' condition such as independence of irrelevant alternatives:[15] 'For Bergson, one and only one of the ... possible patterns of individuals' orderings is

---

15. That the condition of independence was the real bone of contention was disputed by Samuelson (1967), p. 47, but only because of the confusion that 'if the ordering is transitive, it *automatically* satisfies the condition called "independence of irrelevant alternatives" ' (Samuelson, 1967, p. 43). On this see Sen (1977b, pp. 1562–4) [pages 251–3 in this volume].

needed' (Samuelson, 1967, pp. 48–9).[16] But the main use of this interprofile condition in Arrow's impossibility theorem lies in precipitating welfarism, or—to be more precise—strict-ranking-welfarism, effectively ruling out the use of non-utility information for social judgements. But that feature of welfarism, in the context of single-profile judgements, seems to be incorporated *directly* by Bergson and Samuelson in many of their formulations of social welfare, so that impossibility results will follow even without bringing in more than one profile of individual orderings.

'If the decision', says Bergson, 'is in favour of consumers' sovereignty, the welfare function may be expressed in the form,

$$W = F(U^1, U^2, U^3, \ldots). \tag{1}$$

Here $U^1$, $U^2$, $U^3$, etc., represent the utilities of the individual households as they see them and $W$, the welfare of the community, is understood to be an increasing function of these utilities' (Bergson, 1948, p. 418).[17] This welfarism can be applied over a single profile of individual utilities to get *single-profile inter-pair* welfarism. (E.g., in the case of the $y$ regime discussed in the proof of (T.1) in Section 2, one would be able to conclude *directly* that if $x$ is socially preferred to $y$, then $a$ must be socially preferred to $b$, in a welfarist, ordinal, non-comparable framework.) The Arrow impossibility will then readily translate to the Bergson–Samuelson framework as well (see Parks, 1976; Kemp and Ng, 1976; Hammond, 1976b; Pollak, 1979). And the explanation can be similar to that in the Arrow case, namely the combination of welfarism (ruling out the use of non-utility information) and very poor utility information (ordinal and non-comparable) eliminates all possible rules except some very crude ones, and they can be readily weeded out by the other conditions.

## 5 Richer Utility Information

Not only is the Arrow impossibility theorem a remarkable result, of great analytical beauty, it is also surprisingly robust, *given* the informational constraints. Recent works in weakening the conditions of social transitivity, binariness of social choice, independence conditions and unrestricted domain, have revealed how easy it is to get trapped in an Arrow-like impossibility result as one escapes the exact impossibility pinpointed in Arrow's theorem.[18] On

16. See Johansen's (1970) lucid and illuminating account of the contrast.

17. See also Samuelson (1947), pp. 228–9, 246. See, however, Samuelson (1977) and Kemp and Ng (1977).

18. See Kelly's (1978) excellent critical survey of the Arrow-like impossibility results, and also Pattanaik's (1978) elegant account of the related literature on strategic impossibilities. See also Blair *et al.* (1976).

the other hand, genuine escape routes emerge with real possibility results once the informational constraints are lifted or weakened.[19]

It is, however, easy to establish that dropping 'ordinalism' and permitting, in principle, the use of cardinal utility has no effect on the impossibility result so long as the rest of the Arrow framework is kept unchanged, in particular the exclusion of interpersonal comparability of utility (see Theorem 8*2 in Sen, 1970; see also d'Aspremont and Gevers, 1977). Cardinality *without* interpersonal comparability in Arrow's framework does not widen the real possibilities of informed social welfare judgement.

Interpersonal comparability without cardinality is, however, a way out of the impossibility. Ordinal comparisons of different persons' utilities permit the use of such criteria as Rawls's (1971) 'maximin' interpreted in terms of utilities, focusing on the welfare levels of the worst-off in any group to arrive at a social-welfare ordering. This makes the 'worst-off rank' something like a dictator, and though it is not a personal dictatorship, it is possible to argue that it is a rather extreme approach. It appears that with interpersonal comparability without cardinality, the tendency towards such 'rank-dictatorships' (e.g., the dictatorship of the $m$th rank) is considerable, and it is possible to exclude all *other* possibilities by relatively small extensions of the Arrow conditions, *given* the welfarist (or strict-ranking welfarist) structure (see Gevers, 1979; Roberts, 1976).

Dropping non-comparable utilities *along with* ordinality permits a great many other rules to be considered. Utilitarianism is only one such rule. Many types of interpersonal comparability can be considered (e.g., ordinal, cardinal, ratio-scale, and various intermediate cases of partial comparability) within the generalized format of social welfare *functionals* (see Sen, 1970). Recently the problem of social judgement has been extensively studied axiomatically using alternative informational possibilities.[20]

Rules of social judgement based on richer utility information escape Arrow-type impossibility problems, but in so far as the welfarist (or strict-ranking welfarist) framework is retained, other difficulties can crop up. There are principles of social judgement that require essential use of non-utility information, and while such principles (e.g., liberty, non-exploitation, non-discrimination) are typically not much discussed in traditional welfare economics, they do relate closely to the subject matter of welfare economics. The next two sections are devoted to these issues.

19. Arrow (1963) himself considered the possibility of using interpersonal comparisons of utility based on the approach of 'extended sympathy'—formally explored in a pioneering paper by Suppes (1966)—but concluded that 'it is not easy to see how to construct a theory of social choice from this principle' (Arrow, 1963, pp. 114–15). See, however, Arrow (1977).

20. See Sen (1970; 1977b), Hammond (1976a; 1977), Strasnick (1976), d'Aspremont and Gevers (1977), Arrow (1977), Deschamps and Gevers (1978), Maskin (1978), and Roberts (1978), among others.

## 6   Limitations of Welfarism even with Rich Utility Information

The difficulties with welfarism discussed in Sections 2–4 arose from combining it with poor utility information. I would now like to dispute the acceptability of welfarism *even when* utility information is as complete as it can possibly be. So ordinalism is dropped, and the use of cardinal measures is permitted, and even—more demandingly—ratio scale measures (permitting statements such as: utility $U_1$ is twice $U_2$). To go as far as is logically conceivable, we can even demand that utility numbers be simply unique (and not just unique up to any positive affine transformation as under cardinality, or unique up to any positive homogeneous linear transformation as under a ratio-scale measure). Interpersonal comparisons are also extreme in the sense that each person's utility numbers—unique as they are—correspond naturally to those of others in a one-to-one way. These requirements are very demanding indeed, but since the object is to criticize welfarism *even when* utility information is as good as it can conceivably be, this only makes the exercise more biased in favour of welfarism. If utility information is, in fact, weaker than that, then of course welfarism will be even less (rather than more) acceptable.

Consider a set of three social states $x$, $y$ and $z$, with the following utility numbers for persons 1 and 2 (there are no others).

|                    | $x$ | $y$ | $z$ |
| ------------------ | --- | --- | --- |
| Person 1's utility | 4   | 7   | 7   |
| Person 2's utility | 10  | 8   | 8   |

In $x$ person 1 is hungry while 2 is eating a great deal. In $y$ person 2 has been made to surrender a part of his food supply to 1. While 2 is made worse off, 1 gets more utility, and the sum total of utility happens to be larger (with diminishing marginal utility).

It is clear that $y$ must be judged to be better than $x$ by utilitarianism (since the utility sum is larger for $y$), by the so called 'Rawlsian maximin' or its lexicographic extension 'leximin' (since the worst-off person's utility is larger in $y$ than in $x$), and indeed by virtually all the equity criteria that have been proposed in the literature using utility data (see, for example, Phelps, 1973; Sen, 1973; Hammond, 1976a; d'Aspremont and Gevers, 1977; Deschamps and Gevers, 1978; and Kern, 1978). Let us take $y$ to be better than $x$.

Consider now $z$. Here person 1 is still just as hungry as in $x$, and person 2 is also eating just as much. However, person 1, who is a sadist, is now permitted to torture 2, who—alas—is not a masochist. So 2 does suffer, but resilient as he is, his suffering is less than the utility gain of the wild-eyed 1. The utility numbers in $z$ being exactly the same as in $y$, welfarism requires that if $y$ is preferred to $x$, then so must be $z$. But $y$ *is* socially preferred to $x$. So $z$ is preferred to $x$ as well, thanks to welfarism.[21]

The conclusion that $z$ can be socially preferred to $x$ can, of course, be directly derived using utilitarianism, maximin, leximin, or some utility-based equity criterion. However, we might wonder whether those approaches should be used in the case of judging torture. (Cf. Harsanyi's, 1978, p. 8, rejection of utilitarian calculus in the case of 'sadism, resentment, or malice'.) But the decision to rank $y$ over $x$ by any of these criteria in a choice involving no judgement of torture, will readily translate into a preference for torture-inclusive $z$ over $x$, *due to welfarism*.

Similarly, if our disapproval of the torture leads us to prefer $x$ to $z$ (or at least to a refusal to rank $z$ better than $x$), then welfarism will require that we must rank $x$ above $y$ as well, thereby opposing the food transfer (or at least refuse to approve of the food transfer). Welfarism *is* a demanding restriction.

It is interesting to consider also the ranking of $y$ vis-à-vis $z$. By the Pareto indifference rule, $y$ and $z$ must be judged to be socially indifferent. If instead of passing on some food from rich 2 to poor 1, letting 1 torture 2 gives both exactly the same utilities, then Paretianism obliges us to declare the two alternatives to be exactly as good as each other. If we wish to make a moral distinction between $y$ and $z$ despite their coincidence on utility space, we have to go not merely against welfarism in general, but even against that limited expression of welfarism that we find in the Paretian approach. This issue is pursued further in the next section.

While the subject of torture arouses moral feelings that are very deep, there are also other subjects on which the inadequacy of the utility information—however complete in itself—seems important. Indeed, some moral principles are formulated without making any use of utility information at all, e.g., 'equal pay for equal work', 'non-exploitation',[22] etc., and it is easy to demonstrate that these principles would conflict with welfarism, which makes the utility information decisive. Even Rawls's (1971) 'difference principle' in his theory of justice, in which a person's disadvantage is judged in terms of his access to 'primary social goods', and not in terms of utility as such (as in the apocryphal version popular among economists), will clash violently with welfarism. In its uncompromising rejection of the relevance of non-utility information welfarism is indeed a very limiting approach.

Finally, there is the question of data availability. Often utility information

---

21. It is assumed that there are no indirect consequences of torture, e.g., in attitude formation. These indirect effects do not change the nature of the difficulty, even though they can be properly accommodated only in a much more complex analysis.

22. See Marx (1887). It is, however, important to note that while being sceptical of the utility-based moral calculus, Marx also disputed the normative depth of claims based on labour entitlements; see especially Marx (1875). I have tried to discuss elsewhere (Sen, 1978b) the relationship between the descriptive and evaluative aspects of the labour theory of value, as used by Marx. See also Leinfellner (1978).

is very difficult to obtain both because of problems of measurability and comparability, as well as because of well-known difficulties in inducing honest revelation of preferences (see Gibbard, 1973; Satterthwaite, 1975; Pattanaik, 1978, and others).[23] In contrast some of the non-utility information, e.g., whether 'equal pay for equal work' is being observed, or what primary goods people have, may be a lot easier to obtain. Thus the restriction imposed by welfarism is not only ethically limiting, it can be deeply problematic also from the point of view of data availability, making this restriction 'doubly' regrettable.[24]

## 7   Limitations of Paretianism

Despite their formal independence, there is a sense in which Paretianism can be seen as essentially a weak form of welfarism. Welfarism asserts that non-utility information is *in general* unnecessary for social welfare judgements. Paretianism makes non-utility information unnecessary *in the special case* in which everyone's utility rankings coincide. (It also makes the social welfare judgement mirror the unanimous individual utility rankings, which is an additional feature, but that does not, of course, affect the redundancy of the non-utility information.) If everyone has more utility from $x$ than from $y$, then it does not matter what $x$ and $y$ are like in any other respect; the Pareto principle will declare $x$ to be socially better than $y$ without inquiring further. It was indeed this blindness to non-utility information in such special cases that was used to precipitate strict-ranking welfarism by combining the weak Pareto principle with unrestricted domain and independence in (T.1) in Section 2.

The 'impossibility of the Paretian libertarian', which I have presented elsewhere (Sen, 1970; 1976a),[25] relates closely to the difficulties with welfarism.

23. The problem of data availability will not, of course, arise in this form if individual utility is defined as the *component of social welfare* that is attributed to the conditions of that individual, in a 'separable' social welfare framework (see Hammond, 1977). Indeed, with such a framework and with that definition of individual utility, welfarism would be an analytical requirement of consistency. But welfarism in this case is not a substantial claim, and only shows social welfare to be a function of its own components (e.g., the sum of the parts—to take the simplest form). The really interesting controversial issues will, then, arise in the *correspondence* between individual utility (as the person's own conception of his own well-being) and the component of social welfare that is attributed to him ('utility' in this rather artificial sense).

24. See Sen (1979b).

25. For discussion of various aspects of this problem see—among others—Ng (1971, 1979), Batra and Pattanaik (1972), Ramachandra (1972), Gibbard (1974), Nozick (1974), Bernholz (1974), Blau (1975), Seidl (1975), Farrell (1976), Buchanan (1976), Campbell (1976), Fine (1976), Aldrich (1977), Breyer (1977), Miller (1977), Perelli-Minetti (1977), Suzumura (1978), Karni (1978), Ferejohn (1978), Gaertner and Krüger (1978), Kelly (1978), Stevens and Foster (1978), and Rawls (1978). The earlier of these critiques and extensions—and some others—were reviewed in Sen (1976a).

The result shows the incompatibility of the Pareto principle (even in the weak form) with some relatively mild requirements of personal liberty, for consistent social decisions, given unrestricted domain. The link with welfarism can be seen in the following way. Considerations of liberty require specification of non-utility information as relevant, e.g., whether a particular choice is self-regarding or not (cf. Mill, 1859), or as falling within a person's 'protected sphere' (cf. Hayek, 1960). The claim is that this use of non-utility information goes not merely against welfarism, it can go even against Paretianism (Theorems 6.1, 6.2, and 6.3 in Sen, 1970).

Consider the first example in terms of which I tried to illustrate the result captured formally in the Pareto-libertarian theorems. Two persons, namely, the prude and the lewd, are considering three states of affairs, namely, $p$ (the prude reading *Lady Chatterley's Lover*, $l$ (lewd reading the book), and $o$ (nobody reading it). The prude's personal utility ranking, in decreasing order, is: $o, p, l$, while the lewd ranks them $p, l, o$. The prude likes $o$ (nobody reading the book) best; the lewd likes it least. But both prefer $p$ to $l$, i.e., the prude reading the book rather than the lewd. It is postulated that in $p$ the lewd is overjoyed at the prude's discomfiture in having to read a naughty book, and the prude is less unhappy, having avoided the dire outcome of that lascivious lewd actually reading and enjoying 'such muck'. This leads to the Pareto-libertarian cycle. On libertarian grounds, it is better that the lewd reads the book rather than nobody, since what the lewd reads is his own business and the lewd does want to read the book; hence $l$ is socially better than $o$. On libertarian grounds again, it is better that nobody reads the book rather than the prude, since whether the prude should read a book or not is his own business, and he does not wish to read the book; hence $o$ is better than $p$. On the other hand, both get more utility from the prude reading the book rather than the lewd. The Pareto preference for $p$ over $l$, completes the cycle with the libertarian rankings of $l$ over $o$, and $o$ over $p$.

The 'impossibility of the Paretian libertarian' captures this conflict in the form of a theorem in a general framework. There is then the further question as to how to resolve the conflict. It is not my contention that the libertarian rights should *invariably* prevail over Paretian judgements, but that there are cases when this makes evident sense. The decision may have to be conditional on other features, e.g., the *motivation* underlying the utility rankings (see Sen, 1970; 1976a). I wish to consider now those cases in which we decide to come out against Paretianism on libertarian grounds. The question is: how can this possibly make sense since both parties have more utility in $p$ than in $l$?

In the torture case discussed in the last section a distinction was made between utility arising from getting some food when hungry and that arising from torturing. In the current context, it is possible to make a distinction between utility arising from reading a book one wants to read and that arising from someone else's discomfiture. And between suffering arising from having to read something one hates to read, and suffering arising from the contemplation of someone else enjoying what one regards to be bad stuff. If it is decided to ignore the utility arising from the discomfiture of others, or disutility from the enjoyment of others (or to put a lower weight on these things rather than ignoring them altogether), then distinctions are being made between different kinds of utility, using non-utility information.[26]

Indeed, it is possible that the prude and the lewd *themselves* would make a *moral* judgement in favour of the lewd reading the book—despite its Pareto inferiority. This they can do for the reasons mentioned above, and they can do this even without apologizing for their own actual utility functions. The prude, for example, can argue thus. 'My desire that I rather than the lewd should read the book arises from my dislike of the lewd's enjoyment of certain types of pleasures. As a person of good taste, it is of course natural that I should feel this revulsion: there is nothing illegitimate in that, and I am quite free to feel the way I do. But it is another matter to argue that my revulsion is as relevant in deciding whether the lewd should read the book, as the lewd's own pleasure in reading that book; it is after all a personal matter for him. I am not pretending that I don't care what he does, or that I *should not* care, but I don't think that my caring about what the lewd reads should have the same weight—or perhaps even any weight—as the lewd's own caring about what he does in his personal life.'

This reasoning is also relevant to an interesting objection that has been raised about the formulation of the Pareto libertarian problem. If people always act in a way that would maximize their utilities, then the libertarian solution that the lewd reads the book will not be an equilibrium. It would be foolish for the prude to exercise his right not to read the book, since the alternative (the lewd reading it) is even worse for the prude. Indeed, it will be in the interest of both parties to do a 'trade' and arrive at a contract ensuring that the prude reads the book. This will lead to more utility for both. Doesn't this solve the problem of the Paretian libertarian?[27] Doesn't the possibility of the trade make the allegedly libertarian solution (namely the lewd reading the book) unsustainable and, therefore, unviable? Since a Pareto-inoptimal situation in the circumstances specified would fail to be an equilibrium, doesn't this eliminate the force of the criticism of the Pareto principle?

We may begin by noting that the prude or the lewd may refuse to enter into

26. See Sen (1976a), pp. 235–7. This type of consideration also provides a way of resolving Gibbard's (1974) important problem of consistency of libertarian rights, on which see Suzumura (1978).

27. This way of escaping the problems of the Paretian libertarian (and avoiding the impossibility theorem presented in Sen (1970)) has been explored by several authors. For discussion of the relevant issues, see Gibbard (1974), Bernholz (1974), Buchanan (1976), and Kelly (1978), chapter 9, among others. Paul Grout (1978) has discussed rather similar issues in the context of his critique of Rowley and Peacock (1975), and while the claims made by Rowley and Peacock are quite different from mine—as they have taken pains to explain—the issue of sustainability has cropped up in both contexts.

such a 'trade' despite utility gain, if he is libertarian enough to see no moral gain in the 'trade' (namely the 'deal' involving the prude reading a book that he detests to prevent the lewd reading it with pleasure). Indeed, he can reason with John Stuart Mill.[28]

> There are many who consider as an injury to themselves any conduct which they have a distaste for, and resent it as an outrage to their feelings; ... but there is no parity between the feeling of a person for his own opinion, and the feeling of another who is offended at his holding it; no more than between the desire of a thief to take a purse, and the desire of the right owner to keep it. And a person's taste is as much his own peculiar concern as his opinion or his purse. (Mill, 1859, p. 140)

The possible refusal of the prude or the lewd to 'trade' in this way despite utility gain may perhaps appear puzzling to those 'revealed preference' theorists who can define utility only in terms of what is chosen irrespective of *why* it is chosen. Indeed, if utilities are defined entirely in terms of choice, then a person will be seen as maximizing his utility in every feasible choice. But this assertion, then, is no more than a tautology. If, on the other hand, utility is taken in the traditional sense of happiness, or in the sense of a person's own conception of his well-being, then to identify that utility as invariably the same as the binary relation revealed by his consistent choice, would produce an immensely limited model of human behaviour.[29]

It may be useful to distinguish between three types of cases. First, as outlined above, one or more of the parties may refuse to enter into the 'trade' and reject it on moral grounds. Here the libertarian solution of the lewd reading the book need not fail to be an equilibrium. Second, one or more of the parties may think the 'trade' to be immoral on libertarian grounds, but may decide nevertheless to indulge in the 'trade'; *akrasia* or the weakness of will is not an uncommon problem. Here the libertarian solution will fail to be an equilibrium, but it will not go against a unanimous moral judgement (despite going against a unanimous utility ranking). The rejection of the Paretian ranking in either or both of these cases is adequate for the purpose of rejecting the Pareto principle, since the principle is meant to apply without qualification.

Violation of the Pareto principle would be, however, a good deal more controversial in the third case in which neither party disapproves of the trade

---

28. For an illuminating analysis of Mill's libertarianism especially clarifying Mill's conception of a person's 'interests', see Wollheim (1973).

29. The characterization of human behaviour as being based *exclusively* on the pursuit of one's own happiness (or one's own sense of well-being) irrespective of moral values, social conventions, or ties of class or community, produces a model of breathtaking simplicity. I have tried to analyse elsewhere the consequences of characterizing human beings in this way; see Sen (1977c).

and both in fact would proceed to such a deal.[30] It raises a deeper question, viz., whether *having a right* based on the 'personal' nature of some decisions (in this case the right to read what one likes and shun what one does not wish to read) must invariably imply being free *to trade that right* for some other gain, irrespective of the nature of the gain (in this case the lewd's gain consists in getting pleasure from the prude's discomfiture, and the prude's gain in avoiding the discomfort of knowing that the lewd is reading a book that he— the prude—disapproves of). If the answer to this question is yes, then clearly the criticism of the Pareto principle would not apply to this case. I believe it is possible to question such an affirmative answer, but I resist the temptation to go further into this complex issue, since for the purpose at hand, viz., the rejection of the Pareto principle (given its unconditional character), the other two cases are sufficient.

Before ending this section, I would like to take up two general issues. First, using a deontological approach, it is possible to include considerations of liberty not in the evaluations of states of affairs, but instead in the evaluation of action through a 'non-consequentialist' framework.[31] Robert Nozick's (1974) proposal for the resolution of the Pareto-libertarian conflict takes this form (pp. 164–6). Judgements on action are constrained by a firm system of rights which do not get accommodated in the evaluation of 'end-states'. The Pareto principle is retained in the evaluation of *outcomes*, but it does not get translated into a corresponding assessment of right *action*. The prude reading the book may be higher in the social ordering than the lewd reading it (on Paretian grounds), but the protection of their rights to read what they like, and not read what they don't, would prevent a translation of the Paretian ranking into an immediate judgement of actions. This approach has some clear advantages, not least in giving both the Pareto principle as well as requirements of liberty well-assigned and consistent roles—protecting violations of personal rights while retaining the Pareto principle as a part of the social ordering.[32]

30. There is, however, still the problem of *enforcing* such a deal, and it is not altogether obvious how the lewd could ensure that the prude having got the book would, in fact, read it. This would make the trade that much more difficult to execute. See also Olson's (1965) general discussion of the difficulties of contractive action: 'it does *not* follow, because all of the individuals in a group would gain if they achieved their group objective, that they would act to achieve that objective, even if they were all rational and self-interested' (p. 2). But while trade may fail to take place for such instrumental difficulties, that would not be, it seems to me, a reason for denying that the trade would have been in the interest of social welfare. The actual failure of the trade would not, thus, weaken the force of the Paretian welfare judgement in this situation, and if the Pareto principle has to be rejected in this third case, the argument must be found elsewhere. In fact, the issue of feasibility is a distinct one from that of social desirability, and this has to be borne in mind *both* in criticizing the Pareto principle (say, in case 2) as well as in defending it (say, in case 3).

31. For a general critique of 'consequentialism' see Bernard Williams (1973).

32. See also Ronald Dworkin's (1978) contrast between 'general welfare' and 'rights'. It is also worth noting that Dworkin's contrast between 'personal' and 'external' preferences can be used to throw light on the Pareto-libertarian conflict. See also Farrell (1976).

However, the role that is given to the Pareto principle in this approach may well be very limited (and quite possibly, vacuous) in terms of actual activities. While 'rights do not determine a social ordering but instead set the constraints within which a social choice is to be made', 'a choice can be made by a social choice mechanism based upon a social ordering, if there are any choices left to make!' (Nozick, 1974, p. 166). Furthermore it can be argued that including considerations of liberty and rights in the evaluation of outcomes themselves also has some advantages, especially in dealing with 'third-party moralities', e.g., person 3's moral involvement in letting strong-armed 1 torture, or rape, or exploit, person 2, *when* it is in 3's power to stop it. If the violation of rights were reflected into the evaluation of states of affairs themselves, then a consequence-based analysis of right action would involve 3 directly into the event. If, on the other hand, this violation does not make the state of affairs any worse, and rights merely 'set the constraints within which a social choice is to be made' then it is not immediate that person 3 has any involvement in this episode at all.[33]

Finally, it is perhaps worth remarking that the criticism of the Pareto principle under discussion does not dispute the use of 'dominance' as a way of separating out non-controversial choices, which do not involve conflicting considerations, from choices that do. If utility were accepted to be the only basis of moral claim, then the Pareto principle would indeed reflect 'dominance' of moral claims, and would be—accordingly—quite non-controversial. The difficulty, however, arises from accepting other sources of moral claim. This leads to the specification of claims that do not rest on utility considerations, or which require a revision of the relative weighting of different elements in aggregate utility values (e.g., attaching more weight to the prude's displeasure from having himself to read a book he does not like vis-à-vis his displeasure from the knowledge that *somebody else* is enjoying reading that book). The Pareto principle (i) lists a set of virtues, and (ii) uses dominance of virtues as the criterion. What is in dispute here is the former, not the latter.

## 8   Concluding Remarks

I shall not attempt a summary of the arguments presented in this paper, but will make a few general remarks, to put the discussion in perspective.

First, all the properties on which 'something like a general consensus' seems to exist in traditional welfare economics (Section 1) are eminently questionable.

Second, Arrow's impossibility theorem can be seen as resulting largely from combining 'welfarism' (ruling out the use of non-utility information) with remarkably poor utility information (especially because of the avoidance of interpersonal comparisons) (Sections 2 and 3).

33. I have tried to discuss the question and some related ones in Sen (1978a). Also in Sen (1976a), pp. 230–2.

Third, the power of these combined informational exclusions can be illustrated by noting that in the exercise of aggregating the conflicting interests of the poor vis-à-vis the rich, the exclusions make it, in effect, impossible to give priority to the interest of the poor. The poor cannot be distinguished for this purpose from the rich—neither in terms of utility, nor in terms of income or other non-utility information (Section 3). There are many different ways of avoiding the impasse: dropping welfarism is one, using richer utility information is another (Section 5).

Fourth, the Arrow impossibility result translates readily to the Bergson—Samuelson social welfare function as well, precisely to the extent that it too tries to combine welfarism with poor utility information (Section 4).

Fifth, while welfarism is disastrous when the utility information is poor, it remains a very limiting constraint even when the utility information is very rich (Section 6). This can be brought out by explicitly considering such issues as liberty, discrimination, exploitation, or entitlement to social security. The underlying principles tend to give non-utility information a role of its own (in addition to any relevance it might have as determinant of—or as surrogate for—utility data).

Finally, Paretianism can be seen essentially as a weak version of welfarism—banning any independent use of non-utility information in a class of special cases. Even this apparently mild exclusion of non-utility information has highly restrictive consequences, especially for issues related to liberty (Section 7). While escape from these difficulties has been sought in the possibility of 'trading' one's rights, it is argued that this does not dispose of the case against the Pareto principle.

### References

Aldrich, J. (1977): 'The dilemma of the Paretian liberal: some consequences of Sen's theorem', *Public Choice, 30,* 1–21.

Arrow, K. J. (1951): *Social Choice and Individual Values* (New York: Wiley).

_____ (1963) 2nd edition of Arrow (1951).

_____ (1977): 'Extended sympathy and the possibility of social choice', *American Economic Review, 67,* 219–25.

_____ and Hahn, F. (1971): *General Competitive Analysis* (San Francisco: Holden-Day. Edinburgh: Oliver & Boyd. Distribution taken over by North-Holland, Amsterdam).

Atkinson, A. B. (1970): 'On the measurement of inequality', *Journal of Economic Theory, 2,* 244–63.

Batra, R. N. and Pattanaik, P. K. (1972): 'On some suggestions for having non-binary social choice functions', *Theory and Decision, 3,* 1–11.

Bergson, A. (1938): 'A reformulation of certain aspects of welfare economics', *Quarterly Journal of Economics, 52,* 30–34.

_____ (1948): 'Social Economics'. In *A Survey of Contemporary Economics* (ed. H. S. Ellis) (Homewood, Illinois: Irwin).

Bernholz, P. (1974): 'Is a Paretian liberal really impossible?' *Public Choice*, **19**, 99–107.

Blackorby, C. and Donaldson, D. (1977): 'Utility vs. equity: Some plausible quasi-orderings', *Journal of Public Economics*, **7**, 365–81.

Blair, D. H., Bordes, G., Kelly, J. S. and Suzumura, K. (1976): 'Impossibility theorems without collective rationality', *Journal of Economic Theory*, **13**.

_____ and Pollak, R. A. (1979): 'Collective rationality and dictatorship: The scope of the Arrow theorem', *Journal of Economic Theory*, **21**, 186–94.

Blau, J. H. (1957): 'The existence of a social welfare function', *Econometrica*, **25**, 302–13.

_____ (1959): 'Aggregation of preferences' (abstract), *Econometrica*, **27**, 283.

_____ (1972): 'A direct proof of Arrow's theorem', *Econometrica*, **40**, 61–7.

_____ (1975): 'Liberal values and independence', *Review of Economic Studies*, **42**, 413–20.

_____ (1976): 'Neutrality, monotonicity and the right of veto: A comment', *Econometrica*, **44**, 603.

_____ (1979): 'Semiorders and collective choice', *Journal of Economic Theory*, **21**, 195–206.

Breyer, F. (1977): 'The liberal paradox, decisiveness over issues, and domain restrictions', *Zeitschrift für Nationalökonomie*, **37**, 45–60.

Brown, D. J. (1975): 'Collective rationality', mimeographed, Cowles Foundation Discussion Paper No. 393, Yale University.

Buchanan, J. (1976): 'An ambiguity in Sen's alleged proof of the impossibility of a Paretian libertarian', mimeographed, Virginia Polytechnic.

Campbell, D. E. (1976): 'Democratic preference functions', *Journal of Economic Theory*, **12**, 259–72.

Chipman, J. S. (1974): 'The welfare ranking of Pareto distributions', *Journal of Economic Theory*, **9**, 275–82.

d'Aspremont, C. and Gevers, L. (1977): 'Equity and informational basis of collective choice', *Review of Economic Studies*, **46**, 199–210.

Debreu, G. (1959): *Theory of Value: An Axiomatic Study of Economic Equilibrium* (New York: Wiley).

Deschamps, R. and Gevers, L. (1978): 'Leximin and utilitarian rules: A joint characterization', *Journal of Economic Theory*, **17**, 143–63.

Dobb, M. (1955): *On Economic Theory and Socialism* (London: Routledge & Kegan Paul).

Dworkin, R. (1978): *Taking Rights Seriously* (London: Duckworth).

Farrell, M. J. (1976): 'Liberalism in the theory of social choice', *Review of Economic Studies*, **43**, 3–10.

Ferejohn, J. A. (1978): 'The distribution of rights in society'. In Gottinger and Leinfellner (1978).

Fine, B. (1976): 'Individual liberalism in a Paretian society', *Journal of Political Economy*, **83**, 1277–82.

Fishburn, P. C. (1973): *The Theory of Social Choice* (Princeton University Press).

Fisher, F. M. (1956): 'Income distribution, value judgements and welfare', *Quarterly Journal of Economics*, **70**, 380–424.

Gaertner, W. and Krüger, L. (1978): 'From hand-cuffed Paretians to self-consistent libertarians: A new possibility theorem'. [Revised version, 'Self-supporting

Preferences and Individual Liberty: The Possibility of Paretian Libertarianism', published later in *Economica,* **48** (1981), 17–28.]

Gevers, L. (1979): 'On interpersonal comparability and social welfare orderings', *Econometrica,* **47**, 75–89.

Gibbard, A. (1973): 'Manipulation of voting schemes: A general result', *Econometrica,* **41**, 587–601.

―――― (1974): 'A Pareto-consistent libertarian claim', *Journal of Economic Theory,* **7**, 338–410.

Gottinger, H. W. and Leinfellner, W. (1978) (eds): *Decision Theory and Social Ethics* (Dordrecht: Reidel).

Graaff, J. de V. (1957): *Theoretical Welfare Economics* (Cambridge: Cambridge University Press).

―――― (1977): 'Equity and efficiency as components of the general welfare', *South African Journal of Economics,* **45**, 362–75.

Grout, P. (1978): 'Is there a liberal welfare economics?' Manuscript, Department of Economics, Birmingham University.

Guha, A. (1972): 'Neutrality, monotonicity and the right of veto', *Econometrica,* **40**, 821–6.

Hammond, P. J. (1976a): 'Equity, Arrow's conditions and Rawls' difference principle', *Econometrica,* **44**, 793–804.

―――― (1976b): 'Why ethical measures of inequality need interpersonal comparisons', *Theory and Decision,* **7**, 263–74.

―――― (1977): 'Dual interpersonal comparisons of utility and the welfare economics of income distribution', *Journal of Public Economics,* **6**, 51–71.

Hansson, B. (1972): 'The existence of group preference functions', mimeographed, Working Paper No. 3, The Mattias Fremling Society, Lund University. [Revised version published in *Public Choice,* **28** (1976), 89–98.]

Harsanyi, J. C. (1955): 'Cardinal welfare, individualistic ethics and interpersonal comparisons of utility', *Journal of Political Economy,* **63**, 309–21.

―――― (1978): 'Rule utilitarianism and decision theory'. In Gottinger and Leinfellner (1978).

Hayek, F. A. (1960): *The Constitution of Liberty* (London: Routledge).

Johansen, L. (1970): 'An examination of the relevance of Kenneth Arrow's general possibility theorem for economic planning'. In *Optimation et Simulation de Macro-décisions* (Namur: Gembloux).

Karni, E. (1978): 'Collective rationality, unanimity and liberal ethics', *Review of Economic Studies,* **45**, 571–4.

Kelly, J. S. (1978): *Arrow Impossibility Theorems* (New York: Academic Press).

Kemp, M. C. and Ng, Y. K. (1976): 'On the existence of social welfare functions, social orderings and social decision functions', *Economica,* **43**, 59–66.

―――― (1977): 'More on social welfare functions: The incompatibility of individualism and ordinalism', *Economica,* **44**, 89–90.

Kern, L. (1978): 'Comparative distributive ethics: An extension of Sen's examination of the pure distribution problem'. In Gottinger and Leinfellner (1978).

Kolm, S. (1969): 'The optimum production of social justice'. In *Public Economics* (ed. J. Margolis and H. Guitton) (London: Macmillan).

Laffont, J. J. (1979): *Aggregation and Revelation of Preferences* (Amsterdam: North-Holland).

Leinfellner, W. (1978): 'Marx and the utility approach to the ethical foundations of microeconomics'. In Gottinger and Leinfellner (1978).

Leontief, W. (1966): *Essays in Economics: Theories and Theorizing* (New York: Oxford University Press).

Lerner, A. P. (1944): *Economics of Control* (London: Macmillan).

Little, I. M. D. (1957): *A Critique of Welfare Economics*, 2nd ed. (Oxford University Press).

Marx, K. (1875): *Critique of the Gotha Programme*, English translation of K. Marx and F. Engels, *Selected Works*, vol. II (Moscow: Foreign Languages P.H., 1958).

\_\_\_\_ (1887): *Capital: A Critical Analysis of Capitalist Production*, vol. I (London: Sonnenschein. Re-published Allen & Unwin, 1938).

Maskin, E. (1978): 'A theorem on Utilitarianism', *Review of Economic Studies,* 45, 93–6.

Meade, J. E. (1976): *The Just Economy* (London: Allen & Unwin).

Mill, J. S. (1859): *On Liberty*. Reprinted in J. S. Mill, *Utilitarianism: On Liberty; Representative Government*. Everyman's Library.

Miller, N. R. (1977): ' "Social preference" and game theory: a comment on "The dilemma of the Paretian liberal",' *Public Choice,* 30, 23–34.

Mirrlees, J. A. (1971): 'An exploration in the theory of optimum income taxation', *Review of Economic Studies,* 38, 175–208.

Müellbauer, J. (1974): 'Inequality measures, prices and household composition', *Review of Economic Studies,* 41, 493–504.

Murakami, Y. (1968): *Logic and Social Choice* (London: Macmillan).

Ng, Y. K. (1971): 'The possibility of a Paretian liberal: Impossibility theorems and cardinal utility', *Journal of Political Economy,* 79, 1397–401.

\_\_\_\_ (1979): *Welfare Economics* (London: Macmillan).

Nozick, R. (1974): *Anarchy, State and Utopia* (Oxford: Blackwell).

Olson, M. (1965): *The Logic of Collective Action* (Cambridge: Harvard University Press).

Parks, R. R. (1976): 'An impossibility theorem for fixed preferences: A dictatorial Bergson–Samuelson social welfare function', *Review of Economic Studies,* 43, 447–50.

Pattanaik, P. K. (1971): *Voting and Collective Choice* (Cambridge University Press).

\_\_\_\_ (1978): *Strategy and Group Choice* (Amsterdam: North-Holland).

Perelli-Minetti, C. R. (1977): 'Nozick on Sen: A misunderstanding', *Theory and Decision,* 8, 387–93.

Phelps, E. S. (1973): *Economic Justice* (Harmondsworth: Penguin Books).

Plott, C. R. (1976): 'Axiomatic social choice theory: An overview and interpretation', *American Journal of Political Science,* 20, 511–96.

Pollak, R. A. (1979): 'Bergson–Samuelson social welfare functions and the theory of social choice', *Quarterly Journal of Economics,* 93, 73–90.

Ramachandra, V. S. (1972): 'Liberalism, non-binary choice and Pareto principle', *Theory and Decision,* 3, 49–54.

Rawls, J. (1971): *A Theory of Justice* (Oxford: Clarendon Press).

\_\_\_\_ (1978): 'Primary goods and responsibility for ends', mimeographed, Harvard University.

Robbins, L. (1932): *An Essay on the Nature and Significance of Economic Science* (London: Allen & Unwin).

Roberts, K. W. S. (1976): 'Possibility theorems with interpersonally comparable welfare levels', mimeographed. [Revised version in *Review of Economic Studies,* **47** (1980), 409–20.]

_____ (1978): 'Interpersonal comparability and social choice theory', mimeographed. [Revised version in *Review of Economic Studies,* **47** (1980), 421–39.]

Rowley, C. K. and Peacock, A. T. (1975): *Welfare Economics: A Liberal Restatement* (London: Martin Robertson).

Samuelson, P. A. (1947): *Foundations of Economic Analysis* (Cambridge, Mass.: Harvard University Press).

_____ (1967): 'Arrow's mathematical politics'. In *Human Values and Economic Policy* (ed. S. Hook) (New York University Press).

_____ (1977): 'Reaffirming the existince of reasonable Bergson–Samuelson social welfare functions', *Economica,* **44**, 81–8.

Satterthwaite, M. A. (1975): 'Strategy-proofness and Arrow's conditions: Existence and correspondence theorems for voting procedures and social welfare functions', *Journal of Economic Theory,* **10**, 187–217.

Schwartz, T. (1974): 'Notes on the abstract theory of collective choice', mimeographed (Philosophy Department, Carnegie-Mellon University).

Seidl, C. (1975): 'On liberal values', *Zeitschrift für Nationalökonmie,* **35**, 257–90.

Sen, A. K. (1970): *Collective Choice and Social Welfare* (San Francisco: Holden-Day; Edinburgh: Oliver & Boyd, distribution taken over by North-Holland, Amsterdam).

_____ (1973): *On Economic Inequality* (Oxford: Clarendon Press; New York: Norton).

_____ (1976a): 'Liberty, unanimity and rights', *Economica,* **43**, 387–403. [Essay 14 in this volume.]

_____ (1976b): 'Poverty: An ordinal approach to measurement', *Econometrica,* **44**, 219–31. [Essay 17 in this volume.]

_____ (1976c): 'Real national income', *Review of Economic Studies,* **43**, 19–39. [Essay 18 in this volume.]

_____ (1977a): 'Social choice theory: A re-examination', *Econometrica,* **45**, 53–90. [Essay 8 in this volume.]

_____ (1977b): 'On weights and measures: Informational constraints in social welfare analysis', *Econometrica,* **45**, 1539–72. [Essay 11 in this volume.]

_____ (1977c): 'Rational fools: A critique of the behavioural foundations of economic theory', *Philosophy and Public Affairs,* **6**, 317–44. [Essay 4 in this volume.]

_____ (1978a): 'Welfare and rights'. Text of Hagerstrom Lectures, Philosophy Department, Uppsala University (April). [Parts of the material used later in 'Rights and Agency', *Philosophy and Public Affairs,* **11** (1982).]

_____ (1978b): 'On the labour theory of value: Some methodological issues', *Cambridge Journal of Economics,* **2**, 175–90.

_____ (1979a): 'The welfare basis of real income comparisons: A survey', *Journal of Economic Literature,* **17**, 1–45.

_____ (1979b): 'Strategies and revelation: Informational constraints in public decisions'. In Laffont (1979).

_____ (1979c): 'Social choice theory'. Prepared for the *Handbook of Mathematical Economics* (ed. K. J. Arrow and M. Intriligator). To be published by North-Holland, Amsterdam.

Stevens, D. N. and Foster, J. E. (1978): 'The possibility of democratic pluralism', *Economica,* **45**, 391–400.

Strasnick, S. (1976): 'Social choice theory and the derivation of Rawls' Difference principle', *Journal of Philosophy,* **73**, 85–99.

Suppes, P. (1966): 'Some formal models of grading principles', *Synthese,* **6**, 284–306. Reprinted in his *Studies in the Methodology and Foundations of Science* (Dordrecht: Reidel, 1969).

Suzumura, K. (1978): 'On the consistency of libertarian claims', *Review of Economic Studies,* **45**, 329–42.

Williams, B. (1973): 'A critique of utilitarianism'. In J. J. C. Smart and B. Williams, *Utilitarianism: For and Against* (Cambridge: Cambridge University Press).

Wilson, R. (1975): 'On the theory of aggregation', *Journal of Economic Theory,* **10**, 89–99.

Wollheim, R. (1973): 'John Stuart Mill and the limits of state action', *Social Research,* **40**, 1–30.

# 16

# Equality of What?

Discussions in moral philosophy have offered us a wide menu in answer to the question: equality of what? In this lecture I shall concentrate on three particular types of equality, viz., (i) utilitarian equality, (ii) total utility equality, and (iii) Rawlsian equality. I shall argue that all three have serious limitations, and that while they fail in rather different and contrasting ways, an adequate theory cannot be constructed even on the *combined* grounds of the three. Towards the end I shall try to present an alternative formulation of equality which seems to me to deserve a good deal more attention than it has received, and I shall not desist from doing some propaganda on its behalf.

First a methodological question. When it is claimed that a certain moral principle has shortcomings, what can be the basis of such an allegation? There seem to be at least two different ways of grounding such a criticism, aside from just checking its *direct* appeal to moral intuition. One is to check the *implications* of the principle by taking up particular cases in which the results of employing that principle can be seen in a rather stark way, and then to examine these implications against our intuition. I shall call such a critique a *case-implication critique*. The other is to move not from the general to the particular, but from the general to the *more* general. One can examine the consistency of the principle with another principle that is acknowledged to be more fundamental. Such prior principles are usually formulated at a rather abstract level, and frequently take the form of congruence with some very general procedures. For example, what could be reasonably assumed to have been chosen under the *as if* ignorance of the Rawlsian 'original position', a hypothetical primordial state in which people decide on what rules to adopt without knowing who they are going to be—as if they could end up being any

For helpful comments I am most grateful to Derek Parfit, Jim Griffin, and John Perry.

This essay was delivered as The Tanner Lecture on Human Values at Stanford University, May 22, 1979, and originally published in *The Tanner Lectures on Human Values*, Volume I, by the University of Utah Press and Cambridge University Press, 1980. It is reprinted with the permission of The Tanner Lectures on Human Values, a corporation.

one of the persons in the community.[1] Or what rules would satisfy Richard Hare's requirement of 'universalizability' and be consistent with 'giving equal weights to the equal interests of the occupants of all the roles'.[2] I shall call a critique based on such an approach a *prior-principle critique*. Both approaches can be used in assessing the moral claims of each type of equality, and will indeed be used here.

## 1 Utilitarian Equality

Utilitarian equality is the equality that can be derived from the utilitarian concept of goodness applied to problems of distribution. Perhaps the simplest case is the 'pure distribution problem': the problem of dividing a given homogeneous cake among a group of persons.[3] Each person gets more utility the larger his share of the cake, and gets utility *only* from his share of the cake; his utility increases at a diminishing rate as the amount of his share goes up. The utilitarian objective is to maximize the sum-total of utility irrespective of distribution, but that requires the *equality* of the *marginal* utility of everyone—marginal utility being the incremental utility each person would get from an additional unit of cake.[4] According to one interpretation, this equality of marginal utility embodies equal treatment of everyone's interests.[5]

The position is a bit more complicated when the total size of the cake is not independent of its distribution. But even then maximization of the total utility sum requires that transfers be carried to the point at which the marginal utility gain of the gainers equals the marginal utility loss of the losers, after taking

1. J. Rawls, *A Theory of Justice* (Cambridge: Harvard University Press, 1971), pp. 17–22. See also W. Vickrey, 'Measuring Marginal Utility by Reactions to Risk', *Econometrica,* 13 (1945), and J. C. Harsanyi, 'Cardinal Welfare, Individualistic Ethics, and Interpersonal Comparisons of Utility', *Journal of Political Economy,* 63 (1955).

2. R. M. Hare, *The Language of Morals* (Oxford: Clarendon Press, 1952); 'Ethical Theory and Utilitarianism', in H. D. Lewis (ed.), *Contemporary British Philosophy* (London: Allen & Unwin, 1976), pp. 116–17.

3. I have tried to use this format for an axiomatic contrast of the Rawlsian and utilitarian criteria in 'Rawls versus Bentham: An Axiomatic Examination of the Pure Distribution Problem', in *Theory and Decision,* 4 (1974); reprinted in N. Daniels (ed.), *Reading Rawls* (Oxford: Blackwell, 1975). See also L. Kern, 'Comparative Distributive Ethics: An Extension of Sen's Examination of the Pure Distribution Problem', in H. W. Gottinger and W. Leinfellner (eds), *Decision Theory and Social Ethics* (Dordrecht: Reidel, 1978), and J. P. Griffin, 'Equality: On Sen's Equity Axiom', mimeographed, 1978. [Later published in *Mind,* 50 (1981).]

4. The equality condition would have to be replaced by a corresponding combination of inequality requirements when the appropriate 'continuity' properties do not hold. Deeper difficulties are raised by 'non-convexities' (e.g., increasing marginal utility).

5. J. Harsanyi, 'Can the Maximin Principle Serve as a Basis for Morality? A Critique of John Rawls' Theory', *American Political Science Review,* 64 (1975).

into account the effect of the transfer on the size and distribution of the cake.[6] It is in this wider context that the special type of equality insisted upon by utilitarianism becomes assertively distinguished. Richard Hare has claimed that 'giving equal weight to the equal interests of all the parties' would 'lead to utilitarianism'—thus satisfying the prior-principle requirement of universalizability.[7] Similarly, John Harsanyi shoots down the non-utilitarians (including this lecturer, I hasten to add), by claiming for utilitarianism an exclusive ability to avoid 'unfair discrimination' between 'one person's and another person's equally urgent human needs'.[8]

The moral importance of needs, on this interpretation, is based exclusively on the notion of utility. This is disputable, and having had several occasions to dispute it in the past,[9] I shall not shy away from disputing it in this particular context. But while I will get on to this issue later, I want first to examine the nature of utilitarian equality without—for the time being—questioning the grounding of moral importance entirely on utility. Even when utility is the sole basis of importance there is still the question as to whether the size of *marginal* utility, irrespective of *total* utility enjoyed by the person, is an adequate index of moral importance. It is, of course, possible to define a metric on utility characteristics such that each person's utility scale is coordinated with everyone else's in a way that equal social importance is simply 'scaled' as equal marginal utility. If interpersonal comparisons of utility are taken to have no descriptive content, then this can indeed be thought to be a natural approach. No matter how the relative social importances are arrived at, the marginal utilities attributed to each person would then simply reflect these values. This can be done explicitly by appropriate interpersonal scaling,[10] or implicitly through making the utility numbering reflect choices in situations of *as if* uncertainty associated with the 'original position' under the additional assumption that ignorance be interpreted as equal probability of

6. As mentioned in footnote 4, the equality conditions would require modification in the absence of continuity of the appropriate type. Transfers must be carried to the point at which the marginal utility gain of the gainers from any further transfer is *no more than* the marginal utility loss of the losers.

7. Hare (1976), pp. 116–17.

8. John Harsanyi, 'Non-linear Social Welfare Functions: A Rejoinder to Professor Sen', in R. E. Butts and J. Hintikka (eds), *Foundational Problems in the Special Sciences* (Dordrecht: Reidel, 1977), pp. 294–5.

9. *Collective Choice and Social Welfare* (San Francisco: Holden-Day, 1970), chapter 6 and section 11.4; 'On Weights and Measures: Informational Constraints in Social Welfare Analysis', *Econometrica*, **45** (1977). See also T. M. Scanlon's arguments against identifying utility with 'urgency' in his 'Preference and Urgency', *Journal of Philosophy*, **72** (1975).

10. For two highly ingenious examples of such an exercise, see Peter Hammond, 'Dual Interpersonal Comparisons of Utility and the Welfare Economics of Income Distribution', *Journal of Public Economics*, **6** (1977): 51–7; and Menahem Yaari, 'Rawls, Edgeworth, Shapley and Nash: Theories of Distributive Justice Re-examined', Research Memorandum No. 33, Center for Research in Mathematical Economics and Game Theory, Hebrew University, Jerusalem, 1978.

being anyone.[11] This is not the occasion to go into the technical details of this type of exercise, but the essence of it consists in using a scaling procedure such that marginal utility measures are automatically identified as indicators of social importance.

This route to utilitarianism may meet with little resistance, but it is non-controversial mainly because it says so little. A problem arises the moment utilities and interpersonal comparisons thereof are taken to have some independent descriptive content, as utilitarians have traditionally insisted that they do. There could then be conflicts between these descriptive utilities and the appropriately scaled, essentially normative, utilities in terms of which one is 'forced' to be a utilitarian. In what follows I shall have nothing more to say on utilitarianism through appropriate interpersonal scaling, and return to examining the traditional utilitarian position, which takes utilities to have interpersonally comparable descriptive content. How moral importance should relate to these descriptive features must, then, be explicitly faced.

The position can be examined from the prior-principle perspective as well as from the case-implication angle. John Rawls's criticism as a preliminary to presenting his own alternative conception of justice took mostly the prior-principle form. This was chiefly in terms of acceptability in the 'original position', arguing that in the postulated situation of *as if* ignorance people would not choose to maximize the utility sum. But Rawls also discussed the violence that utilitarianism does to our notions of liberty and equality. Some replies to Rawls's arguments have reasserted the necessity to be a utilitarian by taking the 'scaling' route, which was discussed earlier, and which—I think—is inappropriate in meeting Rawls's critique. But I must confess that I find the lure of the 'original position' distinctly resistible since it seems very unclear what precisely would be chosen in such a situation. It is also far from obvious that prudential choice under *as if* uncertainty provides an adequate basis for moral judgement in *un*original, i.e., real-life, positions.[12] But I believe Rawls's more direct critiques in terms of liberty and equality do remain powerful.

In so far as one is concerned with the *distribution* of utilities, it follows immediately that utilitarianism would in general give one little comfort. Even the minutest gain in total utility *sum* would be taken to outweigh distributional inequalities of the most blatant kind. This problem would be avoidable under certain assumptions, notably the case in which everyone has the *same* utility function. In the pure distribution problem, with this assumption the utilitarian best would require absolute equality of everyone's total

11. See Harsanyi (1955, 1975, 1977).

12. On this, see Thomas Nagel, 'Rawls on Justice', *Philosophical Review,* **83** (1973), and 'Equality' in his *Mortal Questions* (Cambridge: Cambridge University Press, 1979).

utilities.[13] This is because when the marginal utilities are equated, so would be the total utilities if everyone has the same utility function. This is, however, egalitarianism by serendipity: just the accidental result of the marginal tail wagging the total dog. More importantly, the assumption would be very frequently violated, since there are obvious and well-discussed variations between human beings. John may be easy to please, but Jeremy not. If it is taken to be an acceptable prior-principle that the equality of the distribution of total utilities has some value, then the utilitarian conception of equality—marginal as it is—must stand condemned.

The recognition of the fundamental diversity of human beings does, in fact, have very deep consequences, affecting not merely the utilitarian conception of social good, but others as well, including (as I shall argue presently) even the Rawlsian conception of equality. If human beings are identical, then the application of the prior-principle of universalizability in the form of 'giving equal weight to the equal interest of all parties' simplifies enormously. Equal marginal utilities of all—reflecting one interpretation of the equal treatment of needs—coincides with equal total utilities—reflecting one interpretation of serving their overall interests equally well. With diversity, the two can pull in opposite directions, and it is far from clear that 'giving equal weight to the equal interest of all parties' would require us to concentrate only one one of the two parameters—taking no note of the other.

The case-implication perspective can also be used to develop a related critique, and I have tried to present such a critique elsewhere.[14] For example, if person A as a cripple gets half the utility that the pleasure-wizard person B does from any given level of income, then in the pure distribution problem between A and B the utilitarian would end up giving the pleasure-wizard B more income than the cripple A. The cripple would then be doubly worse off: both since he gets less utility from the same level of income, *and* since he will also get less income. Utilitarianism must lead to this thanks to its single-minded concern with maximizing the utility sum. The pleasure-wizard's superior efficiency in producing utility would pull income away from the less efficient cripple.

Since this example has been discussed a certain amount,[15] I should perhaps explain what is being asserted and what is not. First, it is *not* being claimed that anyone who has lower total utility (e.g., the cripple) at any given level of income must of necessity have lower marginal utility also. This must be true

13. The problem is much more complex when the total cake is not fixed, and where the maximization of utility sum need not lead to the equality of total utilities unless some additional assumptions are made, e.g., the absence of incentive arguments for inequality.

14. *On Economic Inequality* (Oxford: Clarendon Press, 1973), pp. 16–20.

15. See John Harsanyi, 'Non-linear Social Welfare Functions', *Theory and Decision,* 6(1976): 311–12; Harsanyi (1977); Kern (1978); Griffin (1978); Richard B. Brandt, *A Theory of the Good and the Right* (Oxford: Clarendon Press, 1979), chapter 16.

for some levels of income, but need not be true everywhere. Indeed, the opposite could be the case when incomes are equally distributed. If that were so, then of course even utilitarianism would give the cripple more income than the non-cripple, since at that point the cripple would be the more efficient producer of utility. My point is that there is no guarantee that this will be the case, and more particularly, if it were the case that the cripple were not only worse off in terms of total utility but could convert income into utility less efficiently everywhere (or even just at the point of equal income division), then utilitarianism would compound his disadvantage by settling him with less income on top of lower efficiency in making utility out of income. The point, of course, is not about cripples in general, nor about all people with total utility disadvantage, but concerns people—including cripples—with disadvantage in terms of both total *and* marginal utility at the relevant points.

Second, the descriptive content of utility is rather important in this context. Obviously, if utilities were scaled to reflect moral importance, then wishing to give priority to income for the cripple would simply amount to attributing a higher 'marginal utility' to the cripple's income; but this—as we have already discussed—is a very special sense of utility, quite devoid of descriptive content. In terms of descriptive features, what is being assumed in our example is that the cripple can be helped by giving him income, but the increase in his utility as a consequence of a marginal increase in income is less—in terms of the accepted descriptive criteria—than giving that unit of income to the pleasure-wizard, when both have initially the same income.

Finally, the problem for utilitarianism in this case-implication argument is not dependent on an implicit assumption that the claim to more income arising from disadvantage must dominate over the claim arising from high marginal utility.[16] A system that gives some weight to both claims would still fail to meet the utilitarian formula of social good, which demands an exclusive concern with the latter claim. It is this narrowness that makes the utilitarian conception of equality such a limited one. Even when utility is accepted as the only basis of moral importance, utilitarianism fails to capture the relevance of overall advantage for the requirements of equality. The prior-principle critiques can be supplemented by case-implication critiques using this utilitarian lack of concern with distributional questions except at the entirely marginal level.

## 2   *Total Utility Equality*

Welfarism is the view that the goodness of a state of affairs can be judged

---

16. Such an assumption is made in my Weak Equity Axiom, proposed in Sen (1973), but it is unnecessarily demanding for rejecting utilitarianism. See Griffin (1978) for a telling critique of the Weak Equity Axiom, in this exacting form.

entirely by the goodness of the utilities in that state.[17] This is a less demanding view than utilitarianism in that it does not demand—in addition—that the goodness of the utilities must be judged by their sum-total. Utilitarianism is, in this sense, a special case of welfarism, and provides one illustration of it. Another distinguished case is the criterion of judging the goodness of a state by the utility level of the worst-off person in that state—a criterion often attributed to John Rawls. (*Except* by John Rawls! He uses social primary goods rather than utility as the index of advantage, as we shall presently discuss.) One can also take some other function of the utilities—other than the sum-total or the minimal element.

Utilitarian equality is one type of welfarist equality. There are others, notably the equality of total utility. It is tempting to think of this as some kind of an analogue of utilitarianism shifting the focus from marginal utility to total utility. This correspondence is, however, rather less close than it might first appear. First of all, while we economists often tend to treat the marginal and the total as belonging to the same plane of discourse, there is an important difference between them. Marginal is an essentially *counter-factual* notion: marginal utility is the additional utility that *would be* generated if the person had one more unit of income. It contrasts what is observed with what allegedly would be observed if something else were different: in this case if the income had been one unit greater. Total is not, however, an inherently counter-factual concept; whether it is or is not would depend on the variable that is being totalled. In case of utilities, if they are taken to be observed facts, total utility will not be counter-factual. Thus total utility equality is a matter for direct observation, whereas utilitarian equality is not so, since the latter requires hypotheses as to what things would have been under different postulated circumstances. The contrast can be easily traced to the fact that utilitarian equality is essentially a consequence of sum *maximization*, which is itself a counter-factual notion, whereas total utility equality is an equality of some directly observed magnitudes.

Second, utilitarianism provides a complete ordering of all utility distributions—the ranking reflecting the order of the sums of individual utilities—but as specified so far, total utility equality does not do more than just point to the case of absolute equality. In dealing with two cases of non-equal distributions, something more has to be said so that they could be ranked. The ranking can be completed in many different ways.

One way to such a complete ranking is provided by the lexicographic version of the maximin rule, which is associated with the Rawlsian Difference Principle, but interpreted in terms of utilities as opposed to primary goods. Here the goodness of the state of affairs is judged by the level of utility of the worst-off person in that state; but if the worst-off persons in two states respectively have the same level of utility, then the states are ranked according to the utility levels of the second worst-off. If they too tie, then by the utility levels of the third worst-off, and so on. And if two utility distributions are matched at each rank all the way from the worst off to the best off, then the two distributions are equally good. Following a convention established in social choice theory, I shall call this *leximin*.

In what way does total utility equality lead to the leximin? It does this when combined with some other axioms, and in fact the analysis closely parallels the recent axiomatic derivations of the Difference Principle by several authors.[18] Consider four utility levels *a, b, c, d*, in decreasing order of magnitude. One can argue that in an obvious sense the pair of extreme points (*a, d*) displays greater inequality than the pair of intermediate points (*b, c*). Note that this is a purely *ordinal* comparison based on ranking only, and the exact magnitudes of *a, b, c*, and *d* make no difference to the comparison in question. If one were *solely* concerned with equality, then it could be argued that (*b, c*) is superior—or at least non-inferior—to (*a, d*). This requirement may be seen as a strong version of preferring equality of utility distributions, and may be called 'utility equality preference'. It is possible to combine this with an axiom due to Patrick Suppes which captures the notion of *dominance* of one utility distribution over another, in the sense of each element of one distribution being at least as large as the corresponding element in the other distribution.[19] In the two-person case this requires that state *x* must be regarded as at least as good as *y*, *either* if each person in state *x* has at least as much utility as himself in state *y*, *or* if each person in state *x* has at least as much utility as the *other* person in state *y*. *If*, in addition, at least one of them has strictly more, then of course *x* could be declared to be strictly better (and not merely at least as good). If this Suppes principle and the 'utility equality preference' are combined, then we are pushed in the direction of leximin. Indeed, leximin can be fully derived from these two principles by requiring that the approach must provide a complete ordering of all possible states no matter what the interpersonally comparable individual utilities happen to be (called 'unrestricted domain'), and that the ranking of any two states must depend on utility information concerning *those* states only (called 'independence').

In so far as the requirements other than utility equality preference (i.e., the

18. See P. J. Hammond, 'Equity, Arrow's Conditions and Rawls' Difference Principle', *Econometrica,* **44** (1976); S. Strasnick, 'Social Choice Theory and the Derivation of Rawls' Difference Principle', *Journal of Philosophy,* **73** (1976); C. d'Aspremont and L. Gevers, 'Equity and Informational Basis of Collective Choice', *Review of Economic Studies,* **44** (1977); K. J. Arrow, 'Extended Sympathy and the Possibility of Social Choice', *American Economic Review,* **67** (1977); A. K. Sen, 'On Weights and Measures: Informational Constraints in Social Welfare Analysis', *Econometrica,* **45** (1977) [Essay 11 in this volume]; R. Deschamps and L. Gevers, 'Leximin and Utilitarian Rules: A Joint Characterization', *Journal of Economic Theory,* **17** (1978); K. W. S. Roberts, 'Possibility Theorems with Interpersonally Comparable Welfare Levels', *Review of Economic Studies,* **47** (1980); P. J. Hammond, 'Two Person Equity', *Econometrica,* **47** (1979).

19. P. Suppes, 'Some Formal Models of Grading Principles', *Synthese,* **6** (1966).

Suppes principle, unrestricted domain, and independence) are regarded as acceptable—and they have indeed been widely used in the social choice literature—leximin can be seen as the natural concomitant of giving priority to the conception of equality focusing on total utility.

It should be obvious, however, that leximin can be fairly easily criticized from the prior-principle perspective as well as the case-implication perspective. Just as utilitarianism pays no attention to the force of one's claim arising from one's disadvantage, leximin ignores claims arising from the *intensity* of one's needs. The *ordinal* characteristic that was pointed out while presenting the axiom of utility equality preference makes the approach insensitive to the magnitudes of potential utility gains and losses. While in the critique of utilitarianism that was presented earlier I argued against treating these potential gains and losses as the only basis of moral judgement, it was *not* of course alleged that these have no moral relevance at all. Take the comparison of $(a, d)$ vis-à-vis $(b, c)$, discussed earlier, and let $(b, c)$ stand for $(3, 2)$. Utility equality preference would assert the superiority of $(3, 2)$ over $(10, 1)$ as well as $(4, 1)$. Indeed, it would not distinguish between the two cases at all. It is this lack of concern with 'how much' questions that makes leximin rather easy to criticise *either* by showing its failure to comply with such prior-principles as 'giving equal weight to the equal interest of all parties', *or* by spelling out its rather austere implications in specific cases.

Aside from its indifference to 'how much' questions, leximin also has little interest in 'how many' questions—paying no attention at all to the number of people whose interests are overridden in the pursuit of the interests of the worst off. The worst-off position rules the roost, and it does not matter whether this goes against the interests of one other person, or against those of a million or a billion other persons. It is sometimes claimed that leximin would not be such an extreme criterion if it could be modified so that this innumeracy were avoided, and if the interests of *one* worse-off position were given priority over the interests of exactly *one* better-off position, but not necessarily against the interests of *more than one* better-off position. In fact, one can define a less demanding version of leximin, which can be called leximin-2, which takes the form of applying the leximin principle *if* all persons other than two are indifferent between the alternatives, but not necessarily otherwise. Leximin-2, as a compromise, will be still unconcerned with 'how much' questions on the magnitudes of utilities of the two non-indifferent persons, but need not be blinkered about 'how many' questions dealing with numbers of people: the priority applies to one person over exactly one other.[20]

---

20. Leximin—and maximin—are concerned with conflicts between positional priorities, i.e., between ranks (such as the 'worst-off position', 'second worst-off position', etc.), and not with interpersonal priorities. When positions coincide with persons (e.g., the *same* person being the worst off in each state), then positional conflicts translate directly into personal conflicts.

Interestingly enough, a consistency problem intervenes here. It can be proved that given the regularity conditions, viz., unrestricted domain and independence, leximin-2 logically entails leximin in general.[21] That is, given these regularity conditions, there is no way of retaining moral sensitivity to the number of people on each side by choosing the limited requirement of leximin-2 without going all the way to leximin itself. It appears that indifference to *how much* questions concerning utilities implies indifference to *how many* questions concerning the number of people on different sides. One innumeracy begets another.

Given the nature of these critiques of utilitarian equality and total utility equality respectively, it is natural to ask whether some *combination* of the two should not meet both sets of objections. If utilitarianism is attacked for its unconcern with inequalities of the utility distribution, and leximin is criticized for its lack of interest in the magnitudes of utility gains and losses, and even in the numbers involved, then isn't the right solution to choose some mixture of the two? It is at this point that the long-postponed question of the relation between utility and moral worth becomes crucial. While utilitarianism and leximin differ sharply from each other in the use that they respectively make of the utility information, both share an exclusive concern with utility data. If non-utility considerations have any role in either approach, this arises from the part they play in the determination of utilities, or possibly as surrogates for utility information in the absence of adequate utility data. A combination of utilitarianism and leximin would still be confined to the box of welfarism, and it remains to be examined whether welfarism as a general approach is *itself* adequate.

One aspect of the obtuseness of welfarism was discussed clearly by John Rawls.

> In calculating the greatest balance of satisfaction it does not matter, except indirectly, what the desires are for. We are to arrange institutions so as to obtain the greatest sum of satisfactions; we ask no questions about their source or quality but only how their satisfaction would affect the total of well-being ... Thus if men take a certain pleasure in discriminating against one another, in subjecting others to a lesser liberty as a means of enhancing their self-respect, then the satisfaction of these desires must be weighed in our deliberations according to their intensity, or whatever, along with other desires ... In justice as fairness, on the other hand, persons accept in advance a principle of equal liberty and they do this without a knowledge of their more particular ends ... An individual who finds that he enjoys seeing others in positions of lesser liberty understands that he has no claim whatever to this enjoyment. The pleasure he takes in other's deprivation is wrong in itself: it is a

---

21. Theorem 8, Sen (1977). See also Hammond (1979) for extensions of this result.

satisfaction which requires the violation of a principle to which he would agree in the original position.[22]

It is easily seen that this is an argument not merely against utilitarianism, but against the adequacy of utility information for moral judgements of states of affairs, and is, thus, an attack on welfarism in general. Second, it is clear that as a criticism of welfarism—and *a fortiori* as a critique of utilitarianism—the argument uses a principle that is unnecessarily strong. If it were the case that pleasures taken 'in other's deprivation' were not taken to be wrong in itself, but simply *disregarded*, even then the rejection of welfarism would stand. Furthermore, even if such pleasures were regarded as valuable, but *less* valuable than pleasures arising from other sources (e.g., enjoying food, work, or leisure), welfarism would still stand rejected. The issue—as John Stuart Mill had noted—is the lack of 'parity' between one source of utility and another.[23] Welfarism requires the endorsement not merely of the widely shared intuition that any pleasure has some value—and one would have to be a bit of a kill-joy to dissent from this—but also the much more dubious proposition that pleasures must be relatively weighed *only* according to their respective intensities, irrespective of the source of the pleasure and the nature of the activity that goes with it. Finally, Rawls's argument takes he form of an appeal to the prior-principle of equating moral rightness with prudential acceptability in the original position. Even those who do not accept that prior-principle could reject the welfarist no-nonsense counting of utility irrespective of all other information by reference to other prior-principles, e.g., the irreducible value of liberty

The relevance of non-utility information to moral judgements is the central issue involved in disputing welfarism. Libertarian considerations point towards a particular class of non-utility information, and I have argued elsewhere that this may require even the rejection of the so-called Pareto principle based on utility dominance.[24] But there are also other types of non-utility information which have been thought to be intrinsically important. Tim Scanlon has recently discussed the contrast between 'urgency' and utility (or intensity of preference). He has also argued that 'the criteria of well-being that we actually employ in making moral judgements are objective', and a person's level of well-being is taken to be 'independent of that person's tastes and interests'.[25] These moral judgements could thus conflict with utilitarian—and more generally (Scanlon could have argued) with welfarist—moralities, no matter whether utility is interpreted as pleasure, or—as is increasingly common recently—as desire-fulfilment.

22. Rawls (1971), pp. 30–1.
23. John Stuart Mill, *On Liberty* (1859), p. 140.
24. Sen (1970), especially chapter 6. Also Sen (1979).
25. T. M. Scanlon (1975), pp. 658–9.

However, acknowledging the relevance of objective factors does not require that well-being be taken to be independent of tastes, and Scanlon's categories are *too* pure. For example, a lack of 'parity' between utility from self-regarding actions and that from other-regarding actions will go beyond utility as an index of well-being and will be fatal to welfarism, but the contrast is not, of course, independent of tastes and subjective features. 'Objective' considerations can count along with a person's tastes. What is required is the denial that a person's well-being be judged *exclusively* in terms of his or her utilities. If such judgements take into account a person's pleasures and desire-fulfilments, but also certain objective factors, e.g., whether he or she is hungry, cold, or oppressed, the resulting calculus would still be non-welfarist. Welfarism is an extremist position, and its denial can take many different forms—pure and mixed—so long as totally ignoring non-utility information is avoided.

Second, it is also clear that the notion of urgency need not work only *through* the determinants of personal well-being—however broadly conceived. For example, the claim that one should not be *exploited* at work is not based on making exploitation an additional parameter in the specification of well-being on top of such factors as income and effort, but on the moral view that a person deserves to get what he—according to one way of characterizing production—has produced. Similarly, the urgency deriving from principles such as 'equal pay for equal work' hits directly at discrimination without having to redefine the notion of personal well-being to take note of such discriminations. One could, for example, say: 'She must be paid just as much as the men working in that job, not primarily because she would otherwise have a lower level of well-being than the others, but simply because she is doing the *same* work as the men there, and why should she be paid less?' These moral claims, based on non-welfarist conceptions of equality, have played important parts in social movements, and it seems difficult to sustain the hypothesis that they are purely 'instrumental' claims—ultimately justified by their indirect impact on the fulfilment of welfarist, or other well-being-based, objectives.

Thus the dissociation of urgency from utility can arise from two different sources. One disentangles the notion of personal well-being from utility, and the other makes urgency not a function only of well-being. But, at the same time, the former does not require that well-being be independent of utility, and the latter does not necessitate a notion of urgency that is independent of personal well-being. Welfarism is a purist position and must avoid any contamination from either of these sources.

### 3   Rawlsian Equality

Rawls's 'two principles of justice' characterize the need for equality in terms of—what he has called—'primary social goods'.[26] These are 'things that every rational man is presumed to want', including 'rights, liberties and opportunities, income and wealth, and the social bases of self-respect'. Basic liberties are separated out as having priority over other primary goods, and thus priority is given to the principle of liberty which demands that 'each person is to have an equal right to the most extensive basic liberty compatible with a similar liberty for others'. The second principle supplements this, demanding efficiency and equality, judging advantage in terms of an index of primary goods. Inequalities are condemned unless they work out to everyone's advantage. This incorporates the 'Difference Principle' in which priority is given to furthering the interests of the worst-off. And that leads to maximin, or to leximin, defined not on individual utilities but on the index of primary goods. But given the priority of the liberty principle, no trade-offs are permitted between basic liberties and economic and social gain.

Herbert Hart has persuasively disputed Rawls's arguments for the priority of liberty,[27] but with that question I shall not be concerned in this lecture. What is crucial for the problem under discussion is the concentration on bundles of primary social goods. Some of the difficulties with welfarism that I tried to discuss will not apply to the pursuit of Rawlsian equality. Objective criteria of well-being can be directly accommodated within the index of primary goods. So can be Mill's denial of the parity between pleasures from different sources, since the sources can be discriminated on the basis of the nature of the goods. Furthermore, while the Difference Principle is egalitarian in a way similar to leximin, it avoids the much-criticized feature of leximin of giving more income to people who are hard to please and who have to be deluged in champagne and buried in caviar to bring them to a normal level of utility, which you and I get from a sandwich and beer. Since advantage is judged not in terms of utilities at all, but through the index of primary goods, expensive tastes cease to provide a ground for getting more income. Rawls justifies this in terms of a person's responsibility for his own ends.

But what about the cripple with utility disadvantage, whom we discussed earlier? Leximin will give him more income in a pure distribution problem. Utilitarianism, I had complained, will give him *less*. The Difference Principle will give him neither more nor less on grounds of his being a cripple. His utility disadvantage will be irrelevant to the Difference Principle. This may seem hard, and I think it is. Rawls justifies this by pointing out that 'hard cases' can 'distract our moral perception by leading us to think of people distant from us whose fate arouses pity and anxiety'.[28] This can be so, but

---

26. Rawls (1971), pp. 60–5.

27. H. L. A. Hart, 'Rawls on Liberty and Its Priority', *University of Chicago Law Review,* **40** (1973); reprinted in N. Daniels (ed.), *Reading Rawls* (Oxford: Blackwell, 1975).

28. John Rawls, 'A Kantian Concept of Equality', *Cambridge Review* (February 1975), p. 96. [My criticism here of Rawls's argument gives a misleading impression of the content of that argument. Rawls is, in fact, justifying *postponing* the question rather than justifying *ignoring*

hard cases do exist, and to take disabilities, or special health needs, or physical or mental defects, as morally irreleant, or to leave them out for fear of making a mistake, may guarantee that the *opposite* mistake will be made.

And the problem does not end with hard cases. The primary goods approach seems to take little note of the diversity of human beings. In the context of assessing utilitarian equality, it was argued that if people were fundamentally similar in terms of utility functions, then the utilitarian concern with maximizing the sum-total of utilities would push us simultaneously also in the direction of equality of utility levels. Thus utilitarianism could be rendered vastly more attractive if people really were similar. A corresponding remark can be made about the Rawlsian Difference Principle. If people were basically very similar, then an index of primary goods might be quite a good way of judging advantage. But, in fact, people seem to have very different needs varying with health, longevity, climatic conditions, location, work conditions, temperament, and even body size (affecting food and clothing requirements). So what is involved is not merely ignoring a few hard cases, but overlooking very widespread and real differences. Judging advantage purely in terms of primary goods leads to a partially blind morality.

Indeed, it can be argued that there is, in fact, an element of 'fetishism' in the Rawlsian framework. Rawls takes primary goods as the embodiment of advantage, rather than taking advantage to be a *relationship* between persons and goods. Utilitarianism, or leximin, or—more generally—welfarism does not have this fetishism, since utilities are reflections of one type of relation between persons and goods. For example, income and wealth are not valued under utilitarianism as physical units, but in terms of their capacity to create human happiness or to satisfy human desires. Even if utility is not thought to be the right focus for the person-good relationship, to have an entirely good-oriented framework provides a peculiar way of judging advantage.

It can also be argued that while utility in the form of happiness or desire-fulfilment may be an *inadequate* guide to urgency, the Rawlsian framework asserts it to be *irrelevant* to urgency, which is, of course, a much stronger claim. The distinction was discussed earlier in the context of assessing welfarism, and it was pointed out that a rejection of welfarism need not take us to the point in which utility is given no role whatsoever. That a person's interest should have nothing directly to do with his happiness or desire-fulfilment seems difficult to justify. Even in terms of the prior-principle of prudential acceptability in the 'orginal position', it is not at all clear why people in that primordial state should be taken to be so indifferent to the joys

---

it. For this misimpression, I must apologize to John Rawls. However, I should also add that I believe that a substantial theory of justice cannot sensibly postpone this question in developing the basic structure of the theory. Need differences—of which 'hard cases' are just extreme examples—are pervasive, and they deserve a more central place in a theory of justice such as Rawls's.]

and sufferings in occupying particular positions, or if they are not, why their concern about these joys and sufferings should be taken to be morally irrelevant.

## 4 Basic Capability Equality

This leads to the further question: Can we not construct an adequate theory of equality on the *combined* grounds of Rawlsian equality and equality under the two welfarist conceptions, with some trade-offs among them. I would now like to argue briefly why I believe this too may prove to be informationally short. This can, of course, easily be asserted *if* claims arising from considerations other than well-being were acknowledged to be legitimate. Non-exploitation, or non-discrimination, requires the use of information not fully captured either by utility or by primary goods. Other conceptions of entitlements can also be brought in going beyond concern with personal well-being only. But in what follows I shall not introduce these concepts. My contention is that *even* the concept of *needs* does not get adequate coverage through the information on primary goods and utility.

I shall use a case-implication argument. Take the cripple again with marginal utility disadvantage. We saw that utilitarianism would do nothing for him; in fact it will give him *less* income than to the physically fit. Nor would the Difference Principle help him; it will leave his physical disadvantage severely alone. He did, however, get preferential treatment under leximin, and more generally, under criteria fostering total equality. His low level of total utility was the basis of his claim. But now suppose that he is no worse off than others in utility terms despite his physical handicap because of certain other utility features. This could be because he has a jolly disposition. Or because he has a low aspiration level and his heart leaps up whenever he sees a rainbow in the sky. Or because he is religious and feels that he will be rewarded in after-life, or cheerfully accepts what he takes to be just penalty for misdeeds in a past incarnation. The important point is that despite his marginal utility disadvantage, he has no longer a total utility deprivation. Now not even leximin—or any other notion of equality focusing on total utility—will do much for him. If we still think that he has needs as a cripple that should be catered to, then the basis of that claim clearly rests neither in high marginal utility, nor in low total utility, nor—of course—in deprivation in terms of primary goods.

It is arguable that what is missing in all this framework is some notion of 'basic capabilities': a person being able to do certain basic things. The ability to move about is the relevant one here, but one can consider others, e.g., the ability to meet one's nutritional requirements, the wherewithal to be clothed and sheltered, the power to participate in the social life of the community. The notion of urgency related to this is not fully captured by either utility or primary goods, or any combination of the two. Primary goods suffers from fetishist handicap in being concerned with goods, and even though the list of goods is specified in a broad and inclusive way, encompassing rights, liberties, opportunities, income, wealth, and the social basis of self-respect, it still is concerned with good things rather than with what these good things *do* to human beings. Utility, on the other hand, *is* concerned with what these things do to human beings, but uses a metric that focuses not on the person's capabilities but on his mental reaction. There is something still missing in the combined list of primary goods and utilities. If it is argued that resources should be devoted to remove or substantially reduce the handicap of the cripple despite there being no marginal utility argument (because it is expensive), despite there being no total utility argument (because he is so contented), and despite there being no primary goods deprivation (because he has the goods that others have), the case must rest on something else. I believe what is at issue is the interpretation of needs in the form of basic capabilities, This interpretation of needs and interests is often implicit in the demand for equality. This type of equality I shall call 'basic capability equality'.

The focus on basic capabilities can be seen as a natural extension of Rawls's concern with primary goods, shifting attention from goods to what goods do to human beings. Rawls himself motivates judging advantage in terms of primary goods by referring to capabilities, even though his criteria end up focusing on goods as such: on income rather than on what income does, on the 'social bases of self-respect' rather than on self-respect itself, and so on. If human beings were very like each other, this would not have mattered a great deal, but there is evidence that the conversion of goods to capabilities varies from person to person substantially, and the equality of the former may still be far from the equality of the latter.

There are, of course, many difficulties with the notion of 'basic capability equality'. In particular, the problem of indexing the basic capability bundles is a serious one. It is, in many ways, a problem comparable with the indexing of primary good bundles in the context of Rawlsian equality. This is not the occasion to go into the technical issues involved in such an indexing, but it is clear that whatever partial ordering can be done on the basis of broad uniformity of personal preferences must be supplemented by certain established conventions of relative importance.

The ideas of relative importance are, of course, conditional on the nature of the society. The notion of the equality of basic capabilities is a very general one, but any application of it must be rather culture-dependent, especially in the weighting of different capabilities. While Rawlsian equality has the characteristic of being both culture-dependent and fetishist, basic capability equality avoids fetishism, but remains culture-dependent. Indeed, basic capability equality can be seen as essentially an extension of the Rawlsian approach in a non-fetishist direction.

## 5 Concluding Remarks

I end with three final remarks. First, it is not my contention that basic capability equality can be the sole guide to the moral good. For one thing morality is not concerned only with equality. For another, while it is my contention that basic capability equality has certain clear advantages over other types of equality, I did not argue that the others were morally irrelevant. Basic capability equality is a partial guide to the part of moral goodness that is associated with the idea of equality. I have tried to argue that as a partial guide it has virtues that the other characterizations of equality do not possess.

Second, the index of basic capabilities, like utility, can be used in many different ways. Basic capability equality corresponds to total utility equality, and it can be extended in different directions, e.g., to leximin of basic capabilities. On the other hand, the index can be used also in a way similar to utilitarianism, judging the strength of a claim in terms of incremental contribution to *enhancing* the index value. The main departure is in focusing on a *magnitude* different from utility as well as the primary goods index. The new dimension can be utilized in different ways, of which basic capability equality is only one.

Last, the bulk of this lecture has been concerned with rejecting the claims of utilitarian equality, total utility equality, and Rawlsian equality to provide a sufficient basis for the equality-aspect of morality—indeed, even for that part of it which is concerned with needs rather than deserts. I have argued that none of these three is sufficient, nor is any combination of the three.

This is my main thesis. I have also made the constructive claim that this gap can be narrowed by the idea of basic capability equality, and more generally by the use of basic capability as a morally relevant dimension taking us beyond utility and primary goods. I should end by pointing out that the validity of the main thesis is not conditional on the acceptance of this constructive claim.†

† [The capability approach has been further explored in the context of the theory of rights in my 'Rights and Agency', *Philosophy and Public Affairs*, **11** (1982), and in relation to judgements of the standard of living in a forthcoming book, *Standard of Living*, Hennipman Lecture, to be published by North-Holland, Amsterdam.]

# Part V

# Social Measurement

# 17

# Poverty: An Ordinal Approach to Measurement

### 1 *Motivation*

In the measurement of poverty two distinct problems must be faced, viz., (i) identifying the poor among the total population, and (ii) constructing an index of poverty using the available information on the poor. The former problem involves the choice of a criterion of poverty (e.g., the selection of a 'poverty line' in terms of real income per head), and then ascertaining those who satisfy that criterion (e.g., fall below the 'poverty line') and those who do not. In the literature on poverty significant contributions have been made in tackling this problem (see, for example, Rowntree [27], Weisbrod [41], Townsend [39], and Atkinson [1]), but relatively little work has been done on problem (ii) with which this paper will be concerned.

The most common procedure for handling problem (ii) seems to be simply to count the number of the poor and check the percentage of the total population belonging to this category. This ratio, which we shall call the head-count ratio $H$, is obviously a very crude index. An unchanged number of people below the 'poverty line' may go with a sharp rise in the extent of the short-fall of income from the poverty line.[1]

The measure is also completely insensitive to the distribution of income among the poor. A pure transfer of income from the poorest poor to those

For helpful comments I am very grateful to Sudhir Anand, Tony Atkinson, Idrak Bhatty, Frank Fisher, Richard Layard, Suresh Tendulkar, and to an anonymous referee of *Econometrica*.

1. Cf. 'Its [the new Poor Law's] only effect was that whereas previously three to four million half paupers had existed, a million of total paupers now appeared, and the rest, still half paupers, merely went without relief. The poverty in the agricultural districts has increased every year' (Engels [10, p. 288]).

From *Econometrica*, **44** (March 1976), 219–31.

who are better off will either keep $H$ unchanged, or make it go down—surely a perverse response. Measure $H$ thus violates both of the following axioms.

MONOTONICITY AXIOM.   *Given other things, a reduction in income of a person below the poverty line must increase the poverty measure.*

TRANSFER AXIOM.   *Given other things, a pure transfer of income from a person below the poverty line to anyone who is richer must increase the poverty measure.*[2]

Despite these limitations, the head-count ratio is very widely used.[3]

Another common measure is the so-called 'poverty gap' (used by the United States Social Security Administration) (see [5, p. 30]) which is the aggregate short-fall of the income of all the poor taken together from the poverty line. This satisfies the monotonicity axiom but violates the transfer axiom.[4]

Though it will not be necessary to use formally the monotonicity axiom and the transfer axiom in deriving the new poverty measure (they will be satisfied anyway, implied by a more demanding axiomatic structure†), the motivation of our search for a new measure can be understood by noticing the violation of these elementary conditions by the poverty measures currently in wide use.

## 2   *Income Short-fall and Poverty*

Consider a community $S$ of $n$ people. The set of $q$ people with income no higher than $x$ is called $S(x)$. If $z$ is 'the poverty line', i.e., the level of income

2. Cf. Dalton's 'principle of transfers' in measuring inequality; see Atkinson [2, pp. 247–9]. See also Dasgupta, Sen and Starrett [9], and Rothschild and Stiglitz [26].

3. The vigorous and illuminting debate on whether or not rural poverty is on the increase in India, which took place recently, was based almost exclusively on using the head-count ratio. See particularly Ojha [24], Dandekar and Rath [8], Minhas [20 and 21], Bardhan [3 and 4], Srinivasan and Vaidyanathan [37], Vaidyanathan [40], and Mukherjee, Bhattacharya and Chatterjee [22]. A remarkable amount of sophistication in correcting consumption data, calculating class-specific deflators, etc., was coupled with the use of this rather crude criterion of measuring poverty.

4. It is also completely insensitive to the *number* of people (or the *percentage* of people) who are poor, sharing a given poverty gap.

† [This is not correct. The poverty measure $P$, which is axiomatically derived here, does not, in fact, invariably satisfy the 'strong' version of the transfer axiom used here; this was noted in 'Social Choice Theory: A Re-examination', *Econometrica,* **45**, January 1977: Essay 8 in this volume, p. 185. The strong version of the transfer axiom takes no note whatsoever of poverty line, which is quite legitimate for a measure of inequality but not perhaps for a measure of poverty. The measure $P$ does satisfy a weaker version of the transfer axiom proposed in Essay 8. The question is discussed in the Introduction to this volume, section 5.1. Further, a minor misstatement in equation (2), also noted in Essay 8, has been corrected here.]

at which poverty begins, $S(z)$ is the set of 'the poor'. $S(\infty)$ is, of course, the set of all, i.e., $S$. The income gap $g_i$ of any individual $i$ is the difference between the poverty line $z$ and his income $y_i$.

$$g_i = z - y_i. \tag{1}$$

Obviously, $g_i$ is non-negative for the poor and negative for others.

For any income configuration represented by an $n$-vector $\mathbf{y}$, 'the aggregate gap' $Q(x)$ of the set $S(x)$ of people with income no higher than $x$ is a normalized weighted sum of the income gaps $g_i$ of everyone in $S(x)$, using non-negative weights $v_i(z, \mathbf{y})$:

$$Q(x) = A(z, q, n) \sum_{i \in S(x)} g_i v_i(z, \mathbf{y}). \tag{2}$$

The specification of $A$ and $v_i$ will depend on a set of axioms to be proposed presently. It should, however, be noted at this stage that the form of (2) is very general indeed, and that $v_i$ has been defined as a function of the vector $\mathbf{y}$, and not of $y_i$ alone (along with $z$). In particular no requirement of additive separability has been imposed.

The index of poverty $P$ of a given income configuration $y$ is defined to be the maximal value of the aggregate gap $Q(x)$ for all $x$:

$$P = \max_x Q(x). \tag{3}$$

Since the weights $v_i$ are all non-negative, it is obvious from (1) and (2) that:

$$P = Q(z). \tag{4}$$

That is, the index of poverty $P$ of a community is given by the value of the weighted aggregate gap of the poor in that community.

## 3    Relative Deprivation and Interpersonal Comparability

In line with the motivation of the transfer axiom, it may be reasonable to require that if person $i$ is accepted to be worse off than person $j$ in a given income configuration $\mathbf{y}$, then the weight $v_i$ on the income short-fall $g_i$ of the worse-off person $i$ should be greater than the weight $v_j$ on the income short-fall $g_j$. Let $W_i(\mathbf{y})$ and $W_j(\mathbf{y})$ be the welfare levels of $i$ and $j$ under configuration $\mathbf{y}$.

AXIOM E (Relative Equity).   *For any pair $i$, $j$: if $W_i(\mathbf{y}) < W_j(\mathbf{y})$, then* $v_i(z, \mathbf{y}) > v_j(z, \mathbf{y})$.

If the individual welfare functions were cardinal, interpersonally fully comparable and identical for all persons, and furthermore if the Benthamite additive utilitarian form of social welfare were accepted, then it would be natural to relate $v_i$ in Axiom E to the marginal utility of income of person $i$.

But in this paper the utilitarian approach is not taken; nor are the assumptions of cardinality and full interpersonal comparability made.[5] Individual welfare is taken to be ordinally measurable and level comparable. There is agreement on who is worse off than whom, e.g., 'poor $i$ is worse off than wealthy $j$', but ho agreement on the values of the welfare differences is required.

While Axiom E can be justified on grounds of a strictly concave interpersonally comparable cardinal welfare function, that is not the only possible justification. The idea that a greater value should be attached to an increase in income (or reduction of short-fall) of a poorer person than that of a relatively richer person can also spring from considerations of interpersonal equity.[6] The appeal of Axiom E is, I believe, much wider than that which can be obtained from an exclusive reliance on utilitarianism and diminishing marginal utility.

Axiom E gives expression to a very mild requirement of equity. Another axiom is now proposed, which incorporates Axiom E, but is substantially more demanding.

AXIOM R (Ordinal Rank Weights).   *The weight $v_i(z, y)$ on the income gap of person $i$ equals the rank order of $i$ in the interpersonal welfare ordering of the poor.*

The method of constructing weights on the basis of rank orders is not new, and since the classic discussion of the procedure by Borda [6] in 1781, it has been extensively analysed and axiomatized in voting theory (see, especially [11; 12, Ch. 13; 14; and 17]). Axiom R is taken as an axiom here, though it can be easily made a theorem derived from more primitive axioms (see Sen [33 and 34]).

There are essentially two ways of doing this. The first is to follow Borda in equidistanced cardinalization of an ordering. If $A$, $B$, and $C$ are ranked in that order in terms of their weights, and if there is no intermediate alternative between $A$ and $B$, and none between $B$ and $C$, 'I say that the degree of superiority that this elector has given to $A$ over $B$ should be considered the same as the degree of superiority that he has accorded to $B$ over $C$' (Borda [7, p. 659], translated by Black [6, p. 157]). We know from Axiom E that if $i$ is worse off than $j$, then the weight on $i$'s income gap should be greater than on $j$'s

5. Alternative frameworks for interpersonal comparability were explored in Sen [29 and 31] in which the possibility of *partial* comparability of cardinal individual welfare functions was also explored. [See Essay 9 in this volume. See also Essay 11, pages 228–30, and Essay 12, pages 272–4.]

6. On various aspects of equity considerations in welfare economics, see Graaff [16], Runciman [28], Kolm [19], Sen [30], and Pattanaik [25].

income gap. Using Borda's procedure combined with appropriate normalization of the origin and the unit, we arrive at Axiom R.

The second is to take a 'relativist' view of poverty, viewing deprivation as an essentially relative concept (see Runciman [28]). The lower a person is in the welfare scale, the greater his sense of poverty, and his welfare rank among others may be taken to indicate the weight to be placed on his income gap.[7] Axiom R can be derived from this approach as well.

We turn now to the relation between income and welfare, since Axioms E and R are in terms of welfare rankings, whereas the observed data are on income rankings. There are, of course, good reasons to think that sometimes a richer person may have lower welfare than a poorer person, e.g., if he is a cripple, and this may raise interesting issues of equity (see [32, Ch. 1]). When dealing with a general measure of poverty for the community as a whole, however, it is not easy to bring such detailed considerations into the exercise. Axiom M proceeds on the cruder assumptions that a richer person is also better off. Furthermore, the individual welfare relation is taken to be a strict complete ordering to avoid some problems that arise with rank-order methods in the case of indifference. This last assumption is less arbitrary than it may at first seem.[8]

AXIOM M (Monotonic Welfare).  *The relation $>$ (greater than) defined on the set of individual welfare numbers $\{W_i(\mathbf{y})\}$ for any income configuration $\mathbf{y}$ is a strict complete ordering, and the relation $>$ defined on the corresponding set of individual incomes $\{y_i\}$ is a sub-relation of the former, i.e., for any i, j: if $y_i > y_j$, then $W_i(\mathbf{y}) > W_j(\mathbf{y})$.*

## 4    Crude Indicators and Normalization

In Section 1, references were made to two measures of poverty currently in use. The 'head-count ratio' is the ratio of the number of people with income $y_i \leqslant z$, to the total population size $n$:

$$H = \frac{q}{n}. \tag{5}$$

The other measure—the poverty gap—is silent on the number of people who share this gap, but can be easily normalized into a per-person percentage

7. This can be axiomatized either in terms of the welfare rank of the person among the poor (as in Axiom R) or in terms of that among the entire population (see Axiom R* in Section 6 below). Both lead to essentially the same result if correspondingly normalized (see Axiom N).

8. The poverty index $P$ to emerge in Theorem 1 is completely insensitive to the way we rank people with the same income. See equation (15) below.

gap $I$, which we shall call the 'income-gap ratio':[9]

$$I = \sum_{i \in S(z)} g_i/qz. \tag{6}$$

While the head-count ratio tells us the percentage of people below the poverty line, the income-gap ratio tells us the percentage of their mean short-fall from the poverty level. The head-count ratio is completely insensitive to the *extent* of the poverty short-fall per person, the income-gap ratio is completely insensitive to the *numbers* involved. Both should have some role in the index of poverty. But $H$ and $I$ together are not sufficiently informative either, since neither gives adequate information on the exact income distribution among the poor. Further, neither measure satisfies the transfer axiom, or the requirement of putting a greater weight on the income gap of the poorer person (axiomatized in Axiom E given Axiom M).

However, in the special case in which all the poor have exactly the *same* income level $y^* < z$, it can be argued that $H$ and $I$ together should give us adequate information on the level of poverty, since in this special case the two together can tell us all about the proportion of people who are below the poverty line and the extent of the income short-fall of each. To obtain a simple normalization, we make $P$ equal $HI$ in this case.

AXIOM N (Normalized Poverty Value).   *If the poor have the same income, then $P = HI$.*

## 5   The Poverty Index Derived

The axioms stated determine one poverty index uniquely. It is easier to state that index if we number the persons in a non-decreasing order of income,[10] i.e., satisfying:

$$y_1 \leqslant y_2 \leqslant \ldots \leqslant y_n. \tag{7}$$

THEOREM 1.   *For large numbers of the poor, the only poverty index satisfying Axioms R, M, and N is given by*:

$$P = H[I + (1 - I)G], \tag{8}$$

*where $G$ is the Gini coefficient of the income distribution of the poor.*

9. Another measure—let us call it $I^*$—is obtained by normalizing the 'poverty gap' on the total income of the community:

$$I^* = Iqz/nm^*, \tag{6*}$$

where $m^*$ is the mean income of the entire population.

10. If there is more than one person having the same income, (7) does not of course determine the numbering uniquely. But the formula for the poverty index specified in Theorem 1 yields the same $P$ no matter which numbering convention is chosen satisfying (7).

*Proof.*    By Axiom M, there is a way of numbering the individuals satisfying (7), such that:

$$W_1(\mathbf{y}) < W_2(\mathbf{y}) \ldots < W_n(\mathbf{y}).\tag{9}$$

For any person $i \leqslant q$, there are exactly $(q + 1 - i)$ people among the poor with at least as high a welfare level as person $i$. Hence by Axiom R:

$$v_i(z, \mathbf{y}) = q + 1 - i.\tag{10}$$

Therefore, from (2) and (4):

$$P = A(z, q, n) \sum_{i=1}^{q} g_i(q + 1 - i).\tag{11}$$

In the special case in which all the poor have the same income $y^*$ and the same income gap $g^* = z - y^*$, we must have:

$$P = A(z, q, n)g^*q(q + 1)/2.\tag{12}$$

But according to Axiom N:

$$P = \left(\frac{q}{n}\right)\left(\frac{g^*}{z}\right).\tag{13}$$

Therefore from (12) and (13):

$$A(z, q, n) = 2/(q + 1)nz.\tag{14}$$

From (11) and (14), it follows that:

$$P = \frac{2}{(q + 1)nz} \sum_{i=1}^{q} (z - y_i)(q + 1 - i).\tag{15}$$

The Gini coefficient $G$ of the Lorenz distribution of incomes of the poor is given by (see Gini [15] and Theil [38]):

$$G = \frac{1}{2q^2m} \sum_{i=1}^{q} \sum_{j=1}^{q} |y_i - y_j|,\tag{16}$$

where $m$ is the mean income of the poor.

Since $|y_i - y_j| = y_i + y_j - 2 \min (y_i, y_j)$, clearly

$$G = 1 - \frac{1}{q^2m} \sum_{i=1}^{q} \sum_{j=1}^{q} \min (y_i, y_j)$$

$$= 1 + \frac{1}{q} - \frac{2}{q^2m} \sum_{i=1}^{q} y_i(q + 1 - i).\tag{17}$$

From (15) and (17), it follows that:

$$P = \frac{1}{(q + 1)nz} \left[zq(q + 1) + q^2m\left(G - \frac{q + 1}{q}\right)\right]$$

which in view of (5) and (6) reduces to:

$$P = H\left[1 - (1 - I)\left(1 - G\left(\frac{q}{q+1}\right)\right)\right]. \tag{18}$$

For large $q$, (18) yields (8). This establishes the necessity part of Theorem 1, and the sufficiency part is easily established by checking that $P$ given by (18), and for large $q$ by (8), does indeed satisfy Axioms R, M, and N.

## 6   Poverty and Inequality

The role of the Gini coefficient of the Lorenz distribution of the incomes of the poor is worth clarifying. This is best done by posing the question: what measure of inequality would follow from the same approach as used here in deriving the poverty measure?

The poverty index was derived by making use of the more primitive concept of the aggregate gap $Q(x)$. It should be noticed that given the weighting system precipitated by Axioms R and M, the value of $Q(x)$ is the same for all $x \geqslant z$, so that $P$ defined by (3) as $\max_x Q(x)$ can be taken to be $Q(x)$ for any $x \geqslant z$ and not merely $x = z$. This is because Axiom R makes the weight on the income gap $g_i$ of person $i$ equal to the number of people *among the poor* who are at least as well off as person $i$. The inclusion of people above the poverty line $z$ does not affect the value of $Q$ since the weight on their income gap $g_i$ is zero in view of Axiom M.

This is reasonable enough in measuring poverty, but if we now shift our attention to the measurement of inequality, we would like to consider the income gaps of people above the poverty line as well. Furthermore, the income gaps should be calculated not from the exogenously given poverty line $z$, but from some internal characteristic of the income configuration y, possibly the mean income. Variations in these lines will transform an absolute poverty measure into a relative measure of inequality.

To do this, we replace $z$ by the mean income $m^*$ of y. Further, the weighting given by Axiom R is modified to include all the people whether poor or not.

AXIOM R*.   *The weight $v_i(z, $ y$)$ on the income gap of person i equals the number of people in S who are at least as well off as person i.*

Axiom R* will require that the weight $v_i$ on the income gap of person $i$ should be $(n + 1 - i)$.

The problem of measurement of inequality and that of poverty can be seen to be two intertwined exercises. The measure of inequality corresponding to the measure of poverty $P$ can be defined in the following way.

*Definition.*   The measure of inequality $\eta$ corresponding to the poverty index $P$ as specified in Theorem 1 is the value obtained in place of $P$ by replacing $q$ (the number of poor) by $n$ (the total number of people in the community), and replacing $z$ (the poverty level) by $m^*$ (the mean income of the community).

THEOREM 2.    *The measure of inequality $\eta$ corresponding to the poverty index approximates the Gini coefficient for large $n$.*

The proof is obvious from (15) and (17) replacing $q$ by $n$, and $z$ and $m$ by $m^*$, in the formulations of $P$ and the Gini coefficient (now redefined for the whole community). This is also checked by putting $H = 1$ and $I = 0$ in $P$ as given by Theorem 1.

Thus the poverty measure $P$ obtained in Theorem 1 is essentially a translation of the Gini coefficient from the measurement of inequality to that of poverty.[11]

A diagrammatic representation of $G$ and $P$ is provided in Figure 1. Line

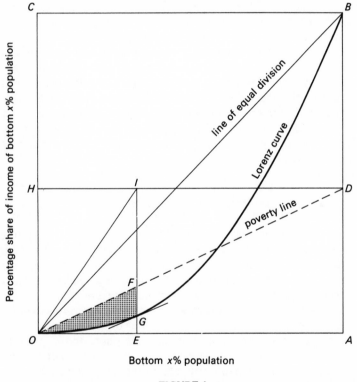

FIGURE 1

11. An axiomatization of the Gini coefficient as a measure of inequality can be found in Sen [34]. The more primitive axiom system used there leads to $R^*$ as a theorem without being taken as an axiom in itself.

$OGB$ is the Lorenz curve, while $OB$ is the line of equal division. The Gini coefficient $G$ is given by area $OGB$ divided by area $OAB$. The slope of the line $OD$ gives 'the poverty line' in these normalized units, and $OE$ is the number of the poor. The poverty measure $P$ can be seen to correspond to area $OGF$ divided by area $OEI$. The difference between the two lies in (i) the slope of line $OD$ ('the poverty line') being different from the slope of line $OB$ (the normalized mean income), and (ii) counting only the poor, i.e., $OE$, in the poverty measure, as opposed to all, i.e., $OA$.

The rank-order weighting form of the Gini coefficient $G$ and the poverty measure $P$ can be understood intuitively by considering the area under the curve $OGB$, which the Gini numerator leaves out, i.e., what $(1 - G)$ includes. The poorest man's income is included at every point and if there are $n$ persons his income comes in $n$ times. On the other hand, the highest income is included in the area under $OGB$ exactly once at the point $A$ when everyone is counted in, i.e., the richest man makes it exactly once more than the camel can get through the eye of a needle. The $i$th poorest man comes in at the $i$th point of observation and has his income included for the remaining $(n - i)$ observations as well, thereby having his income counting in $(n + 1 - i)$ times. This produces the rank order weighting through the mechanism of the Lorenz curve, and it is this remarkable coincidence that makes the Gini coefficient give expression to the normative value judgement of weighting according to ordinal ranks satisfying Axiom R* (and Axiom E) given Axiom M. The same way of intuitively understanding the result regarding the poverty measure can be easily suggested by considering the number of times the gap between the slope of $OD$ (the poverty line) and the slope of $OGB$ (the income of the poor) gets counted in.

## 7   Interpretation and Variations

The poverty index proposed here turns out to have quite an easy interpretation. The measure is made up of the head-count ratio $H$ multiplied by the income-gap ratio $I$ augmented by the Gini coefficient $G$ of the distribution of income among the poor weighted by $(1 - I)$, i.e., weighted by the ratio of the mean income of the poor to the poverty line income level. One way of understanding its rationale is the following: $I$ represents poverty as measured by the proportionate gap between the mean income of the poor and the poverty line income. It ignores distribution *among* the poor, and $G$ provides this information. In addition to the poverty gap of the mean income of the poor reflected in $I$, there is the 'gap' arising from the unequal distribution of the mean income, which is reflected by the Gini coefficient $G$ of that distribution multiplied by the mean income ratio. The income-gap measure thus augmented to take note of inequality among the poor, i.e., $I + (1 - I)G$, is normalized per poor person, and does not take note of the number of people below the poverty line, which could be minute or large. Multiplying $[I +(1 - I)G]$ by the head-count ratio $H$ now produces the composite measure $P$.

While this is perhaps the easiest way of interpreting the poverty index $P$, it must be borne in mind that its justification lies in the axioms used to derive it. The multiplicative form chosen in Axiom N, though simple, is arbitrary. Axiom M, perhaps justifiable in the absence of detailed information on the poor, is objectionable when much is known about individual members of the group, e.g., that cripple Mr $A$ while richer than robust Mr $B$ is less well off in some sense (see [32, pp. 17–20]). Finally, Axiom R follows Borda's procedure of cardinalizing an ordering by treating rank numbers as weights. This is, of course, also arbitrary, though frequently used in other contexts as the popularity of several variants of the rank order procedures of voting indicates. The justification can be either in terms of intensity of preference being surmised from rankings only by using a version of 'insufficient reason' (following Borda), or in terms of an essentially relativist conception of poverty. Axiom R may not be acceptable to many since there is arbitrariness in making the weight on person $i$'s income gap equal his poverty rank. Even with a *given* level of income, a person's poverty weight will go down if a richer poor becomes poorer than him. The advantages and defects of the rank-order system are clear enough.

A few properties of $P$ may be worth pointing out. It lies in the closed interval $[0, 1]$, with $P = 0$ if everyone has an income greater than $z$, and $P = 1$ if everyone has zero income. In practice, of course, $P$ will never equal unity, both because there are subsistence requirements (so that for each $i$: $y_i > 0$) as well as because even in very poor economies the class system ensures the prosperity of some (so that for some $i$: $y_i > z$).

Note also that when all the poor have the same income, i.e., $G = 0$, the lower the income of the poor, the closer will $P$ approach the head-count measure $H$, and the larger the proportion of the poor, the closer will $P$ approach the income-gap measure $I$.

Some variations of the normalization procedures may be worth considering. First, if the weights on income gaps are all reduced by one-half, i.e., the income gap $g_i$ of the $i$th poorest is taken to be $(q - i + \frac{1}{2})$, then (8) holds not only for large $q$ but for any $q$. However, for measuring poverty of any sizeable community, the two procedures do not make any real difference.

Second, even retaining the weighting procedure, the normalization reflected in Axiom N can be changed. In particular, the poverty measure can be made to depend also on the *ratio* of the mean income of the poor to the mean income of the entire community (Sen [33, equations (8) and (9)]). This would give the poverty measure wider coverage. For example, exactly the same number and income distribution of the poor will have a *higher* poverty index if the income of some people above the poverty line falls even without taking them below the poverty line.[12] In contrast, the measure $P$ is completely invariant with respect to changes in the income of people *above* the poverty line and depends only on the incomes of the poor. This does not, of course, prevent us from defining the poverty line $z$ taking note of the entire distribution of income (e.g., a higher $z$ for the United States than for India), but once the poverty line has been specified, the poverty measure $P$ depends only on the incomes of the poor.

## 8    *Concluding Remarks*

(i) The measure of poverty $P$ presented here uses an ordinal approach to welfare comparisons. The need for placing a greater weight on the income of a poorer person is derived from equity considerations (Axiom E) without necessarily using interpersonally comparable *cardinal* utility functions. Ordinal level comparability is used to obtain rank order weighting systems (Axiom R) given a monotonic relation between income and welfare (Axiom M).

(ii) The poverty measure $P$ obtained axiomatically in Theorem 1 corresponds to the Gini measure of inequality in the sense that replacing the poor by the entire population and replacing the poverty threshold of income by the mean income would transform $P$ into $G$. This poverty measure $P$ contrasts sharply with the crude measures of poverty used in the statistical literature on the subject and in policy discussions. Unlike $H$ (the percentage of people below the poverty line), $P$ is not insensitive to the extent of the short-fall of income of the poor from the poverty line. Unlike $I$ (the percentage average short-fall of the income of the poor from the poverty line), $P$ is not insensitive to the number below the poverty line.[13] And unlike any conceivable function $\Psi(H, I)$ of these crude measures, $P$ *is* sensitive to the exact pattern of distribution of the incomes of the poor.

(iii) Throughout this paper income has been taken to be a homogeneous magnitude represented by a real number. The framework developed here can be extended to multicommodity cases as well, evaluating the consumption of commodity $j$ by person $i$ in terms both of the price of $j$ and the income rank of $i$, basing the calculation on Fisher's [13 and 18] 'commodity matrices'.[14]

(iv) If one accepts the ordinal welfare interpretation of the rationale of the Gini coefficient (Axiom R*), then one might wonder about the significance of the debate on the non-existence of any 'additive utility function which

12. Consider the 'mean-dependent measure' $P^* = Pz/m^*$.

13. The alternative definition of the income-gap measure $I^*$ is sensitive to the number below the poverty line, but it is also sensitive to the incomes of people *above* the poverty line. Furthermore, $I^*$ is insensitive to the *distribution* of income among the poor.

14. The use of such an approach has been explored, as an illustration of a general system of real income comparisons with explicit treatment of distribution, in Sen [35].

ranks income distributions in the same order as the Gini coefficient' (see Newbery [23, p. 264], Sheshinski [36], Dasgupta, Sen, and Starrett [9], and Rothschild and Stiglitz [26]). Evidently $-G$ is not an additive function of individual incomes, nor is it strictly concave or strictly quasi-concave (as is obvious from equation (17)). Axiom E and specifically Axiom R* precipitate the equality-preferring result noted in [9 and 26]; but the ordinal weighting of the Gini coefficient cannot be cast into the strictly concave utilitarian framework, or into any other social welfare function that makes marginal weights sensitive to the exact values of income (as opposed to their ordinal ranks). The same applies to the poverty measure $P$ proposed here.

(v) Finally, it should be pointed out that any system of measurement that takes note only of *ordinal* welfare information must be recognized to be deficient by an observer who is convinced that he has access to cardinal interpersonally comparable welfare functions. If such cardinal information did obtain, the fact that $P$ should throw away a part of it and use only the ordering information must be judged to be wasteful. On the other hand, it is much more difficult to agree on interpersonally comparable cardinal welfare functions than to find agreement on welfare rankings only. The approach proposed here, while deficient in the sense described, also demands less. It is a compromise in much the same way as the Borda method of voting is, in making do with rankings only and in slipping in an assumption of equidistance to get numerical weights. The data requirement in estimating the poverty measure $P$ is, as a consequence, quite limited.

## References

[1] Atkinson, A. B.: *Poverty in Britain and the Reform of Social Security* (Cambridge: Cambridge University Press, 1970).

[2] ____ 'On the Measurement of Inequality', *Journal of Economic Theory, 2* (1970), 244–63.

[3] Bardhan, P.: 'On the Minimum Level of Living and the Rural Poor', *Indian Economic Review, 5* (1970).

[4] ____ 'On the Minimum Level of Living and the Rural Poor: A Further Note', *Indian Economic Review, 6* (1971).

[5] Batchelder, A. B.: *The Economics of Poverty* (New York: Wiley, 1971).

[6] Black, D.: *The Theory of Committees and Elections* (Cambridge: Cambridge University Press, 1958).

[7] Borda, J. C. de: 'Mémoire sur les Élections au Scrutin', in *Histoire de l'Académie Royale des Sciences* (Paris, 1781); extracts translated in English in D. Black, *The Theory of Committees and Elections* (Cambridge: Cambridge University Press, 1958), chapter XVIII.

[8] Dandekar, V. M., and N. Rath: *Poverty in India* (Poona: Indian School of Political Economy, 1971).

[9] Dasgupta, P., A. K. Sen, and D. Starrett: 'Notes on the Measurement of Inequality', *Journal of Economic Theory, 6* (1973), 180–7.

[10] Engels, F.: *The Condition of the Working Class in England*, 1892 (London: Panther, 1969).

[11] Fine, B., and K. Fine: 'Social Choice and Individual Ranking', *Review of Economic Studies*, 41 (1974), 303–22, 459–75.

[12] Fishburn, P. C.: *The Theory of Social Choice* (Princeton, NJ: Princeton University Press, 1973).

[13] Fisher, F. M.: 'Income Distribution, Value Judgements, and Welfare', *Quarterly Journal of Economics*, 70 (1956), 380–424.

[14] Gärdenfors, P.: 'Positional Voting Functions', *Theory and Decision*, 4 (1973), 1–24.

[15] Gini, C.: *Variabilità e Mutabilità* (Bologna, 1912).

[16] Graaff, J. de V.: *Theoretical Welfare Economics* (Cambridge: Cambridge University Press, 1967).

[17] Hansson, B.: 'The Independence Condition in the Theory of Social Choice', *Theory and Decision*, 4 (1973), 25–50.

[18] Kenen, P. B., and F. M. Fisher: 'Income Distribution, Value Judgements, and Welfare: A Correction', *Quarterly Journal of Economics*, 71 (1957), 322–4.

[19] Kolm, S. Ch.: 'The Optimal Production of Social Justice', in *Public Economics*, ed. by J. Margolis and H. Guitton (London: Macmillan, 1969).

[20] Minhas, B. S.: 'Rural Poverty, Land Redistribution, and Development', *Indian Economic Review*, 5 (1970).

[21] ____ 'Rural Poverty and the Minimum Level of Living', *Indian Economic Review*, 6 (1971).

[22] Mukherjee, M., N. Bhattacharya, and G. S. Chatterjee: 'Poverty in India: Measurement and Amelioration', *Commerce*, 125 (1972).

[23] Newbery, D. M. G.: 'A Theorem on the Measurement of Inequality', *Journal of Economic Theory*, 2 (1970), 264–6.

[24] Ojha, P. D.: 'A Configuration of Indian Poverty', *Reserve Bank of India Bulletin*, 24 (1970).

[25] Pattanaik, P. K.: *Voting and Collective Choice* (Cambridge: Cambridge University Press, 1971).

[26] Rothschild, M. and J. E. Stiglitz: 'Some Further Results on the Measurement of Inequality', *Journal of Economic Theory*, 6 (1973), 188–204.

[27] Rowntree, B. S.: *Poverty: A Study of Town Life* (London: Macmillan, 1901).

[28] Runciman, W. G.: *Relative Deprivation and Social Justice* (London: Routledge, 1966).

[29] Sen, A. K.: 'Interpersonal Aggregation and Partial Comparability', *Econometrica*, 38 (1970), 393–409. [Essay 9 in this volume.]

[30] ____ *Collective Choice and Social Welfare* (San Francisco: Holden-Day, 1970).

[31] ____ 'Interpersonal Aggregation and Partial Comparability: A Correction', *Econometrica*, 40 (1972), 959.

[32] ____ *On Economic Inequality* (Oxford: Clarendon Press, 1973).

[33] ____ 'Poverty, Inequality, and Unemployment: Some Conceptual Issues in Measurement', *Economic and Political Weekly*, 8 (1973), 1457–64.

[34] ____ 'Informational Bases of Alternative Welfare Approaches: Aggregation and Income Distribution', *Journal of Public Economics*, 4 (1974), 387–403.

[35] ____ 'Real National Income', *Review of Economic Studies*, 43 (1976), 19–39. [Essay 18 in this volume.]

[36]  Sheshinski, E.: 'Relation between a Social Welfare Function and the Gini Index of Inequality', *Journal of Economic Theory,* **4** (1972), 98–100.

[37]  Srinivasan, T. N. and A. Vaidyanathan: 'Data on Distribution of Consumption Expenditure in India: An Evaluation', mimeographed, I.S.I. Seminar on Income Distribution, New Delhi, 1971.

[38]  Theil, H.: *Economics and Information Theory* (Chicago: Rand McNally, 1967).

[39]  Townsend, P.: 'Measuring Poverty', *British Journal of Sociology,* **5** (1954), 130–7.

[40]  Vaidyanathan, A.: 'Some Aspects of Inequalities in Living Standards in Rural India', mimeographed, I.S.I. Seminar on Income Distribution, New Delhi, 1971.

[41]  Weisbrod, B. A., (ed.): *The Economics of Poverty* (Englewood Cliffs, NJ: Prentice-Hall, 1965).

# 18

# Real National Income

## 1 Introduction

Real national income comparison is one of the most frequently performed exercises in empirical economics. While the welfare implications of such comparisons are often not spelt out, there is little doubt that the significance that is attached to comparisons of real national income depend greatly on their implicit welfare content. This also influences the statistical procedures that are chosen, and as has been observed, 'the basic conventions that have been adopted by the statisticians of most countries for purposes of GNP-measurement are still founded on some notion of what measure of economic activity can best represent the contribution of that activity to welfare' (Beckerman [2], p. 80).

The welfare theory of real national income comparisons is, however, incomplete in several important ways, despite outstanding contributions by several distinguished economists, including Hicks [17], [18], Scitovsky [40], Kuznets [24], Samuelson [38], [39], Little [26] and Graaff [12], among others. Perhaps the most serious difficulty is with the treatment of income distribution.

The starting point of this paper lies in treating the same commodity going to two different persons as two different goods. The weighting of 'goods', thus defined, will incorporate distributional judgements. (The approach presented in this paper is best seen in the context of Graaff's [12] analysis of the need to 'dispense with the time-honoured device of drawing a distinction between the size and the distribution of the national income and saying that welfare depends upon them both', and his penetrating observation that

For helpful comments on an earlier version of this paper, I am most grateful to Franklin Fisher, Terence Gorman, Jan Graaff, Peter Hammond, Geoff Heal, Tapas Majumdar, John Muellbauer, Richard Portes, and the anonymous referees of [Review of Economic Studies].

Based on the Zakir Husain Memorial Lectures given at Jawaharlal Nehru University, New Delhi, in November 1973, and Special Lectures given at Manchester University in May 1974; published in Review of Economic Studies, 43 (February 1976), 19–39.

welfare 'depends (if we must use the term) on size only—and we do not know what the size is until we know the distribution' ([12], p. 92).) This will permit a welfare interpretation of real income comparisons without the usual restrictive assumptions, e.g., leaving out distributional considerations explicitly (cf. Hicks [17], [18]), or making the peculiarly unrealistic assumption that distribution is made 'optimal' by lump-sum transfers (cf. Samuelson [38], pp. 28−9, [39]). The important point to note is that typically social welfare can be seen to be a function of the vector of 'goods' as defined here, but not as a function of the vector of commodities in the usual sense (i.e., irrespective of who gets them).

Another departure lies in the explicit recognition of the fact that real national income comparisons involve different groups of people.[1] In this, these comparisons differ from traditional welfare economics (e.g., the use of 'Pareto Optimality' or of 'Compensation Tests'), collective choice theory (e.g., the use of Arrovian 'social welfare functions'), and the standard theory of national planning (e.g., 'cost-benefit analysis', or 'optimal growth theory'), which are concerned with comparing *alternative* positions of the *same* group of people. One way of avoiding the complex problems of inter-group contrasts is to confine real income comparisons to contrasting the actual position of a group with what its position 'would have been' if it were placed in the position of another group. (Cf. Pigou: 'If the German population with German tastes were given the national dividend of England, ...' [34], pp. 52−3.) But this problem is ill-defined. For two groups of $n$ people each, there are $n!$ different ways of placing one group in the position of another. And, for two groups of different sizes, the interpretation of such 'as if' comparisons is totally ambiguous.

This paper is aimed at tackling both these problems, taking distribution as an integral part of real income evaluation, and providing a rigorous treatment of the alternative interpretations of real income comparisons arising from inter-group differences. The approach presented is very general, but to demonstrate its possible applicability, in Section 9 the approach is illustrated with an explicit set of fairly demanding axioms involving distribution and population size. The results of that exercise are then used for inter-state comparisons of real income in India (see the Appendix), providing an empirical example of a particular case of the general approach developed in this paper.

## 2   The Basic Theorem of Constant-weight Comparisons

In Sections 2−5 the problem of distribution-dependent weights is explored

1. International or interregional comparisons obviously involve different groups. So do intertemporal comparisons (e.g., 'the British were better off last year than this year'), because people die and others are born, and also because the same person at different points of time may have quite different welfare characteristics.

without going into the question of population differences, which is tackled in Sections 6–8.

Consider a community of $n$ persons, $i = 1, \ldots, n$. There are $m$ commodities, $j = 1, \ldots, m$. Using a term employed by Hahn [13] in a different context, commodity $j$ going to person $i$ will be called a 'named good', $ij$, the amount of which is denoted by $x_{ij}$. There are, obviously, $mn$ named goods, and a 'named good vector' $x$ indicates the amount of each named good $x_{ij}$, i.e., the amount of each commodity $j$ going to each person $i$, which can, of course, be zero. The amount of each commodity consumed by person $i$ is given by the 'personal basket' $i(x)$. It should be clear that $x$ is an $mn$-vector, while each $i(x)$ is an $m$-vector, and the $n$ personal baskets together give the same information as $x$. (Note also that the vector $x$ gives exactly as much information as Fisher's [7] 'commodity matrix'.) The total amount of each commodity $j$ is given by $c_j$, and the $m$-vector $c$ of (anonymous) commodities is called the 'commodity vector'. It is obvious that:

$$c = \Sigma_i i(x) = (\Sigma_i x_{i1}, \ldots, \Sigma_i x_{im}). \tag{1}$$

The interpretation of named goods is easier for consumer goods than for investment goods, and in some sense it may be more convenient to think of the comparison as one of 'real consumption' rather than of 'real income'. This is so in the traditional real income theory as well (e.g., Hicks [17], [18], Samuelson [38], [39], Little [26]), and the evaluation of investment in national income involves quite different issues of inter-temporal allocation (see, for example, Weitzman [52]). However, in so far as having an owner-ship right over an investment good is a source of direct or indirect gratification for a person,[2] the approach of named goods may well be thought to be appropriate for investment goods also.

The set $X$ of possible vectors of named goods $x$ is a subset of the non-negative orthant of the $mn$-dimensional real space. It will be assumed that $X$ is convex; this is entirely for the purpose of simplifying the axioms to be proposed (in particular, Axiom V), and it can be easily removed and the axioms correspondingly restated without upsetting the results. Let $R$ stand for the weak binary relation of social preference ('at least as good as') with $P$ and $I$ standing respectively for its asymmetric and symmetric parts. The symbol $\geqslant$ stands for the strict partial ordering of vector dominance in the sense that $x \geqslant y$ if and only if $x_k \geqslant y_k$ for all $k$, and $x_k > y_k$ for some $k$. Finally, the set of named good vectors in $X$ that are at least as good as $x$ according to $R$ is called $R(x)$.

$$R(x) = \{ y \in X \mid yRx \}. \tag{2}$$

2. Investment goods have to be viewed not merely as a source of future income, but also as one of current privilege, e.g., a capitalist being a 'boss', while a labourer without any means of production must seek a job as a 'wage slave'. Cf. 'Every individual capital is a larger or smaller concentration of means of production, with a corresponding command over a larger or smaller labour-army' (Marx [27], p. 639).

Three axioms are now proposed.

AXIOM C (*Complete Ordering*).   *R completely orders X.*

AXIOM V (*Convex Preference*).   *For each x in X, R(x) is convex.*

AXIOM M (*Strict Monotonicity*).   *For any x, y in X: if x $\geq$ y, then xPy.*

Axiom M makes social preference respect vector dominance, and is in fact a condition of social non-satiation. In the special case of the 'individualistic' social welfare function respecting the Pareto principle, M follows from the non-satiation of the individuals, in the absence of externalities.[3] Axiom V is a condition of quasi-concave welfare (e.g., the usual 'non-increasing rates of indifferent substitution'[4]). In the individualistic case, it can be derived from combining convex preferences of 'self-centred' individuals with a social preference for the averaging process (see Samuelson [39], and Gorman [11], who calls the latter 'moderation').[5] Axiom V is, in fact, a bit weaker than this since these assumptions are sufficient but not strictly necessary for the convexity of $R(x)$. Axiom C requires that $R$ be transitive and complete over $X$, and if real income comparisons are to reflect social preference, it is reasonable to require that social preference should satisfy some systematic properties. However, both transitivity and completeness can be significantly weakened without upsetting the results.[6]

An elementary result to be obtained from Axioms C, V and M, can be taken to be the basic theorem of constant-weight real income comparison as a guide to social preference.

(T.1)   *Axioms C, V and M together imply that for any x in X there exists a weight vector p such that for all y in X: if px > py, then xPy.*

*Proof.* By Axiom M, $x$ is not interior to $R(x)$, and since $R(x)$ is convex, it follows from a well-known theorem of Minkowski that there is a hyperplane $H$ through $x$ bounding $R(x)$. If the normal of the hyperplane $H$ is $p$, then for all $z$ in $R(x)$: $pz \geq px$. Hence if for some $y$: $px > py$, then $y$ is not in $R(x)$. By Axiom C, $xPy$.

Note that (T.1) permits social preference to take note of income distribution (in fact, of distribution of real commodities) in any way we like, reflecting

3. If people take pleasure at other's welfare, this will not affect M. Even negative externalities can be permitted provided they are 'mild' enough not to outweigh the direct gain of the person getting more (see Graaff [12], p. 51, on externalities being 'excessive').

4. Note that 'diminishing' rates are not being required, and $R(x)$ need not be *strictly* convex.

5. See also Fisher's [7] condition of a 'distribution value judgement' being 'non-troughed', which is a condition of convexity applied to different distributions of the same bundle of commodities.

6. In fact, transitivity of $R$ is not directly used, and it comes in only in so far as convexity of $R(x)$ already implies transitivity over specific parts of the domain. Completeness can be dropped by defining $R(x)$ as vectors 'no worse' than $x$, and reinterpreting the axioms accordingly.

distributional judgements through the shape of $R(x)$, and thus through the normal $p$. If social welfare can be taken to be a function of the commodities enjoyed by each person, then (T.1) does provide a justification for the constant-weight real-income procedure under a set of fairly reasonable assumptions. Since social welfare is not independent of distribution, a similar justification does not obtain for comparisons of anonymous commodity vectors, contrary to usual practice. The procedure is a natural method of ranking named good vectors and does not, in fact, extend to anonymous vectors except through some special assumptions (see Section 4 below).

## 3  Real Income Partial Orderings

It should be observed that (T.1) shares the general limitation of constant-price real income analysis of getting a sufficient but not a necessary condition for an increase in social welfare. The procedure is based on checking whether the point $y$ with which $x$ is to be compared lies below a *hyperplane* bounding the convex region $R(x)$, rather than below the convex region $R(x)$ *itself*.

A characteristic of real income comparisons is that it yields a ranking that is neither necessarily complete, nor necessarily transitive, but satisfies the property of 'acyclicity', which only requires that if $x^1 P x^2, x^2 P x^3, \ldots, x^{k-1} P x^k$, then *not $x^k P x^1$*.[7]

*Real income ranking.*  $xP^*y$ if and only if there exists a hyperplane $H$ through $x$ bounding $R(x)$ such that for the normal $p$ of $H$: $px > py$.

(T.2)  *Given Axioms C, V and M:*
    (i) *$P^*$ is a sub-relation of strict social preference P;*
    (ii) *the relation of vector dominance on X is a sub-relation of $P^*$;*
    (iii) *$P^*$ is asymmetric and acyclic, but not necessarily complete or transitive.*

(T.1) guarantees (i). Axiom M ensures (ii). It follows from (i) and Axiom C that $P^*$ must be asymmetric and acyclic. That $P^*$ need not be complete is obvious from the argument presented above. That $P^*$ need not be transitive is illustrated in Figure 1, where $xP^*y$ and $yP^*z$, whereas not $xP^*z$. The consistency condition satisfied by $P^*$ is the weaker one of acyclicity permitting an extension into a transitive, complete ordering, but not transitivity in itself.

It is in fact quite easy to extend the asymmetric, acyclical ranking $P^*$ into a strict partial ordering $P^{**}$ represented by the closure, or the 'ancestral', of $P^*$.[8]

*Real income strict partial ordering.*  $xP^{**}y$ if and only if there is a finite sequence $xP^*z^1, z^1P^*z^2, \ldots, z^{k-1}P^*z^k, z^kP^*y$. It is obvious that:

---

7. Acyclicity rules out cycles of strict preference of finite length. See Herzberger [16].
8. Cf. Houthakker's [19] concept of indirect revealed preference; see also Herzberger [16].

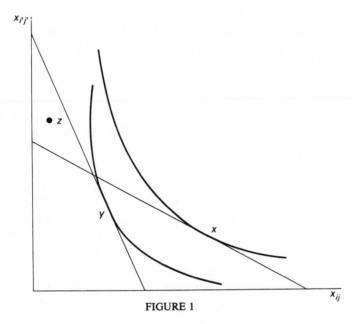

FIGURE 1

(T.3)   *Given Axioms C, V and M: P\*\* is a strict partial ordering (asym-*
        *metric and transitive) and a sub-relation of social strict preference P.*


## 4   Anonymous Commodity Prices and Distributional Differences

The main contributions to the theory of real income comparisons have all
been based on the 'individualistic approach', making social welfare a function
of individual welfares satisfying the Pareto principle. The framework used in
this paper permits the applications of non-individualistic approaches as well,
though there is no compulsion to do this.

The individualistic approach gives immediate guidance about the relative
values of different commodities going to the same person, if it is assumed in
addition that (i) each person's welfare depends only on what he purchases,
that (ii) the buyers are all price-takers, and that (iii) each buyer is rational in
the sense that his choice function is 'binary' and the binary relation revealed
by his choices is also his welfare ranking.[9] The use of market prices for intra-

---

9. Assumption (i) rules out consumption externalities, but this can be relaxed somewhat to
permit 'goodwill'. If commodities were to include investment goods also, then assumption (i)
will be even more restrictive. Assumption (ii) rules out market imperfections on the buyer's side,
even though imperfections on the sellers' side are not necessarily absent. While the limitations of
both these assumptions are widely acknowledged, assumption (iii) seems to be more commonly
accepted. However, on its limitations, see Scitovsky [41] and Sen [45].

personal commodity weighting is usually justified in terms of such a framework of assumptions.[10] Without knowing anything more about individual preferences $R_1, \ldots, R_n$, the assumptions quoted would justify the deduction that for any Pareto-inclusive social welfare function $f(R_1, \ldots, R_n) = R$, the intra-personal commodity weights should coincide with market prices. Let $q$ be the $m$-vector of market prices in the situation in which $x$ was chosen.

AXIOM X (*Efficient Exchange*).    *Given Axioms C, V and M, for each $x$, the normal $p$ of some hyperplane $H(x)$ through $x$ bounding $R(x)$ satisfies for all $i, j, h$:*

$$p_{ij}/p_{ih} = q_j/q_h. \tag{3}$$

The market, however, throws little light on the relative valuation of the same good going to two different persons. In order to keep this problem also within the set-up of market prices, an additional assumption is invoked by Samuelson, viz., optimal redistributions of income are made 'to keep the ethical worth of each person's marginal dollar equal' ([39], p. 21).

AXIOM D (*Optimal Distribution*).    *Given Axioms C, V, M and X, for each $x$, the normal $p$ of some hyperplane $H(x)$ through $x$ bounding $R(x)$ and satisfying the condition specified in Axiom X, also satisfies for all $i, g$ and $j$:*

$$p_{ij} = p_{gj}. \tag{4}$$

It is immediately clear that:[11]

(T.4)    *Given Axioms C, V, M, X and D, if $c(x)$ and $c(y)$ are two (anonymous) commodity vectors corresponding respectively to two named good vectors $x$ and $y$, then $qc(x) > qc(y)$ implies that $xPy$.*

The distributional assumption underlying Axiom D is, however, extraordinarily unrealistic. While one can certainly defend Samuelson's claim that the development of the Bergson 'social indifference curves' defined on the (anonymous) commodity space on the basis of the optimal-distribution assumption implies that 'the foundation is laid for the "economics of a good society"' ([39], p. 22), not much can be said about any *actual* society using these social indifference curves.

In the absence of Axiom D, must we give up constant-price judgements based on anonymous weighting? The answer, in general, is yes, but a couple of exceptions are worth recording.

First, it should be noted that while the use of market prices is a case of anonymous weighting, it implies something more than that, viz., the weights on commodities should equal market prices. If the interpersonal distribution

10. Perhaps the best discussion is to be found in Samuelson [38], [39].
11. Cf. Samuelson's theorem ([38], pp. 28–9), corrected by Graaff ([12], pp. 162–3). Note, however, that the assumptions that 'diminishing returns prevail' and 'prices equal marginal costs' (Graaff [12], p. 162) are quite redundant, as is obvious from (T.4).

of commodities remains the same in relative terms, anonymous weighting could be justified given the other axioms, but the weights will not, typically, be proportional to market prices. Denote the amount of commodity $j$ in the commodity vector $c(x)$ as $c(x)_j$. For any $x$, define $D_x$ as the subset of $X$ such that:

$$D_x = \{ y \mid y \text{ in } X \text{ and for all } i, j: x_{ij}/c(x)_j = y_{ij}/c(y)_j \}. \qquad (5)$$

$D_x$ is the subset of named good vectors in $X$ with the same percentage distribution of each commodity as in $x$. (In the terminology of Fisher [7], $D_x$ is the subset of $X$ with the same 'distribution matrix' as $x$.)

(T.5)  *Given Axioms C, V and M, there exists an m-vector of (anonymous) commodity prices u such that if $uc(x) > uc(y)$ for any y in $D_x$, then xPy.*

*Proof.* Let $d_{ij}$ be the proportionate share of commodity $j$ going to person $i$ in the named good vector $x$, i.e., $d_{ij} = x_{ij}/c(x)_j$. By (T.1), there exists an $mn$-vector $p$ such that $px > py$ implies that $xPy$. Note that:

$$px = \Sigma_j(\Sigma_i p_{ij} d_{ij})c(x)_j \qquad (6)$$

$$py = \Sigma_j(\Sigma_i p_{ij} d_{ij})c(y)_j, \text{ since } y \text{ belongs to } D_x. \qquad (7)$$

Putting $u_j = \Sigma_i p_{ij} d_{ij}$, (T.5) follows directly from (6) and (7).

Even when the relative interpersonal distribution of commodities changes, the procedure involved in (T.5) can be used as an intermediate step to be combined with what Fisher [7] calls 'distribution value judgments'. For any anonymous commodity vector $c$, let $A_c$ be the set of all named good vectors with the same aggregate amounts of each commodity, given by $c$.

$$A_c = \{ x \mid \text{ for all } j: \Sigma_i x_{ij} = c_j \}. \qquad (8)$$

It is obvious that the intersection of $D_x$ and $A_{c(y)}$, for any two *named* good vectors $x$ and $y$ is a unit set, and let that unique element be called the distributional equivalent of $x$ for $y$, denoted $\eta(x, y)$, itself a *named* good vector. Clearly $\eta(x, y)$ is the commodity vector corresponding to $y$, with each commodity distributed interpersonally in the same relative proportions as $x$.

*Distributional non-inferiority.* A named good vector $x$ is distributionally non-inferior to another named good vector $y$ if and only if $\eta(x, y)Ry$.[12]

(T.6)  *Given Axioms C, V and M, there exists an m-vector of (anonymous) commodity prices u such that for any two named good vectors x*

---

12. Note that the fact that $x$ is distributionally non-inferior to $y$, does not preclude the possibility that $y$ is also distributionally non-inferior to $x$. Indeed there is no contradiction even in strictly preferring $\eta(x, y)$ to $y$ and also strictly preferring $\eta(y, x)$ to $x$, since our ranking of relative distributions need not be independent of the 'level' of income, i.e., may depend on the total amount of commodities to be thus distributed. Cf. Kenen and Fisher [20].

*and y, with x distributionally non-inferior to y, if uc(x) > uc(y), then xPy.*

*Proof.*  Noting that $c(y) = c(\eta(x, y))$, it follows from (T.5) that there is a *u* such that $uc(x) > uc(y)$ implies $xP\eta(x, y)$. Since *x* is distributionally non-inferior to *y*, clearly $\eta(x, y)Ry$. Hence (T.6).

(T.6) is, in some ways, similar to Little's [26] 'double criterion', and is indeed inspired by it. The similarity lies in the use of an intermediate point to compare *x* and *y*, and those who find the use of such intermediate points unhelpful or misleading,[13] are unlikely to see much merit in (T.6). But the intermediate point $\eta(x, y)$ does permit a constant-price real-income judgement over the space of anonymous commodities (between $c(x)$ and $c(y)$) to be supplemented by a judgement over different distributions of the same anonymous commodity-vector (between $\eta(x, y)$ and *y*), to arrive at an over-all judgement on the space of *named* commodities (between *x* and *y*). It should, incidentally, be noted that while similar in *spirit* to Little's 'double criterion', the criterion used in (T.6) is in fact different from it in several important respects.

(i)   The points to be compared *x* and *y* need not be on the respective 'utility possibility frontiers', and the intermediate point $\eta(x, y)$ need not be on the 'utility possibility frontier' through *y*; in the Little criterion they are all assumed to be.

(ii)  The intermediate point $\eta(x, y)$ need not be Pareto-comparable to *x*;[14] in the Little criterion the intermediate point on the frontier of *y* must be Pareto-inferior to *x*.

(iii) The anonymous commodity prices *u* used in the real-income comparison between *x* and $\eta(x, y)$ need not be market prices; in the Little criterion the commodity prices are the competitive market prices ruling when *y* was chosen.

(iv)  The judgement between *y* and $\eta(x, y)$ is a 'distribution value judgement' in the sense of Fisher [7], viz., the alternatives are different interpersonal distributions of the same commodity vector $c(y) = c(\eta(x, y))$—a restriction not imposed by Little.

## 5   *Intertemporal Comparisons*

Contrast the two following statements of the superiority of *x* over *y* for a

---

13. See, for example, Kennedy [21] and Graaff [12], pp. 161–2. See, however, Little [26], Chapter VI.

14. Recall that while *x* and $\eta(x, y)$ have the same distribution matrix in Fisher's [7] sense, the total supply of some commodities may be larger in *x* and that of others in *y*, and it is possible that someone might be better off at *x* and another person at $\eta(x, y)$.

given group of people:

(A) The group is better off with $x$ than it *would have been* with $y$.
(B) The group is better off with $x$ than it *was* with $y$.

In so far as real income comparisons are made in terms of a particular social welfare relation $R$, statements like (A) are easier to examine than those like (B), which would have to take note of welfare functions at both points of time. There are two types of problem with (B):

(1) The social preference relation $R$ may not remain unchanged over time.
(2) Even if $R$ does remain unchanged, it does not follow that a statement like (B) can be made.

The social preference relation $R$ may be defined as a function of individual orderings (as in the Arrovian [1] framework), in which case $R$ will change if individual orderings change. While this is the traditional assumption in collective choice theory, the function determining $R$ may also be made to take note of individual cardinal welfare functions (e.g., Nash [31]), or interpersonal rankings of welfare levels (e.g., Rawls [36], Suppes [48], Sen [43], Hammond [14]), or interpersonal correspondence of cardinal welfare (e.g., Harsanyi [15], Kolm [22], Sen [42], Pattanaik [33]), which can change even when individual orderings do not. The function determining $R$ may itself change over time (e.g., a community of Benthamites may turn Rawlsian). The stationarity of $R$ is a severe requirement.

Turning now to the second problem, suppose $xRy$ at both $t^1$ and $t^2$. It does not follow from this that $x$ at $t^1$ is preferable to $y$ at $t^2$. The social preference map may have remained unchanged, but it tells us nothing about the desirability of $x$ at $t^1$ *vis-à-vis* $y$ at $t^2$. Things could have changed between $t^1$ and $t^2$ without affecting the preference map over $x$ and $y$, e.g., 'people have lost their natural joyfulness', 'no one feels safe in the streets any more', 'boy, do I feel alienated!' The constancy of the preference map is quite insufficient for making intertemporal welfare comparisons.[15]

In view of the importance of this problem, it is remarkable how little attention this problem has received.[16] Essentially, comparisons of type (A) come naturally out of the collective choice basis of real income comparisons, while statements of type (B) if made on the basis of real income analysis involve a

15. Cf. Graaff ([12], pp. 157–8): 'Let us suppose that it is $W^*$ on the basis of the first year's tastes, and $W^{**}$ on the basis of the second year's ... It may easily happen that $W_2^{**} > W_1^{**}$ and $W_2^* < W_1^*$, so that we have an ambiguity.' The sad fact is that even if we have $W_2^{**} > W_1^{**}$ *and* $W_2^* > W_1^*$, we *still* have an ambiguity, since nothing about the relative magnitudes of $W_2^{**}$ and $W_1^*$ can be deduced from comparing $W_2^{**}$ with $W_1^{**}$ and $W_2^*$ with $W_1^*$.

16. See, however, Gintis [10], and Fisher and Shell [8], p. 3. See also Graaff ([12], pp. 157–8), whose presentation of this problem is, however, somewhat obscured by his insistence on seeing it in terms of the classic dichotomy between ordinal and cardinal conceptions of welfare.

host of *additional* assumptions—a great deal more than an unchanging social preference map $R$ over $X$.

## 6  Differences in Population: Composition

In the last section the group involved was assumed to be the same. Two separate problems need to be distinguished in comparing the position of two different communities: (i) the *people* involved are different; and (ii) the *number* of people varies.

The former problem is tackled first for the special case in which the two communities have exactly the same *number* of people. The case of variable numbers, which raises issues of a somewhat different type, is taken up in the next section.

In line with questions (A) and (B) discussed in the last section, two types of questions can be raised in making welfare comparisons between two communities 1 and 2 enjoying $x$ and $y$ respectively.

(A\*)  Is community 1 better off with $x$ than it *would have been* with $y$?

(B\*)  Is community 1 better off with $x$ than community 2 *is* with $y$?

Just as (B) was seen to be in some ways a more difficult question than (A), so is (B\*) a more difficult query to answer than (A\*). But in fact (B\*) incorporates some additional complications over (B) since the persons involved are different and the cutting power of the *individualistic* conception of social welfare reduces dramatically. In fact, the Pareto principle yields nothing whatsoever; the question of somebody being better off and nobody worse off simply does not arise.

Question (A\*) does not, however, involve this problem, but—on the other hand—suffers from a serious ambiguity concerning its meaning. How do we translate the distribution of commodities between persons in community 2 reflected in $y$ into a distribution enjoyed by community 1? We have to establish a correspondence between the persons in the two communities, and there are $n!$ different one-to-one correspondences between two groups of $n$ people each. While questions of type (A\*) are frequently asked, there is a serious specification problem in interpreting them.[17]

Let $J^1$ and $J^2$ be two sets of $n$ people in communities 1 and 2 respectively. Let the individuals $i$ in each community be arbitrarily numbered from 1 to $n$. A named good vector $x$ is now a '*numbered* good vector', and is interpretable for both communities. Define $M$ as the set of one-to-one correspondences $\mu$

17. This specification problem becomes transparent if the analysis is done in terms of named good vectors but is present in any case. It usually escapes attention in the tradition of talking in terms of a representative individual enjoying the *per capita* average income (see, for example, Usher's [5] otherwise admirable comparison of the British and Thai national income).

from the set of positive integers $(1, \ldots, n)$ to itself, so that a $\mu$ can be used either to establish a one-to-one correspondence between members of the two communities, or to reflect a renumbering of the members of the same community. Let a renumbered $x$ according to $\mu$ be denoted by $x(\mu)$; for all $i$ and $j$, $x(\mu)_{ij} = x_{\mu(i)j}$. Person $i$ in $x(\mu)$ is the same as person $\mu(i)$ in $x$.

We cannot any longer interpret $xRy$ without first specifying in terms of which correspondence the statement is being made. To permit a variety of interpretations of $R$, a new social preference relation $R^0(\mu)$—to be called $R^0$ when there is no ambiguity—is introduced now which makes the comparison simply by assigning to person $i$ in community 1 the personal basket of $\mu(i)$ in community 2. In $x$, while person $i$ gets $i(x)$, in $y$ he gets $\mu(i)(y)$. $R^0$ is thus well defined, and by considering different $\mu(\cdot)$ functions, all the possible assignments can be explored. The symmetric and asymmetric factors of $R^0$ are called $I^0$ and $P^0$ respectively.

The interpretation of social preference $R$ between $x$ and $y$ now depends on what we wish to assume about who takes whose position. One approach is to specify some particular correspondence which would catch best the usual meaning of community 1 being placed in the position of community 2. Another is to try all correspondences, while a third is to check whether the relation holds for any correspondence at all. While various intermediate cases can also be considered, the following may be particularly interesting to explore.

(1) *The Distinguished Approach*: $x$ is socially better than $y$, denoted $xP(\mu^*)y$, if and only if for some distinguished correspondence $\mu^*$ in $M$, $xP^0y(\mu^*)$.

(2) *The Existential Approach*: $x$ is socially better than $y$, denoted $xP(\exists)y$, if and only if there exists some $\mu$ in $M$ such that $xP^0y(\mu)$.

(3) *The Universal Approach*: $x$ is socially better than $y$, denoted $xP(\forall)y$, if and only if for all $\mu$ in $M$, $xP^0y(\mu)$.

Note that social preference $P$ can either be taken to be $P(\mu^*)$ for some given $\mu^*$, or $P(\forall)$, or $P(\exists)$. These are not variations of preference, and indeed for $x$ and $y$ enjoyed by the same community, $xPy$ is unambiguously defined. The problem arises only when community 1 gets $x$, while community 2 gets $y$, and we find ourselves investigating whether community 1 is better off with $x$ than it 'would have been' with $y$—a question that occurs frequently in international comparisons. The difficulty is in interpreting the *meaning* of community 1 getting $y$.

Considering the approach of separating out some distinguished correspondence $\mu^*$ in $M$ for particular attention, it may be observed that it is quite common to compare two communities by looking at the relative position of 'comparable' classes or ordinal income groups in the two communities, e.g., Kuznets' comparison of 'top ordinal groups', 'intermediate groups', 'low ordinal groups', etc. ([25], pp. 423–6). This type of ordinal group comparison can be extended to establish a one-to-one correspondence between two equi-sized communities.

Let $e_i(x, q)$ be the aggregate income of the person numbered $i$ in the numbered good vector $x$ at commodity prices $q$:

$$e_i(x, q) = qi(x). \tag{9}$$

*Ordinal correspondence.* An ordinal correspondence is a one-to-one correspondence $\theta$ between two equi-numbered communities $J_1$ and $J_2$ enjoying $x$ and $y$ respectively, such that for all $i$, $g$ in $J_1$: $e_i(x, q) > e_g(x, q)$ implies $e_{\theta(i)}(y, q) \geqslant e_{\theta(g)}(y, q)$.

An ordinal correspondence relates the members of the two communities in terms of relative opulence, placing a richer man in one community in the position of a richer man in the other. If the numbering of persons is in a weak order of aggregate income $e_i$, so that $i > j$ implies that $e_i \leqslant e_j$, then a 'numbered good vector' can also be called a '*ranked* good vector'. For two ranked good vectors, the identity mapping $\mu(i)$ is an ordinal correspondence. Note that an ordinal correspondence is not necessarily unique.

The question of which prices to use for doing the ranking of aggregate income is a serious one. From the point of view of data it is obviously easier to rank the aggregate incomes at local prices in each economy. However, the motivation of question (B*) may make such a procedure suspect. The contrast is between community 1 in one situation (viz., $x$) *vis-à-vis* the *same* community with all its tastes and values in another situation (viz., $y$), and it seems natural to use the same notion of opulence prevalent in community 1 in both cases. We shall typically interpret the prices $q$ referred to in the definition of ordinal correspondence as the ruling market prices in the actual experience of community 1, but alternative interpretations are possible without upsetting the results.

An ordinal correspondence being accepted as the natural basis of comparison is a special case of a more general approach in which there exists some distinguished correspondence in terms of which the interpretation is made.

AXIOM N (*Natural Correspondence*). *Between any two equi-numbered communities enjoying $x$ and $y$ respectively, there is a distinguished interpersonal correspondence $\mu^*$ such that if $xP^0y(\mu^*)$, then $xPy$.*

Axiom N makes the 'distinguished approach' the appropriate one. An alternative axiom is now introduced which makes the different approaches coincide.

AXIOM S (*Personal Symmetry*). *Between any two equi-numbered communities enjoying $x$ and $y$ respectively, if for some $\mu$ in $M$: $x = y(\mu)$, then for all $\rho$ in $M$: $xI^0y(\rho)$.*

(T.7)   *If R is transitive and satisfies Axiom S, then $P(\forall) = P(\exists) = P(\mu^*)$*
        *for all $\theta^*$ in M.*

*Proof.*   It follows from Axiom S that for all $\mu$, $\rho$ in $M$: $y(\mu)I^0y(\rho)$. If,
therefore, $xP(\exists)y$, and there exists $\mu$ in $M$ such that: $xP^0y(\mu)$, then $xP^0y(\rho)$ for
all $\rho$ in $M$ by the transitivity of $R^0$. Hence $xP(\forall)y$.

Axiom S requires that if for some renumbering of the members of community 2, $x$ and $y$ are identical vectors of numbered goods, then for every
interpersonal correspondence $x$ and $y$ are equally good for community 1. It is
not particularly attractive, since it ignores all interpersonal differences
among members of community 1, and in the special case of individualistic
social welfare function, must require that the individual welfare functions be
identical if social welfare is to be a symmetric function of individual welfares.
    Under Axiom S, the scope of real income comparisons expands radically.
Social preference $P$ can be taken to be either $P(\forall)$ or $P(\exists)$, since $P(\forall) = P(\exists)$.

(T.8)   *If R satisfies Axioms C, V, M and S, then there exists a price vector*
        *p such that if there is any $\mu$ in M for which $px > py(\mu)$, then $xP(\forall)y$.*

From (T.1), a $p$ exists such that $px > py(\mu)$ implies that $xP^0y(\mu)$. Hence
$xP(\exists)y$. By Axiom S, $xP(\forall)y$.
    Since the constant-price real-income method generates an incomplete
ranking for reasons discussed in Section 2, this method of expanding the
observed comparability by considering every possible interpersonal permutation is useful. (See Section 8 for an illustration.)

## 7   Differences in Population: Size

The assumption that both communities have the same number of members
should now be relaxed. There are some complex philosophical issues about
the dependence of social welfare on the *size* of the population.
    Consider a fanciful case first. Suppose community 1 is replicated $b$ times
to form community 2, so that for each person in community 1, there are $b$
such persons (with identical individual welfare functions) in community 2.
Further let the commodity basket enjoyed by each of these $b$ persons in 2 be
exactly identical to that enjoyed by the corresponding person in 1. Suppose
also that there are no externalities, so that each of these $b$ persons in 2 is
exactly as well off as the corresponding person in 1.
    Consider now the two following questions: (i) Does community 2 have
greater *total* social welfare than community 1? (ii) Is the *standard* of welfare
in community 2 higher than in community 1?[18] There have been many debates

---

18. The two questions relate to two different types of choice: (i) Given the choice of having
community 1 and having community 2—as described—which one should one choose? (ii) Given

on (i), e.g., the Sidgwick–Meade position being to say 'yes' and the Cannan–Wicksell position being to deny it (see Dasgupta [4] for an important and useful analysis of the issue and its implications), but (ii) would seem to be relatively less controversial. It seems reasonable to argue that the standard of welfare (the welfare version of the standard of living) is the same in community 2 as in community 1. In so far as real income comparisons are concerned with *standards* of welfare, we can avoid entering into the Sidgwick *vs.* Cannan controversy. The assumption of 'scale independence' will be built into the properties of the relation $R^s$ of welfare standard.[19]

This property has to be translated to the space of numbered good vectors. For any $x$, an $mn$-vector of numbered goods with $m$-commodities and $n$ persons, and for any positive integer $b$, define the $b$-fold replica of $x$, called $r(x, b)$, as the $bmn$-vector of numbered goods with $m$ commodities and $bn$ persons satisfying:

$$\forall i: \{ \forall g: (1 + (i - 1)b \leq g \leq bi) \Rightarrow g(r(x, b)) = i(x) \}. \tag{10}$$

That is the $b$ persons numbered $1 + (i - 1)b$ to $bi$ all have the same personal basket $i(x)$ as enjoyed by $i$ in $x$. (Note that the procedure of numbering the persons used in (10) is such that if $x$ is a *ranked* good vector, then so would be $r(x, b)$. For any set of given prices, in the enlarged community, the $bn$ persons are numbered in a weak order of money income, if the $n$ persons in the community enjoying $x$ are.) Let $R^s$ stand for the weak relation of welfare standard with $P^s$ and $I^s$ being its asymmetric and symmetric parts respectively.

AXIOM I (*Size Independence*). *For all $mn$-vectors $x$ of numbered goods and all positive integers $b$: $x I^s r(x, b)$.*

Axiom I may, at first sight, appear to be more appealing than is justified. First, the replication is defined for 'personal baskets' of commodities, but if the persons enjoying them are markedly different, the replication may not be complete in welfare terms. The appeal of Axiom I depends, therefore, on the context in which it is used. As it happens, in this paper Axiom I will be used only in the context of a hypothetical replication to generate an intermediate point for comparison, so that there are no great difficulties in assuming complete replication, including personal characteristics.

Second, if welfare depends not merely on the person's own basket, but also on the consumption of others, it is possible that a $b$-fold replication of a given person—consumption basket, personalities and all—may still not lead to a $b$-fold replication of welfare levels. A million-fold multiplication of a

the choice of being any member—unknown which particular one—of community 1 and any member—unknown which—of community 2, what should one choose? The latter question relates to the normative framework of Harsanyi [15] and Rawls [36], among others, though the Harsanyi position would convert the 'ignorance' clause into 'equi-probability' of being anyone in the respective community. See also Pattanaik [33].

19. Cf. 'the Symmetry Axiom for Population' in Dasgupta, Sen and Starrett [5] and Sen [44].

basket including Christian Dior's latest dress may lead to some dampening of the enthusiasm of the proud owners. Axiom I is unashamedly obtuse about such subtleties.

Armed with Axiom I, the basic theorem (T.1) of real income comparisons can now be extended to the case of variable population size. If we interpret the comparison of the standard of welfare in line with (B*), the difficulties of different welfare functions of the two different groups of people—discussed earlier—must be faced. This is a particularly difficult issue to tackle when dealing with people belonging to different cultures and ways of life, and as was noted before, questions of the type of (A) or (A*) belong more naturally to the approach of real income comparisons than (B) or (B*) do.

Even with (A*), however, we have a serious problem, viz., that of interpretation. What can one mean by saying that the standard of welfare of community 1 with $n$ members is higher from its named good vector $x$ than what would have been the case if it had $x'$, the named good vector in fact enjoyed by community 2 with $n'$ members, $n \neq n'$?

Given Axiom I, a natural interpretation can be found in considering replicas of $x$ and $x'$ which have the same number of people. Consider the $n'$-fold replica of $x$ and the $n$-fold replica of $x'$. Both extended communities have $nn'$ people who could be put into a one-to-one correspondence *vis-à-vis* each other. And as in Section 6, welfare comparisons can be based on some distinguished correspondence, or on all correspondences, or on any correspondence, leading to preference relations $P(\mu^*)$, $P(\forall)$ and $P(\exists)$ respectively. And by virtue of Axiom I, the replicas of $x$ and $y$ yield identical standards of welfare as $x$ and $y$ respectively.

While Axiom I is defined explicitly in terms of $R^s$, the same is not true of the other axioms, which are all defined for social preference for a given population size. $R^s$ can be now required to 'take on' these axioms in the special case of comparisons involving a given population.

*R and $R^s$.* $R^s$ coincides with $R$ for all comparisons involving a given population, and $R^s$ is taken to satisfy any of the Axioms C, V, M, X, D, N and S if and only if all the corresponding $R$ and $R^0$ satisfy it.

(T.9) *If $R^s$ satisfies Axioms C, V, M, N and I, then there exists a price vector p such that $pr(x, n') > pr(x', n)(\mu^*)$ for some distinguished correspondence $\mu^*$ implies that $xP^s x'$.*

*Proof.* By (T.1), $pr(x, n') > pr(x', n)(\mu^*)$ implies that $r(x, n')P^0 r(x', n)(\mu^*)$, and if the chosen $\mu^*$ is the one referred to in Axiom N, then it also implies that $r(x, n')Pr(x', n)$. Hence $r(x, n')P^s r(x', n)$. (T.9) now follows from Axiom I since $xI^s r(x, n')$ and $x' I^s r(x', n)$.

Consider next the case in which Axiom N does not hold. The interpretation of $P^s$ now involves a problem. Suppose the universal approach is followed.

(T.10)   If $R^s$ satisfies Axioms C, V, M and I, then there exists a set $\Delta$ of
         $nn'!$ price vectors $p(\mu)$ such that if for all $p(\mu)$ in $\Delta$: $p(\mu)r(x, n')$ >
         $p(\mu)r(x', n)(\mu)$, then $xP^sx'$.

The possibility of practical use of the universal approach is not very great.
There are $nn'!$ one-to-one correspondences between the $nn'$ members of the
two extended communities. (The dimension of the problem can be somewhat
reduced by taking replicas of $x$ and $x'$ such that each have as many members
as the lowest common multiple $\lambda$ of $n$ and $n'$, but $\lambda!$ is typically a very large
number as well.) The main interest in (T.10) lies in the analytical insight it
provides rather than in practical use.

The picture simplifies enormously if the Axiom of Personal Symmetry is
used.

(T.11)   If $R^s$ satisfies Axioms C, V, M, I and S, then there exists a price
         vector $p$ such that if there is any correspondence $\mu$ for which
         $pr(x, n')$ > $pr(x', n)(\mu)$, then $xP^sx'$.

*Proof.*   By (T.1), there exists $p$ such that $pr(x, n')$ > $pr(x', n)(\mu)$ implies
that $r(x, n')P^0r(x', n)(\mu)$, and therefore by Axiom S, for all $\mu$: $r(x, n')P^0$
$r(x', n)(\mu)$. Hence $r(x, n')P^sr(x', n)$. (T.11) now follows from Axiom I.


## 8   Ordinal Weighting: an Illustration

The analysis in the last few sections has been in very general terms. In order
to make any practical use of the real income procedure, something about the
shape of the preference structure $R$ would have to be specified. This is perhaps
most conveniently done through the specification of the supporting hyperplanes at the relevant points. In Section 4 two specific axioms, viz., X and D,
were considered, which yielded the special case of evaluation at market
prices. While both the axioms were seen to be limited, Axiom D was found to
be particularly obnoxious.

In what follows it will be assumed throughout that social preferences satisfy
Axioms C, V and M. This will not be repeated in the statements of (T.12)–
(T.16).

Let $e_i$ be the money income of person $i$ at the ruling market prices.

AXIOM E (*Ordinal Equity*).   *For each x, the normal p of some hyperplane*
$H(x)$ *through x bounding $R(x)$ and satisfying the condition specified in
Axiom X, also satisfies for all i, g and j:*

$$\text{if } e_i > e_g, \text{ then } p_{ij} < p_{gj}. \tag{11}$$

Axiom E taken in conjunction with Axiom X means that a poorer person's
dollar will receive a larger weight than a richer man's dollar, in contrast with

Axiom D which weights everyone's dollars equally.[20] The ordering of weights on dollars is inverse to the ranking of people's income.

A particular case satisfying Axiom E is to make the weights equi-distanced, e.g., making the weight on a dollar of the $i$th richest man equal his income rank $i$. (If more than one person has the same total income, they can be ranked in any arbitrary order. It should be noted that for real income comparisons using Axiom R to be proposed presently, it would not matter which particular rank ordering is chosen in this case.) Such an approach has been used for the measurement of inequality and poverty (see Sen [46], [47], the first of which also provides an axiomatic breakdown of this procedure).

Its motivation can be compared with that of Borda's famous rule of rank-order voting, which is in fact frequently used in practice and has been extensively analysed in the recent collective choice literature. The following axiom is defined for ranked good vectors so that $i$ stands for the person's income rank.

AXIOM R (*Rank Order Weighting*).   *For each $x$, an mn-vector of ranked goods for n persons and m commodities, the normal $p$ of some hyperplane $H(x)$ through $x$ bounding $R(x)$ satisfies for all $i$ (the income rank of a person at $q$) and $j$:*

$$p_{ij} = Aiq_j, \tag{12}$$

*where $A > 0$ is some constant.*

Note that Axiom R incorporates both Axiom X and Axiom E, but goes somewhat further. Given Axiom R the ratio of the weights on two ranked goods $ij$ and $gh$ are given by the ratio of their respective market prices each multiplied by the income rank of the person enjoying the commodity:

$$p_{ij}/p_{gh} = (iq_j/gq_h). \tag{13}$$

Let ranked good vectors $x$ and $x'$ enjoyed by two equi-numbered communities 1 and 2 yield mean money incomes $e$ and $e'$ and Gini coefficients $G$ and $G'$ respectively, all at $q$ prices referred to in Axiom R.

(T.12)   *Given Axiom R, for all equi-numbered large communities ($n$ large), if $e(1 - G) > e'(1 - G')$, then $xP(\theta)x'$, where $\theta$ is any ordinal correspondence.*

*Proof.*   The value of the Gini coefficient is given by (see Gini [9], Theil [49]):

$$G = (\Sigma_i \Sigma_g \mid e_i - e_g \mid)/2n^2e. \tag{14}$$

It is easily checked that:

---

20. See Sen [44]. See also Muellbauer [29] for an illuminating discussion of this issue in the context of constructing price indices.

$$G = 1 + 1/n - 2(\Sigma_i i e_i)/n^2 e. \tag{15}$$

Hence

$$\Sigma_i i e_i = en(n + 1 - Gn)/2. \tag{16}$$

Given Axiom R, the value of $px$ is given by:

$$px = A\Sigma_i i \Sigma_j q_j x_{ij} = A\Sigma_i i e_i. \tag{17}$$

Therefore:

$$px = An^2 e((n + 1)/n) - G)/2. \tag{18}$$

Note that for a given large $n$, this can be written as:[21]

$$px = Ke(1 - G), \quad \text{with } K \text{ a constant.} \tag{19}$$

It is clear that $e(1 - G) > e'(1 - G')$ implies that $px > px'$. Since $p$ is the normal of a supporting hyperplane of $R(x)$ through $x$, it is clear that $xP(\theta)x'$ under any ordinal correspondence $\theta$.

(T.12) is a theorem using the distinguished approach. What about the existential and the universal approaches?

(T.13)  *For equi-numbered large communities, if not $e(1 - G) > e'(1 - G')$, then given Axiom R there is no interpersonal correspondence $\mu$ such that $px > px'(\mu)$.*

*Proof.*  Note that $px = A\Sigma_i i e_i$, and $px' = A\Sigma_i i \mu(i) e_i'$. Since $i < g$ implies that $e_i' \geqslant e_g'$, it is clear that the value of $px'$ is minimized if $\mu(i) = i$, i.e., if $\mu$ is an ordinal correspondence. Hence if $px > px'(\mu)$ for any $\mu$, then $px > px'$, and so by (19), $e(1 - G) > e'(1 - G')$.

Hence to be covered by the real-income procedure under the existential approach satisfying $R$, the best bet is the comparison of the values of $e(1 - G)$. (Note also that (T.13) demonstrates that ordinal correspondence at the *same* prices $q$ for both numbered good vectors $x$ and $x'$ maximizes the scope of constant-price real-income comparisons in this framework, and ranking the members of $J_1$ and $J_2$ in terms of the respective local prices will reduce (at least not increase) the possibility of the real-income inequality being satisfied.)

(T.14)  *Given Axioms R and S, for equi-numbered large communities if $e(1 - G) > e'(1 - G')$, then $xP(\forall)x'$.*

This follows directly from (T.7) and (T.12).

Notice that the combination of (T.13) and (T.14) indicates how comparison of the values of $e(1 - G)$ squeezes out as much juice as possible from constant-price real-income comparison under rank order weighting. To demonstrate

---

21. Note also that the requirement that $n$ be large would have been unnecessary if we had taken the weights $p_{ij} = A(i - \frac{1}{2})q_j$, instead of (12). See Sen [47].

$xP(\forall)x'$, we need to demonstrate $xP(\mu)x'$ for some $\mu$, and that can be done if and only if $e(1 - G) > e'(1 - G')$. For other correspondences $\rho$, it could be the case that $px \leqslant px'(\rho)$, but still $xP^0x'(\rho)$, by virtue of symmetry. The comparison of $e(1 - G)$ being the condition most likely to be satisfied on purely analytical grounds does point towards the most extensive partial ordering.[22]

We turn now to the problem of extension of this approach to international comparisons involving nations of different size.

AXIOM R FOR $R^s$:    $R^s$ satisfies Axiom R if and only if $R^0$ for any two equisized communities satisfies Axiom R.

Let $x$ and $x'$ be two ranked good vectors enjoyed by two communities not necessarily of the same size but with the same types of commodities. At $q$ (the market prices referred to in Axiom R), $e$ and $e'$ are the respective mean per capita incomes and $G$ and $G'$ the respective Gini coefficients of the two income distributions of the two communities.

(T.15)    If $R^s$ satisfies Axioms R, S and I, then $e(1 - G) > e'(1 - G')$ implies that $xPx'$.

*Proof.* Let $n$ and $n'$ be the respective numbers of people in communities 1 and 2. Consider $r(x, n')$, the $n'$-fold replica of $x$, and $r(x', n)$, the $n$-fold replica of $x'$. First check that at any set of market prices $q$, specified in Axiom R, the mean incomes of $r(x, n')$ and $r(x', n)$ are also $e$ and $e'$ respectively, and furthermore, the respective Gini coefficients are also the same as for $x$ and $x'$, i.e., $G$ and $G'$ respectively. Therefore, by (T.14), if $e(1 - G) > e'(1 - G')$, then $r(x, n')P(\forall)r(x', n)$. Hence $r(x, n')P^s r(x', n)$. But by Axiom I, $xI^s r(x, n')$ and $x'I^s r(x', n)$. Hence $xP^s x'$.

Finally, it should be noted that Axiom S can be dropped if some distinguished correspondence is accepted as natural in comparing the numbered good vectors $r(x, n')$ and $r(x', n)$, i.e., in deciding who takes whose position in the $nn'$ people of the first extended community being placed in the position of the second. In particular, the procedure of ordinal correspondence, defined in Section 6 is adequate.

(T.16)    If $R^s$ satisfies Axioms R and I, then under the distinguished approach using any ordinal correspondence, $e(1 - G) > e'(1 - G')$ implies that $xP^s x'$.

22. Note also that under the assumption of symmetry, the procedure of using values of $e(1 - G)$ can also be used for *intertemporal* comparisons of social welfare for the same community. If $e(1 - G)$ at the final year weights is greater in the final year, then under Axioms R and S, there is a rise in social welfare. The comparison may involve some interpersonal permutation (the $i$th richest man in the final year being placed in the position of the $i$th richest man in the initial year and the two need not be the same person). In this the procedure has some similarity with Suppes' [48] 'grading principles'; see also Hammond [14].

The proof, which is close to that of (T.15), is omitted.

The axioms used in this section illustrate one possible application of the general framework for real income comparisons developed earlier in this paper. Since these axioms—in particular, Axiom R—may be quite controversial, it is worth emphasizing that the use of the general framework is by no means conditional on this particular set of axioms being accepted. The general framework involves a structure for generating welfare partial orderings based on constant-weight real income comparisons taking explicit note of distribution and of the composition and the size of the population. (T.10)–(T.16) merely explore one particular case within this general framework, and the relevance of these results depends, of course, on the acceptability of the value judgements explicitly used in the axioms. (For a breakdown of Axiom R into more primitive axioms, see Sen [46].) Alternative axiom structures can also be used within the general framework explored in (T.1)–(T.9).

## 9    Concluding Remarks

In this paper a general approach to real income comparisons has been presented which makes distribution an integral part of such comparisons. This permits the treatment of real national income comparison as generating a partial ordering of a complete welfare indicator rather than a complete ordering of a partial welfare indicator (leaving out 'distribution').[23]

Since various types of comparisons are relevant, involving rather different specific problems within the same general framework, Figure 2 presents a partitioning of problems, also indexing which problem has been discussed where in this paper.

The approach of real national income comparisons yields partial rankings (extendable to partial orderings) based on the general strategy of making global judgements using locally relevant weights (Sections 2, 3). Under very special assumptions these weights will be given by the market prices (Section 4), but a concern with distribution will require an alternative approach. This general approach, presented in this paper, has been illustrated with a particular procedure (Section 8). An empirical application is presented in the Appendix. In general making the weights on commodities depend on the persons to whom they go is a distinctive feature of the approach of this paper.

Some of the biggest problems in real national income comparisons seems to arise from difficulties of interpretation. Are we comparing the welfare of one nation with that of another, or the welfare of one nation with what the

23. For an example of the latter, see Kuznets [23]. An important recent contribution in the latter tradition is Nordhaus and Tobin [32]. Note also that in the traditional pure theory of real income comparison (e.g., Hicks [17], [18]), the incomplete nature of the national income ranking was clearly noted, so that that approach can be viewed as generating a partial ordering of a partial welfare indicator.

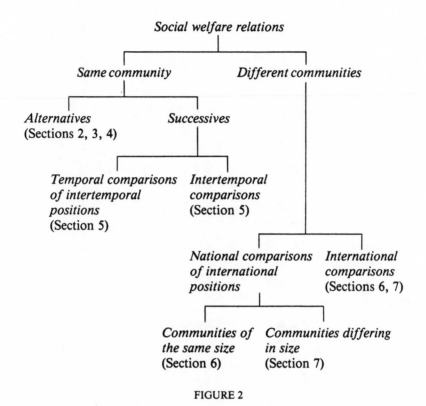

FIGURE 2

welfare of that nation *would have been* if it were placed 'in the position of' the other nation? While the former involves difficult issues of inter-group welfare comparison, there are serious problems of interpretation in the latter question when distribution of commodities among individuals have to be taken into account and when population size of the two nations vary. A substantial part of this paper has been devoted to sorting out these issues.

## APPENDIX   INTER-STATE DISPARITIES IN PER CAPITA RURAL CONSUMPTION IN INDIA

In this Appendix an attempt is made to apply the procedure of real income comparison of named good vectors to study regional differences in the rural standard of living in India. The welfare axioms used are Axiom R (Rank-order Weighting) and Axiom I (Independence of Size) presented in Section 9 to illustrate the named good approach. The comparisons are made in terms of questions of type (A*), i.e., in terms of the welfare relation R of the rural

TABLE 1   Values of $e(1 - G)$ of rural consumption of each state (column) at prices of every state (row) 1961−62*

| | Andhra Pradesh | Assam | Bihar | Gujarat | Jammu and Kashmir | Kerala | Madhya Pradesh | Madras | Maha-rashtra | Mysore | Orissa | Punjab | Rajas-than | Uttar Pradesh | West Bengal |
|---|---|---|---|---|---|---|---|---|---|---|---|---|---|---|---|
| Andhra Pradesh | 13.61 | 16.49 | 12.24 | 18.17 | 19.54 | 14.04 | 18.31 | 14.75 | 16.34 | 20.25 | 13.49 | 24.11 | 19.63 | 19.24 | 14.87 |
| Assam | 14.52 | 16.87 | 12.81 | 19.88 | 21.00 | 14.44 | 19.09 | 15.54 | 16.42 | 20.71 | 13.97 | 26.80 | 21.22 | 19.15 | 15.42 |
| Bihar | 13.87 | 16.43 | 11.51 | 18.30 | 19.45 | 14.11 | 17.81 | 14.90 | 15.44 | 19.81 | 13.32 | 24.52 | 19.51 | 18.59 | 14.59 |
| Gujarat | 13.21 | 15.98 | 11.53 | 16.84 | 19.23 | 14.07 | 17.54 | 14.19 | 15.19 | 19.41 | 12.64 | 24.99 | 19.47 | 19.10 | 14.25 |
| Jammu and Kashmir | 12.84 | 15.51 | 10.99 | 17.60 | 17.88 | 14.64 | 16.64 | 13.96 | 14.62 | 18.74 | 12.35 | 24.17 | 18.50 | 18.24 | 13.76 |
| Kerala | 15.87 | 18.29 | 14.11 | 21.59 | 22.71 | 14.26 | 21.02 | 16.54 | 17.92 | 22.58 | 15.24 | 28.61 | 23.41 | 22.16 | 16.85 |
| Madhya Pradesh | 12.64 | 15.35 | 10.65 | 17.40 | 18.23 | 13.57 | 15.13 | 13.91 | 13.83 | 18.55 | 11.96 | 23.61 | 18.14 | 17.53 | 13.34 |
| Madras | 14.41 | 17.20 | 12.94 | 19.39 | 20.67 | 14.64 | 19.20 | 15.07 | 16.50 | 20.84 | 14.08 | 26.02 | 21.13 | 20.51 | 15.63 |
| Maharashtra | 13.17 | 16.06 | 11.48 | 17.93 | 19.01 | 15.06 | 17.19 | 14.27 | 14.36 | 19.13 | 12.77 | 24.75 | 19.13 | 18.96 | 14.15 |
| Mysore | 13.19 | 15.92 | 11.57 | 17.73 | 18.70 | 14.02 | 17.58 | 14.21 | 15.00 | 18.11 | 12.87 | 24.08 | 19.00 | 18.65 | 14.41 |
| Orissa | 12.66 | 15.32 | 10.85 | 17.87 | 18.35 | 13.30 | 16.72 | 13.69 | 14.48 | 18.60 | 11.80 | 24.33 | 18.51 | 17.72 | 13.49 |
| Punjab | 12.85 | 15.60 | 11.06 | 17.44 | 18.23 | 14.75 | 16.65 | 13.94 | 14.48 | 18.62 | 12.13 | 21.46 | 18.36 | 18.05 | 14.20 |
| Rajasthan | 11.94 | 14.45 | 9.97 | 16.31 | 17.12 | 13.72 | 15.33 | 12.94 | 13.40 | 17.27 | 11.09 | 22.64 | 16.11 | 16.67 | 12.66 |
| Uttar Pradesh | 12.52 | 15.01 | 10.58 | 17.19 | 17.88 | 13.74 | 16.94 | 13.58 | 14.17 | 18.38 | 11.63 | 23.09 | 17.79 | 15.93 | 13.25 |
| West Bengal | 14.86 | 17.99 | 12.97 | 19.96 | 21.22 | 16.14 | 19.18 | 16.02 | 16.57 | 21.16 | 14.33 | 26.27 | 21.00 | 20.17 | 15.58 |

*Two types of assumptions have been chosen to close some holes in the data. The first deals with covering some gaps in the price data; for the specific assumptions made, see Rath [35], pp. 338−44. The second concerns the 1960−61 Gini coefficients at local prices separately estimated for each state by Vaidyanathan [51]. We use these estimates for our 1961−62 weighting, on the presumption that (i) the price variations between the states would not materially change the values of the state Gini coefficients if revalued at the prices of other states (even though the opulence ranking of the particular persons in each state may change), and (ii) the 1961−62 Gini coefficients would have been similar to the 1960−61 values. See also Mukherjee [30] and Bhattacharya and Chatterjee [3].

community of any given state putting that community in the position of the rural population of every other state respectively. This is done for each state, and since 15 states are covered, $15 \times 14 = 210$ pairwise comparisons are involved. The interpretation of 'putting in the position' is taken to be in line with the 'extended community' presentation outlined in Section 7. As far as the interpersonal correspondences of equi-sized extended communities are concerned, we use any 'ordinal correspondence', $\theta$, interpreting social preference as $P(\theta)$, using (T.16). Or alternatively, we use the existential approach, involving $P(\exists)$, which comes to the same thing, as is obvious from (T.13). A third alternative is to bring the powerful Axiom S (Personal Symmetry) and use the most exacting universal approach, involving $P(\forall)$, which again leads to the same formula as is clear from (T.15). The results of

TABLE 2   Comparative picture 1961–62

| Reference State | Has a higher standard of rural welfare than it would have if placed in the position of the rural community in the following States |
|---|---|
| Bihar | None |
| Kerala Orissa | Bihar |
| Andhra Pradesh | + Orissa |
| West Bengal | + Andhra Pradesh |
| Madras | + Kerala |
| Maharashtra | – Kerala<br>+ Madras<br>+ West Bengal |
| Assam Madhya Pradesh | + Kerala<br>+ Maharashtra |
| Gujarat Uttar Pradesh | + Assam |
| Jammu and Kashmir Mysore Rajasthan | + Gujarat<br>+ Madhya Pradesh |
| Punjab | + Jammu and Kashmir<br>+ Mysore<br>+ Rajasthan<br>+ Uttar Pradesh |

the empirical exercise can be interpreted in either of these three possible ways.

Our calculations are based on the rural consumption studies by Rath [35] and Vaidyanathan [51], using the National Sample Survey, 16th and 17th Rounds, relating respectively to 1960–61 and 1961–62. (See also the pioneering work of Nikhiles Bhattacharya and G. S. Chatterjee [3]. An alternative basis for the statistical exercise in this Appendix could have been found in the estimates of Bhattacharya and Chatterjee who use a more disaggregated commodity structure.)

Table 1 presents the 225 values of $e(1 - G)$ of rural consumption for each state at the prices of every state. Each row specifies the state the prices of which are being used, while the columns indicate the numbered vector of which is being evaluated. Following our procedure, comparisons are made row-wise. If the value of the diagonal element for any state 1 is larger than the value in the same row for another state 2, then we conclude that in terms of consumption, state 1 has a higher rural standard of welfare (under Axioms R and I) than it would have had if it were placed in the position of state 2.

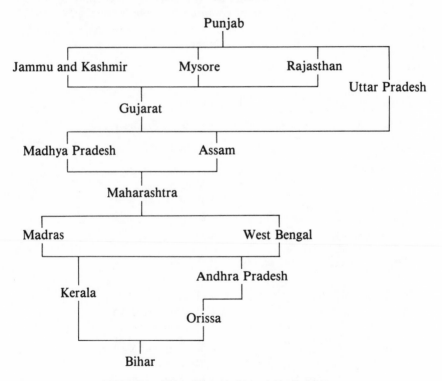

FIGURE 3   *Hasse diagram of summarized rankings*

Of course, it is in principle perfectly possible for state 1 to 'beat' state 2 in this sense while state 2 'beats' state 1, since the first comparison is made in terms of the welfare relation of state 1 and the second in terms of that of state 2. As it happens this does not occur here at all, and no evidence for crucial differences in preference emerge.

In Table 2, we specify for each state the other states compared with which it has a higher rural standard of welfare in terms of its own welfare relation. At one end is Bihar without a single 'victory', and at the other end is Punjab, which 'beats' all the other states.

A pithy representation of the results of the 210 pair-wise comparisons is given in Figure 3, which is a 'Hasse diagram' with a downward path indicating superiority in the standard of welfare in sense (A*).[24] This should not, however, be taken to be an inter-state ranking of the standards of welfare in the more demanding sense (B*), unless the additional assumption is made that all states have the same basic welfare function $W(\cdot)$, defined over the numbered good space of the equi-numbered replicas.

## References

[1] Arrow, K. J.: *Social Choice and Individual Values* (New York: Wiley, 1951; 2nd ed. 1963).

[2] Beckerman, W.: *In Defence of Economic Growth* (London: Jonathan Cape, 1974).

[3] Bhattacharya, N. and Chatterjee, G. S.: 'Consumer Prices and Per Capita Household Consumption in Rural India', *Economic and Political Weekly,* 6 (30 October, 1971).

[4] Dasgupta, P.: 'On Optimum Population Size', in A. Mitra (ed.), *Economic Theory and Planning: Essays in Honour of A. K. Dasgupta* (Calcutta: Oxford UP, 1974).

[5] Dasgupta, P., Sen, A. K. and Starrett, D.: 'Notes on the Measurement of Inequality', *Journal of Economic Theory,* 6 (1973).

[6] Debreu, G.: *Theory of Value* (New York: Wiley, 1959).

[7] Fisher, F. M.: 'Income Distribution, Value Judgements and Welfare', *Quarterly Journal of Economics,* 70 (1956).

[8] Fisher, F. M. and Shell, K.: *The Economic Theory of Prices Indices* (New York and London: Academic Press, 1972).

---

24. This representation is possible in this case because the rankings viewed together satisfy not merely two-term consistency but also acyclicity and Houthakker's [19] condition of 'semi-transitivity', permitting an extension to a partial order. Note, however, that all the extensions were already present in the directly observed relations, with one exception, viz., Maharashtra beats Madras, which beats Kerala, but Maharashtra and Kerala are not ranked *vis-à-vis* each other by direct comparison. If the rankings represented the same underlying welfare function for all states then taking the 'ancestral' $P^{**}$, i.e., the transitive closure of the directly observed preference relation $P^*$, would be a perfectly legitimate interpretation of social preference (see Section 3).

[9] Gini, C.: *Variabilità e mutabilità* (Bologna, 1912).
[10] Gintis, H.: *Alienation and Power: Towards a Radical Welfare Economics*, Harvard University Ph.D. dissertation, 1969.
[11] Gorman, W. M.: 'Are Social Indifference Curves Convex?' *Quarterly Journal of Economics,* **73** (1959).
[12] Graaff, J. de V.: *Theoretical Welfare Economics* (Cambridge UP, 1957).
[13] Hahn, F. H.: 'Equilibrium with Transaction Costs', *Econometrica,* **39** (1971).
[14] Hammond, P. J.: 'Equity, Arrow's Conditions and Rawls' Difference Principle', mimeographed, September 1974.
[15] Harsanyi, J. C.: 'Cardinal Welfare, Individualistic Ethics, and Interpersonal Comparisons of Utility', *Journal of Political Economy,* **63** (1955).
[16] Herzberger, H. G.: 'Ordinal Preference and Rational Choice', *Econometrica,* **41** (1973).
[17] Hicks, J. R.: 'Valuation of Social Income', *Review of Economic Studies,* **7** (1940).
[18] ____ 'Measurement of Real Income', *Oxford Economic Papers,* **10** (1958).
[19] Houthakker, H. S.: 'Revealed Preference and the Utility Function', *Economica,* **17** (1950).
[20] Kenen, P. B. and Fisher, F. M.: 'Income Distribution, Value Judgements and Welfare: A Correction', *Quarterly Journal of Economics,* **71** (1957).
[21] Kennedy, C. M.: 'The Economic Welfare Function and Dr. Little's Criterion', *Review of Economic Studies,* **20** (1952–53).
[22] Kolm, S. Ch.: 'The Optimal Production of Social Justice', in J. Margolis and H. Guitton (eds), *Public Economics* (London: Macmillan, 1969).
[23] Kuznets, S.: *National Income and Its Composition: 1919–1938* (New York: NBER, 1941).
[24] ____ 'On the Valuation ot Social Income: Reflections on Professor Hicks' Article', *Economica,* NS, **15** (1948).
[25] ____ *Modern Economic Growth* (New Haven and London: Yale UP, 1966).
[26] Little, I. M. D.: *A Critique of Welfare Economics* (Oxford: Clarendon Press, 1950; 2nd ed., 1957).
[27] Marx, K.: *Capital,* Vol. I, tr. by S. Moore and E. Aveling (London: Allen & Unwin, 1887; re-set, 1946).
[28] Mirrlees, J.: 'The Evaluation of National Income in an Imperfect Economy', *Pakistan Development Review,* **9** (1969).
[29] Muellbauer, J.: 'The Political Economy of Price Indices', mimeographed, Birkbeck College Discussion Paper No. 22, 1974. [Revised version, 'Distributional Aspects of Price Comparisons', in R. Stone and W. Peterson (eds), *Economic Contributions to Public Policy* (London: Macmillan, 1978).]
[30] Mukherjee, M.: 'Size and Area Distribution of the Level of Living in India', *Sankhya,* Series B, **31** (1969).
[31] Nash, J. F.: 'The Bargaining Problem', *Econometrica,* **18** (1950).
[32] Nordhaus, W. and Tobin, J.: 'Is Growth Obsolete?' in NBER, *Economic Growth,* Fifth Anniversary Colloquium (New York: NBER, 1972).
[33] Pattanaik, P. K.: *Voting and Collective Choice* (Cambridge UP, 1971).
[34] Pigou, A. C.: *The Economics of Welfare* (London: Macmillan, 4th ed., 1952).
[35] Rath, N.: 'Regional Variation in Level and Cost of Living in Rural India', *Artha Vijnana,* **15** (1973).

[36] Rawls, J.: *A Theory of Justice* (Cambridge, Mass.: Harvard UP, and Oxford: Clarendon Press, 1971).

[37] Samuelson, P. A.: *Foundations of Economic Analysis* (Cambridge, Mass., 1947).

[38] ____ 'Evaluation of Real National Income', *Oxford Economic Papers*, 2 (1950).

[39] ____ 'Social Indifference Curves', *Quarterly Journal of Economics*, 70 (1956).

[40] Scitovsky, T.: 'A Note on Welfare Propositions in Economics', *Review of Economic Studies*, (1941).

[41] ____ 'A Theory of the Quality of Life', mimeographed, 1974. [Revised version published as *The Joyless Economy* (Oxford University Press, 1976).]

[42] Sen, A. K.: 'Interpersonal Aggregation and Partial Comparability', *Econometrica*, 38 (1970); 'A Correction', *Econometrica*, 40 (1972). [Essay 9 in this volume.]

[43] ____ *Collective Choice and Social Welfare* (San Francisco: Holden-Day, and Edinburgh: Oliver & Boyd, 1970).

[44] ____ *On Economic Inequality* (Oxford: Clarendon Press, 1973).

[45] ____ 'Behaviour and the Concept of Preference', *Economica*, 40 (1973). [Essay 2 in this volume.]

[46] ____ 'Informational Bases of Alternative Welfare Approaches: Aggregation and Income Distribution', *Journal of Public Economics*, 4 (1974).

[47] ____ 'Poverty: An Ordinal Approach to Measurement', *Econometrica*, 44 (1976). [Essay 17 in this volume.]

[48] Suppes, P.: 'Some Formal Models of Grading Principles', *Synthese*, 6 (1966); reprinted in P. Suppes, *Studies in the Methodology and Foundations of Science* (New York: Humanities Press, 1969).

[49] Theil, H.: *Economics and Information Theory* (Amsterdam: North-Holland, 1967).

[50] Usher, D.: *The Price Mechanism and the Meaning of National Income Statistics* (Oxford: Clarendon Press, 1968).

[51] Vaidyanathan, A.: 'Some Aspects of Inequalities in Living Standards in Rural India', mimeographed, 1972.

[52] Weitzman, M.: 'Aggregation and Disaggregation in the Pure Theory of Capital and Growth: A New Parable', Cowles Foundation Discussion Paper No. 292, 1970.

# 19

# Ethical Measurement of Inequality: Some Difficulties

## 1 *Introduction*

In studies of the language of morals it is common to distinguish between a 'prescriptive' term, which has prescriptive meaning 'whether or not it has descriptive meaning', and an 'evaluative' term, which has 'both kinds of meaning' (Hare, 1952; 1963). That it is not easy to view 'inequality' as a purely descriptive concept seems to be widely accepted by now;[1] it relates to the notion of 'equity' which—as Tinbergen points out in his paper presented at the same conference (see Krelle and Shorrocks, 1978)—must be seen to be 'normative', being 'based on a value judgement'. But, at the same time, inequality cannot be seen to be a *purely* prescriptive concept either, since it also has descriptive meaning from which the concept cannot be easily divorced.[2] I shall try to show in Section 2 that this duality has very damaging consequences for the 'ethical measurement' of inequality, initiated by Dalton (1920), and recently widely explored in a number of contributions, most notably in the path-breaking and elegant paper of Atkinson (1970).

There is a second issue closely related to this. In one of the traditional formulations of the Bergson–Samuelson social welfare function, social welfare $W$ is taken to be a function of the vector of individual utilities (see Samuelson, 1947 and Graaff, 1967).[3]

---

My greatest debt is to Tony Atkinson, since my thinking on this subject has been largely inspired by his contributions, even though this has led me to a position rather different from his.

1. For an engaging (and illuminating) dissent, see Wiles (1974), who feels able 'to *banish welfare economics from the process of measurement,* and to restore the strictest objectivity to our actual measures' (page xi).
2. See Bentzel (1970), Sen (1973), Wiles (1974), Hansson (1977) and Atkinson (1976).
3. There is an ambiguity in the form of this representation (1) since it is possible to take $W$ and $(U_1, \ldots, U_n)$ not to be a real number and a vector of real numbers respectively, but to be a real-

---

From Krelle, W. and Shorrocks, A. A. (eds), *Personal Income Distribution* (Amsterdam: North-Holland, 1978).

$$W = f(U_1, \ldots, U_n). \qquad (1)$$

While it is not possible in general to split up the ethical judgements implicit in $f(\cdot)$ into assessment of total *size* and that of *distribution*, under special circumstances such identifications are possible. Since—to quote Tinbergen again—'equity is not the only aim of a social order', it is not really surprising that a measure of inequality that is derived from *over-all* ethical judgements may incorporate the influence of size in addition to that of distribution. What may be less obvious is that, under some specified circumstances when the size-distribution split up is possible and the ranking of size is exactly the opposite of the ranking of distribution, the ethical measures of inequality may reflect the ranking of size only, ignoring distribution altogether. ·

It is possible to use *personal* welfare functions rather than *social* welfare functions in inequality assessment. This may not necessarily lead to a complete measure (i.e., a measure that generates a complete ordering over all distributions of income). On the other hand, under standard assumptions, it certainly does generate an important partial ordering (see Section 3), and permits us to focus directly on the question of the distribution of personal welfares. Interpersonal comparisons of utility need be no more than *ordinal* for this purpose.

Finally, the question is raised as to whether it is sensible to think of social welfare as a function of individual welfares only, i.e., to assume what I have elsewhere called 'welfarism' (Sen, 1977a). Concepts of rights implicit in such diverse notions as liberty and exploitation militate against a welfarist approach. If welfarism is abandoned, the consequent broadening of the ethical framework raises some additional difficulties in the ethical measurement of inequality. These are briefly discussed in Section 4.

## 2   *Contradictions*

First a description of the ethical measures of inequality. Let social welfare be taken to be an increasing, symmetric and quasi-concave function $g(\cdot)$ of the vector of individual incomes:[4]

valued function and an $n$-tuple of real-valued functions respectively, each defined over the environment $X$ of social states. The distinction turns out to be crucial in assessing the applicability of Arrow-like impossibility theorems to the Bergson–Samuelson social welfare functions (see Sen, 1977a). It seems clear, however, that this interpretation of $f(\cdot)$ as a 'functional' is not intended in the formulations in question (see the operations in Samuelson, 1974, p. 246, equation (31) and Graaff, 1967, p. 51, figure 7(b)). However, these impossibility theorems arise only when interpersonal comparisons of utility are ruled out, which makes rather little sense for ethical measures of inequality, and leads to disastrous results (see Hammond, 1976a).

4. These assumptions are not strictly necessary for the approach to be used. It is sufficient that, for each total income, social welfare should be maximized by equal distribution. For this, $S$-concavity of function $g(\cdot)$ is sufficient (see Kolm, 1972 and Dasgupta, Sen and Starrett, 1973).

$$W = g(y_1, \ldots, y_n). \tag{2}$$

The level of inequality of a given vector y of incomes can be measured under the normative approach

*either* (i) by comparing the level of social welfare generated by y with the social welfare that would be generated if the same total income were equally distributed (the Dalton measure);

*or*    (ii) by comparing the total income of y with the total income that would generate the same social welfare if it were equally distributed (the Atkinson measure).

In fact, Atkinson also assumed additionally that $g(\cdot)$ was an additively separable function of individual incomes, and Dalton went further in assuming that $g$ must be strictly utilitarian (and there were no externalities):[5]

$$W = \sum_{i=1}^{n} U(y_i), \quad \text{with } U(\cdot) \text{ concave.} \tag{3}$$

We do not *need* these additional assumptions for the use of the Dalton– Atkinson ethical approach and their measures can be translated into the general form of (2). But, of course, utilitarianism is perfectly *compatible* with the approach, and since it will simplify the presentation of the point at issue, we may as well begin with this case.

To simplify further, let the individual utility function be of the following form (with constant elasticity of marginal utility):[6]

$$U = C + \frac{1}{\eta} (y_i)^{\eta}, \quad \text{with } \eta \leqslant 1. \tag{4}$$

Atkinson's measure of inequality $X$ can now be seen to be given by:

$$A = 1 - \frac{e}{m}, \tag{5}$$

when $m$ is the mean income of the individual incomes vector, and $e$ is 'the equally distributed equivalent income':

$$e = \left[ \frac{1}{n} \sum_{i=1}^{n} (y_i)^{\eta} \right]^{1/\eta}. \tag{6}$$

---

5. Atkinson's formulation looks similar to (3), but the set of $U$-values need not be interpreted as 'utilities'.

6. This class of utility functions was much explored in contributions to the optimum growth literature in the 1960s (see Chakravarty, 1970). Note that with $\eta < 0$, the second term on the right hand side of (4) must always be negative, and the responsibility for making total utility non-negative for the relevant values of $y_i$ falls on $C$ being positive and sufficiently large. In fact the 'subsistence' level may then be defined by $y^*$:

$$y^* = (- C\eta)^{1/\eta}. \tag{4'}$$

We now have to check how this ethical measure relates to our ideas on the descriptive notion of inequality. The descriptive notion of inequality is not, however, unambiguous in many comparisons, and therefore we have to concentrate on those special cases in which there is no ambiguity in the descriptive ranking of inequality.

Two types of variations may now be considered:

(I)   variations of the income distribution vector given the degree of concavity of the utility function $g(\cdot)$;
(II)  variations of the degree of concavity of $g(\cdot)$ given the income distribution vector.

Contradictions between the ethical measures and descriptive features of inequality have been noted for variations of type (I) in Sen (1973) and for variations of type (II) in Hansson (1977). The problems in question are analysed below.

An unambiguous case of an increase in income inequality arises when there is a transfer of income from a poorer to a richer person. This obviously also leads to an increase in the inequality of personal welfares if both persons share the same increasing utility function relating personal welfare to personal income. It is clearly reasonable to require that this must lead to an increase in the measure of inequality, and this is indeed the so-called 'Pigou–Dalton criterion'. This mild test is, in fact, passed by the ethical measure $A$ for $\eta < 1$. But if $\eta = 1$ (a possibility admitted above and by Atkinson, 1970), we do have a violation, since this would make $e = m$, and the Atkinson measure of inequality becomes zero for all distributions. Contradictions of this type between the ethical and the descriptive notions of inequality are worrying, since 'it would be odd to describe (0, 10) and (5, 5) as having the same degree of inequality' (Sen, 1973).

One can argue that the source of this problem lies in ignoring the difference between the two following statements:

(A)  'there *is no social welfare loss* from inequality',
(B)  'there *is no* inequality'.

Ethical measures of the class specified by Dalton and Atkinson take the two statements to be the same, but in an obvious sense (A) and (B) are saying quite different things.

If the difficulty in question were confined only to the extreme case of $\eta = 1$, then one might try to dismiss it as merely a curiosum. But the problem is much deeper. As the value of $\eta$ is raised parametrically, the impact of the transfer (from the pool to the rich) on the ethical measure becomes smaller and smaller until it vanishes altogether in the extreme case of $\eta = 1$. On the other hand, the impact on inequality enhancement in income terms remains the same (obviously so, since we keep looking at the *same* income transfer), and the impact on inequality enhancement in terms of personal welfares goes on *increasing*. Thus as the welfare inequality responds *more and more* to the transfer of income, the ethical measure of inequality responds *less and less*.

The reason for this difference is not far to seek. In the case of a transfer from the poor to the rich, the impact on social welfare, with which the ethical measure is concerned, is given under utilitarianism by:

$$\text{social welfare loss} = U'(y_p) - U'(y_r), \tag{7}$$

where $U'(y_p)$ and $U'(y_r)$ are the marginal utility of income of the poor and rich respectively. On the other hand, the extent of enhancement of personal welfare inequality between the rich and the poor is given *not* by the *difference* between the marginal utilities, but by their *sum*:

$$\text{enhancement of inequality} = U'(y_p) + U'(y_r). \tag{8}$$

It is, therefore, not surprising that as the social value of $\eta$ is raised, the reduction of social welfare loss is accompanied by an increase in inequality enhancement. The extreme case of $\eta = 1$, which yields the minimal social welfare loss of 0 and the maximal enhancement of inequality of 2, is simply the end of this chain of a perverse relationship. The problem is fundamental and *not* a curiosum.

I turn now to Hansson's problem, viz., the effect of variations of type (II) on the extent of inequality of a *given* distribution of income. As the value of $\eta$ is raised towards unity, the ethical measure of inequality *goes down* monotonically. But since the rise of $\eta$ leads to a *widening* of the range of, and the gaps between, the welfare values, in an obvious sense the inequality of the welfare distribution is *increased*. Thus as the degree of concavity is changed through variation of $\eta$, the ethical measure of inequality seems to head in the opposite direction to the description of inequality.

The contrast can be brought out graphically by taking a two-person case with a given income distribution, say $y_p$ and $y_r$ with $y_p < y_r$. In Figure 1 three alternative values of $\eta$ are considered, and as $\eta$ is raised, the value of the parameter $C$ is reduced to keep $U(y_p)$ unchanged. (It may be remarked that the value of $C$ does not affect the value of the ethical measure $A$ given by (5) and (6).) It is clear that the inequality of personal utilities *increases* as $\eta$ is raised, and in the extreme case of linearity ($\eta = 1$), the welfare inequality for the given income distribution reaches its peak. In contrast, the ethical measure of inequality *goes down* monotonically, becoming zero with $\eta = 1$.

This contrast can, of course, arise even when the utility function is not of the constant elasticity form, but takes some other form, e.g., that obtained by van Praag (1968, 1971) and van Praag and Kapteyn (1973). In fact, what the preceding discussion shows is that *even within the family of constant-elasticity utility functions*, we can find two utility functions such that a change from one to the other unambiguously *increases* inequality of personal welfares, while the ethical measure records a clear *decline*.

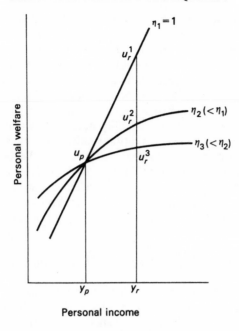

FIGURE 1

Furthermore, these conflicts are not confined only to utilitarian social welfare functions. It is easy to find non-utilitarian and non-additively-separable social welfare functions $f(\cdot)$ that also show a direction contradiction between the ranking of inequality by the ethical measures and the descriptive rankings of inequality of personal welfares.

The attempt to identify 'greater inequality' with 'lower social welfare' leads to contradictions arising from the fact that both inequality and social welfare are 'primitive' notions, and they cannot be arbitrarily declared to be identical without some genuine loss of meaning. The ranking of 'social welfare' of alternative distributions cannot be simply *defined* to be the ranking of 'equality', since they stand for distinct concepts. There is, of course, an often-articulated view that anyone is free to define anything as he likes. But people's interest in the measurement of inequality depends on the accepted meaning of inequality, and will not necessarily survive if the term inequality were redefined.

While the contradictions between ethical measures and descriptions of inequality are not confined to utilitarian social welfare functions, they are particularly acute under utilitarianism. This is because utilitarianism is concerned only with the utility *sum* irrespective of distribution of that sum.[7] Thus, when the ethical measures are combined with utilitarianism, this produces a peculiarly perverse situation: 'inequality' ranking is defined entirely in terms of the 'social welfare' ranking, and the 'social welfare' ranking is entirely unconcerned with distribution as such! This is why in the example considered earlier with a given income distribution, as $\eta$ was raised and the personal welfare distribution turned more and more unequal while the loss of welfare *sum* from inequality became less and less, the ethical measure of inequality based on utilitarianism recorded an *unequivocal* decline (despite growing inequality of welfare levels). While the difficulty in identifying the inequality ranking with the social welfare ranking is present in any case, it becomes especially severe when the social welfare ranking couldn't care less about distribution as such and puts all its weight on total *size* only.

### 3   Description and Prescription: Minimal Partial Orderings

Following the publication of Robbins' classic discussion of interpersonal comparisons of utility (see Robbins, 1938), the fashionable view among economists was, for a long time, that such comparisons must be based on value judgements. The conceptual confusion implicit in that view has been discussed by Little (1950) and others, and it is fair to say that that view is not so common now. Had that view been adhered to, it would have been, of course, absurd to seek a *descriptive* measure of interpersonal welfare inequality. Quite a number of contributions in recent years have been concerned with the meaning and use of interpersonal welfare comparisons, defined frequently in terms of hypothetical choices about being one person rather than another (see, among many others, Vickrey, 1945; Harsanyi, 1955; Rawls, 1958; 1971; Suppes, 1966; Kolm, 1969; 1972; Sen, 1970; 1973; 1976b; 1977a; Hammond, 1976b; 1977; Maskin, 1976; d'Aspremont and Gevers, 1977; Deschamps and Gevers, 1976a; Roberts, 1976 and Arrow, 1977).

Nevertheless, there are difficulties in applying descriptive measures of inequality to personal welfare data, since the extent of measurability of welfare information is typically taken to be much weaker than that of income data. Depending on the type of 'invariance restriction' applied to the welfare information, particular mathematical operations to which the magnitudes of incomes may be subjected may or may not be usable for personal welfare data (see Sen, 1977a). Perhaps the most difficult case arises when it is taken that welfare comparisons—whether for the same person or between persons— must be purely *ordinal*. This would rule out the use of the standard descriptive

---

7. On the far-reaching implications of this feature of utilitarianism, see Sen (1973). For some controversies on this, see Harsanyi (1975), Sen (1976c), Harsanyi (1977), Sen (1977b).

measures of inequality (e.g., the variance) for expressing welfare inequality. Would this at all permit any interesting statements to be made about descriptive inequality of personal welfares? Would such statements not be entirely arbitrary?

Before turning to answering these questions, it may be useful to note that statements on even ethical measures of inequality tend to have an element of arbitrariness arising from the difficulty of choosing a particular social welfare function $g(\cdot)$ from a wide class.[8] It is to avoid this problem of arbitrariness that a number of recent contributions have been concerned with the question of generating a partial ordering of ethical measures that would correspond to the entire class of plausible social welfare functions satisfying certain general properties (see Kolm, 1969; Atkinson, 1970; Sheshinski, 1972; Dasgupta, Sen and Starrett, 1973; Rothschild and Stiglitz, 1973; Sen, 1973 and others). The 'unambiguous' ethical measurement that emerges from these works is confined to the case of Lorenz-dominance only. It transpires that if income distributions $y$ Lorenz-dominates income distribution $x$, then $y$ must have a lower ethical measure of inequality than $x$ for all social welfare functions $g(\cdot)$ that satisfy symmetry and strict quasi-concavity (more weakly—and therefore more generally for this sufficiency theorem—strict $S$-concavity). Furthermore, we can be sure that $y$ has a lower ethical measure of inequality than $x$ *only if* $y$ Lorenz-dominates $x$, when all we know about the social welfare function $g(\cdot)$ is that it satisfies symmetry and strict quasi-concavity (more strictly—and therefore more generally for this necessity theorem—symmetry, strict concavity and additivity). Thus, for the familiar class of social welfare functions (even when rather narrowly defined), the only 'safe' ethical ranking of inequality is the Lorenz partial ordering.

Is there a similar 'safe' partial ranking for the descriptive measurement of inequality of personal welfares, even when no more than *ordinal* comparisons of utility are permitted? The answer is: yes, and it is exactly the same partial ordering, viz., that given by the Lorenz-dominance relation.

Consider a ranking of four utility values in the following order: $a > b \geqslant c > d$. There is clearly no 'cardinal' assumption involved in declaring that the pair $(a, d)$ has more inequality of welfare than $(b, c)$. This type of comparison of 'ordinal intensity' permits us to rank alternative distributions without using anything other than *ordinal* welfare information (see Sen, 1976c).

It is easy to combine the above requirement with the condition that a permutation of utility numbers among persons must not change the descriptive measure of inequality. And it can also be combined with a requirement of 'separability' so that the presence of other welfare numbers (when matched

---

8. Note, however, that there is no one-to-one correspondence between ethical measures of inequality and social welfare functions (see Esteban, 1976). There are, however, more complex correspondences (see Blackorby and Donaldson, 1977).

in terms of 'indifference') should not affect the description of inequality.[9] Thus if two $n$-vectors of utility $x$ and $y$ match each other exactly except for two numbers each (say, $x_1$, $x_2$, and $y_1$ and $y_2$), and these remaining numbers are ranked $x_1 > y_1 \geqslant y_2 > x_2$, or $x_1 > y_2 \geqslant y_1 > x_2$, then $x$ is more unequal than $y$.

This criterion was called 'strengthened two-person ordinal inequality criterion'—STOIC for short—in Sen (1976c), and the ordinal inequality ranking was denoted $\theta^*$ (i.e., $y\theta^*x$, in the above case). The transitive closure of $\theta^*$ was denoted $\theta^{**}$, which is the 'ancestral' inequality ranking under ordinal comparisons. The symmetry assumption used in the *ethical* measurement of inequality has its counterpart in the descriptive framework in the assumption that everyone shares the same personal utility function $U(\cdot)$, and furthermore $U(\cdot)$ is assumed to be a monotonically increasing function of the income of the person in question.

The following result holds: the ranking of descriptive inequality of personal welfares obeying STOIC must incorporate the relation of Lorenz-dominance (see (T.1) in Sen, 1976c).[10] For any two distributions $x$ and $y$ of the same total income, $y$ Lorenz-dominates $x$ if and only if $y\theta^{**}x$.

In an important sense it can, therefore, be said that the non-controversial part of the descriptive ranking of welfare inequality is exactly as extensive as the non-controversial part of the ethical ranking. While $U(\cdot)$ is taken to be an increasing function of personal income, it can be *any* increasing function, and nothing more than *ordinal* comparisons are used. In fact, no assumption of *concavity of any kind* is needed for the descriptive theorem, and even increasing marginal utility (if measurable) will not affect the result one iota.

This coincidence of ethical measurement of inequality with the description of welfare inequality happens to hold only for the case of Lorenz-dominance. Even here description and ethical measurement may contradict each other in terms of the relative *sensitivity* of inequality measures to transfers, as discussed in Section 2. (Remember that 'Pigou–Dalton' transfers are covered by the Lorenz-dominance relation.) The coincidence is only of the *ordering* properties of the inequality measures applied to alternative distributions with *given* personal and social welfare functions, and it holds only for the 'unambiguous' *partial* ordering implicit in each.[11]

9. For a critical evaluation of this type of 'separability' in the context of social choice, see Deschamps and Gevers (1976b).

10. The theorem follows essentially from an elementary result noted by Hardy, Littlewood and Polya (1934) that $y$ Lorenz-dominates $x$ (as we define this term) if and only if $y$ can be obtained from $x$ by a non-empty and finite sequence of transfers from a higher to a lower income; see Sen (1976c). In fact, the theorem on the ethical measure of inequality in terms of social welfare involving Lorenz-dominance also follows from exactly the same property.

11. In fact, as discussed in Section 2, under utilitarianism with $\eta = 1$, which is a permitted case, this Lorenz-dominance strict partial ordering would not, in fact, be incorporated in the ethical measurement of inequality. But this is an extreme case at the end of a perverse chain (see Section 2).

When cases not covered by Lorenz-dominance are considered, the exercise of ethical measurement and that of description part company, and much will then depend on the exact social welfare function chosen and the exact personal utility function and descriptive measure selected. There is, of course, quite a wide family of decriptive measures,[12] which can be combined with a particular specification of personal utility functions (e.g., obtained by quantifying parameters $C$ and $\eta$ for the constant-elasticity functions (4), or $\mu$ and $\sigma$ for van Praag's formulation). However, depending on the 'invariance requirements' imposed by the measurability conditions of personal welfare, some particular measures may be rendered inadmissible (see Sen, 1977a). The relationship between these 'invariance requirements' and admissible measures of welfare inequality will not be further pursued in this paper. The important point to note in the present context is that once the Lorenz-dominance relation has been separated out, any *additional* ranking based on ethical measurement can coincide with descriptive ranking only accidentally, since the two types of exercises are essentially unlike each other (see Section 2).

## 4    Welfare and Welfarism

In Section 2 we considered parametric variations in the personal utility function in the form of changes in the value of $\eta$ and examined its consequences on (i) ethical and descriptive measures of inequality for a *given distribution* of income, and (ii) the sensitivity of these measures to a *given transfer* of income. The discussion having been rather formal, one might wonder what is the real content of this type of exercise.

Perhaps an illustration will help. Suppose a utilitarian economist has sent around a questionnaire of the type used by van Praag (1971), and it has turned out that the answers lead to a good estimation of $C$ and $\eta$. (I am sticking to the constant-elasticity form since it is easier to interpret.) Suppose also that calculations reveal a rather rapid move towards 'satiation' thanks to a low value of $\eta$. The boss of the research project promptly uses equations (5) and (6) to obtain the ethical measure of inequality $A$, and the result is, of course, reported in *The Times*.

Then, suddenly, it transpires that some mistake was made in the calculation, and—after firing the old research assistant (without changing the income distribution)—it is now estimated that $\eta$ is, in fact, much higher, and satiation takes place much more slowly than was thought earlier. The utilitarian boss promptly recalculates the ethical measure of inequality $A$ and it is, of course, now substantially lower. The correction is duly published in *The Times* with the following explanation: 'The recalculation shows that satiation from income increments is reached more slowly. Hence the rich are, in fact, quite

12. See Atkinson (1970), Sen (1973, Chapter 2), Muellbauer (1974), Mehran (1976), Stoft (1975).

efficient in transforming income into utility (happily, their own). So the loss of aggregate welfare from inequality is less than we thought earlier. Obviously, there is less inequality in this country.'

The research assistant, who is now a man of leisure, writes a letter to his former boss saying that since the interpersonal gaps in levels of well-being have been revised *upwards* by the change, there clearly must be *more* inequality, not less. 'Isn't there a mistake?' The boss feels vindicated in having fired the former assistant, since the poor chap clearly does not understand that the increase in welfare gaps between persons has got *nothing* to do with the measure of inequality $A$! ('Probably reading a lot of Wiles!', the boss was overheard to mutter.)

The contradiction between the directions of movement of the ethical and descriptive measures arises in this case out of a cognitive revision, viz., that concerning facts about satiation and the true personal welfare function. Exactly a similar contrast will hold between the assessments of inequality increase arising from a *transfer* from a poorer to a richer person under these circumstances. After $\eta$ has been revised upwards, a lower impact of the transfer on social welfare will now be observed (see (7)) and the ethical measure $A$ will be less affected by it. On the other hand, the extent of enhancement of welfare gaps by such transfers will now be larger (see (8)), suggesting the opposite in terms of description of inequality of personal welfares. These contrasts reflect contradictory responses to a factual revision.

It is worth noting in this context that while a social welfare function is essentially an ethical concept, the same is not true of personal welfare functions. Whatever arbitrariness there may be in the latter, it is an arbitrariness of description rather than of prescription. The revision of parameters like $\eta$ (or van Praag's $\mu$ and $\sigma$) are factual corrections. It is the contradictory handling of such factual corrections that is at the root of the inability of ethical measures of 'inequality' to reflect inequality as description.

The contrast is, of course, most sharp with a utilitarian social welfare function since under that approach $f(u)$ is concerned only with the utility *sum*. If the form of the function is made more unfavourably inclined to features of inequality captured in descriptive measures of welfare inequality, the contradictions will, obviously, tend to be reduced. But the question of the right ethical approach raises a more fundamental issue: should social welfare $W$ be at all taken to be a function *only* of personal utilities?

I have tried to argue elsewhere that a function $f(u)$ is *informationally* very restrictive (Sen, 1977a). It assesses social states *entirely* in terms of the *personal welfare* features of the respective states; the approach may thus be described as 'welfarism'.[13] Such ethical concepts as 'exploitation', 'justice' and 'liberty', cannot be accommodated in $f(u)$, since they typically require information

---

13. In collective choice theory, this is the condition of 'neutrality' (see Arrow, 1963, Sen 1970, 1977a).

that go beyond personal welfare data, e.g., dated labour inputs, past promises, specification of 'personal' protected spheres, etc. To take the notion of 'exploitation' as an illustration, two *identical* distributions of personal welfares may receive *different* treatments in the Marxian system depending on how the personal incomes are related to the respective labour inputs.[14] Similarly, the formulation of the 'liberty' to do certain things requires detailed specification of pairs of social states over which a person is given freedom to choose. Two *identical* distributions of personal welfares may receive *different* treatments in a framework granting the right to personal liberty, if one case involves the violation of that liberty and the other does not.[15]

While these non-welfaristic concepts have great relevance to political discussions and practical judgements, they are completely left out in those Bergson–Samuelson social welfare functions which make social welfare a function only of the personal welfare data. It is important for the progress of normative economics, and—in particular—the analysis of distributive justice, that attention be paid to acknowledgement of 'rights', involving sucn notions as 'claim' (see Kanger, 1957; 1972; Hart, 1961 and Dworkin, 1977).[16]

The enrichment of the ethical framework involved in this broadening of the informational base will militate against both welfarism ($W = f(u)$) and the treatment of social welfare as a function of the vector of individual incomes ($W = g(y)$). But if such a 'broader' social welfare function is used, then two vectors of individual incomes cannot be compared with each other in terms of social welfare *without* bringing in further information, and the ethical measures would cease to be well-defined. One would no longer be able to answer clearly such questions as: what total income, if distributed equally, would lead to just as much social welfare as the current income distribution? The answer can be quite different depending on a variety of factors that have not been specified (e.g., what types of production structure, what systems of remuneration, what types of redistribution policy, etc., will be used to bring about the counter-factual equal distribution of income).

This basic difficulty is analytically most damaging to the approach of ethical measurement of inequality. But it only accentuates what we knew already (see Section 2), viz., the ethical approach involves an identification, in specified contexts, of two quite distinct 'primitive' concepts, viz., 'social welfare' and 'equality'. While the latter is an important constituent of the former (in terms of prevailing notions of social welfare), it is not the only constituent, even when we focus our attention on the distribution of a given total income. (Indeed, for some ethical systems, particularly utilitarianism,

14. See Marx (1887). A more welfaristic approach, Marx reserved exclusively for the 'ultimate stage of communism' (see Marx, 1875). [For a recent reinterpretation of the Marxian theory of exploitation, see J.E. Roemer, *A General Theory of Exploitation and Class* (Cambridge, Mass.: Harvard University Press, 1982).]

15. See Sen (1970, 1976a), Rawls (1971), Nozick (1974).

16. For a helpful exposition of the analytical formulations involved, see Lindahl (1977).

there is no role given to equality of personal *utilities*, and even the role of *income* equality in enhancing social welfare is not intrinsic but entirely context-dependent.) Thus, even under welfarism and even when $W$ is taken to be a function of $y$, the ethical measurement of 'inequality' can go totally against the notion of inequality as a description of the distribution of personal incomes and of personal welfares.

## 5  Concluding Remarks

It is certainly true that the descriptive notion of inequality is not an exact one, and we may often have to settle for a partial ordering based on the intersection of the orderings generated by a set of descriptive criteria. What is at issue is whether this incompleteness should lead us to use instead a complete 'ethical' ordering obtainable from a specified social welfare function. It must be recognized, however, that there is ambiguity also in the 'ethical' measurement arising from the choice of a particular social welfare function out of an 'acceptable' family, and the 'unambiguous' partial ordering corresponding to the usual ethical restrictions is not more extensive than the 'unambiguous' partial ordering of description of inequality (see Section 3).

But this is not the only difficulty in using the ethical approach. A more fundamental difficulty arises from the fact that our ethics, when more fully specified, may incorporate elements that go well beyond a concern for reducing inequality, even when we examine alternative distributions of a given total income, which does not, of course, imply a given *sum* of personal welfares. The extra-egalitarian concerns are patent with utilitarian ethics (see Section 2), as well as with many others, e.g., those involving concepts of rights, dealing with such issues as non-exploitation and liberty (see Section 4). This makes the ethical approach yield in many cases clearly perverse results from the point of view of description of inequality (Section 2), while in other cases the ethical measure is rendered unusable (Section 4).

The idea of measuring inequality on the basis of an over-all social welfare function is fundamentally misconceived. It leads to a clearcut answer but to a question different from the one that was posed.

## References

Arrow, K. J. (1963): *Social Choice and Individual Values*, 2nd ed. (New York: Wiley).
_____ (1977): 'Extended Sympathy and the Possibility of Social Choice', *American Economic Review*.
Atkinson, A. B. (1970): 'On the Measurement of Inequality', *Journal of Economic Theory*.
_____ (1976): *The Economics of Inequality* (Oxford: Clarendon Press).
Bentzel, R. (1970): 'The Social Significance of Income Distribution Statistics', *Review of Income and Wealth*.

Blackorby, C. and D. Donaldson (1977): 'Measures of Relative Equality and Their Meaning in Terms of Social Welfare', *Journal of Economic Theory*.

Burk, R. and W. Gehrig (1976): 'Indices of Income Inequality and Societal Income, An Axiomatic Approach', mimeographed, Universität Karlsruhe.

Chakravarty, S. (1970): *Capital and Development Planning* (Cambridge, Mass.: MIT Press).

Dalton, H. (1920): 'The Measurement of the Inequality of Incomes', *Economic Journal*.

Dasgupta, P., A. K. Sen and D. Starrett (1973): 'Notes on the Measurement of Inequality of Incomes', *Journal of Economic Theory*.

d'Aspremont, C. and L. Gevers (1977): 'Equity and the Informational Basis of Collective Choice', *Review of Economic Studies*.

Deschamps, R. and L. Gevers (1976a): 'Leximin and Utilitarian Rules: A Joint Characterization', *Journal of Economic Theory*, forthcoming. [In fact, published in 1978.]

Deschamps, R. and L. Gevers (1976b): 'Separability, Risk-bearing and Social Welfare Judgements', mimeographed. [Revised version published in J.-J. Laffont (ed.), *Aggregation and Revelation of Preferences* (Amsterdam: North-Holland, 1979).]

Dworkin, R. (1977): *Taking Rights Seriously* (London: Duckworth).

Esteban, J. M. (1976): 'Social Welfare Functions and Inequality Measures', mimeographed, Economia W. P. 76, Universitat Autónama de Barcelona.

Gevers, L. (1976): 'On Interpersonal Comparability and Social Welfare Orderings', mimeographed, Faculté des Sciences Économiques et Sociales, Namur.

Graaff, J. de V. (1967): *Theoretical Welfare Economics* (Cambridge: Cambridge University Press).

Hammond, P. J. (1976a): 'Why Ethical Measures of Inequality Need Interpersonal Comparisons', *Theory and Decision*.

_____ (1976b): 'Equity, Arrow's Conditions and Rawls' Difference Principle', *Econometrica*.

_____ (1977): 'Dual Interpersonal Comparisons of Utility and the Welfare Economics of Income Distribution', *Journal of Public Economics*.

Hansson, B. (1977): 'The Measurement of Social Inequality', text of invited lecture at the Congress of Logic, Philosophy and Methodology of Science, London, Ontario, 1975; in R. Butts and J. Hintikka (eds), *Logic, Methodology and Philosophy of Science* (Dordrecht: Reidel).

Hardy, G., J. Littlewood and G. Polya (1934): *Inequalities* (London: Cambridge University Press).

Hare, R. M. (1952): *The Language of Morals* (Oxford: Clarendon Press).

_____ (1963): *Freedom and Reason* (Oxford: Clarendon Press).

Hart, H. L. A. (1961): *The Concept of Law* (Oxford: Clarendon Press).

Harsanyi, J. (1955): 'Cardinal Welfare, Individualistic Ethics and Interpersonal Comparisons of Utility', *Journal of Political Economy*.

_____ (1975): 'Non-linear Social Welfare Functions, or Do Welfare Economists have a Special Exemption from Bayesian Rationality', *Theory and Decision*.

_____ (1977): 'Non-linear Social Welfare Functions: A Rejoinder to Professor Sen', in R. Butts and J. Hintikka (eds), *Logic Methodology and Philosophy of Science* (Dordrecht: Reidel).

Kanger, S. (1957): *New Foundations for Ethical Theory*, Part 1, Stockholm.

_____ (1972): 'Law and Logic', *Theoria*.

Kanger, S. and H. Kanger (1966): 'Rights and Parliamentarism', *Theoria*.

Kolm, S-Ch. (1969): 'The Optimum Production of Social Justice', in J. Margolis and H. Guitton (eds), *Public Economics* (London: Macmillan).

___ (1972): *Justice et equité* (Paris: CNRS).

___ (1976): 'Unequal Inequalities', *Journal of Economic Theory*.

Krelle, W. and A. A. Shorrocks (eds) (1978): *Personal Income Distribution* (Amsterdam: North-Holland).

Little, I. M. D. (1950): *A Critique of Welfare Economics* (Oxford: Clarendon Press).

Lindahl, L. (1977): *Position and Change: A Study in Law and Logic* (Dordrecht: Reidel).

Marx, K. (1958): *Critique of the Gotha Programme*, 1875. English translation in K. Marx and F. Engels, *Selected Works, vol. II* (Moscow: Foreign Languages Publishing House).

___ (1887): *Capital: A Critical Analysis of Capitalist Production*, vol. I (London: Sonnenschein; Republished London: Allen & Unwin, 1938).

Maskin, E. (1976): 'Decision-making under Ignorance with Implications for Social Choice', mimeographed, Jesus College, Cambridge. [Revised version published later in *Theory and Decision, 11* (1979).]

Mehran, F. (1976): 'Linear Measures of Income Inequality', *Econometrica*.

Muellbauer, J. (1974): 'Inequality Measures, Prices and Household Composition', *Review of Economic Studies*.

Nozick, R. (1974): *Anarchy, State and Utopia* (Oxford: Blackwell).

Rawls, J. (1958): 'Justice as Fairness', *Philosophical Review*.

___ (1971): *A Theory of Justice* (Cambridge, Mass.: Harvard University Press and Oxford: Clarendon Press).

Robbins, L. (1938): 'Interpersonal Comparisons of Utility', *Economic Journal*.

Roberts, K. W. S. (1976): 'Interpersonal Comparability and Social Choice Theory', mimeographed, St John's College, Oxford. [Revised version published later in *Review of Economic Studies, 47* (1980).]

Rothschild, M. and J. E. Stiglitz (1973): 'Some Further Results on the Measurement of Inequality', *Journal of Economic Theory*.

Samuelson, P. A. (1947): *Foundations of Economic Analysis* (Cambridge, Mass.: Harvard University Press).

Sen, A. K. (1967): 'The Nature and Classes of Prescriptive Judgements', *Philosophical Quarterly*.

___ (1970): *Collective Choice and Social Welfare* (San Francisco: Holden-Day and Edinburgh: Oliver & Boyd).

___ (1973): *On Economic Inequality* (Oxford: Clarendon Press and New York: Norton).

___ (1976a): 'Liberty, Unanimity and Rights', *Economica*. [Essay 14 in this volume.]

___ (1976b): 'Interpersonal Comparisons of Welfare', mimeographed, forthcoming in a festschrift for Tibor Scitovsky, 1976b. [Published later: M. Boskin (ed.), *Economics and Human Welfare: Essays in Honor of Tibor Scitovsky* (New York: Academic Press, 1979). Essay 12 in this volume.]

___ (1976c): 'Welfare Inequalities and Rawlsian Axiomatics', text of invited lecture at the Congress of Logic, Philosophy and Methodology of Science, London, Ontario, 1975, in *Theory and Decision*. (Also in R. Butts and J. Hintikka (eds), *Logic, Methodology and Philosophy of Science* (Dordrecht: Reidel), 1977.)

_____ (1977a): 'On Weights and Measures: Informational Constraints in Social Welfare Analysis', *Econometrica*. [Essay 11 in this volume.]

_____ (1977b): 'Non-linear Social Welfare Functions: A Reply to Professor Harsanyi', in R. Butts and J. Hintikka (eds), *Logic, Methodology and Philosophy of Science* (Dordrecht: Reidel).

Sheshinski, E. (1972): 'Relation between a Social Welfare Function and the Gini Index of Income Inequality', *Journal of Economic Theory*.

Stoft, S. (1975): 'A New Positive Measure of Inequality', mimeographed, University of California, Berkeley.

Suppes, P. (1969): 'Some Formal Models of Grading Principles', *Synthese*, 1966; reprinted in P. Suppes, *Studies in the Methodology and Foundations of Science* (Dordrecht: Reidel).

Tinbergen, J. (1970): 'A Positive and Normative Theory of Income Distribution', *Review of Income and Wealth*.

Van Praag, B. M. S. (1968): *Individual Welfare Functions and Consumer Behaviour* (Amsterdam: North-Holland).

_____ (1971): 'The Welfare Function of Income in Belgium: An Empirical Investigation', *European Economic Review*.

Van Praag, B. M. S. and A. Kapteyn (1973): 'Further Evidence on the Individual Welfare Function of Income: An Empirical Investigation in the Netherlands', *European Economic Review*.

Vickrey, W. (1945): 'Measuring Marginal Utility by Reactions to Risk', *Econometrica*.

Wiles, P. (1974): *Distribution of Income: East and West* (Amsterdam: North-Holland).

# 20

# Description as Choice

## 1

Description is sometimes contrasted with prescription, and at other times with prediction. While the former differentiates descriptive statements from value judgements and imperatives, the latter differentiates it from predictive statements. Philosophical discussions in the social sciences have tended to concentrate on prescriptive and predictive exercises, and as a consequence the methodological issues involved in description have remained largely unexplored. The object of this paper is to take up some of these issues.

Boundaries are not always clear-cut between prescription and description, nor between prediction and description. The ambiguities have given philosophers scope for interesting and amusing arguments, while bemusing and befuddling the no-nonsense practical man eager to get on with the job. Some of the discussion in this paper will touch on these boundary questions, but I shall not be directly concerned with these classificatory problems.

I believe that boundary questions are sometimes taken to be more important than they are. Intellectual interest in these issues may distract attention from the fact that imprecision of boundaries can still leave vast regions without ambiguity. It is indeed possible to say a good deal about China and India without asserting that there are no ambiguities as to where the boundary between the two countries lies.

For critical comments on an earlier draft, I am most grateful to John Hicks and Tim Scanlon. I have also benefited from discussions with John Fischer, Dieter Helm, Eric Hobsbawm, Isaac Levi, and Henry Wan, Jr.

A revised version of the text of a public lecture given on 30 May 1979, at the Canadian Learned Societies' Conference held at the University of Saskatchewan, Saskatoon, published in *Oxford Economic Papers,* **32** (1980), 353–69.

## 2

It is fair to say that description as an intellectual activity is typically not regarded as very challenging. To characterize a work in the social sciences as 'purely descriptive' would not normally be regarded as high praise. The reason for this—at least in part—must rest in the idea that description is largely a matter of mere observation and reporting, or reading other people's reports and summarizing—at best systematizing. Whether a descriptive statement is acceptable could be thought to be dependent on its correctness, and that could be resolved simply by observing.

I would like to begin with what I think is a moderate claim, reserving the right to be controversial later on. Description isn't just observing and reporting; it involves the exercise—possibly difficult—of selection. For example, in judging F. M. Eden's 1797 study *The State of the Poor*, or Frederich Engels' *The Condition of the Working-Class in England in 1844*, or John and Barbara Hammonds *The Village Labourer 1760–1832*, a good deal more is involved than just checking the truth of the individual facts recorded. In fact, description can be characterized as choosing from the set of possibly true statements a subset on grounds of their relevance. Truth is—at best—a necessary but not sufficient condition for good description. It is perhaps not an exaggeration to say that any conscious act of description contains some theory—usually implicit—about the relative importance of the various statements dealing with the subject matter.[1] I shall call this the 'choice basis of description'. I might add in passing that recent developments in formal choice theory can be fruitfully used for studying the regularities of description, but I shall not pursue this suggestion in this lecture.[2]

## 3

A description can be accurate without being a good description. It could be unhelpful, even useless. We question the expert on the level of factory wages in India. He answers: 'Oh, it varies from place to place'. True enough, of course. We ask for more description, demanding precision. The expert now goes into details. 'The integer approximation of the national average wages in rupees', he says, 'is a prime number'. I won't belabour the point further. Clearly, truth isn't a sufficient condition for a description to be good.

1. See Koopmans (1947) and Hicks (1979), p. ix.
2. The literature on general choice theory is quite vast. Discussion of some of the main issues can be found in Herzberger (1973) and Sen (1977b, Section 4). Herzberger's recent concern with choice-theoretic approaches to semantics relates closely to the choice basis of description, as defined here.

Is it a necessary condition? It might appear that the answer must be yes. How can a false description be good? The issue is, however, more complex than that, and there are at least two distinct sources of difficulty.

First, departures from literal truth may not be immediately dismissable as untrue. Indeed, approximations, metaphors, simplifications, etc., have important roles in conveying the truth. Your child asks you: 'How large is China?', and you reply: 'Very large—it has 900 million people'. You may have enlightened him, but you have also almost certainly made a statement that is untrue in terms of the exact number. 900 million may convey the size more efficiently—shorn of unimportant detail—than 876,493,179, even if that happens to be the exact number at the moment you spoke. Even that old summary statement: 'Every fifth person born on earth is Chinese' has communicated something about the size of China in the past, despite pitfalls in the literal interpretation of that statement and feeble jokes about the fifth child in an English family being called Chang. In so far as truth is a necessary condition of good description, the concept of truth must be a broad one.

The second problem is, I think, a good deal more complex. Description may have objectives the pursuit of which can be helped by departures from truth—even in the broad sense. Milton Friedman (1953), in particular, has argued powerfully in favour of departing from truth in describing reality in the context of economic models, judging the merits of the assumptions not in terms of accuracy but in the light of their predictive usefulness. I shall have something to say presently on Friedman's methodological observations, and on Paul Samuelson's critique of Friedman and the '$F$-twist',[3] but at this stage I would simply note that Friedman has drawn our attention to the important possibility that an unrealistic assumption giving an inaccurate description may nevertheless be a useful one for the purpose for which the description is intended. Friedman restricts his attention to predictive usefulness only, but the point can be generalized, and objectives other than predictive success might also lead to a case for departing from the truth. Examples can be constructed such that truth of descriptions conflicts with usefulness for prescriptive exercises, or even for communication.

## 4

A distinction must, however, be made between a description of something being good in the sense of being a good one *to give* and it being a good description of *that* thing. The aspiring murderer demands from you a description of where his would-be victim has gone, and as you point at the wrong road he proceeds in that direction with a roar. That description of where the would-be victim has gone is, I would agree, a good one to give, but it can hardly be

3. Samuelson (1963), pp. 231–6; reprinted in Stiglitz (1966), pp. 1772–8.

accepted as a good description of where the would-be victim has gone. The goodness of a description can be judged in terms of many alternative criteria, but in calling a description a good description of something, truth—in the broad sense—would seem to be a necessary condition.[4]

There isn't anything very puzzling here, even though the distinction has been frequently overlooked. A good description of something reflects reality about that thing in some straightforward sense, rather than distorting it. This is so even when distortion is a commendable activity in terms of some *other* objective, and furthermore also commendable taking *everything* into account. A cook who helps the arrest of a mass murderer by mixing a sleeping drug with his food might well be doing good, but that does not make his cooking good, nor does it make him an outstanding cook.

5

I turn now to the methodological dispute between Friedman and Samuelson.[5] Friedman argued that the appropriateness of an assumption must be judged not by its realism but by its predictive usefulness. Furthermore, Friedman saw an inverse relationship between realism of assumptions and its predictive contribution.

> Insofar as a theory can be said to have 'assumptions' at all, and insofar as their 'realism' can be judged independently of the validity of predictions, the relation between the significance of a theory and the 'realism' of its assumptions is almost the opposite of that suggested by the view under criticism. Truly important and significant hypotheses will be found to have 'assumptions' that are widely inaccurate descriptive representations of reality, and, in general, the more significant the theory, the more unrealistic the assumptions (in this sense).[6]

Characterizing the approach as '*F*-twist', Samuelson has attacked Friedman's position sharply. 'If the abstract models contain empirical falsities, we must jettison the models, not gloss over their inadequacies'. 'The empirical harm done by the *F*-twist is this. In practice it leads to Humpty-Dumptiness. Lewis Carroll had Humpty-Dumpty use words any way he wanted to. I had in mind something different: Humpty-Dumpty uses the *F*-twist to say, "What I choose to call the admissible amount of unrealism and empirical invalidity is the tolerable amount of unrealism".'[7]

4. In terms of M. A. Slote's (1966) 'theory of important criteria', truth can be seen to be an important criterion of a description being a good description of something.

5. See also Nagel (1963).

6. Friedman (1953), p. 14.

7. Samuelson (1963), p. 236.

I am not presently concerned with whether Friedman is correct in thinking that an inverse relationship tends to exist between accurate assumptions and predictive success. The important point to note is that if such an inverse relationship were to obtain, Friedman would be quite willing to sacrifice accuracy.

Stanley Wong (1973) has pointed out that Samuelson's critique takes insufficient note of the 'instrumental' nature of Friedman's methodological position, and the latter's overriding concern with prediction.[8] This, I believe, is indeed the case, but the two views of description differ on an issue that goes well beyond the question of the predictive focus. No matter what the aim happens to be, as long as it is not—or does not include—making only accurate statements about observed facts, a conflict can conceivably arise between descriptive accuracy and the aim of the description. The issue is a good deal more general than the so-called 'F-twist', and concerns the conflict between aims of description and the truth of statements that can be used to further these aims.

6

Another different motivation is involved in Nicholas Kaldor's[9] advocacy of departure from truthful description, in favour of what he calls 'stylized facts'. These aren't facts in the sense of being true, but they communicate rapidly certain things that are close enough to being true, but avoid a plethora of details. An example: that in the Western economies the capital−output ratio remained stationary over many decades and so did the share of wages in national income. Not exactly true for *all* the alluded economies. In fact, not exactly true for *any* of the alluded economies. Still, if the variations are relatively small in comparison with other, related variables, the simplification will have certain obvious advantages.

I have to report that in this case the advantages were probably rather unequally shared, with the biggest share going to Kaldor himself, who used these stylized facts to illustrate his well-known models of growth and distribution. But that wasn't all there was to it, and some of the stylized facts undoubtedly succeeded in enhancing comprehension, drawing attention to important observed regularities, even though they were not quite accurate. However, the important issue here isn't whether these particular simplifications were all informative without being misleading but that the method of using 'stylized facts' can indeed have this property.

There is nothing exceptional to economics in making stylized facts a possible and potentially efficient method of understanding reality. Fiction is a general

8. See also Boland (1979).
9. See Kaldor (1960a, 1960b).

method of coming to grip with facts. There is nothing illegitimate in being helped by *War and Peace* to an understanding of the Napoleonic wars in Russia, or by *Grapes of Wrath* to digesting aspects of the Depression. There is no reason why descriptive statements in economics have to aspire after mechanical accuracy even when it conflicts with comprehension and absorption. There is, of course, an obvious objection to presenting non-facts dressed up as facts, but there is no need to do this once non-facts are accepted as legitimate descriptive instruments themselves. Such a description of something will be good in the sense of being useful, but—as already explained— must not be confused with its being a good—or realistic—description of that thing.

7

Samuelson's argument that 'we must jettison the models' that 'contain empirical falsities' seems to be based on a very narrow view of objectives of description. However, Samuelson wasn't only objecting to the use of empirical falsities in models, but also disputing Friedman's use of words. The reference to Humpty-Dumptiness deals with this. This relates closely to our distinction between a description that is good and a good description of something. Friedman not only defends the use of inaccurate assumption in predictive theory, but also employs a new concept of realism. It is 'the test by prediction' in classifying alternative assumptions 'as more or less realistic' that Friedman embraces and which he sees others being 'necessarily driven' to accept (p. 33).

The predictive usefulness of an inaccurate description may well justify the choice of that description, but why does it make it a more *realistic* description? The 'instrumental' nature of Friedman's position may be adequate in defending the choice of such an assumption, but to call it 'realistic' is a separate assertion, violating the important criterion that a description must be true, in the broad sense, to be realistic. Samuelson's objection to this violation cannot be dismissed by a pointer to the 'instrumental' character of Friedman's economic methodology.

The defence that Friedman provides of this characterization of 'realism' mainly takes the form of denying the viability of any alternative conception.

A theory or its 'assumptions' cannot possibly be thoroughly 'realistic' in the immediate descriptive sense so often assigned to this term. A completely 'realistic' theory of the wheat market would have to include not only the conditions directly underlying the supply and demand for wheat but also the kind of coins or credit instruments used to make exchanges; the personal characteristics of wheat-traders such as the colour of each trader's hair and eyes, his antecedents and education, the number of members in his family, their characteristics, antecedents, and education, etc.; the kind of soil on which the wheat was grown, its physical and chemical characteristics, the weather prevailing during the growing season; the personal characteristics of the farmers growing the wheat and of the consumers who will ultimately use it; and so on indefinitely. Any attempt to move very far in achieving this kind of 'realism' is certain to render a theory utterly useless.[10]

In assessing this objection it is necessary to consider the distinction between realism in the sense of 'nothing but the truth' and that in the sense of 'the whole truth'. An assumption can be realistic in that it is true without the claim being made that it is exhaustive in capturing all aspects of the reality. Advocates of realism in the sense of 'nothing but the truth' need not demand 'the whole truth'. The dissatisfaction with Friedman's position on the part of critics such as Samuelson does not arise from Friedman's rejection of 'the whole truth', but from his rejection of 'nothing but the truth'.

The distinction is important for Friedman's discussion of departures from realism and the criteria of acceptability of such departures.

What is the criterion by which to judge whether a particular departure from realism is or is not acceptable? Why is it more 'unrealistic' in analysing business behaviour to neglect the magnitude of businessmen's costs than the colour of their eyes? The obvious answer is because the first makes more difference to business behaviour than the second; but there is no way of knowing that this is so simply by observing that businessmen do have costs of different magnitudes and eyes of different colour. Clearly it can only be known by comparing the effect on the discrepancy between actual and predicted behaviour of taking one factor or the other into account. Even the most extreme proponents of realistic assumptions are thus necessarily driven to reject their own criterion and to accept the test by prediction when they classify alternative assumptions as more or less realistic.[11]

I shall have something to say presently on the predictive focus. What is, however, more important in the present context is to note that 'to neglect' the colour of businessmen's eyes need not involve any departure from 'nothing but the truth'. The fact that a model does not bring in the colour of businessmen's eyes does not imply that it is being assumed that businessmen have eyes of the same colour. This neglect would not, thus, be a 'departure from realism' in the sense of making untrue statements. The need to neglect some aspects of the truth and thereby departing from the whole truth does not

10. Friedman (1953), p. 32.
11. Friedman (1953), pp. 32–3.

establish the necessity of departing from nothing but the truth, and Friedman's dismissal of the viability of the traditional view of realism seems over-hasty.

8

While the preceding argument disputes Friedman's treatment of realism, it does not disestablish Friedman's rejection of truth as a necessary condition of acceptability of a description. An untrue description of something may not be a good description of that thing—nor a realistic description. But it can serve some other objective efficiently, and if so, could well be chosen on that ground.

However, Friedman's concentration on predictive success as the only objective he considers, also makes his treatment of the choice basis of description a very limited one. Description may well be geared to some objective other than prediction, e.g., normative analysis, or efficient communication, or even satisfying idle curiosity. Even the preference for concentrating on businessmen's costs rather than on the colour of their eyes—to return to Friedman's example—may arise from some non-predictive motivation. For example, within the normative perspective, the businessmen's costs might be relevant to some notion of desert, e.g., a person deserves to get a reward for the costs he has undertaken, and this may give no place at all to the colour of the person's eyes.

The nature of economic questions reflects a variety of interests that the subject has to cater to. Has the distribution of income turned more unequal in country $x$? Are the residents of country $y$ better fed today than before? Is modern technology getting easily absorbed in country $z$? Has trade unionism influenced the distribution of income under capitalism? Are there business cycles still in the Western economies? How large is the Soviet Union's international trade? How should we plan the use of exhaustible resources? Does progressive taxation affect incentives? Will the expansion of money supply—this one in honour of Milton Friedman—expand prices proportionately? This bag of assorted questions reflects a plurality of motivation that is not reducible to some kind of single 'ultimate objective'. They represent predictive investigation, normative concern as well as curiosity related to a variety of interests from sympathy to satisfying one's spirit of inquiry. A monolithic characterization of the objective of description will leave us with a methodology ill-suited to the subject.

9

The multiplicity of motivation has been discussed so far in the particular context of departures from accuracy, but it is of course a much more central issue than this particular context might suggest. Even when no departures from truth are involved, there is—as already discussed—the problem of selection, choosing from the set of true statements a subset of relevant ones. Criteria of relevance are crucial to this choice basis of description going well beyond the issue of truth.

Methodological discussions in economics have tended to concentrate on predictive and prescriptive concerns, and seem to have had the effect of ignoring other motivations that stimulate inquiry.[12] This bias has had a rather impoverishing role on the descriptive traditions in economics.

The choice basis of description may relate to the curiosity that precipitates inquiry, and this curiosity need not reflect predictive or prescriptive interests. Indeed, even the use of language can relate to selection based on other types of curiosity. In response to the question: 'Is China a large country?', we accepted the answer: 'Yes, it has 900 million people', basing the notion of the size of country on the size of its population. However, China has less surface area than Canada, fewer tigers than India, fewer polar bears than the Soviet Union, and—according to some early enthusiastic accounts—no flies at all. The case for describing China as larger than Canada, India or the Soviet Union clearly rests in our greater interest in human beings than in square miles, tigers, polar bears and flies. But it is *not* a reflection of some greater predictive merit, *nor* of some obvious prescriptive interest. The view of human beings having no interests whatever other than predictive and prescriptive concerns does some injustice to the species.

The non-predictive, non-prescriptive motivations are particularly important to bear in mind in understanding the role of 'theories of value' in economics, particularly the labour theory of value. The labour theory can, in fact, be given various interpretations related to the motivations involved. One is that of a predictive theory—in particular that of relative prices and distribution, and it encompasses the so-called 'law of value'. Another is normative, providing a theory of entitlements. A third, which is frequently missed, is a way of discriminating between different features of production and exchange by focusing on elements of human involvement.[13] Value, in Marx's (1887) words, is 'a relation between persons expressed as a relation between things' (p. 45).

The last interpretation is frequently taken to be 'metaphysical', as Joan Robinson (1964) puts it, describing it also as 'a mere rigmarole of words' (p. 39). Why so? Because it picks up from the description of production and exchange only some features as being specially significant, leaving the rest untouched? The discrimination makes the description arbitrary, as many

12. In this there is unity between members of widely different schools of economic philosophy, e.g., Milton Friedman (1953), Gunnar Myrdal (1954), Joan Robinson (1964).

13. This has been best discussed by Maurice Dobb (1937).

critics have seen it. But, as I have already tried to argue, any description involves discrimination and selection, and the real question is the relevance of the selection process to the objectives of description.

I have claimed elsewhere[14] that the methodological issue can be more easily understood by looking at other descriptive statements in which the discrimination involved cannot be reduced entirely to predictive or prescriptive interests. Consider the statement 'Michelangelo produced the statue of David'. There is an obvious sense in which this would be accepted as a realistic description, despite its being informationally selective and the selection process not being primarily motivated by prediction or prescription. The production process in making the statue actually involved not merely Michelangelo, but his helpers, a huge block of stone, chisels, scaffoldings, etc., but the description quoted focuses on Michelangelo only as the most relevant bit of information. Note that the discrimination cannot be based on any marginal productivity consideration in the usual neoclassical sense. Without Michelangelo, no statue, but without stone, no statue either! But this does not give the same status to the two statements 'Michelangelo produced the statue of David' and 'this stone produced the statue of David' (or 'this stone quarry produced the statue of David'). The selection process reflects other motivations, in particular, that of capturing the source of the imagination displayed in the statue.

The labour theory of value, in its descriptive interpretation, shows a similar— but not the same—type of discrimination, focusing—in this case—on the human effort directly and indirectly involved in the process of production and exchange of commodities. In assessing the labour theory of value as a description of production and exchange, it is the cogency of this focus that has to be assessed, including its ability, if any, to capture our interest compared with other methods of discrimination. Examining only the theory's predictive success, or its normative relevance, will not even begin to provide a complete assessment of the labour theory of value. And to call it metaphysical because it is informationally discriminating involves a total failure to perceive the nature of description as an activity.

## 10

I turn now to the other of the two great theories of value, viz., the utility theory. Again, utility descriptions have predictive and normative interest, but once again they do not exhaust the descriptive motivations. The joys and sufferings of human beings and their deprivations and fulfilments have interest of their own. Even classical political economists were much concerned with

14. Sen (1978a), pp. 176–8.

related—though not identical—features in their interest in use value.[15] It is this part of the descriptive motivation that has been least well served by recent developments of utility theory, most notably by the theory of revealed preference. Focusing only on predicting behaviour, the richness of human psychology has been substantially ignored, refusing to see anything in utility or happiness other than choice. As the 'father' of revealed preference theory, Paul Samuelson, puts it: behaviour is to be 'explained in terms of preference, which are in turn defined only by behaviour'.[16]

This has led to an approach that is—despite some predictive merits—remarkably mute about human joys and sufferings in which economists used to take a lot of interest. The result is a descriptive impoverishment from *many* perspectives, *including*—among others—normative relevance, since many of the common norms do relate precisely to the ignored descriptive features.[17] Attempts at overcoming this lacuna by defining utility not in terms of choice but independently, say, as a person's own concept of his own well-being, but assuming that people do *in fact* choose according to their respective utilities, raise other difficulties. In particular, this yields a view of man totally uncommitted to anything other than maximizing his own well-being irrespective of political values, class interests, community spirits and social conventions, except in so far as these things affect his perception of his own well-being. This extraordinary model of man—the 'rational fool'[18]—has been widely used in economics with very little empirical testing.

Insularity has permitted this theory to remain in vogue, despite conspicuous failure to account for many types of human behaviour, e.g., why people vote in large elections, why people are ready to fight for and even die for a cause, or why so many seem convinced that they do many things out of a sense of commitment rather than pure pursuit of self interest. Predicting future choice on the basis of past choice is not in itself a bad predictive strategy (despite some well-known problems). But if that is used as the only focus of the theory of utility, then there is *either* silence on many important issues (when 'utility' is treated as just another name for a numerical reflector of choice), *or* there is a good deal of senseless noise.

While there have been some attempts recently to break away from this highly limited model, e.g., in the works of Hirsch (1976), Hirschman (1977), Leibenstein (1976), Scitovsky (1976), and a few other authors, the dominant

15. This is especially true of Karl Marx, and as he himself put it: 'use-value plays a far more important part in my economics than in economics hitherto' (Marx, 1879–80, p. 39). In the subject index of volume I of *Capital* (Marx, 1887, edited by Engels, the first reference to 'use-value' is to pages 1–114. This aspect of Marx's concern seems to be frequently overlooked in characterizations of Marx's 'treatment of value'.

16. Samuelson (1947), pp. 90–1.

17. See Hicks (1958, 1974).

18. For a critique of the propensity of economic theory to rely on the 'rational fool', see Sen (1977a). For a 'balanced' account of the issues involved, see Hahn and Hollis (1979), 'Introduction'.

tradition of behaviour studies in economics remains largely shackled to that model. We have, thus, the strange spectacle of two great theories of 'value'— each rich in descriptive features in their original formulation—reduced to descriptive penury or to factual irrelevance. The labour theory of value is dismissed as 'metaphysical', or at best an imperfect intermediate product in a theory of price and distribution. The delimitation of utility theory to one of silence choice—no questions asked as to what lies behind choice—stifles descriptive inquiry into human joys and sufferings. The dominant methodology in economics with is extraordinarily narrow interpretation of objectives of description has produced molehills out of mountains.

11

Descriptive economics has suffered for a long time from the imperialism of *predictive* economics. Recently it has suffered a certain amount also from the new and expanding empire of *prescriptive* economics. Prescriptive economics had itself a rather hard time earlier in the positivist heyday. The debunking of welfare economics that can be seen in such works as Lionel Robbins' *The Nature and Significance of Economic Science*[19] kept prescriptive studies somewhat immersed in a pool of apology from the mid-thirties until relatively recently. Welfare economics was for a long time the 'untouchable' in the community of economics and when economists spoke 'qua economist'—to use that lovely expression brought into circulation by positivism—they tried to speak in a value-free 'scientific' language, with 'expletives' deleted. Welfare economics was seen as the subject, if not of expletives, at least of emotive utterances, which the cool positivist scientists found 'meaningless' in terms of their narrow theory of meaning.

The balloon did ultimately burst, and prescriptive economics has certainly emerged in recent years as a vigorous field—both in the traditional forms of welfare economics and political economy as well as in the shape of the new discipline of social choice theory. Debates on prescriptive matters are no longer treated as just a case of 'thy blood or mine', to quote Lionel Robbins' influential characterization. But while freeing itself from the positivist prison, prescriptive economics has, I would now like to argue, quite often imposed its own shackles on the discipline of description.

There has been the proposition that every factual statement involves implicit values. In its original formulation and use, this claim, which I believe is false, may have played a challenging part in the dialectics with positivism. 'So you want facts only, no values, because they are illegitimate', the argument ran, 'but you can't have facts without values. Touché!'

19. Robbins (1932).

But why must every factual statement involve values? The basis of the claim seems to rest uneasily on the belief, which is correct, that any description involves some selection. What is not correct is the further belief that the selection must be based on some explicit or implicit prescriptive criterion. The criteria used for selection, as I have been arguing, may be aimed at objectives *other than* prescription, e.g., catering to curiosity. Cosmologists or historians take this for granted. There is, of course, a sense in which this too involves a judgement, to wit, it is right to cater to people's curiosity in the choice basis of description.[20] But this does not imply that the selection has to be done in terms of normative interests. Prescription is one of several possible objectives of descriptive selection, and to assert its omnipresence is to replace the imperialism of predictive economics by that of prescriptive economics.

12

The enormous success of Gunnar Myrdal's *Political Elements in the Development of Economic Theory* owes not a little to this spirit of hunting for values in factual statements. While Myrdal entered the exercise as a positivist, looking for contraband values, he ended up asserting something close to the impossibility of prescription-free descriptive statements (see Myrdal, 1958). There was, however, some haste and a good deal of unestablished assertion in detecting underneath each bed a surreptitious prescriptive head.

The chief source of confusion here rests in confounding the need for *selection* in the choice basis of description with the need to cater to *prescriptive* ends in particular. One consequence of this illegitimate identification is the growth of the recent tendency to convert descriptive questions into *as if* prescriptive ones. To take an example, consider the question of measurement of inequalities of income. While there is little doubt that prescriptive interest provides one reason for inquiring into economic inequality, the question 'How much inequality of incomes is there?' cannot be fully captured by a prescriptive interpretation. But in a paper published in 1920, Hugh Dalton,[21] in effect, reinterpreted the question in ethical terms to mean: 'How much loss of social welfare is there from inequality?'

This prescriptive re-interpretation remained subdued under the positivist hegemony established shortly after Dalton's paper was published, but with the prescriptive backlash, this has now re-emerged in the front line. Tony Atkinson's (1970) ethical index of economic inequality measures inequality in terms of the same approach as that of Dalton, but does it more elegantly

---

20. Even the choice of words reflects judgements, when 'a cluster term' is used, as to 'what is or is not important' (Slote, 1966, p. 223).

21. Dalton (1920). For an uncompromising and forceful rejection of this approach, see Wiles (1974).

and more economically through measuring the social welfare loss in terms of equivalent income. This has the consequence that the descriptive features of income inequality are all drowned in a normative flood, producing some rather extraordinary consequences. An income distribution of (99,1) has to be declared as perfectly equal if social welfare is taken to be the sum of individual utilities given by a linear function of individual incomes, since there is no social welfare loss from inequality in this case. Other odd consequences—some more serious than others—have been pointed out.[22]

A hard-headed prescriptivist would perhaps remain unaffected by these consequences if he really does believe that income inequality has no independent descriptive meaning at all, and would probably say something like: 'Why not describe (99,1) as equal if there is no social welfare loss from this inequality, I mean, discrepancy?' But inequality does seem to have descriptive meaning too which people acknowledge,[23] and to jettison all that impoverishes the subject. One of the ironies of the situation is that Tony Atkinson's own works on descriptive features of inequality in Britain (works which in depth and relevance remain, in my opinion, quite unexcelled anywhere), cannot be captured at all within the arena of the Dalton–Atkinson measures. Nor can ethical measurement provide the appropriate background for checking such relations as that between inequality and crime.

We are back again at the question of realism. Friedman discussed its claim on the ground that the only way of telling realism is *predictive* relevance; the Dalton–Atkinson approach to the measurement of inequality amounts to dismissing it on the ground that the only criterion is *prescriptive* relevance. Neither seems correct, but both have a good deal of following.

There are two distinct objections to the ethical indexes of inequality. First, ethical concern is not the only motivation behind measuring inequality, and might not even be the most important motivation in many cases. Second, even if ethical concern were the dominant motivation, a distinction still has to be made between a description of inequality that is useful and a good description of inequality (as discussed in Section 4). Even if we are interested in inequality primarily because of the loss of social welfare from it, the questions 'How much inequality is there?' and 'How much *loss of social welfare* is there from inequality?' are not identical queries. There may be no loss of social welfare from a distribution (99,1), but it is absurd to call it an equal distribution.

---

22. See Hansson (1977) and Sen (1978b) [Essay 19 in this volume].

23. This is, however, not the same as asserting that there are no ambiguities in the descriptive meaning, nor that it must yield a *complete* ordering. These issues have been discussed in Sen (1978b), which shows, among other things, that the partial ordering of unambiguous ethical ranking (given the commonly used value frameworks) is *not* more extensive than the partial ordering of unambiguous descriptive ranking (in terms of the commonly accepted descriptive criteria). [See pages 422–5 in this volume.]

13

A related, though not exactly parallel, problem has arisen in the conceptualization of poverty. The distinguished American sociologist Mollie Orshansky (1969) has not been alone in arguing that 'poverty is a value judgement', and the approach is well-reflected by her often-quoted aphorism: 'Poverty, like beauty, lies in the eye of the beholder' (p. 37). Does it really? Orshansky's view is an amalgam of taking a prescriptive view of description (of poverty, in this case), and—additionally—a subjectivist view of prescription. Both assertions have superficial plausibility, but neither claim is, I believe, easy to sustain.

Here we are really concerned with the former claim, viz., that poverty is a value judgement. This assertion suffers from difficulties rather similar to those that apply to ethical measurement of inequality. Poverty description—like any description—involves selection. Furthermore even if prescription were the only reason for which people take an interest in poverty—this I believe is not the case but assuming that this were the case—poverty description will then *reflect* socially held value judgements rather than *be* value judgements themselves.

As Marx (1887) had argued, discussing the concept of 'subsistence', while the notion of 'the so-called necessary wants' have 'a historical and moral element', 'nevertheless in a given country, at a given period, the average quantity of the means of subsistence is practically known' (p. 150). For the social scientist studying poverty, the exercise is not one of unleashing one's morals on the statistics of deprivation. Rather it is the exercise of assessing these statistics in line with socially held views as to what counts as poverty. These views may or may not themselves be moral ones, but even when they are moral, for the person *studying* these views, they are matters of fact, viz., that such views are held.[24] To describe what prescriptions are made is a description, not a prescription.

14

The view that poverty is a value judgement has often had the peculiar consequence of leading to attempts to avoid the use of the word 'poverty' in social communication. In Indian official documents—including planning papers—the words 'poor' and 'unemployed' have been replaced fairly uniformly by the expression: 'the weaker section of the Indian population'. This may have

24. While typically the exercise may be concerned with views held in the community in which poverty is being measured, this need not always be the case. For example, 'international standards' are sometimes used for the measurement of 'national' poverty.

been morally well-motivated, but it has not been descriptively very illuminating. As it happens, people drawn from this 'weaker section of the Indian population' do the heavy work in India, varying from breaking stones and bending iron to carrying heavy loads on their heads. However, it has been possible to avoid being constantly reminded of the facts of overwhelming poverty in India by the peculiar terminology. Of course, this practice has to be distinguished from the spirit of Mollie Orshansky's claim, but the view that poverty is nothing but a value judgement does open up many possibilities. It also eases the way to achieving what the late Daniel Thorner (1956) had characterized—in a paper on Indian censuses—as 'Agrarian Revolution by Census Redefinition'. Indeed, we have very little hard facts about, say, the plight of the 'untouchables' in India because not content with calling them by the morally superior name 'Harijan'—'children of God'—as Mahatma Gandhi had renamed them, the census authorities proceeded to discontinue data collection on the morally offensive subject of the practice of untouchability.

To return to my general theme, the prescriptive tradition in the social sciences—freed at last from the shackles of positivist dismissal—has started exercising an imperialism of its own.


## 15

Finally, a few concluding remarks.

First, description inevitably involves selection. It can be usefully seen as a choice of a subset from a set of possible statements.

Second, truth is clearly not a sufficient condition for a description to be good.

Third, nor is it a necessary condition. Friedman's defence of departures from truth in choosing factual assumptions is a special case of a general argument in favour of judging description by its usefulness. Friedman considers only predictive usefulness, but there are other objectives which lead to the same conclusion. Samuelson's assertion of the need to 'jettison' models that contain 'empirical falsities' seems to take a very narrow view of description as an activity.

Fourth, Friedman's attack on traditional notions of realism is based on a misunderstanding. His own suggestion about judging realism by 'the test by prediction' seems to confound usefulness of a description with its realism. A description of something can be a good one to give without being a good description of that thing.

Fifth, description can be motivated by predictive interest or by prescriptive interest, but it may also have other motivations, and to confine attention only to predictive or prescriptive interest impoverishes the traditions of descriptive economics.

Finally, such impoverishment can be seen in recent developments in many different fields of economics, varying from interpretations of theories of 'value' to the measurement of inequality and poverty. The richness of descriptive motivations seems to have been sacrificed for consistency within an arbitrarily narrow conception of these motivations, or—to be more exact—for consistency respectively within *two* arbitrarily narrow conceptions of motivations. This, I have argued, has been an unequal exchange: confounding the nature of description as an activity and unnecessarily weakening the theoretical underpinning of many legitimate and useful activities in the social sciences.

## References

Atkinson, A. B. (1970): 'On the Measurement of Inequality', *Journal of Economic Theory*, 2.

____ (1976): *The Economics of Inequality* (Oxford: Clarendon Press).

Boland, L. A. (1979): 'A Critique of Friedman's Critics', *Journal of Economic Literature*, 17.

Butts, R. and Hintikka, J. (eds) (1977): *Logic, Methodology and Philosophy of Science* (Dordrecht: Reidel).

Dobb, M. H. (1937): *Political Economy and Capitalism* (London: Routledge).

Friedman, M. (1953): *Essays in Positive Economics* (Chicago: Chicago University Press).

Hahn, F. and Hollis, M. (eds) (1979): *Philosophy and Economic Theory* (Oxford: Oxford University Press).

Hansson, B. (1977): 'The Measurement of Social Inequality'. In Butts and Hintikka (1977).

Harris, H. (ed.) (1979): *Scientific Models and Man* (Oxford: Clarendon Press).

Herzberger, H. G. (1973): 'Ordinal Preference and Rational Choice', *Econometrica*, 41.

Hicks, J. R. (1958): 'The Measurement of Real Income', *Oxford Economic Papers*, 10.

____ (1974): 'Preference and Welfare', in A. Mitra (ed.), *Economic Theory and Planning: Essays in Honour of A. K. Dasgupta* (London: Oxford University Press).

____ (1979): *Causality in Economics* (Oxford: Blackwell).

Hirsch, F. (1976): *Social Limits to Growth* (Cambridge, Mass.: Harvard University Press).

Hirschman, A. O. (1977): *The Passions and the Interests* (Princeton, NJ: Princeton University Press).

Kaldor, N. (1960a): *Essays on Value and Distribution* (London: Duckworth).

____ (1960b): *Essays on Economic Stability and Growth* (London: Duckworth).

Koopmans, T. (1947): 'Measurement without Theory', *Review of Economics and Statistics*, 29.

Krelle, A. and Shorrocks, A. (eds) (1978): *Personal Income Distribution* (Amsterdam: North-Holland).

Leibenstein, H. (1976): *Beyond Economic Man: A New Foundation for Micro-economics* (Cambridge, Mass.: Harvard University Press).

Marx, K. (1887): *Capital*, vol. I, 1867; English translation (London: Sonnenschein).

____ (1879–80): 'Marginal Notes on A. Wagner'; published in *Marx–Engels Werke*, vol. 19, Dietz Verlag. English translation by A. Hussain, *Theoretical Practice*, Issue 5, Spring 1972.

Myrdal, G. (1953): *Political Elements in the Development of Economic Theory*, ed. by P. Streeten (London: International Library of Sociology).

____ (1958): *Value in Social Theory*, with an Introduction by P. Streeten (London: Allen & Unwin).

Nagel, E. (1963): 'Assumptions in Economic Theory', *American Economic Review*, **53**.

Orshansky, M. (1969): 'How Poverty is Measured', *Monthly Labor Review*.

Robbins, L. (1932): *An Essay on the Nature and Significance of Economic Science* (London: Macmillan, 2nd ed., 1935).

Robinson, J. (1964): *Economic Philosophy* (Harmondsworth: Penguin Books).

Samuelson, P. A. (1947): *The Foundations of Economic Analysis* (Cambridge, Mass.: Harvard University Press).

____ (1963): 'Problems of Methodology: Discussion', *American Economic Review*, **53**; reprinted in Stiglitz (1966).

Scitovsky, T. (1976): *The Joyless Economy: An Inquiry into Human Satisfaction and Consumer Dissatisfaction* (London: Oxford University Press).

Sen, A. K. (1977a): 'Rational Fools: A Critique of the Behavioural Foundations of Economic Theory', *Philosophy and Public Affairs*, vol. 6. [Essay 4 in this volume.]

____ (1977b): 'Social Choice Theory: A Re-examination', *Econometrica*, **45**. [Essay 8 in this volume.]

____ (1978a): 'On the Labour Theory of Value: Some Methodological Issues', *Cambridge Journal of Economics*, **2**.

____ (1978b): 'Ethical Measurement of Inequality: Some Difficulties', in Krelle and Shorrocks (1978). [Essay 19 in this volume.]

____ (1979): 'Utilitarianism and Welfarism', *Journal of Philosophy*, **76**.

Slote, M. A. (1966): 'The Theory of Important Criteria', *Journal of Philosophy*, **63**.

Stiglitz, J. E. (ed.) (1966): *The Collected Scientific Papers of Paul A. Samuelson* (Cambridge, Mass.: MIT Press).

Thorner, D. (1956): 'Agrarian Revolution by Census Redefinition', *Indian Economic Review*, **3**; reprinted in D. Thorner and A. Thorner, *Land and Labour in India* (Bombay: Asia Publishing House, 1962).

Wiles, P. (1974): *Distribution of Income: East and West* (Amsterdam: North-Holland).

Wong, S. (1973): 'The "F-twist" and the Methodology of Paul Samuelson', *American Economic Review*, **63**.

# Name Index

450

# Subject Index

457